"Composed in the style of the great medieval *catenae*, this new anthology of patristic commentary on Holy Scripture, conveniently arranged by chapter and verse, will be a valuable resource for prayer, study and proclamation. By calling attention to the rich Christian heritage preceding the separations between East and West and between Protestant and Catholic, this series will perform a major service to the cause of ecumenism."

AVERY CARDINAL DULLES, S.J.
Laurence J. McGinley Professor of Religion and Society
Fordham University

"The initial cry of the Reformation was *ad fontes*—back to the sources! The Ancient Christian Commentary on Scripture is a marvelous tool for the recovery of biblical wisdom in today's church. Not just another scholarly project, the ACCS is a major resource for the renewal of preaching, theology and Christian devotion."

TIMOTHY GEORGE
Dean, Beeson Divinity School, Samford University

"Modern church members often do not realize that they are participants in the vast company of the communion of saints that reaches far back into the past and that will continue into the future, until the kingdom comes. This Commentary should help them begin to see themselves as participants in that redeemed community."

ELIZABETH ACHTEMEIER
Union Professor Emerita of Bible and Homiletics
Union Theological Seminary in Virginia

"Contemporary pastors do not stand alone. We are not the first generation of preachers to wrestle with the challenges of communicating the gospel. The Ancient Christian Commentary on Scripture puts us in conversation with our colleagues from the past, that great cloud of witnesses who preceded us in this vocation. This Commentary enables us to receive their deep spiritual insights, their encouragement and guidance for present-day interpretation and preaching of the Word. What a wonderful addition to any pastor's library!"

WILLIAM H. WILLIMON
Dean of the Chapel and Professor of Christian Ministry
Duke University

"Here is a nonpareil series which reclaims the Bible as the book of the church by making accessible to earnest readers of the twenty-first century the classrooms of Clement of Alexandria and Didymus the Blind, the study and lecture hall of Origen, the cathedrae of Chrysostom and Augustine, the scriptorium of Jerome in his Bethlehem monastery."

GEORGE LAWLESS
Augustinian Patristic Institute and Gregorian University, Rome

"Few publishing projects have encouraged me as much as the recently announced Ancient Christian Commentary on Scripture with Dr. Thomas Oden serving as general editor. . . . How is it that so many of us who are dedicated to serve the Lord received seminary educations which omitted familiarity with such incredible students of the Scriptures as St. John Chrysostom, St. Athanasius the Great and St. John of Damascus? I am greatly anticipating the publication of this Commentary."

FR. PETER E. GILLQUIST
Director, Department of Missions and Evangelism
Antiochian Orthodox Christian Archdiocese of North America

"The Scriptures have been read with love and attention for nearly two thousand years, and listening to the voice of believers from previous centuries opens us to unexpected insight and deepened faith. Those who studied Scripture in the centuries closest to its writing, the centuries during and following persecution and martyrdom, speak with particular authority. The Ancient Christian Commentary on Scripture will bring to life the truth that we are invisibly surrounded by a 'great cloud of witnesses.'"

FREDERICA MATHEWES-GREEN
Commentator, National Public Radio

"For those who think that church history began around 1941 when their pastor was born, this Commentary will be a great surprise. Christians throughout the centuries have read the biblical text, nursed their spirits with it and then applied it to their lives. These commentaries reflect that the witness of the Holy Spirit was present in his church throughout the centuries. As a result, we can profit by allowing the ancient Christians to speak to us today."

HADDON ROBINSON
Harold John Ockenga Distinguished Professor of Preaching
Gordon-Conwell Theological Seminary

"All who are interested in the interpretation of the Bible will welcome the forthcoming multivolume series Ancient Christian Commentary on Scripture. Here the insights of scores of early church fathers will be assembled and made readily available for significant passages throughout the Bible and the Apocrypha. It is hard to think of a more worthy ecumenical project to be undertaken by the publisher."

BRUCE M. METZGER
Professor of New Testament, Emeritus
Princeton Theological Seminary

ANCIENT CHRISTIAN
COMMENTARY ON SCRIPTURE

NEW TESTAMENT
I*b*

MATTHEW 14-28

EDITED BY
MANLIO SIMONETTI

GENERAL EDITOR
THOMAS C. ODEN

InterVarsity Press
Downers Grove, Illinois

InterVarsity Press
P.O. Box 1400, Downers Grove, IL 60515-1426
World Wide Web: www.ivpress.com
E-mail: mail@ivpress.com

InterVarsity Press® is the book-publishing division of InterVarsity Christian Fellowship/USA®, a student movement active on campus at hundreds of universities, colleges and schools of nursing in the United States of America, and a member movement of the International Fellowship of Evangelical Students. For information about local and regional activities, write Public Relations Dept., InterVarsity Christian Fellowship/USA, 6400 Schroeder Rd., P.O. Box 7895, Madison, WI 53707-7895, or visit the IVCF website at <www.ivcf.org>.

Scripture quotations, unless otherwise noted, are from the Revised Standard Version of the Bible, copyright 1946, 1952, 1971 by the Division of Christian Education of the National Council of the Churches of Christ in the U.S.A., and are used by permission.

Cover photograph: Scala/Art Resource, New York. View of the apse. S. Vitale, Ravenna, Italy.

Spine photograph: Byzantine Collection, Dumbarton Oaks, Washington, D.C. Pendant cross (gold and enamel). Constantinople, late sixth century.

ISBN 0-8308-1469-8

Printed in the United States of America ∞

Library of Congress Cataloging-in-Publication Data

Matthew 14-28/edited by Manlio Simonetti.
    p. cm.—(Ancient Christian commentary on Scripture. New Testament; 1b)
    Includes bibliographical references and index.
    ISBN 0-8308-1469-8 (alk. paper)
    1. Bible. N.T. Matthew XIV-XXVIII—Commentaries. I. Simonetti, Manlio. II. Series.
    BS2575.53 M38 2001
    226.2'077'09—dc21   2001039411

| P | 25 | 24 | 23 | 22 | 21 | 20 | 19 | 18 | 17 | 16 | 15 | 14 | 13 | 12 | 11 | 10 | 9 | 8 | 7 | 6 | 5 | 4 | 3 |
| Y | 23 | 22 | 21 | 20 | 19 | 18 | 17 | 16 | 15 | 14 | 13 | 12 | 11 | 10 | 09 | 08 | 07 | 06 | 05 | 04 |

ANCIENT CHRISTIAN COMMENTARY PROJECT RESEARCH TEAM

GENERAL EDITOR
Thomas C. Oden

ASSOCIATE EDITOR
Christopher A. Hall

OPERATIONS MANAGER
Joel Elowsky

RESEARCH AND ACQUISITIONS DIRECTOR
Michael Glerup

TRANSLATIONS PROJECTS DIRECTOR
Joel Scandrett

EDITORIAL SERVICES DIRECTOR
Warren Calhoun Robertson

ORIGINAL LANGUAGE VERSION DIRECTOR
Konstantin Gavrilkin

GRADUATE RESEARCH ASSISTANTS

Chris Branstetter	*Scott Kisker*
Jeffrey Finch	*Sergey Kozin*
Steve Finlan	*Hsueh-Ming Liao*
J. Sergius Halvorsen	*Dennis McManus*
Patricia Ireland	*Michael Nausner*
Alexei Khamine	*Robert Paul Seesengood*
Vladimir Kharlamov	*Baek-Yong Sung*
Susan Kipper	*Elena Vishnevskaya*

TRANSLATORS

Jim Carr	*Allen Kerkeslager*
Brian Cherer	*Alexei Khamine*
Joel Elowsky	*Jim Marks*
Jeffrey Finch	*Thomas B. Mueller*
Brian Glenney	*Robert Paolucci*
Robert Paul Seesengood	

ADMINISTRATIVE ASSISTANT
Judy Cox

CONTENTS

General Introduction

The Ancient Christian Commentary on Scripture has as its goal the revitalization of Christian teaching based on classical Christian exegesis, the intensified study of Scripture by lay persons who wish to think with the early church about the canonical text, and the stimulation of Christian historical, biblical, theological and pastoral scholars toward further inquiry into scriptural interpretation by ancient Christian writers.

The time frame of these documents spans seven centuries of exegesis, from Clement of Rome to John of Damascus, from the end of the New Testament era to A.D. 750, including the Venerable Bede.

Lay readers are asking how they might study sacred texts under the instruction of the great minds of the ancient church. This commentary has been intentionally prepared for a general lay audience of non-professionals who study the Bible regularly and who earnestly wish to have classic Christian observation on the text readily available to them. The series is targeted to anyone who wants to reflect and meditate with the early church about the plain sense, theological wisdom and moral meaning of particular Scripture texts.

A commentary dedicated to allowing ancient Christian exegetes to speak for themselves will refrain from the temptation to fixate endlessly upon contemporary criticism. Rather, it will stand ready to provide textual resources from a distinguished history of exegesis that has remained massively inaccessible and shockingly disregarded during the last century. We seek to make available to our present-day audiences the multicultural, multilingual, transgenerational resources of the early ecumenical Christian tradition.

Preaching at the end of the first millennium focused primarily on the text of Scripture as understood by the earlier esteemed tradition of comment, largely converging on those writers that best reflected classic Christian consensual thinking. Preaching at the end of the second millennium has reversed that pattern. It has so forgotten most of these classic comments that they are vexing to find anywhere, and even when located they are often available only in archaic editions and inadequate translations. The preached word in our time has remained largely bereft of previously influential patristic inspiration. Recent scholarship has so focused attention upon post-Enlightenment historical and literary methods that it has left this longing largely unattended and unserviced.

This series provides the pastor, exegete, student and lay reader with convenient means to see what Athanasius or John Chrysostom or the desert fathers and mothers had to say about a particular text for preaching, for study and for meditation. There is an emerging awareness among Catholic, Protestant and Orthodox laity that vital biblical preaching and spiritual formation need deeper grounding beyond the scope of the historical-critical orientations that have governed biblical studies in our day.

Hence this work is directed toward a much broader audience than the highly technical and specialized scholarly field of patristic studies. The audience is not limited to the university scholar concentrating on the study of the history of the transmission of the text or to those with highly focused philological interests in textual morphology or historical-critical issues. Though these are crucial concerns for specialists, they are not the paramount interest of this series.

This work is a Christian Talmud. The Talmud is a Jewish collection of rabbinic arguments and comments on the Mishnah, which epitomized the laws of the Torah. The Talmud originated in approximately the same period that the patristic writers were commenting on texts of the Christian tradition. Christians from the late patristic age through the medieval period had documents analogous to the Jewish Talmud and Midrash (Jewish commentaries) available to them in the *glossa ordinaria* and catena traditions, two forms of compiling extracts of patristic exegesis. In Talmudic fashion the sacred text of Christian Scripture was thus clarified and interpreted by the classic commentators.

The Ancient Christian Commentary on Scripture has venerable antecedents in medieval exegesis of both eastern and western traditions, as well as in the Reformation tradition. It offers for the first time in this century the earliest Christian comments and reflections on the Old and New Testaments to a modern audience. Intrinsically an ecumenical project, this series is designed to serve Protestant, Catholic and Orthodox lay, pastoral and scholarly audiences.

In cases where Greek, Latin, Syriac and Coptic texts have remained untranslated into English, we provide new translations. Wherever current English translations are already well rendered, they will be utilized, but if necessary their language will be brought up to date. We seek to present fresh dynamic equivalency translations of long-neglected texts which historically have been regarded as authoritative models of biblical interpretation.

These foundational sources are finding their way into many public libraries and into the core book collections of many pastors and lay persons. It is our intent and the publisher's commitment to keep the whole series in print for many years to come.

Thomas C. Oden
General Editor

A Guide to Using This Commentary

Several features have been incorporated into the design of this commentary. The following comments are intended to assist readers in making full use of this volume.

Pericopes of Scripture

The scriptural text has been divided into pericopes, or passages, usually several verses in length. Each of these pericopes is given a heading, which appears at the beginning of the pericope. For example, the first pericope in the commentary on Matthew 14—28 is "14:1-12 The Death of John the Baptist." This heading is followed by the Scripture passage quoted in the Revised Standard Version (RSV) across the full width of the page. The Scripture passage is provided for the convenience of readers, but it is also in keeping with medieval patristic commentaries, in which the citations of the Fathers were arranged around the text of Scripture.

Overviews

Following each pericope of text is an overview of the patristic comments on that pericope. The format of this overview varies within the volumes of this series, depending on the requirements of the specific book of Scripture. The function of the overview is to provide a brief summary of all the comments to follow. It tracks a reasonably cohesive thread of argument among patristic comments, even though they are derived from diverse sources and generations. Thus the summaries do not proceed chronologically or by verse sequence. Rather they seek to rehearse the overall course of the patristic comment on that pericope.

We do not assume that the commentators themselves anticipated or expressed a formally received cohesive argument but rather that the various arguments tend to flow in a plausible, recognizable pattern. Modern readers can thus glimpse aspects of continuity in the flow of diverse exegetical traditions representing various generations and geographical locations.

Topical Headings

An abundance of varied patristic comment is available for each pericope of these letters. For this reason we have broken the pericopes into two levels. First is the verse with its topical heading. The patristic comments are then focused on aspects of each verse, with topical headings summarizing the essence of the patristic comment by evoking a key phrase, metaphor or idea. This feature provides a bridge by which modern readers can enter into the heart of the patristic comment.

Identifying the Patristic Texts

Following the topical heading of each section of comment, the name of the patristic commentator is given. An English translation of the patristic comment is then provided. This is immediately followed by the title of the patristic work and the textual reference—either by book, section and subsection or by book-and-verse references.

The Footnotes

Readers who wish to pursue a deeper investigation of the patristic works cited in this commentary will find the footnotes especially valuable. A footnote number directs the reader to the notes at the bottom of the right-hand column, where in addition to other notations (clarifications or biblical cross references) one will find information on English translations (where available) and standard original-language editions of the work cited. An abbreviated citation (normally citing the book, volume and page number) of the work is provided except in cases where a line-by-line commentary is being quoted, in which case the biblical references will lead directly to the selection. A key to the abbreviations is provided on page xv. Where there is any serious ambiguity or textual problem in the selection, we have tried to reflect the best available textual tradition.

Where original language texts have remained untranslated into English, we provide new translations. Wherever current English translations are already well rendered, they are utilized, but where necessary they are stylistically updated. A single asterisk (*) indicates that a previous English translation has been updated to modern English or amended for easier reading. The double asterisk (**) indicates either that a new translation has been provided or that some extant translation has been significantly amended. We have standardized spellings and made grammatical variables uniform so that our English references will not reflect the odd spelling variables of the older English translations. For ease of reading we have in some cases edited out superfluous conjunctions.

For the convenience of computer database users the digital database references are provided to either the Thesaurus Linguae Graecae (Greek texts) or to the Cetedoc (Latin texts) in both the appendix found on pages 315-16 and the bibliography found on pages 331-32.

Abbreviations

ACW	Ancient Christian Writers: The Works of the Fathers in Translation. Mahwah, N.J.: Paulist, 1946-.
ANF	A. Roberts and J. Donaldson, eds. Ante-Nicene Fathers. 10 vols. Buffalo, N.Y.: Christian Literature, 1885-1896. Reprint, Grand Rapids, Mich.: Eerdmans, 1951-1956; Reprint, Peabody, Mass.: Hendrickson, 1994.
CCL	Corpus Christianorum. Series Latina. Turnhout, Belgium: Brepols, 1953-.
CS	Cistercian Studies. Kalamazoo, Mich.: Cistercian Publications, 1973-.
FC	Fathers of the Church: A New Translation. Washington, D.C.: Catholic University of America Press, 1947-.
GCS	Die griechischen christlichen Schriftsteller. Berlin: Akademie-Verlag, 1897-.
MKGK	*Matthäus-Kommentare aus der griechischen Kirche*. Edited by Joseph Reuss. Berlin: Akademie-Verlag, 1957.
NPNF	P. Schaff et al., eds. A Select Library of the Nicene and Post-Nicene Fathers of the Christian Church. 2nd series (14 vols. each). Buffalo, N.Y.: Christian Literature, 1887-1894; Reprint, Grand Rapids, Mich.: Eerdmans, 1952-1956; Reprint, Peabody, Mass.: Hendrickson, 1994.
PG	J.-P. Migne, ed. Patrologiae cursus completus. Series Graeca. 166 vols. Paris: Migne, 1857-1886.
PL	J.-P. Migne, ed. Patrologiae cursus completus. Series Latina. 221 vols. Paris: Migne, 1844-1864.
PL Supp	A. Hamman, ed. Patrologia Latinae Supplementum. Paris: Garnier Frères, 1958-.
PO	Patrologia Orientalis. Paris, 1903-.
SC	H. de Lubac, J. Daniélou et al., eds. Sources chrétiennes. Paris: Editions du Cerf, 1941-.
SSL	Spicilegium Sacrum Lovaniense: Études et documents. Université Catholique. Louvain, 1922-

THE GOSPEL ACCORDING TO MATTHEW

14:1-12 THE DEATH OF JOHN THE BAPTIST

¹At that time Herod the tetrarch heard about the fame of Jesus; ²and he said to his servants, "This is John the Baptist, he has been raised from the dead; that is why these powers are at work in him." ³For Herod had seized John and bound him and put him in prison, for the sake of Herodias, his brother Philip's wife;[l] ⁴because John said to him, "It is not lawful for you to have her." ⁵And though he wanted to put him to death, he feared the people, because they held him to be a prophet. ⁶But when Herod's birthday came, the daughter of Herodias danced before the company, and pleased Herod, ⁷so that he promised with an oath to give her whatever she might ask. ⁸Prompted by her mother, she said, "Give me the head of John the Baptist here on a platter." ⁹And the king was sorry; but because of his oaths and his guests he commanded it to be given; ¹⁰he sent and had John beheaded in the prison, ¹¹and his head was brought on a platter and given to the girl, and she brought it to her mother. ¹²And his disciples came and took the body and buried it; and they went and told Jesus.

l Other ancient authorities read *his brother's wife*

OVERVIEW: After King Herod's death the Romans divided his kingdom into a tetrarchy, and one part of the tetrarchy went to his son, who was called Herod the tetrarch (THEODORE OF MOPSUESTIA). Herod imagined that John had risen from the dead after he had been beheaded and was acting in the person of Jesus, the continuation of Elijah's spirit (ORIGEN). Thinking that the Baptist had risen from the dead, Herod began to be afraid of him, as though John had become all the more powerful (THEODORE OF HERACLEA). Herod's fantasies reveal a combination of conflicting emotions: vanity and fear (CHRYSOSTOM). While fear is able to restrain the power to sin, it is unable to remove the will to sin. Hence it makes those whom it has re-strained from crime all the more eager to return to crime (PETER CHRYSOLOGUS). John preferred to incur the king's anger rather than ignore God's commandments (JEROME). Virtue is undesirable to those who are immoral; integrity is a hardship for those who are corrupt; mercy is intolerable to those who are cruel (PETER CHRYSOLOGUS).

Herod is said to be afraid due to his oath and guests, but he should have been far more afraid of that which is more fearful (CHRYSOSTOM). The house is converted into an arena, the table changes into a stall at the amphitheater, the birthday guests turn into spectators, the food ripens into carnage, the wine transforms into blood, the birthday mutates into a funeral

1

(PETER CHRYSOLOGUS). Herod's former willingness is incompatible with his present unwillingness, and the annoyance he now feels is contrary to the elation he felt before (HILARY OF POITIERS). Now that the time of the law is over and buried with John, his disciples (JEROME) announce to the Lord these events as they leave the law and come to the gospel (HILARY OF POITIERS).

14:1 Herod Hears of Jesus' Works

HEROD THE TETRARCH. THEODORE OF MOPSUESTIA: Herod the king is one person, Herod the tetrarch, his son, is another. After King Herod's death the Romans divided his kingdom into a tetrarchy, and one part of the tetrarchy went to his son. This is the man who beheaded the Forerunner and who, for this reason, received his due punishment not long afterward.[1] FRAGMENT 77.[2]

14:2 John's Powers at Work

THE ANALOGY OF THE REAPPEARANCE OF ELIJAH. ORIGEN: The Jews had different opinions about the resurrection. Some of them were false. The Sadducees did not believe in the resurrection of the dead or in the existence of angels. They believed those things that were written about them were only to be interpreted figuratively but had no reality in point of fact.[3] Other Jewish views of the resurrection were true, such as were taught by the Pharisees about the resurrection of the dead—that they rise.

We must now therefore inquire about the opinion regarding the soul, which was mistakenly held by Herod and some from among the people. It ran something like this: John, who a little earlier had been slain by him, had risen from the dead after he had been beheaded. This person who had risen was the same person under a different name, one now called Jesus. Herod imagined that Jesus possessed the same powers that formerly worked in John. If the

powers that worked in John had passed over to Jesus, Jesus was thus thought by some to actually be John the Baptist.

The return of Elijah fueled this idea. Here is the line of argument. It was the spirit and power of Elijah that had returned in John. "This is Elijah who is to come."[4] The spirit in Elijah possessed the power to go into John. So Herod thought that the powers John worked in baptism and teaching had a miraculous effect in Jesus, even though John did not do miracles. It may be said that something of this kind was the underlying thought of those who said that Elijah had appeared in Jesus or that one of the old prophets had risen. COMMENTARY ON MATTHEW 10.20.[5]

THINKING THE BAPTIST HAD RISEN. THEODORE OF HERACLEA: Thinking that the Baptist had risen from the dead, Herod began to be afraid of him, as though John had become all the more powerful. He was alarmed lest John should employ against him even more of his caustic freedom of speech, which was a terror to him, frustrating him by revealing his crooked deeds. FRAGMENT 93.[6]

THE IMAGINATIONS OF VANITY AND FEAR. CHRYSOSTOM: Do you see the intensity of his fear? Herod did not dare speak of it openly, but he still speaks apprehensively to his own servants. Yet this whole opinion was absurd. It savored of the jittery soldier. Even though many were thought to have risen from the dead, no one had done anything like what was imagined of John. Herod's words seem to me to be the language both of vanity and of fear. For such is the nature of unreasonable souls; they often accept a

---

[1]Herod Antipas was deposed by Emperor Caligula and sent into exile in Gaul. [2]MKGK 123-24. [3]Origen means that the Sadducees, not believing in the existence of angels, interpreted allegorically the passages of the Pentateuch (the only Scriptures that they accepted) in which angels are mentioned. [4]Mt 11:14. In the time of Christ it was a common belief among the Jews that Elijah would return to earth to announce the coming of the Messiah before the end of the world. [5]GCS 40:26-28; ANF 9:427. [6]MKGK 82.

mixture of opposite passions. THE GOSPEL OF MATTHEW, HOMILY 48.2.[7]

14:3 Herod Had Imprisoned John

JOHN'S ADMONITION. HILARY OF POITIERS: We have frequently advised that all diligence must be applied to the reading of the Gospels, for in the narration of the different events one may arrive at a deeper understanding. There is indeed an order to the narration of all the works, but the underlying cause behind the effects of the narrated events is preestablished, as with Herod and John.

John, as we frequently noted, preferred the form of the law, because the law foretold Christ and John proceeded from the law, announcing Christ from the law. Herod, on the other hand, was the prince of the people, and the prince of the people embraces the name and interests of his subjects. John accordingly advised Herod not to take to himself his brother's wife. There were and there are two peoples: one people of the circumcision and the other of the Gentiles. But the law admonished Israel not to ally itself with the works of the Gentiles and with infidelity. Infidelity is associated with the Gentiles, as if by a bond of conjugal love. Because of the truth of this stern admonition by John, he was confined in prison like the law. ON MATTHEW 14.3, 7.[8]

14:4 John's Rebuke of Herod

IT IS NOT LAWFUL FOR YOU TO HAVE HER. JEROME: Ancient history tells us that Philip the son of Herod the Great (under whom the Lord fled into Egypt), the brother of that Herod under whom Christ suffered, took as his wife Herodias the daughter of King Phetrai. Later his father-in-law, after a rivalry between him and his son-in-law, took his daughter and, to the great chagrin of the first husband, Herod his enemy united with her in marriage. As to just who this Philip was, Luke the Evangelist notes

clearly, "In the fifteenth year of the reign of Tiberias Caesar, and Herod being tetrarch of Galilee, and his brother Philip tetrarch of the region of Ituraea and Trachonitis."[9]

Therefore John the Baptist, who had come in the spirit and power of Elijah, with the same authority whereby the latter had rebuked Ahab and Jezebel, upbraided Herod and Herodias because they had entered into an unlawful marriage. He did so because it is not lawful to take the wife of one's own living brother. John preferred to incur the king's anger rather than, through fawning, be unmindful of God's commandments. COMMENTARY ON MATTHEW 2.14.4.[10]

INTEGRITY IS A HARDSHIP FOR THE CORRUPT. PETER CHRYSOLOGUS: John aroused Herod by his moral admonitions, not by any formal accusation. He wanted to correct, not to suppress. Herod, however, preferred to suppress rather than be reconciled. To those who are held captive, the freedom of the one innocent of wrongdoing becomes hateful. Virtue is undesirable to those who are immoral; holiness is abhorrent to those who are impious; chastity is an enemy to those who are impure; integrity is a hardship for those who are corrupt; frugality runs counter to those who are self-indulgent; mercy is intolerable to those who are cruel, as is loving-kindness to those who are pitiless and justice to those who are unjust. The Evangelist indicates this when he says, "John said to him, 'It is not lawful for you to have the wife of your brother Philip.' " This is where John runs into trouble. He who admonishes those who are evil gives offense. He who repudiates wrongdoers runs into trouble. John was saying what was proper of the law, what was proper of justice, what was proper of salvation and what was proper certainly not of hatred but of love. And look at the reward he received from the ungodly

---

[7]PG 58:488; NPNF 1 10:297. [8]SC 258:12, 16-18. [9]Lk 3:1. [10]CCL 77:117.

for his loving concern! SERMONS 127.6-7.[11]

14:5 Herod Feared the People

TURNING FROM JUSTICE. PETER CHRYSOLO-GUS: "And though he wanted to put him to death, he feared the people." That person readily turns away from justice who, in matters at issue, fears not God but people. Such fear can restrain the power to sin but is unable to remove the will to sin. Hence, those whom it has restrained from crime, it makes all the more eager to return to crime. It is only the fear of God that can set minds straight, repel criminal actions, preserve innocence and give steadfast power. But let us focus on the passionate intensity of blessed John. SERMONS 127.7.[12]

14:6 Herod's Birthday

THE DAUGHTER OF HERODIAS DANCED. HILARY OF POITIERS: On Herod's birthday—that is, amid the delights of corporeal things—the daughter of Herodias danced. With every enticing movement she made, she exuded sensual pleasure as though from the infidelity that arose through all the joys of Israel. The people gave themselves over to this. All were corrupted by an oath. Through sin and the pleasures of the world, the Israelites sold the gifts of eternal life. The girl requested of her mother—who herself had a knack for infidelity—that the head of John, symbolizing the glory of the law, be brought to her. For the law had exposed incestuous Israel with the authority of the divine commandments. ON MATTHEW 14.7.[13]

THE DANCE. PETER CHRYSOLOGUS: You have heard, brothers, that sensual pleasure may give birth to great cruelty. "And his head was brought on a platter."[14] The house is converted into an arena, the table changes into a stall at the amphitheater, the birthday guests turn into spectators, the feast grows into a furor, the food ripens into carnage, the wine transforms into

blood, the birthday changes into a funeral, sunrise evolves into sunset, the banquet is altered into a bloody killing, and musical instruments perform the tragedy of the ages. A creature enters the room, not a girl; a lynx, not a maiden, moves to the music. She has the mane of an animal, not hair, sprouting up from the crown of her head. She spreads out her limbs with twists and turns; she steadily grows in ferocity. She becomes cunning in cruelty, not in body. And this extraordinarily wild animal lets out a growl. She gnashes her teeth. She does not take up a sword but produces one. "Prompted by her mother," the Evangelist says, and taking an arrow from her mother's heart, this uncanny creature, with contempt for the prize of John's body, slithers through the hall to have his head cut off. SERMONS 127.9.[15]

14:7-9 Herod's Oath

NOW HE IS SORRY. HILARY OF POITIERS: Shortly before, Herod indicated that he wanted to kill John. He hesitated for fear of the people, because they considered him to be a prophet. But now, upon the request for John's death, since Herod was bound formally by the ritual of an oath, how is it that he suddenly becomes sorry? His former willingness is incompatible with his present unwillingness, and the annoyance he now feels is contrary to what he felt before. Previously there was an orderly sequence to what transpired, but now the situation has gotten out of hand. Sensual pleasure springing up from infidelity has seized the glory of the law. But the people, aware of the good things in the law, wink at the pleasurable circumstances not without misgivings as to their own peril. They know it is inappropriate for them to turn away from the glory of the commandments. Yet four factors cause them to give in to sin: an oath, fear of the leaders, the allurements of pleasure and a

---

[11]CCL 24b:784-85. [12]CCL 24b:785. [13]SC 258:18-20. [14]Mt 14:11. [15]CCL 24b:786-87.

bad example. On Matthew 14.8.[16]

Because of His Oaths and His Guests.
Jerome: It is customary in the Scriptures for the historian to narrate the opinion of many, as it was held by them at the time. Even as Joseph is called the father of Jesus by Mary herself, Herod now is said to be exceedingly sad because his guests thought that he was. An artful deceiver and a skilled assassin, he preferred to show a sad face when his mind registered joy. Commentary on Matthew 2.14.9.[17]

14:10-11 John's Execution

John Beheaded. Chrysostom: And she being instructed beforehand by her mother, said, "Give me here John the Baptist's head on a platter."

Her reproach is twofold: first, that she danced, then that she pleased him and so pleased him as to obtain even murder for her reward.

Do you see how savage he was, how senseless, how foolish? He puts himself under the obligation of an oath while to her he gives full power over her request.

But when Herod saw the evil actually ensuing, "he was sorry," it is said. Yet in the first instance he had put him in prison. Why then is he sorry? Such is the nature of virtue. Even among the wicked admiration and praises are its due. But alas for her madness! When she also ought to admire, yes, to bow down to him for trying to redress her wrong, she rather even helps to arrange the plot, lays a snare and asks a diabolical favor.

But he was afraid "for the oath's sake," it is said, "and those that sat with him at dinner." Why did he not fear that which is far more fearful? Surely if Herod was afraid of having witnesses to perjury, much more should he fear having so many witnesses of a murder so lawless. The Gospel of Matthew, Homily 48.4.[18]

14:12 John's Disciples Go to Jesus

The Law Is Buried with John. Hilary of Poitiers: Amid the other enjoyments of the profligate company, the head of John is brought on a platter. Thus the pleasures of the body and worldly extravagance reach the point where the girl carries the head to her mother. And so shameful Israel surrenders the glory of the law to the pleasure and infidelity of its Herodian household, who were formerly Gentiles. Now that the time of the law is over and buried with John, his disciples announce to the Lord the events that transpired, as they leave the law and come to the Gospels. On Matthew 14.8.[19]

His Disciples Came. Jerome: Josephus relates that in a certain town of Arabia John's head had been cut off.[20] As to the words that follow, "and his disciples came and took the body," we presume these people are the disciples of both John and the Savior. Commentary on Matthew 2.14.12.[21]

---

[16]SC 258:18-20. [17]CCL 77:118. [18]PG 58:489; NPNF 1 10:298. [19]SC 258:20. [20]Josephus *Antiquities of the Jews* 18.5. [21]CCL 77:119.

14:13-21 JESUS FEEDS THE FIVE THOUSAND

[13]*Now when Jesus heard this, he withdrew from there in a boat to a lonely place apart. But when the crowds heard it, they followed him on foot from the towns.* [14]*As he went ashore he saw*

a great throng; and he had compassion on them, and healed their sick. ¹⁵When it was evening, the disciples came to him and said, "This is a lonely place, and the day is now over; send the crowds away to go into the villages and buy food for themselves." ¹⁶Jesus said, "They need not go away; you give them something to eat." ¹⁷They said to him, "We have only five loaves here and two fish." ¹⁸And he said, "Bring them here to me." ¹⁹Then he ordered the crowds to sit down on the grass; and taking the five loaves and the two fish he looked up to heaven, and blessed, and broke and gave the loaves to the disciples, and the disciples gave them to the crowds. ²⁰And they all ate and were satisfied. And they took up twelve baskets full of the broken pieces left over. ²¹And those who ate were about five thousand men, besides women and children.

OVERVIEW: When Jesus heard of John's death, he withdrew to a lonely place. This was not for fear of death but to spare his enemies from compounding one murder with another or to defer his death to the day of Passover (JEROME). He withdrew because he did not want to make his identity known at this point (CHRYSOSTOM). They had only five loaves and two fish, namely, the five books of the law and the prophets and John (HILARY OF POITIERS). Even at this point the disciples are not yet awakened but still reason as if with a man (CHRYSOSTOM). Although this was a deserted place, he that is here is ready to feed the world (EUSEBIUS OF EMESA). The one who is speaking is not subject to time, even though it was said to be late in the day (CHRYSOSTOM). Jesus looked up to heaven that he might teach them to keep their eyes focused there. And he broke the bread. If the bread had been left intact and not broken into pieces, they would have been unable to feed the great crowds of men, women and children (JEROME). By the word of God coming from the law and the prophets, the multitude was satisfied and an abundance of divine power, reserved for the Gentiles from the ministry of the eternal food, was left over for the twelve apostles (HILARY OF POITIERS).

14:13-14 Jesus Has Compassion on the Throng

TO A LONELY PLACE APART. CHRYSOSTOM: We

see him on many occasions "departing." We see this when John was imprisoned[1] and killed and when the Jews heard that he was making more disciples.[2] For it was his will to live his life in an ordinary rhythm of interaction and solitude. The time had not yet come for him to reveal his divine glory plainly. This is why Jesus told his disciples to "tell no one that he is the Christ."[3] His will was that this should be better known after his resurrection. During this time he was not very severe with those who were obstinate in their unbelief. Rather, he was prone to be indulgent with them.

On retiring, he departs not into a city but into a wilderness. He leaves in a boat so that no one would follow him.

But note how the disciples of John had by now become more attached to Jesus. For it was they who told him of the event. They in fact had left everything and taken refuge in John. In their calamity Jesus makes provision for them, and in doing so he does them no small benevolence.

But why did he not withdraw before they brought the news to him? Didn't Jesus know the fact of John's death even before they reported it to him? He did not want to make his identity known at this point. The divine economy did not require it. For it was not by his appearance only but by his actions that Jesus would have his identity confirmed. He knew the devil's craft

[1]Mt 4:12. [2]Jn 4:1-3. [3]Mt 16:20.

and that he would leave nothing undone to destroy Christ's revelation.

This is why Jesus withdrew. But the crowds do not withdraw from him. They try to follow him, as if riveted to him. Not even John's tragic end diverted or frightened them. So great a thing is earnest desire, so great a thing is love, that it overcomes and dispels all dangers. THE GOSPEL OF MATTHEW, HOMILY 49.[4]

HE WITHDREW. JEROME: They announced the death of the Baptist to the Savior. When Jesus heard this, he withdrew to a lonely place apart, but not, as some people think, for fear of death. He withdrew to spare his enemies from compounding one murder with another or to defer his death to the day of Passover on which a lamb is ritually offered up and doorposts are sprinkled with the blood of the faithful. Or else he withdrew in order to give us an example of avoiding the foolhardiness of those who betrayed him, because not everyone perseveres amid torments with the same constancy they had when they offered themselves to be tortured. For this reason in another place he gave this admonition: "When they persecute you in this city, flee to another."[5] It was also fitting that the Evangelist did not say "he fled to a lonely place" but "he withdrew," so that he avoided his persecutors rather than feared them. COMMENTARY ON MATTHEW 2.14.13.[6]

14:15-16 You Give Them Something to Eat

YOU GIVE THEM. CHRYSOSTOM: Note carefully the Teacher's skill. Observe with what discretion he draws them toward believing. Observe how deliberately this unfolds. For he did not simply say, "I will feed them." The deeper significance of that would have not been easily understood. So what does he say? "They need not go away; you give them something to eat."

He did not say "I give them" but "you give them." For at this point their regard for him was essentially as to a man. They said to him, "We have only five loaves here and two fish." At this point Mark adds, "They did not understand the saying, for their heart was hardened."[7] For they were continuing to crawl like babies. THE GOSPEL OF MATTHEW, HOMILY 49.[8]

SEND THEM AWAY? CYRIL OF ALEXANDRIA: Let us examine carefully what this sending away of the crowds is all about. Some of those who followed Christ were afflicted by evil spirits and begged to be delivered from them. Others were afflicted with various sicknesses from which they sought relief. Therefore, because the disciples knew that Jesus had only to consider what those who were suffering longed for and it would be accomplished, "they sent them away." They did this not so much because they thought Jesus' time was too valuable but because they had a love for the crowds and, as though already having an understanding of pastoral care, they began to care for the people. FRAGMENT 175.[9]

14:17 Five Loaves and Two Fish

THE FIVE LOAVES OF THE FIVE BOOKS OF THE LAW. HILARY OF POITIERS: When the disciples advised that the crowds be sent away into the neighboring villages to buy food, he answered, "They do not need to go away." This signaled that these people whom he healed with the food of teaching, teaching that was not for sale, had no need to go back to Judea and buy food. He ordered the apostles to give them something to eat.

But was Jesus unaware there was nothing to give? Did he not know the disciples possessed a limited amount of food? He could read their minds, so he knew. We are invited to explain things by reasoning according to types. It was not yet granted to the apostles to make and administer heavenly bread for the food of eternal life. Yet their response reflected an ordered reasoning about types: they had only five loaves

---

[4]PG 58:495-97; NPNF 1 10:303-4. [5]Mt 10:23. [6]CCL 77:119-20. [7]Mk 6:52. [8]PG 58:497; NPNF 1 10:304. [9]MKGK 210.

and two fish. This means that up to then they depended on five loaves—that is, the five books of the law. And two fish nourished them—that is, the preaching of the prophets and of John. For in the works of the law there was life just as there is life from bread, but the preaching of John and the prophets restored hope to human life by virtue of water.[10] Therefore the apostles offered these things first, because that was the level of their understanding at the time. From these modest beginnings the preaching of the gospel has proceeded from them, from these same apostles, until it has grown into an immense power. ON MATTHEW 14.10.[11]

14:18 Bring Them

FEEDING THE WORLD IN A DESERTED PLACE. CHRYSOSTOM: Finally he said to them, "Bring them here to me." Although this was a deserted place, he that is here is ready to feed the world. The one who is speaking to you is not subject to time, even though "the day is now over."

In John's Gospel it is further related that these were loaves of barley.[12] This is not mentioned accidentally but with the object of teaching us to trample under foot[13] the pride of costly living. Such was also the diet of the prophets. THE GOSPEL OF MATTHEW, HOMILY 49.1.[14]

14:19 Blessing and Breaking the Loaves

EVANGELICAL FOOD. HILARY OF POITIERS: Having taken the bread and the fish, the Lord looked up to heaven, then blessed and broke them. He gave thanks to the Father that, after the time of the law and the prophets, he himself was soon to be changed into evangelical food. After this the people were ordered to sit on the grass but not to lie down. Supported by the law, each one was covered as it were with the fruit of his works as with the grass on the ground. ON MATTHEW 4.11.[15]

HE LOOKED TO HEAVEN. JEROME: They are or-

dered to sit down on the grass and, according to another Evangelist, to recline in groups of hundreds and of fifties. In this way from the repentance of the fifty,[16] they ascended toward the perfect summit of one hundred.[17]

He looked up to heaven that he might teach them to keep their eyes focused there. He then took in hand five loaves of bread and two fish; he broke the loaves and gave the food to the disciples. By the breaking of the bread, he makes it into a seedbed of food—for if the bread had been left intact and not pulled apart and broken into pieces, they would have been unable to feed the great crowds of men, women and children. The law with the prophets are therefore pulled apart and broken into pieces. Mysteries are made manifest, so that what did not feed the multitude of people in its original whole and unbroken state now feeds them in its divided state. COMMENTARY ON MATTHEW 2.14.19.[18]

HE BROKE AND GAVE THE LOAVES. CHRYSOSTOM: In this miracle Jesus was teaching them humility, temperance, charity, to be of like mind toward one another and to share all things in common. He did so in his choice of location, by providing nothing more than loaves and fishes, by setting the same food before all and having them share it in common and by affording no one more than another. THE GOSPEL OF MATTHEW, HOMILY 49.3.[19]

14:20 All Were Satisfied, and Food Was Left

THEY WERE SATISFIED. HILARY OF POITIERS: The loaves were given to the apostles, for through them the gifts of divine grace were to be administered. The crowds were then fed with the five loaves and two fish, and they were satis-

---

[10]The water of baptism. [11]SC 258:20-22. [12]Jn 6:9. [13]As barley is crushed. [14]PG 58:497; NPNF 1 10:304. [15]SC 258:22. [16]A number symbolizing repentance, in reference to the Hebrew jubilee year, which recurred every fifty years and during which all debts were remitted. [17]A number signifying perfection. [18]CCL 77:122. [19]PG 58:499; NPNF 1 10:306.

fied. The leftover fragments of bread and fish, after the people had their fill, amounted to twelve baskets. Thus, by the word of God coming from the teaching of the law and the prophets, the multitude was satisfied; and an abundance of divine power, reserved for the Gentiles from the ministry of the eternal food, was left over for the twelve apostles. ON MATTHEW 4.11.[20]

TWELVE BASKETS FULL OF BROKEN PIECES. CHRYSOSTOM: And not even here does he hold back on the miracle, but it continues as the loaves become fragments. The broken pieces signify that of those loaves, some remained unreceived. This was in order that those who were absent might also learn what had been done.

For this providential purpose, then, Jesus indeed permitted the crowds to get hungry in order that no one might suppose what took place to be as illusion.

For this purpose he also caused just twelve baskets to remain over: That Judas, too, might bear one. He wanted all the disciples to know his power. He fed their hunger. In Elijah's case something similar also took place.[21] THE GOSPEL OF MATTHEW, HOMILY 49.3.[22]

THE DIVINE ECONOMY. CYRIL OF ALEXANDRIA: So that by every means the Lord might be known to be God by nature, he multiplies what is little, and he looks up to heaven as though asking for the blessing from above. Now he does this out of the divine economy, for our sakes. For he himself is the one who fills all things, the true blessing from above and from the Father. But, so that we might learn that when we are in charge of the table and are preparing to break the loaves, we ought to bring them to God with hands upraised and bring down upon them the blessing from above, he became for us the beginning and pattern and way. FRAGMENT 177.[23]

LIKE MANNA. CYRIL OF ALEXANDRIA: It is possible to see these new miracles concurring with more ancient ones and as being activities of one and the same power. The manna once remained in the wilderness for those of Israel. Now, behold, again in the desert he has provided ungrudgingly for those in want of food, as though bringing it down from heaven. For to multiply what is little and to feed such a multitude as though out of nothing would not be out of keeping with the former miracle. At that time Israel was to partake according to need; they had not received food in order to take it away with them, even though many fragments were left. This is, again, a good symbol for measuring use according to need and of not introducing an acquisitiveness that goes beyond what is needful. FRAGMENT 178.[24]

THE UNSEEN APPEARS THROUGH WHAT IS SEEN. EUSEBIUS OF EMESA: The miracle of the bread revealed the one through whom the soil, when planted with seed, multiplies. What was done invisibly, once brought to light, proclaimed who it is that always works invisibly. It was not only at that time that Jesus with five loaves does many great things. In the world he was not idle or inactive but was always at work feeding everyone and taking nothing for himself. Because he was unknown, therefore, he came feeding, *eating* and feeding, so that through those things that are seen, he who was unseen might appear. HOMILY 8.12.[25]

14:21 Numbering the Multitude

FIVE THOUSAND MEN. HILARY OF POITIERS: The same number of those eating proved to be the number of those who believed. As noted in the book of Acts, out of the countless people of Israel five thousand men believed.[26] Once the people had been satisfied, when they took up the loaves that had been broken into pieces with the fish, there was enough left over to match the

---

[20]SC 258:22-24. [21]1 Kings 17:16. [22]PG 58:499; NPNF 1 10:306. [23]MKGK 210-11. [24]MKGK 211. [25]SSL 26:205. [26]Acts 4:4.

number of believers and apostles to be filled with heavenly grace. Thus both the measure suited the number and the number the measure. Within its bounds the calculation was keyed to the proper effect and depended on the guidance of divine power. ON MATTHEW 4.11.[27]

[27]SC 258:24.

14:22-36 JESUS WALKS ON WATER

[22]*Then he made the disciples get into the boat and go before him to the other side, while he dismissed the crowds.* [23]*And after he had dismissed the crowds, he went up on the mountain by himself to pray. When evening came, he was there alone,* [24]*but the boat by this time was many furlongs distant from the land,*[m] *beaten by the waves; for the wind was against them.* [25]*And in the fourth watch of the night he came to them, walking on the sea.* [26]*But when the disciples saw him walking on the sea, they were terrified, saying, "It is a ghost!" and they cried out for fear.* [27]*But immediately he spoke to them, saying, "Take heart, it is I; have no fear."*

[28]*And Peter answered him, "Lord, if it is you, bid me come to you on the water."* [29]*He said, "Come." So Peter got out of the boat and walked on the water and came to Jesus;* [30]*but when he saw the wind,*[n] *he was afraid, and beginning to sink he cried out, "Lord, save me."* [31]*Jesus immediately reached out his hand and caught him, saying to him, "O man of little faith, why did you doubt?"* [32]*And when they got into the boat, the wind ceased.* [33]*And those in the boat worshiped him, saying, "Truly you are the Son of God."*

[34]*And when they had crossed over, they came to land at Gennesaret.* [35]*And when the men of that place recognized him, they sent round to all that region and brought to him all that were sick,* [36]*and besought him that they might only touch the fringe of his garment; and as many as touched it were made well.*

m Other ancient authorities read *was out on the sea*   n Other ancient authorities read *strong wind*

OVERVIEW: Jesus retreats to the mountain to teach us the benefit of solitude when we are praying (CHRYSOSTOM). His solitude, the boat and his dismissal of the crowds all have a symbolic meaning, anticipating his final return and glory (HILARY OF POITIERS). The miracle of walking on water was prophesied long before. It points to one who could walk on the water as well as on the ground, for he is truly human and yet God's only begotten Son (CHROMATIUS). He did not come quickly to the disciples' rescue. He was training them by their fears and instructing them to be ready to endure. Gently and by degrees he excites and urges the disciples on toward greater responsiveness (CHRYSOSTOM). The fourth watch of the night also has typological significance in relation to four phases of the history of revelation: the law, the prophets, the incarnation and the return of the Lord (HILARY OF POITIERS) or variously interpreted, Adam to

Noah, Noah to Moses, Moses to the Savior, with the fourth watch marking the time when the Son of God was born in the flesh and suffered (CHROMATIUS). Through the feebleness of the flesh and the fear of death, even the boldness of Peter fails (CHRYSOSTOM). But he cries out and asks the Lord to save him, and that cry is the groan of his repentance (HILARY OF POITIERS).

14:22 Jesus Sends Away the Disciples

THE PLAIN AND SPIRITUAL MEANING. HILARY OF POITIERS: The spiritual significance of this must be discerned, comparing the temporal order with the coming revelation. The historical event of his solitude in the evening anticipates a future event: his solitude at the time of the Passion, when everyone else had fled in fear.

He then orders his disciples to get into the boat and cross the sea while he dismisses the crowds. Once they are dismissed, he goes up on the mountain. This prefigures that he is on the sea and within the church. He orders that he be carried throughout the world until he returns in a dazzling second advent to all who are left from the house of Israel, when he will bring salvation and forgive sins.

Finally, in dismissing the crowds, the Lord is symbolically permitting them to enter into the kingdom of heaven. Then he proceeds to give thanks to God the Father, which anticipates his taking his place in glory and in majesty. ON MATTHEW 14.13.[1]

14:23 Jesus Dismisses the Crowd

INTO THE HILLS. CHRYSOSTOM: For what purpose does he go up into the hills on the mountain? To teach us that solitude and seclusion are good, when we are to pray to God. With this in view, you see, we find him continually withdrawing into the wilderness. There he often spends the whole night in prayer. This teaches us earnestly to seek such quietness in our prayers as the time and place may afford. For the wilderness is the mother of silence; it is a calm and a harbor, delivering us from all turmoils. THE GOSPEL OF MATTHEW, HOMILY 50.1.[2]

14:24 The Boat Beaten by Waves

MANY FURLONGS DISTANT FROM THE LAND. CHRYSOSTOM: The disciples are tossed on the waves again. They are in a storm, fully as bad as the previous one. Gently and by degrees he excites and urges the disciples on toward greater responsiveness, even to the point of bearing all things nobly. Whereas in the previous storm they had him with them in the ship, now they were alone by themselves. Even when he was asleep in the boat in the previous situation, he was ready to give them relief from danger. But then he was present to them.

Now he is leading them into a greater degree of challenge. Now he is not even present to them. He has departed. In midsea he permits a storm to arise. This was all for their training, that they might not look for some easy hope of preservation from any earthly source. He then allows them to be tossed by the storm all night! This had the purpose of awakening their stony hearts in a most complete way. This is how Jesus dealt with the nature of their fear, which the rough weather and the timing had produced. He cast them directly into a situation in which they would have a greater longing for him and a continual remembrance of him. THE GOSPEL OF MATTHEW, HOMILY 50.1.[3]

THE WIND WAS AGAINST THEM. AUGUSTINE: Meanwhile the boat carrying the disciples—that is, the church—is rocking and shaking amid the storms of temptation, while the adverse wind rages on. That is to say, its enemy the devil strives to keep the wind from calming down. But greater is he who is persistent on our behalf, for

---

[1]SC 258:26. [2]PG 58:503-4; NPNF 1 10:310. [3]PG 58:504-5; NPNF 1 10:310.

amid the vicissitudes of our life he gives us confidence. He comes to us and strengthens us, so we are not jostled in the boat and tossed overboard. For although the boat is thrown into disorder, it is still a boat. It alone carries the disciples and receives Christ. It is in danger indeed on the water, but there would be certain death without it. Therefore stay inside the boat and call upon God. When all good advice fails and the rudder is useless and the spread of the sails presents more of a danger than an advantage, when all human help and strength have been abandoned, the only recourse left for the sailors is to cry out to God. Therefore will he who helps those who are sailing to reach port safely, abandon his church and prevent it from arriving in peace and tranquility? SERMON 75.4.[4]

14:25 He Came to Them, Walking on the Sea

THE MIRACLE FORESEEN IN PROPHECY. CHROMATIUS: Who was able to walk on the sea if not the Creator of the universe? He, indeed, about whom the Holy Spirit had spoken long ago through blessed Job: "Who alone stretched out the heavens and walked on the sea as well as the earth."[5] Solomon spoke about him in the person of Wisdom: "I dwelt in the highest places and my throne was in a pillar of cloud. I orbited the heavenly sphere alone and walked on the waves of the sea."[6] David likewise declared in his psalm: "God, your way was through the sea, your path through the great waters."[7] So too Habakkuk noted, "The raging waters swept on; the deep gave forth its voice."[8]

What is more evident than this testimony, what is more clear? It points to him walking on the water as well as on the ground. This is God's only begotten Son, who long ago according to the will of the Father stretched out the heavens and at the time of Moses in a pillar of cloud showed the people a way to follow. TRACTATE ON MATTHEW 52.2.[9]

THE FOUR WATCHES OF THE HISTORY OF

REVELATION. HILARY OF POITIERS: In the meantime, however, the disciples are harassed by wind and by sea. Amid all the disturbances of the world, in conflict with the unclean spirit, they are tossed about. But the Lord comes in the fourth watch. For the fourth time, then, he will return to a roving and shipwrecked church. In the fourth watch of the night, the measure of his concern is found to be just as great. The first watch was that of the law, the second of the prophets, the third of the Lord's coming in the flesh and the fourth of his return in splendor. But he will find the church in distress and beleaguered by the spirit of the antichrist and by disturbances throughout the world. He will come to those who are restless and deeply troubled. And since, as we may expect from the antichrist, they will be exposed to temptations of every kind, even at the Lord's coming they will be terrified by the false appearances of things and crawling phantasms with eyes. But the good Lord will then speak out and dispel their fear, saying, "It is I." He will dispel the fear of impending shipwreck through their faith in his coming. ON MATTHEW 14.14.[10]

THE SPIRITUAL MEANING OF THE FOURTH WATCH OF THE NIGHT. CHROMATIUS: Let us focus on the meaning of this fourth watch in which the Lord comes to his disciples who were caught in the storm. The first watch of the night—that is, of the present world—is understood to be from Adam to Noah, the second watch from Noah up until Moses, through whom the law was given. The third watch was from Moses up to the coming of the Lord and Savior. In these three watches the Lord, even before coming in the flesh, with the vigilance of the angels defends the encampments of his saints from the snares of the enemy—that is, the devil and his angels, who from the begin-

---

[4]PL 38:475-76; NPNF 1 6:337-38 (Sermon 25). [5]Job 9:8. [6]Sir 24:4-5. [7]Ps 77:19 (76:19 LXX). [8]Hab 3:10. [9]CCL 9a:454-55. [10]SC 258:28.

ning of the world plotted against the salvation of the righteous. In the first watch, protection is given to Abel, Seth, Enos, Enoch, Methuselah and Noah. In the second watch, to Abraham, Melchizedech, Isaac, Jacob and Joseph. In the third watch, to Moses, Aaron, Joshua the son of Nun and, after that, to the other righteous men and prophets. The fourth watch marks the time when the Son of God was born in the flesh and suffered, the time he promised his disciples and his church that he would be eternally watchful after his resurrection, saying, "I will be with you even to the consummation of the world."[11] TRACTATE ON MATTHEW 52.5.[12]

14:26-27 Take Heart; Have No Fear

IT IS A GHOST! CHRYSOSTOM: "When the disciples," it is said, "saw him walking on the sea, they were troubled, saying, It is a spirit! And they cried out for fear." This is the way he constantly deals with our fears. He does not hesitate to bring on worse things, even more alarming than those before.[13] They were troubled here not only by the storm but also by the distance from the land. Note that he did not too easily remove the darkness. He did not come quickly to their rescue. He was training them, as I said, by the continuance of these fears and instructing them to be ready to endure. THE GOSPEL OF MATTHEW, HOMILY 50.1.[14]

BEARING ALL CHALLENGES. CHRYSOSTOM: Accordingly, neither did he present himself to them at once. For it is written that "in the fourth watch of the night he came to them, walking on the sea." He was instructing them not too hastily to seek for deliverance from their pressing dangers but to bear all challenges courageously. In any case, just when they looked to be delivered, their fear was again heightened. THE GOSPEL OF MATTHEW, HOMILY 50.1.[15]

THEY SAW HIM WALKING ON THE WATER.

AUGUSTINE: The fourth watch of the night marks the end of the night. One watch consists of three hours. This means that at the end of the world the Lord will come to the rescue, and he will be seen walking on the water. Although this ship is tossed by the storms of temptation, it sees the glorified Lord walking upon all the billows of the sea—that is, upon all the powers of this world. For through the voice of his Passion he gave an example of humility according to the flesh. Those waves of the sea to which he willingly submitted for our sake were stilled, in accordance with the prophecy: "I came to the height of the sea, and the storm swallowed me up."[16] SERMON 75.7.[17]

14:28 Peter Asks to Walk to Jesus

PETER'S BOLDNESS. JEROME: Peter is found to be of ardent faith at all times. When the disciples are asked who people say that Jesus is, Peter declares him to be the Son of God. Though mistaken in wanting to follow Christ to his Passion, he is not mistaken in his affection. He does not desire the death of him who a short time before he declared to be the Son of God. Peter is among the first to go up the mountain with the Savior and is the only one to follow him in his Passion. With bitter tears he immediately washes away the sin of denial that sprang up from fear. After the Passion when they were fishing in Lake Gennesaret, the Lord was standing on the beach, while the others were slowly sailing in the boat. He hesitated not for a moment. He put on his overgarment and plunged into the sea. And now, with the same ardor of faith he always had, the other apostles gazing in awe, he believes that he can do by the will of the Master what the latter could do by nature. "Bid me come to you on the

---

[11]Mt 28:20. [12]CCL 9a:457-58. [13]This procedure resembles what behavior therapists call implosive therapy for desensitization of phobic responses. [14]PG 58:505; NPNF 1 10:310. [15]PG 58:505; NPNF 1 10:310. [16]Ps 69:2 (68:2 LXX). [17]PL 38:476-77; NPNF 1 6:338 (Sermon 25).

water." Just say the word, and immediately the waves will become solid. The body which of itself is heavy will become light. COMMENTARY ON MATTHEW 2.14.28.[18]

LORD, IF IT IS YOU, BID ME COME. AUGUSTINE: What is signified by the fact that Peter dared to come to him upon the water? Peter indeed has the principal role in the church. And what is the meaning of those other words: "Lord, if it is you, bid me come to you on the water," if not, Lord, if you are truthful and never lie at all, let your church be glorified also in this world, for prophecy declared this about you? Let it walk upon the water, and it shall come to you, to whom it was said, "The rich among the people shall entreat your favor."[19] SERMON 75.10.[20]

14:29 Peter Walks on the Water

PETER GOT OUT OF THE BOAT. CHRYSOSTOM: Why then did Christ permit Peter to come? Suppose he had said, "No, you cannot come." With his boldness Peter might have protested again. But when Peter saw the sea and wind, he became dizzy and was afraid, and beginning to sink he cried out, "Lord, save me."

In relating this same situation, John remarks that "then they were willing to take him into the boat, and immediately the boat reached the shore where they were heading."[21] This implies that when they were on the point of arriving at the land, he entered the ship. Peter then having come down from the ship went to Jesus, not rejoicing so much in walking on the water as in coming to him. THE GOSPEL OF MATTHEW, HOMILY 50.2.[22]

14:30 Peter Fears the Wind

FEAR OF THE LESSER DANGER. CHRYSOSTOM: The sea caused his dizziness, but the fear was caused by the wind. The sea was the greater threat, the wind the less. As Peter was struggling with the sea, he was on the point of suffer-

ing more anxiety from the violence of the wind. Such is human nature that we so often feel exposed to the lesser danger but experience it as the greater. THE GOSPEL OF MATTHEW, HOMILY 50.2.[23]

PETER BEGAN TO SINK. HILARY OF POITIERS: The fact that out of all those in the boat, only Peter speaks up and asks that he be ordered to come to the Lord on the water demonstrates the force of his will at the time of the Passion. Then coming back alone and following the Lord's footsteps, with contempt for the turmoil of the world as of the sea, Peter is attended by strength equal to disdaining death itself. His timidity, however, gives an inkling of his weakness in the face of future temptation. For though he ventured forth, he began to sink. Through the feebleness of the flesh and the fear of death, he is brought to the point of denial. But he cries out and asks the Lord to save him. That cry is the groan of his repentance. Though the Lord did not yet suffer, Peter has recourse to confession and in due course receives forgiveness for his denial. Christ was then about to suffer for the redemption of all people. ON MATTHEW 14.15.[24]

14:31 Jesus Rescues Peter

JESUS REACHED OUT HIS HAND. AUGUSTINE: While human praise does not tempt the Lord, people are often ruffled and nearly entranced by human praise and honors in the church. Peter was afraid on the sea, terrified by the great force of the storm. Indeed, who does not fear that voice: "Those who say you are happy place you in error and disturb the path of your feet"?[25] And since the soul struggles against the desire for human praise, it is good for it to turn to prayer and petition amid such danger, lest one who is charmed by praise be overcome by criti-

---

[18]CCL 77:125. [19]Ps 45:13 (44:13 LXX). [20]PL 38:418; NPNF 1 6:339 (Sermon 25). [21]Jn 6:21. [22]PG 58:506; NPNF 1 10:311. [23]PG 58:506; NPNF 1 10:311. [24]SC 258:28-30. [25]Is 3:12, Vulgate.

cism and reproach. Let Peter, about to sink in the waves, cry out and say, "Lord, save me!" The Lord reached out his hand. He chided Peter, saying, "O man of little faith, why did you doubt?"—that is, why did you not, gazing straight at the Lord as you approached, pride yourself only in him? Nevertheless he snatched Peter from the waves and did not allow him who was declaring his weakness and asking the Lord for help to perish. SERMON 75.10.[26]

14:32 The Wind Ceased

PEACE RESTORED. HILARY OF POITIERS: Once he got into the vessel, the wind and the sea calmed down. After the return of eternal splendor, peace and tranquility are in store for the church. And with his arrival made manifest, with great wonder they will all exclaim, "Truly you are the Son of God." All people will then declare absolutely and publicly that the Son of God has restored peace to the church, not in physical lowliness but in heavenly glory. ON MATTHEW 4.18.[27]

14:33 Worshiping the Son of God

THEY WORSHIPED HIM. CHROMATIUS: In the face of the storm the Lord got into the boat and the wind ceased. Those who were in the boat came and worshiped him. This signifies that Our Lord and Savior, once the storm of persecution had passed, would come again in the last days to his disciples and his church. For this he made holy Peter the first of the apostles and commended his sheep to him, saying, "Feed my sheep."[28] When the apostles in the church of believers, positioned in the vessel as it were, beheld the glory of the Lord's resurrection, adoring our Lord and Savior, they declared to the human race that he was truly the Son of God. TRACTATE ON MATTHEW 52.8.[29]

THE SON OF GOD. CHRYSOSTOM: Do you see how by degrees Jesus was leading them all higher and higher? For by his walking on the sea, and by his commanding another to do so and by preserving Peter in jeopardy, their faith was henceforth great. On that occasion he rebuked the sea. But now he is not rebuking the sea, but in another sense his power is still being abundantly demonstrated. For this reason the believers worship him and say, "Truly you are the Son of God." Did Jesus refuse to accept this confession? No, on the contrary, he rather confirmed what they said and with even greater authority healed such as approached him. THE GOSPEL OF MATTHEW, HOMILY 50.2.[30]

14:34-35 Bringing the Sick

THEY BROUGHT HIM ALL WHO WERE SICK. CHRYSOSTOM: For neither did they approach him as before, dragging him into their houses and seeking a touch from his hand and directions from him in words. But now in a far higher pattern, and with greater self-denial and with a more abundant faith, they tried to win themselves a cure. By now the woman who had the issue of blood[31] had taught them all to be constrained in seeking wisdom. And the Evangelist, also implying that at long intervals Jesus visited the various neighborhoods, said, "When the men of that place recognized him, they sent round to all that region and brought to him all that were sick." Far from abolishing their faith, this interval of miracles had made it even greater and preserved it vigorously. THE GOSPEL OF MATTHEW, HOMILY 50.2.[32]

14:36 Touching His Garment

THE FRINGE OF HIS GARMENT. HILARY OF POITIERS: Many things came in the way that, after the gathering of five thousand men who were filled to satiety, dampened our effort to

---

[26]PL 38:478-79; NPNF 1 6:339 (Sermon 25). [27]SC 258:32. [28]Jn 21:17. [29]CCL 9a:459. [30]PG 58:506-7; NPNF 1 10:312. [31]The reference to the hemorrhaging woman (Mt 9:20) was suggested by the detail of the touching of Jesus' robes, common to both episodes. [32]PG 58:507; NPNF 1 10:312.

give a proper account. Our understanding on this point, however, remains the same. The time of the law was over, and five thousand men were brought into the church from Israel.[33] The believing people now hastened from the law, saved through their faith. They offered to God the remaining persons among them who were feeble and ill. These offered persons wanted to touch the hem of his garment to be made whole through faith. As from the hem of the entire garment, the whole power of the Holy Spirit came forth from our Lord Jesus Christ. This power was given to the apostles, who were also going out as it were from the same body, and it afforded healing to those who wished to touch the garment. On Matthew 14.19.[34]

[33]Acts 4:4. [34]SC 258:32.

15:1-9 THE TEACHERS FROM JERUSALEM

[1]Then Pharisees and scribes came to Jesus from Jerusalem and said, [2]"Why do your disciples transgress the tradition of the elders? For they do not wash their hands when they eat." [3]He answered them, "And why do you transgress the commandment of God for the sake of your tradition? [4]For God commanded, 'Honor your father and your mother,' and, 'He who speaks evil of father or mother, let him surely die.' [5]But you say, 'If any one tells his father or his mother, What you would have gained from me is given to God,[o] he need not honor his father.' [6]So, for the sake of your tradition, you have made void the word[p] of God. [7]You hypocrites! Well did Isaiah prophesy of you, when he said:

[8]'This people honors me with their lips,
but their heart is far from me;
[9]in vain do they worship me,
teaching as doctrines the precepts of men.' "

o Or an offering   p Other ancient authorities read law

Overview: The motive of the scribes was their fear that someone might take away their power. They wanted others to be afraid of them (Chrysostom). Keeping food laws is not as important as guarding our speech (Origen). God is less concerned with whether people wash hands ceremonially than whether they have kept their hearts washed and their consciences clean from evil. People are defiled not from the food that enters their mouths but from the perverse thoughts of their minds that proceed from their hearts (Chromatius). Blindness can symbolize a lack of proper understanding about the teaching of the gospel. Persons who lack such an understanding should not be followed (Origen). Erroneous teachings will be uprooted, even though they may extend their branches of infidelity for a short season (Chromatius). The disciples were piously disregarding a tradition of the elders so as not to transgress a commandment of God (Origen).

15:1 *The Scribes and Pharisees*

THE SCRIBES CAME FROM JERUSALEM. ORIGEN: Pharisees and scribes came to him from Jerusalem. They did not come because they were amazed at the power in Jesus that healed people even if they "only touched the edge of his cloak."[1] Instead, they came with a faultfinding attitude and brought an accusation before the teacher. The accusation did not concern the transgression of a commandment of God but rather the transgression of one tradition of the Jewish elders. Probably the charge of the faultfinders itself displays the piety of the disciples of Jesus, because they offered no grounds at all for criticism by the Pharisees and scribes in regard to transgressing the commandments of God. The Pharisees and scribes would not have brought the charge of transgressing the commandment of the elders against the disciples of Jesus if, indeed, they were able to get a firm hold on the ones who were being accused and were able to show that they were transgressing a commandment of God. COMMENTARY ON MATTHEW 11.8.[2]

WHEN AND WHERE. CHRYSOSTOM: It says that the Pharisees and scribes came to him "then." When? When he had worked thousands of signs, when he had healed the sick with the touch of his tassel.[3] It is for this reason that the Evangelist indicates the time, so that he might show that their unspeakable wickedness is second to none. But what is intended by the phrase "the scribes and Pharisees from Jerusalem"? They were scattered everywhere throughout the tribes and were divided into twelve parts. But the ones who were in charge of the mother city were more wicked than the others, because they enjoyed more honor and had become extremely arrogant. THE GOSPEL OF MATTHEW, HOMILY 51.1.[4]

15:2 *The Traditions of the Elders*

WHY TRANSGRESS THE TRADITION? CHRYSOSTOM: Now consider with me how they are convicted even by the very act of asking the question. For they do not say, "Why do they transgress the law of Moses?" Instead they say, "Why do they transgress the tradition of the elders?" From this it is clear that the priests were instituting many new practices, even though Moses with great fear and with dreadful words had commanded that one should neither add nor take away anything. For he says, "Do not add to this word that I am commanding you today, and do not take away from it."[5] But this did not at all stop them from instituting new practices. The issue here provides an example: eating with unwashed hands, which they thought unlawful. They focused inordinately on the outward rites of washing cups and things made of bronze and the rules for washing themselves. By this time they should have been released from needless observances. God's timing had moved forward to that point. But just at that point they bound people up with many more observances. Why did they turn things upside down? Because they were afraid that someone might take away their power. They wanted others to be more afraid of them. They themselves had become the lawgivers. The issue of transgressing the traditions of the elders had gotten so inverted that they were insisting that their own commandments be kept even if God's commandment was violated. They exercised so much obsessive control that the issue finally became a matter of formal legal accusation. But the indictment would instead fall against them in two ways. They themselves were instituting new practices and were devising punishments in regard to their own observances while placing no value on those instituted by God. THE GOSPEL OF MATTHEW, HOMILY 51.1.[6]

---

[1]Mt 9:20; 14:36. [2]GCS 40:46; ANF 9:437. [3]Cf. Mt 9:20; 14:36. The Greek word for the edge of the cloak sometimes refers to the tassel attached to the clothing when the word is used in the plural; cf. Num 15:38-41; Deut 22:12; Mt 23:5. But in this verse the word is used in the singular. So it probably refers only to the hemmed border of the cloth. [4]PG 58:509-10; NPNF 1 10:314. [5]Cf. Deut 4:2; 13:1, neither of which gives exactly the form of the quotation here. [6]PG 58:509-10; NPNF 1 10:314-15.

They Do Not Wash Their Hands. Chromatius: Among other observations, some of the Jewish elders ruled that a person should not take or eat food unless he first washed his hands. This observation, however, reveals a particular custom that is human and produces no beneficial effect. Therefore this tradition of the elders is practically useless, for it does not benefit a person's health. No justification is gained from this tradition, and no harm is done in disregarding it. For God is not concerned whether a man washes his hands before eating but whether he has kept his heart washed and his conscience clean from the filth of sin. Truly, what good is it to wash your hands and to have a defiled conscience? The Lord's disciples were clean of heart and were guided by an untainted conscience. Hence they were not overly concerned with washing their hands. They had washed them once in baptism with their whole body, in accord with our Lord's words to Peter: "He who has bathed needs only to wash, and he is clean all over, as you are clean."[7] Tractate on Matthew 53.1.[8]

15:3-4 Transgressing the Commandment of God

Why Do You Transgress the Command of God? Origen: The Savior summarized and explained two commandments of the law, one from the Decalogue in Exodus, the other from Leviticus or one of the other books in the Pentateuch.[9] We have already described how they set aside the word of God that says, "Honor your father and your mother." They say, "One should not honor one's father or mother if one has said to one's father or mother, 'Anything by which you might have derived benefit from me has been dedicated as a gift to God.'" But now someone might ask, Is not the next statement just an unrelated addition when it says, "Let the one who speaks maliciously against one's father or mother die under the death penalty. For it may be granted that one does not honor one's father and mother when one has dedicated by the formula called Corban the things that would be given for the honor of father and mother"?[10] But how does the tradition of the Pharisees also set aside the statement, "Let the one who speaks maliciously against one's father or mother die under the death penalty"? Perhaps the answer is that it is just as if one was heaping malicious accusations on one's father or mother if one has said to them, "Anything by which you might have derived benefit from me has been dedicated as a gift to God." It is as if one is saying that the parents are temple robbers if they receive the things dedicated by the Corban formula from the one who has dedicated them by that formula. For this reason if any person's sons say, "Anything by which you might have derived benefit from me has been dedicated as a gift to God," Jews punish them as the law demands as if they were speaking maliciously against their father or mother. But you, Jesus says, are setting aside two commandments of God by your one tradition. Then you are not even ashamed when you accuse my disciples when they are not transgressing any commandment. For they were walking blamelessly in all the commandments and ordinances.[11] Commentary on Matthew 11.10.[12]

15:5-6 Making Void the Word of God

Mistaken Ends. Theodore of Mopsuestia: The scribes were entirely preoccupied with

---

[7]Jn 13:10. [8]CCL 9a:461. [9]The first is from Ex 20:12 and Deut 5:16. The second is from Ex 21:17. The wording in Lev 20:9 is slightly different. [10]Jews often introduced a vow by the formula *Corban* ("I hereby dedicate the following to God as a gift"). The word *Corban* is not found in Matthew's version of this saying. It is derived from Mark's version (Mk 7:11). Origen's use of Mark's version may be explained if Origen is relying partly on memory at this point. But it may also indicate Origen's use of the Diatessaron, an ancient harmony of the Gospels that included quotations from all four Gospels. The Hebrew word *Corban* (and its Aramaic cognate) referred to a gift or offering dedicated to God for use in the temple or in other religious service. The word was used as a formula for making a strong vow. [11]Lk 1:6. [12]GCS 40:50; ANF 9:439.

something else. The Lord instead was teaching them to take care of the needs of the body, so long as they were encouraged to cultivate virtue. When the Pharisees observed his disciples unconcerned about washing, they censured him on the grounds that he had not taught them with enough care that it was a matter of utmost importance that they not eat what they had not washed. What reply, then, does the Lord make to this? "Why do you transgress the commandments of God for the sake of your tradition?" Thus he reframes the question into an even graver accusation. They had not only broken God's command but also misused it for mistaken ends. The metaphor shifts: God had commanded that parents be honored by their children. That honor was owed to them to such an extent that whichever of their children sinned stubbornly against them merely by word would be condemned.[13] "But you say, 'If any one tells his father or his mother, What you would have gained from me is given to God, he need not honor his father. You say that it is up to the children whether to honor their parents or not. You imply that a son says nothing out of bounds to a father when he says, "I will give a thank offering instead of taking care of you, my own father, and no further care is to be taken of you."[14] In this way, by your own peculiar traditions, you yourselves are dishonoring the gifts of almighty God. Fragment 79.[15]

15:7-8 Hearts Far from God

Their Heart Is Far from Me. Origen: I have previously quoted[16] some of the words of Isaiah that precede the verse quoted in the Gospel and some of the words that follow the verse quoted in the Gospel.[17] In this way we may show the way in which the word promises that it will close "the eyes" of those of the people who were "out of their senses" and "drunken" and who had been given to drink a "spirit of stupefaction." The word also promises to "close the eyes both of their prophets and their rulers" who claim to

"see the hidden things."

I suppose that these very things happened after the Savior had dwelt with these people. For "all the words," the words of the Scriptures in their entirety and also those of Isaiah, became to them "as the words of a sealed book." Now the word *sealed* was said as if the book was sealed with obscurity and not opened with clarity. The book is unclear to those who right from the start are "not able to read it" simply because "they are illiterate." It is also equally unclear to "those who are literate" because they do not understand the meaning in the things that have been written.

Hence the word rightly adds to these things that the people would "fall into unconsciousness" because of their sins and would be "out of their senses" with madness against the word.[18] The word also adds that the people would "be drunk" against it "with a spirit of stupefaction." The Lord would give them this "spirit of stupefaction" to drink when he "closed their eyes," because they were unworthy of seeing. This would happen to the eyes of "both their prophets and their rulers" that claimed to "see the hidden things" of the mysteries in the divine Scriptures. The word says that when all these things had happened and when their eyes had been closed, then the prophetic words[19] would be sealed and concealed from them. This is exactly what the people experienced along with those who did not believe in Jesus as Messiah. Commentary on Matthew 11.11.[20]

15:9 Teaching Human Precepts

---

[13]Deut 21:18-21. [14]On Corban see p. 18 n. 10. [15]*MKGK* 124-25. [16]Consult Is 29 in more detail to make the connection between what Origen says and what Matthew says. [17]Mt 15:8-9 is a quotation from Is 29:13. Origen argues, however, that all of the words in Is 29:9-14 apply to the people Jesus was addressing, not just what Isaiah said in Is 29:13. These allusions are to Is 29:9-14. [18]The phrase is literally either "with madness against it" or "with madness against him." The pronoun could be either "it" (the word) or "him" (Jesus). The same ambiguity applies in the next sentence when it refers to being drunk "against it" or "against him." The previous lines refer to "the book" and the following lines refer to the "Scriptures" and the "prophetic words." [19]Is 29:11. [20]GCS 40:51; ANF 9:439-40.

In Vain Do They Worship Me. Chrysostom: Did you notice that prophecy agrees exactly with what was said here and that it long ago predicted their evil? For this very thing with which the Messiah now indicts them was also said long ago by Isaiah. Isaiah said that they despise the things of God: "They worship me in vain."[21] But Isaiah also said that they place great value on their own concerns: "They teach as commandments the teachings of human beings."[22] Therefore, it was on reasonable grounds that the disciples did not keep these teachings. Jesus thus strikes them with a mortal blow. He does this on the basis of the circumstances, on the basis of their own covenant to which they had consented, and on the basis of the prophet who had intensified the grounds of the accusation. He does not talk with the scribes at all because they had ceased to accept any more correction. Instead, he directed his message to the crowds so that he could introduce doctrine that is high and great and full of philosophical insight. He took this as his starting point and finally wove in that which was greater, even throwing out the observance of kinds of food. But note when in the sequence of events this happens. When he has cleansed the leper; when he has nullified the Sabbath; when he has displayed himself as king of land and sea; when he has instituted laws; when he has forgiven sins; when he has raised dead people; when he has supplied them with many examples of his deity. It is then that he talks with them about food laws. For all of Judaism is held together by this; and if you take this away, you also have taken away the whole thing. The Gospel of Matthew, Homily 51.2-3.[23]

---

[21]Jesus quoted Is 29:13 in Mt 15:8-9. But the full significance of this quotation can best be understood by referring to the entire context of the verse from Isaiah rather than just the verse itself. [22]Chrysostom follows a word order with a slightly different meaning from what is found in either Mt 15:9 or Is 29:13. [23]PG 58:512-13; NPNF 1 10:316. This quotation from Chrysostom is highly instructive because it epitomizes a number of key points that early developed into what later became "Christian" anti-Semitism (a phrase that should have been an oxymoron): a claim that the Israelite prophets foretold the demise of Jewish tradition; the transformation of the internal Jewish debate between Jesus and his opponents into a debate between Gentile Christians and Judaism as a whole; the image of a non-Jewish Jesus who rejects Judaism and Jewish tradition; the notion that Jews were so incorrigible that they and their belief system had to be eliminated and replaced; the legitimation of vituperation and hostility toward Jews.

15:10-20 THE THINGS THAT MAKE A PERSON UNCLEAN

[10]*And he called the people to him and said to them, "Hear and understand:* [11]*not what goes into the mouth defiles a man, but what comes out of the mouth, this defiles a man."* [12]*Then the disciples came and said to him, "Do you know that the Pharisees were offended when they heard this saying?"* [13]*He answered, "Every plant which my heavenly Father has not planted will be rooted up.* [14]*Let them alone; they are blind guides. And if a blind man leads a blind man, both will fall into a pit."* [15]*But Peter said to him, "Explain the parable to us."* [16]*And he said, "Are you also still without understanding?* [17]*Do you not see that whatever goes into the mouth passes into the stomach, and so passes on?*[q] [18]*But what comes out of the mouth proceeds from the heart, and*

this defiles a man. ¹⁹For out of the heart come evil thoughts, murder, adultery, fornication, theft, false witness, slander. ²⁰These are what defile a man; but to eat with unwashed hands does not defile a man."

q Or *is evacuated*

OVERVIEW: Wash yourself to what degree is fitting, but above all wash with virtues and not with water only (CHRYSOSTOM). Food cannot defile a person. It also cannot make a person holy. Thus eating the bread of the Lord's Supper cannot in itself make a person holy. In addition, evil actions themselves defile a person only because they share in the defilement produced by evil thoughts. The real source of actions that defile a person is the heart, where the evil thoughts begin that lead to evil acts (ORIGEN). Jesus teaches that there is a difference between what proceeds from the heart and what proceeds from the stomach: one remains; the other does not (CHRYSOSTOM). That which does not reach to the heart is not able to cause the person to become unclean (CYRIL OF ALEXANDRIA). The food laws were given to curb immoderate appetites so that the people of God might be more easily disciplined (CHROMATIUS). The soul or principle of action is not according to Plato in the brain but according to Christ in the heart. We should repudiate those who believe that thoughts are introduced by the devil and do not originate from our own will (JEROME).

15:10 Hearing and Understanding

HE CALLED THE PEOPLE TO HIM. CHRYSOSTOM: He does not simply reveal to them what he has to say but first makes his message easy to receive by respect and courtesy. For the Evangelist showed this when he said, "Jesus called the crowd to himself." Then he also makes his message easy to receive by its timing. For it comes after the rebuttal of his critics, his victory over them and the accusation cited from the prophet. It is then that he begins the process of instituting a law, when the things that he is saying were

even more easily accepted.

In addition, he does not simply call them to himself but also makes them more attentive. For he says, "Take notice," that is, "Start thinking, wake up." For the law he was about to enact was such that it required attention. "For you listened when the Pharisees and scribes from Jerusalem nullified the law because of their own tradition and at the wrong time. Since this is so, much more should you listen to me as I lead you into a greater philosophy at the appropriate time."

He also did not say, "The observance of food laws is nothing," or "Moses did a poor job of making laws," or "Moses only made these laws as a way of coming down to your level." Instead, he speaks to them on the level of advice and counsel and took the testimony of natural phenomena. He does this when he says, "Not what goes into the mouth defiles a man, but what comes out of the mouth, this defiles a man." In this statement he appeals to nature itself both in the process of instituting law and in the process of revealing what he has to say. THE GOSPEL OF MATTHEW, HOMILY 51.3.[1]

15:11 What Comes Out of the Mouth

NOT WHAT ENTERS INTO THE MOUTH MAKES ONE HOLY. ORIGEN: Now anyone who has come to this place in the text can agree that it is "not what goes into the mouth that defiles a man, but what comes out of the mouth, this defiles a man," even if it is considered to be defiling by Jews. In exactly the same way it is "not what enters into the mouth" that makes the person holy. This is so even if that which is called the bread of the Lord is considered to

[1]PG 58:513; NPNF 1 10:316-17.

make the person holy by some of the more impeccable disciples. The two cases are similar. It is not the food but the conscience of the one who eats with doubt about its propriety that defiles the person who has eaten. For "the one who doubts is condemned if one eats, because one is not eating from faith."[2] It is also like the case in which "nothing is pure to the one who is defiled and unbelieving."[3] The thing involved is impure not because of itself but because of the person's defilement and unbelief. In the same way, that which is "made holy through the word of God and prayer" does not on its own account make the one who uses it holy.[4] For if it did, it would also make holy the one who eats of the Lord "in an unworthy manner" and no one would become "weak" or "sickly" or would "sleep" because of this food. For this is what Paul showed in the statement, "Because of this many among you are weak and sickly and a significant number are falling asleep."[5] Therefore, in the case of the bread of the Lord, the one who uses it derives benefit when one shares in the bread with a mind that is undefiled and a conscience that is pure. COMMENTARY ON MATTHEW 11.14-15.[6]

THE SPRING OF SINS. ORIGEN: We are accused by the Jews and Ebionites[7] of being violators of the laws that we read in Leviticus and Deuteronomy concerning clean and unclean food. But by means of what is said in this passage we are clearly taught by the Savior not to think that the simple meaning of these laws is the aim intended in the Scripture. For Jesus says, "Not that which enters into the mouth defiles a person but that which comes out of the mouth." Especially significant is what is said in the Gospel of Mark: "Thus he declared all foods clean."[8] Since all this is so, it is obvious that we are not defiled when we eat things that are said to be unclean by Jews, who want to serve the letter of the law. Instead, we are defiled when we say whatever happens to be on our mind and we talk about things that we should not talk about, even though our lips

should be bound "with perception" and we should make for them "a measuring balance and a standard of measure." The spring of sins comes to us from such talking. COMMENTARY ON MATTHEW 11.12.[9]

FOOD AS SUCH DOES NOT DEFILE. CHROMATIUS: The Lord wanted to show up the uncalled-for offense taken by the scribes and the Pharisees about unwashed hands. So he beckoned the crowd to him and said, "What goes into the mouth does not defile a man; but that which comes out of the mouth, that defiles a man." He explained that a man is defiled not from the food that enters his mouth but from the perverse thoughts of his mind, which proceed from his heart. For the food we receive for eating was created and blessed by God to sustain human life. So, it cannot defile a man. Indeed, wicked and perverse thoughts that proceed from the heart, as the Lord himself noted—"murder, adultery, fornication, theft, false witness, blasphemy,"[10] the author of which is the devil—these are the things that really defile a man. TRACTATE ON MATTHEW 53.2.[11]

15:12 Offending the Pharisees

THE PHARISEES WERE OFFENDED. CHRYSOSTOM: The disciples were saying these things not only because they felt pain on behalf of the Pharisees but also because they themselves were a little confused. But since they did not dare to say this out of concern for their own confusion, they hoped to learn further by listening to Jesus' own elaboration of this issue. To show that this is so, listen to what is said after these things by Peter, who was hotheaded and everywhere arriving before the rest. He says, "Explain this para-

---

[2]Rom 14:23. [3]Tit 1:15. [4]1 Tim 4:5 (cf. 1 Tim 4:3-5). [5]1 Cor 11:30. [6]GCS 40:57-58; ANF 9:443. [7]Christians of strongly Jewish tendencies. From the end of the second century they were considered heretics. [8]Mk 7:19. [9]GCS 40:52-53; ANF 9:440. [10]Mt 15:19. [11]CCL 9a:463.

ble to us."[12] By this he reveals the confusion in his soul. He does not dare to say openly, "I take offense at this," but he expects that he will be released from his confusion by the interpretation of the parable. So he too was rebuked. THE GOSPEL OF MATTHEW, HOMILY 51.4.[13]

15:13 Rooting Up What God Has Not Planted

THEIR OWN PRECEPTS. CHROMATIUS: Since the scribes and Pharisees had burst forth in great arrogance and transgressed the divine law, they "planted" their own precepts but not God's. They wanted these to be observed as divine law. So, not without good reason, did they too, with this planting of their own doctrine, deserve to be uprooted by the Lord. And so the Lord said, "Every plant that my heavenly Father has not planted will be rooted up." Indeed, that plant was not of God but of people. Any iniquitous plant, not only of the scribes and Pharisees but also of all heretics, shall be uprooted by the Lord. Though it may extend its branches of infidelity in due season, it cannot be firmly rooted, for such a plant is not of God but of the devil. Furthermore, it must be uprooted and consigned to perpetual fire, since it yields no fruit of faith and wholesomeness. TRACTATE ON MATTHEW 53.7.[14]

GOD'S PLANTINGS. CHRYSOSTOM: Why therefore does Messiah say, "Every plant that my heavenly Father did not plant will be uprooted"? Those who are diseased with the ideas of the Manichaeans say that this was said about the law.[15] But what Jesus had said before this shuts their mouths. For if he were speaking about the law, why did he earlier make a defense on its behalf and fight for it when he said, "Why are you transgressing the commandment of God because of your tradition?" And why does he bring in the prophet [Isaiah] in front of everyone?[16] Contrary to what the Manichaeans say, Jesus says these things about the Pharisees

themselves and their traditions. For God said, "Honor your father and your mother." This statement from God surely is a plant of God.[17] THE GOSPEL OF MATTHEW, HOMILY 51.4.[18]

GOD GIVES GROWTH TO HIS PLANTINGS. JEROME: Even what seems to be clear in the Scriptures presents many problems. Christ said, "Every plant that my heavenly Father has not planted will be uprooted." Does this mean, therefore, that there will be uprooted also that plant which the apostle speaks of when Paul says, "I have planted, Apollos watered"? The problem is solved, however, from the words that follow: "But God has given the growth."[19] He also says, "You are God's field, God's building."[20] And in another place we read, "We are God's coworkers";[21] therefore, if we are his coworkers, with Paul planting and Apollos watering, God plants and waters with his workers. COMMENTARY ON MATTHEW 2.15.13.[22]

15:14 Blind Guides

BLIND LEADERS OF THE BLIND. ORIGEN: "They are blind guides of blind people." Who are these blind guides? The Pharisees, whose minds "the god of this age has blinded" because they are "unbelieving," since they did not believe

---

[12]The statement that Jesus makes in Mt 15:11 is not what the modern reader may think of as a parable. But the word *parable* did not just apply to short illustrations like those found in Mt 13. It also referred to any wise saying, example or proverb by which a point was taught. [13]PG 58:514; NPNF 1 10:317. [14]CCL 9a:467. [15]The Manichaeans were the followers of a teacher named Mani (216-276 A.D.). Mani and his followers believed that the world was radically divided into two independent principles of light and darkness. Mani taught that the good God was characterized by light, while the material world was inherently dark and corrupt. Mani believed that Jesus and other teachers came to release souls of light from prison in material bodies. Because so many of the Old Testament laws concerned physical practices, Mani believed that the Old Testament laws were the product of the forces of darkness. Thus the Manichaeans believed that Jesus and other teachers taught that the Old Testament law was "a plant that the heavenly Father would uproot." [16]This refers to the quote from Is 29:13 in Mt 15:8-9. [17]Ex 20:12; Deut 5:16. [18]PG 58:515; NPNF 1 10:317-18. [19]1 Cor 3:7. [20]1 Cor 3:9. [21]1 Cor 3:9. [22]CCL 77:130.

in Jesus Christ. The god of this age has blinded them "so that the light of the gospel of the glory of God in the face of Christ would not shine on them."[23] We ought to avoid being guided by those blind persons. Not only should we do this, but we certainly should also listen with caution in the case of those who claim to lead in the way of healthy teaching and ought to apply healthy judgment to what they say. We should do these things so that we ourselves do not appear to be blind because we do not see the meaning of the Scriptures. We would become blind like this if we were guided by the ignorance of people who are blind and people who do not perceive the issues of healthy teaching. If we were led by such people, both the one who leads and the one who is led would fall into the pit.[24] COMMENTARY ON MATTHEW 11.14.[25]

LET THEM ALONE. CHROMATIUS: He then goes on to say, "Let them alone; they are blind guides of blind men. But if a blind man guide a blind man, both fall into a pit." These words were intended to expose the scribes and Pharisees, who were blinded by the error of their unbelief. Not only were they unable to recognize the light of truth—not believing in Christ—but also they were attracting others into the pit of death. Nevertheless the words also apply to heretics.[26] Denying that Christ is the "true light from true light, and God from God,"[27] they too were steeped in blindness. Because of their perverse doctrine, they also proved to be guides and leaders to those adrift. TRACTATE ON MATTHEW 53.8.[28]

15:15-16 Still Without Understanding

WITHOUT UNDERSTANDING. CYRIL OF ALEXANDRIA: "Without understanding" is what the Lord calls those who, like the Pharisees, make a fuss about external matters and have not yet discovered the inner life. Meats, therefore, he says, have to do with filling up the body, but they do not reach into the heart. But that which does

not reach to the heart is not able to defile the faithful [genuine] man or cause him to become unclean. FRAGMENT 185.[29]

15:17 What Passes On

WHY FOOD LAWS WERE GIVEN. CHROMATIUS: The Pharisees, as Peter made clear, begrudgingly grasped the dictum of the Lord which says, "It is not what enters the mouth that defiles a man." God indicated through Moses long ago that not everything about the use of food must be considered clean. He declared that certain things were clean and other things were unclean. But now we must ask why God prohibited the people long ago to eat these things. Since all things created by God to be used as human food were blessed at the very beginning and they remain no less so by their very nature, why is it that divine law later prescribed to the Jewish people certain things as lawful for eating because they were clean and certain things as unlawful because they were unclean? First, precepts of this type were given by the Lord because of the dissipation and immoderate appetite of the people. For since they were overly concerned with eating and drinking, these people began to overlook God's precepts. They made for themselves a molten calf in Horeb, about which it was written, "The people sat

---

[23]2 Cor 4:4. [24]In some translations the Greek word used here is translated "ditch," but the word is a generic word for any deep pit or hole. The word usually referred to wells or cisterns dug to collect rainwater. Often these pits were cut deep into solid rock. Wells and cisterns were typically at least as deep as 13 feet, and many were two or three times this deep. From the wide bottom the sides often gradually sloped closer together like the sides of a bottle as one moved upward. The opening at the surface of the ground was often only a couple of feet wide. Channels cut in the rock at the surface of the ground directed water into the cistern in the winter, and the small opening prevented evaporation in the summer. If the cistern was not covered or marked properly, the small opening that appeared on the surface of the ground created a hazard that might go unnoticed even by someone who could see (cf. Jer 38:6). [25]GCS 40:56; ANF 9:442. [26]Chromatius had in mind the Arians, reflecting analogically from his time to the time of Matthew. [27]Nicean-Constantinopolitan Creed. [28]CCL 9a:467. [29]MKGK 213-14.

down to eat and drink and rose up to play."[30] Those necessary things were forbidden by the Lord, so that with the best food having been denied and their immoderate appetites mortified, the people might abide more easily by the discipline of divine observance. It was only after their disobedience with the molten calf that we find those things were prohibited. Concerning them, as though to rebuke this stiff-necked people, the Lord made a mild and merciful pronouncement: "They shall be unclean to you." Not that they are in themselves unclean, but "shall be." Nor did he say "to all" but "to you." He thus made it clear that neither were they unclean nor would they be unclean to people other than themselves. And certainly they deserved this prohibition of many foods, for these people preferred the meats of Egypt, as well as cucumbers and muskmelons, to heavenly manna. TRACTATE ON MATTHEW 53.3.[31]

15:18 What Proceeds from the Heart

THE STOMACH COMPARED WITH THE HEART. CHRYSOSTOM: Note how sharply he deals with them and how he delivers his rebuke. He rebukes with a view to their cure. He appeals to our common human nature when he says, "Whatever goes into the mouth passes into the stomach, and so passes on." Even if it did abide for a while, it would not make one unclean. Yet they were not able to hear this. Because of this the lawgiver allows just so much time for the law to have effect. After it has gone through one's system, it is dispelled. At evening he asks you to wash yourself and so be clean. The time of digesting and excreting is a limited time. But in matters of the heart, they abide within. He is not making a refutation of the goodness of the nature of things. Rather, Jesus is speaking of the difference between what proceeds from the stomach and what proceeds from the heart. One does not remain; the other does. One enters in from the outside. The other goes out from the inside, and having gone forth it may defile, and

the more it goes out the more it defiles. They were not yet able to be taught these things. THE GOSPEL OF MATTHEW, HOMILY 51.4.[32]

15:19 Evil Thoughts

OUT OF THE HEART. JEROME: "Out of the heart," he said, "come evil thoughts." Therefore the soul or principle of action is not in the brain according to Plato but in the heart according to Christ.[33] On this point, those who believe that thoughts are introduced by the devil and do not originate from our own will are to be repudiated. The devil can aid and abet evil thoughts but he cannot originate them, even though, ever lying in wait, he kindles a small spark of our thoughts with his tinder. We must not hold the opinion that the devil can also probe the depths of our heart. However, he can judge from our demeanor and gestures what we are thinking about. For example, if he sees us gazing often at a beautiful woman, he surmises that our heart has been wounded with the dart of love. COMMENTARY ON MATTHEW 2.15.19.[34]

15:20 What Defiles and What Does Not

THESE ARE WHAT DEFILE. ORIGEN: These things are what "defiles the person" when they come out from the heart and, after they have gone out from it, go through the mouth. Thus if they did not occur outside of the heart but were held by the person somewhere around the heart, not being allowed to be spoken through the mouth, they would very quickly disappear and the person would not be defiled any longer. Therefore the source and beginning of every sin is "evil reasonings." For if these reasonings did not prevail, there would be neither murders nor acts of adultery nor any other of such things.

[30]Ex 32:6. [31]CCL 9a:463-64. [32]PG 58:515-16; NPNF 1 10:318. [33]To understand this observation, one should keep in mind that contemporary schools of philosophy debated whether the rational and directive faculties of the soul resided in the brain or in the heart. [34]CCL 77:131-32.

Because of this each one ought to keep one's own heart with all watchfulness. Commentary on Matthew 11.14-15.[35]

Wash Yourself with Virtue. Chrysostom: "To eat with unwashed hands does not defile a man." Let us learn then what are the things that defile the person. Let us learn them and flee from them. For even in the church we still see such a custom prevailing among many that gives great attention to what we are wearing and whether we have our hands washed. But as to presenting a clean soul to God, they make no account. I say wash to what degree is fitting, but above all wash with virtues and not with water only. No one is forbidding the washing of the hands or mouth, but the real filth of the mouth is evil speaking, blasphemy, reviling, angry words, filthy talking, inordinate laughter and immature jesting. If you are not conscious of yourself doing these things or of being defiled with this filth, then draw near with confidence. But if you have often done these things and received these stains, why do you think that washing your tongue with water is going to change anything? You labor in vain to wash it out externally, while you are still inwardly carrying such deadly and hurtful filth. The Gospel of Matthew, Homily 51.4-5.[36]

---

[35]GCS 40:57-58; ANF 9:443-44. [36]PG 58:515-16; NPNF 1 10:318-19.

15:21-28 A WOMAN'S FAITH

[21]And Jesus went away from there and withdrew to the district of Tyre and Sidon. [22]And behold, a Canaanite woman from that region came out and cried, "Have mercy on me, O Lord, Son of David; my daughter is severely possessed by a demon." [23]But he did not answer her a word. And his disciples came and begged him, saying, "Send her away, for she is crying after us." [24]He answered, "I was sent only to the lost sheep of the house of Israel." [25]But she came and knelt before him, saying, "Lord, help me." [26]And he answered, "It is not fair to take the children's bread and throw it to the dogs." [27]She said, "Yes, Lord, yet even the dogs eat the crumbs that fall from their masters' table." [28]Then Jesus answered her, "O woman, great is your faith! Be it done for you as you desire." And her daughter was healed instantly.

Overview: This woman is the mother of the Gentiles. The Lord had left Jewish territory, and the Canaanite woman had come out from her Gentile territory. He left the Jews behind, and the woman was leaving behind idolatry. What the Gentiles had lost, she found through her faith (Epiphanius the Latin). She was appealing on behalf of her daughter, who was a type for all the Gentile peoples. Since she knew the Lord from the law, she addressed him as Son of David (Hilary of Poitiers). Jesus himself opened the way for the Gentiles after nullifying the food laws that separated Jews from Gentiles. His contact with the Gentile woman was not his reason for being in the area of Tyre, but his compassionate nature prevented him from turning her away (Chrysostom). That he came first to Israel does not imply that salvation was not to be imparted also to the Gentiles (HILARY OF POITIERS). Jesus was unwilling to give his detractors an opportunity to accuse him. He was reserving a fully accomplished salvation for the Gentiles at the time of his Passion and resurrection (JEROME). He had to manifest in due sequence to Israel first, his birth, the display of miracles and then the power of his resurrection (AUGUSTINE). The Canaanite woman was in effect saying, You came to the Jews, and they didn't want you. What they turned down, give to us (EPIPHANIUS THE LATIN). He postponed giving her a reply that she might cry aloud with this word, and thereby he would show her to be worthy of a thousand crowns (THEODORE OF MOPSUESTIA). See how this woman who was a Canaanite—who came from the Gentiles and represented a type, a figure of the church—is highly praised for her humility, while others are puffed up with pride (AUGUSTINE).

15:21 Going to Tyre and Sidon

THE MOTHER OF THE GENTILES. EPIPHANIUS THE LATIN: After our Lord departed from the Jews, he came into the regions of Tyre and Sidon. He left the Jews behind and came to the Gentiles. Those whom he had left behind remained in ruin; those to whom he came obtained salvation in their alienation. And a woman came out of that territory and cried, saying to him, "Have pity on me, O Lord, Son of David!" O great mystery! The Lord came out from the Jews, and the woman came out from her Gentile territory. He left the Jews behind, and the woman left behind idolatry and an impious lifestyle. What they had lost, she found. The one whom they had denied in the law, she professed through her faith. This woman is the mother of the Gentiles, and she knew Christ through faith. Thus on behalf of her daughter (the Gentile people) she entreated the Lord. The daughter had been led astray by idolatry and sin and was severely possessed by a demon. INTERPRETATION OF THE GOSPELS 58.[1]

HE WITHDREW TO THE REGION OF TYRE AND SIDON. AUGUSTINE: She was apparently not from the people of Israel, from whom came the patriarchs, the prophets and the parents of Our Lord Jesus Christ according to the flesh; from whom came the Virgin Mary, who brought forth Christ. Clearly this woman was not from that people but from the Gentiles. For, as we read, the Lord withdrew into the regions of Tyre and Sidon; and then the Canaanite woman, having gone beyond those borders, insistently sought help to heal her daughter who was beset by the devil. Tyre and Sidon were not cities of the people of Israel but of the Gentiles, although they were close to that people. She therefore cried out, eager to get help, and kept insisting. But she was ignored, not that mercy might be denied but that desire might be enkindled; not only that desire might be enkindled but, as I said before, that humility might be praised. SERMON 77.1.[2]

15:22 A Canaanite Woman Cries Out to Jesus

THE GENTILES CRY FOR THE SON OF DAVID. HILARY OF POITIERS: To grasp the inner motive of the Canaanite woman for obtaining what came to pass, we must reflect on the impact of her words. There is a firm belief that there was and still is in Israel a community of proselytes who passed over from the Gentiles into the works of the law. They had left behind their previous life and were bonded by the religion of a foreign and dominating law as though from home. The Canaanites were inhabiting the lands of present-day Judea. Whether absorbed by war or dispersed to neighboring places or brought into servitude as a vanquished people, they carried about their name but lacked a native land. Intermingled with the Jews, therefore, these people came from the Gentiles. And since a portion of those among the crowds who believed were proselytes, this Canaanite woman most

---

[1]PL Supp 3:953. [2]PL 38:483; NPNF 1 6:342 (Sermon 27).

likely had left her territory, preferring the status of a proselyte—that is, coming out from the Gentiles to the community of a neighboring people. She was appealing on behalf of her daughter, who was a type for all the Gentile people. And since she knew the Lord from the law, she addressed him as Son of David. For in the law, the king of the eternal and heavenly kingdom is referred to as the "rod out of the stem of Jesse and the son of David."[3] This woman, who professed Christ as both Lord and Son of David, did not need any healing. Rather, she was begging for help for her daughter—that is, the Gentile people in the grips of unclean spirits. ON MATTHEW 15.3.[4]

FROM THAT REGION. CHRYSOSTOM: Mark says that Jesus was not able to escape notice after he had come into the house.[5] But why did he go away to these parts of the region at all? When he released them from the observance of food laws, then he finally also opened a door to the Gentiles as he proceeded on the road. This anticipates the similar act of Peter, who first received a command to put an end to this law and then was sent to Cornelius.[6]

But if anyone should say, "Why then does he allow this woman to approach him when he says to the disciples, 'Do not go in the way of the Gentiles'?"[7] We first note that he himself, being who he is, was not, strictly speaking, required to obey the command that he gave to the disciples. We observe, second, that Jesus was not going there to preach. This is the very point that Mark implies when he says both that Jesus hid himself and that he could not escape notice. The fact that he did not run to them first was consistent with the order of the tasks set before him. In exactly the same way, driving away people who were coming to him was unworthy of his love for humanity. For if one should pursue those who are trying to escape, much more should one not try to escape those who are pursuing. THE GOSPEL OF MATTHEW, HOMILY 52.1.[8]

15:23 Jesus Ignores the Woman

SEND HER AWAY. EPIPHANIUS THE LATIN: Therefore this woman besought the Lord on behalf of her daughter, the church of the Gentiles. "But he did not answer her a word." It was not that the Lord was unwilling to heal her but that he might reveal her great faith and humility. Then the disciples were moved to mercy and pleaded with the Lord, saying, "Send her away, for she is crying after us." But he answered and said, "I was not sent except to the lost sheep of the house of Israel." Now he said this to the crowd of Jews that they might have no excuse on the day of judgment, when they might pretend to say, "He wanted to come to the Gentiles rather than to us." INTERPRETATION OF THE GOSPELS 57.[9]

15:24 Only to the House of Israel

I WAS SENT TO ISRAEL. HILARY OF POITIERS: The Lord remains patiently silent, reserving the privilege of salvation for Israel. And the pitying disciples join in a plea. But he, holding in his hands the secret of his Father's will, answers that he was sent to the lost sheep of Israel. It thus became absolutely clear that the daughter of the Canaanite woman represented a type of the church when the woman kept asking for what was bestowed upon the others. Not that salvation was not to be imparted also to the Gentiles, but the Lord had come to his own and among his own, awaiting the first fruits of faith from those people he took his roots from. The others subsequently had to be saved by the preaching of the apostles. And so he said, "It is not fair to take the children's bread and throw it to the dogs."[10] The Gentile people are dubbed with the name of dogs. But the Canaanite woman is saved because of her faith. Certain of the inner mystery, she responds by talking about

[3]Is 11:1. [4]SC 258:36-38. [5]Mk 7:24. [6]Acts 10:1-48. [7]Mt 10:5. [8]PG 58:517-19; NPNF 1 10:321. [9]PL Supp 3:953-54. [10]Mt 15:26.

crumbs that fall from the table, to be eaten by little dogs. The disparagement of "dogs" was mitigated by the blandishment of a diminutive name. On Matthew 15.4.[11]

Unwilling to Give Detractors an Opportunity to Accuse Him. Jerome: Jesus did not say this to accord with the pride of the Pharisees or the arrogance of the scribes but lest he seem to contradict the instruction he had earlier given: "Go nowhere among the Gentiles, and enter no town of the Samaritans."[12] For he was unwilling to give his detractors an opportunity to accuse him and was reserving a fully accomplished salvation for the Gentiles at the time of his Passion and resurrection. The disciples, yet unaware of the mysteries of the Lord or having been moved to mercy, beseeched the Lord on behalf of the Canaanite woman (whom the other Evangelist calls a Syro-Phoenician). Or else they wanted to be rid of this importuning woman, for she repeatedly called upon him loudly, not as though he were a kind but an austere physician. Commentary on Matthew 2.15.23.[13]

The Lost Sheep. Augustine: A question arises here on that point: How is it that we have come from the Gentiles to the sheepfold of Christ if he was sent only to the lost sheep of the house of Israel? What is the meaning of this puzzling dispensation? The Lord knew why he came—certainly to have a church among all the Gentiles—and he yet said that he was sent only to the lost sheep of the house of Israel? We accordingly understand that he had to manifest in due sequence to that people first the presence of his body, his birth, the display of miracles and then the power of his resurrection. It had thus been predetermined from the beginning, such and such had been foretold and fulfilled, that Christ Jesus had to come to the Jewish people and to be seen and killed and to win for himself those whom he knew beforehand. The Gentiles were not to be condemned but to be winnowed

like grain. A multitude of chaff was there, the hidden dignity of grain was there, burning was to take place there, and a storehouse to be filled there. In fact, where were the apostles if not there? Where was Peter? Where were the rest? Sermon 77.2.[14]

15:25-26 Giving the Children's Bread to the Dogs

A Strange Transformation. Epiphanius the Latin: Then, in face of the Jews who were rejecting him, this Gentile woman asked him to heal her daughter. But the Lord turned a deaf ear to her. She fell down at his feet and adored him, saying, "Lord, help me." The Lord then said to her, "It is not fair to take the children's bread and throw it to the dogs." What have the Jews to say to this? Plainly he implied that they were children and called the Gentiles "dogs." The woman agreed, saying to the Savior, "Yes, Lord." That is to say, I know, Lord, that the Gentile people are dogs in worshiping idols and barking at God. "Yet even the little dogs eat the crumbs that fall from their masters' table." In other words, you came to the Jews and manifested yourself to them, and they didn't want you to make exceptions. What they rejected, give to us who are asking for it. Knowing the importunate faith of this woman, our Lord said, "O woman, your faith is great! Let it be done for you as you desire." Faith accepts what work does not merit, and through faith the Gentiles were made children out of dogs. As the Lord spoke through the prophet: "In the place where it was said to them, 'You are not my people' it shall be said to them, 'Sons of the living God.' "[15] On the other hand, the unreceptive Jews were made loathsome dogs out of children, as the Lord himself said in his Passion through the prophet: "Many dogs surround me; a company of evildoers encircle me."[16] Inter-

---

[11]SC 258:38. [12]Mt 10:5. [13]CCL 77:132-33. [14]PL 38:483; NPNF 1 6:342-43 (Sermon 27). [15]Hos 1:10. [16]Ps 22:16 (21:17 LXX).

PRETATION OF THE GOSPELS 58.[17]

15:27 Even the Dogs Eat Crumbs

CRUMBS FROM THEIR MASTERS' TABLE.
CHRYSOSTOM: See her humility as well as her
faith! For he had called the Jews "children," but
she was not satisfied with this. She even called
them "masters," so far was she from grieving at
the praises of others. She said, "Yes, Lord, yet
even the dogs eat the crumbs that fall from their
masters' table." Behold the woman's wisdom!
She did not venture so much as to say a word
against anyone else. She was not stung to see
others praised, nor was she indignant to be reproached. Behold her constancy. When he answered, "It is not fair to take the children's bread
and throw it to the dogs," she said, "Yes, Lord."
He called them "children," but she called them
"masters." He used the name of a dog, but she
described the action of the dog. Do you see this
woman's humility?

Then compare her humility with the proud
language of the Jews: "We are Abraham's seed
and were never in bondage to any man."[18] "We
are born of God."[19] But not so this woman.
Rather, she calls herself a dog and them masters.
So for this reason she became a child. For what
does Christ then say? "O woman, great is your
faith."

So we might surmise that this is the reason
he put her off, in order that he might proclaim
aloud this saying and that he might crown the
woman: "Be it done for you as you desire." This
means "Your faith, indeed, is able to effect even
greater things than these. Nevertheless be it
unto you even as you wish." This voice was at
one with the voice that said, "Let the heaven be,"
and it was.[20]

"And her daughter was made whole from that
very hour."

Do you see how this woman, too, contributed
not a little to the healing of her daughter? For
note that Christ did not say, "Let your little
daughter be made whole," but "Great is your

faith, be it done for you as you desire." These
words were not uttered at random, nor were
they flattering words, but great was the power
of her faith, and for our learning.

He left the certain test and demonstration,
however, to the issue of events. Her daughter
accordingly was immediately healed. THE GOS-
PEL OF MATTHEW, HOMILY 52.3.[21]

15:28 Be It Done As You Desire

GREAT IS YOUR FAITH. THEODORE OF MOP-
SUESTIA: Having seen her advocates unsuccess-
ful, the woman then appeals for herself and
does not stop but in effect says to the Lord,
"Help me, I haven't been asking this for my
own sake." Then the Savior in turn says, "It is
not good to take the children's bread and to cast
it to dogs." He uses the term *dog* on account of
the Gentiles' unclean lifestyle and proneness to
idolatry, while he calls the Jews children on
account of the fact that they appeared to be
devoted to God. But he uses the word *bread* not
only to speak of his teaching, which was
through words, but also of that which nourished the faithful by means of signs. But in this
case the word preceded the condemnation of
the Jews, since when life in the Lord had been
given to them as bread, they did not accept it.
The woman does not complain, even when
insulted. What does the Savior do? By his
answer, he showed what he had premeditated
from the outset. For it was for this reason that
he postponed giving a reply: that the woman
might cry aloud with this word. Thereby he
would show her to be worthy of a thousand
crowns. For it was not because he did not want
to give her the gift that he delayed but because
he sought and took care beforehand to reveal
her faith. With his accolades he honors her as
presenting a type of the church that is from the
Gentiles. Note that he did not say, "Let your

---

[17]PL Supp 3:954. [18]Jn 8:33. [19]Jn 8:41. [20]Gen 1:1. [21]PG 58:521;
NPNF 1 10:323.

child be healed," but "Be it done for you as you desire," in order to show that it was the power of her faith that elicited the healing. Even if she were worthy of even greater things, nevertheless that which she wanted was what was given to her. FRAGMENT 83.[22]

HER DAUGHTER WAS HEALED INSTANTLY. AUGUSTINE: See, brothers, how in this woman who was a Canaanite—who came from the Gentiles and represented a type (namely, a figure of the church)—how her humility is highly praised. Indeed, the Jewish people, as castigated in the Gospel, were puffed up with pride because they were chosen to receive the law, because the patriarchs proceeded from that people, the prophets appeared and God's servant Moses performed great miracles in Egypt, which we hear about in the Psalms.[23] He led the people through the Red Sea with the waters receding, and he received the law, which he gave to the same people. These were the grounds for extolling the Jewish people. Because of that pride, they were unwilling to respond to Christ the author of humility, the restrainer of swellheadedness, the physician God who, because he was God, became man that as a man he might know himself as man. What great medicine! If this medicine does not cure pride, what could possibly cure it? I do not know. God became a man. He put aside his divinity. That is to say, in a certain measure he kept out of sight—he hid what was his own, while it was evident what he had taken upon himself. He became a man, even though he is God. Yet man does not yet recognize that he is a man, that he is mortal; he does not recognize that he is weak, a sinner, sick, and that being a sick person, he should seek a physician! What is even worse, he sees himself as being healthy!

Because of this, that people did not draw near—that is, because of their pride. And they were called from the olive tree—that is, from that people begotten of the patriarchs—broken natural branches (namely, Jews by right, barren in the spirit of pride). And in that olive tree a wild olive shoot was grafted. This wild olive shoot represents the Gentile people. But the apostle says that the wild shoot was grafted into the olive tree but the natural branches were broken.[24] They were broken because of pride; the wild olive shoot was grafted in because of humility. The woman manifested this humility, saying, "Yes, Lord, I am a dog. I desire crumbs." Jesus found favor also with the centurion, who had this humility. After he asked the Lord to cure his servant, the Lord said, "I will come and cure him." He responded, "Lord, I am not worthy that you should come under my roof; but only say the word, and my servant will be healed. I am not worthy that you should come under my roof."[25] He did not receive the Lord under his roof; he received him in his heart. The more humble a person is, the more receptive and full he becomes. Hills repel water; valleys are filled up. What did the Lord reply, after the centurion said, "I am not worthy that you should enter under my roof"? He said, "Truly, I say to you, not even in Israel have I found such faith"[26]—that is, among those people to whom I have come, "I have not found such faith." What is the meaning of the word *such*? So great. In what way great? To say the least, great in humility. "I have not found such faith": like a grain of mustard seed—the smaller it is, the more potent it is. The Lord therefore grafted the wild olive shoot into the olive tree. He did this when he said, "Truly, I say to you, not even in Israel have I found such faith." SERMON 77.11-12.[27]

---

[22]*MKGK* 126-27. [23]Ps 106 (105 LXX). [24]Rom 11:17-24. [25]Mt 8:7-8. [26]Mt 8:10. [27]PL 38:487-88; NPNF 1 6:345-46 (Sermon 27).

15:29-39 JESUS HEALS AND FEEDS MANY PEOPLE

[29]*And Jesus went on from there and passed along the Sea of Galilee. And he went up on the mountain, and sat down there.* [30]*And great crowds came to him, bringing with them the lame, the maimed, the blind, the dumb, and many others, and they put them at his feet, and he healed them,* [31]*so that the throng wondered, when they saw the dumb speaking, the maimed whole, the lame walking, and the blind seeing; and they glorified the God of Israel.*

[32]*Then Jesus called his disciples to him and said, "I have compassion on the crowd, because they have been with me now three days, and have nothing to eat; and I am unwilling to send them away hungry, lest they faint on the way."* [33]*And the disciples said to him, "Where are we to get bread enough in the desert to feed so great a crowd?"* [34]*And Jesus said to them, "How many loaves have you?" They said, "Seven, and a few small fish."* [35]*And commanding the crowd to sit down on the ground,* [36]*he took the seven loaves and the fish, and having given thanks he broke them and gave them to the disciples, and the disciples gave them to the crowds.* [37]*And they all ate and were satisfied; and they took up seven baskets full of the broken pieces left over.* [38]*Those who ate were four thousand men, besides women and children.* [39]*And sending away the crowds, he got into the boat and went to the region of Magadan.*

OVERVIEW: What follows immediately after the Gentile people are prefigured in the daughter of the Canaanite woman? The crowd offers to the Lord those afflicted with different kinds of diseases. The faithless and the sick are instructed by believers to fall down and adore, and they are made well again. All the functions of mind and body are restored for hearing, gazing and praising (HILARY OF POITIERS). In the case of the Canaanite woman Jesus delayed healing in order to manifest her constancy. To the crowds he bestowed the gift immediately to stop the mouths of unbelievers and cut away every excuse (CHRYSOSTOM). Even those who simply come to the feet of Christ are healed (ORIGEN).

Jesus provides for the needs of both body and soul (THEODORE OF HERACLEA). Jesus did not feed the four thousand on the first or second day but only when all the provisions had all been consumed (CHRYSOSTOM). Lest his people weaken in the course of their workaday world, he wants now to feed them with his food and

fortify them with his mystery of his bread. In this way they can complete the formidable task of their entire journey (HILARY OF POITIERS). The Lord himself is the one who earlier had fed Israel in the desert (THEODORE OF HERACLEA). The fact that four thousand men gather together suggests a multitude of countless people from the four corners of the earth, who come to the Lord to receive the gift of heavenly food (HILARY OF POITIERS). Each one partook according to need. They did not receive food in order to take it away with them. Fragments were left as a symbol for measuring use according to need (THEODORE OF MOPSUESTIA). Significant differences remain in the various narratives of the feeding of the multitudes (ORIGEN).

15:29 Going to the Hills

JESUS WENT UP INTO THE HILLS. CHRYSOSTOM: Now he goes to the mountain awaiting those who are diseased. The lame are brought up the mountain. They are no longer merely touching the edge of his garment. They have advanced a higher step. They are being brought to his feet! Therein they are showing their faith doubly, first by struggling up the mountain even though lame, then by wanting nothing else but only to be cast at his feet. THE GOSPEL OF MATTHEW, HOMILY 52.4.[1]

15:30 Great Crowds Come to Jesus

THEY PUT THE LAME AT HIS FEET. ORIGEN: Again Jesus went up on the mountain where he sat down. Not only people who were healthy but also those suffering from various disorders went up on the mountain where Jesus was sitting. Think of this mountain to which Jesus went up and sat as the church. It has been set up through the word of God over the rest of the world, and all sorts of people come to it. To this assembly have come not only the disciples, as if they were leaving behind the multitudes, as they did in the case of the Beatitudes. Rather, there are great crowds here, many of whom are deaf or suffer from many afflictions. Look at the crowds who come to this mountain where the Son of God sits. Some of them have become deaf to the things that have been promised. Others have become blind in soul, not looking toward the true light.[2] Others are lame and not able to walk according to reason. Others are maimed and unable to work profitably. Each of these who are suffering in soul from such things go up along with the multitudes into the mountain where Jesus sits.

Some who do not draw near to the feet of Jesus are not healed. But those who are brought by the multitude and cast at his feet are being healed. Even those who come only to the edges, just the extremities of the body of Christ, who feel themselves unworthy to obtain such things, are being healed. So now you come into the congregation of what is more commonly called the church.

See the catechumens? They are, as it were,

cast in the far side or back of those who are the extreme end of the body, as if they were coming merely to the feet of the body of Jesus—the church. They are coming to it with their own deafness and blindness and lameness and crookedness. In time they will be cured according to the Word. Observing this you would not be wrong in saying that these people have gone up with the multitudes into the church, up to the mountain where Jesus sits, and have been cast at his feet and are being healed. And so the multitudes are astonished at beholding the transformations that are taking place. They behold those who are being converted from such great evils to that which is so much better. COMMENTARY ON MATTHEW 11.18.[3]

15:31 Glorifying God

FROM THE PROMISE TO THE GENTILES TO THE HEALING OF THE MULTITUDES. HILARY OF POITIERS: Remember that the context is the plea of the Canaanite woman. Remember that the Lord's silence with her had proceeded from a consideration of the gradual timing of revelation and not from any problem of her volition. So when he said, "O woman, great is your faith,"[4] she is now certain of being saved. Indeed, he also comes to the whole Gentile community, when those who accordingly believe will at once be freed like the girl from any power of the unclean spirits. And faith in the deed therefore follows. What follows immediately after the Gentile people are prefigured in the daughter of the Canaanite woman? Those afflicted with different kinds of diseases are offered by the crowd to the Lord on the mountain. That is, the faithless and the sick are instructed by the believers to fall down and adore. They are made well again, and all the functions of mind and body

---

[1]PG 58:523; NPNF 1 10:323. [2]The hermeneutic *ratio* of Origen interprets the material aspects of Jesus' life as symbolic of spiritual realities. In this sense the various diseases of the body symbolize the different sins of the soul. [3]GCS 40:65; ANF 9:447. [4]Mt 15:28.

are being restored for hearing, contemplating, praising and following the Lord. ON MATTHEW 15.5.[5]

THE REQUEST OF THE CANAANITE WOMAN AND THE HEALING OF THE CROWDS. CHRYSOSTOM: Great was the marvel and strange, to see them that were carried walking, the blind having no need for any to lead them by the hand. Yes, both the multitude of the healed and their rapid cure amazed them.

Remember how long Jesus had delayed healing the Canaanite woman. But now he heals these immediately. This is not because these are better than she; indeed, she was more faithful than they. In her case he defers and delays in order to manifest her constancy. In the case of these, he bestows the gift immediately to shut the mouths of unbelievers and cut away from them every excuse. For the greater the favors one has received, so much the more is one held accountable and liable if unresponsive. This is why we see the rich turning more wicked and being more severely punished than the poor. Why? They have not been softened, even by their prosperity. THE GOSPEL OF MATTHEW, HOMILY 52.3.[6]

THEY GLORIFIED THE GOD OF ISRAEL. CYRIL OF ALEXANDRIA: They had not yet thoroughly understood the Lord's dignity as God but supposed him to be a mere man. For this reason they offered up glory to the God of Israel. FRAGMENT 188.[7]

15:32 Lest They Faint on the Way

UNWILLING TO SEND THEM AWAY HUNGRY. THEODORE OF HERACLEA: In this way, by his speech, Christ had so disposed their souls that they had even become self-forgetful and had taken no care to provide for food or other inevitable needs. They had not grown weary, even in the desert, of being with Christ. But Christ understood the weakness of our nature and that

we require food for the health of our bodies. He makes preparation even for this, that it might be evident that he is concerned not only about our souls but about our bodies as well. For he himself is the Creator of both soul and body. He is not merely the Lord of one or the other, as the lunacies of the Manichaeans hold.[8] They teach different creators, one for the soul and another for the body. FRAGMENT 97.[9]

15:33 Finding Enough Bread

THE BREAD OF THE PASSION IS FOR GENTILES AS WELL AS JEWS. HILARY OF POITIERS: This was in response to everything that had happened before. So we must probe the corresponding reason for this entire situation and especially of the relation of Jews and Gentiles. We will then see that the promises that had earlier applied to the Jewish people were to be received by the Gentile people.

There is an order, then, in the Lord's words that holds true in the receiving of grace. Those who approach baptism declare first that they believe in the Son of God and in his Passion and resurrection; a commitment is then made to this sign of profession. In this way a certain truth about the things themselves may result from this verbal promise. Those who devote the entire time in fasting to commemorate the Lord's Passion are joined to the Lord in a sort of fellowship of compassion. Therefore both by the sign of their promise and by their fasting, they spend all the time involved in the Lord's Passion with the Lord.

Do you see the mystery? The Lord has compassion on this hopeful following of believers and says they have been with him for three days! Lest they weaken in the course of their worldly lives, in their workaday world, he wants now to

---

[5]SC 258:38-40. [6]PG 58:522; NPNF 1 10:323-24. [7]MKGK 214. [8]In the complicated Manichaean mythology, the creation of the world occurred in several stages and was the work of beings different from the supreme God of creation in the Hebrew and Christian religions. [9]MKGK 83.

feed them with his food and fortify them with his bread. In this way they can complete the formidable task of the entire journey, for the disciples were complaining that there was no bread in the desert. Indeed, they had previously imbibed the lesson that nothing is impossible with God. But what is signified by certain events can exceed the measure of our understanding. Indeed, how greatly favored the apostles were in saving Israel is told in the epistles of blessed Paul. And so, with the same devotion but now in the gathering of Gentiles, both the multiplying of bread and the silence of fasting are introduced. ON MATTHEW 15.7-9.[10]

15:34 Seven Loaves and a Few Small Fish

HOW MANY LOAVES HAVE YOU? CHRYSOSTOM: Why had he earlier said to his disciples, "Send away the multitude," but now he does not send them away, even though three days had passed? It may be that they themselves had changed and improved by this time. Or it may be that since the people were glorifying God for what had been done, they had no great sense of hunger.

Observe in this instance that he does not proceed immediately to the miracle but calls them out even into the desert. The multitudes who had come for healing were not even daring to ask for food. But he is here seen to be the benevolent and provident one who gives even to those that do not ask. He said to his disciples, "I have compassion and will not send them away hungry." And lest someone might say that they came having provisions for the way, he noted, "They have been with me now three days and have nothing to eat, so that even if some came with provision, it has by now been consumed." Therefore Jesus did not do this on the first or second day but only when everything had been entirely consumed, in order that having first been in need, they might more eagerly receive the miracle of food. He offered them compassion, saying, "Lest they faint in the way"; he implied that both the distance to food was great

and that they had nothing left. Then disciples asked, if you are not willing to send them away hungry, "Where are we to get bread enough in the desert to feed so great a crowd?" Jesus responded, in order to stimulate their faith and make them more compassionate: "How many loaves have you?" But even then they did not fully understand the motive of his question. Hence afterwards he said to them, as Mark relates, "Are your hearts so hardened? Having eyes, do you not see? Having ears, do you not hear?"[11] GOSPEL OF MATTHEW, HOMILY 53.1.[12]

15:35 The Crowd Commanded to Sit Down

DIFFERENCES BETWEEN THE NARRATIVES OF THE LOAVES AND FISHES. ORIGEN: Be attentive to the difference between those things that are written in the various places in regard to the loaves.[13] I think that this passage belongs to a different order than the others. Note the differences. Those were fed on a mountain, these in a desert place. These were fed after they had continued three days with Jesus, but those one day, on the evening of which they were fed. Is there an implication that those to whom Jesus shows kindness are superior when he fed them on the spot to demonstrate his kindness? And according to John, the twelve baskets contained leftovers of barley loaves,[14] but nothing of this kind is said here. Is one preferred to another? In the one case he healed the sick, but in this case he is healing, along with the multitudes, those who are blind, lame, deaf and maimed. Note that the four thousand marveled, but no such thing is said about the sick. And I think we can distinguish those who ate of the seven loaves, for

---

[10]SC 258:42-44. [11]Mk 8:18. [12]PG 58:525; NPNF 1 10:326-27. [13]Cf. Mt 14:13-21; Mk 6:30-44; 8:1-10; Lk 9:10-17; Jn 6:1-13. Origen interprets in an allegorical manner the two accounts of the multiplication of the loaves, finding in the seven thousand beneficiaries of the second account a superior level of perfection to the five thousand of the first; the number seven is the symbol of perfection, whereas five is the symbol of the senses (see *Matthew 1-13* [ACCS], p. 260 n. 4). To this he adds other details, which confirm this superiority. [14]Jn 6:13.

which thanks were given, from those who ate of the five loaves, which were blessed. These who ate the few little fishes are distinguished from those who ate of the two. Those who sat down upon the ground are distinguished from those who sat down on the grass. Note that those from fewer loaves left twelve baskets, but these from a greater number left seven baskets. Perhaps they were able more fully to receive. COMMENTARY ON MATTHEW 11.19.[15]

15:36 Distributing the Food

THE DISCIPLES DISTRIBUTED FOOD TO THE CROWDS. THEODORE OF MOPSUESTIA: The Lord wanted to provide by means of this food a miraculous work for the sake of their faith. This was his will and they perceived it. This is seen even in their questioning him: "Where are we to get bread enough"? Jesus wanted his disciples' souls to be exercised in believing in his divine power. It was not only with words that he taught his followers but also with deeds. He then says that he "gave them to the disciples, and the disciples gave them to the crowds." It was fitting that this should be observed both by the disciples and by the Lord. It was appropriate that the ministry should redound to the glory of those who serve, according to what pertains to the service of discipleship. The goodness shown to those who are most in need, by means of the service of the saints, is kept as though it were an individual act of obedience. Note that they partook according to their need. They did not receive food in order to take it away with them. Fragments were left, as a symbol for measuring use according to need, rather than introducing acquisitiveness that goes beyond what is needful. FRAGMENTS 86, 87.[16]

15:37 All Ate and Were Satisfied

SEVEN BASKETS. HILARY OF POITIERS: They brought forward seven loaves of bread. The Gentiles received no salvation from the law and the prophets. However, they live because of the grace of the Spirit whose sevenfold light, as noted by Isaiah, is a gift.[17] Therefore through faith in the Spirit the Gentiles receive salvation. They recline on the ground, for they were not subject to any works of the law or the flesh but were called in their earthly condition to the Spirit of the sevenfold light. The indefinite number of fish signifies the variety and dispensing of gifts and charisma, by which a diversity of graces satisfied the faith of the Gentiles. Moreover, the fact that seven baskets are filled indicates the overflowing and multiplied abundance of the Spirit of sevenfold light. What he generously gives, abounds. Having been satisfied, the gift becomes ever more richly endowed and full. The fact that four thousand men gather together refers to a multitude of countless people from the four corners of the earth. In terms of the future, a calculated number of people are satisfied in as many thousands of places as there are thousands of believers who hasten to receive the gift of heavenly food. Having been fully fed, the crowd is dismissed. And since the Lord remains with us all the days of our life, a great number of Gentile believers go on board the ship—namely, the church. ON MATTHEW 15.10.[18]

15:38-39 Four Thousand Men, Plus Women and Children

HE FED ISRAEL IN THE WILDERNESS. THEODORE OF HERACLEA: He does this not only once but also a second time, in order that we should know his strength. This strength by which he feeds the multitudes when he wishes and without bread finds its source in his divinity. He does this in order to bring them to believe that he himself is the one who earlier had fed Israel for forty years in the wilderness.[19]

---

[15]GCS 40:68; ANF 9:449. [16]MKGK 127-28. [17]Is 30:26. [18]SC 258:44-46. [19]Christ as Logos, as Son of God who preexists the incarnation, is already the divine agency of the fortunes of Israel in the Old Testament.

And Jesus not only fed them with a few loaves of bread, but he even produced a surplus of seven baskets, so that he might be shown as incomparably surpassing Elijah, who himself also caused a multiplication of the widow's small quantity of oil and flour.[20] Nevertheless, when Jesus produced a multiplication of seven baskets from seven loaves, he did not go beyond what was needed, lest the difference between these miracles should again be forgotten by the disciples. FRAGMENT 98.[21]

[20]1 Kings 17:8-16. [21]MKGK 84.

16:1-12 THE DEMAND FOR A SIGN

¹*And the Pharisees and Sadducees came, and to test him they asked him to show them a sign from heaven. ²He answered them,ʳ "When it is evening, you say, 'It will be fair weather; for the sky is red.' ³And in the morning, 'It will be stormy today, for the sky is red and threatening.' You know how to interpret the appearance of the sky, but you cannot interpret the signs of the times. ⁴An evil and adulterous generation seeks for a sign, but no sign shall be given to it except the sign of Jonah." So he left them and departed.*

⁵*When the disciples reached the other side, they had forgotten to bring any bread. ⁶Jesus said to them, "Take heed and beware of the leaven of the Pharisees and Sadducees." ⁷And they discussed it among themselves, saying, "We brought no bread." ⁸But Jesus, aware of this, said, "O men of little faith, why do you discuss among yourselves the fact that you have no bread? ⁹Do you not yet perceive? Do you not remember the five loaves of the five thousand, and how many baskets you gathered? ¹⁰Or the seven loaves of the four thousand, and how many baskets you gathered? ¹¹How is it that you fail to perceive that I did not speak about bread? Beware of the leaven of the Pharisees and Sadducees." ¹²Then they understood that he did not tell them to beware of the leaven of bread, but of the teaching of the Pharisees and Sadducees.*

r Other ancient authorities omit the following words to the end of verse 3

OVERVIEW: Jesus exposed the rashness of the questions of the scribes (THEODORE OF MOPSUESTIA), who though doctors of the law, were without discernment (JEROME). Had they come with any readiness to believe, he would have given such a sign. His coming in this present time is different from the way he will come in the future. Now Jesus comes as a physician to heal, but then he shall come as a judge to call accounts (CHRYSOSTOM). As for the sign of Jonah, just as that whale was not able to digest Jonah, so too voracious Death assuredly received the Lord but was unable to devour him, regurgitating him on the third day (CHROMATIUS). He did not immediately admonish the disciples for forgetting to bring bread, but rather he took their own thoughtlessness as the occasion for teaching them (CHRYSOSTOM). They are warned not to involve themselves in the disputes of the Jews. The works of the law are now to be viewed in the light of faith (HILARY OF POITIERS). Leaven, if mixed with flour, will grow into something larger and draw to its own essence the whole loaf. So too heretical doctrine, if it ignites even a tiny spark in one heart, in a short time grows into a huge flame and draws to itself the whole person (JEROME). Leniency is not always a good thing. As Jesus sometimes allows his followers freedom for their opinions, at other times he reproves them. By this variable nurturing he provides for their salvation (CHRYSOSTOM).

16:1 Asking for a Sign from Heaven

THEY CAME TO TEST HIM. CHRYSOSTOM: Their inquiry was rightly deserving of anger and great displeasure. Yet the benevolent and provident one is not angry. He pities them even as they tempt him. He laments them as incurably diseased after so full a demonstration of his power.

They did not seek him out in order to believe but to lay hold of him. Had they come with any readiness to believe, he would have given such a sign. For he who said to the woman, "It is not fair,"[1] and afterwards gave, much more would he have shown his bounty to these officials.

But since they did not seek to believe, he therefore calls them hypocrites, because in another place they said one thing and meant another. If they had believed, they would not even have asked. It is evident that they did not believe, since when reproved and exposed, they did not remain with him, nor did they admit "We are ignorant and seek to learn."

But for what sign from heaven were they asking? Either that he should stay the sun, or curb the moon, or bring down thunderbolts, or work a change in the air, or some other such thing. THE GOSPEL OF MATTHEW, HOMILY 53.3.[2]

16:2 Predicting the Weather

THE DOCTORS OF LAW CANNOT FORECAST THE SAVIOR. JEROME: This is not found in many codices.[3] The meaning is clear from the order and harmony of the elements. Both fair and rainy days can be forecast. But the scribes and Pharisees, who were viewed as doctors of the law, could not discern the coming of the Savior from what the prophets had predicted. COMMENTARY ON MATTHEW 2.16.3.[4]

THE RASHNESS OF THEIR QUESTION. THEODORE OF MOPSUESTIA: He exposes the rashness of their question, saying, "You regard the air as moving according to a certain order, so that by means of signs you are able to predict when the weather will be fair and when stormy. But in the case of miracles you recognize no order at all. You do not recognize any occasions on which doing or not doing wonders is appropriate. You assume that such a thing happens completely without order and without any reason." FRAGMENT 89.[5]

16:3 Not Understanding Signs of the Times

YOU CANNOT INTERPRET THE SIGNS. CHRYSOSTOM: What then does he say to all this? "You know how to interpret the appearance of the sky, but you cannot interpret the signs of the times." Observe Christ's meekness and moderation.

Even earlier he did not just refuse and say "no sign shall be given." And so now he goes further and states the reason why he gives them no sign, even though they were not asking for information.

What then was the cause? It is much as in the sky, he says, where one thing is a sign of a storm and another of fair weather. No one when he saw the sign of foul weather would expect a calm, nor in calm and fair weather would one expect a storm. So you would do well also to

---

[1]Mt 15:26. [2]PG 58:529; NPNF 1 10:328. [3]Verses 2 (from "when it is evening") and 3 are lacking in part of the tradition; modern editors generally consider them to be interpolations. [4]CCL 77:136-37. [5]MKGK 128.

think with regard to me. My coming in this present time is different from the way in which I shall come in the future. Now there is need of these signs which are on the earth. But those in heaven are stored up against that time. Now as a physician I have come to heal. Then I shall come as a judge. Now I am seeking out those who have gone astray. Then I will demand an account. Now I have come in a hidden manner. Then I will come much more publicly, folding up the heaven, hiding the sun, not permitting the moon to give its light. Then "the very powers of the heavens shall be shaken,"[6] and the manifestation of my coming shall imitate lightning that appears suddenly. THE GOSPEL OF MATTHEW, HOMILY 53.3.[7]

16:4 Seeking a Sign

EVIL AND ADULTEROUS. ORIGEN: Now he called them evil because their wicked deeds had made them evil people (evil because of deliberate wickedness) and adulterous because when the Pharisees and Sadducees left their metaphoric spouse, the true word, they committed adultery, with falsehood and the law of sin.[8]

Assume there are two laws: the law of our bodies, which is in conflict with the law of our mind. We might say then that the law of the mind (that is, the law of the Spirit) is the husband to whom the soul was betrothed by God as wife according to the Scripture; a wife is married to a man by God.[9] But the other law is a seducer of the soul and as such is called "adulterous." COMMENTARY ON MATTHEW 12.4.[10]

THE SIGN OF JONAH. CHROMATIUS: Just as that whale was not able to digest Jonah nor was able to keep him alive inside himself for long, so too voracious Death assuredly received the Lord. But since he was not able to keep him alive and in custody inside himself, Death regurgitated him on the third day, just as the whale had regurgitated Jonah. For Death, though accustomed always to eat and digest the dead, was nauseated and vomited out the Lord alive. Truly he was not able to digest him, for he was a rock—as the apostle says: "Moreover, Christ was a rock."[11] And indeed the whale gulped and expelled only Jonah. But Death in ingesting the Lord cast out not that very one alone but many with him. For we read that many corpses of the holy had risen up with the Lord. TRACTATE ON MATTHEW 54.3.[12]

NO SIGN FOR AN ADULTEROUS GENERATION. HILARY OF POITIERS: But he descended from the sky and established for these an earthly sign that he might preserve among them a conviction of bodily humility, saying that the sign was to be given by Jonah. The Lord compares himself by means of like appearance with this one whom he had dispatched to Nineveh to accomplish the coming suffering for the proclamation of repentance. Indeed, Jonah was thrown from the ship by furiously raging winds and was devoured by the whale. After the space of three days he was cast out alive, not retained by the monster. He was not digested as food, but contrary to the nature of the human body, he escaped whole and unharmed into the open air. He prefigured the Lord. Therefore Jesus demonstrated that this sign of his own power had been divinely constituted, thus proclaiming in himself the forgiveness of sins through repentance. For he was soon to be cast out of Jerusalem and the synagogue by the blast of unclean spirits and by the power of Pontius Pilate. ON MATTHEW 16.2-3.[13]

16:5 The Disciples Lack Bread

CROSSING TO THE OTHER SIDE. ORIGEN: The bread that they had before they crossed the lake was no longer of any use to them when they

---

[6]Mt 24:29. [7]PG 58:529; NPNF 1 10:328-29. [8]Origen explains in which sense Jesus refers to the Pharisees and the Sadducees as adulterers and then generalizes the explanation: The soul is the bride of moral law and becomes an adulteress if it follows the inclination to sin. [9]Prov 19:14. [10]GCS 40:73-74; ANF 9:451. [11]1 Cor 10:4. [12]CCL 9a:470. [13]SC 258:48-50.

reached the other side. They needed one kind of bread[14] before they crossed and a different kind afterward. They forgot to take any loaves with them because they were careless about carrying bread. The disciples of Jesus had also crossed to another side. They had passed from the material to the spiritual, from the sensory to the intellectual. This is why Jesus said to them after the crossing, be careful and be on your guard.

The Pharisees and Sadducees offered a different dough of teaching, a truly ancient yeast restricted to the bare letter[15] and therefore not free from evil. Jesus does not want his disciples to eat of it any longer. Instead, he mixed a new spiritual dough when he himself offered to any who would abandon the yeast of the Pharisees and Sadducees and come to him, the living bread which came down from heaven and gives life to the world.[16] Anyone intending no longer to use the yeast and dough of the Pharisees and Sadducees' teaching must first "be careful." He must "be on guard" that he will not use the old leaven either accidentally or due to shortages. So Jesus tells his disciples first, "be careful," and second, "be on your guard." Commentary on Matthew 12.5.[17]

The Disciples Had Forgotten to Bring Any Bread. Chrysostom: Why did he not say plainly, "Beware of their teaching?" His purpose is rather to remind them of what had just been done—the feeding of the multitude—for he knew they had already forgotten its significance. But Christ did not immediately admonish them. Rather, he took their own thoughtlessness as the occasion for reproof. Remember that he had not reproved them when they had earlier said, "Where are we to get bread enough in the desert to feed so great a crowd?"[18] It seemed better now to say to them what he says here. He did not want to rush hastily on to another miracle. He did not admonish them before the multitude, nor did he seek to elevate himself in their eyes. He might have been much harsher with them after their forgetfulness following the miracle of

the loaves. All of these considerations gave his reproof a greater meaning. The Gospel of Matthew, Homily 53.4.[19]

16:6 The Leaven of the Sadducees

Take Heed. Hilary of Poitiers: The apostles are ordered to watch out for the leaven of the Pharisees and Sadducees. They are warned not to be involved in the disputes of the Jews. The works of the law are now to be viewed in the light of faith. They are forewarned that they, into whose time and age the truth had appeared incarnate, should judge nothing except which lies within the position of hope in likeness of the truth that is revealed. They are warned against allowing the doctrine of the Pharisees, who are unaware of Christ, to corrupt the effectiveness of the truth of the gospel. On Matthew 16.3.[20]

16:7-8 Men of Little Faith

No Need for the Yeast of the Pharisees. Origen: After Jesus said this, the disciples thought to themselves (not aloud but in their hearts), "We did not bring bread." Then they said something else, like "If we had bread, then we wouldn't need the yeast from the Pharisees and Sadducees, but since we don't have bread, we are at risk of taking their yeast. The Savior does not want us to return to their tutelage, so he told us 'be careful and be on your guard against the yeast of the Pharisees and Sadducees.'" Or they reasoned similar things.

But Jesus, seeing into their hearts and hearing their inner arguments, reproves them as the Shepherd of the heart because they did not understand nor remember the bread which they had received from him. Because of what they had received, even when they appeared to lack

---

[14]To pass beyond the sea signifies progressing spiritually and thus having no further need of the nutrition of the past. [15]The bad leaven of the Pharisees signifies for Origen only the literal interpretation of the Scriptures. [16]Jn 6:51. [17]GCS 40:75-76; ANF 9:452. [18]Mt 15:33. [19]PG 58:529; NPNF 1 10:329. [20]SC 258:50.

bread, they did not need the yeast of the Pharisees and Sadducees. COMMENTARY ON MATTHEW 12:5.[21]

O MEN OF LITTLE FAITH! CHRYSOSTOM: Note how intense is his displeasure. Nowhere else does he appear to have rebuked them so much. How does he do this? He is challenging their prejudices about food laws. Already he had said, "Are you still without understanding?"[22] Now in this place, with a strong rebuke he says, "O men of little faith." THE GOSPEL OF MATTHEW, HOMILY 53.4.[23]

16:9-10 Not Yet Perceiving

THE SUBTLETY OF THE ADMONITION. CHRYSOSTOM: Leniency is not always a good thing. Christ sometimes allows the disciples freedom for their opinions. At other times he reproves them. By this variable nurturing he provides for their salvation. Note how at the same time his reproof is strong and yet mild. For all but excusing himself to them for his severe reproofs to them, he says, "Do you not yet perceive? Do you not remember the five loaves of the five thousand, and how many baskets you gathered? Or the seven loaves of the four thousand, and how many baskets you gathered?" He specifies the numbers and the fragments, so as to bring them to a clear recollection of what had just happened and making them more attentive to the future.

And to teach you how great is the power of his reproof, and how it roused up their slumbering mind, hear what the Evangelist says. For Jesus having reproved them said no more but added this only: How is it that you fail to perceive that I did not speak about bread? Beware of the leaven of the Pharisees and Sadducees. Then they understood that he did not tell them to beware of the leaven of bread but of the teaching of the Pharisees and Sadducees.

See how much good his admonition conveyed. For it both led them away from the Jewish food observances and, when they were remiss, made them more attentive and delivered them from the neglect of faith. So they were not afraid nor in alarm about having no food or about starving. THE GOSPEL OF MATTHEW, HOMILY 53.4.[24]

16:11 Not Bread but Teaching

TEACHING IS LEAVEN. ORIGEN: Some were distracted by the use of bread and yeast. In order to clarify and enlighten them in a still symbolic way that he was not speaking about literal bread but about yeast as representing teaching, Jesus adds, "How is it that you do not understand that I was not talking to you about bread? Beware of the yeast of the Pharisees and Sadducees." Even though he still had not exposed the literal meaning of his words but continued as before, the disciples would have understood the Savior as referring to the teaching of the Pharisees and Sadducees as leaven.

When Jesus said "beware of the yeast," the disciples understood that he did not tell them to watch out for bread but instead for the teaching of the Pharisees and Sadducees. You, of course, are aware that whenever yeast is used in the law or in the Scripture which follows the law, it refers to teaching. Perhaps then yeast should not be burnt on an altar. Prayers should not have the form of teachings but should be only supplications for good things from God.

Now, someone might ask, based on what has been said about the disciples crossing over to the other side, how can anyone who has reached the other side be rebuked as a person with little faith, not yet understanding or remembering what Jesus did? It is not difficult, I think, to answer this. That which has only a part will be done away with before that which is perfect. Little faith is all the faith we can have. Accordingly, we who know in part do not yet fully understand or remember.[25] Therefore we are not able

---

[21]GCS 40:76; ANF 9:453. [22]Mt 15:16. [23]PG 58:529; NPNF 1 10:329. [24]PG 58:529-30; NPNF 1 10:329-30. [25]Cf. 1 Cor 13:12.

to achieve a mind sufficient and capable of attaining the magnitude and nature of such speculations. COMMENTARY ON MATTHEW 12.6.[26]

16:12 Then They Understood

BEWARE OF FALSE TEACHING. JEROME: This was a favorable opportunity for instruction which was ordered by the Savior. He said, "Beware the leaven of the Pharisees and the Sadducees." He taught them what the five loaves and seven that had nourished five thousand and four thousand men in the desert signified. He showed that there is a spiritual understanding underlying these events, even if the import of the sign is clear. For if the leaven of the Pharisees and the Sadducees indicated not physical bread but twisted narratives and heretical teaching, then might not also the food by which the people of God were nourished signify the true and complete doctrine?

Someone might inquire, "How is it that they do not have the loaves? For they immediately boarded the boat after the seven baskets had been filled." But the Scripture testifies to the fact that they had forgotten to take food with them.

Remember the leaven about which even the apostle speaks when he writes, "A little leaven spoils the whole dough."[27] The sort of leaven of which he speaks is something like the kind that Marcion and Valentinus[28] and all heretics exhibited. It is to be avoided by all means.

Leaven has this power, that, if mixed with flour, that which seemed small would grow into something larger and draw to its own essence the whole loaf. So too with heretical doctrine, if it tosses even a tiny spark into your heart, in a short time a huge flame grows beneath and draws to itself a person's entire substance. It was then that they finally understood that he had not meant them to beware simply of the leaven of bread but of the teaching of the Pharisees and Sadducees. COMMENTARY ON MATTHEW 2.16.6-12.[29]

---

[26]GCS 40:77-78; ANF 9:453. [27]Cf. 1 Cor 5:6; Gal 5:9. [28]Marcion and Valentinus were heretics of the second century. Valentinus was the most important Gnostic teacher; Marcion originated the heresy that took his name. [29]CCL 77:137-38.

16:13-20 PETER'S CONFESSION OF THE CHRIST

[13]*Now when Jesus came into the district of Caesarea Philippi, he asked his disciples, "Who do men say that the Son of man is?"* [14]*And they said, "Some say John the Baptist, others say Elijah, and others Jeremiah or one of the prophets."* [15]*He said to them, "But who do you say that I am?"* [16]*Simon Peter replied, "You are the Christ, the Son of the living God."* [17]*And Jesus answered him, "Blessed are you, Simon Bar-Jona! For flesh and blood has not revealed this to you, but my Father who is in heaven.* [18]*And I tell you, you are Peter,ˢ and on this rockᵗ I will build my church, and the powers of deathᵘ shall not prevail against it.* [19]*I will give you the keys of the kingdom of heaven, and whatever you bind on earth shall be bound in heaven, and whatever you*

loose on earth shall be loosed in heaven.” [20]*Then he strictly charged the disciples to tell no one that he was the Christ.*

s Greek *Petros*　t Greek *petra*　u Greek *the gates of Hades*

OVERVIEW: Our Lord did not examine his own disciples as to his identity within the borders of Judea but did so in the territory of the Gentiles, so that it would be revealed to the Gentiles through Peter what flesh and blood had not unveiled. All of this would in due time occur in the faith of Cornelius, who was first among the Gentiles to believe (EPIPHANIUS THE LATIN). By the title Son of man, Jesus showed that he himself not only appears to be but in fact unchangeably is man, without ceasing to be true God (THEODORE OF HERACLEA). He signifies how earnestly he desires the triune economy to be duly confessed when he says, "Who do men say the Son of man is?" for he thereby denotes his true deity (CHRYSOSTOM). He asked about a secret that the faith of those who believe ought to penetrate (HILARY OF POITIERS). Peter is the rock upon whose confession the church will be built (THEODORE OF MOPSUESTIA). If Christ is the Son of God, he is also God. If he is not God, he is not the Son of God. But he himself is the Son and as the Son takes up all things from the Father, and so we hold him in our hearts (EPIPHANIUS THE LATIN). He was unwilling to be proclaimed Jesus Christ prior to his suffering and resurrection (JEROME). It was still necessary that this be hidden from the rulers, so that Christ, by suffering and rising again, might transform in himself human life and recreate it, changing it back to the state in which it was prior to its corruption (THEODORE OF MOPSUESTIA). When the things that offend would be taken out of the way and the cross accomplished, then his true identity could be engraved pure and immovable in the mind of believing hearers (CHRYSOSTOM).

16:13 Who Do People Say I Am?

INTO CAESAREA PHILIPPI. CHRYSOSTOM: Why does he mention Philip, the founder of the city? Because there was another city, Caesarea Stratonis.[1] He does not go there, but rather he leads them far away from Judea, so that being freed from all alarm, they might speak with boldness all that was in their mind. THE GOSPEL OF MATTHEW, HOMILY 54.1.[2]

THE QUESTION ASKED OUTSIDE JUDEA. EPIPHANIUS THE LATIN: Caesarea Philippi is outside Judea in the region of the Gentiles. Why therefore did our Lord not examine his own disciples within the borders of Judea? Why did he go far north into the territory of the Gentiles? But as our insignificance [as Gentiles] works against us, he questioned the disciples in Gentile territory. The result was that by the true and everlasting conviction of the blessed apostle Peter—what flesh and blood had not unveiled, the Father revealed from the heavens. Through faith the Gentiles rather than the Jews would come to acknowledge the Son of God. This indeed occurred in the city of Caesarea—Cornelius who was first among the Gentiles to believe with all his own household, through the holy apostle Peter. The Lord was not inclined to question his own disciples in Judea, when the Jews did not believe that he was the Son of God but regarded him merely as the son of Joseph. INTERPRETATION OF THE GOSPELS 28.[3]

SON OF MAN, SON OF GOD. THEODORE OF HERACLEA: Jesus asks this in order that we might know what opinions about him were current among the Jews. [He also asks] so that we might learn to inquire intently into what people are saying about him, and if it is bad, to remove

---

[1]In reality considerably more than two cities bore the name Caesarea. [2]PG 58:531-32; NPNF 1 10:332. [3]PL Supp 3:868-69.

the causes, or if complimentary, to increase them. But he said "Son of man" in order to show that he himself not only appears to be but in fact unchangeably is man, and again, is true God. [It is] not as if he were divided into different species, one part God and one part man; rather one may address him as Son of man with no doubt that this very same one is also the Son of God.[4] FRAGMENT 101.[5]

16:14 The Opinions of the Multitude

WHO DO PEOPLE SAY THAT THE SON OF MAN IS? CHRYSOSTOM: Note that he is not asking them their own opinion. Rather, he asks the opinion of the people. Why? In order to contrast the opinion of the people with the disciples answer to the question "But who do you say that I am?" In this way, by the manner of his inquiry, they might be drawn gradually to a more sublime notion and not fall into the same common view as that of the multitude.

Note that Jesus does not raise this question at the beginning of his preaching but only after he had done many miracles, had talked through with them many lofty teachings, and had given them many clear proofs of his divinity and of his union with the Father. Only then does he put this question to them.

He did not ask "Who do the scribes and Pharisees say that I am?" even though they had often come to him and discoursed with him. Rather, he begins his questioning by asking "Who do men say the Son of man is?" as if to inquire about common opinion. Even if common opinion was far less true than it might have been, it was at least relatively more free from malice than the opinions of the religious leaders, which was teeming with bad motives.

He signifies how earnestly he desires this divine economy to be confessed when he says, "Who do men say the Son of man is?" for he thereby denotes his godhead, which he does also in many other places. THE GOSPEL OF MATTHEW, HOMILY 54.1.[6]

SOME SAY JEREMIAH. THEODORE OF MOPSUESTIA: In the same way they had supposed that Christ was Jeremiah. Perhaps they knew that the Lord had wisdom from his birth and was without peer in his teaching. Something similar was thought of Jeremiah, in that as a child he was singled out for prophecy and that without human training he was the prophet of a greater prophet who was to follow.[7] FRAGMENT 91.[8]

ONE OF THE PROPHETS. ORIGEN: Just look at the differences of opinion among the Jews about Jesus. Some, following corrupt thinking, said he was John the Baptist (for example, Herod the tetrarch, who asked his servants, "Is this John the Baptizer now risen from the dead and, because of this, with powers at work in him?") Others said that Elijah is now the one called Jesus. He has either been born a second time or he has been alive somewhere all along and is now appearing again. Some suggested Jeremiah was Jesus, and not that Jeremiah was a type of Christ. This comes perhaps from a mistaken interpretation of a passage in the beginning of Jeremiah about Christ's prophecy unfulfilled in the time of the prophet but beginning to be fulfilled in Jesus, whom God set up over nations and kingdoms "to root up, and to build up, and to transplant."[9] COMMENTARY ON MATTHEW 12.9.[10]

16:15 What Do You Say?

THE MESSIANIC SECRET. HILARY OF POITIERS: When they had presented diverse human origins concerning him, he asked what they them-

---

[4]Theodore observes that the person of Christ being one alone, man and God together, the titles "Son of man" and "Son of God" both define his divinity and humanity. [5]MKGK 85. [6]PG 58:532-33; NPNF 1 10:332. [7]As it appears in Jeremiah 1:5, Jeremiah had already in his mother's womb been chosen by God as a prophet. [8]MKGK 129. [9]Jer 1:10. In Origen's view these words, which the Lord speaks to Jeremiah, go beyond the mission entrusted to the prophet and are instead meant for Christ, of whom Jeremiah had therefore been a prophetic prefiguration. [10]GCS 40:81-82; ANF 9:455.

selves thought about him. Peter answered, "You are the Christ, the Son of the living God." But Peter had pondered the nature of the question. For the Lord had said, "Whom do men say that the Son of man is?" Certainly his human body indicated he was a Son of man. But by adding "Who do you say that I am?" Jesus indicated that they should consider something besides what he seemed in himself, for he was a Son of man. Therefore what judgment concerning himself did he desire? It was a secret he was asking about, into which the faith of those who believe ought to extend itself. ON MATTHEW 16.6.[11]

PROBING FOR ANOTHER JUDGMENT. CHRYSOSTOM: Then, since they said, "Some John the Baptist, some Elijah, some Jeremiah, or one of the prophets," and set forth their mistaken opinion, he next added, "But who do you say that I am?" He was calling them on by his second inquiry to entertain some higher mental picture, indicating that their former judgment falls exceedingly short of his dignity. Thus Jesus probes for another judgment from them. He poses this second question that they might not fall in with the multitude who, because they saw his miracles as greater than human, accounted him a man indeed but one that, as Herod had thought, may have appeared after a resurrection. To lead them away from such notions, he says, "But who do you say that I am?"—that is, you who are always with me, and see me working miracles and have yourselves done many mighty works by me. THE GOSPEL OF MATTHEW, HOMILY 54.1.[12]

16:16 You Are the Christ

CHRIST, THE SON OF THE LIVING GOD. EPIPHANIUS THE LATIN: Did the Lord not know what people called him? But by questioning he brought forth the conviction of the apostle Peter and left for us in the future a strong affirmation of faith. For the Lord questioned not only Peter but all the apostles when he said, "Who do you say that I am?" Yet one on behalf of all answered

the King, who is in due time to judge the whole world. He is God, both God and man. How miserable does this make those who are false teachers and strangers now, and to be judged in eternity. If Christ is the Son of God, by all means he is also God. If he is not God, he is not the Son of God. But since he himself is the Son, and as the Son takes up all things from the Father, let us hold this same one inseparably in our heart because there is no one who escapes his hand. INTERPRETATION OF THE GOSPELS 28.[13]

ONE CHRIST. CYRIL OF ALEXANDRIA: Peter did not say "you are a Christ" or "a son of God" but "the Christ, the Son of God." For there are many christs by grace, who have attained the rank of adoption [as sons], but [there is] only one who is by nature the Son of God.[14] Thus, using the definite article, he said, the Christ, the Son of God. And in calling him Son of the living God, Peter indicates that Christ himself is life and that death has no authority over him. And even if the flesh, for a short while, was weak and died, nevertheless it rose again, since the Word, who indwelled it, could not be held under the bonds of death. FRAGMENT 190.[15]

16:17-18 On This Rock I Will Build My Church

UPON THIS ROCK. THEODORE OF MOPSUESTIA: This is not the property of Peter alone, but it came about on behalf of every human being. Having said that his confession is a rock, he stated that upon this rock I will build my church. This means he will build his church upon this same confession and faith. For this reason, addressing the one who first confessed him with this title, on account of his confession

---

[11]SC 258:52-54. [12]PG 58:533; NPNF 1 10:332. [13]PL Supp 3:869. [14]*Christ* signifies "anointed," and in the Old Testament many people were *christs*: kings, priests and prophets. Hence the dignity of Jesus is defined by the association of the name *Christ* with the term *Son of God*. [15]MKGK 215.

he applied to him this authority, too, as something that would become his, speaking of the common and special good of the church as pertaining to him alone. It was from this confession, which was going to become the common property of all believers, that he bestowed upon him this name, the rock. In the same way also Jesus attributes to him the special character of the church, as though it existed beforehand in him on account of his confession. By this he shows, in consequence, that this is the common good of the church, since also the common element of the confession was to come to be first in Peter. This then is what he says, that in the church would be the key of the kingdom of heaven. If anyone holds the key to this, to the church, in the same way he will also hold it for all heavenly things. He who is counted as belonging to the church and is recognized as its member is a partaker and an inheritor of heaven. He who is a stranger to it, whatever his status may be, will have no communion in heavenly things. To this very day the priests of the church have expelled those who are unworthy by this saying and admitted those who have become worthy by repentance. FRAGMENT 92.[16]

16:19 What Is Bound or Loosed

THE KEYS OF THE KINGDOM. EPIPHANIUS THE LATIN: For Christ is a rock which is never disturbed or worn away. Therefore Peter gladly received his name from Christ to signify the established and unshaken faith of the church. . . . The devil is the gateway of death who always hastens to stir up against the holy church calamities and temptations and persecutions. But the faith of the apostle, which was founded upon the rock of Christ, abides always unconquered and unshaken. And the very keys of the kingdom of the heavens have been handed down so that one whom he has bound on earth has been bound in heaven, and one whom he has set free on earth he has also set free in heaven. INTERPRETATION OF THE GOSPELS 28.[17]

16:20 Jesus Charges the Disciples to Tell No One

HE STRICTLY CHARGED THEM. CHRYSOSTOM: And why did he charge them? That when the things which offend are taken out of the way, the cross is accomplished and the rest of his sufferings fulfilled, and when there is nothing any more to interrupt and disturb the faith of the people in him, the right opinion concerning him may be engraven pure and immovable in the mind of the hearers. For in truth his power had not yet clearly shone forth. Accordingly it was his will then to be preached by them when both the plain truth of the facts and the power of his deeds were pleading in support of the assertions of the apostles. For it was by no means the same thing to see him in Palestine, now working miracles and now insulted and persecuted, especially when the very cross was presently to follow the miracles that were happening, and then to behold him everywhere in the world, adored and believed, and no more suffering anything such as he had suffered. THE GOSPEL OF MATTHEW, HOMILY 54.4.[18]

THE PROHIBITED PROCLAMATION. JEROME: For the purpose of proclaiming, he had sent his disciples before him and ordered them to announce his arrival. But he advised them lest they say publicly that he was Jesus Christ. It seems to me to be one thing to proclaim him to be Christ, another thing to proclaim him to be Jesus Christ. Christ is a common term for the messianic dignity,[19] while Jesus is the proper name for the Savior. It is possible that for this reason he had been unwilling to be proclaimed Jesus Christ prior to his suffering and resurrection in order that he might afterwards, when the obligation of blood had been fulfilled, at an opportune time say to his apostles, "Go and teach all nations"[20] and the rest. And lest anyone

---

[16]MKGK 129. [17]PL Supp 3:869-70. [18]PG 58:535; NPNF 1 10:334. [19]Cf. p. 45 n. 14. [20]Mt 28:19-20.

think that this is merely our opinion and not the perceptions of the Evangelist, then what follows explains further the reasons for the prohibited proclamation. COMMENTARY ON MATTHEW 3.16.20.[21]

TELL NO ONE. THEODORE OF MOPSUESTIA: When the disciples had received the Spirit, then the teaching concerning the divinity of the Son was shown to them perfectly and the Spirit himself bore witness through the miracles that were done in his name. Yet it was still necessary that

this be hidden from the rulers, the elemental powers of this world,[22] so that Christ, by suffering and rising again, might transform in himself human life and recreate it, changing it back to the state it was in at the beginning of its corruption. This perhaps is the reason why of necessity this instruction had not yet been given them. FRAGMENT 93.[23]

---

[21]CCL 77:142-43. [22]Eph 6:12. [23]MKGK 130.

16:21-28 JESUS SPEAKS ABOUT HIS SUFFERING AND DEATH

[21]*From that time Jesus began to show his disciples that he must go to Jerusalem and suffer many things from the elders and chief priests and scribes, and be killed, and on the third day be raised.* [22]*And Peter took him and began to rebuke him, saying, "God forbid, Lord! This shall never happen to you."* [23]*But he turned and said to Peter, "Get behind me, Satan! You are a hindrance*[v] *to me; for you are not on the side of God, but of men."*

[24]*Then Jesus told his disciples, "If any man would come after me, let him deny himself and take up his cross and follow me.* [25]*For whoever would save his life will lose it, and whoever loses his life for my sake will find it.* [26]*For what will it profit a man, if he gains the whole world and forfeits his life? Or what shall a man give in return for his life?* [27]*For the Son of man is to come with his angels in the glory of his Father, and then he will repay every man for what he has done.* [28]*Truly, I say to you, there are some standing here who will not taste death before they see the Son of man coming in his kingdom."*

v Greek *stumbling block*

OVERVIEW: When Peter objects to Christ's talk of future suffering, Jesus explains that if Peter had listened to his teachings rightly, he would know that this, of all things, is most fitting to him. Now it becomes ever more clear how correct Jesus was in forbidding them not to declare his identity publicly. For if it so confounded the disciples, who knows what the response of others might have been (CHRYSOSTOM)? After Jesus had warned of the cross to be borne, the soul to be ruined and eternal life to be exchanged for the loss of the world, he turned toward his disciples and said that some would not taste death until they beheld the Son of man in the glory of his own kingdom (HILARY OF POITIERS). When Peter confessed Christ, Christ praised him. But when he was irrationally terrified, Christ rebuked him (THEODORE OF HERACLEA).

16:21-22 Suffering Many Things

THIS SHALL NEVER HAPPEN TO YOU. CHRYSOSTOM: Peter was examining the issue by human and earthly reasoning. He thought it disgraceful to Jesus as something unworthy of him. Jesus responded sharply, in effect saying, "My suffering is not an unseemly matter. You are making this judgment with a carnal mind. If you had listened to my teachings in a godly way, tearing yourself away from carnal understanding, you would know that this of all things most becomes me. You seem to suppose that to suffer is unworthy of me. But I say to you that for me not to suffer is of the devil's mind." So he repressed Peter's alarm by contrary arguments.

Remember that John, accounting it unworthy of Christ to be baptized by him, was persuaded by Christ to baptize him, saying, "Let it be so now."[1] So we find Peter as well, forbidding Christ to wash his feet. He is met by the words, "If I do not wash you, you have no part in me." Here too Jesus restrained him by the mention of the opposite, and by the severity of the reproof he repressed his fear of suffering. THE GOSPEL OF MATTHEW, HOMILY 54.6.[2]

16:23 A Hindrance to Me

JESUS FORBIDS MAKING HIS IDENTITY PUBLIC. ORIGEN: What he intended when he forbade them to publicly declare him Christ is clarified in part by "From that time Jesus began to show his disciples how he must go to Jerusalem and suffer many things from the elders" and the following thoughts. At the right time and in the right way, he proclaimed to those who knew that Jesus was Christ, Son of the living God (the Father had revealed this to them), that rather than believing in Jesus Christ already crucified,

they should believe in Jesus Christ soon to be crucified. So also, instead of believing in Jesus Christ already risen from the dead, they should believe in "Jesus Christ soon to be raised from the dead."

"Having put off from himself the principalities and powers, he made a show of them openly, triumphing over them in the cross."[3] If anyone is ashamed of the cross of Christ, he is ashamed of the agency by which these powers were defeated. The one who both believes and is assured of these things should, more appropriately, glory in the cross of our Lord and Savior Jesus Christ. Through that cross, when Christ was crucified, the principalities (among them, I think, was also the prince of this world) were publicly humiliated and paraded before the eyes of the believing world. COMMENTARY ON MATTHEW 12.18.[4]

GET BEHIND ME, SATAN! CHRYSOSTOM: Therefore, the rest being troubled and in perplexity, Peter again in his ardor alone ventures to discuss these things. And he does not discuss them openly but only when he had taken him aside. Having separated himself from the rest of the disciples, he says, "God forbid, Lord! This shall never happen to you." What is happening here? The very one who had obtained a revelation, who had been blessed, has now so soon fallen away, so as now to fear the Passion of the Lord, and thereby his faith has been overthrown. It is remarkable that Peter, who had not yet been fully instructed in the course of revelation, should come up with these responses. The larger picture had not yet been revealed to Peter, and he was confused and overwhelmed. Peter had learned that Christ is the Son of God. But he had not learned of the mystery of the cross and the resurrection. It was as yet not manifested to him. It remained hidden. Do you see how correct Jesus was in forbidding them not to

---

[1]Mt 3:15. [2]PG 58:537; NPNF 1 10:335. [3]Col 2:15. [4]GCS 40:110-11; ANF 9:461.

declare his identity publicly? For if it so confounded the disciples, who were being made aware of it, who knows what the response of others might have been.

This is why he rebuked Peter and called him Satan: to signify that he is coming to his future suffering voluntarily. THE GOSPEL OF MATTHEW, HOMILY 54.5-6.[5]

PETER REBUKED. THEODORE OF HERACLEA: When, contrary to what he had hoped, Peter heard this, he was troubled. For the revelation had exhibited Christ as Son of God and the living God, on the one hand. Yet on the other hand, he was found to be preparing for the dreadful events of the Passion. In rebuking Peter, Christ brings to light his own righteous judgment. When Peter confessed Christ, Christ praised him. But when he was irrationally terrified, Christ rebuked him, acting without respect of persons. FRAGMENT 102.[6]

PETER AS SATAN. ORIGEN: Responding to Peter's ignorance as one opposing God, Jesus said, "Satan," which is Hebrew for opponent. If he had not spoken to him from ignorance nor of the living God when he said, "Never, Lord! This must never happen to you!" then he would not have said to him "Get behind me," as if speaking to someone who had given up being behind him and following him. Neither would he have called him "Satan." Satan had overpowered the one following Jesus in order to turn him aside from following him and from being behind the Son of God, to make him, because of ignorant words, worthy of being called "Satan" and a scandal to the Son of God, "not thinking in the ways of God but of humans." COMMENTARY ON MATTHEW 12.21.[7]

16:24 Denying Oneself

LET HIM TAKE UP HIS CROSS. CHRYSOSTOM: When did he teach this? When Peter said, "God forbid, Lord! This shall never happen to you."

And when Peter was told, "Get behind me, Satan," Jesus did not merely rebuke Peter. He was willing to teach him more fully of the benefit of his Passion and about the exceeding confusion in what Peter had said. So he responds in effect: "Your word to me is that this shall never happen to me, but my word to you is 'Not only is this hurtful to you, and destructive, to hinder me and be displeased at my Passion.' But more so it will be impossible for you even to be saved, unless you yourself are continually prepared for death."

So, lest anyone should imagine that his suffering was unworthy of him, he teaches them what great gain will come from it. This applies not only to his former afflictions but also to those yet to come. Later he will teach in John's Gospel that "unless a grain of wheat falls into the earth and dies, it remains alone; but if it dies, it bears much fruit."[8] So he now begins discussing more fully the outworkings of the future, not only with respect to his own suffering and death but with theirs as well. Unwillingness to die is grievous, but to be ready for death is good and of great profit.

Jesus makes this clear by what follows, but for the present he works it out on one side only. Note that he does not say, "You must suffer whether you will it or not." Rather, he says, "If any man would come after me, let him deny himself and take up his cross and follow me." This is as if to say: "I force no one, I compel no one, but each one I make lord of his own choice. So I say, 'If any one will.'" THE GOSPEL OF MATTHEW, HOMILY 55.1.[9]

16:25 Losing One's Life for Jesus' Sake

WHOEVER WOULD SAVE HIS LIFE WILL LOSE IT. CHRYSOSTOM: Then, because he had said, "Whoever would save his life will lose it, and whoever loses his life for my sake will find it,"

---

[5]PG 58:536; NPNF 1 10:335. [6]*MKGK* 85. [7]GCS 40:117; ANF 9:462-63. [8]Jn 12:24. [9]PG 58:539-41; NPNF 1 10:338-39.

Jesus makes a strict distinction between salvation and destruction. This was to prevent anyone from imagining the one destruction and the other salvation to be all the same thing in the last instance. The distance is infinite between destruction and salvation. Then he makes this inference once for all to establish these points: "For what is a man profited if he gains the whole world and loses his own soul?"

Do you see how the wrongful preservation of life amounts to destruction and is worse than all destruction, as being even past remedy from the want of anything more to redeem it? THE GOSPEL OF MATTHEW, HOMILY 55.4[10]

16:26 Forfeiting One's Soul

WHERE IS THE PROFIT? ORIGEN: The first statement is ambiguous. At first it could be taken this way: Someone who loves being alive and thinks the present life is good manages his own life in order to live well according to the flesh, fearing death since by death he loses life. In this way, wanting to save his own life, he will lose it, having removed it beyond the boundaries of blessedness. Yet someone despising the present life because of my teaching and convinced of eternal life, even facing death for the sake of the truth may, because of piety, lose his own life in death. Yet the same one who lost his life because of me will instead save and keep it.

We could interpret the saying, however, in another way. If anyone knows what salvation is and wants to save his own life, after bidding farewell to his life, denying himself and taking up his cross and following me, he will, in terms of the world, have lost his life. But, having lost his life for me and my teaching, he will gain in the end this kind of loss, salvation. COMMENTARY ON MATTHEW 12.26.[11]

WHAT IS A LIFE WORTH? ORIGEN: But what shall a person give in exchange for his life, would seem, if spoken in answer to a query, to indicate a person who trades his life; a person who, after

sin, has given up his substance in order that his property might feed the poor. He would in that way receive salvation. Yet, in a positive light, I think this indicates that there is nothing in a person that he can give in trade for his life that will buy off death. God, however, has ransomed us all with the priceless blood of Jesus[12] so that "we are bought with a price,"[13] "having been purchased not with perishable things like silver and gold but with the priceless blood of the spotless, flawless Lamb,"[14] Christ. COMMENTARY ON MATTHEW 12.28.[15]

THE DISCIPLES' HUMAN WEAKNESS. CYRIL OF ALEXANDRIA: Since the disciples had not yet received power from on high,[16] it was perhaps not unnatural that they should fall occasionally into human weaknesses and, thinking something of this sort, say, "How shall someone deny himself? Or how can someone, by losing his own life, save it?" . . .

Therefore, to lead them away from reasonings of this sort and, so to speak, forge courage anew within them, communicating to them a longing for the glory to come, he says, "There are some standing here," hinting at Peter and the sons of Zebedee; for these were taken up with him at the transfiguration,[17] which Christ calls "the kingdom," as demonstrating the ineffability of [his] authority and the immutable nature of [his] kinship with the Father. And in this [saying] he also hints at the importance and the fearfulness of his second coming, showing this coming to be a prelude and, as it were, a confirmation of that. For he will come "in the glory of God, the Father," not in the humble condition

---

[10]PG 58:543; NPNF 1 10:340-41. [11]GCS 40:127-28; ANF 9:464. [12]1 Pet 1:19. Origen turns the words of Jesus to a more specific and restricted meaning, applying them to the condition of the sinner who, enslaved by sin, cannot pay any price to free his soul. Jesus paid this price freely through his blood, since he was not subject to sin. [13]1 Cor 6:20. [14]1 Pet 1:18-19. [15]GCS 40:131; ANF 9:465. [16]Lk 24:49. [17]The transfiguration immediately follows the prediction of the future coming of the Son of man in his kingly dignity. Hence Origen means that this prediction has come true with the transfiguration itself.

that is commensurate with us. FRAGMENT 195.[18]

16:27 Coming in the Glory of His Father

WITH HIS ANGELS IN THE GLORY OF HIS FATHER. CHRYSOSTOM: Do you see how the glory of the Father and of the Son is all one glory? But if the glory is one, it is quite evident that the substance also is one. For if in one substance there be a difference of glory ("for there is one glory of the sun, and another glory of the moon, and another glory of the stars; for one star differs from another star in glory";[19] although the substance is one), how may the substance of those differ in which the glory is one? For he did not say, "In glory such as the Father's," whereby someone might suppose again some variation between the glory of the Father and the Son. Rather, he implies the entire perfection of the one God: "In that same glory, he will come," for it to be deemed one and the same.

"Why are you afraid, Peter," so he speaks, "as you hear of death? Then you will see me in the glory of the Father. If I am in glory, so are you all. Your interests are no way limited to the present life. Another sort of condition will take you up, a better one." Nevertheless, when he had spoken of the good things to come, he did not neglect to speak also of the fearful things to come. He spoke of the judgment seat, and the inexorable account, and the inflexible sentence and the judgment that cannot be deceived.

Thus Christ's discourse was not intended only to make people feel dismal, but it was tempered with good hope.... He reminded not only the sinners of punishment but also them that have done well of rewards and crowns. THE

GOSPEL OF MATTHEW, HOMILY 55.5.[20]

16:28 The Son of Man Coming in His Kingdom

SOME STANDING HERE WILL NOT TASTE DEATH. HILARY OF POITIERS: The Lord teaches that both deeds and words, and speech and action, equally furnish the faith of our hope. For it might seem that he had imposed a grievous burden upon human infirmity; namely that, when people had begun to have a sense of life by experiencing it, they should let go its enjoyment which is gratifying to their bodies. He taught that they should deny themselves for the sake of themselves—that is, they should not wish to be that which they had once begun to be. These things which are held close are accompanied by the enticements of gratifying joy, but they may lead to a wavering and uncertain hope. Therefore it was necessary by the authority of a real and manifest example that he teach them of the loss of present things and place these in the context of future gains. All of this might seem contrary to the power and perception of current judgment. After he had warned of the cross to be borne and the soul to be ruined and the eternity of life to be exchanged for the loss of the world, he turned toward his disciples and said that some of them would not taste death until they beheld the Son of man in the glory of his own kingdom. Moreover, Jesus himself tasted death and showed the faithful already a taste of death. And so deeds follow words. ON MATTHEW 17.1.[21]

---

[18]MKGK 216-17. [19]1 Cor 15:41. [20]PG 58:544; NPNF 1 10:341-42. [21]SC 258:60-62.

17:1-13 THE TRANSFIGURATION

¹And after six days Jesus took with him Peter and James and John his brother, and led them up a high mountain apart. ²And he was transfigured before them, and his face shone like the sun, and his garments became white as light. ³And behold, there appeared to them Moses and Elijah, talking with him. ⁴And Peter said to Jesus, "Lord, it is well that we are here; if you wish, I will make three booths here, one for you and one for Moses and one for Elijah." ⁵He was still speaking, when lo, a bright cloud overshadowed them, and a voice from the cloud said, "This is my beloved Son,ʷ with whom I am well pleased; listen to him." ⁶When the disciples heard this, they fell on their faces, and were filled with awe. ⁷But Jesus came and touched them, saying, "Rise, and have no fear." ⁸And when they lifted up their eyes, they saw no one but Jesus only.

⁹And as they were coming down the mountain, Jesus commanded them, "Tell no one the vision, until the Son of man is raised from the dead." ¹⁰And the disciples asked him, "Then why do the scribes say that first Elijah must come?" ¹¹He replied, "Elijah does come, and he is to restore all things; ¹²but I tell you that Elijah has already come, and they did not know him, but did to him whatever they pleased. So also the Son of man will suffer at their hands." ¹³Then the disciples understood that he was speaking to them of John the Baptist.

w Or *my Son, my* (or *the*) *Beloved*

OVERVIEW: Peter, James and John accompany Jesus up the mount of transfiguration because of their close and loving relation to him (CHRYSOSTOM). In his transfiguration Jesus is beheld as truly in the form of God while remaining no less truly human (ORIGEN). His body had become spiritual, so that even his garments were transformed (JEROME). Jesus shone as the sun, indicating that he is the light that illuminates everyone who comes into this world (AUGUSTINE), that he may be manifested to the children of light, who have put off the works of darkness and become the sons of day (ORIGEN). By seeking three tabernacles Peter appeared to be comparing incommensurably the two servants with the one Lord (JEROME). The Lord did not reply, for Peter's comparison was inappropriate, not wicked (LEO THE GREAT). The shining cloud gives shade to the righteous and at the same time protects them and gives them light (ORIGEN). The Son is distinguished from his servants, Moses and Elijah. They, along with you, are to prepare a tabernacle for the Lord in the inner sanctum of their heart (JEROME). The Father reveals the Son when the ringing voice from heaven bursts forth loudly, and yet one must not think that the voice of God is necessarily audible (APOLLINARIS). It says, "Listen to him. By his preaching I am manifest. By his humility I am glorified" (LEO THE GREAT). Why did they fall on their faces in awe? Because there was solitude, the height of the mountain, great quietness, a transfiguration full of awe, a pure light and a cloud stretched out (CHRYSOSTOM, CYRIL OF ALEXANDRIA). Human weakness is not strong enough to bear the sight of such great glory but trembles with its whole heart and body and falls to earth (JEROME).

John the Baptist was forerunner of the first advent. He is called by the name Elijah, not because he was Elijah but because he was fulfilling Elijah's ministry. For just as Elijah will be the forerunner of the second advent, so John was of the first (CHRYSOSTOM, THEODORE OF MOPSUESTIA). The Savior too would suffer what the scribes did to Elijah (ORIGEN).

17:1 Jesus Takes Peter, James and John to a High Mountain

AFTER SIX DAYS. HILARY OF POITIERS: Indeed, in this type of event, reason, harmony and example are served. For after six days the appearance of the Lord's glory is revealed. No doubt, with the cycles of six thousand years having unfolded, the glory of the heavenly kingdom is prefigured. And the three were taken up in analogy to the descent of the three, Shem, Ham and Japheth. By this the coming election to divine favor of the people is shown. ON MATTHEW 17.2.[1]

THE COUNTING OF DAYS. JEROME: Now it is asked how after six days he took them and led them separately onto a high mountain, whereas the Evangelist Luke established the number at eight. The answer is easy because in Matthew the days in the middle are counted, but in Luke the first and last are added.[2] For Luke does not say after eight days Jesus took Peter and James and John but "now about eight days after."[3] COMMENTARY ON MATTHEW 3.17.1.[4]

WHY ONLY THREE? CHRYSOSTOM: Why does he take only these three with him? Because each one of these three was elevated above the rest. Peter showed his preeminence by exceedingly loving him; John by being exceedingly loved by him. James showed his superiority by his ready response to his brother: we are able to drink the cup[5] and by his works and by doing what he said. For so earnest was James, and grievous to the Jews, that Herod himself imagined that he had bestowed a great favor on the Jews by killing him.[6] THE GOSPEL OF MATTHEW, HOMILY 56.2.[7]

17:2 Jesus Transfigured Before Them

THE SUN OF RIGHTEOUSNESS. ORIGEN: But some may ask, when he was transfigured before those who were led up by him into the lofty mountain, did he appear to them in the form of God or in the preincarnate form that he earlier had? Did he appear to those left below in the form of a servant, but to those who had followed him after the six days to the lofty mountain, did he have not the form of a servant but the form of God? Listen carefully, if you can, and at the same time be attentive spiritually. It is not simply said that he was transfigured, but with a certain necessary addition. Both Matthew and Mark have recorded this: he was transfigured before them. Is it therefore possible for Jesus to be transfigured before some but not before others?[8]

Do you wish to see the transfiguration of Jesus? Behold with me the Jesus of the Gospels. Let him be simply apprehended. There he is beheld both "according to the flesh" and at the same time in his true divinity. He is beheld in the form of God according to our capacity for knowledge. This is how he was beheld by those who went up upon the lofty mountain to be apart with him. Meanwhile those who do not go up the mountain can still behold his works and hear his words, which are uplifting. It is before those who go up that Jesus is transfigured, and not to those below. When he is transfigured, his face shines as the sun, that he may be manifested to the children of light, who have put off the works of darkness and put on the armor of light.[9] They are no longer the children of dark-

---

[1]SC 258:62. [2]To make the six-day interval in Matthew 17:1 fit with the eight days in Luke 9:28, Jerome holds that Matthew indicates only the whole days, whereas Luke, applying the criterion of the *synecdoche*, includes the incomplete portions of the day before and the day after the six. [3]Lk 9:28. [4]CCL 77:147. [5]Mt 20:22. [6]Cf. Acts 12:1-3: "Herod . . . killed James the brother of John with the sword; and when he saw that it pleased the Jews . . ." [7]PG 58:549-50; NPNF 1 10:345. [8]Origen holds that the Logos has an individual relation to every rational being, which varies according to the moral progress or regress of each being. Thus the Logos always presents itself to each being in a new way, so that the being can derive from this ever differing contact the maximum spiritual benefit. [9]Rom 13:12.

ness or night but have become the children of day. They walk honestly as in the day. Being manifested, he will shine to them not simply as the sun but as he is demonstrated to be, the sun of righteousness. COMMENTARY ON MATTHEW 12.37.[10]

HIS GARMENTS BECAME WHITE AS LIGHT. JEROME: Certainly the Lord was transformed into that glory with which he would afterwards come in his own kingdom. The change accentuated in splendor. It did not diminish his outward appearance. Let it be that his body had become spiritual. Even his garments were changed, which were white to such a high degree that as another Evangelist would say, "And his clothes became dazzling white, as no fuller on earth could bleach them."[11] What the mortal bleacher on earth is able to make is material and subject to touch, not supernatural and heavenly, which mocks the eyes and is only seen in a vision. COMMENTARY ON MATTHEW 3.17.2.[12]

HIS FACE SHONE LIKE THE SUN. AUGUSTINE: Indeed, Jesus himself shone as the sun, indicating that he is the light which illuminates every one who comes into this world.[13] And this is the sun to the eyes of the flesh, that is the sun to the eyes of the heart. His garments are a type of his church. For garments, unless held up by the one having donned them, fall. Paul was like the lowest hem of these garments. For he himself says, "For I am the least of the apostles,"[14] and in another passage, "I am the last of the apostles." On a garment, the hem is the last thing and the least. Just as that woman who touched the Lord's hem was made well, so the church which came out of the Gentiles was saved by means of Paul's preaching. SERMON 78.2.[15]

17:3 Moses and Elijah Appear

READINESS TO DIE. CHRYSOSTOM: He is transfigured to manifest the glory of the cross, to console Peter and the others in their dread of the

Passion and to bring their minds to elevated understanding. Those who went up with him did not hold their peace but were destined to speak of the glory which he was to accomplish at Jerusalem—of his Passion and the glory of the cross.

And not only did Jesus elevate their understanding, but also he brought their virtues to a higher level, so that they could meet the requirements expected of them. He had just said, "If any man would come after me, let him deny himself, and take up his cross, and follow me."[16] He then set before them Moses and Elijah, who were ready to die ten thousand times for God's decrees and for the people entrusted to them. Each of them, having lost his life, found it. For each of them both spoke boldly to tyrants, the one to the Egyptian, the other to Ahab. They spoke on behalf of heartless and disobedient people. They were brought into extreme danger by the very persons who were saved by them. Both desired to lead people away from idolatry. These were not eloquent men. Moses was slow of tongue and dull of speech.[17] Elijah had the crudest sort of appearance.[18] Both were strict observers of voluntary poverty. Moses did not work for worldly gain. Elijah did not possess anything more than his sheepskin. THE GOSPEL OF MATTHEW, HOMILY 56.3.[19]

THERE APPEARED MOSES AND ELIJAH. JEROME: While the scribes and Pharisees were testing him, he was unwilling to give signs from heaven to those demanding them; however, he silenced their perverse demand with a prudent response. Here, indeed, so that he might increase the faith of the apostles, he gave a sign from heaven. Thereupon Elijah descended from the place to which he had ascended. Moses rose from the lower regions. COMMENTARY ON MATTHEW 3.17.3.[20]

[10]GCS 40:152-53; ANF 9:470. [11]Mk 9.3 [12]CCL 77:147. [13]Jn 1:9. [14]1 Cor 15:9. [15]PL 38:490-91; NPNF 1 6:347 (Sermon 28). [16]Mt 16:24. [17]Ex 4:10. [18]2 Kings 1:8. [19]PG 58:551; NPNF 1 10:346. [20]CCL 77:148.

17:4 Offering to Make Three Booths

I Will Make Three Booths. Jerome: You go astray, Peter, just as the other Evangelist attests: you do not know what you are saying. Do not seek three tabernacles. Seek only the tabernacle of the gospel in which the law and the prophets are to be recapitulated.[21] By seeking three tabernacles you appear to be comparing incommensurably the two servants with the one Lord. Seek only the Father and the Son and the Holy Spirit, for in these there is one God, who is to be worshiped in the tabernacle of your heart. Commentary on Matthew 3.17.4.[22]

Peter Said to Jesus. Cyril of Alexandria: Peter didn't know what he was saying, for before the Savior's Passion, resurrection and victory over death and corruption, it was impossible for Peter to be with Christ and to be permitted into the tents which are in heaven. These things would happen only after the Savior's resurrection and ascent into heaven. Fragment 200.[23]

It Is Well That We Are Here. Leo the Great: Excited therefore by these revelations of secret realities, the apostle Peter, spurning the mundane and loathing earthly things, was seized by a certain excess of passion toward a yearning for eternal things. Filled up with the joy of the whole vision, he wished to dwell there with Jesus where he was delighting in Christ's manifested glory. Thus Peter said, "Lord, it is good for us to be here; if you wish, I will make three booths here, one for you and one for Moses and one for Elijah." But the Lord did not reply to this suggestion, for it was not wicked but inappropriate, since the world could not be saved except by Christ's death. And in the Lord's warning the faith of those who believe is called to account. Among the temptations of this life we should understand that we are to ask for endurance before glory. Good fortune in ruling cannot come before a time of enduring. Sermon 38.5.[24]

17:5 Hear My Beloved Son

A Bright Cloud Overshadowed Them. Origen: I think that God, wishing to dissuade Peter from making three tabernacles, under which so far as it depended on his choice he was going to dwell, shows him a better tabernacle, so to speak, and far superior: the cloud. It is the function of a tabernacle to give shade to one who is in it and to shelter him, and the bright cloud overshadowed them. So God made, as it were, a more divine tabernacle, inasmuch as it was bright, that it might be to them a pattern of the resurrection to come. For the shining cloud gives shade to the righteous and at the same time protects them, gives them light and illuminates them. What would the shining cloud that gives shade to the righteous be? Is it perhaps the Father's power, from which comes the Father's voice saying that this is his Son in whom he is well pleased, urging those that are shaded by it to listen to him and to no one else? He speaks—just as of old so also for all times—through those whom he wishes. Perhaps the shining cloud is the Holy Spirit, giving shade to the righteous and announcing the words of God at work within it and saying, "This is my beloved Son in whom I am well pleased." I would even venture to say that the shining cloud is our Savior. Commentary on Matthew 12.42.[25]

This Is My Beloved Son. Jerome: Because Peter had asked imprudently, he does not merit the Lord's answer. But the Father answered for the Son so that the word of the Lord might be fulfilled: "I do not bear witness for myself, but the Father who sent me, he bears witness for me."[26] The cloud appears bright and shades them, so that those who were looking for a material booth made from boughs or tents

---

[21]Jerome's observation is meant to reveal the tight unity between the Old Testament (law and prophets) and the New Testament. [22]CCL 77:148. [23]MKGK 218. [24]SC 74:18-19; NPNF 2 12:163-64. [25]ANF 9:472-73; GCS 40:165-66. [26]Jn 8:18.

might be protected with the shade of a shining cloud. The voice of the Father speaking from heaven is also heard. It provides testimony and teaches Peter the truth with error removed, and in fact through Peter teaches all the apostles: "This is my beloved Son." It is for him that you must build the tabernacle, him you must obey. "My Son" is distinguished from his servants, Moses and Elijah. They, along with you, are to prepare a tabernacle for the Lord in the inner sanctum of their heart. COMMENTARY ON MATTHEW 3.17.5.[27]

FROM PROMISE TO FULFILLMENT. APOLLINARIS: The Father is evidently revealing the Son when the ringing voice from heaven bursts forth so loudly. Through it he reveals to everyone the testimony coming from above. One must not think that the voice of God is audible. Nor can one perceive a bodiless being. Just as no one has ever seen God,[28] so no one has ever heard God. The words "listen to him" have the power of making a necessary distinction. For he says listen to him, rather than to Moses or the prophet who had been introduced, because it was now time to go forward and advance from the introduction to the fulfillment, from the prefiguration to the true reality.[29] FRAGMENT 85.[30]

LISTEN TO HIM. LEO THE GREAT: A voice from the cloud said, This is my beloved Son, with whom I am well pleased; listen to him. I am manifested through his preaching. I am glorified through his humility. So listen to him without hesitation. He is the truth and the life.[31] He is my strength and wisdom. "Listen to him" whom the mysteries of the law foreshadowed, of whom the mouths of the prophets sang. "Listen to him" who by his blood redeemed the world, who binds the devil[32] and seizes his vessels, who breaks the debt of sin and the bondage of iniquity. "Listen to him" who opens the way to heaven and by the pain of the cross prepares for you the steps of ascent into his kingdom. SERMON 38.7.[33]

17:6 The Disciples Filled with Awe

FILLED WITH AWE. CHRYSOSTOM: Why was it that when they heard these words they were dismayed? For previously a similar voice had spoken in Jordan and a crowd was present, but no one felt anything like this; and afterwards, again, when they said that it thundered, they did not feel anything like this.[34] Why then did they fall on their faces on the mountain? Because there was solitude, and the height of the mountain, and great quietness, and a transfiguration full of awe, and a pure light and a cloud stretched out; all of these threw them into great alarm. Amazement arose on every side, and they fell on their faces in both fear and adoration at the same time. THE GOSPEL OF MATTHEW, HOMILY 56.6.[35]

THEY FELL ON THEIR FACES. CYRIL OF ALEXANDRIA: Through their speaking together it shows that the old prophets also spoke the same things as Jesus, even if enigmatically. In great awe the disciples fell on their faces, and the Savior raised them up. This shows that if Jesus had not been incarnate and had not been Mediator between God and humanity and strengthened his own nature, he would not have endured to hear the voice of God. FRAGMENT 199.[36]

17:7 Rise, and Have No Fear

JESUS CAME AND TOUCHED THEM. JEROME: For three possible reasons they were petrified with fear: either because they knew they had sinned or because the bright cloud covered them or because they had heard the voice of God the Father speaking. Human weakness is not strong enough to bear the sight of such great glory but

---

[27]CCL 77:148-49. [28]Jn 1:18; 1 Jn 4:12. [29]The Old Testament prefigured, both symbolically and prophetically, the New Testament; hence the progress from one to the other is defined as progress from the *typos* to the truth. [30]MKGK 26-27. [31]Jn 14:6. [32]Rev 20:2. [33]SC 74:20; NPNF 2 12:164. [34]Jn 12:28-29. [35]PG 58:554; NPNF 1 10:348. [36]MKGK 218.

trembles with its whole heart and body and falls to earth. . . . "And Jesus came up and touched them." Because they were lying down and could not rise, he mercifully came up and touched them so that through his touch he might put to flight their fear and strengthen their weakened limbs. "And he said to them, 'Rise, and don't be afraid.'" Those whom he had healed with his hand, he heals with his command, "Have no fear." First fear is expelled so that afterwards doctrine may be imparted. COMMENTARY ON MATTHEW 3.17.6-7.[37]

17:8 When They Lifted Their Eyes

THEY SAW JESUS ONLY. ORIGEN: Consider the details of this passage. See if you can also say this: The disciples understood that the Son of God had been speaking with Moses. It was Moses who had said of God, "No one shall see my face and live."[38] The disciples understood the testimony of Moses about God. They were not able to endure the radiance of the Word. They humbled themselves under the mighty hand of God.

But after the touch of the Word, they lifted up their eyes. They saw Jesus only and no other. Moses, the law and Elijah the prophet had become one with the gospel of Jesus. They did not abide as they formerly were as three, but they became one. Think of these things in a spiritual sense. COMMENTARY ON MATTHEW 12.43.[39]

17:9 Tell No One the Vision

UNTIL JESUS IS RAISED FROM THE DEAD. CHRYSOSTOM: For the greater the things said about him, the harder it was for the many at that time to accept them. And the offense of the cross increased all the more thereby. Therefore he told them to be silent about the transfiguration. He again reminded them of the Passion, and he almost mentioned the reason why he told them to be silent. For he did not command them never to tell anyone but "[to wait] until he is

raised from the dead." Saying nothing about the painful part, he told them only of the good. What then? Were they not going to be offended after this? Not at all. For the silence that was being demanded was only for the time before the crucifixion. After this they were thought better prepared to receive the Spirit. They had the voice of the miracles advocating for them, and everything that they said from then on was easier to receive. For the course of events announced his power more clearly than a trumpet, and no stumbling block interrupted these events. THE GOSPEL OF MATTHEW, HOMILY 56.6.[40]

TELL NO ONE. JEROME: The preview of the future kingdom and the glory of his triumph had been shown on the mountain. So he does not want this to be told to the people in case it should be deemed incredible because of its greatness and also so that after such great glory the event of the cross that follows should not cause untaught minds to stumble. COMMENTARY ON MATTHEW 3.17.9.[41]

17:10 First Elijah Must Come

THE SCRIBES' TEACHING. JEROME: Unless we know the reasons why the disciples asked about the name of Elijah, their questioning seems foolish and extraordinary. For what does asking about Elijah's arrival have to do with what was written above? The Pharisees' tradition, following the prophet Malachi of the twelve minor prophets, is that Elijah comes before the end.[42] He turns the hearts of the fathers to their children and the hearts of children to their fathers and restores everything to its ancient state. So the disciples think that the transfiguration of glory is the one that they have seen on the mountain and say, "If you now have come in glory, why does your precursor not appear?"

---

[37]CCL 77:149. [38]Ex 33:20. [39]ANF 9:473; GCS 40:167-68. [40]PG 58:554; NPNF 1 10:348-49. [41]CCL 77:150. [42]Mal 4:5-6.

especially since they had seen Elijah disappear. But when they say, "The scribes say that Elijah must first come," by the word *first* they are saying that unless Elijah comes, it is not the advent of the Savior according to the Scriptures. Commentary on Matthew 3.17.10.[43]

17:11 Restoring All Things

He Is to Restore All Things. Theodore of Mopsuestia: Therefore there will be a forerunner of his second coming about the time of the consummation. Also this time he is to restore all to true knowledge, restoring everyone who obeys him. The scribes deceived the people when they said that Elijah comes before the advent of the Christ. And this word was reported also among the ignorant crowd; that is what the disciples now ask. How then does he resolve it? Fragment 94.[44]

17:12 Elijah Has Already Come

They Did Not Know Him. Origen: The disciples who went up with Jesus remembered the traditions of the scribes concerning Elijah, that before the advent of Christ, Elijah would come and prepare for him the souls of those who would receive him. But the vision on the mountain, in which Elijah appeared, did not seem to be harmonized with what had been said, since Elijah seemed to them to have come with him rather than before him. So they say this thinking that the scribes were wrong. To this the Savior replies, not denying what was handed down about Elijah but saying that there was another coming of Elijah before that of Christ unknown to the scribes. In [this coming] "they did not know him but did to him whatever they pleased," as though they too were accomplices in his imprisonment by Herod and execution by him. Then he says that he too will suffer what they did to Elijah. The disciples asked these questions as though about Elijah and the Savior replied. But hearing the Savior's words, "Elijah has already come," and what followed, they took it as a reference to John the Baptist. Commentary on Matthew 13.1.[45]

Fulfilling Elijah's Ministry. Chrysostom: They did not know this from the Scriptures, but the scribes used to tell them, and this saying was reported among the ignorant crowd, as also about Christ. Therefore the Samaritan woman also said, "The Messiah is coming; when he comes, he will show us all things."[46] And they themselves asked John, "Are you Elijah or the prophet?"[47] For this opinion was strong, as I said, both the one about Christ and the one about Elijah, but they did not interpret it as it should have been. For the Scriptures speak of two comings of Christ, both this one that has taken place and the future one. Paul spoke of these when he said, "For the grace of God has appeared for the salvation of men, training us to renounce irreligion and worldly passions, and to live sober, upright and godly lives in this world."[48] Behold the first advent, and listen to how he declares the coming advent: "Awaiting our blessed hope, the appearing of the glory of our great God and Savior Jesus Christ."[49] The prophets also mention both advents; of the one that is second they say that Elijah will be the forerunner; John was forerunner of the first, John whom Christ also called by the name Elijah, not because he was Elijah but because he was fulfilling Elijah's ministry. For just as Elijah will be the forerunner of the second advent, so John was of the first. But the scribes, confusing these things and perverting the people, mentioned that coming alone, the second one, to the people, and said, "If this is the Christ, Elijah ought to have come first." That is why the disciples also say, "Then why do the scribes say that first Elijah must come?" The Gospel of Matthew, Homily 57.1.[50]

---

[43]CCL 77:150-51. [44]MKGK 130. [45]GCS 40:171-72; ANF 9:474. [46]Jn 4:25. [47]Jn 1:21. Cf. p. 2 n. 3. [48]Tit 2:11-12. [49]Tit 2:13. [50]PG 58:557-59; NPNF 1 10:352.

17:14-23 JESUS HEALS A BOY WITH A DEMON AND SPEAKS AGAIN ABOUT HIS DEATH

[14]And when they came to the crowd, a man came up to him and kneeling before him said, [15]"Lord, have mercy on my son, for he is an epileptic and he suffers terribly; for often he falls into the fire, and often into the water. [16]And I brought him to your disciples, and they could not heal him." [17]And Jesus answered, "O faithless and perverse generation, how long am I to be with you? How long am I to bear with you? Bring him here to me." [18]And Jesus rebuked him, and the demon came out of him, and the boy was cured instantly. [19]Then the disciples came to Jesus privately and said, "Why could we not cast it out?" [20]He said to them, "Because of your little faith. For truly, I say to you, if you have faith as a grain of mustard seed, you will say to this mountain, 'Move from here to there,' and it will move; and nothing will be impossible to you."[x]

[22]As they were gathering[y] in Galilee, Jesus said to them, "The Son of man is to be delivered into the hands of men, [23]and they will kill him, and he will be raised on the third day." And they were greatly distressed.

x Other ancient authorities insert verse 21, "But this kind never comes out except by prayer and fasting"   y Other ancient authorities read *abode*

OVERVIEW: Every disease and weakness that our Savior cured corresponds to different symptoms in the soul (ORIGEN). Nothing is impossible to those who have total faith (CHRYSOSTOM). The mountains mentioned here are the hostile powers that have their being in a flood of great wickedness, such as are settled down, so to speak, in some souls. But when one has total faith such that one no longer disbelieves in anything found in holy Scripture, possessing faith like that of Abraham, then one has complete faith like a grain of mustard seed (ORIGEN). All power not only for defeating demons, but even for raising the dead, has been given to the faith of the apostles (HILARY OF POITIERS). If one can pray so that one may cast out another demon, how much more should one pray that one's own demons be cast out (AUGUSTINE).

The disciples knew that the Son of man would die, having heard it continually. But what kind of death was to occur, that release from death would come quickly and that death would work innumerable blessings they did not yet understand (CHRYSOSTOM). Whenever the Lord speaks of future disaster, he always teaches its close connection with the happiness of redemption, so that when disasters suddenly come they do not terrify but may be borne by hearts that have premeditated them (JEROME). It was necessary for him to undergo his saving Passion for us (CYRIL OF ALEXANDRIA).

17:14-15 Lord, Have Mercy on My Son

THE BOY SUFFERS TERRIBLY. ORIGEN: If every disease and weakness which our Savior cured at that time among the people represents different symptoms in the soul, it stands to reason that by the paralytics are symbolized the palsied in soul, who keep it lying paralyzed in the body. By those who are blind are symbolized those who are blind in respect of things seen by the soul alone,[1] and these are really blind. And by the deaf are symbolized those who are deaf in regard

---

[1]Cf. p. 33 n. 2.

59

to the reception of the word of salvation. On the same principle it will be necessary that the matters regarding the epileptic should be investigated. This disease attacks those who suffer from it at considerable intervals, during which time he who suffers from it seems in no way to differ from the man in good health, at the season when the epilepsy is not working on him. You will find some souls that are often considered to be healthy suffering from symptoms like these in their chastity and the other virtues. But there comes a time when they are attacked by a kind of epilepsy, and then they seem to fall from their solid foundation and are seized by the deceits and other desires of this world. COMMENTARY ON MATTHEW 13.4.[2]

17:16 The Disciples Could Not Heal Him

HELP MY UNBELIEF. CHRYSOSTOM: The Scripture shows that this man is very weak in faith. This is evident from many things: from Christ's saying, "All things are possible to him who believes,"[3] and from the fact that the man himself as he approached said, "Help my unbelief."[4] And it is evident from Christ's ordering the demon "never to enter him again"[5] and from the man's saying again to Christ, "If you can."[6] But you will say, "If his unbelief was the reason why the demon had not gone out of the boy, why does he blame the disciples?" To show that they can often cure the sick, even though no one brings them in with faith. For just as the faith of the one bringing in the sick was often sufficient for receiving a cure even from lesser ministers, so the virtue of the minister was also sufficient to achieve a miracle even without the faith of those bringing them in. Both of these are demonstrated in the Scriptures; for those around Cornelius drew to them the power of the Spirit by their faith. And in the time of Elisha, when no one believed, a dead man was raised.[7] THE GOSPEL OF MATTHEW, Homily 57.3.[8]

17:17 A Faithless and Perverse Generation

O PERVERSE GENERATION. ORIGEN: When the Savior says, "O faithless and perverse generation," he shows that wickedness has entered us through perversity, that it is contrary to nature and makes us perverse. And I think that he was irked at the whole human race on earth for its wickedness. So he said, "How long am I to bear with you?" COMMENTARY ON MATTHEW 13.7.[9]

HOW LONG AM I TO BEAR WITH YOU? CHRYSOSTOM: Note this man's lack of sense in another instance: in full view of the crowd he pleads to Jesus against his disciples, saying, "I brought him to your disciples, and they could not cure him." But Jesus dismissed these complaints before the people and blamed him the more, saying, "O faithless and perverse generation, how long am I to be with you?" He is not addressing this person alone, so as not to upset him, but he is addressing all the Jews. For it is likely that many had been offended and thought ill of the disciples.

But when he says, "How long am I to be with you?" he shows how welcome death is to him and his desire of passing on from here. He longs for his departure. It is being with them, and not so much the crucifixion, that is grievous.

He did not put up with their complaints, but what does he say? "Bring him here to me." And he himself further asks him, "How long has this been this way?" He is thereby both defending the disciples and leading the man to a better hope, that he should believe that there will be an end to his troubles. And Jesus lets him be convulsed, not for display (for when the crowd gathered he rebuked the demon) but for the father's sake, that when he saw the demon being put to flight at Christ's mere call, so at least, if in no other way, he might be led to believe the coming miracle. THE GOSPEL OF MATTHEW, Homily 57.3.[10]

---

[2]GCS 40:187-89; ANF 9:477. [3]Mk 9:23. [4]Mk 9:24. [5]Mk 9:25. [6]Mk 9:22. [7]2 Kings 13:21. [8]PG 58:561; NPNF 1 10:354. [9]GCS 40:196-97; ANF 9:479. [10]PG 58:561; NPNF 1 10:354.

17:18 *The Boy Cured Instantly*

JESUS REBUKED HIM. JEROME: Note that it was not the suffering victim but the demon who had to be directly rebuked. It may be that he indirectly rebuked the boy and the demon went out of him because it was owing to his sins that the demon had oppressed him. COMMENTARY ON MATTHEW 3.17.18.[11]

17:19 *The Disciples Question Jesus Privately*

WHY COULD NOT WE CAST IT OUT? HILARY OF POITIERS: The disciples are surprised that they could not throw out the demon. All power, not only of besting demons but even of raising the dead, had been given them.[12] Furthermore, because the law was soon to be transcended, Jesus says, "O faithless and perverse generation, how long am I to be with you?" He does not seem to be saying this to those whom he had set apart. Those who did not have faith were going to lose the very law that they had. If they had had this faith within them, they would have been like the grain of mustard seed. By the power of the Word they would have thrown out this burden of sins and the heavy mass of their unbelief. They would have transferred it, like a mountain into the sea, to the activity of the pagans and secular people. ON MATTHEW 17.8.[13]

PRAYING TO CAST OUT ONE'S OWN DEMONS. AUGUSTINE: In this chapter the Lord urged us to pray when he said, "Because of your little faith you could not cast out this demon." For urging us to prayer he thus concluded, "This kind does not go out except by prayer and fasting."[14] If a man prays so that he may throw out someone else's demon, how much more so that he may cast out his own avarice? How much more so that he may cast out his own drunkenness? How much more so that he may cast out his own dissipation? How much more so that he may cast out his own impurity? How great are the sins in human beings! If they persevere in

them, they do not allow them to enter the kingdom of heaven! SERMON 80.3.[15]

17:20 *Because of Your Little Faith*

FAITH AS A GRAIN OF MUSTARD SEED. ORIGEN: The mountains here spoken of, in my opinion, are the hostile powers that have their being in a flood of great wickedness, such as are settled down, so to speak, in some souls of various people. But when someone has total faith, such that he no longer disbelieves in anything found in holy Scripture and has faith like that of Abraham, who so believed in God to such a degree that his faith was reckoned to him as righteousness,[16] then he has all faith like a grain of mustard seed. Then such a man will say to this mountain—I mean in this case the deaf and dumb spirit in him who is said to be epileptic—"Move from here to another place." It will move. This means it will move from the suffering person to the abyss. The apostle, taking this as his starting point, said with apostolic authority, "If I have all faith, so as to remove mountains."[17] For he who has all faith—which is like a grain of mustard seed—moves not just one mountain but also more just like it. And nothing will be impossible for the person who has so much faith.

Let us examine also this statement: "This kind is not cast out except through prayer and fasting."[18] If at any time it is necessary that we should be engaged in the healing of one suffering from such a disorder, we are not to adjure nor put questions nor speak to the impure spirit as if it heard. But [by] devoting ourselves to prayer and fasting, we may be successful as we pray for the sufferer, and by our own fasting we may thrust out the unclean spirit from him. COMMENTARY ON MATTHEW 13.7.[19]

---

[11]CCL 77:152. [12]Mt 10:8. [13]SC 258:68. [14]Cf. Mk 9:29; Augustine is quoting a variant from Mt 17:20. [15]PL 38:495; NPNF 1 6:350 (Sermon 30). [16]Gen 15:6. [17]1 Cor 13:2. [18]Mk 9:29 KJV. [19]GCS 40:197-98; ANF 9:479.

SAY TO THIS MOUNTAIN: MOVE. CHRYSOS-
TOM: The disciples seem to me to be in anxiety
and fear that they had lost the grace with which
they had been entrusted. For they had received
power over unclean demons. So they approached him in private and asked him the question, not out of shame (for if the matter had got
out and they were criticized, it would have been
superfluous for the future to have been ashamed
of admitting it in their words) but because what
they were going to ask him was secret and of
great moment.

What, then, does Christ say? "Because of
your little faith. For truly, I say to you, if you
have faith as a grain of mustard seed, you will
say to this mountain, 'Move from here to there,'
and it will move; and nothing will be impossible
to you." But if you say "Where did they move a
mountain?" I will say that they did things much
greater than that in raising up innumerable
dead. For moving a mountain and moving death
from a body are not at all comparable. After
them other saints, far inferior to the disciples,
are said to have moved mountains when necessity demanded. It is clear that the disciples also
would have done so had necessity demanded.
But if there was never need at that time, do not
find fault with them. THE GOSPEL OF MAT-
THEW, HOMILY 57.4.[20]

17:22-23 Jesus Speaks of His Death and Resurrection

**THE DISCIPLES WERE GREATLY DIS-
TRESSED.** CHRYSOSTOM: In case they say "Why
do we delay here so long?" again he tells them
about his Passion. Hearing of it, they did not
even want to see Jerusalem. . . . Peter had been
rebuked, those around Moses and Elijah had
spoken with him and had called the thing glory,
and . . . the Father had spoken from above; after
so many miracles had taken place and the resurrection was close by (for he said that he would
not long remain in death but would rise on the
third day)—not even thus could they endure it.

But "they were distressed," and not simply "distressed" but "greatly distressed." This happened
because they did not yet recognize the power of
what he said. But Mark and Luke imply it; the
former saying that "they did not understand the
saying and they were afraid to ask";[21] the latter
saying that "it was concealed from them that
they should not perceive it, and they were afraid
to ask him about this saying."[22] Yet if they did
not know it, why were they distressed? Because
they were not totally ignorant.

They knew that he would die, having heard it
continually. But as yet they did not know clearly
what kind of death this was to be, or that there
would be a speedy release from it, or that it
would work innumerable blessings, or what this
resurrection might be. They did not know it,
and so they were distressed, for they greatly
adored their Master. THE GOSPEL OF MAT-
THEW, HOMILY 58.1.[23]

HE WILL BE RAISED. JEROME: Whenever the
Lord speaks of future disaster, he always teaches
its close relation with the happiness of redemption, so that when disasters suddenly come they
do not terrify the apostles but may be borne by
hearts that have premeditated them. If it sad-
dens them because he is going to be killed, it
ought to make them rejoice that it says, "On the
third day he will arise again." Further, their distress, in fact their great distress, does not come
from lack of faith—elsewhere also they knew
that Peter had been rebuked because he did not
consider what belonged to God but what
belonged to men—but because their love of
their Master does not let them hear anything
ominous or humiliating. COMMENTARY ON
MATTHEW 3.17.23.[24]

THE NECESSITY OF HIS PASSION. CYRIL OF
ALEXANDRIA: Therefore he brought the disciples to the mountain and showed them the glory

---

[20]PG 58:562; NPNF 1 10:355. [21]Mk 9:32. [22]Lk 9:45. [23]PG 58:565-
66; NPNF 1 10:358. [24]CCL 77:153-54.

with which he will shine on the universe in the future. Then coming down from the mountain he freed a person from a rough and evil spirit. It was altogether necessary for him to undergo his saving Passion for us and to suffer the violence of the Jews. When this happened, it was quite likely that the disciples would be alarmed and would ponder it and say among themselves: "He has raised so many from the dead by divine power, he commands the seas and winds, he overwhelms Satan with his words—how has he now been taken and fallen to the noose of his murderers? Then maybe we were deceived when we thought that he was God?" So that they should know the future fully and completely, therefore, he foretells to them the mystery of the Passion. FRAGMENT 209.[25]

THEY WILL KILL HIM. ORIGEN: I think we have an obligation to examine this, too: that Jesus was delivered into the hands of men, not by men into the hands of men but by powers to whom the Father delivered his Son on behalf of us all. In the very act of being delivered and coming under the power of those to whom he was delivered, he "destroyed him who had the power of death." For "through death he destroyed him who has the power of death, that is, the devil, and delivered all those who through fear of death were subject to lifelong bondage."[26] COMMENTARY ON MATTHEW 13.8.[27]

---

[25]MKGK 221. [26]Heb 2:15-16. [27]GCS 40:203; ANF 9:479.

17:24-27 PAYING THE TEMPLE TAX

[24]*When they came to Capernaum, the collectors of the half-shekel tax went up to Peter and said, "Does not your teacher pay the tax?"* [25]*He said, "Yes." And when he came home, Jesus spoke to him first, saying, "What do you think, Simon? From whom do kings of the earth take toll or tribute? From their sons or from others?"* [26]*And when he said, "From others," Jesus said to him, "Then the sons are free.* [27]*However, not to give offense to them, go to the sea and cast a hook, and take the first fish that comes up, and when you open its mouth you will find a shekel; take that and give it to them for me and for yourself."*

OVERVIEW: The half-shekel was the amount that the law had established for those serving in the temple for the redemption of soul and body, and for rich and poor alike (HILARY OF POITIERS, CYRIL OF ALEXANDRIA). The giving of the half-shekel is a symbol of true redemption, and the shekel is for the redeemed soul (APOLLINARIS). Rightly understood, the Lord is free from paying tribute, and yet he must fulfill all righteousness (CHRYSOSTOM). We are like fish caught by the apostles, in whose mouths we display Christ the royal coin, who rendered payment of our debt for two things, our soul and our body (CYRIL OF ALEXANDRIA). It was no small thing to predict that the fish carrying the tribute would be the first one caught in those depths or that the net thrown into the deep would obey his command and would bring in the fish carrying the coin (CHRYSOSTOM). Since Jesus is the image of God the unseen and did not have stamped upon him the image of Caesar, he took the image of Caesar from a suitable place in the sea, so as to pay it to the kings of the earth as the contribution of himself and his disciple. He did this so that those taking the half-shekel might not suppose Jesus to be in debt either to them or to the kings of the earth (ORIGEN).

17:24 Does Not Your Teacher Pay the Tax?

THE HALF-SHEKEL INTERPRETED CHRISTOLOGICALLY. APOLLINARIS: This tax of the half-shekel was the law, defined by Moses, who said, "Each will give as redemption of his soul to the Lord, a half shekel."[1] The Jews collected this from everyone, and the half-shekel was paid as redemption for two souls according to the law. The rich man was not demanded more, nor the poor man less. The half-shekel is sacred, intimating nothing else than the true divine-human Mediator, since everything foreshadowed this. The true redemption was the Lord who had the Father in himself, since his nature is divine.[2] The giving of the half-shekel is a symbol of his self-giving, and the shekel is for the redeemed soul. No one is allowed to pay more than the half, not even if he is rich. Thus it is said, "For in him all the fullness of God was pleased to dwell,"[3] that is, all the fullness of divinity, which is offered in his mediatorial work on the cross, abides in his dual nature as God-man. The richness of his divinity and the poverty of his humanity are fully integrated in one person. The half-shekel is interpreted here as his divinity, under question by the tax collectors. FRAGMENT 87.[4]

A SYMBOL FORESHADOWING OUR REDEMPTION. HILARY OF POITIERS: The Lord is asked to pay a half-shekel. For this was the amount that the law had established for those serving in the temple for the redemption of soul and body. But the law, as we know, is the foreshadowing of the future (for it was not the value of the coin that God desired so that with such a small expense redemption of soul and body might be granted for sins). Therefore the offering of this

half-shekel was established[5] so that we might offer ourselves certified and professed and enrolled in the name of Christ, in Christ who is the true temple of God, and it was established as testimony of the Son of God. ON MATTHEW 17.10.[6]

NOT PAYING THE TAX? JEROME: After Caesar Augustus, Judea was made a tributary state and all the people were registered in the census. So Joseph and his kinswoman Mary had set off for Bethlehem. Once again, since Jesus had been brought up in Nazareth, which is a town of Galilee lying close to Capernaum, he is asked to pay taxes. Because of the magnitude of the miracles he had done, those who demanded this tax do not dare to ask him. Instead, they meet a disciple and maliciously ask whether he should pay taxes or defy Caesar's will. COMMENTARY ON MATTHEW 3.17.24.[7]

17:25-26 From Whom Do Earthly Kings Take Tribute?

THE SONS ARE FREE. CHRYSOSTOM: So that Peter should not think that he said it after hearing it from others, he forestalls him by showing this very thing and giving Peter, a man who up to now shrank from speaking about these things, freedom to speak about it. What he says is something like this: "I am free from paying tribute. For if the kings of the earth do not take it from their sons but from their subjects, much more ought I to be free of this demand, being the Son not of an earthly king but of the king of heaven and myself a king as well." Do you see how he has distinguished the sons from them

---

[1]Ex 30:13. [2]Roman coins normally carried an image (*charactēr*) of the emperor stamped on their obverse alongside titles ascribing divine status to the Roman emperor. The Jewish half-shekel (the coin used to pay the temple tax) bore no human image or text inscription, yet it was considered by its use as holy. Apollinaris is contrasting the conventions to comment on Christ's dual nature. To make the point more obvious, he refers to Jesus' character, or nature (*charactēr*), as divine (*theikos*). [3]Col 1:19. [4]*MKGK* 27. [5]Ex 30:13. [6]SC 258:70. [7]CCL 77:154.

that are not sons? And if he were not a son, he brought in the example of the kings without purpose. Someone may say, "Yes, he is a son but not trueborn." Then he is not a son, and if he is not a son or trueborn he does not belong to God but to someone else. But if he belongs to someone else, then the comparison does not have its proper strength. For he is speaking not of sons generally but of truly begotten sons, their very own sons, of sons who share the kingdom with their parents. And so by way of contrast he mentioned "the sons of others," calling those that are born of themselves "their own" and those not born of themselves "of others." THE GOSPEL OF MATTHEW, HOMILY 58.2.[8]

IMMUNITY FROM TAXES. JEROME: Our Lord was the son of a king both according to the flesh and according to the spirit, begotten either from the stock of David or from the Word of the almighty Father. Therefore as the son of a king he did not owe tax, but as one who had assumed the humility of the flesh he has to fulfill all justice. We unfortunates, who are enrolled under Christ's name and do nothing worthy of such great majesty, for us he both underwent the cross and paid our tax. But we do not pay him tribute in return for his honor and like the sons of a king we are immune from taxes. COMMENTARY ON MATTHEW 3.17.26.[9]

DO KINGS TAKE TRIBUTE FROM THEIR SONS? HILARY OF POITIERS: Is it not clear that the sons of kings are not subject to tax and those who are the heirs of a kingdom are free from service? But his words have inner meaning. A drachma was demanded of the people. Now the law moves toward that faith which was to be revealed through Christ. Therefore by the custom of the law this same drachma was demanded from Christ as though from an ordinary citizen. But to show that he was not subject to the law and to demonstrate the glory of his Father's dignity in himself, he offered as an example of earthly privilege the fact that kings'

sons are not subject to census and tax. He is the Redeemer of our soul and body. Nothing should be demanded of him for his redemption, because it was necessary that a king's son be distinguished from the common lot. Therefore the king's son offers a stumbling block to the tax law in order to do away with it, he being free from the duty of the law. ON MATTHEW 17.11.[10]

17:27 *Fishing for a Shekel*

THE FISH A FIGURE FOR THE CHURCH. APOLLINARIS: He establishes himself as lord and master of the sea, of the things in it and of all the elements, as the true Son of God the Father. For this fish provides a type of the church: once [it was] held by the brine of faithlessness and superstition, submerged in the depths of the sea and swamped by the storms and distress of worldly pleasures. But now [it is] raised up by the apostles' hook of teaching and the fishing nets of the Word to the knowledge of God, of him "who calls us from darkness to his amazing light."[11] FRAGMENT 88.[12]

FIND A SHEKEL IN THE FISH'S MOUTH AND GIVE IT. CHRYSOSTOM: Elsewhere, however, he despises the offense,[13] when he was talking about foods,[14] teaching us to know the times when we must take account of those being offended and when to disregard them. And in the manner of giving or paying the tax, he discloses himself again. Why does he not tell Peter to give of what they have laid up? So that, as I said, in this too he might show that he is God of all and that he rules even the sea. He had already demonstrated this when he rebuked it and by his commanding Peter to walk on the waves.[15] Now again he signifies the same thing, though in another way, yet so as to cause great amazement. For it was not a small thing to pre-

---

[8]PG 58:567; NPNF 1 10:358-59. [9]CCL 77:155. [10]SC 258:70-72. [11]1 Pet 2:9. [12]MKGK 28. [13]*Scandalon*, stumbling block. [14]Mt 15:11-20. [15]Mt 14:29.

dict that the fish carrying the tribute would be the first one caught in those depths or that the net thrown into the deep would obey his command and would bring in the fish carrying the coin. Thus it is an act of divine and unutterable power. THE GOSPEL OF MATTHEW, HOMILY 58.2.[16]

GIVE IT TO THEM FOR ME AND FOR YOURSELF. ORIGEN: This coin was not in Jesus' house but happened to be in the mouth of a fish in the sea. This too, I think, was a result of God's kindness. It was caught and came up on the hook belonging to Peter, who was the fisher of men. That which is figuratively called a fish was caught in order that the coin with the image of Caesar might be taken from it, that it might take its place among those which were caught by them who have learned to become fishers of men. Let him, then, who has the things of Caesar render them to Caesar,[17] that afterwards he may be able to render to God the things of God. But since Jesus is the image of God the unseen and did not have the image of Caesar (for there was nothing in him that had anything to do with the prince of this world),[18] he therefore took the image of Caesar from a suitable place in the sea, so as to pay it to the kings of the earth as the contribution of himself and his disciple. Jesus did this so that those taking the half-shekel might not suppose Jesus to be in debt either to

them or to the kings of the earth. For he paid the debt, one he had never taken on or possessed or used to buy anything or made his personal possession, to prevent the image of Caesar ever being alongside the image of the invisible God. COMMENTARY ON MATTHEW 13.10.[19]

GO TO THE SEA. CYRIL OF ALEXANDRIA: He was also able to take the coin out of the earth, but he did not do so. [Instead he] made the miracle out of the sea, so that he might teach us the mystery rich in contemplation. For we are the fish snatched from the bitter disturbances of life. It is just as if we have been caught out of the sea on the apostles' hooks. In their mouths the fish have Christ the royal coin, which was rendered in payment of debt for two things, for our soul and for our body. Also for two peoples, the Jews and the Gentiles. Also in the same way for the poor and the wealthy, since the old law clearly demanded the payment of the half-shekel from both rich and poor alike. FRAGMENT 212.[20]

---

[16]PG 58:567; NPNF 1 10:359. [17]Mt 22:21. [18]In sharp contrast to Apollinaris (cf. p. 64. n. 2), Origen interprets the Roman emperor as a symbol of the devil, the prince of this world. Christ is the fish, and the coin found in its mouth signifies the ransom that he has paid the devil to free humankind, which through sin had become the devil's slave. The fact that the coin was found in the sea (symbolic of the world) indicates that Christ did not take it from his dominion but from that of the devil, to show that he was not the devil's slave as was his disciple Peter, who here symbolizes humanity set free by Christ. [19]GCS 40:207-8; ANF 9:481. [20]MKGK 222-23.

18:1-5 WHO IS THE GREATEST?

At that time the disciples came to Jesus, saying, "Who is the greatest in the kingdom of heaven?" [2]And calling to him a child, he put him in the midst of them, [3]and said, "Truly, I say to you, unless you turn and become like children, you will never enter the kingdom of heaven. [4]Whoever humbles himself like this child, he is the greatest in the kingdom of heaven.

[5]"Whoever receives one such child in my name receives me."

OVERVIEW: Because the disciples had observed that the same tax had been paid for Peter and the Lord, they inferred that Peter might have been set over all the other apostles. Thus they asked who is greater in the kingdom of heaven (JEROME, CHRYSOSTOM). The child called by Jesus into the middle of the disciples is analogous to the lowly work of the Holy Spirit (ORIGEN). What children are in their simplicity, let us become through a holy way of life: as children innocent of sin and thus as one who is great in the kingdom of heaven (JEROME, EPIPHANIUS THE LATIN). One who receives such a person will receive Christ (JEROME).

18:1 Who Is Greatest in the Kingdom of Heaven?

WHETHER PETER IS FIRST. JEROME: We must seek for reasons for individual sayings and actions of the Lord. After the coin was found, after the tribute paid, what do the apostles' sudden questions mean? Why precisely "at that time" did the disciples come to Jesus saying, "Who is the greatest in the kingdom of heaven?" Because they had seen that the same tax had been paid for both Peter and the Lord. From the equal price they inferred that Peter may have been set over all the other apostles, since Peter had been compared with the Lord in the paying of the tax. So they ask who is greater in the kingdom of heaven. Jesus, seeing their thoughts and understanding the causes of their error, wants to heal their desire for glory with a struggle for humility. COMMENTARY ON MATTHEW 3.18.1.[1]

WHY THEY WERE UPSET. CHRYSOSTOM: The disciples experienced some human weakness; therefore the Evangelist also shows this, adding "in that hour," when he honored Peter more than all others. For though Peter was a firstborn son along with James and John, he did nothing similar for them. Then being ashamed to admit what they felt, they did not openly say, "Why have you honored Peter above us?" or "Surely he is not greater than us?" When they became ashamed, they asked less definitely, "Who then is greater?" When they had seen the three honored above the rest, they had felt nothing of the kind. But when one took the highest honor, then they were hurt. Apparently it was not for this alone but piling up many feelings they became incensed. For Jesus had said to Peter, "I will give you the keys,"[2] and "You are blessed, Simon Bar-Jonah,"[3] and to Peter here he instructed, "Give it to them for me and for yourself." And seeing the great freedom allowed him elsewhere they were upset. THE GOSPEL OF MATTHEW, HOMILY 58.3.[4]

18:2 A Child in the Midst of Them

THE IMAGE OF INNOCENCE. JEROME: He called a child to him to ask its age or to show the image of innocence. Or perhaps he actually set a child in their midst—he himself, who had not come to be served but to serve—to show them an example of humility. COMMENTARY ON MATTHEW 3.18.2.[5]

18:3 Unless You Become Like Children

THINK OF THE HOLY SPIRIT AS A CHILD. ORIGEN: Beside this obvious explanation[6] let another be given as well. As an act of theological and ethical reflection, let us ask what sort of a child Jesus called to him and has set in the midst of the disciples. Think of it this way: The child called by Jesus is the Holy Spirit, who humbled himself. He was called by the Savior and set in the middle of the disciples of Jesus. The Lord wants us, ignoring all the rest, to turn to the examples given by the Holy Spirit, so that we become like the children—that is, the disci-

---

[1]CCL 77:156. [2]Mt 16:19. [3]Mt 16:17. [4]PG 58:568; NPNF 1 10:359. [5]CCL 77:156. [6]Previously Origen proposed the literal interpretation of the Gospel text, identified as "more sound" (*haplousteros*), because it was suitable for believers who were still beginners in the faith.

ples—who were themselves converted and made like the Holy Spirit. God gave these children to the Savior according to what we read in Isaiah: "Behold, I and the children whom the Lord has given me."[7] To enter the kingdom of heaven is not possible for the person who has not turned from worldly matters and become like those children who had the Holy Spirit. Jesus called this Holy Spirit to him like a child, when he came down from his perfect completeness to people, and set it in the middle of the disciples. COMMENTARY ON MATTHEW 13.18.[8]

18:4 Humble as a Child

RETURN TO THE SIMPLICITY OF CHILDREN. HILARY OF POITIERS: The Lord teaches that we cannot enter the kingdom of heaven unless we revert to the nature of children, that is, we must recall into the simplicity of children the vices of the body and mind. He has called children all who believe through the faith of listening. For children follow their father, love their mother, do not know how to wish ill on their neighbor, show no concern for wealth, are not proud, do not hate, do not lie, believe what has been said and hold what they hear as truth. And when we assume this habit and will in all the emotions, we are shown the passageway to the heavens. We must therefore return to the simplicity of children, because with it we shall embrace the beauty of the Lord's humility. ON MATTHEW 18.1.[9]

HUMBLING ONESELF. JEROME: "Whoever humbles himself like this child, he is the greatest in the kingdom of heaven." Just as this child whose example I show you does not persist in anger, does not long remember injury suffered, is not enamored inordinately by the sight of a beautiful woman, does not think one thing and say another, so you too, unless you have similar innocence and purity of mind, will not be able to enter the kingdom of heaven. Or it might be taken in another way: "Whosoever therefore

humiliates himself like this child is greater in the kingdom of heaven," so as to imply that anyone who imitates me and humiliates himself following my example, so that he abases himself as much as I abased myself in accepting the form of a servant, will enter the kingdom of heaven. COMMENTARY ON MATTHEW 3.18.4.[10]

18:5 Receiving Christ

WHO RECEIVES SUCH A CHILD. JEROME: Whoever receives one such child in my name receives me. Whoever lives so as to imitate Christ's humility and innocence, in him Christ is taken up. And he is careful to add—so that when the apostles heard of it, they would not think that they had been honored—that they would not be taken up for their merit but for the honor of the master. COMMENTARY ON MATTHEW 3.18.5.[11]

WHAT IT MEANS TO BECOME A CHILD. EPIPHANIUS THE LATIN: Here the Lord not only repressed the apostles' thoughts but also checked the ambition of believers throughout the whole world, so that he might be great who wanted to be least. For with this purpose Jesus used the example of the child, that what he had been through his nature, we through our holy living might become—innocent, like children innocent of every sin. For a child does not know how to hold resentment or to grow angry. He does not know how to repay evil for evil. He does not think base thoughts. He does not commit adultery or arson or murder. He is utterly ignorant of theft or brawling or all the things that will draw him to sin. He does not know how to disparage, how to blaspheme, how to hurt, how to lie. He believes what he hears. What he is ordered he does not analyze. He loves his parents with full affection. Therefore what children are in their simplicity, let us

[7]Is 8:18. [8]GCS 40:226-27; ANF 9:485. [9]SC 258:74-76. [10]CCL 77:157. [11]CCL 77:157.

become through a holy way of life, as children innocent of sin. And quite rightly, one who has become a child innocent of sin in this way is greater in the kingdom of heaven. And whoever

receives such a person will receive Christ. Interpretation of the Gospels 27.[12]

[12]PL Supp 3:866-67.

18:6-9 TEMPTATIONS TO SIN

[6]"But whoever causes one of these little ones who believe in me to sin,[z] it would be better for him to have a great millstone fastened round his neck and to be drowned in the depth of the sea.

[7]"Woe to the world for temptations to sin![a] For it is necessary that temptations come, but woe to the man by whom the temptation comes! [8]And if your hand or your foot causes you to sin,[z] cut it off and throw it away; it is better for you to enter life maimed or lame than with two hands or two feet to be thrown into the eternal fire. [9]And if your eye causes you to sin,[z] pluck it out and throw it away; it is better for you to enter life with one eye than with two eyes to be thrown into the hell[b] of fire."

z Greek causes . . . to stumble   a Greek stumbling blocks   b Greek Gehenna

Overview: The millstone stands for blind toil, for pack animals that are driven around in the circle with their eyes closed (Hilary of Poitiers). When temptations come unaware, the situation is analogous to a sick person enjoying excellent care but refusing to follow the physician's regimen (Chrysostom). Woe is pronounced upon those who voluntarily subject themselves to temptations. But the disciples, who are not attached to the things of the world, do not voluntarily enter into these temptations (Origen). The whole world is not equally full of temptation to sin, but it is all filled with the possibility of fruitful action. It is "the world who knew him not" upon which woe is pronounced, not the world which Christ has reconciled to himself. To say figuratively it is full of chaff does not imply that it contains nothing good (Augustine).

The metaphor of cutting off limbs is really about friends and relatives who constantly cause temptation. For nothing is so harmful as bad

company (Chrysostom). If at some time it happens that the eye so changes that it becomes a temptation to sin for the whole body, it would be better for it to be ripped out from the whole body than for the whole body together with the soul to be condemned (Origen). If the hands or feet of the church (that is, any priest or deacon), either through heretical faith or depraved living, has brought temptations to sin on the church, the Lord orders that such be plucked from the body of the church and thrown out (Chromatius).

18:6 Causing a Believer to Sin

A Spiritual Understanding of the Millstone. Hilary of Poitiers: These important items of comparison are not idle. Such an offender is to be sunk in the sea with both a millstone[1] and an asses' pack load,[2] and even

[1]Mola. [2]Asinaria.

this is better[3] for him! What is better in the accepted sense of the word is always beneficial. What then is the utility of being sunk with an asses' millstone hung around one's neck? So harsh a death will profit him in terms of future punishment. In some way it will be beneficial to meet that death which is the ultimate of evils.

But how should we understand this spiritually? That is the deeper question. The millstone stands for blind toil, for pack animals are driven around in a circle with their eyes closed. And we frequently find the Gentiles referred to under the name *ass*. The Gentiles do not know what they do. They are in ignorance, and their life's work is like blind labor. Not so the Jews. For them the path of knowledge has been set forth in the law. Insofar as they gave offence to Christ's apostles, it was more just for them to be sunk in the sea with an asses' millstone tied to their neck. ON MATTHEW 18.2.[4]

IT WOULD BE BETTER FOR WHOM? JEROME: This can be viewed as a general sentence against all who raise a stumbling block. Yet according to the context of the discourse, it can also be understood as spoken against the apostles. In asking who was greater in the kingdom of heaven, they seemed to have just previously been contending among themselves for honor. If they persisted in this misbehavior they could lose those whom they were calling to the faith, if they should see the apostles fighting among themselves for honor.

But when Jesus said, "It would be better for him to have a great millstone fastened around his neck," he is following the rite of the province and telling how among ancient Jews this was the punishment for major crimes, that they be sunk in the deep with a rock attached to them. It is better for him, because it is much better to receive a short, quick punishment for one's sin than to be reserved for eternal tortures. For the Lord will not punish the same fault twice. COMMENTARY ON MATTHEW 3.18.6.[5]

18:7 Temptations to Sin

WOE TO THE WORLD. ORIGEN: Jesus pronounced "woe for temptations to sin" on people scattered throughout the whole world who are subject to temptations. But the disciples, who do not contemplate the things that are seen, are not of the world. Neither is their Master of the world. Therefore the "woe for temptations to sin" does not apply to Jesus' faithful disciples. Rather, "great peace have those who love your law; nothing can make them stumble."[6] But there are some who appear to be disciples yet are still of the world. They love the world, and they love inordinately what is in it. They love the life that is led in these earthly places or the money which is in them, or the possessions or any resources whatsoever. The words "they are not of the world" do not apply to them. But "woe for temptations to sin" will apply to them since they are indeed of the world. COMMENTARY ON MATTHEW 13.21.[7]

NECESSARY THAT TEMPTATIONS COME. CHRYSOSTOM: Perhaps one of our adversaries may think, If it is necessary that temptations come, why does he call woe down on the world when he ought to help it and offer a hand? For this is the task of the physician and the protector. Cursing the world is what the man in the street does. So what are we to reply to this shameless questioner? What equal of this therapy do you seek? For though he is God, he was made man for you, took on the form of a servant, suffered all the harshest treatment and still did not fail in anything that was assigned him. But because nothing further happened among ungrateful people, for this reason he calls woe down on them, because after so much fostering care they continued in their unsoundness. It is just as if some sick man were enjoying fine care but refused to follow his physician's regimen.

[3]*Expediens*. [4]SC 258:76-78. [5]CCL 77:157-58. [6]Ps 119:165 (118:165 LXX). [7]GCS 40:237-38; ANF 9:487-88.

Suppose someone lamented the patient, saying, "Woe to that man for his sickness, which he has increased by his own laxity!" But in that case no benefit comes from the lament. Here, however, there is also a kind of therapy, in that Jesus foretells what will happen and laments it. THE GOSPEL OF MATTHEW, HOMILY 59.1.[8]

WOE TO THE ONE BY WHOM TEMPTATIONS COME. AUGUSTINE: Of what world are we speaking when we say "Woe to the world for temptations to sin"? We speak of that world of which it is said, "And the world knew him not."[9] We are not speaking of that world of which it is said, "God was in Christ reconciling the world to himself."[10] There is an evil world, and there is a good world. In the evil world are all the evil ones of this world. In the good world are all the good ones of this world. We often hear it said of a field: his field is full. Of what? Of wheat. Yet we say also, and say truly too, his field is full of chaff. So with a tree, one says that it is full of fruit while another says it is full of leaves. Both speak truly. The supply of leaves has not usurped the place of the fruit, nor has the supply of fruit driven out the mass of leaves. The tree is full of both. But one thing is plucked by the wind; the other is picked by the harvester. So therefore when you hear, "Woe unto the world because of offenses," do not be afraid. Love the law of God, and you will have no temptation to sin. SERMON 81.3.[11]

18:8 Cutting Off Causes to Sin

CUT IT OFF. CHRYSOSTOM: He is not saying this about human limbs. Far from it. This is said about friends, about relatives, whom we regard in the rank of necessary limbs. Jesus also said this earlier,[12] and now he says it again. For nothing is so harmful as bad company.

For what relationship cannot do, often friendship can do, both for harm and for benefit. So he orders us with great emphasis to cut off those who are harmful to us, implying that these are people who supply temptations to sin.

Do you see how he checks the future damage from temptations? First he predicts that they will happen, so that no one should be lazy, but everyone should be awake expecting them. Then he predicts that the evils will be very great. For Jesus did not simply say, "Woe to the world for temptations to sin," but showed their great damage. For when he says, "But woe to that man by whom temptation comes," he indicates a great punishment. He does not only mention this, but he increases the fear by adding a comparison.

And he supplies incontrovertible reasoning. If they remain your friends, you will not benefit them and you will destroy yourself. If you cut them off, at least you will preserve your own salvation.

Then, not content with this, he shows us the way by which we can escape temptations to sin. What is that? The wicked, he says, even if they are very friendly to you, cut them off from your friendship. Therefore if someone's friendship harms you, cut him off from you. For if at times we cut off our limbs when they are incurable and are doing damage to our other members, how much more should we do this in the case of friends. If the limbs were evil by nature, all this advice and counsel would be useless; the warning of what is preached would be superfluous. If it is not superfluous, as in fact it is not, then it is clear that wickedness comes from the will. THE GOSPEL OF MATTHEW, HOMILY 59.4.[13]

18:9 Plucking Out an Eye

BETTER ONE EYE. ORIGEN: If somebody, in the whole body of the congregations of the church, is industrious and handy for practical action and he changes and his hand causes him to sin, the eye should say to this hand, "I have no need of you." And after it has said it, let him cut it off

---

[8]PG 58:573; NPNF 1 10:364. [9]Jn 1:10. [10]2 Cor 5:19. [11]PG 38:501; NPNF 1 6:354* (Sermon 31). [12]Mt 5:29. [13]PG 58:578; NPNF 1 10:367.

and throw it from him. All will still be well if his head is still blessed and his feet worthy of his blessed head, so that the head, doing its duty, may not be able to say to the feet, "I have no need of you." But if some foot is found which is a temptation to sin for the whole body, the head should say to this foot, "I have no need of you," and should cut it off and throw it away from him. It is far better for the rest of the body to go on into life lacking the foot or hand that offers temptation to sin than for the whole body to be exposed to temptation and to be sent into eternal fire with two whole feet or hands. Likewise it is good if what could be the eye of the whole body shows itself worthy of Christ and of the whole body. But if at some time it happens that this eye so changes that it becomes a temptation to sin for the whole body, it will be better for it to be ripped out and thrown from the whole body . . . than for the whole body together with the soul to be condemned. COMMENTARY ON MATTHEW 13.24.[14]

FORBIDDING CORRUPT CHURCH LEADERS. CHROMATIUS: This sentence of the Lord can faithfully be understood about any one of us. Yet in cutting off a hand or foot or in plucking out an eye, it is clear that family relations or unbelieving ministers and leaders of the church are signified.

And so by "hand" we understand that priests are signified; like a hand their work in every area is necessary to the body of the church, about whom we find it written in the Song of Solomon: "his arms"—that is, the body of the church—"are rounded gold set with jewels."[15] By "foot" we recognize that deacons are signified. In busying themselves with the sacred mysteries of the church they serve the body like feet, about which it is written in the same Song of Solomon: "His legs are alabaster columns, set upon bases of gold."[16] And so, if hands or feet of this sort, that is, any priest or deacon, either through heretical faith or through depraved living, has become a stumbling block to the church, the Lord orders that such a man be plucked from the body of the church and thrown out. The example of his life and heretical doctrine endangers all the body of the church, that is, the whole people, when it follows or imitates such doctrine. TRACTATE ON MATTHEW 56.2-4.[17]

---

[14]GCS 40:245-46; ANF 9:489. [15]Song 5:14. [16]Song 5:15. [17]CCL 9a:478-80.

18:10-14 THE PARABLE OF THE LOST SHEEP

[10]"See that you do not despise one of these little ones; for I tell you that in heaven their angels always behold the face of my Father who is in heaven.[c] [12]What do you think? If a man has a hundred sheep, and one of them has gone astray, does he not leave the ninety-nine on the mountains and go in search of the one that went astray? [13]And if he finds it, truly, I say to you, he rejoices over it more than over the ninety-nine that never went astray. [14]So it is not the will of my[d] Father who is in heaven that one of these little ones should perish."

c Other ancient authorities add verse 11, For the Son of man came to save the lost   d Other ancient authorities read your

OVERVIEW: Do not hate those who have been excommunicated, since it is possible for them to change (THEODORE OF HERACLEA). Not one of these little ones who believe in Christ should be despised. For their sake the Son of God came down from heaven and saved them by his Passion. It was for this that he took on the body of our human weakness (CHROMATIUS, CHRYSOSTOM). Though the height of the body depends on the seed, the largeness of our souls depends upon our own agency, actions and character (ORIGEN). The will in its weakness could not be safe amid so many forceful attacks of the enemy if it is not strengthened by the help of the angels (CHROMATIUS). The first man strayed from the company of the angels by sinning. Through him all people strayed from God. Our Lord seeks to recall the whole human race from death to life (EPIPHANIUS THE LATIN). The shepherd seeks the missing sheep to make the flock complete (APOLLONARIS).

18:10 Do Not Despise These Little Ones

DO NOT HATE THOSE CUT OFF. THEODORE OF HERACLEA: But see, he says, that you do not at all despise those forced out of the church for wickedness.[1] He does not want them to be cast out with any hatred or curse. But he spares those who are guilty of some damage or disorder and often hardened in their own depravity. It is as if it were possible to see even these change again for the better. By "little ones" he means those imperfect in their knowledge or those recently baptized. He does not want these to be looked down upon as ignorant in his teaching. FRAGMENT 105.[2]

LARGENESS OF SOUL. ORIGEN: The bodies of people differ from each other in size, so that some are short, some are tall, and some are in between. Again the short are different in their shortness since they are more short or less short, and the same likewise of the tall, and again of those in between. So it is also in human

souls, it seems to me: There is something which distinguishes their shortness, and again, so to speak, their tallness, and, again analogous to the bodily differences, their moderateness. But the bodily difference does not depend on the individuals themselves but on the nature of the seed. So this person becomes tall, that one short and another in between. But with our souls, our own agency that is our actions and our character causes one to be large or small or belonging to those in the middle. And it is in our power whether we grow in stature and receive an increase in size or do not grow and remain small. For we must believe that to attain to manhood and mature manhood at that[3] depends on the person within: passing out of the times of childhood and advancing to manhood and putting aside the stuff of childhood and perfecting the stage of manhood. Just so we must suppose that there is still some measure of spiritual growth to which the most perfect soul can advance in glorifying the Lord and so become great. COMMENTARY ON MATTHEW 13.26.[4]

THE LITTLE ONES. CHROMATIUS: And rightly the Lord has said, "The Son of man has come to save what had perished,"[5] so that all the more he might show that not one of these little ones who believe in Christ should be despised. For their sake the Son of God came down from heaven and saved them by his Passion. It was for this that he took on the body of our human weakness, so that he might in every way save this one who had perished. For the elements of the world have kept the law given them by the Lord. Humanity alone has been found the transgressor. Alone we had fallen from immortality into death. And for this reason to save us the Son of God at a mature time descended from heaven according to the will of the Father. Hence, quite

---

[1]Theodore here limits the meaning of *little ones* considerably to indicate the sinners who had been sent away from the communion of the church until repenting of their sin. [2]MKGK 86. [3]Eph 4:13. [4]GCS 40:250-51; ANF 9:490. [5]Cf. Lk 19:10.

rightly Solomon speaks of a time of destroying and a time of saving.[6] There was a time when the devil destroyed humankind. But again there came a time when the Son of God, the only begotten Son of God, saved the human race for life. TRACTATE ON MATTHEW 57.4.[7]

WHO IS THE LITTLE ONE? ORIGEN: Another may say that among these children "little" means perfect, recalling that the one who is less among you all is greater.[8] Some may argue that the child shown by Jesus is the person who humbles himself and becomes a child among the whole mass of the faithful. This is so even if he is an apostle or bishop. He may become like a nurse taking care of her children.[9] He is like an angel worthy of looking upon the face of God. COMMENTARY ON MATTHEW 13.29.[10]

THEIR ANGELS BEHOLD THE FACE OF MY FATHER. CHROMATIUS: For just as the Lord commands that unbelieving and treacherous persons who are a stumbling block to the body of the church should be cut off or plucked out, so he also warns us not to despise any of the little children, that is, humble people in the laity who simply and faithfully believe in the Son of God. For it is not right to despise anyone who believes in Christ. A believer is called not only a servant of God but also a son though the grace of adoption, to whom the kingdom of heaven and the company of the angels is promised. And rightly the Lord adds, "For I tell you that in heaven their angels always behold the face of my Father who is in heaven." How much grace the Lord has toward each one believing in him he himself declares when he shows their angels always beholding the face of the Father who is in heaven. Great is the grace of the angels toward all who believe in Christ. Finally, the angels carry their prayers to heaven. Hence the word of Raphael to Tobias: "When you prayed along with your daughter-in-law Sara, I offered the memory of your prayer in the sight of God."[11] Around them there is also the strong guard of

the angels; they help each of us to be free from the traps of the enemy. For a human in his weakness could not be safe amid so many forceful attacks of that enemy if he were not strengthened by the help of the angels. TRACTATE ON MATTHEW 57.1.[12]

18:12 Searching for One Stray Sheep

THE ONE LOST SHEEP. JEROME: When he said, "See that you do not despise one of these little ones," he is calling us to be merciful. Then he adds the parable of the ninety-nine sheep left in the mountains and the one stray that because of its great weakness could not walk. The good shepherd carried it on his shoulders to the rest of the flock. This, some say, is the shepherd "who, though he was in the form of God, did not count equality with God a thing to be grasped but emptied himself, taking the form of a servant, being born in the likeness of men. And being found in human form he humbled himself and became obedient unto death, even death on a cross."[13] For that reason he descended to earth: to save the one sheep that had perished, that is, the human race. Others think that by the ninety-nine sheep should be understood the number of the righteous and by the one sheep the number of the sinners, according to what he said in another place: "I have come not to call the righteous but the sinners; for it is not the healthy who have need of the physician but those who are ill."[14] COMMENTARY ON MATTHEW 3.18.12.[15]

18:13 Rejoicing About the One Sheep

HE REJOICES OVER THE ONE. CHRYSOSTOM: Do you see in how many ways he leads us to care for our worthless brothers? Don't therefore say, "The fellow's a smith, a cobbler, a farmer; he's

---

[6]Eccles 3:3. [7]CCL 9a:486. [8]Lk 9:48. [9]1 Thess 2:7. [10]GCS 40:259; ANF 9:492. [11]Tob 12:12. [12]CCL 9a:483. [13]Phil 2:6-8. [14]Mt 9:13. [15]CCL 77:160-61.

stupid," so that you despise him. In case you suffer the same, see in how many ways the Lord urges you to be moderate and enjoins you to care for these little ones. He placed a little child in the midst and said, "Become like children," and, "Whoever receives one such child, receives me." But "whoever causes one of these to sin" will suffer the worst fate. And he was not even satisfied with the example of the millstone, but he also added his curse and told us to cut off such people, even though they are like a hand or eye to us. And again, through the angels to whom these small brothers are handed over, he urges that we value them, as he has valued them through his own will and passion. When Jesus says, "The Son of man came to save the lost,"[16] he points to the cross, just as Paul also says, writing about his brother for whom Christ died.[17] It does not please the Father that anyone is lost. The shepherd leaves the ones that have been saved and seeks the one lost. And when he finds the one that has gone astray, he rejoices greatly at its discovery and at its safety. THE GOSPEL OF MATTHEW, HOMILY 59.4.[18]

ADAM'S STRAYING. EPIPHANIUS THE LATIN: For anyone who has sheep is a shepherd. No one is more truly a shepherd than Christ our God. One of his sheep has strayed. It is not the fault of the shepherd but of the sheep that had strayed from its flock. This one sheep is the man Adam, whom in the beginning the Lord had created in his image and likeness. This one strayed from the company of the angels by sinning, and through him the entire human race strayed from God. Our Lord seeks to recall all humanity from death to life. For it was for us that he went to death, so that he might make us alive, these who had died. For he rejoiced even more over the hundredth sheep that was lost than over the ninety and nine. The patriarch of a hundred years, Abraham, had faith in God, and from his faith was held righteous. He received back his one and only son Isaac. Thus Abraham was called, because of his faith, father of the nations.

So he crossed from the left onto the right, the number one hundred being viewed as held on the right.[19]

Therefore, beloved, the hundredth sheep is the congregation of the nations—but only those who believed and served the Lord in the same way as Abraham did, so that they merit to be placed on the right side. This is just as the Lord himself says: "Then he will set up the sheep on the right but the goats on the left."[20] The "goats" are in this case the unbelieving Jews or infidels and sinners. To those who will be on the left, the Lord will say, "Depart from me, accursed ones, into the eternal fire which my Father has prepared for the devil and his angels."[21]

Thus God wills "that not one of these little ones perish." But if your brother sins against you, rebuke him. The Lord commands us to rebuke the sinner until he is corrected. But if he cannot be corrected, he is to be considered as a heathen. For our Lord acted as he taught. In his own person he rebuked the people of the Jews straying in the desert. He rebuked them again and again through the law and the prophets. Finally, in his own person in the presence of all the congregation of the saints he chastised the Jewish people. INTERPRETATION OF THE GOSPELS 27.[22]

18:14 *That They Not Perish*

TO MAKE THE FLOCK COMPLETE. APOLLINARIS: The sheep that became lost is the sinner lost from the flock of a hundred. This could refer to the number of the heavenly powers.[23] These powers are capable of speech and reasoning. The one sheep is counted as being among

---

[16]Lk 19:10. [17]Rom 14:15. [18]PG 58:579; NPNF 1 10:368. [19]Epiphanius here alludes to the method of counting on the fingers, according to which one counted to one hundred with the fingers of the left hand and thereafter with the fingers of the right. His interpretation relies on the positive significance of the right. [20]Mt 25:33. [21]Mt 25:41. [22]PL Supp 3:867-68. [23]In biblical typology, the number one hundred often symbolizes a completed cycle or a perfected number. Since the powers that comprise the heavenly hosts are such a completed cycle, they are symbolized by one hundred.

the flock, a part of a great number, as if among "a hundred sheep." His wandering is the consequence of Adam's fall. He is searched for. He is of like nature to those who stay at God's side. He is necessary for their full complement, so that the shepherd may not be deficient and wanting. The summing up of what Paul calls "the whole in Christ"[24] involves the regaining of the deficient part, since the composition of the whole in Christ is not complete because of the deficient and absent one. FRAGMENT 89.[25]

---

[24]Cf. 1 Cor 12:12-31. [25]MKGK 28.

18:15-17 A CHRISTIAN WHO SINS

[15]"If your brother sins against you, go and tell him his fault, between you and him alone. If he listens to you, you have gained your brother. [16]But if he does not listen, take one or two others along with you, that every word may be confirmed by the evidence of two or three witnesses. [17]If he refuses to listen to them, tell it to the church; and if he refuses to listen even to the church, let him be to you as a Gentile and a tax collector."

OVERVIEW: We should immediately reprove our brother, if he has lost his shame, so that he does not remain in sin. If he refuses to listen, we should summon a brother, and then another, and finally the congregation if he remains recalcitrant (JEROME). A less caring response might have been to let him be if he persisted uncorrected from the first meeting. But instead Jesus shows us how to seek his cure once, twice and many times: first alone, then with two, then with many more (CHRYSOSTOM). Do not make his behavior worse by intensifying defensiveness and rationalization. Seek behavioral change, not shame for itself (AUGUSTINE).

18:15 Telling About a Fault Privately

THE ART OF RECONCILIATION. CHRYSOSTOM: He does not say "accuse him" or "punish him" or "take him to court." He says "correct him." For he is possessed, as it were, by some stupor, and drunk in his anger and disgrace. The one who is healthy must go to the one who is sick. You must conduct your judgment of him privately. Make your cure easy to accept. For the words "correct him" mean nothing other than help him see his indiscretion. Tell him what you have suffered from him.

What then if he does not listen, if he stubbornly flares up? Call to your side someone else or even two others, so that two witnesses may corroborate all that's said. For the more shameless and boldfaced he is, so much the more must you be earnest toward his cure, not toward satisfying your anger and hurt feelings. For when a physician sees the sickness unyielding, he does not stand aside or take it hard but then is all the more earnest. That then is what Christ orders us to do. You appeared too weak since you were alone, so become stronger with the help of others. Two are sufficient to reprove the wrongdoer. Do you see how he seeks the interest not of the aggrieved party alone but also that of the one who caused the grief? For the person injured may be the one who is more taken captive by passion. He becomes the one that is diseased and weak and infirm.

This effort may occur many times, as he attempts to lead him first alone and then with others. If he persists, then make the effort with the whole congregation. "Tell it," he says, "to the church." If he had sought the interest of the aggrieved alone, he would not have told him to approach the sick individual seventy-seven times.[1] He would not have attempted so many times or brought so many treatments to the malady. He might have just let him be if he persisted uncorrected from the first meeting. But instead he shows us how to seek his cure once, twice, and many times: first alone, then with two, then with many more. The Gospel of Matthew, Homily 60.1.[2]

18:16 Confirmed by Two or Three Witnesses

SEEK AMENDMENT, SPARING SHAME. AUGUSTINE: If someone has done you injury and you have suffered, what should be done? You have heard the answer already in today's Scripture: "If your brother sins against you, go and tell him his fault, between you and him alone."[3]

If you fail to do so, you are worse than he is. He has done someone harm, and by doing harm he has stricken himself with a grievous wound. Will you then completely disregard your brother's wound? Will you simply watch him stumble and fall down? Will you disregard his predicament? If so, you are worse in your silence than he in his abuse.

Therefore, when any one sins against us, let us take great care, but not merely for ourselves. For it is a glorious thing to forget injuries. Just set aside your own injury, but do not neglect your brother's wound. Therefore "go and tell him his fault, between you and him alone," intent upon his amendment but sparing his sense of shame. For it might happen that through defensiveness he will begin to justify his sin, and so you will have inadvertently nudged him still closer toward the very behavior you desire to amend. Therefore "tell him his

fault between you and him alone. If he listens to you, you have gained your brother," because he might have been lost, had you not spoken with him. SERMON 82.7.[4]

18:17 Tell It to the Church

WHEN SIN IS AGAINST GOD. JEROME: If our brother has sinned against us and damaged us in anything, we have the power of dismissing it, in fact the obligation to do so, since we are commanded to forgive our debtors their debts. But if anyone sins against God, it is not in our control. Divine Scripture says, "If a man has sinned against a man, the priest will pray for him; but if he sins against God, who will speak for him?"[5] But we, on the contrary, are lenient over a sin against God but act out our hatred when we ourselves are insulted. Yet we should immediately reprove our brother, if he has once lost his shame and innocence, so that he does not remain in sin. And if he listens, we profit his soul, and through the salvation of another we too acquire salvation. But if he refuses to listen, we should summon a brother; and if he does not listen to him either, yet a third should be summoned in the hope of either correcting him or meeting him with witnesses. Then if he refuses to listen even to these, the congregation must be told, so that they may curse him. Then the one who could not be saved through shame may be saved through their approbation. But since it is said, "Let him be to you as a heathen and a publican," the person who under the name of faith does an infidel's works is shown to be more cursed than those who openly are heathen. Publicans, figuratively speaking, are those who pursue the profits of the secular world and exact taxes by business, fraud, theft, crimes and false oaths. COMMENTARY ON MATTHEW 3.18.15-17.[6]

---

[1]Mt 18:22. [2]PG 58:584-85; NPNF 1 10:372-73. [3]Mt 18:5. [4]PL 38:508-9; NPNF 1 6:359. [5]1 Sam 2:25. [6]CCL 77:161-62.

Telling the Church. Augustine: But "if he does not listen," that is, if he chooses to justify his sin as if it were a just action, "take one or two others along with you, that every word may be confirmed by the evidence of two or three witnesses. If he refuses to listen to them, tell it to the church; and if he refuses to listen even to the church, let him be to you as a Gentile and a tax collector."[7] Don't consider him now in the number of your brothers. But not even so is his salvation to be neglected. For even the heathen, that is, the Gentiles and pagans, we do not consider in the number of our brothers, yet we constantly pray for their salvation. Sermon 82.7.[8]

---

[7]Mt 18:16-17, i.e., as one who has chosen to be an outsider among the covenant people. [8]PL 38:509; NPNF 1 6:359 (Sermon 32).

18:18-20 PROHIBITING AND PERMITTING

[18]"Truly, I say to you, whatever you bind on earth shall be bound in heaven, and whatever you loose on earth shall be loosed in heaven. [19]Again I say to you, if two of you agree on earth about anything they ask, it will be done for them by my Father in heaven. [20]For where two or three are gathered in my name, there am I in the midst of them."

Overview: The authorization of the church to discipline its members comes from Christ and promises to be binding in heaven (Augustine). People who do not want to be loosed from the bond of sin but draw sin to themselves so as to become alienated from the saints are alienated also from the church in heaven (Theodore of Mopsuestia). When people have been duly bound and condemned, they remain bound insofar as none of those in heaven rescinds the judgment of the one by whom they were bound (Origen). It is not the one who has called for accountability that is to blame but the one who is unwilling to be admonished (Chrysostom). How important a place the unanimity and harmony of Christians hold with God! We can know this from the fact that the Lord has clearly said that when two or three pray in unanimity, the Father grants everything (Chromatius). The reason we do not achieve our desires and prayers is our own fault, when we do not agree together either in our thoughts or in our way of life (Origen). Individual members have their own duty of personal prayer, but they will not be able to fulfill that duty if they come to common worship, to the beauty of that perfect body, still wrapped up in themselves (Peter Chrysologus).

18:18 Bound on Earth and in Heaven

The Confirming Judgment of Heaven. Origen: After stating that the one judged is viewed as a heathen and tax collector, something else is added which is well put: "Truly, I say to you"—clearly to those judging someone to be as a heathen and tax collector—"whatever you bind on earth shall be bound in heaven." For he who has three times admonished him and not been heard has justly bound him, and that man is then to be thought judged as a heathen and tax collector. Therefore when a man like this has been bound and condemned by someone, he remains bound insofar as none of those in heaven rescinds the judgment of the man by whom he was bound. So too the man who has once been warned and does things worthy of being won back is released through the warning of the one who wins him back. He is no longer bound by the bonds of his sins for which he was warned and bound; he will be judged by those in heaven as set free. COMMENTARY ON MATTHEW 13.31.[1]

WHATEVER YOU BIND ON EARTH. AUGUSTINE: This then is what we have heard the Lord advising, and with such great particularity that he himself adds, "Truly, I say to you, whatever you bind on earth shall be bound in heaven, and whatever you loose on earth shall be loosed in heaven." So the very moment you begin to hold your brother as an outsider to the covenant community, "you bind him on earth." But see to it that you bind him justly. For unjust bonds will by justice soon be burst apart. . . . When you have admonished him and have been "reconciled to your brother," you have thereby "loosed him on earth." And when "you shall have loosed him on earth, he shall be loosed in heaven" also. So this is a weighty matter. You do this not for yourself but for him. For the harm he has done is not primarily to you but to himself. SERMON 82.7.[2]

WHATEVER YOU LOOSE ON EARTH. THEODORE OF MOPSUESTIA: Well introduced were the words "whatever you loose," since he shows that if they loose those who repent, their action has power, since the church in heaven and on earth is one. Anyone who does not want to be loosed from the bond of his sin but draws it to himself by the alienation of the saints is alienated also from the church in heaven and accordingly is also bound by it. Hence, if one is earnest about being loosed and receives the loosing of the saints when they "ratify their love for him,"[3] as Paul teaches, he will belong in the heavenly church and be loosed from the bondage of the judgment. FRAGMENT 96.[4]

THE CALL TO ACCOUNTABILITY. CHRYSOSTOM: He did not say to the leader of the church, "bind him" but "if you bind him," leaving the whole entire decision to the one aggrieved. Only after a due process do the bonds remain unbreakable, and so he will suffer the worst fate. It is not the one who has called for accountability that is to blame but the one who had not been willing to be persuaded. Do you see how Christ has bound him with a twofold constraint, both by the chastisement here and by the punishment hereafter? He threatens the one punishment to prevent the other from happening. Thus, by fearing both rejection from the church and the threat of being bound in heaven, he may become better behaved. And knowing these things, if not at the beginning, at any rate through so many judgments he will put off his anger. For this reason, Jesus set up a first and a second and a third judging. He does not immediately cut him down, so that if he does not obey the first, he may still yield to the second. But if he rejects that too, he may still respect the third. But if he takes no account of this third danger, let him be terrified of future punishment, of God's sentence and vengeance. THE GOSPEL OF MATTHEW, HOMILY 60.2.[5]

18:19 Done for Them by the Heavenly Father

EARTH AND HEAVEN IN HARMONY. ORIGEN: Concord occurs in two kinds: first, in agreement of thought, when two minds think the same ideas (as the apostle called it) and have the same thoughts. Second, in agreement of will, in living similar lives. But since "If two of you agree on earth about anything they ask, it will be done for them by Jesus' Father in heaven," if something is asked of the Father in heaven and is not granted, it is clear that the two here on earth are not in harmony. The reason why we do not

---

[1]GCS 40:268-69; ANF 9:493.　[2]PL 38:509; NPNF 1 6:359 (Sermon 32).　[3]Cf. 2 Cor 2:8.　[4]MKGK 130-31.　[5]PG 58:585; NPNF 1 10:373-74.

achieve our desires and prayers is our own fault: we do not agree either in our thoughts or in our way of life. Besides, if we are the body of Christ and "God arranged the members in the body, each one of them . . . so that the members may have the care for one another, and if one member suffers all suffer together; if one member is honored all rejoice together,"[6] then we must practice the harmony that comes from God's music, so that when we are gathered in Christ's name, Christ may be in our midst, who is God's word and wisdom and power. COMMENTARY ON MATTHEW 14.1.[7]

IF TWO OR THREE PRAY TOGETHER. CHROMATIUS: How important a place the unanimity and harmony of brothers hold with God! We can know from this very fact that the Lord has clearly said that when two or three pray in unanimity, the Father grants everything from heaven. For with God nothing is more pleasing than brotherly peace, nothing better than unanimity and harmony, according to what is written: "Behold, how good and pleasant it is when brothers dwell in unity."[8] And again: "There is great peace among those who love your name,[9] and there is no stumbling block for them."[10] And in another place: "The God who makes us live in harmony in the house."[11] So Isaiah also testified: "Lord," he said, "our God, give us peace. For you have given us everything."[12] That this harmony of brothers is pleasing to God, the Holy Spirit declared through Solomon, saying, "There are three things which are pleasing to God and men: harmony of brothers, love of one's neighbors and the union of man and woman."[13] So quite rightly the Lord in this passage testifies that when two or three come together on earth, whatever they ask for, all is granted by the Father. TRACTATE ON MATTHEW 59.1.[14]

18:20 Where Two or Three Gather in My Name

TWO OR THREE. CYRIL OF ALEXANDRIA: Christ

gives to those who are allotted the duty of teaching the power to loose and to bind. So when those who have once fallen do not convert to the pursuit of virtue, they must fear the voices of the saints, even if they are not many who make the petition to bind or loose. For Christ has assured us of this, saying that there will be strength in the prayers of many, but that even if only two in number harmoniously and deliberately define their requests, they will come to their goal. "For I will be with you," he says, "and will support you if only two are gathered, because of me." For it is not the number of those gathered but the strength of their piety and their love of God that is effective. FRAGMENT 215.[15]

THE BEAUTY OF THE WHOLENESS OF THE BODY. PETER CHRYSOLOGUS: There are those who presume that the congregation of the church can be disregarded. They assert that private prayers should be preferred to those of an honorable assembly. But if Jesus denies nothing to so small a group as two or three, will he refuse those who ask for it in the assemblies and congregation of the church? This is what the prophet believed and what he exults over having obtained when he states, "I will confess to you, O Lord, with my whole heart, in the council and congregation of the righteous."[16] A man "confesses with his whole heart" when in the council of the saints he hears that everything which he has asked will be granted him.

Some, however, endeavor to excuse under an appearance of faith the idleness that prompts their contempt for assemblies. They omit participation in the fervor of the assembled congregation and pretend that they have devoted to prayer the time they have expended upon their household cares. While they give themselves up to their own desires, they scorn and despise the

---

[6]1 Cor 12:18, 25-26. [7]GCS 40:276-77; ANF 9:495. [8]Ps 133:1 (132:1 LXX). [9]According to Codex Alexandrinus. [10]Cf. Ps 119:165 (118:165 LXX). [11]Cf. Ps 68:6 (67:7 LXX). [12]Is 26:12. [13]Sir 25:1. [14]CCL 9a:492. [15]MKGK 224. [16]Ps 111:1 (110:1 LXX).

divine service. These are the people who destroy the body of Christ. They scatter its members. They do not permit the full form of its Christlike appearance to develop to its abundant beauty—that form which the prophet saw and then sang about: "You are beautiful in form above the sons of men."[17]

Individual members do indeed have their own duty of personal prayer, but they will not be able to fulfill it if they come to the beauty of that perfect body wrapped up in themselves.

There is this difference between the glorious fullness of the congregation and the vanity of separation that springs out of ignorance or negligence: in salvation and honor the beauty of the whole body is found in the unity of the members. But from the separation of the viscera there is a foul, fatal and fearful aroma. SERMON 132.4-5.[18]

---

[17]Cf. Is 52:14. [18]CCL 24b:811-12; FC 17:217-18.

18:21-35 THE PARABLE OF
THE UNFORGIVING SERVANT

[21]Then Peter came up and said to him, "Lord, how often shall my brother sin against me, and I forgive him? As many as seven times?" [22]Jesus said to him, "I do not say to you seven times, but seventy times seven.[e]

[23]"Therefore the kingdom of heaven may be compared to a king who wished to settle accounts with his servants. [24]When he began the reckoning, one was brought to him who owed him ten thousand talents;[f] [25]and as he could not pay, his lord ordered him to be sold, with his wife and children and all that he had, and payment to be made. [26]So the servant fell on his knees, imploring him, 'Lord, have patience with me, and I will pay you everything.' [27]And out of pity for him the lord of that servant released him and forgave him the debt. [28]But that same servant, as he went out, came upon one of his fellow servants who owed him a hundred denarii;[g] and seizing him by the throat he said, 'Pay what you owe.' [29]So his fellow servant fell down and besought him, 'Have patience with me, and I will pay you.' [30]He refused and went and put him in prison till he should pay the debt. [31]When his fellow servants saw what had taken place, they were greatly distressed, and they went and reported to their lord all that had taken place. [32]Then his lord summoned him and said to him, 'You wicked servant! I forgave you all that debt because you besought me; [33]and should not you have had mercy on your fellow servant, as I had mercy on you?' [34]And in anger his lord delivered him to the jailers,[h] till he should pay all his debt. [35]So also my heavenly Father will do to every one of you, if you do not forgive your brother from your heart."

---

e Or seventy-seven times f This talent was more than fifteen years' wages of a laborer g The denarius was a day's wage for a laborer h Greek torturers

OVERVIEW: The beautiful mystery of seventy-seven is this: in that special number all sins of all generations were symbolized as having been forgiven. Since no generation was omitted, no generation misses out on the full gift of divine forgiveness in the cross. So also should we learn to forgive each other to the same extent that God has fully forgiven us. The frequency of pardon shows us there is never a time for anger, since God pardons us for all sins in their entirety by his gift rather than by our merit (HILARY OF POITIERS). The number six is full of toil and labor, reflecting the work of creation, but seven encompasses rest, which points to forgiveness (ORIGEN).

In the parable, the unmerciful servant had lost a vast amount. Much had been loaned and entrusted to him, but he had brought no gain to his master (ORIGEN). The master's teaching purpose was to show him with all justice precisely how much debt he was going to free him from. In this way at least he might in due time become more gentle toward his fellow servant. Yet, even having learned of the weight of his debt and the greatness of the forgiveness, he continued to seize his fellow servant by the throat (CHRYSOSTOM). The forced sale of his wife and family portrays metaphorically utter separation from the joys of God (CYRIL OF ALEXANDRIA). God created us from nothing and made the whole visible world for us. To us alone he breathed a living soul. Yet after all this, when humanity proved ungrateful toward its benefactor, God thought us worthy of an even greater gift: forgiveness (CHRYSOSTOM). God forgives our immense debt of ten thousand talents on the proviso that we ourselves release our fellow servants from the paltry hundred denarii, from the few minor faults they have committed against us (CYRIL OF ALEXANDRIA). The king in the parable is the Son of God, and the kingdom belongs to the one who incomparably defines kingship itself and makes it possible (ORIGEN). Compare the two servants: one was indebted for ten thousand talents, the other for a pittance. One was merely dealing

with his fellow servant, while the other was dealing with his lord. The one received entire forgiveness, the other asked for delay (CHRYSOSTOM). The story demands two things of us: to remember our own faults and not to bear a grudge against one who stumbles (APOLLINARIS).

18:21-22 How Often Shall I Forgive?

NO TIME FOR ANGER. HILARY OF POITIERS: When Peter asked him whether he should forgive his brother sinning against him up to seven times, the Lord replied, "Not up to seven times but up to seventy times seven times." In every way he teaches us to be like him in humility and goodness. In weakening and breaking the impulses of our rampant passions he strengthens us by the example of his leniency, by granting us in faith pardon of all our sins. For the vices of our nature did not merit pardon. Therefore all pardon comes from him. In fact, he pardons even those sins that remain in one after confession.

The penalty to be paid through Cain was established at sevenfold, but that sin was against a man, against his brother Abel, to the point of murder.[1] But in Lamech the penalty was established at seventy times seven times,[2] and, as we believe, the penalty was established on those responsible for the Lord's Passion.[3] But the Lord through the confession of believers grants pardon for this crime. By the gift of baptism he grants the grace of salvation to his revilers and persecutors. How much more is it necessary, he shows, that pardon be returned by us without measure or number. And we should not think how many times we forgive, but we should cease to be angry with those who sin against us, as often as the occasion for anger exists. Pardon's

---

[1]Gen 4:8. [2]Gen 4:24. [3]It did not miss the eye of rabbinic interpreters that Cain would be avenged seven times and Lamech seventy-seven. Lamech lived 777 years. Lamech boasted of his vengeful killing of a young man, so it is pride that is being corrected. Such pride was attributed by Hilary of Poitiers to those who killed the Savior (cf. Gen 4:18-24).

frequency shows us that in our case there is never a time for anger, since God pardons us for all sins in their entirety by his gift rather than by our merit. Nor should we be excused from the requirement of giving pardon that number of times [i.e., seventy times seven], since through the grace of the gospel God has granted us pardon without measure. ON MATTHEW 18.10.[4]

THE SEVENTY-SEVEN GENERATIONS FROM ADAM TO CHRIST.

AUGUSTINE: What then does "seventy times seven" mean? Listen, my friends, to this great mystery, this wonderful gift. When the Lord was baptized, Luke the holy Evangelist there noted down his ancestry, in what order, series and stems that generation had been reached in which Christ was born. Matthew began from Abraham and came as far as Joseph in descending generations.[5] But Luke began to count by going back up in ascending order. Why does the one reckon in a descending and the other in an ascending order? Because Matthew set forth the generations of Christ by which he came down to us, and so he began to reckon when Christ was born from a descending order.[6] Luke begins to reckon in reverse from when Christ was baptized. In this is the beginning of an ascension, for he begins to reckon in an ascending order. Note that in his account he enumerates seventy-seven generations![7] With whom did he begin his reckoning? Note carefully! He began to reckon from Christ up to Adam himself, who was the first sinner and who parented us into bondage to sin. Luke reckoned up to Adam, and so there are enumerated in toto seventy-seven generations— from Christ up to Adam and from Adam up to Christ. Note seventy-seven! So then if no generation was omitted, there is no exemption of any trespass that ought not to be forgiven. For therefore did he reckon up his seventy-seven generations, which number the Lord mentioned as to the forgiveness of sins; since he begins to reckon from the baptism, where all sins are remitted.[8] SERMON 83.5.[9]

18:23 A King Settling Accounts

WHICH KING? WHOSE KINGDOM? ORIGEN: If the comparison is to a king like this—and to one who acts like this—of whom must we be speaking if not the Son of God? For he is the king of the heavens. Just as he is wisdom itself and justice and truth, is he not kingship itself? The kingdom does not belong to any of those below, nor a part of those above, but to all those above, whatever is called the heavens. If you are curious about the beatitude "theirs is the kingdom of heaven,"[10] you can just as well say "theirs is Christ," since Christ is the kingdom. COMMENTARY ON MATTHEW 14.7.[11]

SETTLING ACCOUNTS WITH HIS SERVANTS. ORIGEN: The servants in this case are the dispensers of the word.[12] When he demands an account of the servants, the king also asks those who have borrowed from the servants, whether a hundred measures of grain or a hundred jars of oil or whatever those outside the king's stewardship have received. For the fellow servant of the unjust steward, according to the parable, will not be found to be the one who owes a hundred measures of grain or a hundred jars of oil, as is clear from the words "How much do you owe my master?" Consider that each good and fitting deed is like a profit and a gain, but each bad one is like a loss. And just as one gain can be a gain of more money and another of less and there is a difference between the more and the less, so in the case of good deeds there is a kind of valuing of greater or lesser gains. COMMENTARY ON MATTHEW 14.8.[13]

DEGREES OF SIN. CHRYSOSTOM: Do you see

---

[4]SC 258:84-86. [5]Mt 1:1. [6]Cf. NPNF 1 6:257-58. [7]Lk 3:23. [8]Augustine followed Hilary of Poitiers and others in assuming that Jesus' word about unlimited forgiviness may be a conscious allusion to the song of Lamech (Gen 4:24). [9]PL 38:516-17; NPNF 1 6:364* (Sermon 33). [10]Mt 5:3-10. [11]GCS 40:289; ANF 9:498. [12]*Word* means the Christian message, which is identified with Christ himself, the divine Word (Logos). [13]GCS 40:293-94; ANF 9:499.

how great a difference there is between sins against humanity and sins against God? As much a difference as between ten thousand talents and a hundred denarii; no, much greater in fact. This comes about from the difference of the persons and from the frequency of the sins. For when someone is watching, we hold off and do not dare to sin. But God is watching all the time, and yet we are not afraid; in fact, we even say and do everything quite brazenly. THE GOSPEL OF MATTHEW, HOMILY 61.1.[14]

18:24 One Who Owed Ten Thousand Talents

WHEN HE BEGAN THE RECKONING. ORIGEN: The moment of beginning the reckoning starts with the household of God, as is it written in Ezekiel: "Begin at my sanctuary."[15] This judgment begins as quickly as the twinkling of an eye.[16] In thinking of the demanding of accounts, let us not forget what we have said before, that these accounts are spiritually conceived. And the moment of demand begins understandably with those who owe the most. This is why the passage does not begin generally with a reckoning of all accounts but a specific one: one was brought to him. Here is the moment. He is beginning to demand an account of one who owed him ten thousand talents! It is as if the servant had lost a vast amount and much had been loaned and entrusted to him but had brought no gain to his master. Rather, he ended up losing a vast sum so as to owe him an incredible debt of talents. Remembering the prophet Zechariah, it may be that he owed so many talents for this reason: he had often sought out the woman hidden in a barrel with a lead cover, whose name is Iniquity.[17] COMMENTARY ON MATTHEW 14.10.[18]

18:25 His Lord Ordered Payment to Be Made

HE ORDERED HIM SOLD WITH HIS WIFE AND CHILDREN. CHRYSOSTOM: "His lord ordered

him to be sold, with his wife and children." Why? Not out of cruelty or inhumanity, for the punishment concerned the steward—his wife was already trapped like a slave to his folly. Rather, this discipline occurred in order to effect his transformation. His purpose is to frighten him by this threat so that he may come to supplication, and not merely that they all be sold. For if the lord had done this with unmitigated punishment in mind, he would not have granted his request, nor would he have bestowed upon him a special favor. He did not dismiss the debt, and he called for an accounting. Why? His teaching purpose was to show him with all justice precisely how much debt he was going to free him from! In this way at least he might in due time become more gentle toward his fellow servant. Yet, even having learned of the weight of his debt and the greatness of the forgiveness, he continued to take his fellow servant by the throat. If the master had not disciplined him beforehand with such attempted medicines, how much worse might his cruelty have been than the shocking extent that it actually turned out to be? THE GOSPEL OF MATTHEW, HOMILY 61.3.[19]

FORCED SALE. CYRIL OF ALEXANDRIA: The sale of his wife and the rest of his family shows the complete and utter separation from the joys of God. For the sale shows quite clearly alienation from God. Those alienated from God are those who hear those bitter, fearful words, "Depart from me, you workers of iniquity, for I do not know you."[20] FRAGMENT 217.[21]

18:26-27 The Servant's Plea, the Lord's Mercy

THE REDEMPTIVE MOTIVE OF THE MASTER.

---

[14]PG 58:589-90; NPNF 1 10:376. [15]Ezek 9:7. [16]1 Cor 15:52. [17]Zech 5:7-8, a vision in which wickedness was personified as a woman entrapped in a measuring barrel with a heavy lead cover. [18]GCS 40:298-99; ANF 9:520. [19]PG 58:592; NPNF 1 10:378. [20]Mt 7:23; Lk 13:27. [21]MKGK 225.

CHRYSOSTOM: Do you see again how generous he was? The servant asked only for an extension of time, but he gave him more than he asked for, remission and forgiveness of the entire debt. He wanted to give him this from the start, but he did not want the giving to be on his side only. He wanted the servant to learn from it and to ask for mercy, in order than he not be under an illusion of innocence. For that the whole was the Lord—even if the servant fell on his knees and implored—is demonstrated by the motive for the remission, for it says, "Out of pity the lord released him." In this way he also wanted the servant to take some responsibility, to prevent him being too much put to shame, and so that he might learn from his own case and be lenient to his fellow servant, and schooled in his own calamities. THE GOSPEL OF MATTHEW, HOMILY 61.3.[22]

THE LORD FORGAVE THE DEBT. CHROMATIUS: So we recognize that in the person of this king is signified the Son of God, who held the whole human race guilty in the infinite debt of sin, since through the original sin we were all debtors of sin and death. In the ten thousand talents the serious sins of the human race are signified. And though all men by natural law were debtors to this heavenly king and guilty—since the apostle says about the same natural law that "all men, both Jews and Greeks, are under the power of sin"[23]—yet in this debt of sin the people of the Jews were particularly held guilty. After so many great benefits they could not keep the law received through Moses. Since they did not have the wherewithal to repay such debt, that is, how to make it good, the lord had ordered them to be tormented, along with their wives and children. That is, this same people along with their synagogue and all their offspring were to be thrashed, to the point of death. But in no way could either the people of the Jews, who had received the law, nor the Gentiles, that is, we ourselves, pay off such a great debt of sin. Hence the heavenly King,

moved by pity and mercy, forgave us all our sins. And what are these sins? Those that every day in our prayers we ask to be forgiven, saying, "Forgive us our debts, as we forgive our debtors." Therefore, since in no way—that is, with no satisfaction and no worthy penitence—could we pay off this debt of sin and eternal death, that eternal King came down from heaven and by remitting the human race its sins forgave all the debt of every one who believes in him. How he forgave it the holy apostle clearly shows when he says, "having canceled the bond which stood against us with its legal demands; this he set aside, nailing it to the cross."[24] For we are held in sin-guilt as if under the debt of some creditor note. The Son of God has annulled this note written against us by the water of baptism and the drops of his blood. TRACTATE ON MATTHEW 59.5.[25]

18:28 Pay What You Owe

TEN THOUSAND TALENTS OWED, A HUNDRED DENARII COLLECTED. CYRIL OF ALEXANDRIA: The God of all releases us from the difficulties of our faults, according to the parable. This is what is signified by the ten thousand talents.[26] But this happens on the proviso that we ourselves release our fellow servants from the hundred denarii, that is, from the few minor faults they have committed against us. The angels who stand over us and are under the same yoke of service as we are make accusations before God. They do not speak to God as if God does not know—for God knows everything. Rather, in the interest of justice, they demand the proper punishment for those who choose to despise and dishonor the command that we love one another. When we meet our proper deserts, either we receive punishment in our present life, such as being visited with some pain or trouble or infirmity, or if not, we will certainly be pun-

---

[22]PG 58:592-93; NPNF 1 10:378. [23]Rom 3:9. [24]Col 2:14. [25]CCL 9a:495-96. [26]Mt 18:24.

ished in the future life. God punishes the obstinate, intractable person with a view to improving and changing him for the better. This is easy to see. Holy Scripture is pertinent here, in these wisely spoken words: "the Lord disciplines those he loves, and he punishes everyone he accepts as a son,"[27] and again: "Abide instruction."[28] FRAGMENT 216.[29]

18:29 His Fellow Servant Pleads

I WILL PAY YOU. CHRYSOSTOM: And so our sins become greater, and not only from this but also from the benefits and honor which we enjoy from them. If you want to learn how our sins against God are like ten thousand talents, or more in fact, and even much more, I will try to show you briefly. But I fear, lest to those who are inclined to wickedness and love continually to sin, I should appear to provide them with still greater security; or that I might drive the meeker sort to despair, and that they should repeat the despairing question of the disciples: "Who then can be saved?"[30] But nevertheless I will continue on in the hope that I may make those who pay attention more secure and more amenable. For those who suffer an incurable disease and feel no pain are untouched by these words and do not change from their natural wickedness and inertia. And even if in the future they derive from my words greater occasion for contempt, that should be attributed not to this kind of argument but to their own insensibility. What I will say ought to be able to arouse them if only they attend to it and let it prick their hearts. But the meeker sort, when they see the profusion of their sins and learn the power of repentance, will of themselves pay more attention, I hope. And so it is necessary that I speak. In speaking of our sins, I will distinguish between those we commit against God and against other persons. I will set forth not each person's own but what are common. But then I will ask individuals to add their own sins according to an examination of their conscience. I will do this,

having first set forth the good deeds of God to us. What then are God's good deeds? He created us from nothing; he made the whole visible world for us, the heaven, the sea, the earth, animals, plants and seeds. I must be brief because of the infinite number of his works. Into us alone of all that are on earth he breathed a living soul. He planted a garden for us. He gave us a helpmate and set us over all the brute species, and he crowned us with glory and honor.

And yet after all this, when humanity turned out ungrateful toward its benefactor, he thought us worthy of an even greater gift—forgiveness. THE GOSPEL OF MATTHEW, HOMILY 61.1.[31]

18:30 He Refused to Show Mercy

UNJUST AND CRUEL. CHROMATIUS: When Peter asked this, the Lord commanded that the sinning brother should be forgiven not seven times but seventy times seven. He then added a parable, making the comparison of a king and his servant. The servant, though unworthy, had received such mercy from his master that even an immense debt was forgiven him. But he himself refused to show mercy to a fellow servant for his small debt. So, quite rightly, he was handed over to the torturers and received the just punishment of condemnation. For what would such a wicked servant not deserve to suffer? Though he had experienced such pity from his master, he was himself unjust and cruel to his fellow servant. By this example, we are clearly instructed and advised that if we do not forgive our fellow servants—that is, the brothers who sin against us— the debt of their sins, we will be condemned with like punishment. And though the comparison may seem to have been introduced for the present occasion, yet the parable itself has within it an integral logic and manifest truth. TRACTATE ON MATTHEW 59.4.[32]

---

[27]Heb 12:6; Prov 3:12. [28]Prov 4:13; cf. Prov 19:20, Sir 41:14. [29]*MKGK* 225. [30]Mt 19:25. [31]PG 58:589-90; NPNF 1 10:376. [32]CCL 9a:495.

18:31-33 Should Not You Have Had Mercy?

MERCY AND LACK OF MERCY. CHRYSOSTOM:
Do you see the mercy of the lord? Do you see
contrasted the lack of mercy of the servant? Listen, all you who do such things for money: one
should not act like this because it is a sin. But it
is much worse to act like this for money. How
then does he plead? "Have patience with me, and
I will pay you everything." But he did not even
respect the very words through which he had
himself been saved. With these words he himself had been freed from a debt of ten thousand
talents! He did not even recognize the harbor by
means of which he had escaped shipwreck. Even
the gesture of supplication did not remind him
of his master's kindness.

Casting all these out of his mind in his greed,
cruelty and rancor, he was more brutal than any
wild beast in seizing his fellow servant by the
throat.

What are you doing, O my beloved? Do you
not see that you are making such a demand upon
yourself? You are deceiving yourself. You are
thrusting a sword into yourself! You are revok-
ing both the sentence and the gift. But he considered none of this, nor did he remember his
own case, nor did he yield at all. Yet the requests
were not on the same order. Compare them.
One was for ten thousand talents, the other for
a pittance: a hundred denarii. One was merely
dealing with his fellow servant. But the other
was dealing with his lord. The one received
entire forgiveness; the other asked for delay, and
not so much as this did he give him, for "he cast
him into prison." THE GOSPEL OF MATTHEW,
HOMILY 61.4.[33]

18:34 Delivered to the Jailers

**TILL HE SHOULD PAY ALL HIS DEBTS. APOL-
LINARIS:** When they do not tolerate our wickedness, our fellow servants are angels who accuse us
before God. They do not accuse to God as to one
who does not know of our sins but because of

their anger at those who break the laws of human
love. By "jailers" he means the angels entrusted
with our punishment. "Till he should pay all his
debts" means in effect that he has handed him
over to be punished for all time. For he could
never pay it back. For when he corrects a person
in the present life, God hands him over to bonds,
sickness and tortures, but in the future he hands
him over to anguish without remission for all
time. He did not say, "So also will your Father do
to you," but "my Father." For such people are
unworthy to be called sons of God. So the parable
describes in summary the indescribable love of
God. Anyone who does not imitate this love as
far as he can will suffer severe punishment from
the just Judge. Even though it has been said, "Not
to be regretted are God's blessings," yet wickedness is so strong that it blocks out these words.
So the story demands two things of us: to remember our own faults and not to bear a grudge on
one who stumbles. FRAGMENT 92.[34]

18:35 If You Do Not Forgive

**SO MY FATHER WILL DO TO YOU. CHRYSOS-
TOM:** "In anger his lord delivered him to the jailers, till he should pay all his debt."[35] This means
forever, since he will never pay it. For since you
did not become better by receiving blessings, it
remains for you to be corrected by punishment.
For since you have not become better by the
kindness shown to you, it remains that you will
be corrected only by vengeance. Although it is
said that the blessings and gifts of God are irre-
vocable,[36] our recalcitrance may frustrate even
this intention of God. For what, then, can be a
more grievous thing than to be vengeful, especially when it appears to overthrow so great a
gift of God. The text does not simply say they
"delivered him" but "in anger delivered him." For
when he had earlier commanded him to be sold,
his were not the words of wrath but, rightly

---

[33]PG 58:593; NPNF 1 10:379. [34]MKGK 29. [35]Mt 18:34. [36]Rom 11:29.

understood, a moment of great mercy. He did not in fact show wrath at that point. But in this case it is a sentence of great anger, punishment and vengeance. So what does the parable mean? "So also my heavenly Father will do to you," he says, "if you do not forgive your brother from your heart." Note that he did not say "your Father" but "my Father." For it is not proper for God to be called the Father of one who is so wicked and malicious. THE GOSPEL OF MAT-THEW, HOMILY 61.4.[37]

---

[37] PG 58:594; NPNF 1 10:379-80.

19:1-15 JESUS TEACHES ABOUT DIVORCE AND BLESSES THE CHILDREN

Now when Jesus had finished these sayings, he went away from Galilee and entered the region of Judea beyond the Jordan; [2]*and large crowds followed him, and he healed them there.*

[3]*And Pharisees came up to him and tested him by asking, "Is it lawful to divorce one's wife for any cause?"* [4]*He answered, "Have you not read that he who made them from the beginning made them male and female,* [5]*and said, 'For this reason a man shall leave his father and mother and be joined to his wife, and the two shall become one flesh'?* [6]*So they are no longer two but one flesh. What therefore God has joined together, let not man put asunder."* [7]*They said to him, "Why then did Moses command one to give a certificate of divorce, and to put her away?"* [8]*He said to them, "For your hardness of heart Moses allowed you to divorce your wives, but from the beginning it was not so.* [9]*And I say to you: whoever divorces his wife, except for unchastity,*[j] *and marries another, commits adultery."*[k]

[10]*The disciples said to him, "If such is the case of a man with his wife, it is not expedient to marry."* [11]*But he said to them, "Not all men can receive this saying, but only those to whom it is given.* [12]*For there are eunuchs who have been so from birth, and there are eunuchs who have been made eunuchs by men, and there are eunuchs who have made themselves eunuchs for the sake of the kingdom of heaven. He who is able to receive this, let him receive it."*

[13]*Then children were brought to him that he might lay his hands on them and pray. The disciples rebuked the people;* [14]*but Jesus said, "Let the children come to me, and do not hinder them; for to such belongs the kingdom of heaven."* [15]*And he laid his hands on them and went away.*

---

j Other ancient authorities, after *unchastity*, read *makes her commit adultery*   k Other ancient authorities insert *and he who marries a divorced woman commits adultery*

OVERVIEW: Jesus left Galilee, where he had been born, as though the sun were climbing higher in the east. He came to Judea, the place where he was going to die, as though the sun were setting in the west (INCOMPLETE WORK ON MATTHEW). There is a great difference between those who follow at a distance like the great multitudes and those who have left everything and followed, giving up all that was formerly theirs (ORIGEN). His miracles accompanied and confirmed his teaching (CHRYSOSTOM).

If a man loves his wife, he does not even think about a law for dissolving marriage. Such a law seems unnecessary (INCOMPLETE WORK ON MATTHEW). On this matter, Jesus' detractors tried to ambush him by trapping him into saying something against the law. Hence the question on divorce took a deceptive form. The motive of his detractors was to stir the crowd of husbands against him (CHRYSOSTOM).

Jesus reminded them of how God had said "male and female," so that a woman should think that no man has been made in the world except one and a man should think that no woman has been made in the world except one (INCOMPLETE WORK ON MATTHEW). Man "puts asunder" when he dismisses the first wife in desire of a second (JEROME). If God had wanted Adam to dismiss this wife and marry another, when he made one man, he would have made many women. But as it is, he shows both by the manner of her creation and the form of the commandment that one man must dwell with one woman continually and never break off from her (CHRYSOSTOM).

Just as faithfully as God relates to the church, so should we relate to our spouse. God will never abandon his people, unless they of their own will fall away into recalcitrant alienation (INCOMPLETE WORK ON MATTHEW). God did not simply bring the woman to her husband but ordered her also to leave her father and mother; and he not only ordered the man to go to the woman but also to cling to her, showing by his way of speaking that they should not be separated (CHRYSOSTOM). God, who created humanity in the beginning according to his image, who being in the form of God created the Savior male and the church female, bestowed on both the same humanity according to his image. The Lord, becoming man, left his Father on ac-count of the bride, the church, when he was "in the form of God."[1] He also left his mother, since he was the son of the heavenly Jerusalem, and became joined to the woman who had fallen down here (ORIGEN). Unless we receive the help of divine grace, we have no power on our own account to avoid inordinate passions. Grace cannot achieve anything without the will, nor can will have any power without grace (CHRYSOSTOM, INCOMPLETE WORK ON MATTHEW). The will frequently sins without action. The continence that brings glory is the will of holy intention (JEROME, INCOMPLETE WORK ON MATTHEW).

Jesus then laid his hands on the children so as to signify the arming of God's power. Those qualities that the child has by nature God wishes us to have by choice: simplicity, forgetfulness of wrongs done us, love of our parents (APOLLINARIS). Children are ignorant of wickedness, do not know how to return evil for evil, do not know how to fornicate or to rob. What they hear, they believe. What they are by the gift of nature, we should become by the fear of God, a holy way of life and love of the heavenly kingdom (EPIPHANIUS THE LATIN).

19:1 Jesus Entered Judea Beyond the Jordan

HE ENTERED JUDEA. INCOMPLETE WORK ON MATTHEW: Therefore, when he had completed these discourses, Jesus shifted his ministry from Galilee to Judea. He thus showed that the Lord of all loves some servants in such a way that he does not despise others. For just as they all owe him glory, as being Lord, so he renders to all of them mercy, as being servants. For if one place were to keep him all the time, he would not now be the possessor of all people but of some. "He went away from Galilee and entered the region of Judea." He left Galilee his homeland, the place where he had been born, as though the sun were climbing higher in the east. He came to

---

[1]Phil 2:6.

Judea, the place where he was going to die, as though the sun were setting in the west, as if reclining in the peace transcending his Passion. He did this so that again from another place he might show us a new sunrise by his resurrection. And so we may say with the apostle: "the old has passed away, behold, the new has come."[2] And many crowds followed him. HOMILY 32.[3]

THE BORDERS OF JUDEA. CHRYSOSTOM: He had often before left Judea because of the people's hostility. Now he returned there at last, as the time of his Passion was near. But he did not go up to Jerusalem yet, but to the borders of Judea. THE GOSPEL OF MATTHEW, HOMILY 62.1.[4]

19:2 Large Crowds Followed

LARGE CROWDS. CHRYSOSTOM: Entering Judea, "large crowds followed him, and he healed them there." And he did not spend all his time either teaching or performing miracles, but at one time taught, at another time healed. Thus Jesus worked for the salvation of those remaining close by him and following him, so as through the miracles to appear, in what he said, a teacher worthy of belief, and to add the gain coming from the miracles to the teaching of his words. In this way he was leading them by the hand to the knowledge of God. But look at this with me. See how the disciples treat briefly whole multitudes in one word, not recording by name all the individuals who were healed. For they did not say "so and so, and so and so" but "many," teaching us not to be boastful. Christ healed them, benefiting them and through them many others. For the healing of their sickness becomes for others the moment of recognition of God. THE GOSPEL OF MATTHEW, HOMILY 62.1.[5]

THEY FOLLOWED HIM. ORIGEN: Note that there is a distinction here between the crowds who simply followed and Peter and the others who "left everything and followed" and Matthew, who arose and followed him—he did not simply follow but "having arisen"; for "having arisen" is an important addition. There are always those, then, who follow at a distance like the great multitudes yet who have not arisen that they may follow, nor have they given up all that was theirs formerly. But they are few who have arisen and followed, who also, in the regeneration, shall sit on twelve thrones.[6] Only, if one wishes to be healed, let him follow Jesus. COMMENTARY ON MATTHEW 14.15.[7]

19:3 The Pharisees' Question About Divorce

WHY ASK ABOUT DIVORCE? INCOMPLETE WORK ON MATTHEW: To one who is chaste, marriage is good. Love that is wholesome and complete does not even perceive vices. If a man loves his wife, he does not even think about a law for dissolving marriages. Such a law seems unnecessary.

But when someone begins inquiring about law aimed at dissolving marriage, there is already some sense of alienation present. Where alienation is found, fornication is lurking in the wings. Suppose you see someone who is searching out physicians. You probably would conjecture that he is sick. In the same way also, when you see either man or woman searching out information on the laws of dissolving marriages, you might not be far from wrong in conjecturing that some alienation has occurred between them and that one or the other may be wanton.

So does the question of this passage arise out of alienation. HOMILY 32.[8]

THEY TESTED HIM BY ASKING. CHRYSOSTOM: Note their craftiness from the very form of their questioning. They did not say to him, "You told him not to dismiss his wife," for he had already

---

[2]2 Cor 5:17. [3]PG 56:799. [4]PG 58:595; NPNF 1 10:381. [5]PG 58:595; NPNF 1 10:381. [6]Mt 19:28. [7]GCS 40:317-18; ANF 9:505. [8]PG 56:799.

spoken about this law.[9] They did not mention those words but started off from that point. Thinking to make the ambush greater and wanting to trap him into saying something against the law, they did not say, "Why did you command such and such?" But, as if nothing had been said, they asked, "Is it lawful?" expecting that he would have forgotten what he had said. And they were ready if . . . he said, "It is lawful to put away," to bring against him the things he himself had spoken and to say, "Why did you say the opposite?" And if he repeated what he had earlier said, they were ready to challenge him with the words of Moses. THE GOSPEL OF MATTHEW, HOMILY 62.1.[10]

19:4 God Made Male and Female

GOD MADE THEM MALE AND FEMALE. INCOMPLETE WORK ON MATTHEW: "Male and female." Not male and many females, so that a man is allowed to possess many wives, nor males and a female, so that one woman is allowed to have many husbands. No, he said male and female, so that a woman should think that no man has been made in the world except one, and a man should think that no woman has been made in the world except one. For it was not two or three ribs that he took from the side of man; and he did not make two or three women. When, therefore, a second or a third wife stands before your face, as then Eve stood before Adam, how could you say to them, "This is bone from my bones"? For even if that woman is truly a rib, it is still not yours. If you have not said this to her, you do not affirm that she is your wife; but if you have said it, you lie. HOMILY 32.[11]

FROM THE BEGINNING. CHRYSOSTOM: Look carefully at the wisdom of the teacher. For being asked, "Is it allowed?" he does not immediately say, "It is not allowed," lest they should be disturbed and break out in an uproar. Before Jesus made his own statement he made it clear through his opening remarks that what he had

to say came from his Father's commandment. In commanding this he was not in opposition to Moses but fully in agreement with him. Notice how he validates covenant sexuality not from the creation alone but from God's commandment. For he did not say that God had made only one man and one woman but that God had also commanded that the one man should be joined to the one woman.

If God had wanted Adam to dismiss this wife and marry another, when he made one man, he would have made many women. But as it is, he shows both by the manner of her creation and the form of the commandment that one man must dwell with one woman continually and never break off from her. And see how he says, "He who made them at the beginning made them male and female," that is, they sprang from one root and came together as one body, "or the two shall be one flesh." THE GOSPEL OF MATTHEW, HOMILY 62.1.[12]

19:5-6 Two Becoming One Flesh

WHAT GOD HAS JOINED. CHRYSOSTOM: Then he showed that it is a fearful thing to tamper with this law. When establishing this law, he did not say, "Therefore, do not sever or separate." but "What God has joined together, let man not separate." If you quote Moses, I will quote the God of Moses, and with him I am always strong. For God from the beginning made them male and female. This law is very old, even if it appears human beings have recently discovered it. It is firmly fixed. And God did not simply bring the woman to her husband but ordered her also to leave her father and mother. And he not only ordered the man to go to the woman but also to cling to her, showing by his way of speaking that they could not be separated. And not even with this was God satisfied, but he sought also for another greater union: "for the

---

[9]Mt 5:31-32. [10]PG 58:596-97; NPNF 1 10:381-82. [11]PG 56:800. [12]PG 58:597; NPNF 1 10:382.

two shall be one flesh." THE GOSPEL OF MAT-
THEW, HOMILY 62.1.[13]

LET NOT MAN PUT ASUNDER. JEROME: "What
therefore God has joined together, let no man
put asunder." God "has joined" in making one
flesh of man and woman; this no man can put
asunder, unless perhaps God alone. Man "puts
asunder" when we dismiss our first wife in
desire of a second; God, who also had joined
together, puts asunder, when by consent for
God's service, we so have our wives as though
not having them.[14] COMMENTARY ON MAT-
THEW 1.19.6.[15]

THE UNION OF CHRIST AND THE CHURCH.
ORIGEN: The apostle understands "the two shall
become one flesh," as referring to Christ and the
church. So we must say that Christ did not dismiss the former (so to speak) wife, that is, the
former synagogue, for any other cause than that
the wife committed fornication, being made an
adulteress by the evil one. Along with him she
plotted against her husband and gave him over
to death, saying, "Away with such a fellow from
the earth, crucify him, crucify him."[16]

It was she, the synagogue, therefore who left
him, rather than that her husband divorced her
and sent her away. Therefore it says in Isaiah,
rebuking her for this divorce: "Where is your
mother's bill of divorce, with which I put her
away?"[17] COMMENTARY ON MATTHEW 14.17.[18]

19:7 A Certificate of Divorce

THE COMMAND OF MOSES. ORIGEN: Now,
keeping in mind what we said above in regard to
the passage from Isaiah about the bill of divorce,
we will say that the mother of the people separated herself from Christ, her husband,[19] without having received the bill of divorce.

Afterward, however, when an unseemly
thing was found in her, she did not find favor in
his sight, and the bill of divorce was written out
for her. When the new covenant called those of

the Gentiles to the house of him who had cast
away his former wife, it virtually gave the bill of
divorce to her who formerly separated from her
husband—the law and the Word. Therefore, he
also having separated from her, married, so to
speak, another, having given into the hands of
the former wife the bill of divorce. So they can
no longer do what was ordered to them under
the law because of the certificate of divorce. And
a sign that she has received the bill of divorce is
that Jerusalem was destroyed along with what
they called the sanctuary of the things in it
which were believed to be holy, the altar of
burnt offerings and all the rites contained in it.
And a further sign of the bill of divorce is this,
that they cannot keep their feasts, even though
the letter of the law specifically commanded
them [to be celebrated] in the place that the
Lord God appointed for keeping feasts. At
present the whole synagogue cannot stone those
who have committed such and such sins; and
thousands of other instructions are proof of the
certificate of divorce. Add to this the fact that
"there is no longer any prophet" and that they
say, "We do not see any signs."[20] COMMENTARY
ON MATTHEW 14.19.[21]

THE MOTIVE OF JESUS' DETRACTORS. CHRY-
SOSTOM: They ought not to have brought this
up to him but rather he to them. Nevertheless
he does not take advantage of them, nor does he
say, "I am not now bound by this," but he
explained this, too. In fact, if he had been alien
from the old law, he would not have argued on
Moses' side, nor would he have argued from the
original events in the beginning; nor would he
have striven to show that his views agreed with

---

[13]PG 58:597; NPNF 1 10:382. [14]1 Cor 7:29. [15]CCL 77:166. [16]Jn
19:15. [17]Is 50:1. [18]GCS 40:325-26; ANF 9:506. [19]Extending to
divorce the allegorical interpretation of marriage, Origen sees the
Jewish people as the repudiated wife; the divorce decree is indicated
by the destruction of Jerusalem and the temple by the Romans,
which signified that the Jewish religion, since it had denied Christ,
had by now completed its mission. [20]Ps 74:9 (73:9 LXX). [21]GCS
40:329-30; ANF 9:507-8.

the old ones. In fact, Moses gave many other commandments, about foods to eat, about the sabbath. Why do they not challenge Jesus with Moses anywhere else, as they do here? The motive of his detractors was that they wanted the crowd of husbands to be stirred up against him. For divorce was viewed as a matter of considerable indifference among the Jews. Yet when so many things had been said on the mount, they remembered this commandment only now. THE GOSPEL OF MATTHEW, HOMILY 62.2.[22]

19:8 For Your Hardness of Heart

THE ACCUSERS AT FAULT. CHRYSOSTOM: Nevertheless, with unspeakable wisdom he makes a defense even for these things, saying that "Moses for the hardness of your hearts" had thus made that law. And he does not let Moses remain accused, since it was he himself who had given Moses the law, but he frees him from blame and turns the whole matter onto their heads, as he does everywhere. Just as when they accused the disciples while they were gleaning grain, he showed the accusers themselves to be at fault.[23] When they charged them with eating with unwashed hands, Jesus proved that they themselves were the transgressors; and the same happened over the sabbath. So it happened here too. THE GOSPEL OF MATTHEW, HOMILY 62.2.[24]

19:9 No Divorce Except for Unchastity

HE COMMITS ADULTERY. APOLLINARIS: To commit adultery is to have relations with a woman who is not one's proper spouse. A man commits adultery if he brings another woman in, instead of the one to whom he was lawfully bound. The law forbade obvious adultery, which is when another man seduces the woman in the house. But the Savior includes also that adultery that has not become known to everyone or that has not been proven as having occurred physically, because it is still adultery. Moreover, Christ agrees that the unfaithful wife has

rebelled because she herself has destroyed the natural yoking and is no longer treated as a wife by her husband. FRAGMENT 94.[25]

SEPARATION OF THE WILL. INCOMPLETE WORK ON MATTHEW: In adultery, every thing is destroyed by the very causes through which it is born. For marriage is not made by intercourse but by will. Therefore it is not destroyed by bodily separation but by separation of the will. Thus he who dismisses his wife and does not take another is still a husband. For although he has now been separated in the body, yet he is still joined in will. When he takes another wife, then he fully dismisses the first. So it is not the man who dismisses his wife who is an adulterer but the one who takes another wife. And just as the man who dismisses a chaste wife is cruel and unjust, so he who keeps a prostitute is foolish and unjust. . . . Therefore we ought to be imitators of God: just as faithfully as God relates to the church, so should we relate to our wife. God will never abandon his people unless they of their own will cross over to the heathen or to heresy. HOMILY 32.[26]

19:10 Not Expedient to Marry

IS IT NOT EXPEDIENT TO MARRY? CHRYSOSTOM: What then was Christ saying? He did not say, "Yes, marriage would be easier; that is what you must do." He did not want the disciples to consider this as a commandment. So he added, "Not all receive this word but only those to whom it is given." He raises up the matter of marriage and shows that it is important, both drawing them toward chastity and encouraging them. THE GOSPEL OF MATTHEW, HOMILY 62.3.[27]

19:11 Few Can Receive This Saying

---

[22]PG 58:598; NPNF 1 10:382-83. [23]Mt 12:1-7. [24]PG 58:598; NPNF 1 10:383. [25]MKGK 30. [26]PG 56:802. [27]PG 58:599; NPNF 1 10:383.

Not All Willing to Receive This Saying.
Incomplete Work on Matthew: Then the
Lord did not say that it was expedient, but instead he agreed that it was not expedient. But
looking to the weakness of the flesh he said,
"Not all men can receive this precept but only
those to whom it is given." The meaning is that
not all men in fact do receive this, even if they
are able to. All can indeed receive it, but not all
are willing to receive it.

The prize of glory has been laid out. Anyone
who desires glory does not think about the toil.
No one would win if all were afraid of the danger of the battle. Some are unable and fall from
the goal of continence, but we ought not for that
reason to become less earnest about the virtue of
chastity. For if some who fall in the fight do not
dispirit the others but say to them that that is
their given lot, they do not apply the matter to
the fight but to the person. All the more ought
we to impute their fall to the negligence of the
fallen and not to the difficulty of virginity.

But he says, "To whom it is given." By this he
does not mean that to some it is given and to
some it is not given. Rather, Jesus shows that
unless we receive the help of divine grace, we
have no power on our own account. But since
grace is not denied to those who are willing, the
Lord says in the Sermon on the Mount: "Ask,
and it will be given you; seek, and you will find.
Knock and it will be opened to you. For every
one who asks, receives, and every one who
seeks, finds, and to him who knocks it will be
opened."[28] We must first will to ask, and then
grace follows. For grace cannot achieve anything
without will, nor can will have any power without grace. The earth too does not germinate
unless it receives rain, nor does rain bring forth
fruit without the earth. Homily 32.[29]

19:12 Eunuchs for the Sake of the Kingdom

The Grace to Live a Chaste Life. Jerome:
There are three kinds of eunuchs, two carnal
and the third spiritual. One group are those who

are born this way. Another are those who are
made into eunuchs by captivity or for pleasuring
older women. The third are those who "have
made themselves eunuchs for the kingdom of
heaven" and who become eunuchs for Christ
though they could be whole men. The last group
are promised the reward. The other two, for
whom chastity is not a matter of willing but
necessity, are due nothing at all. We can put it
another way. There are eunuchs from birth who
are of a rather frigid nature and not inclined to
lust. There are others who are made eunuchs by
men, those who are made so by philosophers,
others who are made weak toward sex from
their worship of idols, and still others who by
heretical persuasion feign chastity so as to
falsely claim the truth of religion. None of the
above is receptive to the kingdom of heaven.
Only the person who for Christ seeks chastity
wholeheartedly and cuts off sexual impurity
altogether [is the genuine eunuch]. So he adds,
"He who is able to receive this, let him receive
it," so that each of us should look to his own
strength as to whether he can carry out the commands of virginity and chastity. Chastity in
itself is agreeable and alluring; but one must
look to one's strength so that "he who is able to
receive this may receive it." It is as if the Lord
with his words were urging on his soldiers to the
reward of chastity with these words: He who is
able to receive this let him receive it; he who is
able to fight, let him fight and conquer. Commentary on Matthew 3.19.12.[30]

Willing and Acting Chastely. Incomplete Work on Matthew: As if someone
should say, "What are you saying, Lord? If for
whatever reason a man happened not to have a
wife, will he receive the reward of chastity?" Not
always. For just as without will an action cannot
cause sin, so justice is not achieved merely by
the action unless there is the will. For many try
to be chaste in body but commit adultery in

---

[28]Mt 7:7-8. [29]PG 56:803. [30]CCL 77:168-69.

their will. If fornication were not committed through the will alone, the Lord never would have said, "Everyone who looks at a woman lustfully has already committed adultery with her in his heart."[31] Therefore the will frequently sins without action. The continence that brings glory is not the continence that a weakness in our bodies compels us to keep; rather it is the one which we embrace with the will of our holy intention. Therefore he says, "There are eunuchs who have been so from birth; there are eunuchs who have been made eunuchs by men." These are kept chaste by necessity, but the third group, those "who have made themselves eunuchs for the sake of the kingdom of heaven," are crowned by their willing it. HOMILY 32.[32]

19:13 Children Brought to Jesus

THE CHILDREN PREFIGURE THE GENTILES. HILARY OF POITIERS: The children prefigure the Gentiles, to whom salvation is given through faith and the simple word. But since the goal was first to save Israel, they were at first prevented by the disciples from approaching. The action of the apostles is not about their personal desires but rather their serving as a type or prefiguring of the future proclamation of the gospel to the Gentiles. The Lord says that the children should not be prevented because "theirs is the kingdom of heaven"; for the grace and gift of the Holy Spirit was going to be bestowed on the Gentiles by the laying on of hands, when the work of the law ceased. ON MATTHEW 19.3.[33]

CHILDREN WERE BROUGHT TO HIM. INCOMPLETE WORK ON MATTHEW: "Then"—that is, when the Lord was preaching about chastity and saying that eunuchs were blessed. For when the Lord was speaking about the glory of chastity and saying, "There are eunuchs who have made themselves eunuchs for the kingdom of heaven,"[34] some of those listening offered him their infants, boys of the purest chastity. For they thought that the Lord was praising those

who were pure in body only, not those also pure in will. They did not know that the Lord did not call blessed those eunuchs made chaste by the necessity of youth but those made chaste by the virtue of continence. "But the disciples rebuked the people." O flesh, friend of wickedness and not of goodness! Because it does not delight in the good, it easily forgets the good.[35] But whatever evil it hears, it retains forever as though naturally planted in the heart. For a man can never forget what he loves nor remember what he hates.

Only a little before, when receiving a child, Christ had said, "Unless you become like this child here, you will not enter the kingdom of heaven." But now look at how the disciples had immediately forgotten the innocence of children and had kept them back as though they were not worthy to come to Christ, even though the disciples themselves had been invited to be like children.[36] Who would merit to approach Christ if innocent children are kept back from him? The disciples thought they were doing honor to Christ, while actually they were diminishing his glory. For just as it is a loss to a physician if the sick are kept away from him, so it is a loss to Christ not to have those he may save. HOMILY 32.[37]

19:14 Let the Children Come to Me

TO SUCH BELONGS THE KINGDOM. EPIPHANIUS THE LATIN: Why did the disciples keep the children back? Not because of the children's wickedness but because it was not the right time. They did not want the Lord to be tired by the great crowd. To them he said, "Let the children come to me and do not hinder them, for to such belongs the kingdom of heaven." For children are ignorant of wickedness. They do not

---

[31]Mt 5:28. [32]PG 56:803-4. [33]SC 258:90-92. [34]Mt 19:12. [35]The disciples rebuked the people for overvaluing the goodness of creation. Jesus rebuked the disciples for failing to value the goodness of creation. [36]Mt 18:4. [37]PG 56:804.

know how to return evil for evil or how to do someone an injury. They do not know how to be lustful or to fornicate or to rob. What they hear, they believe. They love their parents with complete affection. Therefore, beloved, the Lord instructs us that what they are by the gift of nature, we should become by the fear of God, a holy way of life and love of the heavenly kingdom; for unless we are alien to all sin just like children, we cannot come to the Savior. INTERPRETATION OF THE GOSPELS 25.[38]

19:15 He Laid His Hands on Them

CHILDLIKE QUALITIES. APOLLINARIS: Only the wickedness and corruption of the creature stands in the way of our approaching the Creator. Lack of wisdom should not prevent it. He seeks completeness, and your approach is welcome to him for this completeness. Therefore the words "For to such belongs the kingdom of heaven" are accurate. He did not say "of these"

but "to such," since lack of wisdom is a property of children. For the same reason the apostle said, "Do not be children in your thinking; be babes in evil."[39] And Mark also examines the cause, speaking and interpreting as follows: "To such belongs the kingdom of heaven" and "Truly I say to you, whoever does not receive the kingdom of God like a child shall not enter it."[40] Luke also said the same as Matthew above: "Whoever humbles himself like this child, he is the greatest in the kingdom of heaven."[41] For those qualities which the child has by nature, God wishes us to have by choice: simplicity, forgetfulness of wrongs done to us, love of our parents, even if struck by them. He laid his hands on the children because the laying on of hands signifies the arming of God's power. FRAGMENT 96.[42]

---

[38]PL Supp 3:862. [39]1 Cor 14:20. [40]Mk 10:14. [41]Mt 18:4. [42]MKGK 31-32.

19:16-30 THE RICH YOUNG MAN

[16]And behold, one came up to him, saying, "Teacher, what good deed must I do, to have eternal life?" [17]And he said to him, "Why do you ask me about what is good? One there is who is good. If you would enter life, keep the commandments." [18]He said to him, "Which?" And Jesus said, "You shall not kill, You shall not commit adultery, You shall not steal, You shall not bear false witness, [19]Honor your father and mother, and, You shall love your neighbor as yourself." [20]The young man said to him, "All these I have observed; what do I still lack?" [21]Jesus said to him, "If you would be perfect, go, sell what you possess and give to the poor, and you will have treasure in heaven; and come, follow me." [22]When the young man heard this he went away sorrowful; for he had great possessions.

[23]And Jesus said to his disciples, "Truly, I say to you, it will be hard for a rich man to enter the kingdom of heaven. [24]Again I tell you, it is easier for a camel to go through the eye of a needle than for a rich man to enter the kingdom of God." [25]When the disciples heard this they were greatly astonished, saying, "Who then can be saved?" [26]But Jesus looked at them and said to

them, "With men this is impossible, but with God all things are possible." [27]Then Peter said in reply, "Lo, we have left everything and followed you. What then shall we have?" [28]Jesus said to them, "Truly, I say to you, in the new world, when the Son of man shall sit on his glorious throne, you who have followed me will also sit on twelve thrones, judging the twelve tribes of Israel. [29]And every one who has left houses or brothers or sisters or father or mother or children or lands, for my name's sake, will receive a hundredfold,[1] and inherit eternal life. [30]But many that are first will be last, and the last first.

1 Other ancient authorities read *manifold*

OVERVIEW: The law is the beginning of the route to the good life but not its completion (APOLLINARIS). When Jesus says no one is good, he means no one among humanity, and he says it not to exclude people from goodness but to make a comparison of human goodness with the goodness of God. That the rich man went away sorrowful is an indication that he did not come to Jesus with evil intent, but he did come with too weak a will (CHRYSOSTOM). Christ did not answer him as he expected but simply pointed him to the law, not because the law is perfection but because the life lived according to law is a kind of introduction to eternal life and an education toward Christ (CYRIL OF ALEXANDRIA). Jesus sent the young man back to the law so that he might understand that in the very thing in which he takes pride, he has as yet done no righteous work. He put his trust in the law but did not really comply with it (HILARY OF POITIERS).

Learn therefore to seek eternal life, when you will not face these worldly troubles but will reign with God forever (AUGUSTINE). Even though we may be practiced in the other virtues, avarice may bring all the others to ruin (CHRYSOSTOM). One who fails in only one of the law's commandments cannot enter into life (ORIGEN). If you are not willing to do the greater commandments, do the lesser ones. The greater commandments are "Sell everything that you have and give to the poor and follow me." The lesser are "You shall not commit murder; you shall not commit adultery; you shall not bear false witness; you shall not steal; honor your fa-

ther and mother; love your neighbor as yourself" (AUGUSTINE). One may abandon wealth and still not follow the Savior (JEROME). One does not instantly lose rage or inordinate desire the moment one has sold all and given to the poor (ORIGEN). If not being generous with one's own wealth is an impediment to gaining the kingdom, think how much fire is amassed for stealing another's wealth (CHRYSOSTOM).

The incarnate Word is viewed under the analogy of a needle: sharp, subtle, straight and enabling that which is torn to be sewn together without making a deep wound (INCOMPLETE WORK ON MATTHEW). God knew that even if the disciples had been endowed with much wealth they would still not have been distracted by it. Nor would their desire to follow Jesus have been thwarted by it (ORIGEN). The disciples, though simple, unpolished sinners, could recognize him, but the priests and scribes, who had Scriptures before their eyes, could not recognize him. Almost the whole race was ignorant of him whom Twelve knew (INCOMPLETE WORK ON MATTHEW). The hundredfold harvest is the same as that which is filled with heavenly joy at the hundredth sheep (HILARY OF POITIERS, THEODORE OF HERACLEA). The synagogue was first to be called to salvation, but it was enfeebled due to a lack of faith. Then the church, rising in the house of its father—that is, the law—out of the weakness of its sins came to Christ and overcame its feebleness with faith. The church took from the synagogue the grace thus passed on (INCOMPLETE WORK ON MATTHEW).

19:16 *Having Eternal Life*

WHAT MUST I DO TO INHERIT ETERNAL LIFE? CHRYSOSTOM: And, behold, one came and said to him, "Good Master, what deed must I do to inherit eternal life?" Some criticize this young man as dissembling and wicked, approaching Jesus to put him to the test. I would not hesitate to say that he is avaricious and greedy since Christ also showed him up as such. Yet I would by no means call him a dissembler, because it is not safe to venture on things uncertain and especially in a case of blame. Such is also true because Mark has taken away the suspicion of dissembling. For Mark says, "A man ran up and kneeling before him asked him" and "Jesus looking upon him loved him."[1] The tyranny of money is a powerful thing, as is clear here. Though we are practiced in the other virtues, avarice brings the others to ruin. THE GOSPEL OF MATTHEW, HOMILY 63.1.[2]

19:17 *If You Would Enter Life*

OVERCONFIDENCE UNDER THE LAW. INCOMPLETE WORK ON MATTHEW: With good reason we should ask here: when the young man had asked Christ, "Teacher, what good deed must I do to have eternal life?" and the Lord had finished his explanation, why did he add at the end "But many that are first will be last and the last first"? No one doubts that it was said about the Jews and Gentiles. It is not by chance, therefore, that this young man is introduced as immature in the mystery. He is boasting and frivolous, showing features of a life lived too confidently under the law. Christ usually does this when he is going to speak about the mystery of some subject. First he introduces someone physically, so as to find an opportunity for reflecting spiritually out of the physical situation. He then explains the meaning of the matter. For example, when he was going to talk about restraining the pride of the Pharisees,[3] he first introduced

the man with dropsy and healed him; the passage ends in midsentence but goes on: so that in the physical tumor of the man with dropsy the swollen pride of the Pharisees might be pricked. HOMILY 33.[4]

ONE WHO IS GOOD. CHRYSOSTOM: Why therefore did Christ reply to him in these words: "No one is good"? Because he considered Jesus a mere man and one of the crowd, and a Jewish teacher. For this reason he spoke as a man to him. For often he answers the hidden thoughts of the questioner, as when he says, "We worship what we know"[5] and "If I bear witness of myself, my testimony is not true."[6] Therefore when he says, "No one is good," he does not say this to show that he is not good; far from it. For he does not say, "Why do you call me good? I am not good" but "No one is good," that is, no human being. When he says this, he does not mean to exclude men from goodness but to make a comparison with the goodness of God. Therefore he adds, "Except God alone." THE GOSPEL OF MATTHEW, HOMILY 63.1.[7]

KEEP THE COMMANDMENTS. APOLLINARIS: The teaching of the law is good, and Christ does not criticize it, but he says, "If you would enter life, keep the commandments," indicating the beginning of this route but not its completion. Through this he shows that the law is not alien to himself, but perfection comes from himself. FRAGMENT 97.[8]

SEEK THE LIFE THAT ENDURES. AUGUSTINE: The Lord said to a certain young man, "If you would enter life, keep the commandments." He did not say "If you would have life" but "If you would enter life," defining that life as eternal life. Let us first consider then the love of this life. For this life is loved, whatever its quality; and however troubled it is, however wretched,

---

[1]Mk 10:17, 21. [2]PG 58:603; NPNF 1 10:387. [3]Lk 14. [4]PG 56:805-6. [5]Jn 4:22. [6]Jn 5:31. [7]PG 58:603; NPNF 1 10:387. [8]MKGK 32.

people are afraid to end it. Hence we should see, we should consider, how much eternal life is to be loved, when this miserable life that must at some time be ended is so loved. Consider, brothers, how much that life is to be loved when it is a life you never end. You love this life, where you work so much, run, are busy, pant. In this busy life the obligations can scarcely be counted: sowing, plowing, working new land, sailing, grinding, cooking, weaving. And after all this hard work your life comes to an end. Look at what you suffer in this wretched life that you so love. And do you think that you will always live and never die? Temples, rocks, marbles, all reinforced by iron and lead, still fall. And a person thinks that he will never die? Learn therefore, brothers, to seek eternal life, when you will not endure these things but will reign with God forever. SERMON 84.1.[9]

19:18 Listing the Commandments

KEEP WHICH COMMANDMENTS? CHRYSOSTOM: Note how prepared the young man is to obey the commandments. For he says, "What must I do to have eternal life?" He seems ready to do what he would be told. If his purpose had been to put Jesus to a test, the Evangelist would have given some indication of this as he does in other cases, for instance, in the case of the lawyer.[10] If the young man had remained silent or been deceptive, Jesus would have easily exposed that and brought it into the open. If the young man had come to test him, he would not have retreated downcast at what he heard. This never happened to any of the Pharisees. When refuted they were all the more angry. This man was not angry. He went away in sorrow, which is no little signal that he did not come to him with evil intent. But he did come with too weak a will. Truly he did desire life but was held in the grip of a serious moral infirmity. When therefore Christ said, "If you would enter life, keep the commandments," he said "Which?" not putting him to the test—far from it—but because he

thought that there were some other ones beside those in the law which could bring him life. So he seems to be quite earnest. THE GOSPEL OF MATTHEW, HOMILY 63.1.[11]

CHRIST AND THE LAW. CYRIL OF ALEXANDRIA: When Christ says to him, "If you would enter life, keep the commandments," the man expects him to add immediately, "my commandments." "Which ones?" he asks. He was quite deceived in his expectation. For Christ did not answer him as he expected but simply pointed him to the law. This is not because the law is perfection, for "no one is justified by the law,"[12] as it is written, but because the life lived according to law is a kind of introduction to the eternal life, briefly acquainting trainees to the things above. "For the law was put in charge to lead us to Christ."[13] The law is the starting point for social justice. Christ is the perfection. For the beginning of good is to act justly, he says. Just action then is shown by the law, but goodness is shown by Christ. The law taught us to repay those who wish to harm us, as in "eye for eye, tooth for tooth."[14] But Christ taught us to let go such balanced vengeance with a view to the greater good, teaching that "if anyone strikes you on the right cheek, turn to him the other also; and if anyone would sue you and take your coat, let him have your cloak as well."[15] FRAGMENT 218.[16]

KNOWLEDGE OF THE LAW DOES NOT IMPLY OBEDIENCE. HILARY OF POITIERS: This young man has grown impudent from studying the law. He is worried about his salvation. Jesus sends him back to the law so that he might understand that, in the very thing in which he takes pride, he has as yet done no righteous work. For the Lord answered him with the words of the law. But the young man, like the boastful and impu-

---

[9]PL 38:519; NPNF 1 6:365-66 (Sermon 34). [10]Mt 22:35. [11]PG 58:604; NPNF 1 10:387-88. [12]Gal 3:11. [13]Gal 3:24. [14]Lev 24:20. [15]Mt 5:39-40. [16]MKGK 225-26.

dent people of whom he is a type,[17] put his trust in the law, but he did not really comply with it at all. For they had been ordered not to kill, yet they had killed the prophets. They knew they were not to commit adultery, yet they had brought corruption on the faith and adultery on the law and had worshiped other gods. They knew not to steal, yet by stealth they had dissolved the commandments of the law, before Christ restored the freedom of believing in the faith. They knew not to bear false witness, yet they denied that Christ rose from the dead. They were ordered to honor father and mother, yet they had separated themselves from the family of God the Father and their mother the church. They were ordered to love their neighbor as themselves, yet they persecuted Christ, who had assumed the body of us all and had become neighbor to each one of us by the condition of the assumed body; they persecuted him to the punishment of the cross. So the young man was ordered to cast off and cut out all these vices and to return to the law. ON MATTHEW 19.5.[18]

THE LAW AND LIFE. ORIGEN: These commandments are sufficient for someone entering on the ground level of the path of eternal life. But they are not sufficient to lead one to the higher life, and certainly not to perfection. One who fails in just one of these commandments cannot even enter the beginnings of life. Anyone who wishes to enter the early stages of the path of life must be free from adultery and murder and any kind of theft. For just as the adulterer and murderer will not enter into life, so neither will the thief. Many of those who are said to believe in Christ are guilty of this sin. Just look at their daily business and the way money is entrusted to them and the crafts they practice. COMMENTARY ON MATTHEW 15.13.[19]

19:19-20 What Do I Still Lack?

THE GREATER AND LESSER COMMANDMENTS.

AUGUSTINE: The rich young man claimed to have kept the commandments. Then he heard the greater commandment: "If you wish to be perfect, you still lack one thing: sell all that you have and give it to the poor"; you will not lose it, but "you will have treasure in heaven; and come, follow me." What good does it do you if you follow the law and do not follow me? He went away sad and sorrowful, as you have heard, for he had great wealth.

What he heard, we too have heard. The Word of Christ is the gospel. He sits in heaven, but he does not cease to speak on earth. Let us not be deaf, for he shouts. Let us not be dead, for he thunders. If you are not willing to do the greater commandments, do the lesser ones. If the burden of the greater is too much for you, take up the lesser. Why are you slow to do either? Why do you oppose both? The greater commandments are "Sell everything that you have and give to the poor and follow me."[20] The lesser are "You shall not commit murder; you shall not commit adultery; you shall not bear false witness; you shall not steal; honor your father and mother; love your neighbor as yourself."[21] So do these things. Why do I shout to you that you must sell your possessions when I cannot get you to admit that you should not take someone else's? You have heard, "You shall not steal." You rob. Before the eyes of so great a judge, I now hold you not a thief but a robber. Spare yourself; pity yourself. This life still gives you time. Don't reject reproof. Yesterday you were a thief; do not also be one today. Perhaps you have also been one today? Do not be one tomorrow. Sometime end your sin and expect good reward. You want to have your goods, but you are unwilling to be good. Your life is contrary to your hopes. If it is a great good to have a good house, how great an evil is it to have an evil soul? SERMON 85.1.[22]

---

[17]The reference here is to the Jewish leaders who were resistant to the gospel. [18]SC 258:94. [19]GCS 40:383. [20]Mt 19:21. [21]Mt 19:18-19. [22]PL 38:520-21; NPNF 1 6:366-67 (Sermon 35).

19:21 *Sell, Give, Follow*

SELL WHAT YOU POSSESS. JEROME: It is in our power whether we wish to be perfect. Yet whoever wishes to be perfect ought to sell what he has—and not sell them in part, as Ananias did and Sapphira,[23] but to sell it all. When he has sold it to give it all to the poor, he has begun to prepare for himself a treasure in the kingdom of heaven. Nor is this sufficient for perfection unless after despising riches he follows the Savior, that is, abandons evil and does good. For more easily is a little purse despised than one's will. Many abandon their wealth but do not follow the Savior. To follow the Savior is to be an imitator of him and walk in his steps. Anyone who says that he believes in Christ must himself also walk in the steps he walked in. COMMENTARY ON MATTHEW 3.19.21.[24]

IF YOU WOULD BE PERFECT. ORIGEN: Someone might ask, If a perfect person is one who possesses all the virtues and no longer acts out of malice, how can the person who sells all his possessions and gives it to the poor then be perfect? For granted someone has done this, how will he go forth instantly without rage if he has previously been subject to rage? How will he instantly be immune to grief and rise above all the worries that can beset someone and cause him grief? How can he be free from all fear, whether of troubles or of death or those things which can upset the still imperfect soul? How will it be that anyone who sells his possessions and gives them to the poor will lack all desire?

More wisely a believer would seem to meet the question by keeping to the literal meaning and not expounding it allegorically. You decide for yourself whether what is said is worthily said according to its context or not. Some will say that anyone who gives to the poor is helped by their prayers. He takes for his salvation the abundance of the spiritual goods of those who are poor in material possessions to meet his own lack, as the apostle suggests in the second letter to the Corinthians.[25] Who else would have this happen to him and be so greatly helped? For God listens to the prayers of so many poor people who have been relieved. Among them perhaps are people like the apostles or at any rate a little inferior to them, poor in material effects but rich in spiritual gifts. COMMENTARY ON MATTHEW 15.16-17.[26]

19:22 *The Young Man Went Away Sorrowful*

ARRESTED ADOLESCENCE. HILARY OF POITIERS: But the young man, when he heard this, "went away sorrowful." For he put great trust in wealth. And in him we observe the rational working out of a metaphor. This was a young man. He himself said that since his youth he had obeyed the commandments that are contained in the law. Yet an arrested adolescence remains within his youth, whatever age he may be.[27] ON MATTHEW 19.7.[28]

19:23-24 *A Camel Through the Eye of a Needle*

THE INCARNATE WORD AS NEEDLE. INCOMPLETE WORK ON MATTHEW: The needle is the Word of God, which is the Son of God himself. The tip of the needle is sharp and subtle: subtle according to his divinity and sharp as to his incarnation. The needle is straight and without curve, that is, without scruple. Through the wound of his Passion the Gentiles now have entered eternal life. Only this needle, the cross, can stitch wounds together. He sewed together once again the tunic of immortality, which had been torn by Adam. It is the needle that sewed the flesh to the spirit. This needle joined together the Jewish people and that of the Gen-

---

[23]Acts 5:1-2. [24]CCL 77:170-71. [25]2 Cor 8:14. [26]GCS 40:395, 397-98. [27]His optimism about himself may be evidence of an adolescent idealism whose hopes were stultified, so that even as a young man he is still trapped in immaturity. [28]SC 258:96.

tiles; the apostle says of it, "For he is our peace who has made us both one."[29] This is the needle that joined the broken friendship of angels and human beings. This is the needle that pierces and passes through but does not wound. HOMILY 33.[30]

THE METAPHOR OF THE CAMEL. HILARY OF POITIERS: The arrogant young man, when told to make good his failure to obey the law, is downcast and sad. To the people of which he is a prototype,[31] the cross and Passion are a stumbling block. There is no salvation for this young man there. But he glories in the law, despises the Gentiles and refuses to cross into the freedom of the gospel; therefore it will be difficult for him to enter the kingdom of heaven. For few of them—and compared with the multitude of the Gentiles they are very rare—were those Jews who would believe. It was difficult for them to bend their will, long hardened under the law, to the gospel's preaching of humility. But more easily will the camel pass through the eye of a needle. A camel cannot fit into the eye of a needle, nor can the bulk of the huge beast be received by the narrow mouth of the tiny hole. In the beginning of this book in discussing John's clothing I pointed out that the camel signifies the Gentiles. For this beast obeys the word, is restrained by fear, is tolerant of fasting and kneels to take on its burden with a kind of ordered discipline. In this comparison the wildness of the Gentiles has been tamed by obedience to God's commandments. These then enter the very narrow path of the heavenly kingdom, that is, the needle, which is the preaching of the gospel word. By it the wounds of the body are stitched together, the torn clothing is rewoven, and death itself is pricked. Therefore this is the route of this new preaching. Into it the weakness of the Gentiles will enter with less difficulty than the opulence of the rich man, that is, of the one taking pride in the law. ON MATTHEW 19.10-11.[32]

CYRIL OF ALEXANDRIA: By "camel" here he means not the living thing, the beast of burden, but the thick rope[33] to which sailors tie their anchors. He shows this comparison to be not entirely pointless (as a camel would be), but he makes it an exceedingly difficult matter; in fact, next to impossible. FRAGMENT 219.[34]

19:25 Who Can Be Saved?

THE RICH AND THE KINGDOM. CHRYSOSTOM: What then did Christ say? "How difficult it will be for the rich to enter the kingdom of heaven." He was not criticizing money itself but the wills of those who are taken captive by it. If it will be difficult for the rich, how much more so for the avaricious! For if stinginess with one's own wealth is an impediment to gaining the kingdom, think how much fire is amassed for taking someone else's. But why does he say that it is hard for the rich man to enter the kingdom, to the disciples, who were poor and had nothing? He teaches them not to be ashamed of their poverty and, as it were, gives the reason why he did not allow them to possess anything. After saying it is hard, he also shows them that it is impossible, and not simply impossible but even in an exaggerated way impossible. He shows this from the comparison of the camel and the needle: "It is easier for a camel to pass through the eye of a needle than for a rich man to enter the kingdom of heaven." Hence Christ demonstrates that there is a significant reward for the wealthy who can practice self-denial. He also said that this had to be the work of God, that he might show that great grace is needed for anyone who is going to achieve it. THE GOSPEL OF MATTHEW, HOMILY 63.2.[35]

---

[29]Eph 2:14. [30]PG 56:812. [31]The leaders of the Jews. [32]SC 258:98-100. [33]This interpretation—"rope" (*kamilos*) and not "camel" (*kamēlos*)—rests on the homonymic character of the two words in Greek and has been variously followed even by modern exegetes. It is, however, unacceptable (cf. TDNT 3:593-94). [34]MKGK 226. [35]PG 58:605; NPNF 1 10:388-89.

19:26 All Things Possible with God

READILY APPROACHING GOD. CHRYSOSTOM: When the disciples were upset, he said, "With men this is impossible, but with God all things are possible." But why were the disciples upset since they were poor, in fact very poor? They were upset for others' salvation and because they possessed great love toward them all. Already they were taking on the tenderness of teachers. At least they were in such trembling and fear for the whole world from Jesus' declaration as to need much comfort.

And so after Jesus had made eye contact with them, he said, "With men this is impossible, but with God all things are possible." So with a pleasant and gentle look, he soothed those whose hearts were terrorized and relieved their anguish (for this is what the Evangelist meant by "looking at him"). Then he uplifted them with his words as he focused on the power of God, and thus he gave them faith.

If you also want to learn the way and how the impossible becomes possible, listen. He did not make this statement that what is impossible for man is possible for God merely so you could relax and do nothing and leave it all to God. No, he said this so you could understand the importance of calling upon God to give you help in this rigorous contest and that you might more readily approach his grace. THE GOSPEL OF MATTHEW, HOMILY 63.2.[36]

19:27 What Shall We Have?

WE HAVE LEFT EVERYTHING. CHRYSOSTOM: What is "everything," blessed Peter? Is it your fishing rod? your net? your boat? your skill? Are you telling me these are the "everything"? "Yes," he says, "I am not saying these things to show off but in order that by this question I may embrace the multitude of the poor." For when the Lord said, "If you wish to be perfect, sell what you have and give to the poor and you will have treasure in heaven," one of the poor may say, "What

then? If I have no possessions, can I not be perfect?" Peter asks the question so that you, the poor man, may learn that you are in no way inferior to the disciples. Peter asks the question, not so that you may have doubts if you learn it from Peter (for he was still imperfect and as yet unfilled by the Spirit) but so that you may hear the word from Peter's Master and so believe. When we dispute on behalf of others, we often make their concerns our own. That is what the apostle did when he offered this question to the Master on behalf of the wider world of the poor. THE GOSPEL OF MATTHEW, HOMILY 64.1.[37]

19:28 Judging the Twelve Tribes of Israel

YOU WILL SIT ON TWELVE THRONES. ORIGEN: In gift giving it is not the gift itself that God praises and approves but the will and sincerity of the giver. He excuses and holds more acceptable the one who gave less but gave it with more perfect sincerity than the one who gave more from a fuller store but with less pure affection.[38] Thus, from what is written about the gifts of the wealthy and from the two mites which the widow in the treasury sent for the poor,[39] it is clear that the same also happens to those who leave everything that they possess for the love of God so as to follow undistractedly the Christ of God. They will do everything according to his word. The one who leaves the greater wealth is not more acceptable than the one who leaves the lesser. This is especially so if he leaves the lesser with his whole heart. What Peter left, along with his brother Andrew, was small and of no value, but when they both heard, "Follow me, and I will make you fishers of men, immediately they left their nets and followed him."[40] Yet they were not valued lightly by God, who knew that they had done this with great love. God knew that even if they had been endowed with much wealth they would still not have been distracted

---

[36]PG 58:605; NPNF 1 10:389.   [37]PG 58:609; NPNF 1 10:391.
[38]Mk 12:43-44; Lk 21:3-4.   [39]Mk 12:41-44.   [40]Mt 4:19-20.

by it, nor would their desire to follow Jesus have been thwarted by it. . . . Those who follow the Savior, therefore, will sit on the twelve thrones judging the twelve tribes of Israel and will receive this power in the resurrection of the dead. For this is the regeneration, a new birth, when the new heaven and the new earth are established for those who renew themselves, and a New Testament with its chalice is given. COMMENTARY ON MATTHEW 15.21-22.[41]

THE TWELVE TRIBES OF ISRAEL. CHRYSOSTOM: But what does it mean that they will "judge the twelve tribes of Israel"? It means they will judge them insufficient and convicted. For they are not going to sit as jurymen. But just as he said that the queen of the south is to judge that generation[42] and the Ninevites will condemn them,[43] so will these too. For this reason he did not say "the nations and the world" but "the tribes of Israel." The Jews and the apostles had been brought up in the same laws and customs and political system. When the Jews said that they were not able to believe in Christ because the law forbade them to receive his commandments, he brings forward these people who had received the same law and had believed, and thus he condemns all those others. That is why he had already said, "Therefore they shall be your judges."[44] THE GOSPEL OF MATTHEW, HOMILY 64.2.[45]

YOU WHO HAVE FOLLOWED ME. INCOMPLETE WORK ON MATTHEW: On the day of judgment the Jews will reply, "Lord, we did not know that you were the Son of God incarnate. For what man could see the treasure hidden in the earth[46] or the sun hidden in a cloud? Who suspected that the morning star[47] was born upon earth? Who thought that the woman who shut us out from paradise and prevented us all from entering it should herself become the first door of paradise? Or that the light should go forth through her who had caused the darkness to enter? And so it was not obstinacy of heart that

drove us to injure you, but we were deceived by consideration of the flesh."

You will reply to them, "We too were men just like you, having a similar soul and the same carnal nature, and we lived in one and the same world. We were threatened by the same factions of worldly spirits, helped by the same safeguards of God. Further, you had this advantage over us: we were simple, unpolished men and sinners, and obscure in the crowd, while you were priests and scribes and leaders of the people. We, simple, rustic sinners, could recognize him. You, though priests and scribes, who had Scriptures before your eyes like beacons and pathways, still could not recognize him. Even before witnessing his miracles, we understood him. But you, even after witnessing all his powers, could not understand him? How could it be that almost the whole race was ignorant of him whom Twelve knew? You did not believe him. You did not know that he was the Son of God. What caused you to kill him when you did not find any fault in him? In us the goodwill of our rustic ignorance was like a lantern. But in you, the malice of your knowledge enveloped you like darkness." HOMILY 33.[48]

19:29 *Inheriting Eternal Life*

A HUNDREDFOLD HARVEST. HILARY OF POITIERS: They followed him in the washing of baptism, the sanctification of the faith, in the adoption of the inheritance and in the resurrection from the dead. For this is that regeneration that the apostles received and that the law could not grant. It joined them together above the twelve thrones, judging the twelve tribes of Israel, to the glory of the twelve patriarchs. To others following him in scorn of the secular world, he promises the abundance of hundredfold harvests. This hundredfold harvest is the same as that which is filled with heavenly joy at the hun-

---

[41]GCS 40:410-11, 416. [42]Mt 12:42. [43]Mt 12:41. [44]Mt 12:27. [45]PG 58:610; NPNF 1 10:392. [46]Mt 13:44. [47]Rev 22:16. [48]PG 56:813.

dredth sheep.[49] This hundredfold harvest is that which the fruitfulness of the perfected earth will provide. This honor was also destined to the church in Sarah's name.[50] This honor will be merited through the loss of the law and the faith of the gospel. And thus he says that the first are to be made from the last because the last are made from the first. ON MATTHEW 20.4.[51]

ETERNAL SPIRITUAL JOYS. THEODORE OF HERACLEA: "A hundredfold" means that which is incomparably better as regards the future in heaven. When Mark says he will receive a hundredfold "in this age,"[52] we should understand him as speaking about spiritual joys far exceeding earthly ones, inasmuch as they are pledges of future blessings. FRAGMENT 107.[53]

RECEIVING THE SPIRITUAL. JEROME: So the meaning is this: He who has given up the carnal for the Savior will receive the spiritual. In comparison and merit this will be as if a small number were compared with a number in the hundreds. Hence the apostle, who had given up only a house and his small provincial fields, also says, "As having nothing, and yet possessing everything."[54] COMMENTARY ON MATTHEW 3.19.30.[55]

EVERYONE WHO HAS LEFT ALL. CYRIL OF ALEXANDRIA: So that no one should think that what was said applied only to the disciples, he extended the words to cover all those doing likewise. The rest might not receive the same as the disciples; yet instead of their relatives of the flesh they will have kinship with God and fraternity with the saints. In fact, he means the older men and women of the church, who were, as it were, relatives through love, beloved from disposition, who loved them much more than their relatives of the flesh. They also received money from them to spend as they wished, while the future treasures were laid up in store for them. Instead of their fields they will receive paradise. They will receive paradise instead of their fields. They will receive Jerusalem above, the mother of their firstborn, in place of their houses built of stone. FRAGMENT 221.[56]

19:30 The Last First

THE FIRST WILL BE LAST. INCOMPLETE WORK ON MATTHEW: The synagogue had been first to be called to salvation, but it was enfeebled due to a lack of faith. Then the church, rising in the house of its father—that is, the law—out of the weakness of its sins ran to Christ and overcame its feebleness with faith. The church took from the synagogue the grace thus passed on. But the synagogue, driven more by zeal than faith, saw that the church had not only been cured of its sickness but also made the daughter of God by receiving the Holy Spirit, by which it came to Christ. As the apostle says, "Through their trespass salvation has come to the Gentiles, so as to make Israel jealous."[57] Thus the synagogue, which was the first to be called, was the second to believe. The church, which was the second to be called, obtained the first place of salvation with God. HOMILY 33.[58]

---

[49]Lk 15:3-7. [50]Gen 17:16. [51]SC 258:106. [52]Mk 10:30. [53]*MKGK* 87. [54]2 Cor 6:10. [55]CCL 77:173. [56]*MKGK* 227. [57]Rom 11:11. [58]PG 56:816.

20:1-16 WORKERS IN THE VINEYARD

¹"For the kingdom of heaven is like a householder who went out early in the morning to hire laborers for his vineyard. ²After agreeing with the laborers for a denarius^m a day, he sent them into his vineyard. ³And going out about the third hour he saw others standing idle in the market place; ⁴and to them he said, 'You go into the vineyard too, and whatever is right I will give you.' So they went. ⁵Going out again about the sixth hour and the ninth hour, he did the same. ⁶And about the eleventh hour he went out and found others standing; and he said to them, 'Why do you stand here idle all day?' ⁷They said to him, 'Because no one has hired us.' He said to them, 'You go into the vineyard too.' ⁸And when evening came, the owner of the vineyard said to his steward, 'Call the laborers and pay them their wages, beginning with the last, up to the first.' ⁹And when those hired about the eleventh hour came, each of them received a denarius. ¹⁰Now when the first came, they thought they would receive more; but each of them also received a denarius. ¹¹And on receiving it they grumbled at the householder, ¹²saying, 'These last worked only one hour, and you have made them equal to us who have borne the burden of the day and the scorching heat.' ¹³But he replied to one of them, 'Friend, I am doing you no wrong; did you not agree with me for a denarius? ¹⁴Take what belongs to you, and go; I choose to give to this last as I give to you. ¹⁵Am I not allowed to do what I choose with what belongs to me? Or do you begrudge my generosity?'^n ¹⁶So the last will be first, and the first last."

m The denarius was a day's wage for a laborer   n Or *is your eye evil because I am good?*

OVERVIEW: The vineyard is a place for the cultivation of virtues: gentleness, chastity, patience, and countless other good qualities (INCOMPLETE WORK ON MATTHEW). The workers, who are called to the task at different times of the day— early, at the third hour, at the sixth, at the ninth, at the eleventh—are those who have come forward at different ages and lived justly (CHRYSOSTOM). By "day" Jesus means the whole age during which at different moments since the transgression of Adam he calls just individuals to their pious work, defining rewards for them for their actions. (CYRIL OF ALEXANDRIA). He went out early and summoned Adam and those who were with him; at the third hour Noah and those who were with him; at the sixth hour Abraham; and at the ninth hour Moses and David. At the eleventh hour he calls the Gentiles (INCOMPLETE WORK ON MATTHEW). The Lord justly gives to

all "their single denarius," the grace of the Spirit, perfecting the saints in conformity with God, impressing the heavenly stamp on their souls and leading them to life and immortality (CYRIL OF ALEXANDRIA).

Some grumbled that God's justice is flawed in admitting some into the kingdom in what seemed an untimely way. Even being last in the kingdom of God is an incalculable gift. No one should begrudge God's generosity in allowing some who worked less to come in to the kingdom with some who worked more. God is not less good because we in our distorted perception think we have been unfairly treated. No one can boast of this gift (GREGORY THE GREAT). Heaven is free of envy and jealousy. Just as the one group received greater reward in being the first to receive it, so the other group was more highly honored by the abundance of the gifts (CHRY-

sosto' ... one hires a laborer to work
on¹ ... aborer may eat, so we too have
... Christ not to do only what per-
... our own benefit but to do what pertains
to the glory of God (INCOMPLETE WORK ON MAT-
THEW). The lambs and goats mingle in the
church this side of final judgment, when they
will be separated. On the final day the judge will
separate from the ranks of the humble those
who now exalt themselves on the horns of pride.
This is why fewer are chosen out of so many
who understand themselves to be called (GREG-
ORY THE GREAT).

20:1 A Householder Hires Laborers

THE HOUSEHOLDER. INCOMPLETE WORK ON
MATTHEW: The householder is Christ, to whom
the heavens and the earth are like a single house;
the family is as it were the multitude of creatures both angelic and earthly. It is as if he built
a three-storied house: hell, heaven and earth, so
that those struggling may live upon the earth,
those conquered below the earth, those con-
quering in heaven. We too, set in the middle,
should strive not to descend to those who are in
hell but ascend to those who are in heaven. And
in case perhaps you do not know which one you
ought to shun or which one you ought to aspire
to, he has given you as it were a little taste of
both while you live between light and darkness:
night as a taste of hell, daylight as a taste of
heaven. HOMILY 34.¹

LABORERS FOR HIS VINEYARD. INCOMPLETE
WORK ON MATTHEW: "To hire laborers for his
vineyard." What is the vineyard of God here?
Not men, as elsewhere; for men are called the
cultivators of the vineyard. The vineyard is justice and in it different kinds of virtues are placed
like vines. For example, gentleness, chastity, patience, high-mindedness, and countless other
good qualities which are all in general called virtues. So let us note how earnestly we should cultivate the heavenly vineyard. Adam was put in

paradise to cultivate it and work it, but because
he neglected it he was thrown out of it. We have
been put here to cultivate justice; if we neglect
it, we will be cast out, just as the Jews also were
cast out, of whom it was written: "Add iniquity
to their iniquity, that they may not enter thy
justice."² The fall of those going before should be
a warning for those following. But if we the followers have also fallen into ruin, those who were
the first to fall deserve pardon more than we
who follow. . . . A hired hand placed in the vineyard will not only lose his pay if he neglects it,
but he will also be charged with the loss of the
abandoned vineyard. So we too, if we neglect the
justice committed to us, will not only have no
reward, but we will also be charged for the justice that has been abolished. For God's vineyard
is not outside us but has been planted inside our
very selves. So anyone who commits sin destroys the justice of God within himself; but
anyone who does good works cultivates it in
himself. The well-cultivated justice of God
within you brings forth grapes, that is, Christ.
For those who do just deeds form Christ in
themselves, as is written: "My little children,
with whom I am again in travail, until Christ be
formed in you."³

Anyone who consigns a vineyard to another
to work consigns it not so much for the other's
benefit as for his own; but God, giving his justice to our understanding, gave it not for his
own benefit but for ours. God does not need
our labor, but we who do just work may live because of it. The owner who consigned the vineyard to someone else for his own benefit
expects to receive it back in the same condition
as he handed it over. How then will justice not
be demanded back from us in as immaculate a
condition as he created it in us, particularly as
he gave it not for his own benefit but for our
salvation?

Be aware that we have been hired as laborers.
If we have been hired as laborers, we ought to

---

¹PG 56:817. ²Ps 69:27 (68:27 LXX). ³Gal 4:19.

know what our tasks are, for a hired laborer cannot be without a task. Our tasks are the works of justice, not to till our fields and vineyards; not to amass riches and pile up honors but to benefit our neighbors. And though we can do this tilling and amassing without sin, yet they are not our tasks but our daily occupations.

No one hires a laborer to work only so that the laborer may eat. So we too have been called by Christ to do not merely what pertains to our own benefit but to do what pertains to the glory of God. The hired hand, who only works so that he may fill his belly, wanders purposelessly about the house. So we too, if we do only what pertains to our benefit, live without reason on the earth. And just as the hired hand first looks to his work and then to his wages, so we too are Christ's hired hands and first ought to look at what pertains to God's glory and to the benefit of our neighbors. . . . Charity and true love toward God "does not insist on its own way"[4] but desires to perform everything to the wish of the beloved—then to what pertains to our own benefit. HOMILY 34.[5]

20:2 Negotiating a Wage

THE VINEYARD AND THE WORKERS. CHRYSOSTOM: What then does the parable mean? For it is necessary first to make this clear; then we will unravel the other point. By the vineyard he means the commandments of God, and the time of working refers to the present life. The workers—those called to the task at different times: early, at the third hour, at the sixth, at the ninth, at the eleventh—are those who have come forward at different ages and lived justly. THE GOSPEL OF MATTHEW, HOMILY 64.3.[6]

A DENARIUS A DAY. CYRIL OF ALEXANDRIA: He gives to all "their single denarius," which is the grace of the Spirit, perfecting the saints in conformity with God and impressing the heavenly stamp on their souls and leading them to life and immortality. FRAGMENT 226.[7]

20:3-5 Hiring at Different Times of the Day

THE DAY AS THE HISTORY OF REVELATION. CYRIL OF ALEXANDRIA: Avoiding ambition, the Lord speaks about another householder, being himself the householder and the regulator of the kingdom of heaven. By "day" he means the whole age during which at different moments since the transgression of Adam he calls just individuals to their pious work, defining rewards for them for their actions. And so "around the first hour" are those at the time of Adam and Enoch; "at the third hour" those in the time of Noah and Shem and the righteous descending from them, for the second time is also the second calling, when the laws were also different. The workers called "at the sixth hour" are those in the time of Abraham, the time of the institution of the circumcision; those "at the eleventh hour" are those just before Christ's advent. In their time alone the question is asked, "What are you doing standing the whole day idle?" for they do not have the hope of the Lord. They were godless in the world and idle in every good work; they are like those "standing idle in the market place," not groping in search of anything at all but running through their whole life to no purpose. The Lord admonishes them, "Why do you stand idle?" They answer, "No one has hired us; for neither Moses nor any of the holy men spoke to the Gentiles but to Jerusalem alone." Nevertheless the lord sends them too into the vineyard. There are five callings so that he may show that at each time there were sensible people and aimless ones, like the five wise virgins and the five foolish ones, according to their particular times.[8] Some were found worthy, and some in their folly thought little of the coming age. At the end of life, which is evening (for the time after Christ's sojourn until the consummation is the time after the eleventh hour, as John says: "It is the last hour"),[9] the householder orders their

---

[4]1 Cor 13:5. [5]PG 56:817-18. [6]PG 58:612; NPNF 1 10:394. [7]MKGK 229. [8]Mt 25:2. [9]1 Jn 2:18.

wages to be given, beginning with the last. The householder should be considered the Father using the Son as manager, not as a subsidiary but as colleague; for he orders and regulates everything through him, whatever he wishes. FRAGMENT 226.[10]

20:6 Why Do You Stand Idle?

THE THIRD, NINTH AND ELEVENTH HOURS. INCOMPLETE WORK ON MATTHEW: And just as the hired hand spends the whole day in his lord's work and only one hour feeding himself, so we too ought to spend every hour of our life in the work of God's glory and only a fraction in our own earthly interests. And just as the hired hand is ashamed to enter the house and ask for bread on a day when he has not worked, how will you not be ashamed to enter church and stand before God's gaze when you have done nothing good in God's sight? He went out "early" and summoned Adam and those who were with him; "at the third hour" Noah and those who were with him; "at the sixth hour" Abraham and those who were with him; "at the ninth hour" Moses and those who were with him, or David and those who were with him,[11] for to these he gave the testaments. "At the eleventh hour" understand the Gentiles, because now we stand on the very edge of the world, as John testifies in his letter, saying: "Children, it is the last hour."[12] According to the apostle some part of the twelfth hour has now passed, for he says, "Salvation is nearer to us now than when we first believed."[13] That was the eleventh hour. Now, in our time, the twelfth hour is not yet complete, but without a doubt little time remains. We are in the twelfth hour. HOMILY 34.[14]

20:7-8 Paying All the Laborers

BEGINNING WITH THE LAST. CYRIL OF ALEXANDRIA: The last ones, receiving the generosity of the Master instead of troubles, are first to receive their reward, since all those after the

Lord's coming have become—through baptism and the union with the Spirit—"sharers in God's nature" and are called sons of God. . . . For the prophets too have become sharers in the Spirit, but not in the same way as the faithful, since the Holy Spirit is in some way like a leaven for the souls of the faithful and changes the entire man to another condition of life. And so we have become "participants in God's nature," and openly we cry "Abba, Father." The more ancient peoples did not receive the same grace. So Paul too says, "For you did not receive a spirit that makes you a slave again to fear, but you received the Spirit of sonship."[15] The ancients then received a spirit of slavery without the honor of adoption. Since therefore we really are first to receive a denarius, we must of necessity be said to be honored above the rest. FRAGMENT 226.[16]

20:9 Each Received a Denarius

READY TO OBEY. CHRYSOSTOM: So what was the point of this parable and what does it want to accomplish? To make those who convert in their extreme old age more earnest and to make them better and not to let them think they have less. He introduces others who are angry over the rewards of these elders, not so as to show them pining or eaten with envy—far from it—but to show that the elders enjoy such great honor as even to cause envy in others. This we too often do when we say, "The fellow criticized me because I thought you worthy of such great honor," when we have not been criticized and do not really wish to abuse him but just to show him how large a gift the other enjoyed. But why did he not hire them all at once? As far as concerned him, he did hire

---

[10]MKGK 228-29. [11]The tendency to divide the time of the Old Testament into various chronological ages goes back to the second century; the division into four ages is already attested in Irenaeus. Cf. Auguste Luneau, L'Histoire du salut chez les Pères de l'Église (Paris: Beauchesne, 1964). [12]1 Jn 2:18. [13]Rom 13:11. [14]PG 56:818. [15]Rom 8:15. [16]MKGK 229-30.

all. But if all did not listen at the same time, the time difference was caused by the inclinations of those called. And so some are called early, some at the third hour, some at the sixth, some at the ninth hour and some at the eleventh when they were about to obey. Paul also makes this same point when he says, "When it pleased him, separating me from my mother's womb."[17] When did it please him? When Paul was ready to obey. For God wished it even from the beginning, but Paul would not yield; then it pleased him when he too was ready to obey. In this way too Christ called the thief, though he was able to call him even earlier, but he would not have obeyed.[18] For if Paul at the beginning would not obey, how much less would the thief have obeyed. Some may say, "No one hired us." As I said, we should not busy ourselves too much about every detail in the parables. But here it is not the master of the house who said this but those workers; he does not contradict them, not so as to perplex them but to draw them to him. For that he called all—as far as concerned him—to him from the first, even the parable shows when it says that "he went out early in the morning to hire." THE GOSPEL OF MATTHEW, HOMILY 64.3.[19]

20:10 Each Received the Same

THEY THOUGHT THEY WOULD RECEIVE MORE. CYRIL OF ALEXANDRIA: Among these [workers] the first seem to have toiled more than the last as having been subject longer to the devil's fanaticism—sin and death and corruption not yet being overpowered. If examined on an equal basis, the matter supposes that more is owed to the earlier workers, because they lived their life when death and the devil ruled; for this is "the burden of the day and the scorching heat," when not even the dew of the Spirit was present to help men to righteousness. FRAGMENT 226.[20]

20:11 They Grumbled at the Householder

NOT MURMURING. GREGORY THE GREAT: But we can ask why those who were called, even though late, to the kingdom are said to murmur. No one who murmurs receives the kingdom of heaven, and no one who receives it can murmur. Our ancestors up to the Lord's coming, however righteous their lives, were not let into the kingdom until he came down, who by his death opened up the paradise that had been closed to the human race. Their murmuring means that they lived in such a way as to obtain the kingdom and yet were kept for a long time from obtaining it. . . . We who come at the eleventh hour do not murmur after our labor, and we receive a denarius. After our Mediator's coming into the world, we are led to the kingdom as soon as we leave the body. We obtain with no delay what our ancestors obtained only after waiting a long time. FORTY GOSPEL HOMILIES 19.4.[21]

20:12 The Burden of the Day

YOU HAVE MADE THEM EQUAL WITH US. CHRYSOSTOM: What does this parable wish us to understand? For what is said at the beginning does not agree with what is said at the end but appears totally at odds. For in the first part he shows all enjoying the same rewards and not some being thrown out and some being brought in. And yet he himself, both before the parable and after the parable, said the opposite, that "the first will be last and the last first," that is, first before the original first; [those who worked all day] do not stay first but become last. To show what this means, Jesus adds, "For many are called, but few are chosen"; so in a double way he criticizes one group and encourages and consoles the other. The parable does not say this, but it says that they will be equal with the just and those who have toiled much. "You have made them equal to us," it says, "who have carried the burden and the heat of the

---

[17]Jer 1:5. [18]Cf. Lk 23:40-43. [19]PG 58:613; NPNF 1 10:394. [20]MKGK 229. [21]PL 76:1156; CS 123:81 (Homily 11).

day." THE GOSPEL OF MATTHEW, HOMILY 64.3.[22]

20:13 *You Agreed for a Denarius*

I AM DOING YOU NO WRONG. CHRYSOSTOM: But the question is whether the first ones, who were righteous and pleased God and who shone brightly from their labors through the whole day, at the end are possessed by the lowest vice, envy and jealousy. For they saw the others enjoying the same rewards and said, "These last ones worked only one hour, and you have made them equal to us, who bore the weight and the heat of the day." Even though they were not going to be penalized or to suffer any loss of their own pay, with these words they were angry and displeased at the blessing others received. That was proof of envy and jealousy. And what is more, the master of the house, in justifying and defending himself to the speaker, convicts him of wickedness and the lowest envy, saying, "Did you not agree with me for a denarius? Take what belongs to you and go; I choose to give to this last as I give to you. Is your eye wicked because I am good?" THE GOSPEL OF MATTHEW, HOMILY 64.3.[23]

20:14 *I Choose to Give*

THE POINT OF THE PARABLE. CHRYSOSTOM: What then is to be understood from these words? From other parables also it is possible to see the same point. The son who was righteous is shown to have suffered from this same fault when he saw his prodigal brother enjoying great honor, even more than himself.[24] So just as the one group received greater reward in being the first to receive it, so the other group was more highly honored by the abundance of the gifts; and to these that righteous son bears witness.

What then can we say? In the kingdom of heaven there is no one who justifies himself or blames others in this way; perish the thought! That place is pure and free from envy and jeal-

ousy. For if the saints when they are here give their lives for sinners, how much more do they rejoice when they see them there enjoying rewards and consider their blessings to be their own. For what reason then did he use this figure of speech? A parable is being told, and it is not necessary to examine everything in a parable to the letter. But when we have learned the point of the parable as composed, we should reap this harvest and not be overly particular about further details. THE GOSPEL OF MATTHEW, HOMILY 64.3.[25]

20:15 *Do You Begrudge My Generosity?*

IS YOUR EYE EVIL BECAUSE MINE IS GOOD? GREGORY THE GREAT: The householder said to them, "I wish to give to this last one as I give even to you." And since the obtaining of his kingdom comes from his good will, he properly adds, "Or am I not allowed to do what I wish?" It is always foolish to question the goodness of God. There might have been reason for loud complaint if he did not give what he owed but not if he gives what he does not owe. And so he adds, "Or is your eye evil because I am good?"[26]

But no one should boast of his work or of his time, when after saying this Truth cries out: "So the last will be first and the first last." We know what good things we have done and how many they are; we do not know with what exactitude our judge on high will investigate them. Indeed, we must all rejoice exceedingly to be even the last in the kingdom of God. FORTY GOSPEL HOMILIES 19.4.[27]

20:16 *The First Last*

THE FINAL WINNOWING OF THE ELECT. GREGORY THE GREAT: But what follows after this is

---

[22]PG 58:612; NPNF 1 10:393-94. [23]PG 58:612-13; NPNF 1 10:394. [24]Lk 15:28-30. [25]PG 58:613; NPNF 1 10:394. [26]RSV: "Or do you begrudge my generosity?" [27]PL 76:1156-57; CS 123:81-82 (Homily 11).

dreadful. For many are called, but few are chosen; many come to the faith, and only a few are brought to the heavenly kingdom. See how many have gathered for today's celebration; we fill the church! But yet who knows how few may be numbered in the flock of God's elect. All voices shout "Christ," but not everyone's life shouts it. Many follow God with their voices but flee from him by their conduct. Paul says, "They profess that they know God, but they deny him by their deeds";[28] and James, "Faith without works is worthless";[29] and the Lord says through the psalmist, "O Lord my God, you have multiplied your wonderful works, and in your thoughts there is none who shall be likened to you. I declared and spoke of them. They exceed number."[30] At the Lord's call the faithful were increased more than he could count, because they also come to the faith who do not belong to the number of the elect. In this world they mingle with the faithful through their confession of faith, but in the next they do not merit to be counted in the ranks of the faithful because of their wicked way of life. The sheepfold of our holy church receives goats together with lambs, but as the Gospel bears witness, when the judge comes he will separate the good from the evil as a shepherd sets the sheep apart from the goats. Those who are subject to the pleasures of their bodies here cannot be counted as sheep there. The judge will separate from the ranks of the humble those who now exalt themselves on the horns of pride. Those who share the heavenly faith in this life but seek the earth with their whole desire cannot obtain the kingdom of heaven. FORTY GOSPEL HOMILIES 19.5.[31]

---

[28]Tit 1:16. [29]Jas 2:20. [30]Ps 40:5 (39:6 LXX). [31]PL 76:1157; CS 123:82 (Homily 11).

20:17-19 JESUS SPEAKS A THIRD TIME ABOUT HIS DEATH

[17]*And as Jesus was going up to Jerusalem, he took the twelve disciples aside, and on the way he said to them,* [18]*"Behold, we are going up to Jerusalem; and the Son of man will be delivered to the chief priests and scribes, and they will condemn him to death,* [19]*and deliver him to the Gentiles to be mocked and scourged and crucified, and he will be raised on the third day."*

OVERVIEW: Though a great crowd followed him on the road, he took only the twelve disciples apart in private and to them alone announced the mystery of his death. His motive in telling them about his future death is that when that day of suffering will have arrived, it might disturb them less, having been forewarned that these things were about to happen (INCOMPLETE WORK ON MATTHEW).

20:17 *Taking the Disciples Aside*

SPEAKING TO ONLY THE FEW. INCOMPLETE WORK ON MATTHEW: Therefore, though a great crowd of the faithful followed him on the road, he took only the twelve disciples apart in private and to them alone announced the mystery of his death, because the more precious treasure is always stored in the better vases. There were many men with him, but they were weak on account of the smallness of their faith. There were many women, who, though strong in their faith, were yet less strong physically according to their feminine nature. If they had heard that Christ was going up to Jerusalem so as to be put to death, the men perhaps would be distressed because of the weakness of their faith and the women because of the predilection of their nature. For by nature the mind of woman is gentle and in such a business is quickly reduced to tears. Recall that when Peter himself heard about the death of Christ he was moved by grief and did not fear to rebuke the Lord himself, saying, "God forbid, Lord, this shall never happen to you!"[1] If then Peter was so moved at Christ's death, who else had faith that could sustain the grief of such an evil? If the immovable rock was almost moved, how could the earth bear the onslaught of the storm? HOMILY 35.[2]

20:18 The Son of Man Will Be Condemned to Death

GOING UP TO JERUSALEM. INCOMPLETE WORK ON MATTHEW: "Behold, we are going up to Jerusalem." *Behold*—it is the language of one calling to witness so that they may hide the memory of this foreknowledge in their hearts. It is even more dramatic than if he should say, "Behold, now indeed a third time I predict to you the mystery of my future suffering." Having been repeated more often, it was intended to occupy their thoughts more deeply. HOMILY 35.[3]

CONDEMNED TO DEATH. INCOMPLETE WORK ON MATTHEW: All the glory of God and all the salvation of humanity have been placed in Christ's death. For there is no thing which pertains more to humanity's salvation than Christ's death. Nor is there anything else for which we should thank God more than for his death. HOMILY 35.[4]

20:19 Sufferings Enumerated

WHY DID JESUS PREDICT HIS SUFFERING? INCOMPLETE WORK ON MATTHEW: And why does he predict to them the mystery of his suffering? Because every adversity that arises suddenly for people seems beyond hope and is very serious. But when we prepare ourselves against it, when it overtakes us expecting it, it is found to be lighter than it would have been if it had come unexpectedly. Therefore Jesus announces to them his future death so that when that day of suffering arrives, it might not disturb them, since they were aware that these things were about to happen. Recall that the apostles, who had been so often forewarned about his future death, nevertheless, when he was arrested, were all scandalized and left him. How much more would they have been scandalized if they had not been forewarned? HOMILY 35.[5]

---

[1]Mt 16:22. [2]PG 56:823. [3]PG 56:823. [4]PG 56:822-23. [5]PG 56:823.

20:20-28 A MOTHER'S REQUEST

[20]Then the mother of the sons of Zebedee came up to him, with her sons, and kneeling before him she asked him for something. [21]And he said to her, "What do you want?" She said to him, "Command that these two sons of mine may sit, one at your right hand and one at your left, in

your kingdom." ²²*But Jesus answered, "You do not know what you are asking. Are you able to drink the cup that I am to drink?" They said to him, "We are able."* ²³*He said to them, "You will drink my cup, but to sit at my right hand and at my left is not mine to grant, but it is for those for whom it has been prepared by my Father."* ²⁴*And when the ten heard it, they were indignant at the two brothers.* ²⁵*But Jesus called them to him and said, "You know that the rulers of the Gentiles lord it over them, and their great men exercise authority over them.* ²⁶*It shall not be so among you; but whoever would be great among you must be your servant,* ²⁷*and whoever would be first among you must be your slave;* ²⁸*even as the Son of man came not to be served but to serve, and to give his life as a ransom for many."*

OVERVIEW: The disciples made a salutary error in seeking special privilege. It became the occasion for our learning that to desire a good work is good but to desire honor is not in harmony with the kingdom. When the disciples so readily said "we are able" it was not so much by the boldness of their own hearts as by the ignorance of the trials ahead. To the unknowing, war is a desirable thing. To the inexperienced, the trial of death seems to be a light thing (INCOMPLETE WORK ON MATTHEW). The ecclesiastical histories show that in due time the spirit of martyrdom was not lacking and that James and John did drink the cup of confession (JEROME). Just as James and John would not have made their request if they possessed spiritual understanding, so the ten would not have been saddened if they had understood the spiritual meaning of what had taken place (INCOMPLETE WORK ON MATTHEW). Jesus simultaneously removed the envy of the ten and the arrogance of the two. Eminence within this community is not like status in the world (CHRYSOSTOM). Whoever pursues boasting, while the Lord pursues humility, does not reflect the image of Christ. And one who is a lover of riches in this age, while the Lord is a lover of poverty, repels the likeness of Christ. A person is not a true disciple who does not imitate his or her teacher; nor is it a true image that is not like its creator (INCOMPLETE WORK ON MATTHEW). So you need not be too annoyed if your honor is cast down. No matter how much it is lowered, you will not descend as far as your Lord descended. And yet the deep descent of one has become the ascent of all. His glory shines forth from these very depths (CHRYSOSTOM).

20:20 Asking Jesus for an Honor

THE BEWILDERMENT PRECEDING THE REQUEST. CHRYSOSTOM: Yet none of these things that he had done caused them to be courageous, even when they were continually hearing about his resurrection. It troubled them deeply to hear not only about his death but about him being mocked and scourged and the like. For when they considered his miracles just done, the possessed persons whom he had delivered, the dead whom he had raised, all the other marvelous works which he was doing, and then heard about his death, they were amazed, if it should be the case that he who did these works would then be destined to suffer. Therefore they fell even deeper into bewilderment. They now believed, now disbelieved, and could not understand his sayings. So far at least were they from understanding clearly what he said that the sons of Zebedee simultaneously came to him and spoke to him of precedence. "Command that these two sons of mine may sit, one at your right hand and one at your left, in your kingdom." THE GOSPEL OF MATTHEW, HOMILY 65.2.[1]

---

[1] PG 58:618; NPNF 1 10:398.

THE MOTHER CAME. CHRYSOSTOM: It seems that both the mother and the two sons of Zebedee together came to him, with the purpose of making their supplication stronger and in this way to prevail with Christ. Mark well how Christ responds to them, and you will see better through their motive, since the request was doubtless their own, but they put forward their mother to make it.[2] THE GOSPEL OF MATTHEW, HOMILY 65.2.[3]

20:21 Places in the Kingdom

THESE TWO SONS. HILARY OF POITIERS: The literal sense of this is that the mother begged the Lord for the sake of her two sons. But the spiritual sense is deeper and full of symbolic significance: Think of the analogy as that between the disciples of John the Baptist and the apostles. Both [groups] suffered. Both [groups] were to die. They were the two sons of Israel who were struggling against the Pharisees. After John had suffered and died, some of his disciples came to inquire of the Lord. The supplication is that both [groups] of these callings might be equally treated in the kingdom, since both [groups] believed in the gospel of Christ.[4] ON MATTHEW 20.11.[5]

20:22 Are You Able to Drink the Cup?

THE CUP IS SUFFERING. INCOMPLETE WORK ON MATTHEW: The cup and baptism[6] are not one. For the cup is suffering, but baptism is death itself. Moreover, baptism is said to closely resemble dyed wool. For just as wool, having a natural color, is dipped so that it be colored purple or some other color, so we also descend into death as corporeal beings and rise again as spiritual beings. As the apostle said, "We are sown in infirmity; we rise in strength; we are sown in baseness, we rise in glory; it is sown an animal body, it will rise a spiritual body."[7] Indeed, every death contains in itself suffering, but every suffering does not also contain in itself death. For

there were many who suffered and were not killed; such are the confessors. They all indeed drank the cup of the Lord but were not baptized by his baptism. HOMILY 35.[8]

WE ARE ABLE. INCOMPLETE WORK ON MATTHEW: They say, "We are able." They say this not so much by the boldness of their own hearts as by the ignorance of the trial. For to the unknowing, war is a desirable thing, just as to the inexperienced, the trial of suffering and death seems to be a light thing. For if the Lord, when he had entered into the trial of his suffering, was saying, "Father, if it can be done, let this cup pass from me,"[9] by how much more would the disciples not have said "we are able" if they had known what the trial of death was like? Great indeed is the grief that suffering holds, but death holds even greater fear. HOMILY 35.[10]

20:23 Prepared by the Father

THE ACTUAL DEATHS OF JAMES AND JOHN. JEROME: It is asked how the sons of Zebedee, namely, James and John, drank the cup of martyrdom when Scripture says that such an apostle as James was beheaded by Herod,[11] but John ended life with a natural death. But if we read the ecclesiastical histories, we see it related that even John himself for the sake of martyrdom was sent into a vat of boiling oil and from there proceeded as an athlete to win the crown of Christ.[12] Immediately he was sent away to the

---

[2]Recounting this same episode, Mark 10:35 has only the two sons speak and the mother remain silent. Chrysostom takes this inconsistency, accentuated by the fact that in Matthew the mother makes the request but Jesus answers the two sons, into account and explains it in the manner that follows. [3]PG 58:618; NPNF 1 10:398. [4]Why Hilary of Poitiers here interprets the two sons as analogous to the two dispensations of the Baptist and the Lord is a mystery, but it well illustrates the tendency in patristic exegesis to look for some analogy, even if feeble, when numbers of any sort emerge in the sacred text. [5]SC 258:114-16. [6]It is Mark's Gospel that mentions baptism: "Are you able to drink the cup that I drink or to be baptized with the baptism with which I am baptized?" (Mk 10:38). [7]1 Cor 15:43. [8]PG 56:828. [9]Mt 26:39. [10]PG 56:828. [11]Acts 12:2. [12]See Tertullian *Prescription Against Heretics* 36; ANF 3:260.

island of Patmos. So we shall see that the spirit of martyrdom was not lacking and that John drank the cup of confession, which even the three boys in the furnace of fire drank,[13] although their persecutor did not shed blood. COMMENTARY ON MATTHEW 3.20.23.[14]

FOR THOSE FOR WHOM IT HAS BEEN PREPARED. JEROME: "To sit at my right and at my left is not mine to grant to you, but to those for whom it has been prepared by my Father" must be understood as follows: the kingdom of heaven does not belong to the one giving but to the one receiving. "For there is no respecting of persons with God."[15] But whoever has proven himself in such a way that he is made worthy of the kingdom of heaven will receive what has been prepared, not for a person but for a life. If therefore you are such that you pursue the kingdom of heaven which my Father has prepared for the triumphant and victorious, you also will receive it. Others wish that it was spoken about Moses and Elijah, whom they had seen speaking with him a little earlier on the mountain,[16] but this view does not seem at all plausible to me. The names of those sitting in the kingdom of heaven are not spoken, lest the rest be considered excluded by the few who are named. COMMENTARY ON MATTHEW 3.20.23.[17]

NOT MINE TO GRANT. INCOMPLETE WORK ON MATTHEW: And he says to them: "Indeed you shall drink my cup, and you shall be baptized by the baptism by which I am baptized, but to sit at my right or at my left is not mine to grant to you, but to those for whom it has been prepared by my Father."[18] Did he not have the power to appoint whomever he wished, since it was written, "The Father loves the Son and gave all things into his hand?"[19] But Jesus did not thus reprove their request. He did not want to make them dispirited and fainthearted. For it is not easy to restore one's strength for hoping about the future once one falls from that for which he had hoped. Moreover, the Lord did not wish to

accept their request, in order not to sadden all the others. For it was necessary, to the extent that they even considered such things, to this extent that they be strengthened without the help of the Holy Spirit. If the society of that entire kingdom should be divided among these two, if John is secure at his right and James at his left, what then are we to do? For what do we now hope? For this reason we have followed him, so that we may be found remaining with those chosen from our midst. In labor we have been like them. But it is better that we be not like them in seeking honor. For it was necessary that they who had not yet been made spiritual should think of carnal things. For if their request was not accepted and they all were disturbed, why did they even dare to seek this very thing? How much more would the others have been disturbed if their request had been accepted? Thus he neither said "You will not sit" in order not to confuse the two; nor did he say "You will sit" in order not to anger the rest. But what did he say? "This is not mine to grant to you, but my Father." Although kind and provident, the Father thus arranges and ordains all things so that among like-minded brothers the love of the brotherhood is not broken. See how he neither disturbed any of them or made them hopeful, saying, "It is not mine to grant to you, but my Father." For what is not promised specifically to one or two is hoped for by all. HOMILY 35.[20]

20:24 The Ten Indignant

THE TWO AND THE TEN. INCOMPLETE WORK ON MATTHEW: "And the ten, upon hearing this, were saddened concerning the two brothers." Just as the two carnally sought privilege, so also the ten carnally were saddened for the lack of it. For just as the two, if they had understood spiritually, would not have requested that they be

---

[13]Dan 3:23. [14]CCL 77:178. [15]Acts 10:34. [16]Mt 17:3. [17]CCL 77:178-79. [18]Mk 10:39. [19]Jn 3:35. [20]PG 56:828-29.

put above the others, so also the ten, if they had understood spiritually that some are before them, would not have been saddened. For to wish to be above all is indeed blameworthy, yet to hold up another above oneself is truly glorious. O beneficial error, which absolves the error of the entire world! For if the apostles had not erred thus, where might they have learned that not everything that seems good to desire is good, because it is deceptive? Some might argue that it is bad to desire, bad, just as greed and theft are bad. Now we know indeed that to desire a good work is good. But to covet the first place of honor is vanity. Now we are better able to distinguish between the good of a good work and seeking the first place of honor. For to fulfill a good work is of our will and of our work and labor, on which account the reward is ours. But to pursue the first place intrudes upon the judgment of God. I do not know if we deserve to attain any reward of justice from the first place of honor if we seek it out for ourselves. HOMILY 35.[21]

20:25 Lording It Over Others

HE CALLED THEM ALL TO HIM. CHRYSOSTOM: What then does Christ say? "He called them to him, and said, 'The princes of the Gentiles exercise dominion over them.'" He drew them near to him at the very moment when they were disturbed and troubled, and he calms them by his invitation to come near. Picture the two as standing near him. They had already separated themselves from the company of the ten, pleading their own interests. Therefore Jesus brings all of them near him. By this very unifying act he calms the passions of the two and the ten. He exposes and reveals their plea in the presence of all. THE GOSPEL OF MATTHEW, HOMILY 65.4.[22]

THE RULERS OF THE GENTILES LORD IT OVER THEM. CHRYSOSTOM: And now he corrects them, in a different way than before. Whereas before he brought little children into

their midst and called them to imitate their simplicity and lowliness, now he admonishes them in a sharper way from the opposite direction. He says, "You know that the rulers of the Gentiles lord it over them, and their great men exercise authority over them. It shall not be so among you; but whoever would be great among you must be your servant, and whoever would be first among you must be your slave." Loving the first place is not fitting to us, even though it may be among the nations. Such a passion becomes a tyrant. It continually hinders even great men. So it needs to be treated more severely.

Note how deep the Lord strikes into them by comparing them with the heathen, shaming their inflamed soul. At the same time he removes the envy of the one and the arrogance of the other. In effect he is saying, "When you, the ten, are insulted, do not be moved with such indignation. For James and John harm and disgrace themselves most by seeking the first place. That puts them among the last. For eminence within this community is not like status in the world. For the princes of the Gentiles exercise dominion over others, but here the very last is counted first. And if you want proof that I speak truly, look at what I am doing. Look at what I do and suffer. Let the proof of my teaching be my life. For I have done what I commend." For being King of the powers above, he was willing to become man and submitted himself to be despised and despitefully treated. And not even with this lowliness was he satisfied, but he even came to die. THE GOSPEL OF MATTHEW, HOMILY 65.4.[23]

20:26 Being a Servant

SERVING IN THE IMAGE OF CHRIST. INCOMPLETE WORK ON MATTHEW: With regard to this point, we were made in the image of Christ so that we might become imitators of his will and

[21]PG 56:829. [22]PG 58:622; NPNF 1 10:401. [23]PG 58:622; NPNF 1 10:401.

conduct. How were we created toward the likeness of his greatness? He indeed was able to imitate our flesh, yet we are not able to imitate his divinity. But we are being made in his image so that what seems good to him may also be good to us, and what seems bad to him may also be bad to us. Whoever pursues boasting, while the Lord pursues humility, is not the image of Christ. And he who is a lover of riches in this age, while the Lord is a lover of poverty, repels from himself the likeness of Christ. He is not a true disciple who does not imitate his teacher; nor is it a true image which is not like its creator. HOMILY 35.[24]

20:27-28 Not to Be Served but to Serve

A RANSOM FOR MANY. CHRYSOSTOM: He says, "The Son of man came not to be served but to serve and to give his life as a ransom for many." It is as if he were saying, "I willed not even to stop at death but even in death gave my life as a ransom. For whom? For enemies. For you. If you are abused, my life is given for you. It is for you. Me for you."

So you need not be too picky if you suffer the loss of your honor. No matter how much it is lowered, you will not be descending as far as your Lord descended. And yet the deep descent of one has become the ascent of all. His glory shines forth from these very depths. For before he was made man, he was known among the angels only. But after he was made man and was crucified, so far from lessening that glory, he acquired further glory besides, even that from his personal knowledge of the world.

So fear not then, as though your honor were put down. Rather, be ready to abase yourself. For in this way your glory is exalted even more, and in this way it becomes greater. This is the door of the kingdom. Let us not then go the opposite way. Let us not war against ourselves. For if we desire to appear great, we shall not be great but even the most dishonored of all.

Do you see how everywhere Jesus encourages them by turning things upside down? He gives them what they desire but in ways they did not expect. In the preceding passages we have shown this in many instances. He acted this way in the cases of the covetous and of the proud. So you can see why he asks whether we are giving our alms to be seen by others. To enjoy glory? Do not do this for glory, and you will enjoy it more. Why do you lay up treasures? To be rich? Try laying up no treasures, and then you will be rich. And in this case, why do you set your heart on sitting in the first place? That you may have the honor before others? Try choosing the last place; then you will enjoy the first. That is how things work in the kingdom. If it is your will to become great, then do not seek greatness and you will become great. THE GOSPEL OF MATTHEW, HOMILY 65.4.[25]

---

[24]PG 56:832. [25]PG 58:622-23; NPNF 1 10:401-2.

20:29-34 JESUS HEALS TWO BLIND MEN

[29]And as they went out of Jericho, a great crowd followed him. [30]And behold, two blind men sitting by the roadside, when they heard that Jesus was passing by, cried out,° "Have mercy on us, Son of David!" [31]The crowd rebuked them, telling them to be silent; but they cried out the

more, "Lord, have mercy on us, Son of David!" [32]And Jesus stopped and called them, saying, "What do you want me to do for you?" [33]They said to him, "Lord, let our eyes be opened." [34]And Jesus in pity touched their eyes, and immediately they received their sight and followed him.

o Other ancient authorities insert Lord

OVERVIEW: Let us listen to these blind men, who see better than many. They were not able to see the Lord when he came near to them. They had no one to guide them. Yet they tried to come near to him. Such is the nature of a resolute soul. It is borne up by the very things that hinder it (CHRYSOSTOM). In his bodily, temporal, incarnate life, Jesus was passing by quickly, only for a short time, as is the case with all temporal events—they quickly come to pass. Through the incarnation the Lord passed by us for a brief time in human history. Now we can read about it and believe (AUGUSTINE). To those who view the two blind men symbolically as the Pharisees and Sadducees, let us remember that the apostle advises those of us who are Gentiles not to boast or be haughty against our own roots in the old covenant. For we were the wild olive tree grafted on to a good olive tree. So in no way should we begrudge the salvation of the prior people of the covenant, the Jews (JEROME). In touching their eyes, the Lord Jesus touched also the eyes of the mind of the nations, giving to them the grace of the Holy Spirit. Those nations, when enlightened, followed him with good works, never wholly abandoning him afterwards (INCOMPLETE WORK ON MATTHEW).

20:29-30 Have Mercy on Us, Son of David!

TWO BLIND MEN SITTING BY THE ROADSIDE.
CHRYSOSTOM: But let us keep to the things set before us. Let us listen to these blind men, who see better than many. They were not able to see the Lord when he came near to them. They had no one to guide them. Yet they tried to come near to him. . . . Such is the nature of a resolute soul. It is borne up by the very things that hinder it. THE GOSPEL OF MATTHEW, HOMILY 66.1.[1]

THEY HEARD THAT JESUS WAS PASSING.
AUGUSTINE: The Lord acted according to their faith. He restored their eyes. He has been healing sickness within, deafness within and deadness within. Now he is healing blindness within. The eyes of the heart are closed. Jesus is passing by so that we might shout to him.

What does it mean that Jesus was passing by? He is coming to us in time. Only for a short time is Jesus passing by us.[2] What does it mean that Jesus is passing by? He is acting in a moment that comes to pass. Note how many things he has now done which have already passed by. He was born of the Virgin Mary in time. Is he being born always?[3] As an infant he was nursed. Is he still being nursed? No, he matured through the successive ages of life[4] until he came to adulthood. Is he always growing physically? After infancy came boyhood, after boyhood came youth; after youth he came to full human stature in several developing stages of growth. Even the very miracles that he did have "passed by."[5] Now we read about them and believe. They were written about so that they might be read later. But when they were occurring they were passing by like all temporal events. Finally, not to dwell long on this, he was crucified. Is he still hanging on the cross? In a similar temporal flow, he was buried, he rose again, he ascended into heaven. Now "he cannot die again; death no longer has mastery over him."[6] Now his divinity abides forever; yes, even the immortality of his body now shall never pass away. But nevertheless all those things that were done by him in time have

---

[1]PG 58:625; NPNF 1 10:404. [2]The earthly Jesus passes by us just as any historical event passes by. [3]The nativity is an event in time. [4]Here Augustine echoes the recapitulation then so prominent in Irenaeus *Against Heresies*. [5]Like all historical events. [6]Rom 6:9.

passed by, and having passed by they were written down in order to be read and preached to be believed. In all these things then "Jesus was passing by." Sermon 88.9.[7]

Who Did the Two Blind Men Symbolize?

Epiphanius the Latin: We read in Genesis that Noah, a very just man, had three sons, Shem, Ham and Japheth,[8] with whom he entered into the ark at the time of the flood and departed. From these three sons diverse nations were scattered throughout the entire world. For from the first son of Noah descended the patriarch, Abraham, from whom proceeded, whether for good or ill, all the Jewish people. And from the two [other] sons diverse nations[9] were disseminated. Thus these two blind men had the form of the two sons of Noah. They heard that Jesus was passing by. Now is it not certain that the people of the Gentiles believed in the Savior not by seeing, as did the Jews, but by hearing? And what is the meaning of the phrase that he passed by? Does it not suggest that the messianic event was passing by from the Jews to the nations? Did not the Lord himself say, "I came into this world for judgment so that those who do not see may see and those who see may become blind."[10] Interpretation of the Gospels 30.[11]

20:31 They Cried Out More

The Crowd Told Them to Be Silent.

Chrysostom: Christ permitted the crowd to rebuke them so that their earnestness might all the more appear and that we might learn how worthily they would receive the benefits of a cure. He does not so much as ask, "Do you believe?" as he did with many. For their cry and their struggling to come to him were sufficient to make their faith evident.

Learn this, beloved. Though we may be very vile and outcast, yet when we approach God with utter earnestness, we come closer to what we ask for. Just look at these men. They do not

have any of the apostles to plead for them. Instead, here is the crowd trying to shut them up, telling them to be silent. Yet they were able to overcome all these obstacles and come to Jesus himself. Yet the Evangelist does not attest to any faith in them but only to their importunity. Their earnestness sufficed above all other factors. The Gospel of Matthew, Homily 66.1.[12]

Son of David. Jerome: He calls them blind because they were not yet able to say, "By your light we shall see the light."[13] They were ignorant of Christ's way. They apparently had some knowledge of the law, however inadequately conceived. Some propose a spiritual interpretation here: that the two blind men are to be understood as the Pharisees and Sadducees. Others view one of them as symbolizing the people following natural law without Christ, hence blind, and the other as symbolizing people following the written law of the old covenant in a blinded way.[14] In any event, they were not able to see for themselves. Yet they heard the announcement of the Savior's coming. They proclaimed him Son of David.

But let us suppose that each of the two blind men is blind with respect to the people of the Jews. What might it mean that the crowd rebuked them? It could suggest that the Gentile crowd was rebuking the Jews. Thus let us remember that the apostle advises those of us who are Gentiles not to boast or be haughty against our own roots in the old covenant. For we were the wild olive tree grafted on to a good olive tree.[15] So in no way should we begrudge the salvation of the prior people of the covenant, the Jews. Commentary on Matthew 3.20.31.[16]

---

[7]PL 38:544; NPNF 1 6:382* (Sermon 38). [8]Gen 5:32; 1 Chron 1:4. [9]Apart from the Semites, or sons of Shem. [10]Jn 9:39. [11]PL Supp 3:873. [12]PG 58:625-26; NPNF 1 10:404. [13]Ps 36:9 (35:10 LXX). [14]The "people" discussed here were understood to mean the pagans. The episode of the two blind men was suited to a wide variety of allegorical interpretations, amply illustrated by the selected passages. [15]Rom 11:17-18. [16]CCL 77:180-81.

THEY SHOUTED ALL THE MORE. EPIPHANIUS THE LATIN: Christ is the way. Therefore, the two blind men [the Gentiles] were sitting on the way [yet without seeing the way]. By straying through idols, they had completely wandered from the way of truth. Degenerated in the obscurity of sins, they destroyed the eyes of the heart. Thus those sitting shouted, "Son of David, have mercy on us." But the crowd rebuked them to become silent. But they shouted all the more: "Son of David, have mercy on us." For with the Jews neither believing nor willing, the blinded nations were shouting all the more through faith, saying, "Son of David, have mercy on us." And for us, dearly beloved, whether envy opposes a man or the devil holds him back in darkness, let us therefore shout the more through faith, "Son of David, have mercy on us." INTERPRETATION OF THE GOSPELS 30.[17]

20:32 Jesus Stopped and Called Them

WHAT DO YOU WANT ME TO DO FOR YOU? CHRYSOSTOM: Lest anyone might think that the blind men ask for one thing but Jesus gave them something else, we must examine why he asks them, "What do you want me to do?" It indeed was usual with him on many occasions that he first sought to discover all the highest moral excellences of one he was healing and only then to apply the cure. He did this in order that he might lead others to emulate their good qualities and that he might show that they were receiving the gift of healing in a worthy manner. He did this, for instance, in the case of the Canaanite woman,[18] and also in the case of the centurion[19] and with the woman suffering from bleeding. We especially remember that this marvelous woman even anticipated the Lord's inquiry.[20] But recall that he did not pass her by. Even after her healing he kept looking around to see who had done it.[21] Such earnest care he had on every occasion. He wished to make known the good qualities of those who came to him and to show them to be much greater than they are.

This he also does here.

Then, when they cried out what they desired, he had compassion on them and touched them. For this alone is the cause of their cure. It is the end for which he came into the world. Even though it is filled with mercy and grace, it seeks worthy recipients. THE GOSPEL OF MATTHEW, HOMILY 66.1.[22]

20:33-34 Jesus in Pity Touched Their Eyes

THE GOD-MAN TOUCHES THEIR EYES. INCOMPLETE WORK ON MATTHEW: Therefore Jesus touched their eyes. As truly human, he touched them with the hands of his flesh. As truly God he healed them by the word. He touched them because they called him the Son of David. He healed them because they believed in his power. Thus in one and the same person, God and man, his work of healing both rewarded their faith and admonished their infidelity. HOMILY 36.[23]

IMMEDIATELY THEY FOLLOWED HIM. CHRYSOSTOM: Note that they did not hasten away after their cure, as happened on numerous occasions, with those who were less than grateful after receiving benefits.[24] Not so with these two blind men, whose worthiness to receive is seen both in what they cried out and that they followed. They were persevering before the gift and grateful after the gift. For it says that they followed him. THE GOSPEL OF MATTHEW, HOMILY 66.1.[25]

HE TOUCHED THE EYES OF THE NATIONS. INCOMPLETE WORK ON MATTHEW: While Christ did the healing, they received a good reward. Of what sort? They followed him. For what would a man give back in return to God worthy of his kindness, except that which God

---

[17]PL Supp 3:873. [18]Mt 15:21-28. [19]Mt 8:5. [20]Mt 9:18-26; cf. Mk 5:21-43; Lk 8:40-56. [21]Mk 5:32. [22]PG 58:626; NPNF 1 10:404. [23]PG 56:834. [24]E.g., Mt 9:6-7. [25]PG 58:626; NPNF 1 10:404-5.

himself commends through his prophet: "He has showed you, O man, what is good; and what does the Lord require of you but to do justice, and to love kindness, and to walk humbly with your God?"[26]

In touching their eyes, the Lord Jesus also touched the eyes of the mind of the nations. He was giving to them the grace of the Holy Spirit.

For Christ's touch gives the grace of the Holy Spirit. Those nations, when they were enlightened, followed him with good works, never abandoning him afterward.[27] HOMILY 36.[28]

---

[26]Mic 6:8. [27]Unlike, he goes on to say, the periods of abandonment that sometimes have characterized some periods of Jewish history. [28]PG 58:834.

21:1-17 THE TRIUMPHANT ENTRY INTO JERUSALEM

[1]*And when they drew near to Jerusalem and came to Bethphage, to the Mount of Olives, then Jesus sent two disciples,* [2]*saying to them, "Go into the village opposite you, and immediately you will find an ass tied, and a colt with her; untie them and bring them to me.* [3]*If any one says anything to you, you shall say, 'The Lord has need of them,' and he will send them immediately."* [4]*This took place to fulfil what was spoken by the prophet, saying,*

[5]*"Tell the daughter of Zion,*

Behold, your king is coming to you,

humble, and mounted on an ass,

and on a colt, the foal of an ass."

[6]*The disciples went and did as Jesus had directed them;* [7]*they brought the ass and the colt, and put their garments on them, and he sat thereon.* [8]*Most of the crowd spread their garments on the road, and others cut branches from the trees and spread them on the road.* [9]*And the crowds that went before him and that followed him shouted, "Hosanna to the Son of David! Blessed is he who comes in the name of the Lord! Hosanna in the highest!"* [10]*And when he entered Jerusalem, all the city was stirred, saying, "Who is this?"* [11]*And the crowds said, "This is the prophet Jesus from Nazareth of Galilee."*

[12]*And Jesus entered the temple of God[p] and drove out all who sold and bought in the temple, and he overturned the tables of the money-changers and the seats of those who sold pigeons.* [13]*He said to them, "It is written, 'My house shall be called a house of prayer'; but you make it a den of robbers."*

[14]*And the blind and the lame came to him in the temple, and he healed them.* [15]*But when the chief priests and the scribes saw the wonderful things that he did, and the children crying out in the temple, "Hosanna to the Son of David!" they were indignant;* [16]*and they said to him, "Do you hear what these are saying?" And Jesus said to them, "Yes; have you never read,*

*'Out of the mouth of babes and sucklings
thou hast brought perfect praise'?"*
[17] And leaving them, he went out of the city to Bethany and lodged there.

p Other ancient authorities omit *of God*

OVERVIEW: The children did not understand what they were saying. So Jesus enables their immature tongues to speak through the exercise of his power. Their voices were a prototype of the Gentiles' lisping of the gospel. The children, although immature in their age, uttered things that had a clear meaning in accord with testimony from above. Regarding the events surrounding the triumphal entry into Jerusalem, it might have been possible for these things to have occurred earlier, but the time had not yet come for them. Many miracles now began to occur quickly, and many prophecies were being immediately fulfilled (CHRYSOSTOM). The sending of the two disciples outside of Jerusalem has a deeper spiritual meaning: Jesus is sending them to free the Gentiles who are bound and restricted by error (HILARY OF POITIERS). "Behold" is the expression of one who is showing. It says, "Don't look with physical eyes alone, but look with spiritual intellect. Look upon his virtues, not the external outline of his appearance." The garments are the divine teachings and spiritual grace. For just as the disgrace of nakedness is covered by the garment, so the evils of our flesh are covered by grace (INCOMPLETE WORK ON MATTHEW). The King is gentle. The palm leaves signify victory (SEVERUS).

21:1 They Drew Near to Jerusalem

EARLIER VISITS DIFFERENT. CHRYSOSTOM: He had often entered Jerusalem before, but never with so much at stake. Why were earlier visits different? They came early in the dispensation, when he was not very well known. The time of his Passion had not drawn near. He mixed in without distinction, keeping his identity under wraps. Had he appeared in this mode earlier, he would not have been held in high esteem. He would only have excited them to greater anger. But by now he had given them sufficient proof of his miraculous power. The cross was at the door. He now makes himself more conspicuous. He does not hesitate to do things that were likely to inflame them. All this happens with dramatic impact. It might have been possible for these things to have been done earlier, but it was neither profitable or expedient. THE GOSPEL OF MATTHEW, HOMILY 66.[1]

21:2 Go into the Village Opposite

YOU WILL FIND AN ASS WITH A COLT. CHRYSOSTOM: Note carefully how many miracles occurred so quickly. Observe how many prophecies are fulfilled. For example, when he said, "You will find an ass"[2] he foretold that no man should hinder them but that all, when they heard, should hold their peace. . . . He had already persuaded many who had never known him before to give up their own property and follow him. The Jews of Jerusalem were hardly persuaded, however, even though some of them were present with him when he worked his miracles. THE GOSPEL OF MATTHEW, HOMILY 66.1.[3]

21:3 The Lord Has Need of Them

TWO COMPLEMENTARY VOCATIONS. HILARY OF POITIERS: Two disciples are sent to the village to loosen the ass tied up with its colt and to bring them to him. And should someone ask them why they are doing that, they are to respond that the Lord needs the animals, which

---

[1] PG 58:627; NPNF 1 10:405. [2] Cf. Zech 9:9. [3] PG 58:627; NPNF 1 10:405.

must be released to him without delay.

From the previous sermons[4] we remember that the two sons of Zebedee symbolize the double vocation of Israel. Therefore, now it is fitting to interpret the two disciples sent to release the ass and the colt as the subsequent double vocation of the Gentiles. It applies first of all to the Samaritans, who abandoned the law after their dissent and lived in a state of dependence and servitude. Yet it also applies to the rebellious and ferocious Gentiles.

Therefore the two disciples are sent to loosen those who were bound and arrested by the bonds of error and ignorance. They are sent *from* Jerusalem, since these vocations originated in that city. On the other hand, it was on the way *to* Jerusalem that the Zebedees' mother prayed to the Lord, since it is by the two vocations of the apostles and John, which proceeded from the law, that Israel is saved.

Similarly Samaria (which believed through Philip)[5] and Cornelius (who was brought to Christ by Peter)[6] are the first fruits of the Gentiles. The fact that the disciples are instructed to respond, should someone ask them, that the two animals are needed for the Lord and must be released immediately means that the two preachers of the faith according to the gospel have to give themselves to the Lord as his own nation. Therefore the prophecy that announced the Lord's entering Jerusalem on the ass and colt is fulfilled.[7] ON MATTHEW 21.3.[8]

SERVING THE CREATOR. INCOMPLETE WORK ON MATTHEW: "If anyone says anything to you, you shall say, 'The Lord has need of them,' and he will send them immediately." Do not say "your Lord" or "our Lord" or "the Lord of the beasts of burden," so that they all may understand that I alone am the Lord, not only of animals or only of those who have been set under me but of all humanity, even of those who are against me. For even sinners are mine by right, even though they are the devil's by their own will. "For the world is mine and all its fullness."[9]

Just say, "The Lord has need of them," for it is entirely fitting that the brute creature should serve its own Creator. HOMILY 37.[10]

21:4-5 Your King Is Coming to You

BEHOLD, YOUR KING COMES GENTLE. INCOMPLETE WORK ON MATTHEW: Into the mystery of future nations, sitting upon an ass and its colt, he entered into the temple. In this way he joined together the nations with the Jews. But knowing as a prophet the wickedness of the Jews, that they would speak against Christ ascending into the temple, he therefore predicted that through this sign the Jews would recognize their own kingdom, saying, "Behold, your king comes to you gentle, sitting on an ass and its colt."[11]

"Behold" is the word of the one showing. That is, don't look at your King alone but examine the matter with spiritual intellect. Ponder the works of his virtues, not the external outline of his appearances. For if you look at his outline, you will be disappointed by human nature. If, however, you behold his work, you will be saved by God's own goodness.

A prophet who stood much earlier, however, observing with spiritual vision him who had not yet been born, was saying "behold" in order to show that he, about whom it was spoken, already was before he was born. When therefore you see him in the temple, oh Jews, do not wish to act haughtily toward him, saying, "By what power do you do these things?"[12] Rather, "Behold, your king comes to you gentle, sitting on an ass." Do not consider by what power he does them but only if he is able to do them. Believe. Do not put him to a test. "Behold, your king comes to you gentle, sitting on an ass." Do not say, "We have no king but Caesar only."[13] "Behold, your king comes to you gentle, sitting on

[4]As is his usual practice, Hilary connects the interpretations on contiguous Gospel pericopes one to another. [5]Acts 7:5-12. [6]Acts 10:1-48. [7]Zech 9:9. [8]SC 258:120-22. [9]Ps 24:1 (23:1 LXX). [10]PG 56:836. [11]Zech 9:9. [12]Lk 20:2. [13]Jn 19:15.

an ass." If you understand, he comes to you. If you do not understand, he will come against you. If you understand, he will come in order to save you and to set the nations under your feet, so that you may say with the prophet, "Since God is lofty, terrible and the great king over all the earth, he subjected the peoples to us and the nations under our feet."[14] "He chose us for himself for his inheritance, the image of Jacob, whom he loved."[15] If, however, you do not understand, he will come to destroy you and to expel you from the temple of holiness, and to take another wife more pure from the nations into his bed of holiness. [Then] you, cast forth and standing in the darkness, may say with Solomon, "Do not look at me, since I have been blackened, since the sun has despised me."[16]

Do you wish to know the gentleness of the one who is coming? Consider the image of his arrival. He does not sit on a golden chariot, shining with priceless purple. Nor is he mounted upon a foaming horse, the lover of discord and quarreling, which has a chest filled with glory's boasting, which sniffs out war from afar and rejoices at the sound of the war trumpet and, when it sees a bloody battle, says in its own heart, "It is well done." Rather, he sits upon an ass of tranquility, a friend of peace. HOMILY 33.[17]

THE GENTLE KING. SEVERUS: It is again a prophecy, that of Zechariah, just as that also found in the book of Matthew, which informs us that a donkey's foal was tied to its mother. For the prophecy reads, "Rejoice greatly, daughter of Zion, shout, daughter of Jerusalem; behold, your king comes to you, righteous and having salvation; he himself is humble and mounted on a donkey and on a newly born foal."[18] Now who doesn't, while waiting for a righteous king, immediately understand that the Christ is in view, who prefigured likewise the name of Melchizedek, whose name in translation evokes the "king of justice"?[19] So the prophet himself does not only say "king of jus-

tice," but he added "and redeemer." He did so in order to indicate, in an additional way through this means, the name of Jesus, which when translated means "salvation of God" and "healing." And he added next, "He himself is humble and mounted on a donkey and on a newly born foal." He does so to show in advance he who is written about in the Gospels: "Learn of me, for I am gentle and humble of heart."[20] Now there was never any king, simultaneously just, a redeemer, gentle and seated on a donkey, who came to Jerusalem, unless this is he who alone is King of kings, God and Redeemer, Jesus. He is kind, gentle and abundant in mercy for all those who call upon him,[21] as it is written. CATHEDRAL SERMONS, HOMILY 20.[22]

21:6-7 The Disciples Did As Jesus Told Them

JESUS SAT THEREON. HILARY OF POITIERS: All of these circumstances surrounding his appearance point to the shape of the future. By means of parabolic signs and by the conditions of present things, the form of the future is here suggested. The Lord is taking possession of the nations! His brightness is approaching! He is occupying the minds of the nations— just as the rider of a beast. He is proclaimed by the entire army of his retinue of patriarchs, prophets and apostles. The patriarchs are spreading their garments, which signify their glory, under the Lord. By their generations, names and struggles, the Lord was prophesied. Going to him with all the ornaments of their own worthiness and scattering themselves under his seat, they will show that all their glory had been laid beneath him in preparation for his coming. The prophets are spread-

[14]Ps 47:2-4 (46:3-5 LXX). [15]Ps 47:4 (46:5 LXX). [16]Song 1:6. [17]PG 56:836-37. [18]Zech 9:9. [19]In a passage from Zechariah omitted by Matthew, the Messiah is also defined as just and salvific. Hence the connection with Melchizedek that Severus creates based on the etymology of the latter with "king of justice." [20]Mt 11:29. [21]Ps 86:5 (85:5 LXX). [22]PO 37:51.

ing their own garments under the route of the one who is coming. They predicted this path long ago. They knew that the nations would uphold God. Many had died and offered themselves to stoning. They, in a certain sense, stripped their very bodies and offered their garments upon this path. The apostles are scattering the branches from the cut trees after casting their garments. This is not simply an act of human piety. It might at first seem that the branches might impede the one who is proceeding and might make the journey of the one who is hastening more difficult and entangled. Yet even in this the reasoning of the prophets is preserved and the form of the future announced. These branches are the fruitless nations, or the fruits of the oftentimes faithless nations. These branches are scattered under the route of the Lord by the apostles. They are preparing for the entry of the Savior. ON MATTHEW 21.2.[23]

21:8 The Crowd Spread Garments and Branches

THEY SPREAD THEIR GARMENTS ON THE ROAD. INCOMPLETE WORK ON MATTHEW: The garments are the divine teachings and spiritual grace. For just a garment covers the disgrace of nakedness, so the teachings of divine grace cover the evils of our flesh. "We were by nature children of wrath, like the rest of mankind."[24] Even Adam therefore saw himself naked as a sinner, and so he covered his own nakedness with leaves from a fig tree; that is, with the commands of a harsh law. God is promising his own justice, that he will take his kindness away from the nation of Judea, just as the Lord had said through the prophet Hosea: "And I shall take away my garments and linens, I will show your disgrace to the nations."[25] Therefore they placed their garments over them—that is, they placed over the Jews and Gentiles commands and kindnesses they received from Christ. For Christ would not have been able to rest among them if his com-

mands had not been with them. HOMILY 37.7.[26]

THEY CUT BRANCHES FROM THE TREES. INCOMPLETE WORK ON MATTHEW: "Most of the crowd spread their garments; others, however, cut branches from the trees and spread them on the road." Clearly these garments and trees would be trampled when he comes on the beast of burden. The garments are the commands, just as we said. The leaves, however, are the appearance of piety. Both the commands of the law and the appearances of the Jewish practice were ordered to be treaded upon by Christ on the road. So they spread them then under the feet of the beast of burden on the road. The apostles placed their garments over the beast of burden. The rest of the crowd placed them under the feet of the beast of burden. This means dated legalism is trampled, while the commands of the apostles are spread out. . . .

Yet an entirely different view of this passage is that those who deposited their garments upon the ass are the apostles and teachers. The garments, however, are the beauty and form of glory. Therefore the glory which Christ received from the Father, he gave to his disciples. The disciples, however, receiving it from Christ, gave it to the nations, so that Christ may pleasingly sit among us, just as he himself says: "And the glory which you gave to me I have given to them, so that they may be one, just as we also are one."[27] The crowds, however, who spread their garments on the road, were trusting in circumcision and, upon seeing Christ, cast down the glory that they had from the law. [They are] humbling themselves and saying with the apostle Paul: "In accordance with the justice which is from the law, I was converted without complaint, but whatever gain I had, I counted as loss for the sake of Christ, and I count it as refuse, in order that I may gain Christ as profit."[28] HOMILY 37.8.[29]

---

[23]SC 258:122-24. [24]Eph 2:3. [25]Cf. Hos 2:9 (2:11 LXX). [26]PG 56:837-38. [27]Jn 17:22. [28]Phil 3:6-8. [29]PG 56:838.

21:9 *Hosanna to the Son of David!*

HOSANNA IN THE HIGHEST. HILARY OF POITIERS: Is this the crowd who would applaud his crucifixion? How was their hatred earned from his grace? Even the words of their commendation pointed to the power of redemption. "Hosanna" in Hebrew signifies the redemption of the house of David. They are calling upon the Son of David. They are celebrating the inheritance of the eternal kingdom. They are proclaiming blessing in the name of the Lord. Soon their shouting of "Crucify him!" would be blasphemy. But at present, the deeds he was doing were exhibiting the form of the future. It is granted that the crowd was doing these things with very confused emotions. The things that would follow would be different. Nevertheless they were, inadvertently and without willing it, pointing to heavenly things unfolding. In this way the whole city of Jerusalem was stirred. ON MATTHEW 21.3.[30]

THE SPREADING OF PALM LEAVES AND CLOTHES. SEVERUS: Indeed, on the one hand, the fact that the donkey walks on the branches and leaves of palm trees would make it clearly known that not only he who was mounted upon it but also those who would believe in him were going to subdue all their enemies, trample them under their feet and win a glorious victory. For the branches and leaves of palm trees are the emblems of the victory. On the other hand, the fact that the people took off their coats and threw them on the ground was a proclamation—in an immediate and manifest fashion—to speak of what appeared in reality in the events that followed.

Indeed, when these believers were ridding themselves of all they possessed and even of their clothes, which is a sketch in miniature, they were following the gospel of grace. For it is written in the book of Acts that "all who were owners of land and houses, when they sold them, took the money from what had been sold

and laid it at the feet of the apostles, and one gave to each according to his need."[31] If this were not so, if there were not things mysteriously prefigured in what was coming to pass, the branches and the clothes would have even become an obstacle for the progress of this donkey, by impeding its feet like nets.

"And the crowd that went ahead of him and those that followed were shouting, 'Hosanna to the Son of David.'" This phrase (namely, "Hosanna to the Son of David"), in passing from the Hebrew language to the Greek language, is translated as "praise, or a psalm, to the Son of David." As for Jesus, it does not suit a man to be honored or praised by a psalm. But such does suit him alone who is by nature God, as it is said: "He has placed in my mouth a new song, praise to our God"[32] and "I will sing to my God, as long as I live."[33]

And those who were crying out still added this: "Blessed is he who comes in the name of the Lord! Hosanna in the highest." And certainly it would have been necessary that those who were praising spoke according to custom: "You are the good one who has come." He is like the one who came a first time, or like the ancients greeting the prophet Samuel, asking from the outset, "Do you come in peace, O seer?"[34]

For Jesus' part, the fact that they were crying out "Blessed is he who comes in the name of the Lord! Hosanna in the highest" (Luke as well added, "Peace in heaven and glory in the highest")[35] is the act of those who proclaim his second coming, by which he will come from the heavens with glory. After his coming "he will join by peace earthly things to heavenly things" when "he will likewise judge all the earth with justice,"[36] and he will bring into the kingdom of heaven those who have lived well. This is why indeed it was also very small children who were praising and crying out like this. They were those who entered into the temple with him, for

---

[30]SC 258:124-26. [31]Acts 2:45. [32]Ps 40:3 (39:4 LXX). [33]Ps 104:33 (103:33 LXX). [34]1 Sam 16:4. [35]Lk 19:38. [36]Ps 96:13 (95:13 LXX).

Jesus himself says, "Truly, I say to you, unless you change and become like one of these little children, you will not enter the kingdom of heaven."[37]

Consider still the branches as bearers of victory, by which those who were acclaiming him were honoring the one who was praised in a manner worthy of God. Therefore the Evangelists wrote that already, when he approached and was ready to descend from the Mount of Olives, the crowd began to welcome him and walk in front of him, to praise him and cut branches from the trees. The Evangelists clearly show that these branches were from olive trees. They had to be olive branches because they were growing on the mountain named the Mount of Olives.

Now the olive plant indicates the reconciliation of God and his loving advent to be with us. He accomplished this not because of our righteousness, which did not even exist, but because of his mercy. In the same way indeed it is a dove holding and carrying in its beak the leaves of an olive tree who likewise signaled the end of the flood in the days of Noah and the ceasing of wrath by the mercy of peace which comes from on high.[38] CATHEDRAL SERMONS, HOMILY 20.[39]

21:10 All Jerusalem Was Stirred

ALL THE CITY WAS STIRRED. CHRYSOSTOM: Even when the crowds grasped that something great was happening, their inward thoughts remained uninformed, lowly, unworthy and lacking in understanding. But Jesus did these things in their presence not to display pomp but as I have said, to fulfill prophecy, teach self-denial and to comfort his disciples, who were grieving for his death. He was showing them that he would suffer all these things willingly. Mark well the accuracy of the prophets, how they foretold all these things, some from David's psalms, some from Zechariah. They had proclaimed them beforehand. THE GOSPEL OF MATTHEW, HOMILY 66.3.[40]

21:11-13 A House of Prayer, Not a Den of Robbers

MY HOUSE SHALL BE CALLED A HOUSE OF PRAYER. CHRYSOSTOM: John's Gospel also reported this, but at the beginning of his narrative. But now in Matthew we are coming to the end of the narrative. Thus it is probable that this was done twice and on different occasions. That there was a first cleansing of the temple and then a second is evident from many evidences. In John's Gospel he came at the time of the Passover. Here it was before Passover. In John the Jews said, "What miraculous sign can you show us to prove your authority to do all this?" In Matthew they hold their peace, though reproved, because he was not marveled at among all the population.

If this happened on two different occasions, this becomes a heavier charge against the Jewish leadership. He did it not only once but a second time, and still they continued their buying and selling and called him an adversary of God. They should have learned from the first cleansing to honor his Father and his own power. They could see his works agreeing with his words, and they could behold his miracles. They could hear the prophet pointing to him. They could see the children attesting him in a manner beyond their age. But all this did not persuade them. Instead, "they were indignant." So he brings in Isaiah[41] as their accuser when he says, "My house shall be called a house of prayer." THE GOSPEL OF MATTHEW, HOMILY 67.1.[42]

21:14-17 Perfect Praise from the Mouths of Children

EVEN INFANTS DELIGHTED IN CHRIST'S COMING. INCOMPLETE WORK ON MATTHEW: Columns of a temple that are installed in a perfectly upright manner actually grow more stable when

---

[37]Mt 18:3. [38]Gen 8:11. [39]PO 37:51-57. [40]PG 58:629; NPNF 1 10:406. [41]Cf. Is 56:7. [42]PG 58:631-33; NPNF 1 10:409.

more weight is placed on them, but columns which are at first slightly askew only move farther off center with greater weight. Likewise, if a man's heart is upright, it will be strengthened in wisdom when he sees or hears about the good works of a just man. But the man who begins with a perverse heart will only be provoked to envy and greater perversity by the works of the righteous. In this way also, when the priests of the old covenant saw Christ healing the sick and heard children praising him, they did not thereby come to believe in Christ but were only hardened in their opposition to him, saying, "Do you hear what they are saying?" . . .

"But Jesus said to them, 'Have you not read: out of the mouth of infants and sucklings you brought perfect praise?'"[43] It is as if he had asked rhetorically, "Am I to blame because the children cry out my praise, or is it my fault that the prophet foretold this event so many thousands of years ago?" If we bear in mind how the Gospel said above that "the crowds which preceded him and followed him were shouting,"[44] we can understand that they are called infants because of the simplicity of their hearts, not with respect to their age, for literal "infants and sucklings" can neither understand anything nor give praise. Similarly they were called sucklings because their cries of praise arose from the delight they took in Christ's wondrous works, as though in the sweetest milk, for it is written, "I have lifted up my soul, like a child at its mother's breast."[45] Milk represents the working of miracles, but bread is the teaching of perfect justice, as the apostle says: "My preaching was not with persuasive words of wisdom but in the manifestation of the Spirit and power."[46] And again: "I was not able to speak to you as spiritual persons but as people of the flesh; like the children in Christ you are, I gave you milk, not solid food."[47] Every first introduction to the faith, consisting of simple doctrine, is called milk because it can be assimilated without a great deal of laborious chewing and because it tastes sweet, just like milk. Neither do miracles

require much labor from those who witness them. Moreover they are sweet to behold and provide a winsome invitation to faith. Bread, on the other hand, signifies the teaching of that more perfect justice which no one can assimilate without exerting a great deal of mental effort on spiritual matters, for whoever hears it will need to meditate on it within himself and to analyze it, as though grinding it up with spiritual teeth. HOMILY 38.[48]

OUT OF THE MOUTHS OF BABES. CHRYSOSTOM: Hearing even the children proclaiming, the disciples were ready to stifle them. They remarked, "Do you hear what they are saying?" Jesus said to them, "Yes." The children were singing to him as to God. Since the disciples were speaking against things being revealed, he applies his corrective more in the way of reproof: "Have you never read, 'Out of the mouth of babes and infants you have brought perfect praise'?"[49] For what the children were saying had not reached to their level of understanding. So of his power he gives articulation to their tongues, which are as yet immature.

Their voices were a prototype of the lisping of the Gentiles of the gospel.[50] They were sounding forth great things of faith. The apostles found consolation in this. For they had already been perplexed as to how even the unlearned should be able to publish the gospel. But now they were already finding that the children were anticipating them. The children removed all their anxiety, teaching them that God would grant them utterance, who made even these little ones to sing praises.

This showed that he is Creator of nature. The children, although of immature age, uttered things that had a clear meaning in accordance with testimony from above. But others thought

[43]Ps 8:2 (8:3 LXX). [44]Mt 21:9. [45]Ps 131:2 (130:2 LXX). [46]1 Cor 2:4. [47]1 Cor 3:1-2. [48]PG 56:842-43. [49]Cf. Ps 8:2 (8:3 LXX). [50]This allegorical interpretation by Chrysostom is noteworthy, since he was of the Antiochene school and therefore preferred literal interpretation.

them only to be teeming with frenzy and madness. For such is the nature of wickedness.

So his detractors found many things to provoke them: the multitude, the cleansing out of the buyers and sellers from the temple, the miracles, the children. He once again departs from them, giving room to their swelling frustration,

not yet willing to begin seriously his own teaching, lest boiling with envy they should be all the more displeased at what he would say. THE GOSPEL OF MATTHEW, HOMILY 67.1.[51]

---

[51]PG 58:633; NPNF 1 10:409-10.

21:18-27 JESUS CURSES THE FIG TREE

[18]*In the morning, as he was returning to the city, he was hungry.* [19]*And seeing a fig tree by the wayside he went to it, and found nothing on it but leaves only. And he said to it, "May no fruit ever come from you again!" And the fig tree withered at once.* [20]*When the disciples saw it they marveled, saying, "How did the fig tree wither at once?"* [21]*And Jesus answered them, "Truly, I say to you, if you have faith and never doubt, you will not only do what has been done to the fig tree, but even if you say to this mountain, 'Be taken up and cast into the sea,' it will be done.* [22]*And whatever you ask in prayer, you will receive, if you have faith."*

[23]*And when he entered the temple, the chief priests and the elders of the people came up to him as he was teaching, and said, "By what authority are you doing these things, and who gave you this authority?"* [24]*Jesus answered them, "I also will ask you a question; and if you tell me the answer, then I also will tell you by what authority I do these things.* [25]*The baptism of John, whence was it? From heaven or from men?" And they argued with one another, "If we say, 'From heaven,' he will say to us, 'Why then did you not believe him?'* [26]*But if we say, 'From men,' we are afraid of the multitude; for all hold that John was a prophet."* [27]*So they answered Jesus, "We do not know." And he said to them, "Neither will I tell you by what authority I do these things."*

OVERVIEW: Isn't there something absurd about Jesus literally cursing a tree for not bearing fruit out of season? Everything in Scripture is to be understood either in its literal sense, in its figurative sense or in some combination of these. The lesson figuratively conveyed by this symbolic prophetic action was that it is now time to produce fruit. It is time to end the period of Israel's preparation (AUGUSTINE). When such things are done, whether to places, plants or ani-

mals, we do better not to be overly curious about the divine will. Do not inquire too far into whether it was just that the fig tree withered, or you will lose perspective. This sort of question is trifling. Just behold the miracle and admire and glorify its worker (CHRYSOSTOM). Jesus took no delight in the withering of a tree; he acted this way to produce awe in the disciples, that they should not fail Christ when he is hungry, and that you might hope to be in the coming season of fruit rather than to be in the preparatory season of leaves (AUGUSTINE). Israel had not produced the fruit of righteousness. Even infants delighted in Christ's coming (INCOMPLETE WORK ON MATTHEW).

21:18 As Jesus Returned to Jerusalem

HE WAS HUNGRY. CHRYSOSTOM: How could he who is truly God be hungry in the morning? He is found in human form, so this flesh has ordinary human feelings. THE GOSPEL OF MATTHEW, HOMILY 67.1.[1]

21:19 May No Fruit Ever Come from You Again

THE FIG TREE WITHERED. CHRYSOSTOM: It was not his will to exhibit his anger upon men. Rather upon the plant he furnished the proof of his might in taking vengeance. But when such things are done, whether to places, or to plants, or to brutes, do not be overly curious about the divine will. Do not say, "Was it just that the fig tree withered?" especially if it was not yet the time of figs. This sort of question is the utmost trifling.[2] Just behold the miracle and admire and glorify the worker of it. THE GOSPEL OF MATTHEW, HOMILY 67.1.[3]

NOTHING BUT LEAVES. INCOMPLETE WORK ON MATTHEW: "And seeing a fig tree alongside the path, he approached it and found nothing on it except leaves." The fig tree represents the synagogue, for the great many seeds dwelling within one rind of the fig tree is like the great many faithful men living in the one house of the synagogue, as it is written: "God who causes them to dwell single-mindedly in one house."[4] Observe how the leaves of the fig tree are formed to resemble human hands. The greenness of its leaves is like the mere appearance of holiness among men who are full of religious words but lack the fruit of good works. The sentient tree then [is] the religious

person who professes to be a man of God but fails to perform works of righteousness. [He] is like a leafy tree which bears no fruit, concerning whom the apostle prophesied: "In the last days there will be lovers of self, lusting after money, arrogant, prideful, disobedient to their elders, preferring their own will over the will of God, having the appearance of piety but denying its power."[5] . . . The path along which the fig tree was discovered represents the world. Christ was unable to find any fruit among the Jews because they had been living alongside the world, which is to say that they had been living according to the world. The world is the common path along which everyone travels who has ever been born, as we indicated in our treatment of the parable of the sower. The faithful man, then, the sentient tree, will never be able to bear the fruits of righteousness if he lives in proximity to the world. HOMILY 39.[6]

THE FAILURE TO PRODUCE FRUIT. INCOMPLETE WORK ON MATTHEW: It was not because Christ cursed it that the tree produced no fruit; instead, because the tree first produced no fruit, Christ cursed it to ensure that it would produce no leaves. Likewise, it wasn't because God abandoned them that the Jews squandered his righteousness; rather, because they failed to produce the fruits of righteousness, God abandoned them to ensure that they would not have the appearance or reputation of righteousness. Just as it would have been better had there never been a tree at all than for there to have been a tree which produced no fruit

---

[1]PG 58:633; NPNF 1 10:410. [2]Mark 11:13 points out that it was not yet time for the figs to be mature. Chrysostom notes the apparent contradiction with respect to the observation made in Matthew and resolves it by accusing the disciples of inconsistency in asking whether the fig tree had borne fruit out of season. In fact the episode, easy to interpret allegorically (see the following excerpts from Augustine and the Incomplete Work on Matthew), presents difficulties in the literal sense: Why would Jesus punish the tree if it were natural to have fruit out of season? [3]PG 58:633-34; NPNF 1 10:410. [4]Cf. Ps 68:7 (67:7 LXX). [5]2 Tim 3:1-5. [6]PG 56:844-45.

according to its kind, so also would it have been better had there never been a man of God than for there to have been a man of God who did not live in accordance with God. If those who are not yours in the first place fail to obey you, you suffer nothing. You will suffer severely, however, if the one who belongs to you despises you and serves another instead. In this way, God's wrath was not kindled nearly as much by the fact that people who were strangers to him openly served the devil as it was by the sight of his own possession doing the devil's will. HOMILY 39.[7]

21:20-21 If You Have Faith and Do Not Doubt

A FIGURATIVE, PROPHETIC ACT. AUGUSTINE: Now in order to convey this truth[8] the Lord acted prophetically. By this I mean that in reference to the fig tree, it was not his will merely to exhibit a miracle but rather through this sign to convey an intimation of that which was to come. He often taught and persuaded us by such means. So even when our wills resist, he persuades us and brings us to faith.

We first ask how was it the tree's fault that it had no fruit? Even if it had no fruit in its proper season, its season of mature fruit, still the tree would bear no fault. For the tree is without sense and reason, so it could not be blamed. But to this perplexity is added another, which we read in the narrative of the other Evangelist who expressly mentions this: "It was not the time for that fruit."[9] For this was the time when the fig tree was just shooting forth its tender leaves, which come, as we know, long before the fruit. This sequence has a spiritual meaning. The time for fruit was soon coming with the day of the Lord's Passion, which was at hand. And so to make this clear, the Evangelist, to his credit, notes that "the time of figs was not yet." So then, if it was only a miracle that was being demonstrated and not something to be prophetically prefigured, it would have been much more wor-

thy of the clemency and mercy of the Lord if he had found a withered tree and restored it to life. This would seem more in accord with his healing of the sick, cleansing lepers and raising the dead.

But to the contrary, as though against the ordinary rule of his charity, he found a green tree, not yet bearing fruit, even before its fruit-bearing season but still awaiting the hope of fruit, and what does he do? He withers it straight away! This is a prophetic anticipation of things soon to come, by which he in effect says to us: "I have no delight in the withering away of this tree. By doing so I want to convey to you that I am not acting absurdly but for a lesson you might take more seriously. It is not this literal tree that I have cursed. It is not on an insensible tree that I have inflicted punishment. Rather, I have made you fear, whoever you are who considers this matter, that you should not fail Christ when he is hungry and that you might hope to be in the coming season of fruit than to be in the preparatory season of leaves." . . .

Therefore, beloved, I must tell you and teach you according to my poor abilities that which the Lord has given me for your benefit. I must convey to you what you may hold as a rule in the interpretation of all Scripture. Everything that is said or done is to be understood either in its literal signification, or else it signifies something figuratively; or it may contain both of these at once, both its own literal interpretation and a figurative signification also. . . .

Thus Christ, wishing to convey this lesson to us, wanted us to produce fruit and in this way set forth for us a figurative fiction which is not a deceiving fiction but a fiction worthy of praise. SERMON 89.3-6.[10]

---

[7]PG 56:846. [8]The truth referred to has generally to do with the destiny of the covenant people, about which Augustine had been previously speaking. More specifically it is the truth that now is the time for fruit bearing for Israel. [9]Mk 11:13. [10]PL 38:555-58; NPNF 1 6:389-91* (Sermon 39).

LET THE DEVIL BE CAST INTO THE SEA.
INCOMPLETE WORK ON MATTHEW: Jesus is
referring here to an invisible mountain, one
which produces fruitless trees, a rocky and
rough place where there are steep cliffs, caves
and overhanging crags, not fit for human habitation but only for beasts. There are no level fields
in it for resting peacefully, but the ground is rising or falling away because, among those who
stand against the devil, some rise and some fall.
The devil is called a mountain, not because of
the height of his worthiness, like the holy
angels, but because of the size of his prideful
ego; not on account of the constancy of his virtue but on account of his immovable and incorrigible malice. Remove this mountain from the
midst of the saints, where there is faith, hope
and charity, where there are fields of peace and
beautiful fountains of doctrine, where meadows
abound with the dew of grace, where holy birds
adorn a perpetual springtime with their songs.
"And be cast into the sea." That is, into this
world, where the water is brackish and worthless, which is to say that the people are evil and
add nothing to the glory of God; even the sweet
rivers of every spiritual grace which flows into
them are unable to purify them. Instead, their
brackishness spoils the sweetness of the rivers of
grace flowing into the sea of this world, where
there are perilous battles between conflicting
spirits and where the powerful always rule.
HOMILY 39.[11]

21:22 Whatever You Ask in Prayer

YOU WILL RECEIVE, IF YOU HAVE FAITH.
CHRYSOSTOM: That you might learn that it was
for the disciples' sakes that this was done, that
he might train them in confidence, listen to
what he said afterward: "You also shall do
greater things, if you are willing to believe and
to be confident in prayer."[12] All this was done for
their sakes, that they might not be afraid and
tremble at plots against them. He repeated this
to enable them to cleave to prayer and faith. For

you shall not only do this, but you shall also
remove mountains; and many more things you
shall do, being confident in faith and prayer.
THE GOSPEL OF MATTHEW, HOMILY 67.2.[13]

FAITH NURTURES GOOD WORKS. INCOMPLETE
WORK ON MATTHEW: "And whatever you ask in
prayer with faith, you will receive." God gives
the grace of faith, but humanity nourishes and
strengthens it. Faith then causes one to abstain
from evil and to do good works. The more you
abstain from evil and follow the good, the stronger you will make your faith. The less you
abstain from evil, however, and the more you
neglect good works, the weaker your faith will
become. HOMILY 39.[14]

21:23 Who Gave You This Authority?

THE PHARISEES CONFRONT JESUS. HILARY OF
POITIERS: Prior to this, the Pharisees had seen
many things more worthy to be called great miracles, but now they were deeply troubled and
asked Jesus to identify the authority by which he
performed these works. The great mystery of
the future is included in the consequences of
present deeds. They felt the urge for special
questioning, then, because the prefiguration of
every danger was made known in this event.
The Lord replied that he would tell them by
what authority he did these works if only they
would also reply to his question about whether
they considered John the Baptist to have come
from heaven or from man. They hesitated while
pondering the dangers of responding. If they
confessed John to have come from heaven, they
would be convicted by that very confession for
not believing in the authority of a heavenly witness. They were afraid to say that he was merely
from man, however, because of the large crowd
of people who believed John to be a prophet. So
they answered that they did not know (they did

---

[11]PG 56:846. [12]Jn 14:12. [13]PG 58:634; NPNF 1 10:410. [14]PG
56:846-47.

in fact know him to be from heaven) because they feared that they might be convinced by the truth of their own confession. But they told the truth about themselves, even though it was their intention to deceive; it was only through their infidelity that they did not know John the Baptist to be from heaven. And they could not have known that John the Baptist was from man, because he was not. ON MATTHEW 21.10.[15]

21:24-25 From Where Did John's Baptism Come?

A DARKENED WILL. INCOMPLETE WORK ON MATTHEW: Knowing their irreformable evil, the Lord asked them an entirely rhetorical question, not that they might understand it and respond but that they should be hindered from interrogating him further, for he had commanded, "Do not give what is holy to the dogs,"[16] and it was not fitting that what the Lord commanded should be violated. But it would have profited them nothing, even if he had answered directly, since a darkened will cannot discern what is of the light. What good is it to show something beautiful to a blind man? Spiritual blindness consists of an evil heart, and evil people are not able to understand the mystery of devotion any more than the blind can gaze upon the splendor of the light. When a stealthy hunter sees a place to dig a trap, he also raises a net adjacent to it so that wherever the prey he is seeking to capture attempts to flee, it will either be caught in the net or fall into the pit. Likewise, the Lord set a trap for the chief priests and elders by means of his simple question, in such a way that if they professed John to have come from heaven, he would be able to ask them, "Why, then, did you not believe him?" But if they replied that John was of the world, they would thereby have run into the danger of being stoned to death by the people, as though fleeing into a hunter's trap. It was proper that the Lord teach his interrogator and weaken his tempter in whatever way he could and confound the cleverness of his reproach with rational arguments, while not making known the truth of his own mystery. The Lord did virtually the same thing elsewhere to the devil, who had cited against him a scriptural text without understanding it: "For it is written, 'He will command his angels concerning you, and they will hold you in their hands, lest your foot stumble on a rock.' "[17] The Lord did not respond, "That is not what this Scripture means." Rather, he left the devil ignorant of the true meaning of the text and instead refuted him with another, clearer passage from Scripture in order to confound the devil's arrogance without revealing the prophetic mystery. HOMILY 39.[18]

21:26-27 We Do Not Know

LIARS WILL LIE TO THEMSELVES. INCOMPLETE WORK ON MATTHEW: "They answered Jesus, saying, 'We do not know.' And he said to them, 'Neither will I tell you by what authority I do these things.' " He did not say, "Neither do I know." It was as if he had said, "You know the truth because you are men, but you deny it because you are evil; I know it because I am God, but I will not tell you because you are unworthy." Liars will lie to themselves if they have no one to deceive. Similarly truth will keep itself pure if it finds no one to save. HOMILY 39.[19]

NEITHER WILL I TELL YOU. JEROME: In answering Jesus that they did not know, the chief priests and elders lied. Consequently it would have been appropriate for the Lord to respond by saying, "Neither do I know." The truth cannot lie, however, so he replied instead, "Neither will I tell you." By this he shows both that they knew the answer but were unwilling to say it and that he also knows the answer but will

---

[15]SC 258:134-36. [16]Mt 7:6. [17]Mt 4:5-6; Ps 91:11-12 (90:11-12 LXX). [18]PG 56:848. [19]PG 56:848.

not speak it because they remained silent. Immediately, then, he tells a parable designed to convince them of their own sinfulness and of the necessity that the kingdom of God be trans-ferred to the Gentiles. COMMENTARY ON MATTHEW 3.21.27.[20]

---

[20]CCL 77:193.

21:28-32 THE PARABLE OF THE TWO SONS

[28]"What do you think? A man had two sons; and he went to the first and said, 'Son, go and work in the vineyard today.' [29]And he answered, 'I will not'; but afterward he repented and went. [30]And he went to the second and said the same; and he answered, 'I go, sir,' but did not go. [31]Which of the two did the will of his father?" They said, "The first." Jesus said to them, "Truly, I say to you, the tax collectors and the harlots go into the kingdom of God before you. [32]For John came to you in the way of righteousness, and you did not believe him, but the tax collectors and the harlots believed him; and even when you saw it, you did not afterward repent and believe him."

OVERVIEW: The identity of the two sons in this parable varies with different commentators. For one the older son represents the Gentiles, and the younger son represents the Jews (INCOMPLETE WORK ON MATTHEW). For another the older represents the Pharisees or those influenced by their teaching; the younger represents the publicans and sinners (HILARY OF POITIERS). It is surprising that the publicans and sinners believed in Christ even before the priests, who were too arrogant. To work in the vineyard is to do justice. Lessons drawn from the parable include the point that it is better to do the righteousness of God without promising to do so than it is to promise and then renege (INCOMPLETE WORK ON MATTHEW). The son who first refused to work but afterward repented did the will of the father. The son who said he would go but did not go is reproved. Even after the publicans and harlots had believed, the Jewish leaders had not believed. So they were thereby deprived of all excuses. He is saying, "To you he came first, not to them. You did not believe. They were not offended. They believed. Yet this did not profit you at all" (CHRYSOSTOM).

21:28 Two Sons and a Vineyard

THE TWO SONS. INCOMPLETE WORK ON MATTHEW: Who is this if not the God who created all people and loves them with a fatherly affection, the God who preferred to be loved as a father rather than feared as a lord, even though he was Lord by nature? On this account, at the beginning of the commandments of the law, he did not say, "You shall fear the Lord with all your heart" but "you shall love the Lord with all your heart."[1] To elicit love is not characteristic of a lord but of a father.

Of the two sons in this parable, the older one represents the Gentiles, since they come from their father Noah. The younger son represents

---

[1]Deut 6:5.

the Jews, who come from Abraham. "And approaching the first, he said, 'Son, go and work today in my vineyard.'" "Today" refers to this present age. How did he speak to his sons? He didn't address them face to face like man, but he spoke to the heart, like God. Man only utters words to the ear, but God supplies understanding to the mind. HOMILY 40.[2]

21:29-30 One Son Works, One Does Not

Do Not Promise, Then Renege. INCOMPLETE WORK ON MATTHEW: What does it mean to work in the vineyard? To work in the vineyard is to do justice. We noted above that the vineyard is the justice that God has planted generally in the nature of all people but more particularly in the Jewish Scriptures. Each vine in the vineyard represents a different type of justice, and each person, according to his individual virtues, produces either more or fewer vines. I do not know of anyone, however, who is sufficient to work the entire vineyard.

"And he said, 'I will not.'" How did he say, "I will not"? He said it in his thoughts, for whoever understands the difference between good and evil and abandons the good to follow evil seems to be rebelling against the Lord in his thoughts; for "I will not" is spoken against the faculty of the intellect, which was created by God for himself. No one would ever have been able to sin unless he had first said in his heart "I will not," as the prophet indicates: "Injustice speaks within him that he might sin."[3] The pagans, who abandoned God and his justice from the beginning and converted to the worship of idols and to a life of sin, seem to have rebelled in their thoughts, as though they had said, "We will not do the justice which we learned from you."

"Approaching the other," Jesus asked the same thing, and he replied, "'I will go,' but he did not go." When the Jewish people, represented here by the younger son, were asked both by Moses and by John the Baptist, as though God were speaking through each of them, they

promised that they would do everything the Lord commanded. Afterwards, however, they turned away and lied to God, as the prophet had foretold: "Foreign sons deceived me."[4]

"Which of these two did the will of the Father? They replied, 'the first.'" Notice how, as we have already said above, attracted by the truth of the parable, they turned its meaning against themselves when they said that the first son, who represented the pagan Gentiles, had done the will of the father. It is better to do the righteousness of God without promising to do so than it is to promise and then to renege. HOMILY 40.[5]

21:31 Which Son Did the Will of His Father?

Earlier and Later Responses. HILARY OF POITIERS: The first son represents the people who are from the Pharisees. Urgently admonished by God through the prophecy of John to conform themselves to his commandments, they remained insolent, disobedient and contemptuous to God's warnings.[6] They put their faith in the law and despised repentance from sin, glorying instead in the noble prerogative that they had from Abraham. Later they came to believe through the miracles worked by the apostles after the resurrection of the Lord, and, having returned by a faithful act of the will to evangelical works, they repented and confessed the guilt of their former insolence.

The second son represents the group of publicans and sinners who later returned to the sinful state in which they lived at the time. They were instructed by John to expect salvation from Christ and to be baptized and to believe in him. When the Lord says in the parable that the second son did not go as he promised to do, he shows that these people believed John. But

---

[2]PG 56:849. [3]Ps 36:1 (35:1 LXX). [4]Ps 18:45 (17:46 LXX). [5]PG 56:849-50. [6]It was not easy to interpret the parable of the two sons in relation to the call of the Jews and the Gentiles.

because they were not able to receive the teaching of the gospel through the apostles until after the Lord's Passion (for it was then that the mysteries of human salvation were to be accomplished), they did not go. He didn't say that they refused to go but simply that they did not go. Their failure to go does not make them guilty of disbelief, because to do so would have been very difficult. Therefore it is not that the second son did not want to do immediately what he was ordered to do but rather that he was unable to do it. His will is shown free from guilt by the obstacles of the circumstance. ON MATTHEW 21.13-14.[7]

THE HARLOTS ENTER THE KINGDOM BEFORE YOU. CHRYSOSTOM: If he had said simply, harlots go before you, the word would have seemed to them to be offensive. But now, uttered after their own judgment, it appears to be less harsh. THE GOSPEL OF MATTHEW, HOMILY 67.3.[8]

21:32 The Way of Righteousness

JOHN CAME TO YOU. CHRYSOSTOM: Therefore he adds also another accusation: "John came to you in the way of righteousness, and you did not believe him." John came "to you," he says, not to them. You cannot find fault with him, as if he were some careless person of no value. His life was irreprehensible. His care for you was great, and yet you did not pay attention to him. THE GOSPEL OF MATTHEW, HOMILY 67.3.[9]

THE HARLOTS BELIEVED. CHRYSOSTOM: The word "they go into the kingdom before you" is not meant to emphasize that some were following but as having a hope, if they were willing. For nothing so much as jealousy rouses our passions. Therefore he is forever saying things like "the first shall be last and the last first."[10] Thus he mentioned here both harlots and publicans that they might provoke them to jealousy. Taken together these two represent chief sins engendered by violent lust: the one of sexual desire,

the other of the desire of money. THE GOSPEL OF MATTHEW, HOMILY 67.3.[11]

NO ONE EXPECTED THE PROSTITUTE TO BELIEVE. INCOMPLETE WORK ON MATTHEW: You who are priests, because you know the commandments of Scripture and hold positions of leadership among the people, should have been the first to believe in Christ as an example to the people. Not only did you fail to believe in him, but even after you saw that the publicans and prostitutes believed in him, you were neither ashamed nor repentant. The publicans and prostitutes, whom no one expected to believe, did in fact believe, but you who appeared to be followers of every commandment persisted in your impudence, refusing to repent and believe or even to follow the example of those for whom you ought to have provided an example. Are we to believe that you did not believe in Christ because you were more sinless than those who did believe in him? Quite to the contrary, you did not believe because you were more contemptuous of God, more arrogant, lovers of vainglory, hard-hearted, wanting neither to lead them in faith nor to follow them. Truly great shame has come upon the priesthood and on the whole clergy when the laity can be found more faithful and more just than they are.[12] HOMILY 40.[13]

YOU DID NOT AFTERWARD REPENT. CHRYSOSTOM: And with this there is also still another charge. The publicans were attentive and repented, but even after the publicans and harlots had believed, you did not believe. You should have repented long before they did. But you did not do it. So you are deprived of all excuses. How unspeakable was both the praise of the one and the charge against the other: He

---

[7]SC 258:138-40. [8]PG 58:635-36; NPNF 1 10:411. [9]PG 58:636; NPNF 1 10:411-12. [10]Mt 19:30. [11]PG 58:636; NPNF 1 10:412. [12]The author passes in his criticism from the Jewish to the Christian priests. Like Origen, he is highly sensitive to the theme of dishonesty and corruption in the church hierarchy. [13]PG 56:851.

came to you, and you did not receive him. He did not come to them, and they received him! And you did not even learn from their example. Note in how many ways he shows that some are to be commended and others charged, but in surprising ways, reversing expectations. To you he came first, not to them. You did not believe. They were not offended. They believed. This did not profit you at all. THE GOSPEL OF MATTHEW, HOMILY 67.[14]

WHY PUBLICANS PRECEDE YOU IN THE KINGDOM. INCOMPLETE WORK ON MATTHEW: The Lord's teaching can be paraphrased as follows: "Even if John had not come to you 'in the way of righteousness' but had only preached a baptism of repentance, you should have believed him as priests and wise men who judge impartially and in accordance with the facts, for what relevance is the preacher's way of life to his student? If he lives wickedly, he alone is damned, but if he teaches truthfully, the benefit redounds to everyone who hears him. Even so, however, John came to you in a 'way of righteousness' so clearly manifest that his exemplary conduct and angelic life pierced even the hearts of publicans and prostitutes and converted them with fear and trembling to the faith. Yet he did not affect your hearts at all. You can see then that publicans and prostitutes are rightly said to 'precede you into the kingdom.'" HOMILY 40.[15]

---

[14]PG 58:636; NPNF 1 10:412. [15]PG 56:850.

21:33-46 THE PARABLE OF THE TENANTS IN THE VINEYARD

[33]"Hear another parable. There was a householder who planted a vineyard, and set a hedge around it, and dug a wine press in it, and built a tower, and let it out to tenants, and went into another country. [34]When the season of fruit drew near, he sent his servants to the tenants, to get his fruit; [35]and the tenants took his servants and beat one, killed another, and stoned another. [36]Again he sent other servants, more than the first; and they did the same to them. [37]Afterward he sent his son to them, saying, 'They will respect my son.' [38]But when the tenants saw the son, they said to themselves, 'This is the heir; come, let us kill him and have his inheritance.' [39]And they took him and cast him out of the vineyard, and killed him. [40]When therefore the owner of the vineyard comes, what will he do to those tenants?" [41]They said to him, "He will put those wretches to a miserable death, and let out the vineyard to other tenants who will give him the fruits in their seasons."

[42]Jesus said to them, "Have you never read in the scriptures:
'The very stone which the builders rejected
has become the head of the corner;
this was the Lord's doing,
and it is marvelous in our eyes'?

43Therefore I tell you, the kingdom of God will be taken away from you and given to a nation producing the fruits of it."q

45When the chief priests and the Pharisees heard his parables, they perceived that he was speaking about them. 46But when they tried to arrest him, they feared the multitudes, because they held him to be a prophet.

q Other ancient authorities add verse 44, *"And he who falls on this stone will be broken to pieces; but when it falls on any one, it will crush him"*

OVERVIEW: Many themes are interwoven in this parable: God's providence, the ingratitude of the covenant people, the great care the owner exercised over his property and the extraordinary recalcitrance and violence of the people. The husbandman planted the vineyard, set a hedge around it, dug a wine press in it and built a tower. He left little for them to do but care for what was there and preserve what was given to them. But there was little effort made by them to work the land, even after they had enjoyed such great blessings from him. They killed the owner's son, casting him out of the vineyard, that is, Israel. The stone that the builders rejected has thereby become the head of the corner.

The priests were restrained by the fear of the multitudes. Little attention was paid to the prophet's testimony, their own sentence or the disposition of the people, so entirely had the love of power and the lust for glory blinded them, together with the pursuit of temporal things (CHRYSOSTOM).

Christ is called a stone because his foundation is solid, and the wicked cannot overcome him. Even so, any evil done is done against God. The punishment for evil is proportional to the evil done. Likewise, the glory for good is proportional to the good done. God is unlimited in his range of punishment and glory (INCOMPLETE WORK ON MATTHEW). The chief priests and Pharisees determined to put Jesus to death but still feared the crowd. Such crowds are fickle and easily swayed (JEROME).

21:33 A Householder Planted a Vineyard

HEAR ANOTHER PARABLE. CHRYSOSTOM: This parable suggests many things: God's providence had been at work toward them from the outset; their disposition was murderous from the beginning; nothing had been neglected of whatever pertained to an attentive care for them. even when prophets had been slain, God had not turned away from this people but had sent them his very Son; it is now clear that the God of both the New and the Old Testaments is one and the same; we know that the Son's death will effect great blessings; we here learn that they were to endure extreme punishment for the crucifixion; here we learn of the calling of the Gentiles and the turning aside of the unbelieving Jews.

He presents this parable after the previous one that he may show the charge to be even greater in this case and highly unpardonable. In what way? Although the Jews had received so much care from God, they were now found to be worse than harlots and publicans, and that by a wide margin. THE GOSPEL OF MATTHEW, HOMILY 68.1.[1]

HE SET A HEDGE AROUND THE VINEYARD. CHRYSOSTOM: Observe the great care that the owner took with this place and the extraordinary recalcitrance of the people. He himself did the work the tenants should have done. It was he who planted a vineyard, and set a hedge around it, and dug a wine press in it and built a tower. He left little for them to do. All they had to do was take care of what was there and to preserve what was given to them. Nothing was left undone but all accomplished. But they made lit-

---

[1]PG 58:639; NPNF 1 10:414-15.

tle effort to be productive, even after they had enjoyed such great blessings from him. For when they had come out of Egypt, he gave a law, and set up a city, and built a temple and prepared an altar. Then he "went into a far country." He was patient with them. He did not always keep a close account of their sins. The meaning of "going into a far country" is God's great patience. THE GOSPEL OF MATTHEW, HOMILY 68.1.[2]

21:34-36 The Tenants Kill the Landowner's Servants

HE SENT HIS SERVANTS TO GET HIS FRUIT. CHRYSOSTOM: He sent his servants, that is, the prophets, "to receive the fruit." By fruit he referred to their obedience, demonstrated through their works. But even here they exhibited their wickedness. They not only failed to give the fruit, after having enjoyed so much care, thus displaying their laziness, but also were angry with the servants who came. For those who did not repay what they owed should hardly have been indignant or angry. Rather, they should have asked for the householder's forgiveness. But they not only were indignant; they even bloodied their hands. While deserving punishment, they themselves inflicted punishment. Therefore he sent a second and a third company of servants both to show their wickedness and the love toward humanity of the One who sent them. Why didn't he immediately send his Son? In order that they might repent and condemn themselves for the things they had done to the others. He hoped they would set aside their anger and reverence him when he came. THE GOSPEL OF MATTHEW, HOMILY 68.1.[3]

21:37 Afterward the Landowner Sent His Son

THEY WILL RESPECT MY SON. CHRYSOSTOM: But what does it mean that "it may be that they

will have reverence for my son"? This is not the language of an ignorant man. Away with the thought! Rather, it is the language of one desiring to show the sin to be great and inexcusable. For though he himself knew that they would slay him, he sent him. When he says "they will respect," he states what ought to have been done, that it was their duty to have reverenced him. Elsewhere he says similarly: "whether they hear or refuse to hear."[4] He is not ignorant of their motives. But lest any of the obstinate should say that his prediction was the thing that necessitated their disobedience, therefore he frames his expressions in a particular way, using indeterminate terms like "whether they will" and "it may be." For though they had been obstinate towards his servants, yet they ought to have reverenced the dignity of the Son. THE GOSPEL OF MATTHEW, HOMILY 68.[5]

21:38 The Tenants Kill the Heir

LET US KILL HIM AND HAVE HIS INHERITANCE. CHRYSOSTOM: What then do they do? While they had time to ask for pardon for their offenses and whereas they ought to have run to him to do so, they persist even more strongly in their former sins. They proceed to add even more to their previous pollutions. They always surpass their former offenses by their later ones. This is what he himself declared when he said, "Fill up, then, the measure of your fathers."[6] For from the first the prophets used to charge them with these things, saying, "Your hands are full of blood,"[7] and "They mingle blood with blood,"[8] and "They build up Zion with blood."[9]

But they failed to learn self-control. They had already received the commandment: "You shall not murder." They had already had been commanded to abstain from countless other offenses. They had already been urged by many

---

[2]PG 58:639-40; NPNF 1 10:415. [3]PG 58:640; NPNF 1 10:415. [4]Ezek 2:5. [5]PG 58:640; NPNF 1 10:415. [6]Mt 23:32. [7]Is 1:15. [8]Hos 4:2. [9]Mic 3:10.

and various means to keep these commandments.

Yet, for all that, they did not put aside their evil ways. What did they say when they saw him? "Come, let us kill him." With what motive and for what reason? What possible charge could they lay against him, either small or great? Is it that he honored you, and being God became a human being for your sakes and worked his countless miracles? Or that he pardoned your sins? Or that he called you into a kingdom?

But observe that their disregard for bad was accompanied by great folly, and the cause of his murder was filled with madness. "For let us kill him," it says, "and the inheritance shall be ours." THE GOSPEL OF MATTHEW, HOMILY 68.1.[10]

21:39-41 What Will the Landowner Do?

THE HOUSEHOLDER AND THE VINEYARD.
EPIPHANIUS THE LATIN: The householder in this parable is the Father of our Lord Jesus Christ. The vineyard he planted represents the Jewish people who were begotten from Abraham, Isaac and Jacob, multiplied like the stars in the sky and the sand of the shore, liberated from the land of Egypt and the yoke of slavery, and led through the sea to the promised land, as the prophet said: "You brought a vine out of Egypt; you drove out the nations and planted it."[11] The Lord planted the Jewish people in the promised land, flowing with milk and honey, so that they would bear the fruit of the commandments of God. "He surrounded it with a hedge" means that God fortified it with the protection of angels. The wine press he dug signifies the holy church, where the fruits of righteousness and holiness are gathered; just as the grapes are pressed only with great toil and effort, so also the holy martyrs are crushed like grapes and shed their blood only through great persecutions and tortures. The tower constructed in the middle of the vineyard is our Lord himself, who appeared like a strong tower in the midst of the holy church through the Virgin. Because of his presence, all the saints and martyrs are protected with spiritual weapons from their most wicked enemy, who is the devil. "When harvest time drew near, he sent his servants," that is, the prophets, "to the tenants," who were the teachers of the law, "to collect the fruit of the vineyard." He had already sent the prophets to them repeatedly to collect his fruit, but they were disdainful and rebellious toward the Lord and greeted his prophets with swords, beatings, stonings and other persecutions. They killed Isaiah, stoned Jeremiah, pursued Elijah and beheaded John the Baptist. Every nation that persecutes its teachers and fails to produce the fruit of the gospel is an accomplice to the Jews. "Finally, therefore, he sent his only son to them, saying, 'surely they will respect my son.'" The "only son" of the householder is the Lord, the Son of God, who came by the will of the Father to his vineyard, which is the Jewish people. "But when the tenants," who are the teachers of the law, "saw his son, they said to themselves, 'this is the heir; come, let us kill him, and the inheritance will be ours,' and they threw him out of the vineyard and killed him." They also crucified our Lord outside the city, while they shouted, "Crucify him! Crucify him!" Yet they did not in fact come to possess the inheritance of the law; instead, they sentenced themselves to death, for the Lord asked, "What will the owner of the vineyard do to the tenants when he comes?" They responded, "He will destroy the evil tenants and give the vineyard to other tenants who will produce its fruit in a timely manner." They condemned themselves by their own words, as the Lord implies when he speaks about himself and their faithlessness: "The stone which the builders rejected has become the cornerstone; therefore, I say to you that the kingdom of God will be removed from you and given to a people producing its fruits."[12] INTERPRETATION OF THE GOSPELS 31.[13]

---

[10]PG 58:640-41; NPNF 1 10:415. [11]Ps 80:8 (79:9 LXX). [12]Mt 21:42-43. [13]PL Supp 3:876-77.

THEY CAST HIM OUT OF THE VINEYARD AND KILLED HIM. CHRYSOSTOM: And where do they wish to kill him? "Outside the vineyard." Do you see how he prophesies even the place where he was to be slain? Well, they did cast him out, and they killed him.

And Luke indeed says, "He declared what they must suffer." When they heard this, they said, "God forbid!"[14] He then asks them to remember the testimony of Scripture: "He looked at them and said, 'What then is this that is written: The very stone which the builders rejected has become the head of the corner.' Everyone who falls on that stone will be broken to pieces."[15] Matthew's account does not contradict Luke's. They passed the sentence against themselves, as Matthew says, and again, when they perceived what they had said, they added, "God forbid." By the words of the prophet against them, he sought to persuade them that this certainly would come to pass.

He signified only in a hidden way that he would "give the vineyard to others," not mentioning the Gentiles and not affording his opponents a handle to use to attack him. It was for this reason that he spoke in parables, that they themselves might pass the sentence. THE GOSPEL OF MATTHEW, HOMILY 68.2.[16]

21:42 The Lord's Doing Is Marvelous

CHRIST THE GREAT STONE. INCOMPLETE WORK ON MATTHEW: Christ is called a stone for two reasons. First, because his foundation is solid and no one who stands upon him will fall victim to deceitful charms or be moved by the storms of persecution. Second, Christ is called a stone because in him is the ultimate destruction of the wicked, for just as everything which collides with a stone is shattered while the stone itself remains intact, so also everyone who opposes the Christian faith will himself be ruined, but Christianity will remain untouched. This is the sense in which Christ is the great stone. "Whoever falls on it will be broken to pieces, but it will crush those upon whom it falls."[17] It is one thing to be broken but something else again to be crushed, for sizeable pieces of whatever is broken remain, but whatever gets crushed is reduced to dust and utterly eliminated. The stone does not break those who fall upon it, but they break themselves who fall on the stone. Their destruction therefore is not attributable to the stone's strength but to the violence with which they fall upon it. HOMILY 40.[18]

21:43-45 The Kingdom of God Will Be Taken from You

KILLING GOD TO SIN WITH IMPUNITY. INCOMPLETE WORK ON MATTHEW: The man who commits a grave sin is likely to commit an even worse sin because he no longer hopes in God, as Solomon suggests: "When a wicked man enters the depths of evil, he becomes contemptuous."[19] The sick will abstain from potentially harmful foods until their fever moderates and they begin to have hope that a cure is imminent, but if they are convinced that their disease is incurable, they will eat whatever they like. Likewise, as long as a man sins only venially and retains some hope for salvation, he will abstain from evil as far as possible, but if he begins to despair as a result of committing serious sins, he will come to have no doubt that he has already been done in by the judgment of God. Pathetic is the man who does not realize that there is a gradation of punishments for the evil, each one receiving his punishment according to the measure of his evil, just as there is a gradation of glory for the good, each one receiving a reward according to the measure of his goodness. For God is as unlimited in his range of punishments for the evil as he is in his rewards for the good.

The priests of the old covenant who had

---

[14]Lk 20:16. [15]Lk 20:17-18. [16]PG 58:641; NPNF 1 10:415-16. [17]Lk 20:18; cf. Ps 118:22-23 (117:22-23 LXX); Is 8:14-15. [18]PG 56:858. [19]Prov 18:3.

already ceased to have any hope in God because they were filled with every evil raised their hands against God himself, inasmuch as they knew Christ to be the Son of God, because they had given up on abstaining from evil. Does this astonish you? Truly every evil man, insofar as his will is concerned, raises his hand against God and kills him, for whoever does not hesitate to provoke God's wrath, or despises his commandments, or treats his name with contempt, or utters blasphemies against him, or murmurs against him, or looks toward heaven with an angry countenance or raises his arrogant hand against God in anger, would certainly also kill him if it were possible, just in order to be able to sin with impunity. HOMILY 40.[20]

21:46 The Multitudes Considered Jesus a Prophet

THEY FEARED THE CROWD. JEROME: Although [the chief priests and the Pharisees] were hard of heart and on account of their unbelief and wickedness blunted in their understanding against the Son of God, nevertheless they were unable to deny Jesus' straightforward statements and understood that all the judgments of the Lord were directed against themselves. So they determined indeed to kill him but feared "the crowd, for they considered Jesus to be a prophet." A crowd is always easily moved, not persisting with their will in their resolution. Additionally they are like waves and opposite winds blown to and fro. The one they now honor and revere as a prophet they later shout against: "Crucify, crucify" such a man. COMMENTARY ON MATTHEW 3.21.46.[21]

---

[20]PG 56:858-59. [21]CCL 77:199.

22:1-14 THE PARABLE OF THE WEDDING FEAST

[1]And again Jesus spoke to them in parables, saying, [2]"The kingdom of heaven may be compared to a king who gave a marriage feast for his son, [3]and sent his servants to call those who were invited to the marriage feast; but they would not come. [4]Again he sent other servants, saying, 'Tell those who are invited, Behold, I have made ready my dinner, my oxen and my fat calves are killed, and everything is ready; come to the marriage feast.' [5]But they made light of it and went off, one to his farm, another to his business, [6]while the rest seized his servants, treated them shamefully, and killed them. [7]The king was angry, and he sent his troops and destroyed those murderers and burned their city. [8]Then he said to his servants, 'The wedding is ready, but those invited were not worthy. [9]Go therefore to the thoroughfares, and invite to the marriage feast as many as you find.' [10]And those servants went out into the streets and gathered all whom they found, both bad and good; so the wedding hall was filled with guests.

[11]"But when the king came in to look at the guests, he saw there a man who had no wedding garment; [12]and he said to him, 'Friend, how did you get in here without a wedding garment?' And he was speechless. [13]Then the king said to the attendants, 'Bind him hand and foot, and cast him into the outer darkness; there men will weep and gnash their teeth.' [14]For many are called, but few are chosen."

OVERVIEW: The Lord's table is open to all who are willing correctly to receive it. But it is important that each one examines how he or she approaches. Both good and bad guests are present at this feast. All who excused themselves from this feast are inattentive, but not all those who entered in are good (AUGUSTINE). The graciousness of God toward the people of faith can be compared with a wedding feast. The Father in heaven is making a marriage feast for his Son by joining the church to him through the mystery of his incarnation. The feast is ready, but some who appear are not worthy. This represents the church of this time, in which the bad are present along with the good, only to be separated in final judgment (GREGORY THE GREAT). The proper wedding garment is charity from a pure heart. The wedding garment is not baptism as such but love that comes from a pure heart, a good conscience and a sincere faith (AUGUSTINE). This is what our Creator possessed when he came to the marriage feast to join the church to himself. Meanwhile, prior to the final judgment, the good and bad exist side by side in the church (GREGORY THE GREAT).

22:1-2 The Kingdom of Heaven Is Like a Marriage Feast

INVITATION TO THE FEAST. GREGORY THE GREAT: First we must ask whether this lesson in Matthew is what Luke describes as a dinner, since some details appear inconsistent.[1] Here it is a midday meal, there a dinner; here the one who came to the marriage feast improperly dressed was cast out, and there none of those said to have entered is shown to have been cast out. From Matthew we can infer that in this passage the marriage feast represents the church of the present time, and the dinner in Luke represents the final and eternal banquet. Some who enter the one will leave it, but no one who has once entered the other will later go out. But if anyone argues that it is the same lesson, I think it better to save the faith and yield to another's

interpretation than to give in to strife. Perhaps we can reasonably take it that Luke kept silent about the man Matthew said came without a marriage garment and was thrown out. That one called it a dinner and the other a midday meal does not stand in the way of my interpretation, because when the ancients took their daily midday meal at the ninth hour it was also called a dinner. . . .

A clearer and safer thing to say is that the Father made a marriage feast for his Son by joining the church to him through the mystery of his incarnation. The womb of the Virgin who bore him was the bridal chamber of this bridegroom, and so the psalmist says, "He has set his tent in the sun, and he is like a bridegroom coming forth from his bridal chamber."[2] He truly came forth like a bridegroom from his bridal chamber who, as God incarnate, left the inviolate womb of the Virgin to unite the church to himself.

And so he sent his servants to invite his friends to the marriage feast. He sent once, and he sent again, because first he made the prophets and later the apostles preachers of the Lord's incarnation. He sent his servants twice with the invitation, because he said through the prophets that his only Son's incarnation would come about, and he proclaimed through the apostles that it had.

Because those who were first invited to the marriage banquet refused to come, he said in his second invitation, "See, I have prepared my meal; my oxen and fattened animals have been slain, and everything is ready." What do we take the oxen and fattened animals to be but the fathers of the Old and New Testaments? FORTY GOSPEL HOMILIES 38.1, 3-4.[3]

22:3-4 Come to the Marriage Feast

---

[1]In fact, the parable given in Luke 14:15-35 contains considerable differences from that of Matthew. Gregory harmonizes the two texts, referring the text of Matthew to the current condition of the church and that of Luke to the eschatological banquet. [2]Ps 19:4-5 (19:5-6 LXX). [3]PL 76:1282-83; CS 123:339-41.

EVERYTHING IS READY. AUGUSTINE: All the faithful know the story of the marriage of the king's son, and his feast. They know that the Lord's table is open to all who are willing correctly to receive it. But it is important that each one examines how he approaches, even when he is not forbidden to approach.

The holy Scriptures teach us that there are two feasts of the Lord: one to which the good and evil come,[4] the other to which the evil do not come.[5] So then the feast of which we have just now heard when the gospel was being read has both good and evil guests. All who excused themselves from this feast are evil, but not all those who entered in are good. I now address you, therefore, who are the good guests at this feast. You are taking careful note of the words "For anyone who eats and drinks without recognizing the body of the Lord eats and drinks judgment on himself."[6] It is to you I speak. I plead with you not to look vainly for the good apart from the church but to bear with the evil within it. SERMON 90.1.[7]

22:5-7 Rejecting the Invitation, Persecuting the Messengers

THE KING WAS ANGRY. GREGORY THE GREAT: But they paid no attention and went off, one to his farm, another to his business. To go to your farm is to involve yourself excessively in earthly toil. To go to your business is to long for the gain brought by our worldly activity. One person is concerned with earthly toil, another devoted to the business of this world. Neither takes notice of the mystery of the Lord's incarnation. They are unwilling to live in accordance with it. As if they are proceeding to their farm or business, they refuse to come to the marriage feast of the king. Frequently, and this is a more serious matter, some not only decline the gift of the one calling them but even persecute those who accept it. And so he adds, "The rest seized his servants, and, having insulted them, killed them. But the king, learning of this, sent his armies, destroyed

those murderers and set fire to their city." He destroys the murderers because he has slain the persecutors; he sets fire to their city because not only their souls but even their bodies are tormented by the eternal flames of hell....

But the one who sees himself despised when he issues the invitations will not have the marriage feast of his son the king empty. He sends for others, because although God's word is in danger from some, it will find a place to come to rest. Then he said to his servants, "The marriage feast is ready, but those invited were not worthy. Go therefore into the byroads, and call to the marriage feast everyone you find." If we take the roads in holy Scripture to mean our actions, we interpret the byroads as our failed actions. Often it is those who meet no prosperity in their earthly actions who come readily to God.

And his servants went out into the roads and gathered all whom they found, bad and good, and the marriage feast was filled with guests. The character of those at the banquet reveals clearly that the king's marriage feast represents the church of this time, in which the bad are present along with the good. The church is a thorough mix of various offspring. It brings them all to the faith but does not lead them all to the liberty of spiritual grace successfully by changes in their lives, since their sins prevent it. As long as we are living in this world we have to proceed along the road of the present age thoroughly mixed together. We shall be separated when we reach our goal. Only the good are in heaven, and only the bad are in hell. This life is situated between heaven and hell. It goes on in the middle, so to speak, and takes in the citizens of both parts. The church admits them now without distinguishing them but separates them later when they leave this life. FORTY GOSPEL HOMILIES 38.5-7.[8]

---

[4]Matthew's account. [5]Luke's account. [6]1 Cor 11:29. [7]PL 38:559; NPNF 1 6:392** (Sermon 40). [8]PL 76:1284-85; CS 123:343-44.

22:8 The Invited Guests Unworthy

THOSE INVITED WERE NOT WORTHY. AUGUSTINE: But someone will object, This is strange. What great matter is it that one man among this large crowd does not have a wedding garment? Why rivet attention on this one man? So what if he creeps in unperceived by the servants of the householder? How could it be said that because of just that one, "they invited in both good and bad together"? Attend therefore, beloved, and understand. This man represents a whole class of persons of whom there are many. SERMON 90.4.[9]

22:9-10 Gathering All Whom the Servants Found

GRACE GIVEN TO THE OUTCASTS. APOLLINARIS: This wedding pictures the marriage of the church to the Word. The donation of the gifts of the wealthy provides for the wedding's preparation and is compared with bulls and fattened calves prepared for lavish feasting. For Paul says that "in every way" we have been "enriched" in Christ, in our "speaking and knowledge."[10] The first and second are called servants. The first are those who run ahead in light of the coming of the Lord, fellow laborers and successors[11] of the apostles. But a failure to watch carefully prevents those who are invited from attending. For they "who live their lives according to the flesh"[12] do not follow the divine call which is according to Christ. In the case of the rest, with the calling of the nations there is no longer a separation of a people nor a special honor accorded to Israel. But grace is even [given] to the rejected and outcasts, "to the wise and to the foolish,"[13] as Paul says, to the evil and to the good, as the parable teaches . . . if it is that they really obey the calling to do good, "having clothed themselves with the new humanity."[14] If this proves not to be true, though they were called, they were not chosen. Rather, their calling is even overturned. FRAGMENT 111.[15]

22:11 A Guest with No Wedding Garment

NO WEDDING GARMENT. GREGORY THE GREAT: But since you have already come into the house of the marriage feast, our holy church, as a result of God's generosity, be careful, my friends, lest when the King enters he find fault with some aspect of your heart's clothing. We must consider what comes next with great fear in our hearts. But the king came in to look at the guests and saw there a person not clothed in a wedding garment.

What do we think is meant by the wedding garment, dearly beloved? For if we say it is baptism or faith, is there anyone who has entered this marriage feast without them? A person is outside because he has not yet come to believe. What then must we understand by the wedding garment but love? That person enters the marriage feast, but without wearing a wedding garment, who is present in the holy church. He may have faith, but he does not have love. We are correct when we say that love is the wedding garment because this is what our Creator himself possessed when he came to the marriage feast to join the church to himself. Only God's love brought it about that his only begotten Son united the hearts of his chosen to himself. John says that "God so loved the world that he gave his only begotten Son for us."[16] FORTY GOSPEL HOMILIES 38.9.[17]

22:12 The Guest Speechless

WITHOUT A WEDDING GARMENT. AUGUSTINE: Note that "the master of the house came in to look at the guests."[18] See, my beloved, the servants' business was only to invite and bring in

---

[9]PL 38:560; NPNF 1 6:393** (Sermon 40). [10]1 Cor 1:5. [11]Apollinaris explains what the first servants symbolize but not the second. Given that his text has come down to us via the catenae (cf. introduction to *Matthew 1-13* [ACCS], p. xxxviii), it is clear that the omission is the work of the compiler. [12]Rom 8:4. [13]Rom 1:14. [14]Eph 4:24. [15]MKGK 37-38. [16]Jn 3:16. [17]PL 76:1287; CS 123:346-47. [18]Mt 22:11.

the good and bad. It is not said that the servants took notice of the guests, found among them a man who had no wedding garment and spoke to him. This is not written. The master of the house came in, the master saw him, the master of the house inspected, the master of the house hauled him off and threw him out. It is not fitting to pass over this quickly.[19] But I have undertaken to establish another point, how that one man stands for many. "But when the king came in to look at the guests, he saw there a man who had no wedding garment; and he said to him, 'Friend, how did you get in here without a wedding garment?' And he was speechless." For the one who questioned him was one to whom he could give no deceptive reply. SERMON 90.4.[20]

22:13 Cast into Outer Darkness

BINDING OF HANDS AND FEET. APOLLINARIS: The binding of their feet and hands puts a check on all their activity. . . . The outer darkness speaks of those things far removed from divine virtue and glory. FRAGMENT 111.[21]

CAST HIM OUT. AUGUSTINE: The garment that is required is in the heart, not on the body, for if it had been put on externally, it could not have been concealed even from the servants. But what is the wedding garment that must be put on? We learn it from these words, "May your priests be clothed with righteousness."[22] It is of that garment of righteousness that the apostle speaks when he says, "Because when we are clothed, we are not found naked."[23] In this way the unprepared man was discovered by the Lord of the feast, interrogated, bound and thrown out, one from among the many. SERMON 90.4.[24]

22:14 Many Called, Few Chosen

THOSE WITH THE GARMENT OF CHARITY.

AUGUSTINE: What is that wedding garment, then? This is the wedding garment: "The goal of this command is charity," says the apostle, "which comes from a pure heart and a good conscience and a sincere faith."[25] This is the wedding garment. Not charity of any kind whatever—for very often they who are partakers together of an evil conscience seem to love one another. Those who commit robberies together, who love the destructive arts of witchcraft, and who go to the coliseum together and join together in the shout of the chariot race or the wild beast fight—these too in some sense very often may be said to love one another.

But in these is no charity from a pure heart, a good conscience and a faith unfeigned. The wedding garment is charity such as this: "Though I speak with the tongues of men and of angels and have not charity, I have become like a sounding brass and a tinkling cymbal."[26] Suppose someone who speaks in tongues comes in and is asked, "How did you get in here without a wedding garment?"

Suppose he answers, "But I have the gift of prophecy and understand all mysteries and all knowledge, and I have all faith, so that I could remove mountains." But if he has no charity, he has nothing. Such may be the clothing of those who in fact lack the wedding garment. "Though," he says," I have all these and have not Christ,[27] I am nothing." Is then "the gift of prophecy" nothing? Is then "the knowledge of mysteries" nothing? It is not that these are nothing. But "I, if I have them, and have not charity, am nothing."[28] SERMON 90.6.[29]

---

[19]However we may think we are perceived by humans, in this case the servants, we are perceived accurately by God, who knows the quality of the charity we are wearing. [20]PL 38:560-61; NPNF 1 6:393** (Sermon 40). [21]MKGK 38. [22]Ps 132:9 (131:9 LXX). [23]2 Cor 5:3. [24]PL 38:561; NPNF 1 6:393** (Sermon 40). [25]1 Tim 1:5. [26]1 Cor 13:1. [27]The love of Christ. [28]1 Cor 13:2. [29]PL 38:562; NPNF 1 6:394** (Sermon 40).

22:15-22 THE QUESTION ABOUT PAYING TAXES

¹⁵*Then the Pharisees went and took counsel how to entangle him in his talk.* ¹⁶*And they sent their disciples to him, along with the Herodians, saying, "Teacher, we know that you are true, and teach the way of God truthfully, and care for no man; for you do not regard the position of men.* ¹⁷*Tell us, then, what you think. Is it lawful to pay taxes to Caesar, or not?"* ¹⁸*But Jesus, aware of their malice, said, "Why put me to the test, you hypocrites?* ¹⁹*Show me the money for the tax." And they brought him a coin.*ʳ ²⁰*And Jesus said to them, "Whose likeness and inscription is this?"* ²¹*They said, "Caesar's." Then he said to them, "Render therefore to Caesar the things that are Caesar's, and to God the things that are God's."* ²²*When they heard it, they marveled; and they left him and went away.*

r Greek *a denarius*

OVERVIEW: The Pharisees went off and took counsel together on how to trap Jesus in conversation. Whenever someone wishes to close off a stream of running water, force alone bursts through another path from some new direction. So it was with the evil planning of these men. When cut off in one direction, they simply sought another opening. The Caesar's coin is gold; that of God, humanity. Caesar is seen in his currency; God, however, is known through human beings. And so give your wealth to Caesar but reserve for God the innocence of your conscience, where God is met and beheld. For the hand of Caesar has crafted an image by likenesses and lives each year by renewable decree. However, the divine hand of God has shown his image in the virtues. It is with such inscriptions that God imprints his coins. For Caesar required his image on every coin, but God has chosen the human personality, whom he has created in love, to reflect his glory (INCOMPLETE WORK ON MATTHEW). The passion of hypocrisy is to hide hostility beneath flattery. Paying taxes to Caesar does not prevent one from serving God (SEVERUS).

22:15 The Pharisees Try to Entangle Jesus

THE PHARISEES PLANNED HOW TO ENTANGLE HIM. INCOMPLETE WORK ON MATTHEW: The truth frequently confounds every evil intention but without the intention being thereby reformed. This is especially true of those who intentionally sin by malice rather than out of ignorance. For example, the priests of the old covenant were unable to intimidate the Lord when they asked him, "By what authority do you do these things?"[1] And after the force of his parables further frustrated them, they passed judgment on themselves by saying, "He will utterly destroy those wretches."[2] Since no one bore witness against them, it had to have been their conscience alone which caused them to say this. Yet certainly the fear of sin didn't prick their conscience. Nor did the thought of freedom from sin restrain them. What was it, then? "They went out and planned how to catch him in his words." If anyone attempts to shut off a stream of running water by erecting some sort of blockade, the water will burst through and create a new path in another direction. Similarly the priests' frustrated evil intentions discovered other avenues for themselves. HOMILY 42.[3]

[1]Mt 21:23. [2]Mt 21:41. [3]PG 56:866.

22:16 *Teaching the Way of God*

THEY SENT THEIR DISCIPLES. INCOMPLETE WORK ON MATTHEW: These same Pharisees, hoping to eliminate Christ, accordingly brought him not before the servants of God or truly religious men but before the secularized Herodians, the Gentiles.[4] Such was their plan, and such were the planners. But who had the power to take counsel against Christ, except the devil, the adversary of Christ?

The priests viewed themselves as patterns of the messianic hope. Yet if they went out alone, questioning Christ, no one would believe them. Everyone would know that the Pharisees were Christ's enemy. He had already spoken to the question of whether it was lawful to give tribute to Caesar.

So they joined to their party the Herodians. The witness of enemies is always judged carefully, especially if it is true, since what is suspicious is judged doubly. The Pharisees did not wish to question Christ through the Herodians. But they had a common enemy, Christ. Both parties held Christ in great suspicion. Yet each, being suspect themselves, were afraid that they might not be able to indict Christ. An enemy in the open is far better than one hidden from view. For while the first may be feared, he is easily dealt with. The second, since he is unknown, may prevail. Therefore they sent him disciples, as if still less known and less suspect, so that they might deceive him easily and stealthily, or, if caught, they would at least embarrass themselves less. HOMILY 42.[5]

TEACHER, WE KNOW THAT YOU ARE TRUE. INCOMPLETE WORK ON MATTHEW: They called him teacher, and truly he was. Yet they were only pretending that he was a teacher, one honored and praised. They pretended that he would simply open to them the ministry of his heart, as if they wanted to be his disciples. This is the first power of hypocrites, to simulate praise. They praise those whom they want to destroy.

Their art is to incline human hearts toward simplicity of a kind confession through the delight of praise. They take small steps, a little at a time. HOMILY 42.[6]

YOU TEACH THE WAY OF GOD TRUTHFULLY. SEVERUS: Jesus' opponents expect that one of two outcomes must result for them from Jesus' response. They think they can show clearly that Jesus was acting wrongly against the law of Moses or against the power of the Romans. "Indeed, if he responds that it is necessary for us to pay the tribute," the Pharisees will necessarily slander him alongside those who obey the Romans, saying, "He is guiding us outside the law of Moses away from the service of God. He is leading us to a foreign power and a foreign race." That is indeed why Luke says, "They could not catch him at fault in his teaching before the people."[7] For it is publicly, that is to say, in the midst of the people, that they are questioning him, in order to set the people against him. And if he does not permit the tax to be paid, the Herodians will immediately lay their hands on him as on one who does not submit to the Roman authorities.

Observe what is the passion of hypocrisy, how it has hidden all the hostility and the homicidal thought of the Jews beneath flattery's vile veil, and how those who hate involuntarily honor as they attempt to cause a death. Indeed, those who were saying, "We are the disciples of Moses, but we don't know where that one is from"[8] call him "Master." Those who were calling him a "deceiver" and "seducer" say, "We know that you are truthful." Those who were doing their best to resist with jealousy and with ignorance, saying, "This man does not come from God, because he does not observe the Sabbath" and "he has a demon"[9] witness that he teaches

---

[4]In reality the partisans of King Herod were also Jews, but since the race of Herod is from Idumaea, the author thinks of his supporters as pagans as well. [5]PG 56:866-67. [6]PG 56:867. [7]Cf. Lk 20:26. [8]Jn 9:28-29. [9]Mt 12.

the way of God in all truth. CATHEDRAL SER-MONS, HOMILY 104.[10]

22:17-19 Why Put Me to the Test?

WHOSE LIKENESS IS THIS? SEVERUS: What then does the Wisdom and the Word of God do? Jesus allows all their passion to appear for all to see, without them taking back the words they were speaking to no purpose. And like a skillful physician, he then lances their passion with a deep incision, when he cut with the first word. "Why are you testing me, hypocrites?" And after having shown by a reproach that the skin of deceitful hypocrisy was dead, it is gently, and to speak this way, insensibly and tranquilly that he nipped like the web of a spider their inescapable question. Indeed, he said, "Show me a denarius for the tax." And they presented a coin. And he said to them, "This image and this inscription concern whom?" They said to him, "Caesar." Then he said to them, "Give to Caesar what is Caesar's, and to God what is God's." "If the coin is Caesar's," Jesus says, "because that is what you have said—it is necessary to give it to Caesar himself."

"What then! You permit us to serve a man, and not god? And how is this not a violation of the law?" It will amount to nothing. Indeed, the act of giving tax to Caesar does not prevent the service of God, although you would like to think so. This is why it is necessary for you to give to God equally what is God's, in such a manner that if what is Caesar's is kept for the service of God, it is necessary that God be preferred to him. If you remain a tributary of Caesar, you should attribute this to your sins, not to God. In the same way, Paul similarly applies himself to the same distinction. In sending a letter to the Romans he wrote, "Pay to the world, therefore, what is due to the world; to those you owe taxes, taxes; to those you owe tribute, tribute."[11] CATHEDRAL SERMONS, HOMILY 104.[12]

22:20-22 Render to Caesar the Things That Are Caesar's

THE IMAGE OF GOD. INCOMPLETE WORK ON MATTHEW: The image of God is not depicted on gold but is imaged in humanity. The coin of Caesar is gold; that of God, humanity. Caesar is seen in his currency; God, however, is known through human beings. And so give your wealth to Caesar but reserve for God the sole innocence of your conscience, where God is beheld. For the hand of Caesar has crafted an image by likenesses and lives each year by renewable decree. However, the divine hand of God has shown his image in ten points.

What ten points? From five carnal ones and five spiritual ones[13] through which we see and understand what things are useful under God's image. So let us always reflect the image of God in these ways:

I do not swell up with the arrogance of pride;
nor do I droop with the blush of anger;
nor do I succumb to the passion of avarice;
nor do I surrender myself to the ravishes of gluttony;
nor do I infect myself with the duplicity of hypocrisy;
nor do I contaminate myself with the filth of rioting;
nor do I grow flippant with the pretension of conceit;
nor do I grow enamored of the burden of heavy drinking;
nor do I alienate by the dissension of mutual admiration;
nor do I infect others with the biting of detraction;
nor do I grow conceited with the vanity of gossip.
Rather, instead, I will reflect the image of God in that I feed on love;
grow certain on faith and hope;
strengthen myself on the virtue of patience;

---

[10]PO 25:634-35. [11]Rom 13:7. [12]PO 25:636-37. [13]If human nature is interpreted on the basis of Platonic dualism, the intelligible (spiritual) corresponds to the sensate (corporeal), and consequently the five spiritual senses to the five corporeal senses. The topic of the spiritual senses was much discussed by the mystical doctrine of Origen.

grow tranquil by humility;
grow beautiful by chastity;
am sober by abstention;
am made happy by tranquility;
and am ready for death by practicing hospitality.

It is with such inscriptions that God imprints his coins with an impression made neither by hammer nor by chisel but has formed them with

his primary divine intention. For Caesar required his image on every coin, but God has chosen man, whom he has created, to reflect his glory. HOMILY 42.[14]

---

[14]PG 56:867-68.

22:23-33 THE QUESTION ABOUT THE RESURRECTION

[23]*The same day Sadducees came to him, who say that there is no resurrection; and they asked him a question,* [24]*saying, "Teacher, Moses said, 'If a man dies, having no children, his brother must marry the widow, and raise up children for his brother.'* [25]*Now there were seven brothers among us; the first married, and died, and having no children left his wife to his brother.* [26]*So too the second and third, down to the seventh.* [27]*After them all, the woman died.* [28]*In the resurrection, therefore, to which of the seven will she be wife? For they all had her."*

[29]*But Jesus answered them, "You are wrong, because you know neither the scriptures nor the power of God.* [30]*For in the resurrection they neither marry nor are given in marriage, but are like angels[s] in heaven.* [31]*And as for the resurrection of the dead, have you not read what was said to you by God,* [32]*'I am the God of Abraham, and the God of Isaac, and the God of Jacob'? He is not God of the dead, but of the living."* [33]*And when the crowd heard it, they were astonished at his teaching.*

s Other ancient authorities add *of God*

OVERVIEW: Take away the necessity of death and the usefulness of being born will be found superfluous. Take away the utility of being born and the reason for marriage is explained. The power of present action is in the hope of the future. One who plows does so in order to reap. It is difficult in this world to serve the sanctity of justice if one is deprived of the hope of the resurrection. Take away this hope and the entire practice of piety is undermined (INCOMPLETE WORK ON MATTHEW). To say uncritically that God is the God of the dead is to consign the life

of God to those who have no life (JEROME). He is not the God of those who are not, who are utterly blotted out, and are to rise no more. He did not say "I was" but "I am." He is the God of those that are, those who live (CHRYSOSTOM). As we have seen in previous debates, Jesus takes a proposition from an empty extended hand of a deceiver, searches out its reasons and then presents plausible arguments and answers to it, even though the original question may be absurd. We do well to follow Christ in his argumentation clearly and in good order. In the case of discoursing with the Sadducees, and because of their ignorance in knowing even themselves, he first proposed a rational argument by analogy and then argued according to the authority of Scripture. So today we may use both arguments from reason and the authority of Scripture in our conversations with those who would twist the truth (INCOMPLETE WORK ON MATTHEW).

22:23 The Sadducees Come to Test Jesus

THE SAME DAY THE SADDUCEES CAME. INCOMPLETE WORK ON MATTHEW: On what day? On the day when the Pharisees returned, the Sadducees acquiesced. The Sadducees then returned, and in turn the Pharisees withdrew. So it was one opponent and then another through many days of struggle. They accosted him frequently so that one or the other might be able to best him, or if they were not able to put him down squarely, they might instead subvert others' judgment of him. So they frequented his company. Among the more numerous enemy is found the stronger warrior. While they were not able to put him down simply by words, they all surrounded him. They could not overcome him by strength; they sought to turn everyone against him, with the multitude following. HOMILY 42.[1]

DISTINGUISHING PHARISEES AND SADDUCEES. JEROME: There were two heresies among the Jews: one of the Pharisees and the other of the Sadducees. The Pharisees preferred tradition and the observance of the law, which two things they referred to as "divine service." They preferred them over justice. The Sadducees, however, were thought to be just and punished themselves because they were not. Hence the two parties were thought by the people to be quite different. The Sadducees denied everything about the resurrection. As we find in the Acts of the Apostles, they were opposed to the believers and confessors of the resurrection of the body and soul.[2] These are the two houses

about which Isaiah clearly teaches[3] that because they had climbed high they would surely be knocked down on the ground. COMMENTARY ON MATTHEW 3.22.23.[4]

THEY SAY THERE IS NO RESURRECTION. INCOMPLETE WORK ON MATTHEW: He introduced the heresy of the Sadducees, who said that there was no resurrection of the dead. Of all the propositions to be justly made, he demolished this one. For in everything and in every act, whether corporal or spiritual, the power of action is the hope of future reward. For he who plows does so in order to reap. He who fights does so in order to win. For when it becomes so difficult in this world to serve the sanctity of justice, who would be content to put out such effort against themselves every single day, unless he aspired to the hope of the resurrection? Take away the hope of the resurrection and the entire practice of religion is undermined. For didn't the Sadducees believe that there was marriage after death? There is not. For how could they believe that there was marriage after death when they denied the resurrection? But in defense of their own error they thought that they themselves had found an even more acute reason, speaking this way among themselves: For so it is not possible that she who was the wife of seven men could be the wife of only one or the common wife of all. Thus they thought it not possible that there is a resurrection of the dead. HOMILY 42.[5]

22:24-28 The Law of Levirate Marriage and the Resurrection

TO WHICH OF THE SEVEN WILL SHE BE WIFE? CHRYSOSTOM: Watch him answering these like a deft teacher. For though they deceitfully came to him, yet their question was one of ignorance. Therefore he does not say to them, "You hypocrites."

---

[1]PG 56:868. [2]Acts 23:8. [3]Cf. Is 8:14. [4]CCL 77:204-5. [5]PG 56:869.

To avoid censure for the fact that the seven brothers had one wife, they refer to Moses' authority. However, I believe that their whole story was just a fiction. For the third would not have taken her when he saw the two bridegrooms dead, or if the third, yet not the fourth or the fifth; and if even these, much more the sixth or the seventh would not have come to the woman but have shrunk from her. For such is the custom of the Jews. If they now still have this resistance, how much more did they have it then? They often avoided marrying under these circumstances, even when the law was constraining them. THE GOSPEL OF MATTHEW, HOMILY 70.2.[6]

22:29 Knowing Neither Scripture nor God's Power

YOU ERR. CHRYSOSTOM: What does Christ say? He replies to both, as taking his stand not against their words but their purpose. On every occasion he revealed the secrets of their hearts, at one time exposing them, at another time leaving the refutation of them that question him to their conscience. See, at any rate here, how he proves both points, as well that there will be a resurrection. And it will not be such a resurrection as they suspect.

For what does he say? "You err, not knowing the Scriptures nor the power of God." For since they put forward Moses and the law as if they knew them, he shows that this question is that of men ignorant of the Scriptures. They tempted him because they did not know the Scriptures as they should and because they were also ignorant of the power of God.

"For what marvel then is it," he says, "if you tempt me? I am as yet unknown to you. You do not even know the power of God, although you appear to have had much experience. Yet neither from common sense or from the Scriptures have you become acquainted with it." Even common sense causes us to know this: that to God all things are possible. THE GOS-

PEL OF MATTHEW, HOMILY 70.2.[7]

YOU ARE WRONG. JEROME: On account of these things, they erred since they did not know the Scriptures. Because they were ignorant of the Scriptures, they denied the power of God, that is, Christ, who is the power of God and the wisdom of God. COMMENTARY ON MATTHEW 3.22.29.[8]

22:30 No Marriage in the Resurrection

THEY ARE LIKE ANGELS. ORIGEN: Our Savior does not explain the meaning of the passage from Moses' law, rejecting them as unworthy of the knowledge of such a great mystery. He only represents matters in the simplest way as he speaks and teaches from the divine Scriptures concerning the resurrection of the dead. He teaches that there is no marriage in heaven but that those who are risen from the dead are like the angels in heaven. And, just as the angels in heaven neither marry nor are given in marriage, so he says it is with those who are risen from the dead. But I think he means that only those who are considered worthy of the resurrection of the dead neither marry nor are given in marriage as the angels in heaven. Furthermore, their "humble" bodies are changed to become like the bodies of the angels, ethereal and brilliant. COMMENTARY ON MATTHEW 17.30.[9]

THEY NEITHER MARRY NOR ARE GIVEN IN MARRIAGE. INCOMPLETE WORK ON MATTHEW: Idiots! They thought that this world was like the next. In this world because we die, so there too we die since we are born. Hence we take wives, since in dying this life is made less, but in being born it is increased. Therefore remove the necessity of death and the usefulness of being born will be found superfluous. Remove the utility of being born and the reason for marriage

---

[6]PG 58:657; NPNF 1 10:428. [7]PG 58:657-58; NPNF 1 10:428. [8]CCL 77:205. [9]GCS 40:670-71.

is explained. For this world is of the flesh; that one, of spirits. As the soul in this world is a pilgrim, so the flesh in that world is extraneous. In this world, the soul is subject to the flesh, that is, to human passions, where in the other world, the flesh is subject to the spirit. A particular thing is always stronger in its own country and it overcomes. So if the soul, powerful as it is, can be closed up in this infirm world and so be subdued by the grip of the body, so that nothing by its own efforts is able to grow or increase spiritually in its own nature, then how much more so in that world will our weak and vile flesh become worthy of our spiritual dignity and nothing be able to grow physically or to increase according to its own nature? Homily 42.[10]

22:31 The Resurrection of the Dead

The Chaste Life Is Outside Our Nature. Incomplete Work on Matthew: He has spoken about fasting, almsgiving and certain other spiritual works. Yet we have heard nothing so far about the likeness of the angels. But in speaking of intercourse between men and women, he says, "For in the resurrection they neither marry nor are given in marriage but are like angels in heaven." Why? The work of reproduction is characteristically a fleshly act that we share in common with animals. Just as all carnal powers have affinity with the animals, so also do all spiritual powers have affinity with the angels. This is preeminently so for chastity, an especially angelic practice. For through this characteristic alone, the chaste are distinctively like the angels, and their nature is overcome with virtues. For the same reason he says, "Neither do they marry nor are they given in marriage but are like the angels of God in heaven." For when we marry, because animals have this in common with us, we profess ourselves to be animals. So when we live chastely, because it is outside of our nature, we escape the nature of the flesh and we become coequals with the angels. Homily 42.[11]

22:32 God of the Living, Not of the Dead

I Am God of the Living. Chrysostom: It is again by Moses that he stops their mouths. It is they who had brought forward Moses. Jesus says, "And as for the resurrection of the dead, have you not read what was said to you by God, 'I am the God of Abraham, and the God of Isaac and the God of Jacob'? He is not God of the dead but of the living." He is not the God of those who are not, who are utterly blotted out and rise no more. He did not say "I was" but "I am." I am the God of those that are, those who live. Adam lived on the day he ate of the tree, then died in the sentence. Even though the progeny of Adam died, they live in the promise of the resurrection. How then does he say elsewhere, "That he might be Lord both of the dead and of the living"?[12] But this is not contrary to that. For here he speaks of the dead, who are also themselves to live. Furthermore, "I am the God of Abraham" is another thing from "That he might be Lord both of the dead and of the living." He knew of another death too, concerning which he says, "Let the dead bury their dead."[13]

"And when the multitudes heard this, they were astonished at his teaching." Yet not even here did he persuade the Sadducees. They go away defeated, while the crowd, with less vested interests, reaps the benefit. The Gospel of Matthew, Homily 70.3.[14]

The Eternity of Souls. Jerome: Further, he quotes Moses to explain the eternity of souls: "I am the God of Abraham and the God of Isaac and the God of Jacob," and immediately he adds, "For he is not the God of the dead but of the living." Thereby he shows that souls live after death. To say that God is the God of the dead is to consign the life of God to those who have no life. The nature of the resurrection and how it is the resurrection of both the good and the evil is

---

[10]PG 56:869. [11]PG 56:869-70. [12]Rom 14:9. [13]Mt 8:22; Lk 9:60. [14]PG 58:658; NPNF 1 10:429.

pursued by the apostle Paul more fully in the last part of his first epistle to the Corinthians.[15] COMMENTARY ON MATTHEW 3.22.32.[16]

22:33 The Crowd Astonished at His Teaching

THEY WERE ASTONISHED. INCOMPLETE WORK ON MATTHEW: For if Abraham and Isaac and Jacob might forever perish through death,[17] then God never could be spoken of as their God, the God of those who were no more. As we have seen in previous debates, Jesus takes a proposition from an empty extended hand of a deceiver and then searches out its reasons, and then he presents plausible arguments and answers to it, however absurd it may be. We do well to follow Christ in his ways of presenting arguments clearly and in good order.

In this case Jesus, in discoursing with the Sadducees and because of their ignorance in knowing even themselves, proposed first a rational argument by analogy, saying, "For in the resurrection, they do not marry, nor do they take wives, but they will be like the angels of God in heaven." Then he argues according to the authority of Scripture, saying "I am the God of Abraham, the God of Isaac and the God of Jacob."

So today we may use both arguments from reason and the authority of Scripture in our conversations with those who would twist the truth. However, from whatever source a proposition is put to partners in dialogue, first we outline our argument and then give our authority for it. We are seeking to persuade our hearers by our arguments and then confirm it with legitimate authority. However, our purpose is not merely to convince deceivers but to teach true seekers. Among those prone to deception, even if they understand an argument, they are less likely to consent to it. Yet for people seeking the truth honestly, it suffices only to explain our reasons, so they can understand a proposition, learn it and not deny it. On account of this, the true seekers may come to faith because of the arguments they have heard. HOMILY 42.[18]

---

[15]1 Cor 15:1-58. [16]CCL 77:207. [17]That is, if their death had been absolute and final, without the survival of the soul and the expectation of a future resurrection. [18]PG 56:871.

22:34-40 THE GREAT COMMANDMENT

[34]But when the Pharisees heard that he had silenced the Sadducees, they came together. [35]And one of them, a lawyer, asked him a question, to test him. [36]"Teacher, which is the great commandment in the law?" [37]And he said to him, "You shall love the Lord your God with all your heart, and with all your soul, and with all your mind. [38]This is the great and first commandment. [39]And a second is like it, You shall love your neighbor as yourself. [40]On these two commandments depend all the law and the prophets."

OVERVIEW: Not all who call Jesus Teacher do so appropriately, but only those who have a desire to learn from him. No one is able to say "teacher" properly except a disciple (ORIGEN). The Pharisees joined together as one, seeking to overcome him by force of numbers, since they could not overcome him by rational argument. Yet in the face of the truth, they show themselves to be impotent (Incomplete Work on Matthew). If Christ had not responded to their asking, "What is the greatest commandment of the law?" then we might have concluded that one command was no greater than another. Not only is the greatest commandment to love the Lord, but it is also the first commandment. Worthy is a person, confirmed in all his or her gifts, who exults in the wisdom of God, having a heart full of the love of God, a soul completely enlightened by the lamp of knowledge and a mind filled with the Word of God. Whatever was written in Exodus or Leviticus or Numbers or Deuteronomy depends upon these two commands: to love God and neighbor (Origen). To love God with the whole heart is the cause of every other good (Cyril of Alexandria).

22:34 The Sadducees Silenced, the Pharisees Gather

The Motive Is Envy, Not Understanding the Law. Cyril of Alexandria: After the humiliation of the Sadducees Jesus was highly regarded by the crowds. The Pharisees, filled with envy out of an immeasurable shamelessness, again were testing him, hypocritically asking if he might deliver a ruling concerning the first commandment. By doing so, perhaps Jesus would amend the commandment in a manner that might lead to an accusation against him. Now, Matthew and Luke call the person who asked the question a lawyer, while Mark calls him a teacher of the law. This does not indicate a disagreement.[1] For they both represent the questioner as one learned in the law and as a teacher of the law who is an interpreter of the law to the people. But the Lord publicly reveals their evil. They were not coming to have him interpret the law so that they might benefit but because they were seized by envy. So Jesus teaches that one should not measure out one's devotion, loving God in part but also clinging in

part to the concerns of this world. Through his teaching Jesus said that his commandment was the summary of all the commandments. The lawyer thought he could cast Jesus into danger as one who makes himself out to be God. Jesus failed to respond in the manner he expected, but he ends up praising Jesus, as Mark says.[2] Fragment 251.[3]

The Pharisees Came Together. Incomplete Work on Matthew: They came at him as one, that is, they overcame him as a crowd, since they could not overcome him by argument. In the face of the truth, they show themselves to be naked. Now they arm themselves with a crowd. For they said to him, One speaks for all and all speak for one, as if when one conquers, all seem to be victors. However, just as one may be a victor, one alone may also be confused. O Pharisees, you know and do everything on account of such men! Indeed, because at first you come as one, so must you be conquered by one alone. With one many were conquered. Yet all do not understand that they have all been conquered by one. Do not your own consciences acknowledge that they are confused? For it is a very superficial consolation for the man confused in his own conscience that he is ignored by others. Homily 42.[4]

22:35 A Lawyer Asks a Question

Who Can Rightly Call Him Teacher? Origen: Now let us consider one argument of entrapment: "Teacher," he says, "what is the greater commandment in the law?" He says "teacher" trying to entrap him, since he offers his thoughts not as a disciple of Christ. This however, will be clearer from an example we now offer. Consider: The father of a son is

---

[1]*Diaphōnia* is the technical term for an apparent contradiction between one Gospel and another. See the discussion of Augustine's *Harmony of the Gospels* in *Matthew 1-13* (ACCS), p. l. [2]Mk 12:32-33. [3]MKGK 238. [4]PG 56:872.

indeed the father, and no one else is able to call him father except the son; and the mother of a daughter is indeed her mother, and no one else can call her mother except her own daughter. And so the teacher of a disciple is indeed his teacher, and the disciple of a teacher is truly his disciple. As a result, no one is able to say "teacher" properly except a disciple. And see how, on account of this, that not all who call him teacher do so appropriately but only those who have a desire to learn from him. He said to his disciples, "You call me teacher and lord, and rightly so, for so I am."[5] Therefore disciples of Christ properly indeed address him as teacher, and by this word from the Lord himself his servants rightly call him Lord. Thus the apostle spoke well when he said, "Yet for us there is one Lord Jesus Christ, through whom are all things and for whom we exist."[6] And consider what he says, "It is enough for the discile to be" not simply like a teacher but "like his teacher."[7] Therefore if anyone does not learn something from this word or surrender himself with his whole heart, in order to become his delightful dwelling place but still calls him "teacher," he is brother to the Pharisees attempting to entrap Christ while calling him "teacher." And so all who say "Our Father who art in heaven" ought not to have "the spirit of slavery in fear but a spirit of the adoption of sons."[8] However, whoever does not have "the spirit of adoption of sons" and yet says "Our Father who art in heaven"[9] is lying, since he is not a son of God, while calling God his father. COMMENTARY ON MATTHEW 2.[10]

22:36 Which Is the Great Commandment?

THE GREATEST COMMANDMENT? ORIGEN: The question itself, however, was this: "What is the greatest command of the law?"—a question of great worth which will allow us to explain something of the differences between these commands. For certain commands are very great, but certain others are secondary.

Hence we must look at each right down to the least important of these commands. For if in the baiting of the Pharisees and their asking, "What is the greater commandment of the law?" Christ had not responded, then we would conclude that one command was no greater than another. COMMENTARY ON MATTHEW 2.[11]

22:37 Loving the Lord Your God

LOVE GOD WITH YOUR WHOLE HEART. ORIGEN: However, now as he responds, he says, "Love the Lord your God with your whole heart, your whole soul and your whole mind." This is the greatest and the first commandment. His statement contains something necessary for us to know, since it is the greatest. The others— even to the least of them—are inferior to it. COMMENTARY ON MATTHEW 2.[12]

HEART, MIND AND SOUL. ORIGEN: Worthy is he, confirmed in all his gifts, who exults in the wisdom of God, having a heart full of the love of God, and a soul completely enlightened by the lamp of knowledge and a mind filled with the word of God. It follows then that all such gifts truly come from God. He would understand that all the law and the prophets are in some way a part of the wisdom and knowledge of God. He would understand that all the law and the prophets depend upon and adhere to the principle of the love of the Lord God and of neighbor and that the perfection of piety consists in love. COMMENTARY ON MATTHEW 4.[13]

WITH ALL YOUR HEART. CYRIL OF ALEXANDRIA: Therefore the first commandment teaches every kind of godliness. For to love God with the whole heart is the cause of every good. The second commandment includes the righteous

---

[5]Jn 13:13. [6]1 Cor 8:6. [7]Mt 10:25. [8]Rom 8:15. [9]Mt 6:9. [10]GCS 38.2.11:3. [11]GCS 38.2.11:3-4. [12]GCS 38.2:4. [13]GCS 38.2:8.

acts we do toward other people. The first commandment prepares the way for the second and in turn is established by the second. For the person who is grounded in the love of God clearly also loves his neighbor in all things himself. The kind of person who fulfills these two commandments experiences all the commandments. FRAGMENT 251.[14]

22:38-39 Loving One's Neighbor

THE SECOND IS LIKE IT. ORIGEN: This he adds since the Pharisees have asked truly "What is the greatest commandment in the law?" The Lord himself responds to them and teaches us. Not only is the greatest commandment to love the Lord, but as well it is the first commandment. It is first, however, not in the order of the Scriptures but in the order of virtue. And as this comes from such a source, it must be adhered to, since as with many established commands, Christ says that it is the first and greatest command that "you love the Lord your God with your whole heart and your whole mind and your whole soul," and the second, however, "is like unto" the first; and accordingly, this similitude is also great, "that you love your neighbor as you love yourself." This is how we understand the second one, while another may be third in magnitude and order, or a fourth, and so in order we number the commands of the law, accepting this as wisdom from God, who orders them even to the least. Such is the task of no one else but Christ alone, since he is "the power of God and the wisdom of God."[15] COMMENTARY ON MATTHEW 2.[16]

22:40 These Two Commandments

LAW AND PROPHETS IN SUMMARY. ORIGEN: After this you ask how it is that "all the law and the prophets depend upon these two commands." For it seems that the texts show us that whatever was written in Exodus or Leviticus or Numbers or Deuteronomy depend "upon these two commands." But how is the law which regards lepers or the continual flow of blood or the menstruation of women dependent "upon these two commands"? And still further, how does the prophecy about captured Jerusalem,[17] or the vision of Egypt in Isaiah[18] and the other prophets, or the vision of Tyre[19] or whatever may be prophesied about Tyre or the king of Tyre,[20] or Isaiah's vision of the four-footed beasts in the wasteland[21] "depend upon these two commands"?

It seems to me that the answer is something like this. He who fulfills all that is written concerning the love of God and neighbor is worthy to receive the greatest thanks from God.

Concerning this it has been argued that "the utterance of wisdom [comes] through the Holy Spirit," after which follows "the utterance of knowledge" which is "according to the Spirit."[22] COMMENTARY ON MATTHEW 4.[23]

---

[14]MKGK 238. [15]1 Cor 1:24. [16]GCS 38.2:4. [17]Cf. Is 5:1-30. [18]Cf. Is 19:1-25. [19]Is 23:1-18. [20]Ezek 28:12-19. [21]Is 30:6-7. [22]1 Cor 12:8. [23]GCS 38.2:7-8.

22:41-46 THE QUESTION ABOUT THE MESSIAH

[41]*Now while the Pharisees were gathered together, Jesus asked them a question,* [42]*saying, "What do you think of the Christ? Whose son is he?" They said to him, "The son of David."*

⁴³He said to them, "How is it then that David, inspired by the Spirit,ᵗ calls him Lord, saying,

⁴⁴'The Lord said to my Lord,

Sit at my right hand,

till I put thy enemies under thy feet'?

⁴⁵If David thus calls him Lord, how is he his son?" ⁴⁶And no one was able to answer him a word, nor from that day did any one dare to ask him any more questions.

t Or *David in the Spirit*

OVERVIEW: Pharisees and Sadducees asked their deceptive questions to tempt Jesus, not to learn from him. They appeared to be well-prepared doctors of the law but were not. They were probing him only as tormentors. This is why the Lord chose to put his own questions to those who were professing to have knowledge of the law: that these matters might be argued before the people (ORIGEN). They were being gradually shown that it was not merely a man who was being tempted but God, whom no one is able to tempt. He was neither able to say straightforwardly the truth about himself nor to keep silent. He was not able to speak candidly, lest the Jews, in finding a greater occasion for blasphemy, be all the more enraged. However, it was not possible to silence the truth that had come in him. He propounded this ingenious question to them in order that while he was silent his question itself might reveal his identity and show them that he was not a man but God. So he asks directly, "How is it then that David, inspired by the Spirit, calls him Lord?" For how was it possible for him to be his Lord who was yet to be born from David (INCOMPLETE WORK ON MATTHEW)? He confused them by their own question so that, blushing, they might back away from his directness and thereafter ask him nothing further (ORIGEN). They had supposed that he was a mere man, yet they also said that the Christ is "the Son of David" (CHRYSOSTOM). The incarnate Lord, truly God, truly human, is both David's Son as in a human line of ancestry and David's Lord as truly God (AUGUSTINE). Their mouths were stopped but not their anger. The faults of the jealous are indeed able to be overcome but are difficult to put to rest (JEROME).

22:41 Jesus Questions the Pharisees

THE TABLES ARE TURNED. INCOMPLETE WORK ON MATTHEW: The confusion of the crowd had come about because of the providence of God, the gradual divine economy, which brings all things to ripeness at the proper time. Christ desires not to question those who resist but to teach them in whatever ways he can. Christ desires to teach even further those who already wish to be taught, and for this reason they desired to be questioned. The Lord who sets the limits of the sea is found here boldly setting himself against the devil. He can set such a limit there at any time he wants to. HOMILY 42.[1]

22:42 Whose Son Is the Christ?

WHAT DO YOU THINK OF THE CHRIST? CHRYSOSTOM: Remember how many miracles have preceded this dialogue—after how many signs, after how many questions, after how great a display of his union with the Father in deeds as well as in words—now Jesus asks his own question. After so many previous events, he is now quietly leading them to the point of confessing that he is God. He does this so that they may not be able to say that he is an adversary to the law and a foe to God, even though

[1]PG 56:875.

he has worked mighty miracles.

With his own disciples on the mount of transfiguration he had asked first what the others say and only then what they themselves say. But in this case he did not proceed in this way. For surely they would have said a deceiver and a wicked one, speaking all things without fear. So for this cause he inquires directly for the opinion of these men themselves.

For since he was now about to go on to his Passion, he sets forth the prophecy that plainly proclaims him to be Lord. It is not as if the call to confession has emerged without any precipitating occasion, or from no reasonable cause or as if he had this as his prior aim. For he had already brought the issue to their attention, and they had answered that he was a mere man, in opposition to the truth. Now he is overthrowing their mistaken opinion. This is why he introduces David into the discussion, that his true identity and divinity might be more clearly recognized. For they had supposed that he was a mere man, yet they also say that the Christ is "the Son of David." Hence he now brings in the prophetic testimony to his being Lord, and to the genuineness of his Sonship and his equality in honor with his Father.[2] THE GOSPEL OF MATTHEW, HOMILY 71.2.[3]

22:43 David Calls Him Lord

DAVID INSPIRED BY THE SPIRIT. ORIGEN: It is very worthy for us to consider that our Savior willingly proposed to the Pharisees his question about the Christ, hoping that they might respond in a fitting manner. They were not able to respond adequately. Nonetheless it was the will of the Savior to enter into dialogue with his audacious proponents, the Pharisees, with their many propositions, and similarly with the Sadducees, who placed before him the question of the seven brothers and their one wife.[4] The Pharisees and Sadducees asked their many questions to tempt Jesus, not to learn from him. They appeared to be well-prepared doctors of

the law but were not. This is why the Lord chose to put his own questions to those who were professing to have knowledge of the law: that these matters might be argued openly before the people. The Lord did not give clear responses to his questioners even though he himself responded to all their questions. It was entirely appropriate that the Lord himself, in accordance with the custom of dining with the doctors, show and hand over true divine teaching. They nevertheless did not recognize him as the prophet who was the pinnacle of all prophets. COMMENTARY ON MATTHEW 5.[5]

22:44 Sit at My Right Hand

THE LORD SAID TO MY LORD. INCOMPLETE WORK ON MATTHEW: The judgmental Jewish leaders were tempting Christ the man. They would not have tempted him if they had believed that he were the Son of God. Christ therefore was ready to show himself to them. He knew the dishonesty in their hearts. He was ready to show them that it was not a man who was tempted but God, whom no one is able to tempt. He was not able to say straightforwardly the truth about himself or to keep silent. He was not able to speak openly, lest the Jews, in finding a greater occasion for blasphemy, be all the more enraged. However, it was not possible to silence the truth that had come to him in order that he might let this same truth be known. And it was for this reason that he propounded this ingenious question to them, in order that while he was silent his question itself might show them that he was not a man but God. So he asks directly, "How is it then that David, inspired by the Spirit, calls him Lord?" For how was it possible for him to be his Lord who was yet to be born from David? I think that he posed this question not only against the ancient Pharisees but against our contemporary heretics as well.

[2]Ps 110:1 (109:1 LXX). [3]PG 58:663; NPNF 1 10:432. [4]Mt 22:23-38; Mk 12:28-33; Lk 20:27-33. [5]GCS 38.2:9-10.

For he was the Son of David according to the flesh but Lord according to his divinity. Homily 42.[6]

22:45 How Is He David's Son?

If David Calls Him Lord. AUGUSTINE: Here then there is need for caution, lest Christ himself be thought to have denied that he was the Son of David. He did not deny that he was the Son of David, but he probed his detractors on the particular way this can be. You have said that Christ is the Son of David. I do not deny it. But "if David thus calls him Lord, how is he his Son?" Tell me how he could be his son who is also his Lord? They did not answer him but were dumbfounded.

Let us then answer them by the explanation given by Christ himself. Where given? Through his apostle. By what source can we prove that Christ himself has explained it? The apostle says, "Would you receive a proof of Christ who speaks in me?"[7] So it is through the apostle's voice that Christ has allowed this question to be solved. In the first place, do you remember what Christ said, speaking by the apostle to Timothy? "Remember Jesus Christ, raised from the dead, descended from David. This is my gospel."[8] So it is easy to see that Christ is the Son of David. But how is he also David's Lord? Let the apostle again tell us of the one who, "though he was in the form of God, did not count equality with God a thing to be grasped."[9] Acknowledge David's Lord. If you acknowledge David's Lord, our Lord, the Lord of heaven and earth, the Lord of the angels, equal with God, in the form of God, how is he David's Son? Note what follows. The apostle shows you David's Lord by saying, "Who being in the form of God, thought it not robbery to be equal with God." And how is he David's Son? "But he emptied himself, taking the form of a servant, being made in the likeness of men; and being found in human form, he humbled himself, having become obedient unto death, even the death of the cross. Therefore

God has also highly exalted him."[10] Christ "of the seed of David," the Son of David, rose again because "he emptied himself." How did he empty himself? By taking upon himself that which he was not, not by losing that which he was. He emptied himself. He "humbled himself." Though he was God, he appeared as a man.[11] He was despised as he walked on earth, he who made the heaven. He was despised as though a mere man, as though of no power. He was not only despised but also killed! He was that stone that was laid aside on the ground, which the Jews stumbled against and were shaken. And what does he himself say? "He who falls on this stone will be broken to pieces, but he on whom it falls, it shall grind him to powder."[12] First he was laid low, and they stumbled against him. He shall come from above, and he will "grind" them that have been shaken "to powder."

Thus you have heard that Christ is both David's Son and David's Lord: David's Lord always, David's Son in time. David's Lord, born of the substance of his Father; David's Son, born of the Virgin Mary, conceived by the Holy Spirit. Let us hold fast both. The one of them will be our eternal habitation; the other is our deliverance from our present exile. SERMON 92.2-3.[13]

22:46 No One Was Able to Answer Him

None Dared Question Him. ORIGEN: And so Matthew added, "No one was able to say a word to him, and no one dared from that hour to ask him anything." The reason, however, that they had not dared to ask him even another word was this, that having been asked themselves, they could not respond. For if their question had come from a desire to learn, then they

---

[6]PG 56:875. [7]2 Cor 13:3. [8]2 Tim 2:8. [9]Phil 2:6. [10]Phil 2:6-9. [11]The verb *apparere* here signifies "to show oneself, to make onself seen." It does not at all imply the concept, so widespread in the second and third centuries, that the body assumed by Christ had been merely apparent. [12]Mt 21:44. [13]PL 38:572-73; NPNF 1 6:400-401* (Sermon 42).

would never have proposed their questions to him. They dared not ask him anything now. For they were asking him only as tempters, and for this reason he wanted to confuse them by their own question so that, blushing, they might back away from his directness and thereafter ask him nothing further. We have spoken these things according to an understanding of the plain sense of the text. COMMENTARY ON MATTHEW 5.[14]

NO MORE QUESTIONS. JEROME: The Pharisees and Sadducees had been looking for an opportu-

nity for deceiving him, looking to find some word that might be taken advantage of by the plotters. Yet they had been totally confounded in their conversations. So they asked nothing further. What did they do then? All they could do was turn him over to the custody of the Roman authorities. From this we learn that the faults of the jealous are indeed able to be overcome but are difficult to put to rest. COMMENTARY ON MATTHEW 4.22.46.[15]

---

[14]GCS 38.2:10. [15]CCL 77:210.

23:1-12 JESUS WARNS AGAINST THE TEACHERS OF THE LAW AND THE PHARISEES

[1]*Then said Jesus to the crowds and to his disciples,* [2]*"The scribes and the Pharisees sit on Moses' seat;* [3]*so practice and observe whatever they tell you, but not what they do; for they preach, but do not practice.* [4]*They bind heavy burdens, hard to bear,*[u] *and lay them on men's shoulders; but they themselves will not move them with their finger.* [5]*They do all their deeds to be seen by men; for they make their phylacteries broad and their fringes long,* [6]*and they love the place of honor at feasts and the best seats in the synagogues,* [7]*and salutations in the market places, and being called rabbi by men.* [8]*But you are not to be called rabbi, for you have one teacher, and you are all brethren.* [9]*And call no man your father on earth, for you have one Father, who is in heaven.* [10]*Neither be called masters, for you have one master, the Christ.* [11]*He who is greatest among you shall be your servant;* [12]*whoever exalts himself will be humbled, and whoever humbles himself will be exalted.*

u Other ancient authorities omit *hard to bear*

OVERVIEW: We must admit that the desire for having the first place is found not only among the scribes and Pharisees but also in the church. It is found not only at dinner but also in the front seats of the church. Some rightly hand on the law, but they themselves do not do it. Some lay heavy burdens upon the shoulders of men but do not wish to lift these burdens themselves (ORIGEN). We should

however honor both the good and the bad priests, lest one condemn the good on account of the bad. For it is better to preserve the just with the evil than to subvert the just for the good. Wretched land may produce precious gold. The gold is not despised on account of the wretched land (INCOMPLETE WORK ON MATTHEW). The good pastor ought to be a rigorous and severe judge in things that concern himself. But in the matters of those whom he offers pastoral service, he ought to be gentle and ready to make allowances (CHRYSOSTOM). Mistaken laity may be more easily set straight, but clerics, if evil, are almost impossible to set straight. The seat of Moses does not make the priest, but the priest makes the seat. The place does not sanctify the person, but the person sanctifies the place. Not every priest is holy, but all the holy belong to the spiritual priesthood (INCOMPLETE WORK ON MATTHEW). The priest is eager to please the audience. Whatever they want, he exhibits. If the audience is lacking in enthusiasm and lazy, he also becomes more unconcerned. If the audience delights in ridicule, he becomes one who moves others to ridicule. He is predictable. Without exception, he always does everything with only his audience in mind (CHRYSOSTOM).

No one should be called teacher or father except God the Father and Our Lord Jesus Christ. He alone is the Father, because all things are from him. He alone is the teacher, because through him all things are made and through him all things are reconciled to God (JEROME, ORIGEN, CHRYSOSTOM). Not only does he forbid the disciple to set his heart upon the first place but also he requires him to seek out the last (CHRYSOSTOM). The Lord himself provided the pattern for humility. No matter how great he was, he humbled himself (ORIGEN, CYRIL OF ALEXANDRIA). At the messianic wedding feast, typical protocols are reversed (INCOMPLETE WORK ON MATTHEW).

23:1 Jesus Speaks to the Crowds and His Disciples

THE CROWDS AND THE PHARISEES. INCOMPLETE WORK ON MATTHEW: The Lord had just humbled the disbelieving priests who were flailing against him like wild beasts. With the accuracy of a spear point he gives them a very sharp answer, showing them their own incorrigible condition. Mistaken laity may be more easily set

straight, but clerics, if they are evil, are almost impossible to set straight. After this, he then turned his conversation to the apostles and to the people, saying, "The Pharisees and scribes sit on the throne of Moses." Their confusion there becomes what they end up teaching. HOMILY 43.[1]

23:2 Sitting on Moses' Seat

DISTINGUISHING PRIESTS AND SCRIBES. ORIGEN: Therefore when he speaks "to the crowds and his disciples" he talks about "the scribes and Pharisees who sit upon the throne of Moses." I judge these statements to be referring to the following groups. Those who profess that they interpret the law of Moses and glory in this, or who know the law well and seek to profit by this knowledge—these sit upon the throne of Moses. Those who do not depart from the letter of the law are called scribes. Then there are those who profess to know even more, setting themselves apart because they think they are better than the masses. That is why they are called Pharisees, which interpreted means "to divide or segregate" (for *Phares* translated means "division").[2] COMMENTARY ON MATTHEW 9.[3]

PRIESTS BY NAME. INCOMPLETE WORK ON MATTHEW: What does he say concerning these priests? "The scribes and Pharisees sit upon the seat of Moses.". . . There are many priests by name but few by works. See therefore how you may sit upon it. The chair does not make the priest, but the priest, the chair. The place does not sanctify the man, but the man, the place. Not every priest is holy, but all the holy are priests. Whoever sits well on that throne will receive honor on its account. Whoever sits on it badly causes injury to the throne. And for this

---

[1]PG 56:876. [2]For a further explanation of the term *Pharisee*, see Bauer, Arndt and Gingrich, *A Greek-English Lexicon of the New Testament*, 2nd ed. (Chicago: University of Chicago Press, 1958), p. 853. [3]GCS 38.2:16.

reason, the evil priest is convicted by his priest-hood and not honored by it. HOMILY 43.[4]

23:3 Practice Whatever They Tell You

NOT WHAT THEY DO. JEROME: He is tempted by the Pharisees and surrounded by their lies. According to the psalmist, "The arrows of children are their snares."[5] Nevertheless, on account of the dignity of the priests and their reputation, he encourages the people to obey them, considering not their works but their teaching. What he says is this: "The scribes and Pharisees sit upon the throne of Moses," showing this as a throne of teaching about the law. And we ought to accept this because of what is said in the psalms: "He does not sit in the seat of scoffers"[6] and "He overturned the seats of those who sold pigeons."[7] COMMENTARY ON MATTHEW 4.23.3.[8]

HONOR GOOD PRIESTS AND BAD. INCOMPLETE WORK ON MATTHEW: If they speak well, it is to their credit. If they teach well, it is to yours.[9] Accept therefore what is yours and do not discuss what is another's. For just as the priests teach the unfaithful on account of the faithful, judging better to encourage the evil on account of the good rather than to neglect the good on account of the evil, so also therefore you must honor good priests and bad, lest you condemn the good on account of the bad. For it is better to preserve the just with the evil than to subvert the just for the good. For frequently you will treat the bad man with good faith. Remember that wretched land may produce precious gold. Is the gold despised on account of the wretched land? No! But just as gold is taken and the earth is left behind, so also you must accept their teaching and leave behind their customs. HOMILY 43.[10]

THEY PREACH BUT DO NOT PRACTICE. INCOMPLETE WORK ON MATTHEW: What does he say then to the people? "Whatever you have been told to do, obey and do; just do not imitate their deeds." For you are sitting in the church not only as listeners but also as judges of the priests. You may be learning strange things that would be considered inappropriate. You are judging the priests in comparison with yourselves. You should listen to everything they say, but do not do everything which you hear. Yes, all priests teach, but they do not all practice what they teach. For among men there is a ranking that is quite diverse. But in nature everything is equal. For from the beginning men were created in this same way. Only afterwards are they ranked for your sake. Therefore, on account of this, their nature belongs to them in and of itself, but their ranking is for your benefit. HOMILY 43.[11]

23:4 Binding Heavy Burdens on Others

THEY BIND HEAVY BURDENS. ORIGEN: Therefore up until now the scribes and Pharisees among the Jews have been sitting on the throne of Moses. I am not saying this because only scribes and Pharisees will sit on the seat of Moses. They speak but do not do anything, laying heavy and unsupportable burdens on the shoulders of men. Yet they are not even willing to lift a finger to lighten those burdens. For I judge that those who rightly understand and explain Moses according to his spiritual power are the ones who will indeed sit on the throne of Moses. But these are not the scribes and Pharisees. They are much better. They are the beloved disciples of Christ who interpret his word through the grace of God. They are able to sort out different meanings in different words. Indeed, therefore, before the coming of Christ they sat well on the throne of Moses who inter-

---

[4]PG 56:876. [5]Jerome is referring to Ps 63:8 in the Vulgate. This is not reflected in any of the English translations (Ps 64:7) but does reflect the Septuagint (Ps 63:8). [6]Ps 1:1. [7]Mt 21:12. [8]CCL 77:210. [9]To justify the reverence due to a priest who is morally undeserving, the author observes that the role of the priest is to teach. Hence the faithful must pay heed even if his behavior is reprehensible because for this he is responsible as a man—not as a priest. [10]PG 56:876-77. [11]PG 56:876.

preted the sayings of Moses well and according to reason. However, after the coming of Christ, they sit on the throne of the church, which is the seat and throne of Christ. COMMENTARY ON MATTHEW 9.[12]

NOT WISHING TO MOVE A FINGER. ORIGEN: Just as the scribes and Pharisees wickedly sat upon the throne of Moses, so do some in the church who sit upon the ecclesiastical throne. There are some in the church who have the right understanding of the law and pass it on correctly. They say what each person needs to do, but they themselves do not do it. Some of them lay heavy burdens upon the shoulders of men, but they won't even lift a finger to help. These are the ones the Savior is talking about when he says, "Whoever then relaxes one of the least of these commandments and teaches men so, shall be called least in the kingdom of God."[13] There are others, however, who sit on the throne, who act before they speak and speak wisely, restraining those who are disordered. They place merciful burdens on the shoulders of others. They themselves are the first to lift the heavy burden, for the exhortation of other listeners. It is these of whom the Lord speaks when he says, "He who does so and teaches others to do so, this man will be called great in the kingdom of heaven."[14] COMMENTARY ON MATTHEW 9.[15]

THEY ALLOW THEMSELVES PRIVILEGE. CHRYSOSTOM: He mentions here a twofold wickedness. First they require great and extreme strictness of life, without any indulgence, from those over whom they rule. Yet they are much less stringent with themselves. This is opposite from what the truly good pastor ought to hold. He ought to be a rigorous and severe judge in things that concern himself. But in the matters of those whom he rules, he ought to be gentle and ready to make allowances. What these men do is just the opposite.

For such are all they who practice self-restraint in mere words while being unforgiving

and grievous to bear when they have had no experience of the difficulty in actions. This is no small fault. In no small way does Jesus increase the former charge. THE GOSPEL OF MATTHEW, HOMILY 72.2.[16]

THEY LAY BURDENS ON PEOPLE'S SHOULDERS. INCOMPLETE WORK ON MATTHEW: How great indeed were the heavy burdens and the insupportable demands of the law—attributed to the scribes and the Pharisees—about which Christ spoke and which God most assuredly gave them on account of the sin of the golden calf. The scribes and Pharisees taught [this law], persuading the people to live according to the commands of the law and not to go over to the easy and joyful grace of Christ. Indeed, the Lord spoke above about these very burdensome commands, exhorting the Jews, "Come to me, all you who labor and are burdened, and I will give you rest."[17] And in the Acts of the Apostles, Peter says, "And you, why do you tempt God and wish to impose a yoke on the necks of the disciples which neither we nor our fathers were able to bear?"[18] For there were indeed those who, commending the burdens of the law to their listeners for certain fabled reasons, could not push these things away from themselves, as if chains were binding on their shoulders above their hearts, as if they were constricted by the chains of reason. For the Pharisees and scribes did not fulfill these duties in any moderation. That is to say, they did not do so with full strength nor even with a moderate effort, such as with a finger. Consequently, however, priests who now order justice among their people but who themselves do not serve even moderately are surely not just in doing so, although they may appear to be just teachers. Such are they who impose heavy burdens on those coming to repentance, they who preach but do not practice; and so, while the punishment of sin is placed on those

---

[12]GCS 38.2:16-17. [13]Mt 5:19. [14]Mt 5:19. [15]GCS 38.2:16-17. [16]PG 58:668; NPNF 1 10:436-37. [17]Mt 11:28. [18]Acts 15:10.

present, the punishment of future sin is despised. Homily 43.[19]

23:5 Doing Works to Be Seen by Others

They Make Their Fringes Long. Chrysostom: He then accused them of vanity, from which came their ruin. His previous charges concerned signs of harshness and laziness, but these charges accuse them of a mad desire for glory. This desire drew them away from God. It caused them to make a show in front of others who were watching and corrupted them.

Now that it has become the priest's special interest to please those who are watching, he exhibits whatever they want. If they are noble, he makes a spectacle of confronting conflicts. If they are lacking in enthusiasm and lazy, he also becomes more lackadaisical. If they delight in ridicule, he delights in ridicule, in order to please those watching. If they are earnest and practice self-restraint, he tries to be the same way, since this is the disposition of the one from whom he seeks praise.

It is not that he does some things one way and some things in another way. No, he is far more predictable. He always acts with the spectator in mind, in all things absolutely. Then, having laid bare their vanity, Jesus shows that it is not even about great and necessary things that they are vainglorious. They are vain about things without warmth or worth. These are the proofs of their baseness: the phylacteries and the fringes of their garments. "For they make broad their phylacteries and enlarge the borders of their garments." The Gospel of Matthew, Homily 72.2.[20]

They Make Their Phylacteries Broad. Jerome: They called those phylacteries "little pictures" of the Decalogue, because whoever had them had his own fortification and defense. But the knowledgeable Pharisees did not have them, because these things must be carried in the heart, not the body. They may have children

and treasure boxes and granaries, but they do not have knowledge of God. Even today there are those superstitious ladies who have their "little Gospels." In the absence of the true cross and other such things, they indeed have the zeal of God but no true knowledge of him. Even today, they too do these same kinds of things in front of us by liquefying gnats for drinking and gulping down honey. This is what some see as the small, short fringe mandated by the law. But a better case is the woman with the bloody flow who touched the fringe of the Lord's garment. She was not motivated by the superstitious sentiments of the Pharisees. And what is more, she was healed at his touch. And so when they widened their phylacteries and lengthened their fringes, attracting the honor of the people, they were exposed in their hypocrisies, showing why they seek the first seats at dinners and the front chairs in synagogues. They point out gluttony and glory in public and are hailed by men as rabbi, which in colloquial Latin means "teacher." Commentary on Matthew 4.23.5.[21]

They Do All Their Deeds to Be Seen. Origen: Further, therefore, to the reprehensible Pharisees and scribes who were so concerned about their body and appearance, the Lord said, "They do everything to be seen by other men. For they widen their phylacteries and enlarge the tassels of their clothing." The disciples of Jesus did everything to be seen by God alone. The only ornaments they had bound to their hands were good works. Meditating on divine teaching, they observed the divine commands, always applying them fittingly before the eyes of their souls. Their only tassel was the virtue of Jesus whom they imitated. Commentary on Matthew 11.[22]

23:6-7 Loving the Place of Honor

---

[19]PG 56:877-78. [20]PG 58:669; NPNF 1 10:437. [21]CCL 77:212. [22]GCS 38.2:22.

DEACONS AND BISHOPS WHO LOVE THE PLACE OF HONOR. ORIGEN: What are we to say about those who "love the places of honor at banquets and the front seats in synagogues and the highest respect in public places and to be called rabbi by everyone"? We must first admit that this kind of delight is found not only among the scribes and Pharisees but also in the church of Christ, and not only at dinner, while taking places at the table, but also the front seats in church. These are the deacons, or those who wish to become deacons, yet who "squander the savings of widows, praying for a good opportunity" and yet "will receive a greater judgment."[23] They covet even more avidly the highly visible "first seats" of those called priests. Indeed, however, even they do not put as much effort into their scheming as those who are called bishops, the ones who love "being called rabbi by men." It is they who ought most clearly to understand that a bishop is to be "above reproach" and so on,[24] so that he would be called "bishop" not by men [only] but rather before God. COMMENTARY ON MATTHEW 12.[25]

THE BEST SEATS. CHRYSTOSOM: Everything he accused them of was small and trifling. Yet he was dealing with the cause of all the evils: ambition, the violent seizing of the teacher's chair, and so on. These he brings forward and corrects with diligence, confronting this strongly and earnestly charging them. His own disciples needed to be warned about these matters. THE GOSPEL OF MATTHEW, HOMILY 72.3.[26]

23:8 One Teacher, Many Brothers

YOU HAVE ONE TEACHER. ORIGEN: You are not "to be called rabbi" and especially "not by men," nor are you to love to be called righteous by someone else. "For you have one teacher, and you are all brothers" to each other. For you have been born anew, not only from water but also from the spirit, and you have received the "spirit of adoption," so that it might be said of you that

you were "born not of the flesh, nor of the will of man" but from God.[27] It is hard to imagine this being said of anyone or any son until now. You do not call anyone on earth "Father" in the sense that you say "our Father" of the one who gives all things through all ages and according to the divine plan. Whoever ministers with the divine word does not put himself forward to be called "teacher," for he knows that when he performs well it is Christ who is within him. He should only call himself "servant" according to the command of Christ, saying, "Whoever is greater among you, let him be the servant of all."[28] COMMENTARY ON MATTHEW 12.[29]

NOT TO BE CALLED RABBI. CHRYSOSTOM: "You are not to be called rabbi, for you have one teacher, and you are all brothers." One has nothing more than another. For in respect to his knowledge he knows nothing from himself. This is why Paul says, "For who is Paul, and who is Apollos, but ministers?"[30]—not masters. Again, "call no man your father." This is said in order that they may know whom they ought to call Father in the highest sense. It is not said frivolously as if no one should ever be called father. Just as the human master is not the divine Master, so neither is the father the Father who is the cause of all, both of all masters and of all fathers. THE GOSPEL OF MATTHEW, HOMILY 72.3.[31]

23:9 One Father, Who Is in Heaven

CALL NO MAN YOUR FATHER ON EARTH. JEROME: No one should be called teacher or father except God the Father and our Lord Jesus Christ. He alone is the Father, because all things are from him. He alone is the teacher, because through him are made all things and through him all things are reconciled to God.

But one might ask, "Is it against this precept

---

[23]Mt 12:40. [24]1 Tim 3:22. [25]GCS 38.2:22-23. [26]PG 58:670; NPNF 1 10:438. [27]Jn 1:13. [28]Mk 9:35; 10:43-44. [29]GCS 38.2:23-24. [30]1 Cor 3:5. [31]PG 58:670; NPNF 1 10:438.

when the apostle calls himself the teacher of the Gentiles? Or when, as in colloquial speech widely found in the monasteries of Egypt and Palestine, they call each other Father?" Remember this distinction. It is one thing to be a father or a teacher by nature, another to be so by generosity. For when we call a man father and reserve the honor of his age, we may thereby be failing to honor the Author of our own lives. One is rightly called a teacher only from his association with the true Teacher. I repeat: The fact that we have one God and one Son of God through nature does not prevent others from being understood as sons of God by adoption. Similarly this does not make the terms *father* and *teacher* useless or prevent others from being called father. COMMENTARY ON MATTHEW 4.23.10.[32]

23:10 One Master, the Christ

YOU HAVE ONE MASTER. CHRYSOSTOM: Previously when he had asked, "What do you think of the Christ?" it is worth noting that he did not say, "What do you think of me?" So it is here that he says you have one master, and he does not make this subjective by saying "me" but "the Christ."

Yet note that this passage repeatedly speaks of the one master, the one teacher, repeatedly applying the term *one*.[33] Does this term apply to the Father alone so as to reject the only begotten Son? Is the Father guide? All would agree, and none would challenge it. And yet "one," he says, "is your guide, even Christ." For just as Christ, being called the one guide, does not cast out the Father from being guide, even so the Father, being called Master, does not cast out the Son from being Master. For the expression *one* is spoken in contradistinction to the human way of speaking and within the rest of the creation. THE GOSPEL OF MATTHEW, HOMILY 72.3.[34]

23:11 Humbled and Exalted

WHOEVER HUMBLES ONESELF WILL BE

EXALTED. CHRYSOSTOM: For nothing is as crucial as the practice of modesty. This is why he is continually reminding them of this virtue, both when he brought the children into the midst and now. Even when he was preaching on the mount, beginning the Beatitudes, this is where he began. And in this passage he plucks up pride by the roots, saying, "Whoever humbles himself will be exalted."[35]

See how he draws off the hearer right over to the contrary thing. For not only does he forbid him to set his heart upon the first place but also requires him to follow after the last. For so shall you obtain your desire, he says. So one who pursues his own desire for the first must follow after in the last place: "Whoever humbles himself will be exalted."

And where will we find this humility? Go to the city of virtue, to the tents of the holy men, to the mountains, to the groves.[36] There you may see this height of humility.

For these persons, some illustrious from their rank in the world, some having had wealth, in every way put themselves down, by their vesture, by their dwelling, by those to whom they minister. As if they were written characters, they throughout all things are writing the story of humility.[37] THE GOSPEL OF MATTHEW, HOMILY 72.3.[38]

CULTIVATE HUMILITY. CYRIL OF ALEXANDRIA: Since those who have arrived teaching new beliefs for the most part do so from conceit and arrogance, I will say something concerning the

---

[32]CCL 77:213. [33]Chrysostom's entire reasoning is intended to demonstrate that even though Jesus speaks of one master, one father and one guide, he means to combine himself and God the Father together. Jerome makes more or less the same argument in an even more general sense by emphasizing the distinction between the intrinsic and the figurative sense of a name (e.g., only God is the Father in the strict sense of the word, but in the figurative sense there are many fathers). [34]PG 58:670; NPNF 1 10:438. [35]Lk 14:11. [36]To the ascetic life. [37]Chrysostom evidently alludes to persons of high social rank who had renounced all the prerogatives of their rank to become monks. He himself was one of these. [38]PG 58:670-71; NPNF 1 10:438.

value of the teaching. The Lord cuts short this opinion and way as leading to destruction. He says, "You love glory and the places of first importance." Meanwhile he desires the servant's role and cultivates humility. FRAGMENT 255.[39]

ONE WHO EXALTS WILL BE HUMBLED. ORIGEN: I wish everyone might hear this, and most of all deacons, priests and bishops, especially those who think to themselves that these were not the words written: "He who exalts himself will be humbled." On this basis, they then act as if they do not know that he said, "He who has humbled himself will be exalted." They do not hear him who said, "Learn from me; for I am gentle and lowly of heart."[40] They thought themselves to be self-inspired and through this inspiration fell "into the judgment of the devil."[41] They had not thought of critically examining their false humility. They would have done better to have remembered the word of wisdom that says, "The greater you are, the more you must humble yourself, and you will find grace before God."[42] It was the Lord who provided the pattern for this process. No matter how great he was, he humbled himself. For "though he was in the form of God, [he] did not count equality with God a thing to be grasped but emptied himself, taking the form of a servant, being born in the likeness of men. And being found in

human form he humbled himself and became obedient unto death, even death on a cross. Therefore God has highly exalted him and bestowed on him the name which is above every name."[43] COMMENTARY ON MATTHEW 12.[44]

PROTOCOL REVERSED AT THE MESSIANIC WEDDING BANQUET. INCOMPLETE WORK ON MATTHEW: In this wedding feast, which is the calling of God, the Jews maintained that they should be first to recline at the table. Instead, they were humiliated and put in last place, after the Gentiles. The Gentiles, . . . who understood that their invitation was entirely undeserved, were put ahead of the Jews who preceded them to the feast, for what matters is not the priority of the invitation, but the worthiness of the response. The Jews then were invited only to an ordinary meal, but the Gentiles were invited by the Son himself, for whom the feast was held. The Jews were chosen by God on account of their fathers but the Gentiles because of their faith. Christ says elsewhere of the Jews, therefore, "When you are invited to a wedding feast [that is, to the wedding of Christ], do not seek to recline at the head table."[45] HOMILY 43.[46]

---

[39]MKGK 239. [40]Mt 11:29. [41]1 Tim 3:6. [42]Sir 3:18. [43]Phil 2:6-9. [44]GCS 38.2:24. [45]Lk 14:8. [46]PG 56:880.

23:13-28 JESUS CONDEMNS THE LEGALISTS' HYPOCRISY

[13]"But woe to you, scribes and Pharisees, hypocrites! because you shut the kingdom of heaven against men; for you neither enter yourselves, nor allow those who would enter to go in.[v] [15]Woe to you, scribes and Pharisees, hypocrites! for you traverse sea and land to make a single proselyte, and when he becomes a proselyte, you make him twice as much a child of hell[w] as yourselves.

[16]"Woe to you, blind guides, who say, 'If any one swears by the temple, it is nothing; but if any one swears by the gold of the temple, he is bound by his oath.' [17]You blind fools! For which is greater, the gold or the temple that has made the gold sacred? [18]And you say, 'If any one swears by the altar, it is nothing; but if any one swears by the gift that is on the altar, he is bound by his oath.' [19]You blind men! For which is greater, the gift or the altar that makes the gift sacred? [20]So he who swears by the altar, swears by it and by everything on it; [21]and he who swears by the temple, swears by it and by him who dwells in it; [22]and he who swears by heaven, swears by the throne of God and by him who sits upon it.

[23]"Woe to you, scribes and Pharisees, hypocrites! for you tithe mint and dill and cummin, and have neglected the weightier matters of the law, justice and mercy and faith; these you ought to have done, without neglecting the others. [24]You blind guides, straining out a gnat and swallowing a camel!

[25]"Woe to you, scribes and Pharisees, hypocrites! for you cleanse the outside of the cup and of the plate, but inside they are full of extortion and rapacity. [26]You blind Pharisee! first cleanse the inside of the cup and of the plate, that the outside also may be clean.

[27]"Woe to you, scribes and Pharisees, hypocrites! for you are like whitewashed tombs, which outwardly appear beautiful, but within they are full of dead men's bones and all uncleanness. [28]So you also outwardly appear righteous to men, but within you are full of hypocrisy and iniquity.

v Other authorities add here (or after verse 12) verse 14, *Woe to you, scribes and Pharisees, hypocrites! for you devour widows' houses and for a pretense you make long prayers; therefore you will receive the greater condemnation*   w Greek Gehenna

OVERVIEW: The priests and legalists have laid endless toil upon those for whom they should have been responsible (ORIGEN, JEROME). This should have drawn them toward being more empathic with others' burdens. But the things that we acquire easily we care less about. So even their unfair advantages did not render them gentle. They indulged their own bellies not from the houses of the rich but from the poor. Thereby they aggravated the poverty they should have been relieving. They did not merely eat. They "devoured." All this is for the pretense of making long prayers (CHRYSOSTOM). These imposters of holiness more easily entangled themselves with women, especially widows (INCOMPLETE WORK ON MATTHEW). They lost sight of the advent expected by the prophets. They closed the kingdom of heaven not only for themselves but also for others by hiding the truth in their interpretations of the law (HILARY OF POITIERS).

Jesus showed them that it was equally as absurd to swear by heaven as to swear by the temple or by the altar. In this way he admonished the Pharisees for adding further legalistic complications to these traditions. Spiritually understood, the temple is the Scriptures; the altar is the whole heart. One who rightly swears upon the temple swears upon all the Scriptures and upon the altar—that is, upon the whole heart, which is to say upon an understanding of the sense of the whole of the Scriptures and upon the whole heart. It is not possible for the offering of a person to be more honorable than the heart from which the offering is sent up (ORIGEN). What is lost in their legalism is the hidden dimension of the evil will. The hidden things of the mind bring about these distortions of the law (HILARY OF POITIERS). One is hardly ready to appear in the city above if one remains a sepulcher below (CHRYSOSTOM).

Beyond the plain sense of Jesus' words, their spiritual meaning must be sought (ORIGEN, THEODORE OF HERACLEA). The cup of the soul must be cleansed from the inside to the outside (ORIGEN, APOLLINARIS). Righteousness cannot be feigned (ORIGEN). The Lord requires justice (CYRIL OF ALEXANDRIA), not external pretenses (INCOMPLETE WORK ON MATTHEW).

23:13 Shutting the Kingdom of Heaven Against Humanity

CURSES AND BLESSINGS. ORIGEN: There are those who dare to say that God is not good because of the curses in his law that he places against their sin. And yet the one who is truly the Son of God who gave that same law is also the same one who put blessings into the law. The same God who provides blessings for those who are saved in a similar way applies curses which he placed in the law against sinners. "Woe," he says. Woe to you and to those hearing these things who plead the God of the law and yet do not understand that these words were spoken by God in a kindly way. So we understand why Jesus said, "Woe to you, scribes and Pharisees." They believe that it is in fact a good thing to pronounce these curses against sinners. They consider the arrangement of the law's curses to be a part of God's design. The chiding father frequently urges his advice on his son for his improvement—advice that may seem to be a curse. He does not wish the curses to be actualized, however, but rather he desires to avert him from even more such curses. COMMENTARY ON MATTHEW 13.[1]

WOE TO YOU SCRIBES. HILARY OF POITIERS: "Woe" is a voice of sorrowing. For this reason he says that they close the kingdom of heaven, because they hide in the law the consolation of his truth. They lost sight of the advent expected by the prophets. Through deceptive teachings, they do not allow others to go to heaven either.

They do not adorn the way of eternity. ON MATTHEW 24.3.[2]

YOU NEITHER ENTER NOR ALLOW OTHERS. JEROME: The scribes and Pharisees have the knowledge of the prophets and of the law. They know that Christ is the Son of God. They are not ignorant that he was born of the Virgin. Yet they did not seek to serve the people to whom they were accountable. They themselves were not entering the kingdom of heaven, nor did they permit others who were able to do so. Hosea the prophet declares of them, "The priests have stolen the way, they have killed the [people of] Shechem,"[3] and again, "The priests did not ask where the Lord is."[4] Surely every teacher who misleads his students shuts the gate of the kingdom of heaven before them. COMMENTARY ON MATTHEW 4.23.13.[5]

23:14 Receiving Greater Condemnation

CALLED TO ACCOUNT. HILARY OF POITIERS: These are the poisoners of truth. They are reluctant to undertake the salvation of others. They bolt shut the kingdom of heaven. In their ambition they "devour widows' houses and for pretense make long prayers." By this acquaintance with heaven (achieved with those long prayers), they expect they will persevere in the merits of grace quietly, just as a rich person expects to receive the treasure stored up for him. However, they will receive ample judgment and punishment for their particular sins. They will be called to account for their strange and ignorant practices.[6] ON MATTHEW 24.4.[7]

FOR A PRETENSE YOU MAKE LONG PRAYERS. CHRYSTOSOM: After this, he admonishes them for their gluttony. And it is most grievous that they indulged their own bellies not from rich

---

[1]GCS 38.2:24-25. [2]SC 258:166-68. [3]Hos 6:9. [4]Jer 2:8. [5]CCL 77:213. [6]Verse 14 is included only in a marginal note of the RSV, but is included here due to the Fathers' comments on it. [7]SC 258:168.

men's houses but from the poor. Thereby they aggravated the poverty of the poor, which they should have relieved. They did not merely eat. They "devoured."

The manner of their false piety in overreaching was even yet more grievous: "for a pretense you make long prayers."

It is just for anyone who does evil to receive just retribution. But in this case we have one who is using prayers as a cloak for his own wickedness. And he is deriving even the reason for his avarice as godliness. Sure he is justly liable to a far more grievous punishment. So why did God not stop this and depose them? Because the time had not yet come. He leaves them time for repentance for a while. But by his sayings he tries to avert his own disciples being similarly deceived or to be drawn to emulate these men because of the dignity of their positions. Earlier he said, "Observe whatever they tell you but not what they do."[8] For they do many things amiss. THE GOSPEL OF MATTHEW, HOMILY 73.1.[9]

YOU DEVOUR WIDOWS' HOUSES. INCOMPLETE WORK ON MATTHEW: Imposters of holiness more easily entangle themselves around women. Women are less ready to stand up to such imposters in front of them. These manipulators know that they are softer and more guileless.[10] . . . They loiter especially with widowed ladies for two reasons. First, because women with men are less easily deceived, having the mettle of men and being less ready to give anything from her purse. Widows are in a position in which they are more easily deceived. Second, they more easily involve themselves in things not subject to anyone else's authority. So they are taken advantage of. Jesus here confronts the priests and warns Christian leaders against these temptations. They had best not remain with widowed women any more than with others. For even if the desire to remain with widows is not ill motivated, it still may carry the suspicion of being so. HOMILY 44.[11]

23:15 *Making Proselytes*

THE CORRUPTION OF THE LAITY. CHRYSOSTOM: The scribes and Pharisees have laid endless toil upon others. This should draw them toward being more empathic with others' burdens. But the things that we acquire easily we care less about. So even their unfair advantages do not render them more gentle. Here he lays to the charge of the priests two things. First, that they have been unprofitable for the salvation of many. They have forgotten that they need much toil in order to win over even one. And second, that they were remiss in the preservation of those whom they had won. Not only were they careless but traitors. We see this from the wickedness of their lives, corruption and making others worse. When a disciple sees his teacher to be corrupt, he becomes even more so. He does not stop at his teacher's corruption. THE GOSPEL OF MATTHEW, HOMILY 73.1.[12]

YOU TRAVERSE SEA AND LAND. JEROME: The scribes and the Pharisees were reviewing the whole world on account of the business and diverse profits taken by their disciples. These profits were taken under the pretense of sanctity. COMMENTARY ON MATTHEW 4.23.15.[13]

23:16-17 *You Blind Fools!*

WHICH IS GREATER? HILARY OF POITIERS: Jesus reproached those who by their inane observances detracted from the one who rightly should be honored in worship. He himself was the ground and source of the law. The law did not of itself suffice. The ornaments of the altar and temple were not the primary object of worship but were merely pointing the way for the future of true worship. Gold, silver, bronze,

---

[8]Mt 23:3. [9]PG 58:673; NPNF 1 10:440. [10]The author, in line with a trend then much in vogue among pagans and Christians (e.g., Augustine), contends the weakness of the female sex. [11]PG 56:880. [12]PG 58:673; NPNF 1 10:440. [13]CCL 77:214.

brass, pearl and crystal each embrace a particular meaning from their unique natures as metals. Jesus refuted the premise that the gold of the temple or the gifts of the altar could be venerated as if something in themselves rather than the greater one whom they honor. With the coming of Christ the massive structure of legal obligations became futile. Christ was not in the law, but the law was made holy in Christ. He had placed his seat and throne on the law. One who seeks to be religious should anchor himself rightly in the truth. They were stupid and blind who venerated gifts that were sanctified while they allowed sanctity itself to pass by. ON MATTHEW 24.6.[14]

THE GOLD OR THE TEMPLE. THEODORE OF HERACLEA: Jesus is saying that the gold in the temple, the gold objects dedicated in the temple to the glory of God, whether these be the gold cherubim or the gold jar containing the manna, were considered by the Jews to be worthy of much more honor than the temple.[15] Therefore they were condemned by the Lord. . . . But the saying possesses a figurative meaning directed against them because they are not receiving the truth regarding Christ. Instead, they were judging Moses and the types given through him as more valuable than Christ. . . . They were rejecting the Christ who sanctifies Moses while simultaneously praising the law. Just as the law was praiseworthy, not because it possesses the types and the symbols but because it prefigures the true mystery of worship in Christ, in the same way the gold is precious because of the one who sanctifies the temple, and heaven is beautiful because of the God who sanctifies it and dwells within it. FRAGMENT 115.[16]

23:18 Bound by an Oath

THE TEMPLE OF SCRIPTURES AND THE ALTAR OF THE HEART. ORIGEN: Those who work in the fields of the gospel seek the hidden meaning of these passages of Scripture. We are not sim-

ply confiscating the higher parts of Scripture but rather looking toward its whole sense. As regards swearing, it is intended as a binding action, seeking to confirm the word concerning which something is sworn.

Consider this analogy. Think of the altar as the heart and the temple as the whole of Scripture. The temple of God's glory, spiritually understood, is the divinely inspired Scripture. The gold refers to the meanings it conveys. To swear is to witness to the Scriptures, as a validation and confirmation of the word we speak. Therefore we ought to profess the whole sense of Scripture as a confirmation of the sense which we invoke in all of our words.

Gold found outside the temple is not sanctified. Rather, that gold which is found in the temple is the measure of that which is outside it. Similarly the meaning which is found outside of the Scriptures is not holy, but it is contained in the meaning of the Scriptures. Only that sense of Scripture is sanctified which can be seen from within the temple itself, that is, within the whole of Scripture. The temple, that is, the reading of the Scriptures, makes a great and venerable sense, just as consecrated gold is valuable. So we ought not to swear by our own intellects to confirm our beliefs, as if we were creating witnesses that could judge according to the truth. But let us explore further the analogy of the temple, the gold and the altar. The altar is the place where a vow is sanctified. The altar in this passage is the heart of a man. What happens in the heart happens deeply within a person. Vows and gifts placed on the altar are clearly those placed upon the human heart. When you begin to pray, you place the vow of your prayer upon your heart, as if you had placed something upon the altar, so that you might offer your prayer to God.

---

[14]SC 258:170. [15]Jesus' words against swearing by the gold in the temple are also considered by Apollinaris as indicative of the end of temple worship (p. 64 n. 2), since with the coming of Christ it had exhausted its function as his symbolic preannouncement. [16]MKGK 89.

Suppose you are ready to place an offering of psalms upon your heart, so as to offer to God an offering of psalms, accompanying yourself with a harp. Or suppose you are ready to give alms. You make an offering of alms upon your heart, just as if you had placed something on the altar, as you would offer your alms to God. Suppose you have proposed to fast in order to make an offering of your fasting upon your heart, as if you had placed something upon the altar.

In this way the heart of a man makes vows in a holy and venerable way. It is from the heart, that is, the altar, that the vow is offered to God. Therefore it is not possible for the offering of a man to be more honorable than his heart from which the offering is sent up. COMMENTARY ON MATTHEW 18.[17]

23:19 Which Is Greater?

SWEARING BY THE WHOLE SENSE OF SCRIPTURE. ORIGEN: Anyone who thinks that his own almsgiving, his own fasting, his own psalms and prayers are in themselves great and who, without good judgment, blesses them and does not reflect that it is just from such a heart that his almsgiving or psalms or prayers or fasting are offered—such a man is blind. For indeed his heart is the altar that sanctifies his offering which is the heart of the world. The heart and the conscience of such a man "do not feel remorse but have trust in God,"[18] because his own heart has been rightly formed. He does not rely on his gifts as such or the words of his prayers or of his psalms—although they may seem well composed and chosen from the Scriptures—but on the heart rightly formed. Whoever places his own witness on the altar, that is, his own conscience and the center of his heart, such a man swears by the altar, embracing everything which is contained in it. One who swears according to what we attest to by the temple, that is, "through the whole sense of Scriptures," such a man seems to swear according to the word and the will of God which is contained in

it. Such a man in this sense swears upon the temple (upon all the Scriptures) and upon the altar (upon the whole heart), that is, an understanding of the sense of the whole of the Scriptures and upon the whole heart. The temple is the glory of God, which "we see as in a mirror darkly."[19] The heavens, however, are above the temple of God, in which sits the throne of God, on which we may look "with our face uncovered"[20] when he comes. COMMENTARY ON MATTHEW 18.[21]

23:20 Swearing by the Altar

THE TRADITION OF OATH TAKING. ORIGEN: One of the Pharisaical traditions regarded oath taking. Some were swearing by the temple, others by the gold of the temple; some by the altar, others by the gifts of the altar. The Pharisees were teaching that one who swore by the gold of the altar or by the gift of the altar was obligated, whereas one who swore by the temple or by the altar was not under obligation. Our Savior spoke against these traditions. He wished to call them back from human traditions to divine revelation. Those who hand on such traditions are blind and foolish. They do not see that what is placed in the temple is not sanctified through itself but through the Lord of the temple. That which is placed on the altar is judged already as a gift of God, which is why it is placed on the altar. It seems foolish to argue that one who swears in one way is bound and one who swears in another way is not bound. This assumes that what is sanctified is above the one who sanctifies. It seems foolish to argue that one who swears by heaven is less vulnerable than one who swears by God himself. Jesus showed them that it was equally as absurd to swear by heaven as to swear by the temple or by the altar. It is irrational to assume that one avoids punishment because he is not swearing by God but by the

---

[17]GCS 38.2:33. [18]1 Jn 3:21. [19]1 Cor 13:12. [20]2 Cor 3:16. [21]GCS 38.2:33-34.

throne of God. Thus he spoke to the Jews prohibiting them to follow the Pharisaic tradition. Moreover, he clearly rejected the whole business of swearing at all, as if it were a superior way. COMMENTARY ON MATTHEW 17.[22]

23:21-24 Neglecting Weighty Matters

YOU TITHE MINT, DILL AND CUMMIN. ORIGEN: Not only among the Jews but among ourselves as well, we find people sinning in these ways. They are swallowing camels. People of this type frequently show off their religion even in the smallest of things. They are rightly called hypocrites for wanting to exploit their religiosity before men but being unwilling to undertake that very faith which God himself has justified. Therefore the imitators of the scribes and Pharisees must be dislodged and sent away from us, lest a woe touches us in the same way it touches them. The scribes could be described as those who valued nothing found in the Scriptures except its plain sense interpreted legalistically. Meanwhile they condemn those who look into the very depths of God himself. Mint and dill and cummin are only spices for food but are not themselves substantial food. What substantive food would mean in conversion would be that which is necessary for the justification of our souls—faith and love—unlike these legalisms, which are more like condiments and flavorings. It is as if a meal might be thought to consist more of condiments and flavorings than the food itself. The seriousness of judgment is neglected while great attention is given to minor matters. Spiritual exercises which in and of themselves are hardly justice are spoken of as justice and compassion and faith. It is lacking in justice to treat these small parts as the whole. When we do not offer to God the observance of all that is necessary for worship, we fail altogether. COMMENTARY ON MATTHEW 19-20.[23]

WHAT THE LORD REQUIRES. CYRIL OF ALEXANDRIA: "O Pharisees, you demand," Jesus says, "perhaps the tithes of herbs and the smallest coins while you neglect the commandments, concerning which the violation is greater." And what kind of commandments are these? Justice, that is, to judge uprightly and blamelessly; mercy, that is, genuineness toward God. For justice and mercy and faith toward God are better than the tithe and firstfruits. Therefore the God of all things says through the prophet, "And now, Israel, what does the Lord require from you but to do justice and to love and seek mercy and to be prepared to follow the Lord your God."[24] For the genuine faith of those being saved is seen in their exceeding readiness to follow. FRAGMENT 258.[25]

YOU NEGLECT WEIGHTIER MATTERS OF THE LAW. HILARY OF POITIERS: What is lost is the hidden dimension of the evil will. These hidden things of the mind bring about these distortions of the law. The law prescribes that a tenth be given, so they measure out a tenth of a measure of mint and dill but only in order that they might be thought by other men to fulfill the law. They abandon mercy and justice, faith and every form of benevolence. Yet these are the true duties of man. . . . God laughs at the superficial diligence of those who measure cucumbers. God laughs at our attempts to swallow camels, as if the sins of avoidance were less serious than the sins of consumption. ON MATTHEW 24.7.[26]

23:25-26 Inner and Outer Cleansing

CONGRUENCE OF INNER AND OUTER LIFE. ORIGEN: This passage teaches us that we should hasten to be righteous, not merely to appear so. Whoever strives only to appear righteous will cleanse his exterior and will take great care of what can be seen by others but will neglect his heart and his conscience. He fails to realize that the one who is eager to purify his interior life and his thoughts will also naturally want to give

---

[22]GCS 38.2:31-32. [23]GCS 38.2:35-36. [24]Mic 6:8. [25]*MKGK* 240. [26]SC 258:170-72.

a healthy outward appearance as well. Whoever works hard on the externals but neglects his interior life, however, will inevitably be filled with avarice, lust, malice, and many other kinds of evil. For the one who is solicitous of his own interior salvation also takes care of his external, public reputation. But not everyone who cares first about his public reputation is also solicitous of his interior salvation. In this connection, it is written that "whoever sees a woman and lusts after her has committed adultery with her in his heart."[27] He who refrains from acts of fornication, therefore, but commits fornication by lusting in his heart is like the one who cleanses the outside of the cup and plate while the inside is left full of intemperance. Whoever performs acts of mercy for the purpose of earning human respect, doing his good deeds "to be seen by men," also seems to cleanse only the exterior of the cup and plate but is full of intemperance and lust for vainglory within. COMMENTARY ON MATTHEW 21.[28]

CLEAN INSIDE THE CUP. APOLLINARIS: The law of Moses taught through the use of symbols how to maintain purity throughout life's activities. It was the custom of the Jews, passed on to them from their ancient traditions, to wash carefully their cups and the dish that contained their food. They observed these practices to maintain their purity and to avoid contact with "sinful people." Their aim was that they might flee from fellowship with sinners. . . . How much more through such practices were they preparing themselves to flee from sin itself. And yet those who were carefully observing these practices were themselves acting like robbers and violently making a profit, becoming loathsome by doing so. Therefore Jesus says this: "Flee unrighteousness, O blind Pharisee. For you fail to perceive how you are acting. For what is in the cup and dish are clean if they are not gained in an unrighteous manner. Righteousness cleanses the vessel much better than water." FRAGMENT 117.[29]

THE INWARD AND OUTWARD CUP. ORIGEN: If it is proper to regard everything in the gospel according to the moral sense . . . we can say that it is a sort of spiritual food and spiritual drink that we receive when we read the law and the prophets in Scripture. Indeed, the language through which we take our spiritual drink and the biblical narratives on which we are nourished are the plates and cups for our food and drink. This is why we are warned not to take as much care for their outside as we do for their inside, so that our hearts might be filled with pure understanding, not merely adorned with fine rhetoric and grammar. For "the Kingdom of God does not consist in words but in power."[30] Whoever strives harder to dress his speech in elegant composition than to fill it with saving doctrine has cleaned only the outside, but the inside remains stained with vanity. . . .

We can also say that the very words of the law and the prophets are the cups of spiritual drink for souls and that the plates or bowls of nourishing food for the faithful are their wise authors. The scribes and Pharisees work diligently at discerning only the external, literal meaning of these prophetic cups and plates and bowls, eager to demonstrate that the vessels themselves are pure and holy. The disciples of Christ . . . hasten to purify and sanctify the interior, spiritual meaning by means of knowledge and credible explanations, so that they might eat and drink the law and the prophets whose inside has been purified, desiring as they do to hear and understand the interior, mystical meaning and to go beyond the literal sense of the words. COMMENTARY ON MATTHEW 22-23.[31]

23:27 Whitewashed Tombs

FULL OF DEAD PEOPLE'S BONES. INCOMPLETE WORK ON MATTHEW: The bodies of the just are rightly called temples because their souls reign

---

[27]Mt 5:28. [28]GCS 38.2:37. [29]MKGK 40. [30]1 Cor 4:20. [31]GCS 38.2:38-39.

supreme within them, like God in his temple, or at least because God himself dwells in the bodies of the just. The bodies of sinners, however, are called sepulchers of the dead because their souls are dead within them. For whatever does nothing of a living or spiritual nature with the body is not to be considered truly alive. At the very least, sinners are dead because death itself dwells in their bodies. As long as a sepulcher is closed, it can have a beautiful outward appearance, but if it is opened, it looks horrifying. The case of hypocrites is similar; as long as they are not recognized for who they really are, they can be praiseworthy, but when they are found out, they appear disgusting. Tell me, hypocrite, if it is so good to be good, why do you not strive to be truly what you only appear to be? And if it is so bad to be evil, then why do you allow yourself to be in truth what you would never want to appear to be? What appears to be ugly is even uglier in truth, but what is beautiful in appearance is much more beautiful in reality. Therefore either be what you appear to be or appear to be what you are. Homily 45.[32]

23:28 Full of Hypocrisy and Iniquity

WASH THE CONSCIENCE. INCOMPLETE WORK ON MATTHEW: How men can be compared with a cup and a plate is made clear when Christ adds, "for you are full of robbery and iniquity within." The Jews washed themselves, their clothing and their utensils as often as they entered the temple or offered sacrifices on solemnities, but they never washed themselves from sin. God neither praised cleanliness of the body nor condemned bodily filth. Nevertheless imagine for the moment that God hates filth of the body, of vessels and other such things. If he were to hate the defilement of things like this, which necessarily get soiled during their ordinary use, how much more would he abhor the defilement of the human conscience, which it is possible for us to keep clean continually? It is not the vessels that need washing with water but the conscience that needs washing with prayer.

"O blind Pharisees, first wash the inside of the cup and plate, that the outside might be made clean also." No one notices if the bowl has been cleaned on the inside, but only if it is dirty on the outside does it get washed. A man . . . can never touch a drop of water and yet be perfectly clean before God if he has not been defiled by interior sin. If he were to commit a sin, however, he would be black with filth before God, even though he washes himself in the open sea and in every river of the world. Homily 44.[33]

FEIGNING RIGHTEOUSNESS. ORIGEN: As the scribes and Pharisees were previously called "full of robbery and intemperance,"[34] likewise here they are said to be "full of hypocrisy and iniquity" and are compared with "the bones of the dead and all uncleanness." Hypocrisy, because it is a counterfeit of the good, possesses nothing vital of the good it simulates, but is only its dead bones, so to speak. . . . If we listen with wisdom to what the present passage wants to tell us, we will understand that every simulated righteousness is a dead righteousness, hence no righteousness at all. Just as a dead man can still have the appearance of a man, even though he is in fact no longer a man, so also a dead chastity is no chastity. For any virtue is dead when it is not practiced for God but feigned on account of men. He who feigns righteousness can give the appearance of being righteous even though what he has is not righteousness at all but only a figment of righteousness, much like impersonators who can take on the appearance of another individual without thereby actually becoming the other person. The same is true concerning chastity. Because of this, men who do such things are appropriately compared with "whitewashed tombs which look beautiful from the outside," for they give every external appearance of righteousness, even though they are full of "the

---

[32]PG 56:885. [33]PG 56:885. [34]Mt 23:25.

bones of the dead" within. COMMENTARY ON MATTHEW 24.[35]

LIKE WHITEWASHED TOMBS. CHRYSTOSOM: You have been counted worthy to become temples of God. But you have instead suddenly become more like sepulchers, having the same sort of smell. This is dreadful. It is extreme wretchedness that one in whom Christ dwells and in whom the Holy Spirit has worked such great works should turn out to be a sepulcher, a place for death. What wretchedness is this? What mourning and lamentation does this call for! The members of the body of Christ have become a tomb of uncleanness? Remember your sonship and how you were born. Consider of what things you have been counted worthy. Recall what sort of garment you received in bap-

tism. You were intended to be a temple without fault, beautiful, not adorned with gold or pearls but with the spirit that is more precious than these. You are hardly ready to appear in the city above if you remain a sepulcher below. For if here this is forbidden, much more there. Even here you are an object of scorn. You carry around a dead soul. You are shunned. Be honest. If anyone were to go around carrying about a dead body, wouldn't everyone else rush for cover! Wouldn't they all flee? But this is what you are like. You go about carrying a corpse far more grievous than this. It is a soul deadened by sins, a soul paralyzed. THE GOSPEL OF MATTHEW, HOMILY 73.3.[36]

---

[35]GCS 38.2:39-40. [36]PG 58:676; NPNF 1 10:442.

23:29-36 JESUS PREDICTS THEIR PUNISHMENT

[29]"Woe to you, scribes and Pharisees, hypocrites! for you build the tombs of the prophets and adorn the monuments of the righteous, [30]saying, 'If we had lived in the days of our fathers, we would not have taken part with them in shedding the blood of the prophets.' [31]Thus you witness against yourselves, that you are sons of those who murdered the prophets. [32]Fill up, then, the measure of your fathers. [33]You serpents, you brood of vipers, how are you to escape being sentenced to hell?[w] [34]Therefore I send you prophets and wise men and scribes, some of whom you will kill and crucify, and some you will scourge in your synagogues and persecute from town to town, [35]that upon you may come all the righteous blood shed on earth, from the blood of innocent Abel to the blood of Zechariah the son of Barachiah, whom you murdered between the sanctuary and the altar. [36]Truly, I say to you, all this will come upon this generation.

w Greek Gehenna

OVERVIEW: Jesus pronounces woe upon the scribes and Pharisees because while pretending to condemn those who killed the prophets, they do worse. Yet in no way did this cause them to be corrected. To build the tombs of the prophets

means to interpret prophetic writings only according to the "bodily" (i.e., literal and historical) sense, disregarding the spiritual meaning. Such were the Pharisees who used to kill the prophetic message by separating its body from soul and spirit (ORIGEN). While condemning their ancestors who murdered the prophets, they committed worse crimes, murdering Jesus and the apostles. Fruition of the crime by these last murderers guaranteed them divine punishment for the crimes of all their generation (CYRIL OF ALEXANDRIA). They built the tombs of the prophets to gain human respect, not for the glory of God. Thus they tried to make God their accomplice. As serpents are the cleverest animals, so the hypocrites are the smartest of human beings, yet also the most harmful ones (INCOMPLETE WORK ON MATTHEW). There are different hypotheses on the identity of Zechariah from Matthew 23:35 (JEROME).

23:29 Adorning the Monuments of the Righteous

YOU BUILD TOMBS FOR THE PROPHETS. CHRYSOSTOM: Jesus did not pronounce woe upon them because they blamed others or because they build monuments. Rather, he pronounces woe because while pretending to condemn those who killed the prophets, they do worse. They witness against themselves. As for evidence that their adorning of monuments is a pretense, Luke says, "Woe to you! For you build the tombs of the prophets whom your fathers killed. So you are witnesses and consent to the deeds of your fathers; for they killed them, and you build their tombs."[1] Their purpose was not to honor those that were slain but to make a show of the murders. They are afraid lest, when the tombs had perished by time, the proof of their daring should fade away. They set up these buildings as a kind of trophy, priding themselves in the daring deeds of those men and displaying them. This is what is reproved by the Lord. THE GOSPEL OF MATTHEW, HOMILY 74.1.[2]

23:30 We Would Not Have Shed the Prophets' Blood

WHO SHED THE BLOOD OF THE PROPHETS.

ORIGEN: Once the prophets had departed this life, their bodies were in the tomb but their souls and spirits were in the "realm of the living." Accordingly, the historical narrative of the prophetic writings is to be regarded as the body but their spiritual meaning and the inner truth as the soul and spirit which inhabits history. It is not improper then for us to consider the "tombs of the prophets" to be the letters on the pages of their books, in which the narrative lays as though it were a body placed in a tomb. Those persons therefore who receive and understand the spiritual meaning of the prophetic writings and the truth hidden within them have the soul and spirit of the prophets and are themselves made into a sort of realm of the living prophets. . . . Those who neither seek nor accept the spiritual meaning but attend only to the simple, historical narrative study the bodies of the prophets in the letters and pages of the books, as though in so many tombs. Such persons were the Pharisees, who were rightly called Pharisees (that is, the "separated") because they separated the spiritual meaning of the prophets from their bodily history, as though expelling the prophets' souls from their bodies, killing them and rendering them devoid of soul and spirit. It was also right for the Pharisees to be called "hypocrites," because they built and adorned only the tombs of the prophets which contained their bodily history, which is to say that they studied only the letter of their writings and books. They did not understand that those who study dead bodies (the historical narrative) may seem to act with reverence toward the memory of the prophets but are in fact being most irreverent. Their attempts to defend themselves against the charge of being associated with "those who killed the prophets" and to prove themselves innocent only add to the crimes of "those who killed the prophets," thereby filling up the "measure" of the iniquity of their fathers by not believing in Christ, whom the prophets pro-

---

[1]Lk 11:47-48. [2]PG 58:679; NPNF 1 10:445.

claimed not through the historical sense of their writings but through the spiritual sense. COMMENTARY ON MATTHEW 27.[3]

SONS OF THOSE WHO MURDERED THE PROPHETS: CHRYSOSTOM: And you yourselves continue to do these things in this spirit. Though you may speak to the contrary, you still do them. You say, "If we had lived in the days of our fathers we would not have taken part with them in shedding the blood of the prophets." Yet your own disposition is evident. Even as you are unfolding your intention, you are already expressing it, however disguised. So Jesus adds, "Thus you witness against yourselves, that you are the sons of those who murdered the prophets." If you are the son of a murderer but do not partake of the mind of your father, you yourself are not to blame. But if you do so partake, you have an affinity with his wickedness. THE GOSPEL OF MATTHEW, HOMILY 74.1.[4]

23:31 You Witness Against Yourselves

THE SAME KINDS OF EVIL. CYRIL OF ALEXANDRIA: We will carefully investigate what the Savior says. The forefathers of the Jews killed the holy prophets who were transmitting the divine word to them in those times. They surely have become witnesses for some of them, because the prophets are now revered and honored. They have placed crowns on their heads or assign . . . honor to their tombs as to holy things, for believing the prophets to be holy men, they have become the judges of those who have killed them. For by honoring them in this way, they have spoken against those who killed them, and through these things they accuse them of having acted wickedly. But though they agreed to condemn the murders committed by their own forefathers, they were about to become threshing floors for the same kind of evils, indeed, to things even worse. They "killed the author of life"[5] and added to their impieties against him other murders, those of his holy apostles. For

while one scrutinizes the sins of others, making a decision according to one's innate reason, one sees the wickedness and censures it. . . . He who is led into similar passions is like a blind man carried away. FRAGMENT 260.[6]

THOSE WHO MURDERED THE PROPHETS. HILARY OF POITIERS: The form of judgment is perfect; the understanding and idea of equity are instilled in each of us by nature so that the more fully the ideal of equity is known, the less need there is for the forgiveness of iniquity. The people of the law killed all the prophets. They had become inflamed with hatred toward them because of the harshness of their reproaches, since the prophets had publicly called them thieves, murderers, adulterers and sacrilegious. Moreover, because they had denounced the Jews as unworthy of the kingdom of heaven and because they taught that the Gentiles would be the heirs of the covenant of God, they afflicted the prophets with a variety of other punishments. The descendants, however, repudiated the deeds of their fathers, honoring the prophets' books, decorating their tombs, restoring their sepulchers and attesting by these forms of respect that they were not culpable of the crimes of their fathers. ON MATTHEW 24.8.[7]

23:32 Fill the Measure of Your Ancestors

JUST PIETY. INCOMPLETE WORK ON MATTHEW: Every good deed that is done for God is universally good for everything and everyone. Deeds that are not seen to benefit everything and everyone, however, are done on account of man, as the present matter itself demonstrates. For example, those who build reliquaries and adorn churches seem to be doing good. If they imitate the justice of God, if the poor benefit from their goods and if they do not acquire their goods through violence against others, it is clear that they are building for

---

[3]GCS 38.2:45-46. [4]PG 58:679; NPNF 1 10:445. [5]Acts 3:15. [6]MKGK 241. [7]SC 258:174.

the glory of God. If they fail to observe God's justice, ... and if the poor never benefit from their goods and if they acquire their goods from others by means of violence or fraud, who is so foolish not to understand that they are building for human respect rather than for the glory of God? Those who build reliquaries in a just manner ensure that the poor do not suffer as a result of it. For the martyrs do not rejoice when they are honored by gifts for which the poor paid with their tears. What kind of justice is it to give gifts to the dead and to despoil the living or to drain blood from the poor and offer it to God? To do such things is not to offer sacrifice to God but to attempt to make God an accomplice in violence, since whoever knowingly accepts a gift which was acquired by sinful means participates in the sin. HOMILY 45.[8]

23:33 You Serpents

YOU BROOD OF VIPERS. INCOMPLETE WORK ON MATTHEW: Serpents are the most clever of all the animals, but they use it for evil, not for good, since they are forever scheming to bite something, and, once they've attacked, to conceal themselves. Similarly hypocrites are the cleverest of all people, for while appearing to live innocent lives, they are always planning how to injure their neighbor and then to continue along their way as though they had done no harm to anyone. HOMILY 45.[9]

RESPONSIBILITY FOR MURDER. CYRIL OF ALEXANDRIA: The punishment of all the murders committed in the past will fall on the last generation of murderers according to a certain pattern, although God speaking through the prophet does say that "the fathers will not die for the sins of the children"[10] ... and indeed, "each will die for his own sin."[11] What then should we think about this?[12] How can a later generation be punished for the murders committed by others, concerning whom Christ says these things? Won't Cain be punished for the murder of Abel? ... How is it that these poor souls will be subjected to the punishment due to all these people? For God is not unjust but is the righteous judge, powerful and patient, according to the testimony of the Scripture. Therefore we think there is a certain intention contained within the things that have been spoken that applies to the present case and helps us to fit one thing to another. Let it be taken for granted then that this may be so in the present case. Let us say that they have become robbers in that land. These men were plundering the surrounding villages and killing their inhabitants. But the prince of the realm did not immediately strip them of the ruler's sword. Rather, he was eager to teach them differently through the use of threats. ... But I suppose someone of the last who have been cruelly punished will say that they have received the penalty due to all. ... You will also understand something such as this concerning God. For God was extremely patient in the preceding times until he deemed it necessary to set a boundary on his longsuffering. For it was also necessary that the divine anger fall upon these. On the one hand, they continued to sin against people and their fellow servants. On the other hand, they killed the Lord of all. Not that it is for this reason that he harshly punished the last ones but that it is astonishing that he has borne patiently with them to the present time. FRAGMENT 261.[13]

HOW ARE YOU TO ESCAPE? INCOMPLETE WORK ON MATTHEW: "How will you avoid being sentenced to Gehenna?" They build churches but do not hold the true faith of the churches they build. They read the Scriptures

---

[8]PG 56:885-86. [9]PG 56:889. [10]Deut 24:16. [11]2 Kings 14:6; cf. Jer 31:30; Ezek 18:20. [12]Cyril's explanation aims to harmonize the words of Jesus, which would seem to find the Pharisees of his time also responsible for the crimes of their predecessors, with the numerous scriptural claims that everyone is responsible for their own crimes alone. In agreement with the context, he has no difficulty in demonstrating that the Pharisees of Jesus' time were no less guilty than their predecessors. [13]MKGK 241-42.

but do not believe them. They call upon the prophets, apostles and martyrs but neither imitate their works nor profess their faith. Have you not heard him who said, "It is not those who say to me 'Lord, Lord' who will enter into the kingdom of heaven but those who do the will of my Father"?[14] Just as not all who call upon the Lord are of the Lord but only those who do his will, neither does everyone who extols the apostles, prophets and martyrs thereby venerate them, but only those who imitate their works and hold their faith. HOMILY 45.[15]

23:34 Sending Prophets, Wise Men and Scribes

TONGUES LIKE WHIPS. ORIGEN: The unfruitful scribes of the law are different from the scribes who were sent by Christ on account of the gospel, in whose work the spirit vivifies but the letter does not kill, as does the letter of the law. Those who follow the letter of the law incur faithlessness and vain superstitions. Those who follow the letter of the gospel (i.e., its simple narrative), however, are saved. For the literal story of the gospel itself is sufficient for the salvation of the more simple among us. And if you see scribes of the law and Pharisees acting not only against "wise men" of the gospel and "prophets" of Christ but also against the "scribes" of the new covenant, you will see how (insofar as they are able) they kill the prophets of Christ and crucify the scribes and scourge them with slanderous speech in their synagogues. It is common to hear how the sects, the so-called spiritual men of the Pharisees, use their tongues like whips to scourge Christians with curses and to pursue them "from town to town," sometimes bodily, sometimes spiritually, wanting to expel them from their own town, which is the law and prophets and the gospel and the apostles, and to drive them by deceitful means into another, foreign town, which is another gospel. COMMENTARY ON MATTHEW 27.[16]

23:35 Righteous Blood

THE BLOOD OF ZECHARIAH. JEROME: Because we read about so many Zechariahs in Scripture, we need to inquire into the identity of this particular Zechariah, the son of Barachiah. Lest we mistake him for another, the Gospel specifies "whom you killed between the sanctuary and the altar." Yet there remains a variety of diverse opinions on this question, each of which ought to be considered.[17] Some say that this Zechariah the son of Barachiah is the eleventh of the twelve minor prophets. Although their fathers share the same name, however, they cannot be the same persons because the prophet Zechariah was never said to have been killed between the sanctuary and the altar and especially because the temple had just recently been destroyed in the prophet's time. Others want us to believe that this Zechariah is the father of John the Baptist, killed because he proclaimed the advent of the Savior on the basis of something he had dreamed. Because this theory doesn't have the authority of Scripture, however, it can be disproven as easily as it can be proven. Still others maintain that this is the Zechariah who was killed between the sanctuary and the altar by Joash the king of Judah, as is chronicled in the book of Kings.[18] But that Zechariah was the son of Jehoida the priest, not Barachiah, as the Scripture relates: "Joash did not remember the good which Jehoida, Zechariah's father, had done for him."[19] COMMENTARY ON MATTHEW 4.23.35.[20]

23:36 It Will Come on This Generation

COMMITTING GRIEVOUS ACTS. CHRYSOSTOM: Mark how well he has forewarned them. Even after he has pointed out their hypocrisy, they

---

[14]Mt 7:21. [15]PG 56:890. [16]GCS 38.2:47-48. [17]The difficulty here brought to light by Jerome intrigues modern scholars as well, because from the Old Testament it cannot be deduced with precision who this "Zechariah son of Barachia" actually was. [18]2 Chron 24:20-22. [19]2 Chron 24:22. [20]CCL 77:219-20.

claim that they would not have shed the blood of the prophets. Jesus shamed them thoroughly, saying, "While you condemn them, you do things worse. These things shall not be without punishment." He thus implants in them fear beyond words. He reminds them of hell. Then because that was to come, he brought home to them the terrors as even present. "Truly I say to you, all this will come upon this generation." He added also unspeakable severity to the vengeance, saying that they shall suffer more griev-

ous things than all these. Yet in no way did this cause them to be corrected. But if anyone ask why they will suffer more grievously than all, we would say, Because they have first committed more grievous things than all, and by none of the things that have been done to correct them have they been brought to a sound mind. THE GOSPEL OF MATTHEW, HOMILY 74.2.[21]

---

[21]PG 58:681; NPNF 1 10:446.

23:37-39 JESUS' LOVE FOR JERUSALEM

[37]"O Jerusalem, Jerusalem, killing the prophets and stoning those who are sent to you! How often would I have gathered your children together as a hen gathers her brood under her wings, and you would not! [38]Behold, your house is forsaken and desolate.[x] [39]For I tell you, you will not see me again, until you say, 'Blessed is he who comes in the name of the Lord.' "

x Other ancient authorities omit *and desolate*

OVERVIEW: O Jerusalem, Jerusalem! This is the exclamation of one who at the same time pities, bemoans and greatly loves his beloved. It is like a woman who is much beloved yet who has despised the one who loved her. Now on the point of her punishment, just as the punishment is about to be inflicted, he pleads for her. With what warmth is his affection expressed, as a mother for her brood. This is the language of one who loves earnestly. Jesus is poignantly appealing to the city in relation to the judgment that is to come. He is not merely warning them concerning their past follies. He is now speaking of the future day of his second coming (CHRYSOSTOM). Foreseeing the tribulations and bloodshed to come, he grieves not so much for the saints to be murdered, since he knew the glory prepared for them after death, but for those who were to receive evil in this life and even worse in

the life to come (INCOMPLETE WORK ON MATTHEW). The whole economy of salvation was focused on gathering his people into one, under his protection, symbolized by the wings. Yet they could not bear to remain under his protection and scattered themselves instead (APOLLINARIS). It is only Christ, the Son of the Father, who can come "in the name of the Lord" (CYRIL OF ALEXANDRIA).

23:37 As a Hen Gathers Her Brood

O JERUSALEM, JERUSALEM. CHRYSOSTOM: Then he directs his speech at the city, yet with the intention of correcting his hearers. He says, "O Jerusalem, Jerusalem!" Why the repetition? This is the speech of one who at the same time pities, bemoans and greatly loves this city. The emotive quality is like a woman who is much beloved and forever loved, yet who had despised the one who loved her. Now on the point of her punishment, just as the punishment is about to be inflicted, he pleads for her. The prophets also had similar words when they said, "Turn to me, and she did not return."[1]

Then having called her, he tells also her bloodstained deeds, she who has been "killing the prophets and stoning those who are sent to you! How often would I have gathered your children together as a hen gathers her brood under her wings, but you would not!" In this way Jesus is also pleading his own case. But even with all this you have turned me aside. Yet I have not withdrawn my great affection toward you. It was my desire often to draw you to myself, but you would not.

Jerusalem is defeating itself by its sins. Yet what affection remains. With what warmth is his affection expressed, as a mother for her brood. Everywhere in the prophets is this same image of the wings, both in the song of Moses[2] and in the Psalms,[3] indicating his great protection and care.

"But you would not," he says, so "behold, your house is forsaken and desolate," stripped of the protection which comes from me.

It surely was this same one who had been protecting the city, and holding it together and preserving it, who had found it necessary to chasten his beloved. So now a punishment is appointed, one that brings exceeding dread and implies the entire overthrow of the city. THE GOSPEL OF MATTHEW, HOMILY 74.3.[4]

FOR WHOM WAS THE LORD GRIEVING?

INCOMPLETE WORK ON MATTHEW: The whole future is before the gaze of the Lord, for he foresaw the fall of Jerusalem and the wound which was to be inflicted upon its people by the Roman Empire. It was on account of these things that he raised his mournful lamentation, crying, "Jerusalem, Jerusalem." He was thinking of the blood that flowed from the bodies of his saints, soon to be shed yet again. Nevertheless the Lord

was not grieving over the suffering sustained by these holy ones, for he knew what kind of glory he had prepared for them after death. Instead, he was mourning the destruction of those who were to receive evil in this life and even worse in the life to come. HOMILY 46.[5]

ARDENT CARE FOR HER BROOD. APOLLI-

NARIS: He was soon to rain calamitous blows on Jerusalem because of its bloodthirsty nature. For that very reason Jesus accuses it of possessing a murderous disposition. For he says it kills the prophets and stones the ones sent to it. So often [the city] could have obtained mercy, but it does not desire it. How many times he demonstrated this, on many occasions and to many descendants, as when he brought back the people from captivity. But through their sins they continually scattered themselves. By speaking of wings and shelter Jesus teaches in a way appropriate for God and illustrates the meaning of Moses' words through a human comparison. "He spread his wings and welcomed them."[6] And David: "But the children of men take refuge in the shadow of your wings."[7] For when Satan scattered them on one side into idolatry and on the other into a love for pleasure, he sent prophets to them. Then through himself he came that he might gather them together "into one." But they could not bear to remain under his protection. "For I," he says, "like a loving hen always held you to draw you to myself, but you had no desire for this. You scattered yourself through your constant sinning and drew away from God." But this is a prolific hen who has many children. She ardently loves and cares for her children and willingly gives herself for them. FRAGMENT 121.[8]

23:38-39 A Forsaken and Desolate House

YOU WILL NOT SEE ME AGAIN. CHRYSOSTOM:
"For I tell you, you will not see me again, until

---

[1]Jer 3:7. [2]Deut 32:11. [3]E.g., Ps 91:4. [4]PG 58:682; NPNF 1 10:447. [5]PG 56:894. [6]Deut 32:11. [7]Ps 36:7 (35:8 LXX). [8]MKGK 241.

you say, 'Blessed is he who comes in the name of the Lord.'" This is the language of one that loves earnestly. He is poignantly appealing to them in relation to the judgment that is to come. He is not merely warning them concerning their past follies. He is now speaking of the future day of his second coming.

So did this occur? Did they not see him from that time? He was speaking of the time up to his crucifixion.

They had been continually accusing him of being a foe to God. He can do nothing now but show them who he is, as Son of the Father, in full accord with the Father's will. He indicates himself to be the very one expected by the prophets. This is why he uses the same words as did the prophets. In this way he intimated both his resurrection and his second coming. He made all this plain even to the utterly unbelieving but even more surely to all who would worship him. THE GOSPEL OF MATTHEW, HOMILY 74.3.[9]

THE VISION OF FAITH. CYRIL OF ALEXANDRIA: That which has been spoken possesses an interpretation that comes through the vision of faith. For when "the fullness of the nations come in"[10] and they believe in Christ, then the Jews who believe after these things see the beauty of the divine nature of Christ. They behold the Father in the Son and declare him to be the Redeemer proclaimed through the prophets, whom the prophets previously mentioned as coming in the name of the Lord. For the other prophets did not come in the name of the Lord. For they were saying, "The Lord says these things"[11] and "I am the servant of the Lord, and I worship the God of heaven."[12] FRAGMENT 264.[13]

---

[9]PG 58:683; NPNF 1 10:447-48. [10]Rom 11:25. [11]Jer 14:15. [12]Jon 1:9. [13]MKGK 243.

24:1-14 JESUS SPEAKS OF THE DESTRUCTION OF THE TEMPLE, OF TROUBLES AND PERSECUTIONS

[1]*Jesus left the temple and was going away, when his disciples came to point out to him the buildings of the temple.* [2]*But he answered them, "You see all these, do you not? Truly, I say to you, there will not be left here one stone upon another, that will not be thrown down."*

[3]*As he sat on the Mount of Olives, the disciples came to him privately, saying, "Tell us, when will this be, and what will be the sign of your coming and of the close of the age?"* [4]*And Jesus answered them, "Take heed that no one leads you astray.* [5]*For many will come in my name, saying, 'I am the Christ,' and they will lead many astray.* [6]*And you will hear of wars and rumors of wars; see that you are not alarmed; for this must take place, but the end is not yet.* [7]*For nation will rise against nation, and kingdom against kingdom, and there will be famines and earthquakes in various places:* [8]*all this is but the beginning of the birth-pangs.*

[9]*"Then they will deliver you up to tribulation, and put you to death; and you will be hated by all nations for my name's sake.* [10]*And then many will fall away,*[y] *and betray one another, and*

hate one another. ¹¹*And many false prophets will arise and lead many astray.* ¹²*And because wickedness is multiplied, most men's love will grow cold.* ¹³*But he who endures to the end will be saved.* ¹⁴*And this gospel of the kingdom will be preached throughout the whole world, as a testimony to all nations; and then the end will come.*

y Or *stumble*

OVERVIEW: Everyone who receives the Word of God is a temple. Every sin damages the temple, yet complete departure from God destroys it. Moreover, Jesus meant replacement of the material building of the temple with the unsurpassed mystical temple of Scripture, composed of the inspired words and phrases (ORIGEN). Jesus meant the temple to be destroyed after his crucifixion, not in the consummation of the age (CYRIL OF ALEXANDRIA). In accordance with Jesus' prediction, the Jewish temple stood while Christ and the kingdom of God dwelt among the Jews. When they departed from the Jews to the Gentiles, the temple collapsed (ORIGEN). The temple of Jerusalem was to be destroyed, since the more beautiful and eternal temple, which is every practicing Christian, was being consecrated by the Holy Spirit (HILARY OF POITIERS). The olives that were planted on the Mount of Olives are the Christian churches, which are taken care of by the farmer, the Word of God. It is this farmer who grafts branches of a wild tree, the Gentiles, into the good tree of the righteous (ORIGEN). The disciples asked about the end of the world for our benefit so that we would know the signs of the coming end and would expect it eagerly. These signs, however, are to be interpreted not literally and chronologically but spiritually (INCOMPLETE WORK ON MATTHEW). Jesus foretold the coming wars to strengthen his disciples (CHRYSOSTOM). Interpreted in a moral sense, this passage refers to the spiritual struggle and afflictions of anyone who is about to see the Word of God coming into their soul (ORIGEN). Even the most grievous cooling down of love will not harm the noble and the firm (CHRYSOSTOM). The preaching of the gospel in the whole world is almost accomplished, so no one has the excuse of not knowing it (JEROME). Before the end of the world the church will be seduced by diverse heresies (INCOMPLETE WORK ON MATTHEW).

24:1 The Buildings of the Temple

YOU ARE A TEMPLE. ORIGEN: Everyone who receives the Word of God into himself is a temple. Everyone who does not completely fall away from God after sinning but retains some vestiges of faith and devotion to the commandments of God remains a temple, albeit partially destroyed. Whoever fails to take care of his soul after he sins, however, but continues to walk away from the faith and from the life of the gospel is progressively alienated until he has fully departed from the living God. Then he will be a temple in which "there will not be left one stone" of the teaching of the commandments of God "upon another that will not be destroyed." . . .

The temple of God was a building composed of distinct words, every Scripture from the Old Testament plainly having been constructed according to the historical sense. By their arrangement of words and phrases, Moses and the prophets built it in such a way that the beauty of the stones, that is, the meaning of their carefully chosen sayings, would command the admiration and praise of everyone. When the disciples of Jesus attempted to direct his attention to the structure of the temple, he responded by saying that this first, merely physical building must be destroyed by the Word so that another, more divine, more mystical temple might be constructed in its place. That other temple is the Scripture, as has already been demonstrated. COMMENTARY ON MATTHEW 30-31.[1]

YOU SEE THESE BUILDINGS. CYRIL OF ALEXANDRIA: Some were pointing out to Christ the magnificent things in the temple and how it was adorned by the gifts that had been dedicated to God. For they supposed that Jesus would admire with them all there was to see, although being God he has heaven as his throne! He does offer a teaching concerning them, but he had already predicted that according to the times the temple would utterly fall. The Roman army is being gathered for this very thing, demanding the surrender of Israel itself as all Jerusalem suffers the punishment of the slaying of the Lord. For let me tell you, it came to pass that they suffered these things after the crucifixion of the Savior. But they did not understand the meaning of Jesus' teachings. They supposed his teachings concerned the consummation of the age. FRAGMENT 266.[2]

24:2 One Stone Not Left on Another

THE KINGDOM WILL BE TAKEN FROM YOU. ORIGEN: After Christ predicted everything that was about to happen to Jerusalem, he who had preserved the temple left it, lest it collapse while he was still in it.[3] The temple stood safe and secure as long as the Word and the kingdom of God were with the Jews, as did all things Jewish. Subsequently, however, the kingdom of God was taken from the Jews and given to the Gentiles, as it is written, "The kingdom of God will be taken away from you and given to the nations who produce its fruit."[4] Both Jesus and the kingdom of God were then established among the Gentiles. Therefore neither Jesus nor the kingdom of God is to be found among the Jews, because they were abandoned "like a booth in a vineyard and like a hut in a cucumber field and like a city besieged,"[5] on account of the crime they committed against Christ. COMMENTARY ON MATTHEW 29.[6]

NOT ONE STONE UPON ANOTHER. HILARY OF POITIERS: The magnificent splendor of the temple's design was shown to Christ immediately after he had warned of Jerusalem's desolation, as though to move him. Yet he said that everything had to be destroyed and the scattered stones of its entire foundation demolished, for an eternal temple was being consecrated as a dwelling place of the Holy Spirit. This eternal temple is the man who is made worthy of becoming God's habitation through knowledge of the Son, confession of the Father and obedience to the commandments. ON MATTHEW 25.1.[7]

24:3 What Will Be the Sign of Your Coming?

HE SAT ON THE MOUNT OF OLIVES. ORIGEN: I regard the allegory of the Mount of Olives to refer to the churches of the Gentiles, among whom olive trees were planted. Each church is able to say, "I am like a fruitful olive tree in the house of God."[8] Perhaps also in this Mount of Olives, where the roots of good olive trees live,[9] branches of a wild olive tree were grafted into the good tree in the place of those branches which had been "broken off for their unbelief."[10] The farmer residing on the Mount of Olives is the Word of God as professed in the church, which is Christ, who continually grafts wild olive branches into the good tree of our father Moses and the other prophets, so that having been strengthened by the holy prophets (whose prophecies they understood to refer to Christ), these new branches might offer more abundant, richer fruit than the first olive branches, which had been cut off and made useless on account of

---

[1]GCS 38.2:56-57. [2]MKGK 243-44. [3]According to the exegetical theme already mentioned (cf. p. 92 n. 19), the function of the temple was exhausted with the advent of Christ. In this sense, Christ's distancing himself from it signified its end, which in a short time was actually accomplished by the Roman soldiers. [4]Mt 21:43. [5]Is 1:8. [6]GCS 38.2:55. [7]SC 258:180. [8]Ps 52:8 (51:10 LXX). [9]The symbolic meaning which Origen applies to Jesus' stay on the Mount of Olives springs from the connection with Romans 11:17-24; the pagans are like the wild olive branch grafted onto the good domestic tree (the Jews). [10]Rom 11:20.

the curse which was in the law. COMMENTARY ON MATTHEW 32.[11]

THEY QUESTIONED FOR OUR BENEFIT.
INCOMPLETE WORK ON MATTHEW: Here the disciples were asking, "When will this be that no stone of the temple stands upon another, as you said?" With these questions and others, they asked Jesus also to indicate to them the end of the age, which he had not mentioned. They asked questions about the temple for their own benefit, but those questions concerning the end of the age were asked for our benefit. We never saw the destruction of the temple, nor did they see the end of the age. It was expedient therefore that they hear about the signs of the temple's destruction and that we learn to recognize the signs of the world's consummation. The work's completion is sweet to every laborer, and the traveler eagerly awaits his arrival at home. The mercenary frequently counts the days to year's end, and the farmer constantly looks forward to harvest time. The merchant examines his purse day and night, and an expecting mother continually thinks of her delivery date. In a similar way, the servants of God eagerly anticipate the consummation of the age, for it is written, "Wherever your treasure is, there will your heart be also."[12]

If you have a certain quantity of valuable property stored away in your house, when you come in from the street, you will naturally direct your gaze in the direction of those valuables before you look anywhere else. Likewise, the saints fix their gaze there where their crown has been laid up for them. It is also of some benefit to be able to recognize the end of the age, for when a man is on a journey, the closer he gets to home, the more he begins to celebrate. HOMILY 48.[13]

THE DISCIPLES CAME TO HIM PRIVATELY.
CHRYSOSTOM: Since they meant to inquire about confidential matters, the disciples came to him privately. They were deeply troubled about when the day of his coming would be. They eagerly desired to behold that glory and the countless blessing that will accompany it. Yet they asked him two things. When will these things come to pass—especially the overturning of the temple? And what will be the sign of his coming at the close of the age? THE GOSPEL OF MATTHEW, HOMILY 75.1.[14]

24:4-5 Do Not Be Led Astray

THEY WILL LEAD MANY ASTRAY. ORIGEN: Come up to the moral and spiritual sense of Scripture and see if you can discover an interpretation worthy of the excellence of the knowledge of Christ and of the discernment of the Evangelists, lest you denigrate the dignity of evangelical wisdom with a lesser interpretation. Let us see then if mindful of that which was handed down from above concerning him who said "Many will come in my name saying, 'I am the Christ,' and they will seduce many," we can interpret these things in accordance with their consequences. It is inevitable that everyone who has been made perfect and has been given to see the glorious coming of the Word in his soul, everyone who has destroyed, devoured and crucified the world so that all things worldly are dead to him, and has trained his mind for understanding, will eventually engage doctrinal battles in the course of his search and discernment. He will hear many voices from divergent traditions professing to have the truth. Like a good soldier of the Word, however, his soul shall remain safe from all those opponents of the truth who feign adherence to the truth. In this way, he will be made worthy to receive in his soul the glorious coming of Christ, the Word of God who was "in the beginning with God,"[15] who comes to those who, having recognized him "according to the flesh"[16] and having received the Word who "became flesh,"[17] then ascended far

---

[11]GCS 38.2:57. [12]Mt 6:21. [13]PG 56:900. [14]PG 58:686; NPNF 1 10:450. [15]Jn 1:1. [16]2 Cor 5:16. [17]Jn 1:14.

beyond these things to behold no ordinary glory, but "the glory as of the only begotten of the Father."[18] Commentary on Matthew 35.[19]

24:6 Wars and Rumors of Wars

Interpreting the Signs. Incomplete Work on Matthew: In the interest of acquiring a better understanding of Christ's response, it would seem imprudent to neglect to consider first the apostles' question. The apostles asked two questions. First, they asked, "What will be the sign of the destruction of Jerusalem?" Second, they asked, "What will be the sign of the end of the world?" At the dissolution of the nation of Judea, Jerusalem was destroyed, but what seemed to be Jerusalem was not the true Jerusalem. Likewise, the church will appear to have been forsaken or almost forsaken at the end of the world, but what seemed to be the church was not and is not the true church. The Lord did not differentiate between the signs of the destruction of Jerusalem and the signs of the end of the world, for the signs that pertain to both events are one and the same. This is so because Christ did not respond to his apostles' questions as though he were a historian explaining the chronological order of events but rather in the manner of a prophet foretelling what would have to take place. Prophecies are always communicated through mysteries and properly understood as mysteries.

What does this mean for the passage at hand? If we want to understand them in the full spiritual sense, the signs of which Christ speaks—famine, wars, tremors—could not pertain to the destruction of Jerusalem, because at the time of its capture nation was not rising against nation in the spiritual sense. [That] is to say that heretics were not then fighting among each other, since at the time of the apostles the heresies were still only in their seminal stage but didn't germinate until the time of the Christian king, even though they are now fully grown, powerful forces. Moreover, there was no spiritual famine

at the time of Jerusalem's destruction but great abundance, as the psalmist said, "You visited the earth and watered it and increased its riches."[20]

Again, if we attempted to interpret these signs literally, they would tell us nothing about the end of the world, for there always have been and always will be wars, in the literal sense of the term. The same is true of famines and tremors. Nothing can serve as a sign of future events that already is a normal occurrence. Only something new can properly be called a sign. Just as there is a literal Jerusalem, therefore, which is already conquered figuratively, there is also another, spiritual Jerusalem, the church of Christ, which must be tested at the end of the world and indeed is currently being tested. Therefore the signs of which the Lord spoke must be understood both spiritually and literally. Literally they speak of the destruction of Jerusalem, but spiritually they signify the trial of the church at the consummation of the age. Train your mind on both aspects then, on what occurred before Jerusalem was captured and on what will occur before the final trial of Christ's church. Homily 48.[21]

24:7 Nation Will Rise Against Nation

Famines, Plagues and Tremors. Incomplete Work on Matthew: "And there will be famines and plagues and tremors throughout the land." Anyone who reads Josephus[22] knows what kind of famines, plagues and tremors afflicted Judea before the fall of Jerusalem. Before the spiritual plundering of the church, however, a spiritual hunger for the Word and spiritual tremors and various plagues of carnal sins will undoubtedly afflict the Christian people. So many schisms would never have arisen among Christians had they not already been famished for the Word, nor would they have suffered so many plagues, that is, diseases of

[18]Jn 1:14. [19]GCS 38.2:65. [20]Ps. 65:9 (64:10 LXX). [21]PG 56:900-901. [22]The obvious allusion is to Flavius Josephus Jewish Wars.

189

carnal passion, if they had not been stirred up from without. This is what the Lord taught in the parable of the evil one planting weeds: "While the men were sleeping," that is, when they neglected to guard against sin, "the enemy came and sowed weeds."[23] HOMILY 48.[24]

24:8 All This Is but the Beginning

BIRTH PANGS. CHRYSOSTOM: By "wars and rumors of wars" he refers to the troubles that are coming upon them. They supposed after that war the end would come. But see how he warns them: "But the end is not yet. For nation shall rise against nation, and kingdom against kingdom." He speaks of the preludes to the troubles of the Jews. "All this is but the beginning of the birth pangs," that is, of the troubles that will befall them. "Then they will deliver you up to tribulation and put you to death." This was the season for being candid about what was to come, in order that they might strengthen one another in facing their common miseries. THE GOSPEL OF MATTHEW, HOMILY 75.2.[25]

24:9 Hated for My Name's Sake

YOU WILL BE HATED. CHRYSOSTOM: Then he added, "And you will be hated by all nations for my name's sake. And then many will fall away and betray one another and hate one another. And many false prophets will arise and lead many astray. And because wickedness is multiplied, most men's love will grow cold. But he who endures to the end will be saved." This is the time of greatest evil, when the war becomes internal, for there are many false brothers.

Note that the war is coming from three sources simultaneously: from the deceivers, from the enemies, from the false brothers. Later Paul would lament over the same complications, saying that there were "fightings without, fears within"[26] and "danger from false brothers."[27] Again he wrote, "For such men are false apostles, deceitful workmen, disguising themselves

as apostles of Christ."[28] THE GOSPEL OF MATTHEW, HOMILY 75.2.[29]

24:10 Many Will Fall Away

MANY WILL BETRAY AND HATE. ORIGEN: If we ought to understand this passage in the moral sense, in accordance with how we treated the passages above, then we will explain its meaning as follows. It is necessary that he who is about to see the glorious coming of the Word of God in his soul should, like a great athlete, suffer the snares of his enemies and be given over to afflictions insofar as they advance the perfection of the Word within him. . . .

The manifestation of the qualities of Christ implanted in him, on account of which he is called a Christian, makes him an object of hatred to everyone who has the spirit of the world. This persecution also only tends more and more toward the perfection of the indwelling of Christ.

Few, however, will be left untouched by discussions and questions concerning the fullness of truth. Indeed, many will be "scandalized" and will fall on account of it, having been made betrayers and accusers of one another because of their dissensions over the truth of doctrine, which not everyone is able to learn. This is why they "hate one another." Among the great many who will be engaged in questions of this sort, those "false prophets who deceive many" will report prophecies concerning the future inaccurately and will interpret them incorrectly. Very few will seek the truth. False doctrines in and of themselves cannot overcome the power of truth, but those who have itchy ears will multiply and will take delight in speaking evil contrary to the law. And the tendentious words of many teachers will do such great harm that even those whose charity was once fervent in the simplicity of faith will "grow cold" toward the divine mys-

---

[23]Mt 13:25. [24]PG 56:904. [25]PG 58:688; NPNF 1 10:451-52. [26]2 Cor 7:5. [27]2 Cor 11:26. [28]2 Cor 11:13. [29]PG 58:688; NPNF 1 10:452.

teries and toward the truth. But whoever is able to see all these things and yet to remain in communion with the original purpose of the church's founding and the apostolic tradition will be saved. In this way then the gospel will be preached to every soul and a testimony will be given to every nation, that is, to all the unbelieving thoughts of every single individual. COMMENTARY ON MATTHEW 39.[30]

24:11 Many False Prophets Will Arise

WHY HERESY IS PERMITTED. INCOMPLETE WORK ON MATTHEW: For whom is it said, "Whoever perseveres to the end"? Is this said for the benefit of those who are persecuting Christians or seducing prophets? No, it is not. For just as medicine is administered to the sick rather than to the healthy, so also consolation is given to the endangered, not to the dangerous.

"And the gospel will be proclaimed throughout the whole world." St. Mark clarifies this verse by adding, "First the gospel must be preached." When the literal war was brought against Jerusalem, the gospel had just begun to be preached, but it had not yet extended to the whole world. Prior to the rise of the heresies, however, the proclamation of the gospel had already been completed. For the knowledge of Christ reached everyone either through individual preachers or by one nation evangelizing another continually until the time of the Christian king. If you want to know with certainty, however, that the knowledge of Christ had been extended to the whole world by that time, consider that the very purpose for which the heretical wars began was so that there might be a decision for the better doctrine. Therefore as long as there is still a summons, since a summons is as much an impediment to a final decision as a decision is to a summons, there can be no decisive choice. HOMILY 48.[31]

24:12-14 The Gospel Preached Throughout the World

PREACHED THROUGHOUT THE WHOLE WORLD. CHRYSOSTOM: What is even more terrible than all of these things is that they shall not even have love's consolation. "Most men's love will grow cold." Even all this, however, will in no way harm those who are noble and firm. So do not be afraid. Do not be troubled. If you demonstrate the patience that fits your faith, these dangers will not prevail over you. You will see proof of this when the gospel will be preached everywhere in the world. Then you will be above all these things that would otherwise alarm you. You will preach everywhere. You will not waste away in despair asking whether you will survive. Then he added, "This gospel of the kingdom will be preached throughout the whole world, as a testimony to all nations; and then the end will come." The sign of this final time will be the downfall of Jerusalem. THE GOSPEL OF MATTHEW, HOMILY 75.2.[32]

LEAVING NO EXCUSE. JEROME: The sign of the Lord's coming is that the gospel will be preached throughout the entire world, leaving no one any excuse. We believe that this has already been accomplished or is about to be accomplished, since it appears to me that there remains no nation that does not know the name of Christ. Even if they haven't been visited by an evangelist themselves, certainly they have heard about the Christian faith from neighboring countries. COMMENTARY ON MATTHEW 4.24.14.[33]

THEN THE END WILL COME. INCOMPLETE WORK ON MATTHEW: Both the end of the world and the antichrist must be understood according to the spiritual sense of Scripture, since heresies, famines, epidemics and all such things will precede each of them. Finally, however, the abomination of desolation, which is the army of the antichrist, will stand in the holy place. The army of the antichrist consists principally of

---

[30]GCS 38.2:76-77. [31]PG 56:906. [32]PG 58:688; NPNF 1 10:452. [33]CCL 77:225.

every heresy which finds its way into the church and stands in its holy place that it might appear to be the word of truth, even though it is no word of truth at all, but the abomination of desolation and the army of the antichrist which separates the souls of many from God. Perhaps it was of this that the apostle said, "who opposes and exalts himself against everything which is called God or is worshiped, so that he might be seated in the temple of God, proclaiming himself to be God."[34] In this way, the collective evil of diverse heresies, which at one time were only rumored, will then stand in the holy place and desecrate the church of Christ. Having been given license to go this far, they will then begin to possess the churches entirely. We here announce that reports of war, famines, earthquakes, epidemics, rumors of heresy, deprivation of the Word, the beating of Christians and the corruption of morals have already been preceding these events from the time of Constantine to the reign of Theodosius.[35] HOMILY 49.[36]

---

[34]2 Thess 2:4. [35]Constantine reigned A.D. 306-337; Theodosius reigned A.D. 347-395. [36]PG 56:906-7.

24:15-28 THE DESOLATING SACRILEGE

[15]"So when you see the desolating sacrilege spoken of by the prophet Daniel, standing in the holy place (let the reader understand), [16]then let those who are in Judea flee to the mountains; [17]let him who is on the housetop not go down to take what is in his house; [18]and let him who is in the field not turn back to take his mantle. [19]And alas for those who are with child and for those who give suck in those days! [20]Pray that your flight may not be in winter or on a sabbath. [21]For then there will be great tribulation, such as has not been from the beginning of the world until now, no, and never will be. [22]And if those days had not been shortened, no human being would be saved; but for the sake of the elect those days will be shortened. [23]Then if any one says to you, 'Lo, here is the Christ!' or 'There he is!' do not believe it. [24]For false Christs and false prophets will arise and show great signs and wonders, so as to lead astray, if possible, even the elect. [25]Lo, I have told you beforehand. [26]So, if they say to you, 'Lo, he is in the wilderness,' do not go out; if they say, 'Lo, he is in the inner rooms,' do not believe it. [27]For as the lightning comes from the east and shines as far as the west, so will be the coming of the Son of man. [28]Wherever the body is, there the eagles[z] will be gathered together.

z Or vultures

OVERVIEW: Abomination of desolation signifies either idolatry or worship of antichrist (JEROME). In the end of time there will be no hope of salvation from destruction (CHRYSOSTOM). Prohibition of going from housetop back to the house may be interpreted as prohibition of returning from spiritual life to earthly cares (HILARY OF POITIERS). Not to turn back from the field means not to turn back to the prebaptismal state of sin (ORIGEN). The field represents the church, where the flowers of virtue flourish. Turning back from the field is returning to sin, which obstructs salvation (Epiphanius the Latin). Flight on the sabbath means departing from this life in the state of indolence, while winter signifies the season of spiritual unfruitfulness (Cyril of Alexandria). In accordance with Jesus' prophecy, the terrors and tragedy of the Roman anti-Jewish universal campaign (under Vespasian and Titus) were unprecedented (Chrysostom). Shortening of the days signifies cutting off the doctrines and practices alien to Scripture, which are added by heretics (Origen). Although there were numerous false christs around the time of the Jerusalem siege, Jesus' warning also applies to the end of the world and the war of heretics against the church (Jerome). Antichrist will demonstrate great signs and miracles, and will declare himself God (Epiphanius the Latin). Those who try to lead astray even the elect are preachers of the false doctrine. The signs and miracles they employ are their skillful reasoning and pretentious piety. In Christ's second coming the glory of his divinity will be so apparent that there will be no need to seek him (Incomplete Work on Matthew). Christ, the Word of God, is shining in the whole of Scripture, from the law to the prophets (Origen). The body represents Christ's Passion; the eagles represent the saints (Jerome). The saying about the body and eagles is a metaphoric description of Christ's second coming (Apollinaris).

24:15 Daniel Spoke of the Sacrilege

The Abomination of Desolation. Jerome: Whenever we are urged to use our understanding, the meaning is shown to be mystical. But we read in Daniel this only: "And for half a week my sacrifice and offering will be removed, and the abomination of desolation shall be in the temple until the end of time, and the end will be given in abandonment."[1] The apostle also said in this regard that the man of iniquity, the enemy, would rise up against everything uttered by God and would dare to stand in the temple and be

worshiped as though he were God. After Satan's work is finished, however, Christ's coming will destroy all who raised themselves against him and will return them to the state of divine abandonment. This man of iniquity can be interpreted either simply as the antichrist, or as the image of Caesar which Pilate put in the temple, or as the statue of Hadrian the equestrian which still today stands in the Holy of Holies. Because the Old Testament normally calls the abomination an idol, the word *desolation* is added here to indicate that the idol shall be placed there resulting in the temple's abandonment and destruction. Commentary on Matthew 4.24.15.[2]

24:16 Let Them Flee to the Mountains

Flee to the Mountains. Chrysostom: Having spoken of the ills that were to overtake the city, and of the trials of the apostles, and that they should remain unsubdued, and that they will overcome the whole world, he turns again to the calamities of the Jews. While the gospel dispensation will be gloriously fulfilled, the others will be faced with deepening adversities. He shows how intolerable the war will be, even in every detail.

"Then let those who are in Judea flee to the mountains." When does he mean by "then"? These things will take place, he says, "when you see the desolating sacrilege spoken of by the prophet Daniel,[3] standing in the holy place." He seems to me to be speaking of armies and wars. So flee. There is no hope of safety for you in the cities.

Yet some will say that it has happened again and again that the people of Judah have recovered from terrible times. Think of the conditions under Sennacherib. Remember Antiochus. Remember the time when the armies had come upon them and the temple had been seized and

[1]*Super solitudinem;* see Dan 9:27. [2]CCL 77:225-26. [3]See Dan 9:27; 11:31; 12:11.

the Maccabees rallied to give their affairs an opposite turn! But Jesus forbids them thinking of any such rescue. He does not want to feed them false hopes. For this is different. It is the end time. THE GOSPEL OF MATTHEW, HOMILY 76.1.[4]

24:17 One on the Housetop

THE HOUSETOP AND THE FIELD. HILARY OF POITIERS: The roof is the summit of the house, the noble perfection of the entire dwelling. For one may not even say that a house exists if it does not have a roof. Whoever therefore is established at the summit of his house—that is, in the perfection of his body made new by regeneration, raised high by the Spirit and perfected by the absolution of the divine gift—should not allow himself to be provoked within by bodily enticements and to descend to the sinful desire for the lowly things of this world or fall from the heights of the roof.

"And let whoever is in the field not return to retrieve his tunic," that is, if he is busy fulfilling the commandments, he should not return to his previous cares or desire clothing for this body, lest he restore and wear again the old tunic of sin with which he was once covered. ON MATTHEW 25.5.[5]

24:18 One in the Field

WHAT ROOF? WHAT FIELD? ORIGEN: Whoever is in Judea, that is, "in the letter of the old law," should flee to the mountains of the new things of the Spirit. And whoever is found to have gone up onto the roof, which is the Word, and stands high above his home should not descend to retrieve anything from within his house. For he who remains on the roof and denies himself will never need to come down.

Whoever is in the field must not turn back. If he is in the field in which the treasure is hidden, as the Lord taught in his parable,[6] he must not turn back. If he is in the field to which Jacob was

compared when his father blessed him, saying, "Behold, the smell of my son is like the smell of a bountiful field which the Lord has blessed,"[7] in which everyone who lives according to the law will be blessed with the spiritual blessings of the law, he still must not turn back. As the Scripture says, "You will be blessed in the city and blessed in the field."[8] Whoever therefore is in the field of "every plant which the heavenly Father has planted,"[9] he too must not turn back. Just as he who puts his hand to the plow and turns back is unfit for the kingdom of God,[10] so also the one in the field who turns back on account of those things which he ought to have forsaken will undoubtedly incur the abomination of desolation which is deception. This is especially true of those who had previously stripped off their old tunic (that is, "the old nature with its practices")[11] and return again to retrieve it. COMMENTARY ON MATTHEW 42.[12]

TO TAKE HIS MANTLE. CHRYSOSTOM: Under these conditions one would do well merely to escape with one's naked body. So if anyone is on a housetop, he should not take time to run back into the house to get his clothes. For the evils are inevitable. The calamity is without end. Anyone nearby will surely perish. Therefore he adds also, "if one is in the field," saying, "do not try to take cover or turn back to find your belongings." For if those who are indoors flee, much more ought they that are out of doors not take refuge indoors. THE GOSPEL OF MATTHEW, HOMILY 76.1.[13]

DO NOT TURN FROM THE CHURCH. EPIPHANIUS THE LATIN: The holy reading continues: "Let him in the field not turn back." This field represents the church, as was demonstrated by the blessing our blessed patriarch Isaac gave to his son Jacob: "Behold, the smell of my son is

---

[4]PG 58:693-94; NPNF 1 10:456. [5]SC 258:186. [6]Mt 13:44. [7]Gen 27:27. [8]Deut 28:3. [9]Mt 15:13. [10]Lk 9:62. [11]Col 3:9. [12]GCS 38.2:85-86. [13]PG 58:694; NPNF 1 10:456.

like the smell of a bountiful field which the Lord has blessed."[14] The field was replete with a multitude of flowers and was redolent with the sweetest aroma. Clearly this signifies the church where the Lord's flowers—that is, virginity, chastity, continence, confession, faith, mercy, justice, truth and martyrdom—are perfected. These are the flowers of the field, which is the church; the flowers in which the Son of God rejoices, which have merited God's blessing. Therefore he said, "Let him in the field not turn back." Likewise, the same Lord once said, "Remember Lot's wife."[15] While fleeing the conflagration of Sodom, she looked back and was turned into a pillar of salt, leaving an example of foolishness behind her. Therefore the Lord admonishes us that clinging more fully to his love and faith, we would not turn back, yet rather would save our souls for eternal life. INTERPRETATION OF THE GOSPELS 33.[16]

24:19 Alas for Those with Child

PREGNANCY, INFANCY AND FLIGHT VIEWED SPIRITUALLY. HILARY OF POITIERS: One must not believe that the Lord was drawing our attention to the burden of pregnant women when he said, "Woe to those who are with child." Instead, he wanted to demonstrate the heavy weight of souls filled with sins, a weight which prevents them from escaping the storm of wrath stored up for them, whether they are on the roof or in the field. Suffering naturally accompanies pregnancy, and no one is born into the world without his entire body being shaken by the experience. Souls therefore who are found in a similar condition will continue in their suffering and burdens.

"Woe also to those who are nursing." The weaned infant is no less unfit for flight than is the one who is still nursing. But if the difference in age and status between those who are nursing and those who are weaned is of no importance, how are we to understand "Woe also to those who are nursing"? This warning is meant to show the infirmity of souls who were being taught to know God as though they were being nursed. But in fact they only had a weak foretaste of the knowledge of God and were deprived of the strength which comes from the perfect food. The Lord's woe therefore is said to the souls themselves who are too weighed down to escape the antichrist or too weak to face him because they had not been avoiding sin and because they had not been fed with the true bread.

Therefore we are admonished to pray that our flight does not take place in the winter or on the sabbath. In other words, let us not be found in the coldness of our sins or in the absence of good works. A heavy, intolerable affliction will be visited upon everyone, unless those days are shortened because of the elect of God. ON MATTHEW 25.6-7.[17]

TIES OF SYMPATHY. CHRYSOSTOM: He first mourns for the one weighed down by the burden of pregnancy, who cannot flee easily, who is less mobile. Then he mourns for "those who are nursing." They are bound by ties of sympathy for their children. Yet they cannot protect those who nurse. Who can escape these bonds of natural affection? By comparison, parting with money is nothing. How could the pregnant woman become mobile? How could she that nurses be able to overlook that which she had borne? THE GOSPEL OF MATTHEW, HOMILY 76.1.[18]

TIMES OF TRIBULATION. EPIPHANIUS THE LATIN: The holy reading continues: "Woe to those who are with child and to those who are nursing in those days." This means woe to those who have conceived suffering and begotten iniquity by neglecting the faith. For just as a pregnant woman in flight has no rest but only pain and tribulation, so also sinners and disbelievers in the Christian faith will have nothing but grief

---

[14]Gen 27:27. [15]Lk 17:32. [16]PL Supp 3:882. [17]SC 258:188-90. [18]PG 58:694-95; NPNF 1 10:457.

when the day of judgment comes upon them.

The holy Gospel next says, "Pray that your flight not fall in the winter or on the sabbath, for there will be a tribulation such as has not been from the beginning of the world." These two times, winter and the sabbath, represent two races of people: the Gentiles and the Jews. Just as everything is fruitless, desolate and dead in the winter, so also are the Gentiles. The Lord is hereby warning us therefore not to be found as the Gentiles: desolate, dead and without the fruit of good works on the day of judgment or in the time of persecution. The sabbath . . . is a day reserved entirely for leisure. The Jews do nothing on the sabbath other than rest. We ought to be vigilant then that the time of persecution or the day of judgment does not find us resting. Whoever is found like this will deservedly suffer "a tribulation such as the world has not seen since its beginning." INTERPRETATION OF THE GOSPELS 33.[19]

24:20 The Time of Your Flight

NOT IN WINTER. CHRYSOSTOM: Recall that this discourse is addressed to the Jews. He is speaking here of the ills that should overtake them. He is not speaking primarily to the apostles, who did not keep the Jewish sabbath day.[20] They were nowhere around when Vespasian did these things.[21] Indeed, most of the apostles would soon be dead or in other distant parts of the world.

It is to the Jews that he says "Pray that your flight may not be in winter or on a sabbath." Pray that it not be in winter, because of the difficulty of the season. Pray that it not be on the sabbath day, because of the absolute authority exercised by the law. For they had need of flight, and of the swiftest flight. The Jews would not dare to flee on the sabbath day, because of the law. THE GOSPEL OF MATTHEW, HOMILY 76.1.[22]

A WINTER OF EVILS. CYRIL OF ALEXANDRIA: Perhaps this saying contains a puzzle. It admonishes us to pray that our departure from this body would not happen in the time of rest from good works, which the sabbath signifies, nor in the time of unfruitfullness, which is winter. It is notable, however, that God did not create the winter of misfortunes. Winter means the time that we are possessed by the fleshly passions.[23] FRAGMENT 269.[24]

24:21 Great Tribulation

PRAY AMID THE GREATEST TRIBULATION. CHRYSOSTOM: You must pray, for "then there will be great tribulation, such as has not been from the beginning of the world until now, no, and never will be." Do not let anyone suppose that he is merely speaking in hyperbole. All you need to do is study the writings of Josephus to learn the truth of these predictions. No one who knows the fact of history can say that Christian believers have exaggerated this tragic history or been any part of trying to see that Christ's words were fulfilled. For Jesus himself was a Jew, a determined and faithful Jew, very zealous. And among believers who lived after Christ there were many Jews. What then is this man predicting? That these terrors would surpass all tragedy. And indeed no such similar tragedy has ever overtaken any nation. THE GOSPEL OF MATTHEW, HOMILY 76.1.[25]

24:22 For the Sake of the Elect

NO ONE WOULD BE SAVED. CHRYSOSTOM: This is a tribulation such as never has been before nor will be. He adds, "And if those days had not been shortened, no human being would be saved; but for the sake of the elect those days will be shortened." By this he is indicating that

---

[19]PL Supp 3:882. [20]They celebrated the resurrection on the first day of the week. [21]Vespasian was the Roman emperor A.D. 69-79 and was known for his role in putting down the Jewish rebellion (66-70). [22]PG 58:695; NPNF 1 10:457. [23]In the Mediterranean world severe winds rule and toss the sea during winter. [24]MKGK 244. [25]PG 58:695; NPNF 1 10:457.

they are deserving of a more grievous punishment than any that had previously been experienced. He is speaking now of the days of the war and of the siege. If the war of the Romans against Jerusalem had continued, all the Jews would have perished. By "no human being" in this case he means the Jews. And this doubtless applies to Jews at home and abroad. For the Romans were fighting not only against those in Judea but also against those Jews that were dispersed everywhere. They too were outlawed and banished, because of the Romans' hatred against the Jews of Judea. THE GOSPEL OF MATTHEW, HOMILY 76.1.[26]

THE SHORTENING OF DAYS. ORIGEN: "Those days" refers to the commandments and truths which were placed in Scripture for the illumination of rational souls. Accordingly, every doctrine that comes from "false knowledge"[27] and is joined to the words of Scripture is to be understood as corresponding to additions beyond the natural length of days in Scripture. The good God, however, shortens the addition of these days through whom he chooses. Whenever you see then by the advent of the Word of truth in your mind that the "arrogant who fight against the knowledge of God"[28] are cut off, understand that the days of tribulation are shortened. The extra length is abbreviated which the abomination of desolation always adds in opposition to the natural number of the days of the Lord which are in Scripture. "Those days" will be shortened "for the sake of the elect," so that they will suffer nothing from the desolation of abomination nor from what was added to the true and natural days of Scripture. This assumes that the addition of days has been shortened and that the only remaining light is that of the word of truth. COMMENTARY ON MATTHEW 45.[29]

BELIEVERS IN THEIR MIDST. CHRYSOSTOM: But who in this case does he mean by the elect? He means the believers that were hidden away in the midst of them. In order that Jews may not say that it was because of the gospel and the worship of Christ that these ills took place, he showed that so far from the believers being the cause, if it had not been for them, all Jews would have perished utterly. For if God had permitted the war to be protracted, not so much as a remnant of the Jews would have remained. But lest those of them who had become believers should perish together with the unbelieving Jews, he quickly put down the fighting and allowed an end to the war. THE GOSPEL OF MATTHEW, HOMILY 76.2.[30]

24:23 Ignoring False Reports

DO NOT BELIEVE IT. JEROME: "If anyone says to you, 'Behold, here is the Christ,' or 'There is the Christ,' do not believe him." At the time of the Jewish captivity by Rome, many Jewish elders claimed to be the Christ. There were so many, in fact, that there were three distinct camps of them when the Romans besieged Jerusalem. This saying is better understood as referring to the end of the world, however.

"False Christs and false prophets will arise and perform great signs and wonders so that even the elect might be led into error. Behold, I told you." As I have already noted, this passage is to be explained in one of three ways. It refers either to the Roman siege of Jerusalem or to the end of the world or to the war waged by heretics against the church and by antichrists who oppose Christ under the pretext of false knowledge.

"If, therefore, they say to you, 'Behold, he is in the desert,' do not go out. And if they say 'Behold, he is inside,' don't believe it." If anyone were to tell you that Christ dwells in the wilderness of the pagans or in the doctrine of the philosophers or within the inner chambers of heretics who promise to reveal the secrets of God, do not go out and do not believe them.

---

[26]PG 58:695; NPNF 1 10:457. [27]1 Tim 6:20. [28]2 Cor 10:5. [29]GCS 38.2:93. [30]PG 58:695-6; NPNF 1 10:457.

And lest false prophets find an opportunity for deceiving you at a time of persecution and anxiety, you should not trust just anyone who claims to speak in the name of Christ. Commentary on Matthew 4.24.23-26.[31]

24:24 False Signs and Wonders

False Christs Will Arise. Epiphanius the Latin: We are warned by the Lord so that if anyone were to come to us falsely in his name, none of us would believe in such a person, having already been prepared. Henceforth how great will be the signs by which the faith of the elect is demonstrated! But whoever builds his house on the rock, that is, establishes his faith on Christ, cannot be destroyed by winds or rains. The rock represents Christ, the floods are the kings, and the winds are the kings' orders to persecute the servants of God.[32]

The holy reading continues: "False Christs and false prophets will arise and perform great signs and wonders so that even the elect would be led into error, if possible. Behold, I have told you." You see then, beloved, what great love the Lord displays toward us. He carefully instructs each one of us individually regarding the future so that even if we see all these signs come to pass (having been forewarned by him) we will be wise to the enemy and accept nothing contrary to Christ and the catholic faith. In the Acts of the Apostles, Simon declared himself to be the power of God.[33] Likewise, in the last days, the antichrist will declare himself to be God, as the apostle says, "Thus he will sit in the temple of God, calling himself God . . . whom the Lord Jesus Christ will kill with the breath of his mouth."[34] The day of judgment will come upon the antichrist also, and the Lord will kill him with the sword of his mouth. Interpretation of the Gospels 33.[35]

The Elect. Incomplete Work on Matthew: "That they might lead even the elect into error, if possible." Scripture doesn't say "that they

might deceive even the elect, if possible," but that they might "lead them into error." Commonly, when the saints encounter hidden works of the devil under the appearance of goodness, they cannot understand the enemy's boundless treachery. They are troubled in their hearts and scandalized, asking, "What is happening here?" Yet they are not easily convinced to believe him, for even if their human reason is overcome, they stand firm by faith.

Scripture says "if possible" in order to show the greatness of the signs. How prodigious those signs must have been to deceive even the elect! Yet they were not deceived, because those whom God has preordained to life cannot die. The power of God was shown forth when he forewarned the faithful about these signs for the sake of their salvation. Nevertheless these matters are best understood with regard to the rise of the heresies. False Christs are the false truths of the heresies, and false prophets are preachers of false truths. Their signs consist in doing the same things falsely which the faithful do truthfully. They remain chaste and observe the fasts and practice mercy and fulfill every rule of the church. Do not the devil's signs appear most deceptive when you see him doing the works of God? Homily 49.[36]

24:25-26 I Have Told You Beforehand

Will He Come in the Desert? Incomplete Work on Matthew: He forewarned them lest, having heard of the coming of Christ, they would be seduced by men to step out into the open and either be captured in the desert or imprisoned within the house. Why should the coming of Christ happen in a desert? Does he love isolation more than human community? Is he so afraid of people that he needs to hide in the desert? If he did not fear kings or judges when the time for his Passion had arrived but

---

[31]CCL 77:228. [32]Mt 7:24-25. [33]Acts 8:19. [34]2 Thess 2:4-8. [35]PL Supp 3:883. [36]PG 56:916.

openly preached the word of righteousness to impious people, how is it that he will suddenly be afraid when he comes to judge sinners?

"If anyone says to you, 'Behold, he is inside the house,' do not believe it." You insult the Lord's divinity if you search inside a house for the one who fills all of heaven and earth or if you think him to be hiding who came to resist the proud and to exalt the humble. At his first advent, his divinity was concealed in a body that he might test the faithful. When he comes again, he will be revealed in glory that he might reward their faith. At his first advent, therefore, it was necessary that he be sought out. Now, however, it is not the case that he must be sought in order to be believed. Rather, he himself will seek those by whom he has already been believed. The last times must be interpreted spiritually. Accordingly, there are two kinds of heresies: those which mask their falsehood by attempting to ground it in the divine authority of Scripture and those which are unable to do so because they are so thoroughly contrary to Scripture. The desert therefore represents heresies whose doctrines have forsaken Scripture altogether. The house represents those heresies that are sprinkled with citations from Scripture, thus giving only the appearance of truth. HOMILY 49.[37]

24:27 As the Lightning Comes

TRUTH RADIATES FROM EAST TO WEST. ORIGEN: Christ is shown to be the Word and Truth and Wisdom of God from the very first creature of the world to the last of the writings of the apostles (that is, from Genesis through the apostolic books of the Bible). No Scripture written after these is to be believed in the same way. Because "the law and the prophets prophesied until the coming of John,"[38] the law and the prophets represent the lightning or radiance of truth which "comes from the East and shines as far as the West." The East represents the law, and the West represents the "end of the law,"[39]

which is marked by "the coming of John." The church alone has neither removed one word from this radiance nor added any prophecy of its own. If we were to consider carefully why the Evangelist does not use the singular here but writes of a plurality shining "from the Easts to the Wests,"[40] we would see that the law and the prophets are one thing and Jesus Christ himself is yet another reality which extends from East to West, appearing to the apostle Paul "last of all, as to one untimely born."[41] COMMENTARY ON MATTHEW 47.[42]

ILLUMINATING THE FULLNESS OF TRUTH. THEODORE OF HERACLEA: For it is much the same with lightning. Lightning is figuratively compared with truth. It is likened to the coming of the Son of man, which is explained in every Scripture, whether it concerns the law, prophecy, the gospel or apostolic testimony. It flashes out from the east, the region of principalities and spiritual powers, and shines all the way to the west, the realm of darkness and Satan, in the time of the Passion. Note that if the law is rising in the east, the end of the law is setting in the west. But from Jesus Christ to Paul is a rising and setting. He was revealed to Paul last of all as "to one abnormally born."[43] FRAGMENT 124-25.[44]

24:28 Eagles Gathered Together

WHEREVER THE BODY IS. JEROME: We are taught about the sacrament of Christ by the use of a natural example taken from daily life. Eagles and vultures are said to sense the presence of a carcass all the way across the sea and to gather their food in this way. If therefore these irratio-

---

[37]PG 56:917. [38]Mt 11:13; Lk 16:16. [39]Rom 10:4. [40]Origen highlights the fact that the Greek text of Matthew 24:27 has the plural of *east* and *west*. [41]1 Cor 15:8. Symbolically the spreading of the horizon from east to west signifies both (1) the display of the truth in the entirety of the sacred Scriptures, begun by the will of God with the law and ended with the Passion of Christ, and (2) the story of the origins of Christianity, from Christ himself to Paul. [42]GCS 38.2:96. [43]1 Cor 15:8. [44]MKGK 91.

nal creatures have the natural capacity to know where a small body lies, even though separated by so great a distance across land and sea, how much more ought we and the whole multitude of believers hasten to him whose splendor comes from the east and shines as far as the west!

In Greek the body is called a *ptōma*,[45] but the Latin word for it, *cadaver*, is more illuminating because it comes from the word "to fall," *cadere*, and implies that the body has fallen dead. We can understand this body to refer to the Passion of Christ because wherever Scripture says that we are gathered together, it is for the purpose of coming to the Word of God. For example, "A company of evildoers encircle me; they have pierced my hands and feet,"[46] "like a lamb led to the slaughter,"[47] and in other passages like these. The eagles represent those saints whose youth is renewed like the eagle's[48] and who, according to Isaiah,[49] shall mount up with wings to come to the passion of Christ. COMMENTARY ON MATTHEW 4.24.28.[50]

THE GATHERING OF EAGLES. APOLLINARIS: Jesus spoke in a kind of comparison, as in the form of an illustration and example. For, he says, the appearing of the Son of man will be much the same as when eagles and other flesh-eating birds find a carcass and dead body lying on the ground. They secretly and unexpectedly bear them through the heights and by doing so will provide food for themselves. In the same way, he will appear again on the earth a second and glorious time to judge the world. Ranks of angels will be seen serving as an escort with all the saints rising up "in a moment, in a twinkling of an eye,"[51] according to the last trumpet. . . . But some attempted to explain this text as teaching that at the second coming of the Lord all who conducted themselves uprightly, corresponding with eagles in their lofty and spiritual outlook, will leave paradise behind and be gathered to that place where the fall of Adam occurred. This is the place where Adam violated the commandment and through his disobedience fell into sin. FRAGMENT 126.[52]

---

[45]Actually the Greek *ptōma* derives from *piptein* ("to fall"), and so the correspondence that Jerome notes in Latin can be sustained in Greek as well. [46]Ps 22:16 (21:17 LXX). [47]Is 53:7. [48]Ps103:5 (102:5 LXX). [49]Is 40:31. [50]CCL 77:229. [51]1 Cor 15:52. [52]MKGK 43.

24:29-31 THE COMING OF THE SON OF MAN

[29]*"Immediately after the tribulation of those days the sun will be darkened, and the moon will not give its light, and the stars will fall from heaven, and the powers of the heavens will be shaken;* [30]*then will appear the sign of the Son of man in heaven, and then all the tribes of the earth will mourn, and they will see the Son of man coming on the clouds of heaven with power and great glory;* [31]*and he will send out his angels with a loud trumpet call, and they will gather his elect from the four winds, from one end of heaven to the other.*

OVERVIEW: The sun will be darkened because it is fitting that the day of resurrection would be preceded by the night (INCOMPLETE WORK ON MATTHEW). The powers of heaven will tremble because of the terror of the judgment day (CHRYSOSTOM). As humanity is renewed, the whole of creation is transformed to the new order also (CYRIL OF ALEXANDRIA). At the dread judgment all the sinners will mourn: Jews on account of Christ's crucifixion, Gentiles on account of their false teachings, neglectful Christians on account of their just condemnation. The heretics who deny Christ's divinity will be defeated by seeing him as Judge of the universe (INCOMPLETE WORK ON MATTHEW). The sign of the Son of man, the cross shining brighter than the sun, will appear in the sky (CHRYSOSTOM). Sending the angels by the Son of man clearly demonstrates that he is God (APOLLINARIS). The angels will gather all the elect, who lived in accordance with Scripture, both learned and simple. Moreover, as there were degrees of perfection in the saints' lives, so there will be degrees in their state of blessedness—different heavens, so to speak (ORIGEN).

24:29 After the Tribulation of Those Days

THE SUN WILL BE DARKENED. INCOMPLETE WORK ON MATTHEW: "The sun will be darkened, and the moon will not give its light." Either on account of the undeserved persecution suffered by the saints, for even worse crimes committed by the wicked or to show forth the wrath of God in the last days while the wicked are still living upon the earth, a taste of the infernal darkness will be given. Whatever the reason, it is fitting that a night should intervene between the two days, for a new day of resurrection is about to be born. The days will be separated lest there seem to be one nature belonging both to this world and to the next. For we die in carnal bodies, but we will be raised in spiritual bodies.[1] The day of darkness then serves as a sort of death, indicating that something new will be born. Or it could be that the night represents evil and the daytime righteousness. HOMILY 49.[2]

A GREAT CHANGE WILL COME. CHRYSOSTOM: The sun shall be darkened, not destroyed. It will

be overcome by the light of God's presence. The stars shall fall, for what shall be the need of them thereafter, if there is no night? And "the powers of the heavens will be shaken." For a great change had come to pass. When the stars were made, they trembled and marveled. When the stars were made, all angels praised the Lord with a loud voice.[3] Much more upon seeing all things in course of final change, and their fellow servants giving account, and the whole world standing by that awful judgment seat, and all those who had lived from Adam until his coming having an account demanded of them of all that they did, wouldn't you expect the powers of the heavens to tremble and be shaken? THE GOSPEL OF MATTHEW, HOMILY 76.3.[4]

THE RECAPITULATION OF CREATION. CYRIL OF ALEXANDRIA: How will they not shudder with fear? For heaven and earth are transformed for the sake of God's own discretion (to speak something accurately about such things requires more than one word). The sun and the moon will be darkened, and the stars will fall like flowers. Their very nature is again changed by the One who created them, just as he wills, and the heavenly bodies will be thrown into disorder. For as humanity is renewed the whole creation, which had been created for the sake of humanity, is recapitulated and restored. FRAGMENT 271.[5]

24:30 The Sign of the Son of Man

ALL THE TRIBES OF THE EARTH WILL MOURN. INCOMPLETE WORK ON MATTHEW: "Then all the tribes of the earth will mourn." The Jews will mourn because they will see him living and enlivening whom they thought to be dead. Convicted by the wounds on his body, they will be unable to deny their crime. The Gentiles will mourn because they were deceived

[1]1 Cor 15:44. [2]PG 56:918. [3]Job 38:7 LXX. [4]PG 58:698; NPNF 1 10:459. [5]MKGK 245.

by the vain arguments of the philosophers into thinking it irrational foolishness to worship a crucified God and to attribute the glory of the Creator to a creature. Sinful Christians who loved the world more than they loved Christ will also mourn when they hear him say to them, "I was made man on your account. It is because of you that I was arrested, mocked, beaten and crucified. Where is the fruit of these great injuries I suffered? Consider that the salvation of your souls came at the price of my blood. Where is the service you owe me in return for this? I who am God valued you above my own glory when I became a man. You, however, consider me to be of less worth than anything else you possess. You love the most menial things of the earth more than you love my righteousness and faithfulness." And heretics who say that a mere man was crucified will mourn when they see him whom the Jews pierced return as judge. HOMILY 49.[6]

THE APPEARANCE OF THE SON OF MAN. CHRYSOSTOM: "Then will appear the sign of the Son of man in heaven." The cross will be brighter than the sun. The sun will be darkened and hide itself. The sun will appear at times when it would not normally appear. But why is this sign given? In order that the brazenness of the Jews might be more abundantly silenced. For having the cross as the greatest plea, the Son of man thus comes to that judgment seat, showing not only his wounds but also the reproach of his death. THE GOSPEL OF MATTHEW, HOMILY 76.3.[7]

24:31 The Angels Will Gather the Elect

THE SON OF MAN WILL SEND HIS ANGELS. APOLLINARIS: By saying that the Son of man will send his angels, he demonstrates that the Son of man is God. For they are God's angels, and to send them is solely God's prerogative. The saying "from one end of the heavens to the other" teaches us that the extremes of earth and

heaven are the same. Hence it is necessary to believe in Christ and not to be deceived as though the smallest part of earth, situated in the midst of the heavens, was surpassed by their infinite greatness. FRAGMENT 127.[8]

THE GATHERING OF THE ELECT. ORIGEN: You will understand why the saints are gathered "from the heights of the earth"[9] if you consider the conduct of their lives and the perfection, insofar as possible, of their dealings with others. All who lived uprightly will be gathered not simply from the earth but "from the heights of the earth." After their earthly lives have ended, their conduct in the next life will raise them not simply from the highest point in heaven, as it was from the highest level of earth, but from the "heights of the heavens" because each and every heaven has both a beginning and a conclusion or perfection. After their exemplary lives on earth, the saints' conduct in the first heaven, once they have attained its perfection or conclusion, will elevate them still further. The same is true for the second heaven and the third heaven. It seems to me therefore that there are many heavens, each with its own initiation and perfection. It is from the beginnings and ends of these diverse heavens that God gathers his elect.

"From the heights of the heavens to their ends." It is also possible that the heavens here represent either the divine Scriptures or their authors, in both of which God dwells. In that case, the heights of the Scripture is its beginning, and the perfection of Scripture is its conclusion. To say that the saints will be gathered from "the heights of the heavens" means that they will be found from among those who live in the beginning of Scripture to those who live at

---

[6]PG 56:919. [7]PG 58:698; NPNF 1 10:459. [8]*MKGK* 43-44. [9]Mk 13:27. In the parallel passage in Mark we read "from the uttermost part of the earth to the uttermost part of heaven." Origen links the uttermost part of earth in Mark with the acme of heaven in Matthew and presents the progression toward perfection as a continuous ascent of the rational being from the earth through the various heavens, where *heavens* signifies allegorically the sacred Scriptures.

its conclusion, or, if I may speak more profoundly, from the unskilled to the experts.

The angels who will be sent by the Savior to gather his elect will gather them not just with any ordinary voice but with what Scripture calls a "great trumpet." It won't be an uncertain voice but one that is definite and clear so that all who hear and learn will be established on the way of perfection which leads to the Son of God. COMMENTARY ON MATTHEW 51.[10]

---

[10]GCS 38.2:115-16.

24:32-35 THE LESSON OF THE FIG TREE

[32]"From the fig tree learn its lesson: as soon as its branch becomes tender and puts forth its leaves, you know that summer is near. [33]So also, when you see all these things, you know that he is near, at the very gates. [34]Truly, I say to you, this generation will not pass away till all these things take place. [35]Heaven and earth will pass away, but my words will not pass away.

OVERVIEW: The lesson of the fig tree has to do with the signs of the last time. As the fig tree leaves correlate with the leaves Adam used to cover himself, and thus with sin, so the tree's branch represents antichrist. Greening of the tree signifies the intensification of sin before the end (I HILARY OF POITIERS). By pointing to the fig tree Jesus assured his disciples that his second coming will not be delayed and will surely take place. When it occurs, saints will enjoy their "summer season" of rest, while the sinner suffers the winter season of damnation (CHRYSOSTOM). The fig tree is a metaphor for the church; as the tree contains myriad seeds under one bark, so in the body of the church many Christians are incorporated. Moreover, the fig tree is the only one that produces fruit even in winter, and so the church always produces saints (INCOMPLETE WORK ON MATTHEW). The fig tree represents the "people of circumcision," who did not produce fruit and withered away. Yet later another fig tree, the Gentiles, produced an abundance of fruit (ORIGEN). "This generation will not pass away" refers to the generation of the faithful who will persist until the second coming (CHRY-

sostom). "This generation" refers to both those who suffer temptation and those who cause them, demons. Both groups will persist in their struggle until the end, since temptations are necessary to test faith (INCOMPLETE WORK ON MATTHEW).

24:32 Learn the Lesson of the Fig Tree

FROM THE FIG TREE LEARN ITS LESSON. HILARY OF POITIERS: The parable of the fig tree is offered as a lesson in recognizing the signs of the times. When its branches become tender and green we know that summer is near. Both this fig tree and this summer are very different from those found in nature, however. In nature there is a considerable interval between the onset of summer and the greening of a tree's branches, which begin to grow tender early in the spring. Consequently this parable cannot be about the tree. Indeed, we have already dealt above with the particular meaning of the tree. We saw that Adam had covered himself with its leaves to hide his shameful conscience, which is to say that he was bound under the law as though clothed in sin. The fig tree's branch therefore represents the antichrist, who is a son of the devil, a partaker of sin and protector of the law. When it begins to grow tender and green, then the summer, which here represents the day of judgment, is near. The greening of the tree then refers to the rise of sinners, a time that will be marked by the flowering of slanderers and the popularity of criminals and favor for blasphemers. This signals that summer, the heat of eternal fire, is near. ON MATTHEW 26.2.[1]

HOW LONG A TIME? CHRYSOSTOM: The time is "immediately after the tribulation of those days." After how long a time would it be? They desired to know in particular the very day. So he puts forth the analogy of the fig tree. He indicates that the interval was not great but that in quick succession these things would occur at his advent. He declared this not by the parable of the fig tree alone but by the words that follow. "From the fig tree learn its lesson: as soon as its branch becomes tender and puts forth its leaves, you know that summer is near." He foretells a spiritual summer, a calm for the righteous that would come on that day, after the storm. But to sinners, on the contrary, there would be winter after summer, which he declares in what follows, saying that the day shall come upon them when they are living in luxury. For these two purposes he spoke about the fig tree: in order to declare the short interval and to underscore that these things assuredly will come to pass. It was possible for him to have demonstrated this in other ways, but he chose the fig tree as an example of a necessary series of things occurring in sequence. THE GOSPEL OF MATTHEW, HOMILY 77.1.[2]

YOU KNOW THAT SUMMER IS NEAR. INCOMPLETE WORK ON MATTHEW: Jesus uses the fig tree, rather than another kind of tree, as an illustration for the onset of summer because it commonly happens that after other trees have begun to bloom, a cold snap forces them back into hibernation. Since the fig tree blooms later than almost any other tree, however, its fruitfulness is virtually never interrupted by the cold. In a similar way, the church is a sure sign of the advent of a new age. But let us consider this analogy more carefully. The fig tree begins to produce its leaves at the optimal moment of the spring season, but the church is afflicted with horrible persecutions and driven toward death. The Lord is here correlating the springtime jubilance of the fig tree to the spiritual progress of souls, not to bodily afflictions. For the soul flourishes when the flesh suffers, as the apostle said, "And you received the Word of God in great tribulation, with joy from the Holy Spirit."[3] Just as warm spring winds trigger the trees to begin producing their foliage and fruit, so persecution provokes the human soul to virtue. The fig tree therefore is perennially comparable to the church in the sense that it contains many seeds within a heart of sweetness under one bark, while the church unites many Christians within its heart of love under one body. There is yet another similarity, however. Other trees produce their fruit at approximately the same time of year, for everything ripens and falls to the ground in the space of a few days. Only the fig tree continues to produce fruit unceasingly until winter. While some figs are ready to be harvested, other figs are just beginning to grow. Likewise, the church will never cease to produce saints until the end of time. In every age, while some are dying, others are just being born. HOMILY 49.[4]

24:33 At the Very Gates

HE IS NEAR. ORIGEN: The fig tree may be understood to represent the people of the circumcision. The Lord came to them when he was hungry and, "finding no fruit there"[5] but the appearance of life only, said, "May no one ever

---

[1]SC 258:194. [2]PG 58:701; NPNF 1 10:462. [3]1 Thess 1:6. [4]PG 56:920. [5]Mt 21:19.

eat fruit from you again." At his coming therefore this fig tree, the people of the circumcision, "withered immediately." But the other fig tree, the one which until that time had been barren and was about to be cut down because no one had ever applied himself diligently to its cultivation, began to bear fruit when fertilizer was spread around it. What was formerly a blight upon the earth will now produce fruit in such abundance sufficient even for the entire time in which it was barren. COMMENTARY ON MATTHEW 53.[6]

24:34 Until All These Things Take Place

THIS GENERATION WILL NOT PASS. CHRYSOSTOM: "Truly, I say to you, this generation will not pass away till all these things take place." All these things. What things? Those about Jerusalem, those about the wars, about the famines, about the pestilences, about the earthquakes, about the false Christs, about the false prophets, about the sowing of the gospel everywhere, the seditions, the tumults, and all the other things which we said were to occur until his coming. What does he refer to when he says "this generation"? He is speaking not of the generation then living but of the age of believers. For he is prone to distinguish a generation not by times only but also by the mode of their religious service and practice, as when he says, "Such is the generation of those that seek him."[7] He said "all these things will take place," and yet "the gospel will be preached." These two are not inconsistent. The generation of the faithful shall remain through all things that will surely come to pass. The faithful will not be cut off by any of the things that have been mentioned. For both Jerusalem shall be destroyed and a large part of the Jews shall be decimated, but over this generation— the faithful—shall nothing prevail, not famine, not pestilence, not earthquake, not the tumults of wars, not false Christs, not false prophets, not deceivers, not traitors, not those that cause to offend, not the false brothers, nor any other

such temptation whatever. THE GOSPEL OF MATTHEW, HOMILY 77.1.[8]

MY WORDS WILL NOT PASS AWAY. INCOMPLETE WORK ON MATTHEW: Uncertainty always makes a person careless. We prepare ourselves earnestly only for what we truly believe will happen to us. Therefore, lest his disciples initially prefer certain danger to uncertainty and then, having doubts about its advent, allow themselves to become complacent, the Messiah strengthened his teaching with an oath, saying, "Truly, truly, I say to you, this generation will not pass away until all these things have taken place." Great danger requires great preparation. Great preparation requires diligent admonition and caution. It must be recognized then that Christ did not intend to show his disciples that the coming trial was already beginning but rather that it was altogether in the future. He wasn't addressing only those who had already been born by that time, therefore, but the entire family.[9]

"This generation" refers both to those who suffer temptation and to those who cause it. It refers to sinners among men and to the demons who are at work in them. For neither group will cease being in the world until its consummation. For Christ said, "Depart from me, you cursed, into the eternal fire prepared for the devil and his angels."[10] Moreover, it is necessary that the source of temptation be preserved as long as there is faith which needs testing. It is also possible, however, that "this generation" refers to those mortal Christians who would not pass over into eternal life and be made immortal and impassible "until" all the events about which Christ was speaking had taken place.

"Heaven and earth will pass away, but my words will not pass away" because heaven and

---

[6]GCS 38.2:120. [7]Ps 24:6 (23:6 LXX). [8]PG 58:701-2; NPNF 1 10:462-63. [9]The author means that Jesus spoke of *generatio ista*, including in it not only all the men (and the demons) of his time but their descendants as well. [10]Mt 25:41.

earth were created to serve you, but my words were uttered to govern you. Both heaven and earth are subject to vanity, as the apostle said, "Creation is subject to vanity."[11] Truth, however, is by nature unable to deceive and can never die. HOMILY 49.[12]

---

[11]Rom 8:20. [12]PG 56:920-21.

24:36-44 NO ONE KNOWS THE DAY AND HOUR

[36]*"But of that day and hour no one knows, not even the angels of heaven, nor the Son,[a] but the Father only.* [37]*As were the days of Noah, so will be the coming of the Son of man.* [38]*For as in those days before the flood they were eating and drinking, marrying and giving in marriage, until the day when Noah entered the ark,* [39]*and they did not know until the flood came and swept them all away, so will be the coming of the Son of man.* [40]*Then two men will be in the field; one is taken and one is left.* [41]*Two women will be grinding at the mill; one is taken and one is left.* [42]*Watch therefore, for you do not know on what day your Lord is coming.* [43]*But know this, that if the householder had known in what part of the night the thief was coming, he would have watched and would not have let his house be broken into.* [44]*Therefore you also must be ready; for the Son of man is coming at an hour you do not expect.*

a Other ancient authorities omit *nor the Son*

OVERVIEW: By saying that he does not know the day and the hour, Christ associates himself with his body, the church (ORIGEN). By declaring that no one knows the day, Christ removes from us any need to be concerned about a particular date. This uncertainty is beneficial for our spiritual life (HILARY OF POITIERS). The Lord indicates that he will return unexpectedly, when many will pursue the life of pleasure, luxury and unlawful passions. Yet for the saints it will be a time of tribulations (CHRYSOSTOM). When speaking about those eating and drinking in the time of the deluge, the Lord does not forbid these activities; rather he teaches us to exercise them spiritually, to the glory of God, as opposed to pleasing the flesh. As in the time of Noah only those in the ark were saved, so also in the second coming only those in the church will be saved. The outsiders, the heretics, will perish (INCOMPLETE WORK ON MATTHEW). Those who live according to the gospel do not attempt to find out the date of the end. Rather, knowing that our personal end—death—may happen at any moment, they pursue vigilance (ORIGEN). The second coming will be completely unexpected. Neither occupation or social status will matter for the final judgment (CHRYSOSTOM). Christ's judgment is the final separation between the saints and the sinners (HILARY OF POITIERS). As one has to be always prepared to confront a thief, so one has to be always prepared to face the end of life and the following judgment. To keep us always vigilant and active the Lord does not indicate the precise day of his second coming (CHRYSOSTOM, HILARY OF POITIERS). To be ready means to keep all of the possible entrances (that is, all of the senses) shut to sin and the devil, the thief. Since the date of the second coming as well as the date of personal death are not known to us, every generation should live in the constant expectation of Christ's return (INCOMPLETE WORK ON MATTHEW).

24:36 Of That Time Only the Father Knows

KNOWING THE DAY AND HOUR. ORIGEN: As long as the church, Christ's body, does not know that day and hour, the Son himself is said not to know it in order that he may be understood to learn of that day and hour only when all of his members do. But "to know" is given its own special meaning here (as is customary with sacred Scripture), for only he who remains to meet its arrival will know that day and hour. COMMENTARY ON MATTHEW 55.[1]

WHETHER THE SON KNOWS THE DAY. HILARY OF POITIERS: When Christ taught us that no one knows the day on which the end of time will come, not the angels and not even himself, he removed from us any need to be concerned about its date. O immeasurable mercy of divine goodness! Since the Son said, "All things have been delivered to me by my Father,"[2] we know that the Father did not deny him the knowledge of this day. If anything was denied him, he could not have said that all things were delivered to him. But because the Son has handed on to us everything the Father gave him and the Word of God does not contain in himself as much assurance of the future as of things already accomplished, therefore it was established by God that the date of the end should be indefinite. Thus he could allow us an abundant amount of time for repentance yet still keep us solicitous for fear of the uncertain and so as to avoid giving anyone the idea of a particular day by expressing his will. For just as at the time of the flood, in the normal course of our life, in our activities and in our sufferings,

that great day will suddenly appear. ON MATTHEW 26.4.[3]

THE DAY AND HOUR NO ONE KNOWS. CHRYSOSTOM: He spoke these things in order to show that he would return unexpectedly and suddenly and when many were living luxuriously. For Paul also says this: "When they shall speak of peace and security, then sudden destruction will come upon them."[4] To show just how unexpectedly he uses the metaphor "as travail comes upon a woman with child." THE GOSPEL OF MATTHEW, HOMILY 77.2.[5]

24:37 As Were the Days of Noah

PURSUING PLEASURES. CHRYSOSTOM: What then is meant by "after the tribulation of those days"? If there is to be luxury at that time, and peace and safety, as Paul indicates, how then can he say, "after the tribulation of those days"? If there is luxury, how is there also tribulation? The luxury is spoken of those who are in a state of insensibility and peace. He does not say that there will be peace but rather "when they speak of peace and safety," indicating that their insensibility would be something like those in Noah's time, that even amid such evils they lived in luxury. Yet it will not be a time of peace and luxury for the righteous. The righteous will be passing through this time of tribulation in dejection. He shows that when antichrist has come, the pursuit of unlawful pleasures shall be more eagerly pursued among the transgressors, who have learned to despair of their own salvation. There will then be gluttony, partying and drunkenness. He then offers an example of this. THE GOSPEL OF MATTHEW, HOMILY 77.2.[6]

24:38 Those Days Before the Flood

IN THE DAYS BEFORE THE FLOOD. INCOM-

---

[1]GCS 38.2:126-27. [2]Mt 11:27. [3]SC 258:196-98. [4]1 Thess 5:3. [5]PG 58:703-4; NPNF 1 10:464. [6]PG 58:704; NPNF 1 10:464.

plete Work on Matthew: Christ did not forbid eating, drinking and marrying when he said "As in the days of Noah, they were eating, drinking, marrying, and being given in marriage." He would never destroy what he himself established. Instead, he was commanding that what we do with our bodies, we do spiritually and to the glory of God so that our flesh might be made spiritual on account of the spiritual purposes for which we use it. . . .

Before the flood, people were fleeing from the fear of God and doing nothing for his glory. Everything they did was only for their own flesh. Whenever they ate or drank, they ate and drank only to satisfy their bodily desires, not to glorify God as the apostle had commanded.[7] What Christ wanted to say here is that it will be like this again near the end of the world. . . .

At the end of the world, the destruction will be universal and sudden like it was "in the days of Noah." Just as every creature of the earth was destroyed in the flood, except only those who escaped in the ark, so also at the consummation of the world every heresy will be destroyed, but only one ark will be saved—the church of Christ, composed of the righteous. Everything outside of the ark died in the flood. Likewise, at the end of the world whoever is found to be outside the one true church will perish. Homily 50.[8]

24:39 So Will Be the Coming of the Son of Man

They Did Not Know Until the Flood Came. Origen: All who listen to the depths of the gospel and live it so completely that none of it remains veiled from them care very little about whether the end of the world will come suddenly and all at once or gradually and little by little. Instead, they bear in mind only that each individual's end or death will arrive on a day and hour unknown to him and that upon each one of us "the day of the Lord will come like a thief."[9] It is important therefore to be vigilant,

whether in the evening (that is, in one's youth) or in the middle of the night (that is, at human life's darkest hour) or when the cock crows (at full maturity) or in the morning (when one is well advanced in old age). When God the Word comes and brings an end to the progress of this life, he will gather up the one who gave "no sleep to his eyes nor slumber to his eyelids"[10] and kept the commandment of the One who said, "Be vigilant at all times."[11] . . .

But I know another kind of end[12] for the righteous person who is able to say along with the apostle, "Far be it from me to glory except in the cross of our Lord Jesus Christ, through whom the world is crucified to me and I to the world."[13] In a certain sense, the end of the world has already come for the person to whom the world is crucified. And to one who is dead to worldly things the day of the Lord has already arrived, for the Son of man comes to the soul of the one who no longer lives for sin or for the world. Commentary on Matthew 56.[14]

24:40-41 One Taken, One Left

In the Field, at the Mill. Chrysostom: All these things are demonstrations that he knew what was to come. It would be like the days of Noah: "Then two men will be in the field; one is taken and one is left," so unexpected will it be. It is without thought that they will be taken. "Two women will be grinding at the mill; one is taken and one is left." This is not the employment of those who are contemplating such a calamity.

From both employees and employers some will be taken and some will be left. Among those who are at ease and those who labor, some will

[7]1 Cor 10:3-4. [8]PG 56:922. [9]1 Thess 5:2. [10]Ps 132:4 (131:4 LXX). [11]Lk 21:36. [12]The greek *telos*, like *consummatio* in Latin, signifies completion, thus end and also perfection. Origen, little interested in the matter of the end of the world as a whole, takes the term in the first interpretation to refer to the death of the individual Christian, who must always be prepared for death. In this second interpretation, he reads the term as the perfection one reaches in Christ by dying to the world. [13]Gal 6:14. [14]GCS 38.2:130-31.

be taken, some left. Rank or station will not matter, as it says in the Old Testament: "From him that sits upon the throne to the captive woman who is at the mill."[15] Even though he had said earlier that it is hard for a rich man to be saved, here he shows that not even the rich are altogether lost, neither are all the poor saved, but out of both groups people are saved and lost.

And to me he seems to indicate that the advent will come at night, like a thief, as Luke also indicates. It is amazing how fully he knows all things. THE GOSPEL OF MATTHEW, HOMILY 77.2.[16]

A JUDGMENT COMING. HILARY OF POITIERS: Christ shows that a judgment is coming, since between two people in a field, one is taken up and one left behind. Between two grinding at the mill, one is chosen and one rejected. Between two lying in bed, one departs and one remains. This teaching means that the separation of the faithful from the unfaithful will consist in one being accepted and the other abandoned. For, like the prophet says, when the wrath of God rises, the saints will be hidden in God's chambers but the faithless will be left exposed to celestial fire. The two in the field therefore represent the faithful and the unfaithful, both of whom will be surprised by the day of the Lord in the midst of the world, in the course of their life's work. They will be separated, one taken and the other left. It will be the same for the two grinding at the mill, which represents the work of the law. For only some of the Jews, like Elijah, believed through the apostles that they must be justified by faith. One group will be taken up through the faith that produces good works, and the other group will be abandoned in the fruitless works of the law, grinding in vain at a mill that will never produce heavenly food. The two lying in bed are proclaiming the repose of the Lord after his Passion, which both Catholics and heretics confess alike. But because the truth of the Catholic faith preaches the unity of the Father and the Son, which we call

their deity, whereas the false doctrine of heretics attacks this unity with many different insults, one of the two lying in bed will be taken up but the other will be left behind. For by accepting one and rejecting the other, God's judgment will prove the merit of each confession. ON MATTHEW 26.5.[17]

24:42 You Do Not Know the Day

WATCH THEREFORE. CHRYSOSTOM: But his meaning is like this: If ordinary persons knew when they were going to die, they would surely be striving earnestly at that hour. In order therefore that they may strive, not at that hour only, he does not tell them the hour or day. He wants to keep them on their toes looking for it, that they may be always striving. This is why he made the end of each person's life so uncertain.

In this passage he openly implies that he himself is Lord. Nowhere before has he spoken of this so distinctly. But here he seems to me also to be putting to shame those who remain careless about his lordship. They take much more care about a thief taking their money than about their own soul. Those who care about their house and do not want their possessions stolen take measures against the thief. They watch; they are prepared for the thief. So it is with you. You do not know when he will come. But you know assuredly that he will come. If you do not continue to watch, you will not be ready on that day. You will be unprepared. Destruction will come in your sleep. If the person had known when the thief was coming, he would have been prepared. So be like the one who is prepared at all times, so you will escape free.

Having then mentioned the judgment, he directs his thoughts next to teachers, speaking of honorable and dishonorable actions. His discourse closes with that which is alarming, for he speaks first of those who do right, then of those

[15]Ex 11:5 (variation on LXX). [16]PG 58:704; NPNF 1 10:464. [17]SC 258:198-200.

who continue in sin. THE GOSPEL OF MATTHEW, HOMILY 77.2-3.[18]

24:43 The Householder Would Have Watched

YOU DO NOT KNOW THE TIME. HILARY OF POITIERS: To teach us that our ignorance of the date of his return (which his silence has kept hidden from everyone) is not without its usefulness, Christ warns us to keep all his commandments. We should also be occupied with constant prayer in order to guard against the coming of the thief. For the thief is the devil who seeks to invade our bodily homes with the darts of his thoughts and allurements in order to ruin us while we are sleepy and careless. It is good therefore that we be prepared. Our ignorance of the day of Christ's return should provoke us to be careful as we eagerly await his coming. ON MATTHEW 26.6.[19]

24:44 At an Hour You Do Not Expect

YOU MUST BE READY. INCOMPLETE WORK ON MATTHEW: Does the soul not know when the thief has gained access through one of these entrances? Indeed, it does not know until it has been led into sin.[20] The soul must be vigilant, therefore, and close all its ports of entry. The mouth should be occupied with holy speech, the ears with pious sounds; the eyes with a vision of the wondrous works of God; and the mind with heavenly thoughts. It is not sufficient merely to refrain from speaking, hearing, seeing or thinking evil things. For to do that is only to block the access of good spirits along with the bad. Whoever renounces evil but fails to take up the good is said to have left the gates to his soul open. The enemy enters easily when he finds them vacant. It is necessary therefore that the portals to the soul of the just not only be free of evil but

also be fully occupied with the good, lest evil find a way to gain access. HOMILY 51.[21]

LIVING IN EXPECTATION. INCOMPLETE WORK ON MATTHEW: Why is the date of an individual's death hidden from him? Clearly it is so that he might always do good, since he can expect to die at any moment. The date of Christ's second advent is withheld from the world for the same reason, namely, so that every generation might live in the expectation of Christ's return. This is why when his disciples asked him, "Lord, will you restore the kingdom to Israel at this time?" Jesus replied, "It is not for you to know the times and the seasons which the Father has established by his authority."[22]

"But know this, that if the head of the household had known the hour at which the thief would arrive, he would have been vigilant and would never have allowed his house to be burglarized." The head of the household represents the human soul, the thief is the devil, the house is the body, the doors are the mouth and ears and the windows are the eyes. Like the thief who gains access through the doors and windows to despoil the householder, the devil also finds easy access to the soul of a man through his mouth, ears and eyes to take him captive. This is why Jeremiah wrote, "For death entered through our windows."[23] If you wish to be secure, install a bolt on your door, which is to say, put the law of the fear of God in your mouth so that you can say with the psalmist, "I will guard my ways that I might not sin with my tongue. I will put a guard at my mouth."[24] HOMILY 51.[25]

---

[18]PG 58:705; NPNF 1 10:465. [19]SC 258:200. [20]The careless soul becomes aware of the condition of sin when it is already deeply entangled in it, because it did not notice the insidious beginning of the actions of the thief (the devil) against it. [21]PG 56:925. [22]Acts 1:6-7. [23]Jer 9:21. [24]Ps 39:1 (38:1 LXX). [25]PG 56:924.

24:45-51 THE FAITHFUL AND UNFAITHFUL SERVANTS

[45]"*Who then is the faithful and wise servant, whom his master has set over his household, to give them their food at the proper time?* [46]*Blessed is that servant whom his master when he comes will find so doing.* [47]*Truly, I say to you, he will set him over all his possessions.* [48]*But if that wicked servant says to himself, 'My master is delayed,'* [49]*and begins to beat his fellow servants, and eats and drinks with the drunken,* [50]*the master of that servant will come on a day when he does not expect him and at an hour he does not know,* [51]*and will punish[b] him, and put him with the hypocrites; there men will weep and gnash their teeth.*

b Or *cut him in pieces*

OVERVIEW: Faithful and wise make a rare combination. There are many clever individuals, yet the wise are very few. The good steward is granted authority over all possessions of his master; that is, he is made coheir with Christ and will reign with Christ (ORIGEN). Both wisdom in dispensing the gifts of God and faithfulness to God are the necessary components of good stewardship. This applies both to teachers, entrusted with the distribution of knowledge, and to those entrusted with the greatest and most honorable responsibility over "all possessions" in the life to come (CHRYSOSTOM). The parable of the good and wise steward applies first of all to bishops, who are called to wisely feed their flock with the Word of God and to be constantly ready to give account of their stewardship in Christ's coming (HILARY OF POITIERS). This parable is against the wicked rulers who lead a luxurious life and against negligent teachers. Both of them sin because they do not believe that their judge will ever come. These will be condemned at the last judgment and will be cut off from the grace of God forever (CYRIL OF ALEXANDRIA). Cutting off means separating from the fellowship of Christians and condemning to destruction with the sinners (INCOMPLETE WORK ON MATTHEW). The Holy Spirit is the agent of union with God. Therefore, as Adam after the Fall was cut off from the Spirit, so will be those condemned at the last judgment. Thus cutting off the Spirit means the punishment of separation from God (CYRIL OF ALEXANDRIA).

24:45 Who Is the Faithful and Wise Servant?

THE FAITHFUL AND WISE SERVANTS. ORIGEN: We should understand the phrase "faithful and wise servant" as referring to a person who is faithful in the customary sense of the term, not as referring to those who are wise or clever by natural endowment. Many who are clever and wise are not at all faithful. For instance, whoever considers the great number of people who fancy themselves Christians will discover many who are faithful and who have great zeal for the faith but are not very wise. He will thus conclude that "the sons of this world are wiser in their own generation,"[1] knowing that "God chose the foolish of the world to confound the wise."[2] He will also see that others who are thought to be believers are clever and wise enough but of only limited faith. If they are not unfaithful, they are certainly at least less faithful than the "foolish of the world" whom "God chose." But it is rare for faithfulness and wisdom

---

[1]Lk 16:8. [2]1 Cor 1:27.

to coincide in one person to enable him to "give his fellow servants their food at the proper time." He needs wisdom to give food to the needy "at the proper time" and faith to refrain from keeping the food for himself in time of need. COMMENTARY ON MATTHEW 61.[3]

24:46 Blessed Is That Servant

RESPONSIBLE FOR THE LORD'S GOODS. CHRYSOSTOM: Everyone should make full use of what he has been given for the common advantage of all. If you possess power or wealth or wisdom, do not use it to hurt your fellow servants. If you do, it will be to your own ruin. Since sins come from foolishness, he requires both wisdom and fidelity. One is faithful who has been a good steward of his Lord's goods, not stealing from the Lord, not spending without aim or fruit. One is wise who knows how to dispense the things given him in a fitting way. Indeed, we have need of both these things together, faithfulness and wisdom, and these in conjunction. We are called to exercise our stewardship in a fitting manner, spending carefully. And we must not steal from the Lord. If one of these is lacking, the other is halted. There would be great blame if one were to waste the Lord's goods, spend freely the resources we have been given, even if we never stole anything at all. Similarly there would be heavy charges to make against one who spent his Lord's goods well but occasionally stole something for himself. THE GOSPEL OF MATTHEW, HOMILY 77.3.[4]

A GREAT PROMISE. ORIGEN: "Blessed is the servant whom the Lord will find so doing when he comes." A great promise is extended to the Lord's faithful and wise stewards. It is like the promise he made to those to whom he said, "Take authority over five cities" or "take authority over ten cities."[5] For to be made the head "over all his possessions" is nothing other than to be made an "heir of God and coheir with Christ"[6] and to reign with Christ. The Father

has given him everything he himself possesses, as Christ said, "All authority in heaven and on earth has been given to me."[7] The Son of the good Father who is given authority over all his Father's possessions also shares this honor and glory with his faithful and wise stewards, so they also might be with Christ above every creature and authority. This is what he meant when he said, "Truly I say to you, he will set him over all his possessions." COMMENTARY ON MATTHEW 62.[8]

24:47 Set Over All His Possessions

ENTRUSTED WITH RICHES. CHRYSOSTOM: Let everyone who is entrusted with riches listen carefully. He is not only speaking to teachers but to those who manage money. In both cases they are entrusted with riches. Those who teach are entrusted with a wealth that is far more necessary than those who deal with money. There are times when teachers have difficult times. If in these times you who have money are not willing to demonstrate your generosity, what excuse will you have? You need to exhibit both generosity and honesty, for the two go together.

It is an honor to be entrusted with the responsibility of someone else's resources. This happens to the faithful: "Truly, I say to you, he will set him over all his possessions." What can be equal to this honor? What sort of speech would be fitting to this dignity? What sort of blessedness would accompany it? Here we are speaking of nothing less than the King of heaven who possesses all things. It is he who is setting a person "over all his possessions." This is why he calls him to be wise. He must not spend large sums for small benefits. It is only having been responsible here in this life that he will receive the riches of heaven. THE GOSPEL OF MATTHEW, HOMILY 77.3.[9]

---

[3]GCS 38.2:141. [4]PG 58:706; NPNF 1 10:466. [5]Lk 19:17-19. [6]Rom 8:17. [7]Mt 28:18. [8]GCS 38.2:143. [9]PG 58:706; NPNF 1 10:466.

OVER ALL HIS POSSESSIONS. HILARY OF POITIERS: Although he urged everyone to exercise an indefatigable vigilance, Christ commanded the princes of the people, the bishops, to demonstrate a special attentiveness in expectation of his advent. The bishop is represented in this parable by the faithful and wise servant who was set over the household. He is fully equipped and enabled to care for the people entrusted to him. He needs to be attentive to his instructions and obedient to the commandments. When he speaks the truth and prudently applies doctrine, he will confirm the weak, heal the broken, convert sinners and feed his household with the Word of life—their eternal food. If he is found performing these tasks diligently, he will receive glory from the Lord as a faithful servant and effective steward. He will be set over all his possessions. In other words, he will be established in the midst of the glory of God. Nothing could possibly be better than this. ON MATTHEW 27.1.[10]

24:48-49 The Wicked Servant

BEATING ONE'S FELLOW SERVANTS. CYRIL OF ALEXANDRIA: This teaching is directed against the rulers who are leading a luxurious and leisurely lifestyle. He calls the negligent teacher a wicked and evil servant because he takes advantage of the judge's absence and believes he will not be observed because of the judge's forbearance. So he beats harshly those over whom he holds power and associates with those who are in love with the flesh. They sin both because the judge is not present and because they don't think judgment will ever arrive. By wounding some of them, he points out those who are disabled in soul because of the luxury of their exalted positions. Just as the apostle says, "When you sin against your brothers in this way [you] wound their weak conscience."[11] Therefore he threatens to introduce the most severe punishments to those living self-indulgently. . . .

Those who pretend to understand the princi-

ples of the good life are not thinking as they should but are only clothing themselves in the appearance of virtue. They will be cut into pieces on that fearful day of judgment. This is a judgment from the Spirit and results in a perpetual alienation. . . . Grace will be cut off from all the pollution of his soul, and his part will be reckoned with the hypocrites. Jesus calls hypocrites those who are cut into pieces and yet continue to teach others the way to live. They succeed only in making things worse for those learning the life of discipleship. Further, Jesus teaches that those who have not carried out faithfully the ministry given to them in this present life from the Lord will not receive another from him. . . . For the cutting Jesus reveals is not a bodily one but the stripping of their adoption as sons from the Spirit. Moreover, they are punished because they lived a life of derision. They will gnash their teeth when they consider the reason for their pain and the exceedingly severe character of their punishment. FRAGMENT 277.[12]

24:50-51 Weeping and Gnashing Teeth

THE UNFAITHFUL SERVANT PUNISHED. INCOMPLETE WORK ON MATTHEW: "He will cut him off" means that the Lord will cut him off from the fellowship of Christians. The unfaithful servant will neither be glorified with the saints nor gently punished with those who have committed venial sins. Instead, he will be thrown in with the hypocrites and infidels, where he will suffer the destruction of those whose behavior he imitated. A good priest is glorified above all others, not only on account of his own righteousness but also on account of theirs as well, since he is the cause of their righteousness. In the same way, a sinful priest is punished more severely than anyone else, not only for his own sins, but also for theirs, since he made himself the cause of their sin. The Lord

---

[10]SC 258:202. [11]1 Cor 8:12. [12]MKGK 248.

calls them not only hypocrites but also infidels, because every hypocrite is an infidel, but not every infidel is a hypocrite. Whoever gives the appearance of being in the church and then acts against the church is properly called a hypocrite. HOMILY 51.[13]

THE GIFT OF THE SPIRIT CUT OFF. CYRIL OF ALEXANDRIA: Let us investigate carefully what "to be cut into pieces" means.[14] When in ancient times Adam came into being, God made him a partaker of his own Spirit, giving to his nature a most perfect beauty. For "he breathed on his face the breath of life."[15] For to truly give life is to have the Spirit of life, that is, of Christ. But because Adam was deceived and slipped into sin, he was cut off from the Spirit. For it pleased our God and father "to bring all things together under one head in Christ"[16] and to restore the ancient beauty to human nature. We have received this through grace, but the stealthy entrance of sin stripped it from us. For Christ

breathed into us after the resurrection, restoring ancient beauty to us. "Receive," he says, "the Holy Spirit."[17] And so the Spirit is united to us. For "he who unites himself to the Lord is one with him in spirit."[18] Surely, just as we have been compelled to be zealous in our efforts by a sense of devotion, we are receiving the utmost fullness since we now have the pledge of the Spirit at the appropriate time. We are deprived of that same foretaste of the Spirit when we stand accused in our own sin since the gift of the Spirit is cut off and sent away from us as in the time of the judgment. We affirm that it is this judgment that Jesus speaks of when he mentions cutting something apart. For one such as this who has the Spirit is not delivered over to punishment. FRAGMENT 278.[19]

---

[13]PG 56:928. [14]The act of punishment for which the evil servant is cut off indicates symbolically that the divine Spirit has departed because of sin. Cyril argues that the presence of this Spirit, restored by Christ after the sin of Adam, depends in every person on moral conduct. [15]Gen 2:7. [16]Eph 1:10. [17]Jn 20:22. [18]1 Cor 6:17. [19]*MKGK* 249.

25:1-13 THE PARABLE OF THE TEN VIRGINS

[1]*"Then the kingdom of heaven shall be compared to ten maidens who took their lamps and went to meet the bridegroom.[c] [2]Five of them were foolish, and five were wise. [3]For when the foolish took their lamps, they took no oil with them; [4]but the wise took flasks of oil with their lamps. [5]As the bridegroom was delayed, they all slumbered and slept. [6]But at midnight there was a cry, 'Behold, the bridegroom! Come out to meet him.' [7]Then all those maidens rose and trimmed their lamps. [8]And the foolish said to the wise, 'Give us some of your oil, for our lamps are going out.' [9]But the wise replied, 'Perhaps there will not be enough for us and for you; go rather to the dealers and buy for yourselves.' [10]And while they went to buy, the bridegroom came, and those who were ready went in with him to the marriage feast; and the door was shut. [11]Afterward the other maidens came also, saying, 'Lord, lord, open to us.' [12]But he replied, 'Truly, I say to you, I do not know you.' [13]Watch therefore, for you know neither the day nor the hour.*

c Other ancient authorities add *and the bride*

OVERVIEW: In the final judgment, no one can look to another's praise to help him or her shine. The five virgins are the whole church. The lamps are good works of love done from a pure heart. The wise are those souls who have the catholic faith and seem to demonstrate good works. The lamps of the wise burn with a good conscience, with an inner glory and with inmost charity, yet even they tremble on the last day (AUGUSTINE). The wise virgins are those who, embracing the time available to them, were prepared at the first onset of the Lord's coming (HILARY OF POITIERS). Watchfulness is required, lest Christ come to take the church for his bride at the least expected moment, when some of those waiting are seeking the praise of others (AUGUSTINE).

On the day of the resurrection and judgment, however much people might be rich in good works, they will fear for themselves, lest they not be prepared with faith that has been active in works. The foolish virgins were those who were lazy and unmindful. They were foolish because they were not prepared for the future but only for the present. Thus they were foolish because they did not have works of compassion, for the oil symbolizes compassion (EPIPHANIUS THE LATIN). They troubled themselves only over present matters and, forgetting what God said, did not direct their efforts toward the hope of the resurrection. Because the foolish were not able to go out and meet the bridegroom, for their lamps had gone out, they asked the wise to share their oil. They were not part of the group entering the wedding feast but were late and unworthy of entering. They had lost their opportunity (HILARY OF POITIERS). If our hearts, symbolized by lamps, have in them no sense of the deep reserve of God's graciousness, we are forever running short of oil and forgetting to carry enough ourselves (AUGUSTINE).

25:1 The Kingdom Compared with Ten Maidens

DIVISION BETWEEN GOOD AND BAD. HILARY OF POITIERS: The whole story is about the great day of the Lord, when those things concealed from the human mind will be revealed through our understanding of divine judgment. Then the faith true to the Lord's coming will win the just reward for unwavering hope. For in the five wise and five foolish virgins,[1] a complete separation between the faithful and unfaithful is established. Similarly, Moses had received the Ten Commandments written on two tablets.[2] For it was necessary that all these things be written on each. The double column represented, under a single testament, the division between the good and the bad, between the designation of right and left. ON MATTHEW 27.3.[3]

TO MEET THE BRIDEGROOM. AUGUSTINE: Let us now, beloved, discuss the five wise and the five foolish virgins. They wished to go to meet the bridegroom. What is the meaning of "to go and meet the bridegroom"? To go with all the heart, to eagerly await his coming. SERMON 93.5.[4]

THE TEN MAIDENS. AUGUSTINE: So then let us understand, dearly beloved, that this parable relates to us all, that is, to the whole church together, not to the clergy only, of whom we spoke yesterday, nor to the laity only but generally to all. Why then are the virgins five and five? These five and five virgins are all Christian souls together. But that I may tell you what by the Lord's inspiration I think, it is not souls of every sort but such souls as have the catholic faith and seem to have good works in the church of God. Yet even of them it is said, "Five are wise, and five are foolish." SERMON 93.5.[5]

25:2 Five Foolish, Five Wise

FOOLISH AND WISE. HILARY OF POITIERS:

---

[1]Mt 25:2. [2]Ex 32:15. [3]SC 258:204. [4]PL 38:575; NPNF 1 6:402 (Sermon 43). [5]PL 38:574; NPNF 1 6:401-2 (Sermon 43).

The wise virgins are those who, embracing the time available to them, were prepared at the first onset of the coming of the Lord. But the foolish were those who were lax and unmindful. They troubled themselves only over present matters and, forgetting what God said, did not direct their efforts toward hope for resurrection. ON MATTHEW 27.5.[6]

FIVE SENSES. AUGUSTINE: Every soul that enlivens a body is denoted by the number five, because it makes use of five senses. For there is nothing of which we have perception by the body except through this fivefold gate, either by sight, or hearing, or smelling, or tasting or touching. Whoever abstains from unlawful seeing, unlawful hearing, unlawful smelling, unlawful tasting and unlawful touching, by reason of blamelessness, is here called by the name of virgin. SERMON 93.2.[7]

THE ONLY DISTINCTION. AUGUSTINE: It says that even of these, who were virgins and carrying lamps, some are wise and some foolish. How is this distinction made? By what clue do we tell the difference? Only by whether the oil is present or missing. SERMON 93.4.[8]

25:3-4 Flasks of Oil

WHAT THE OIL SIGNIFIES. AUGUSTINE: It is some great thing, some exceedingly great thing, that this oil signifies. Do you think it might be charity? If we try out this hypothesis, we hazard no precipitate judgment. I will tell you why charity seems to be signified by the oil. The apostle says, "I will show you a still more excellent way."[9] "If I speak with the tongue of mortals and of angels but do not have love, I am a noisy gong or a clanging cymbal."[10] This is charity. It is "that way above the rest,"[11] which is with good reason signified by the oil. For oil swims above all liquids. Pour in water, and pour in oil upon it; the oil will swim above. Pour in oil, pour in water upon it; the oil will swim above. If you

keep the usual order, it will be uppermost; if you change the order, it will be uppermost. "Charity never fails."[12] SERMON 93.4.[13]

TOOK NO OIL WITH THEM. AUGUSTINE: What is the meaning of "took no oil with them"? What is "in their lamps"? In their hearts. For this reason the apostle wrote, "Indeed, this is our glory, the testimony of our conscience."[14] There is the oil, the precious oil. This oil is of the gift of God. We can put oil into our lamps, but we ourselves cannot create the olive. See, I have oil. But did I create the oil? It is of the gift of God. So you have oil. Carry it with you. What does it mean to "carry it with you"? To have it within, where it is pleasing to God. Note: those "foolish virgins, who brought no oil with them," wish to please a human audience by that abstinence of theirs by which they are called virgins, and by their good works, when they seem to carry lamps. But wishing to please human spectators, doing praiseworthy works, they forgot to carry with them the necessary oil. SERMON 93.7-8.[15]

THE FOOLISH DID NOT TAKE OIL. EPIPHANIUS THE LATIN: Those ten virgins, whom the Lord compared with the kingdom of heaven, were set up as an example for all virgins. They went out to meet the bridegroom and the bride. This means that they had received the grace of the Holy Spirit. They had come forth as virgins never stained by sin and had left behind earthly matters to meet Christ and the church. "But five were foolish and five wise. For the wise took oil with them along with their lamps. But the foolish did not take oil." Thus they were foolish, because they were not prepared for the future but only for the present. Thus they were foolish, because they did not have works of compassion.

---

[6]SC 258:208. [7]PL 38:574; NPNF 1 6:402 (Sermon 43). [8]PL 38:575; NPNF 1 6:402 (Sermon 43). [9]1 Cor 12:31. [10]1 Cor 13:1. [11]That more excellent way. [12]1 Cor 13:8. [13]PL 38:575; NPNF 1 6:402 (Sermon 43). [14]2 Cor 1:12. [15]PL 38:577; NPNF 1 6:403-4 (Sermon 43).

For the oil is compassion. But the wise took oil with their lamps. Thus they were wise, because they took these things not on account of people but on account of God. Thus they were wise, because they were virgins not for the sake of the present but the future. Thus they were wise, because they had works of compassion. Thus they were wise, because they were virgins in spirit and body. INTERPRETATION OF THE GOSPELS 36.[16]

THE VIRGINS AND THEIR LAMPS. AUGUSTINE: But if it is good to abstain from the unlawful excitements of the senses, and on that account every Christian soul has received the name of virgin, why then are five admitted and five rejected? They are both virgins, and yet half are rejected. It is not enough that they are virgins but that they also have lamps. They are virgins by reason of abstinence from unlawful indulgence of the senses. But they have lamps by reason of good works. Of these good works the Lord says, "Let your works shine before men, that they may see your good works and glorify your Father who is in heaven."[17] Again he said to his disciples, "Let your loins be girded and your lamps burning."[18] In the "girded loins" is virginity. In the "burning lamps" is good works. SERMON 93.2.[19]

25:5 The Bridegroom Delayed

BOTH BRIDE AND BRIDEGROOM. HILARY OF POITIERS: The bridegroom and bride represent our Lord, God in the flesh. For as the spirit is wedded to the flesh, so the flesh is wedded to the spirit. When the trumpet finally summons us and the bridegroom is at hand, all this will be revealed. Indeed, the two aspects are the corruptible body and the incorruptible soul. ON MATTHEW 27.4.[20]

THEY ALL SLEPT. AUGUSTINE: But he tarried. And "while he tarried, they all slept." What is "all"? Both the foolish and the wise. "All slum-

bered and slept." But is this sleeping good? What does this sleep mean at this time? Might it mean that during the delay of the bridegroom there is an inattentiveness, so that "because of the increase of lawlessness, the love of many will grow cold"?[21] Are we to understand this sleep in this way? I don't like that reading, and I will tell you why. Because among the ten are the five wise virgins. Certainly when the Lord said, "And because of the increase of lawlessness, the love of many will grow cold," he then went on directly to say, "But the one who endures to the end will be saved."[22] So on this premise, where would you place the wise virgins? Are they not among those that will "endure to the end"? They would not be admitted within unless they had "endured to the end." No coldness of love then crept over them. In them love did not grow cold. Love preserves its glow even to the very end. And because it glows even to the end, therefore are the gates of the bridegroom opened to them. So they are told to enter in, just as did that excellent servant[23] to whom it was said, "Enter into the joy of thy Lord."[24]

What then is the meaning of "they all slept"? There is another sleep which no one escapes. Don't you remember the apostle saying, "But I would not have you to be ignorant, brothers, concerning those who are asleep,"[25] that is, concerning those who are dead? For why are they called "those who are asleep," except that they all have died in their own time? Therefore it is said "they all slept." Do you imagine that just because one is wise, she does not have to die? Whether the virgin is foolish or wise, all suffer equally the sleep of death. SERMON 93.5.[26]

THE MOMENT OF LEAST AWARENESS. AUGUSTINE: Why "at midnight"? That is the moment of least expectation. There is no thought of it. It is

---

[16]PL Supp 3:892. [17]Mt 5:16. [18]Lk 12:35. [19]PL 38:574; NPNF 1 6:402 (Sermon 43). [20]SC 258:204. [21]Mt 24:12. [22]Mt 24:13. [23]In the parable of the talents. [24]Mt 25:21, 23. [25]1 Thess 4:13. [26]PL 38:575-76; NPNF 1 6:402-3 (Sermon 43).

a moment of complete unawareness. It is as though one might calculate complacently, . . . "So many years have passed since Adam, and the six thousand years are being completed,[27] and then immediately, according to the computation of certain expositors, the day of judgment will come." Yet these calculations come and pass away, and still the coming of the bridegroom is delayed. So the virgins who had gone to meet him now are sleeping. But just when he is least looked for, when the best calculators are saying, "The six thousand years were waited for, and, look, they are already gone by. So how then shall we know when he will come?"—he comes at midnight. So what is "midnight"? It means when you are least aware. SERMON 93.7.[28]

AT MIDNIGHT, A CRY. HILARY OF POITIERS: The delay of the bridegroom is the time for repentance. The sleep of those waiting is the peaceful rest of believers. The delay has given time for repentance. The cry comes at midnight, when no one yet knows what is happening. The sound of the trumpet of God heralds his coming,[29] rousing all to go out and meet the bridegroom. The taking up of the lamps is the return of souls into their bodies. And the light shining from them is the consciousness of good work, which is contained in our bodies, which are like flasks. ON MATTHEW 27.4.[30]

25:7-8 Preparing to Meet the Bridegroom

THE MAIDENS AROSE. AUGUSTINE: Of what cry are we speaking? That of which the apostle says, "In the twinkling of an eye, at the last trump? For the trumpet shall sound, and the dead shall be raised incorruptible, and we shall be changed"?[31] And so when the cry was made at midnight, "Behold, the bridegroom comes!" what follows? "Then all those maidens arose." But who are "all those" who arose? "The hour will come," said the Lord himself, "when all that are in the graves shall hear his voice and shall come forth."[32] Therefore at the last trumpet they

all arose. "When the foolish took their lamps, they took no oil with them; but the wise took flasks of oil with their lamps."[33] SERMON 93.7.[34]

THEY TRIMMED THEIR LAMPS. AUGUSTINE: Note then, beloved, that before those virgins slept, it is not said that their lamps were extinguished. The lamps of the wise virgins burned with an inward oil, with the assurance of a good conscience, with an inner glory, with an inmost charity. Yet the lamps of the foolish virgins were also still burning. In what way were they burning? They burned because there was no lack of praise among human onlookers. But after that they arose, that is, in the resurrection from the dead. They began to trim their lamps, that is, began to prepare to render to God an account of their works. And because there is then no human beholder to praise them, all persons are wholly employed in their own cause. There is no one then who is not thinking of self. Therefore there were none to sell them oil. SERMON 93.8.[35]

SEEKING THE PRAISE OF OTHERS. AUGUSTINE: So their lamps began to fail, and the foolish plead with the five wise, "Give us of your oil, for our lamps are going out." They sought for what they had been most prone to seek for, to shine, that is, with others' oil, to walk after others' praises. SERMON 93.8.[36]

25:9 Not Enough for Us and for You

PERHAPS THERE WILL NOT BE ENOUGH FOR

---

[27]The belief that the human race would become extinct in six thousand years was widespread among the early Christians, since a millennium was made to correspond with each of the six days of creation, to which was added a seventh millennium as the eschatological day of rest. Augustine rejects these chronological computations and warns his listeners not to base their hopes and expectations on them. [28]PL 38:576; NPNF 1 6:403 (Sermon 43). [29]1 Thess 4:16. [30]SC 258:206. [31]1 Cor 15:52. [32]Jn 5:28-29. [33]Mt 25:3-4. [34]PL 38:577; NPNF 1 6:403 (Sermon 43). [35]PL 38:577; NPNF 1 6:404 (Sermon 43). [36]PL 38:577-78; NPNF 1 6:404 (Sermon 43).

Us. Epiphanius the Latin: "As the bridegroom was delayed, they all slumbered and slept. But at midnight there was a cry, 'Behold, the bridegroom! Come out to meet him.' "[37] Likewise, the blessed apostle, Paul, declared, "For the Lord himself will descend from heaven with a cry of command, with the archangel's call and with the sound of the trumpet of God. And the dead in Christ will rise first; then we who are alive, who are left, shall be caught up together with them in the clouds to meet the Lord in the air; and so we shall always be with the Lord."[38] So those virgins rose and trimmed their lamps. But the foolish said to the wise, "Give us some of your oil, for our lamps are going out."[39] Their spiritual virginity was running out and failing, because they did not have works of religious devotion and compassion. But the wise replied, "Perhaps there will not be enough for us and for you; go rather to the dealers and buy for yourselves." For on the day of the resurrection and judgment, however much anyone might be rich in holy works, he will fear for himself, lest he not have enough. Interpretation of the Gospels 36.[40]

Go to the Dealers and Buy for Yourselves. Augustine: "But the wise replied, 'Perhaps there will not be enough for us and for you; go rather to the dealers and buy for yourselves.' " This is hardly the voice of those who give counsel but rather those who rebuke. Why are they scornful? Because they were wise, because wisdom was in them. For they were not wise by anything that belonged to them. Rather that wisdom was in them of which it is written in a certain Scripture that wisdom shall say to those that despised her, when they have fallen upon the evils which she threatened them, "I will laugh over your destruction."[41] No wonder the wise mock the foolish virgins. And what is this mocking?

"Go rather to the dealers and buy for yourselves," you who never desired to live well but because people praised you, who sold you oil.

Who are these who "sold you oil"? They are the ones who sell praises. Who sells praises, but flatterers? How much better would it have been for you not to have acquiesced to flatterers, and to have carried oil within, and for the sake of a good conscience to have done all good works....

Go then to those who deal in human praise, as you have been accustomed to doing, but do not expect the wise to give you oil at this crucial moment. Why? "Lest there not be enough for us and you." What is "lest there not be enough"? This was not spoken in any lack of hope but in a sober and godly humility. For though the good person have a good conscience, how does he know how the final judge, who is deceived by no one, will judge? He has a good conscience; no sins conceived in the heart argue with him. Yet, though his conscience is good, because of the daily sins of human life, he says to God daily, "Forgive us our debts," on the assumption that he has already done what comes next, "as we also forgive our debtors."[42] He has broken his bread to the hungry from the heart; from the heart has he clothed the naked. Out of that inward oil he has done good works, and yet in that judgment even his good conscience trembles. Sermon 93.8-9.[43]

25:10-11 The Bridegroom's Arrival

While They Went to Buy. Augustine: Now it is no wonder that precisely "while they were going out to buy," while they were seeking for praise from others and found none, while they were seeking for persons by whom to be comforted and found none—just then the shut door opened. Just then "the bridegroom came," and the bride, the church, was glorified then with Christ and all its members gathered together into one. Sermon 93.9.[44]

---

[37]Mt 25:5-6. [38]1 Thess 4:16-17. [39]Mt 25:8. [40]PL Supp 3:892-93. [41]Prov 1:26. [42]Mt 6:12. [43]PL 38:578; NPNF 1 6:404 (Sermon 43). [44]PL 38:579; NPNF 1 6:405 (Sermon 43).

THE DOOR WAS SHUT. HILARY OF POITIERS: Because the foolish were not able to go out and meet the bridegroom, since their lamps had gone out, they asked the wise to share their oil. They replied that they could not give them oil for there would perhaps not be enough. They told them to go to the dealers and buy for themselves.[45] These foolish were not part of the group entering the wedding feast but late and unworthy of entering. They had lost their opportunity. ON MATTHEW 27.5.[46]

THE FOOLISH CAME AFTERWARD. AUGUSTINE: "And those who were ready went in with him to the marriage feast; and the door was shut." Then the foolish virgins came afterward. But had they bought any oil? Had they found any from whom they might buy it? No. Therefore they found the doors shut. They began to knock, but too late. SERMON 93.9.[47]

25:12-13 Not Knowing the Time

I DO NOT KNOW YOU. CYRIL OF ALEXANDRIA: Jesus compares the rulers of the people with virgins. The person who discharges a sacred function must be undefiled in soul and body, just as Paul says, "that she might be devoted to the Lord in both body and spirit."[48] For it is customary for the Scripture to divide the present age into five seasons or times.[49] It assigns to each time both God-fearing and foolish souls, just as each time has wise persons and simpletons, righteous persons and wicked ones. In the parable all the virgins go out with their lamps. Jesus indicates by this that all souls have been illuminated by God through innate and natural laws but also indeed by the laws written by Moses. Now all the virgins went out to meet the bridegroom. All were determined to seek favor with God and to join themselves spiritually to the bridegroom. He sows in the hearts of the faithful the seed of every kind of virtue. Indeed, this is why he is called a bridegroom! Nevertheless some prove to be undistinguished, though they possess an illumination from God. . . . He mockingly calls their drowsiness the death of the flesh, which by necessity will go before both wise and foolish, whom the trumpet of the angels awakes at the time of Christ's second coming. For all who have been rendered powerless by death are awakened, the good and the bad, and all are made ready to present their defense before the judge. This is represented in the parable when each virgin trims her lamp, summing up all that has occurred in her life. The thoughtless virgins have brought no oil with them. Their soul begins to grow gloomy and as if snuffed out departs into a delirious state, so as to think they will be shown mercy through the virtue of the others. They are rejected as the other virgins say there is not enough for us and for you. The virtue of each scarcely suffices for the salvation of the soul, because even those who are very wise transgress in many ways. FRAGMENT 280.[50]

---

[45]Mt 25:8-9. [46]SC 258:208. [47]PL 38:579; NPNF 1 6:405 (Sermon 43). [48]1 Cor 7:34. [49]The five virgins symbolize all of humanity divided into five ages: infancy, childhood, youth, maturity and old age. [50]MKGK 250-51.

25:14-30 THE PARABLE OF THE TALENTS

[14]"For it will be as when a man going on a journey called his servants and entrusted to them his property; [15]to one he gave five talents,[d] to another two, to another one, to each according to

his ability. Then he went away. [16]*He who had received the five talents went at once and traded with them; and he made five talents more.* [17]*So also, he who had the two talents made two talents more.* [18]*But he who had received the one talent went and dug in the ground and hid his master's money.* [19]*Now after a long time the master of those servants came and settled accounts with them.* [20]*And he who had received the five talents came forward, bringing five talents more, saying, 'Master, you delivered to me five talents; here I have made five talents more.'* [21]*His master said to him, 'Well done, good and faithful servant; you have been faithful over a little, I will set you over much; enter into the joy of your master.'* [22]*And he also who had the two talents came forward, saying, 'Master, you delivered to me two talents; here I have made two talents more.'* [23]*His master said to him, 'Well done, good and faithful servant; you have been faithful over a little, I will set you over much; enter into the joy of your master.'* [24]*He also who had received the one talent came forward, saying, 'Master, I knew you to be a hard man, reaping where you did not sow, and gathering where you did not winnow;* [25]*so I was afraid, and I went and hid your talent in the ground. Here you have what is yours.'* [26]*But his master answered him, 'You wicked and slothful servant! You knew that I reap where I have not sowed, and gather where I have not winnowed?* [27]*Then you ought to have invested my money with the bankers, and at my coming I should have received what was my own with interest.* [28]*So take the talent from him, and give it to him who has the ten talents.* [29]*For to every one who has will more be given, and he will have abundance; but from him who has not, even what he has will be taken away.* [30]*And cast the worthless servant into the outer darkness; there men will weep and gnash their teeth.'*

d This talent was more than fifteen years' wages of a laborer

OVERVIEW: Those who do not love lose the love they have (GREGORY THE GREAT). One who is given a gift of preaching or teaching is given it so others may profit from it. If people do not use this gift, they will lose it. But one who uses the gift diligently will gain even more of the gift in abundance, even as the inactive recipient will lose what he or she received (CHRYSOSTOM). The risen Christ, entrusting his gifts to his servants the church, returns to receive an account.

The five talents may be viewed as the gift of the five senses, that is, knowledge of externals by means of sight, hearing, taste, smell and touch. The two talents signify theory and practice; the one talent signifies theory alone. Many in the church resemble the man given one talent, who hides it in the earth, employing abilities in earthly affairs but failing to seek spiritual profit

(GREGORY THE GREAT). One talent is by no means a paltry sum (ORIGEN). Note how sins of omission also are met with extreme rejection. Not only the active doer of evil things, the murderer and the adulterer, but also the one who fails to do good is culpable (CHRYSOSTOM).

Two seems to be an average or mundane number. The servant who received the two talents gained two talents more. This can be viewed either with respect to worldly knowledge or to a higher knowledge. Righteous persons belong to God, who reaps where not he but the righteous person has sown. So we may say that the righteous have scattered and given to the poor. The Lord, however, gathers to himself whatever the righteous person has given to the poor. Reaping what he has not sown and gathering where he has not winnowed, he counts as having been done to himself whatever the faithful have sown or winnowed for the poor (ORIGEN). Let us therefore contribute whatever we have—wealth, diligence, or care giving—for our neighbor's advantage. For the talents here are each person's ability, whether in the way of protection, or in money, or in teaching or in whatever thing one has been given. Let no one say, "I have but one talent and can do nothing with it." For this end God gave us speech, and hands, and feet, and strength of body and mind and understanding, that we might use all these things both for our own salvation and for our neighbor's advantage (CHRYSOSTOM). Who is this man who sets out for foreign parts but our Redeemer, who departed to heaven in the body he had taken on (GREGORY THE GREAT)?

25:14-15 Entrusted with Talents According to Ability

HE ENTRUSTED HIS PROPERTY. ORIGEN: This man, therefore, "like a man going abroad, called his servants and delivered to them" his money with pure words. Indeed, his "words" are "words that are pure, silver refined in a furnace on the ground, purified seven times."[1] COMMENTARY ON MATTHEW 65.[2]

A MAN GOING ON A JOURNEY. GREGORY THE GREAT: Who is the man who sets out for foreign parts but our Redeemer, who departed to heaven in the body he had taken on? Earth is the proper place for his body. It is transported to foreign parts, so to speak, when he establishes it in heaven. FORTY GOSPEL HOMILIES 9.1.[3]

MATTHEW'S NUMBERS DIFFER FROM LUKE'S. CHRYSOSTOM: In Luke[4] the parable of the talents is told differently, and it is indeed different. For there, from the one pound different degrees of increase were made. From one pound one brought five, another ten, one nothing more, and they received recompense accordingly. Here it is different: The one that received two gave two. The one who received five made five more. But in Luke's version, from the same investment, one made the greater and one the less increase, with the reward dispensed accordingly. But in both cases he does not require his investment back immediately. THE GOSPEL OF MATTHEW, HOMILY 78.2.[5]

THE DISTRIBUTOR OF TALENTS. CYRIL OF ALEXANDRIA: The man who is the landowner is actually the Creator and Lord of all. The Word compares the time the landowner spends away from home in the parable to either the ascension of Christ into heaven or at any rate to the unseen and invisible character of the divine nature. Now one must conceive of the property of God as those in each country and city who believe in him. He calls his servants those who according to the times Christ crowns with the glory of the priesthood. For the holy Paul writes, "No one takes this honor upon himself; he must be called by God."[6] He hands over [his property] to those who are under him, to each giving a spiritual gift so that he might have character and aptitude. We think that this distribution of the talents is not supplied to the household servants in equal measure because each is quite different from the other in their understanding. Immediately they head out for their labors, he says, directly indicating to us here that apart from the procrastination of one they are fit to carry out the work of God. Surely those who are bound by fear and laziness will end up in the worst evils. For he buried, Jesus says, the talent given to him in the earth. He kept the gift hidden, making it unprofitable for others and useless for himself. For that very reason the talent is taken away from him and will be given to the one who is already rich. The Spirit has departed from such as these and the gift of the divine gifts. But to those who are

---

[1]Ps 12:6 (11:7 LXX). [2]GCS 38.2:153. [3]PL 76:1106; CS 123:127 (Homily 18). [4]Lk 19:11-28. [5]PG 58:713; NPNF 1 10:471-72. [6]Heb 5:4.

industrious an even more lavish gift will be presented. FRAGMENT 283.[7]

THE FIVE BODILY SENSES. GREGORY THE GREAT: The man setting out for foreign parts entrusted his goods to his servants, for he granted his spiritual gifts to those who believed in him. To one he entrusted five talents, to another two, to another one. There are five bodily senses, sight, hearing, taste, smell and touch. The five talents represent the gift of the five senses, that is, knowledge of externals; the two talents signify theory and practice; the one talent signifies theory alone. FORTY GOSPEL HOMILIES 9.1.[8]

25:16-18 Five Talents, Two Talents, One Talent

TO EACH ACCORDING TO ABILITY. ORIGEN: There is the ability of those to whom "five talents" were given, the ability of those to whom "two talents" were given and the ability of those to whom "one talent" was given. Also, one person did not receive the same amount as the other. And "he who had received the one talent" received by no means a paltry sum, for even one talent from this master is considerable. However, three in number are the servants of him who "set out like a man going abroad," just as in another parable those who bear fruit are three in number: "some" of them. Again "one hundred, some sixty and some thirty."[9] But he who gains thirty is saved. COMMENTARY ON MATTHEW 66.[10]

FIVE TALENTS MORE. GREGORY THE GREAT: The person who received five talents gained another five. There are some who, even without knowing how to probe into inward and mystical matters, use the natural gifts they have received to teach correctly those they can reach to strive for their heavenly home. While guarding themselves from physical wantonness, from striving after earthly things and from taking pleasure in

things they can see, they restrain others too from these things by their counsel. FORTY GOSPEL HOMILIES 9.1.[11]

TWO TALENTS MORE. GREGORY THE GREAT. And there are some endowed with two talents, so to speak, who comprehend both theory and practice. They understand the fine points of interior matters and accomplish astonishing things outwardly. When they preach to others by both theory and practice, their business venture, so to call it, yields a twofold gain. It is good that another five and another two are said to have been gained, since when preaching is provided for both sexes the talents received are so to speak doubled. FORTY GOSPEL HOMILIES 9.1.[12]

HE DUG IN THE GROUND. ORIGEN: The master's words scold him "who had received the one talent" and "hid it in the ground." And I wonder whether those who received "five talents" can be deemed to be more mature than those who study and receive the more noble and sublime context of Scripture. Now those who received "two talents" improved somewhat on the original sum given but were unable to gain more. Those in the third group, however, were unable to capitalize on the amount they had first received. It is entirely a matter of numbers, therefore, in those words that form a fitting discourse of our Lord and Savior—namely, five and two and one. COMMENTARY ON MATTHEW 66.[13]

HE HID THE MONEY. GREGORY THE GREAT: But the person who received one talent went away, dug in the earth and hid his master's money. Hiding a talent in the earth means employing one's abilities in earthly affairs, failing to seek spiritual profit, never raising one's heart from earthly thoughts. There are some

---

[7]MKGK 252-53. [8]PL 76:1106; CS 123:127 (Homily 18). [9]Mt 13:23. [10]GCS 38.2:154. [11]PL 76:1106; CS 123:127-28 (Homily 18). [12]PL 76:1106; CS 123:128 (Homily 18). [13]GCS 38.2:154.

who have received the gift of understanding but have a taste only for things that pertain to the body. The prophet says of them, "They are wise in doing evil, but they do not know how to do good."[14] FORTY GOSPEL HOMILIES 9.1.[15]

25:19 The Master Settled Accounts

THE MASTER CAME TO THEM. ORIGEN: Notice too that the servants did not go to the master so they might be judged and receive their just deserts. Rather, "the master came to them" in due course. "After a long time" he came and "settled accounts with them" on everything they had done, compensating them for the gains of their good works and the losses of their sins. Settling "accounts" and scrutinizing everything, he dealt with each one individually. It behooves us, then, as those who by sinning have done evil and by doing good reaped a profit, to keep a guard on our hearts. In this way, when our Master comes to settle accounts with us, we may not be found to have done evil, even through idle words. COMMENTARY ON MATTHEW 66.[16]

AFTER A LONG TIME. CHRYSOSTOM: In the case of the vineyard, he let it out to farmers and went into a far country. Here he committed to them the talents and took his journey that you might understand his patience and long-suffering. And to me he seems to say these things as an intimation of the resurrection. But here it is no more a vineyard and husbandmen but all farmers. For it is not to rulers only or to Jews but to all that he addresses this discourse. And those who bring a return to him confess frankly, both what is their own and what their Master's. And the one says, "Lord, you gave me five talents," and the other says, "two," indicating that from him they received the source of their gain, and they are very thankful and reckon all to him.[17] THE GOSPEL OF MATTHEW, HOMILY 78.2.[18]

WEIGHING THE GAIN. GREGORY THE GREAT: The Lord who dispensed the talents returns to demand an account, because he who now generously bestows spiritual gifts may at the judgment inquire searchingly into what was achieved; he may take into account what everyone has received and weigh up the gain we bring back from his gifts. FORTY GOSPEL HOMILIES 9.1.[19]

25:20-21 Entering the Joy of the Master

BRINGING FIVE TALENTS MORE. ORIGEN: We earnestly believe that we are incapable of explaining such things, unlike those who infer from the perceptible events of the Scriptures more inspired meanings. These are spiritual meanings that Solomon calls "divine" and which Jeremiah calls "faculties of the heart"[20] and which Paul in his epistle to the Hebrews calls "faculties trained by practice to distinguish good from evil."[21] The persons in the first group are those who in addition to the "five talents" gained five more, trading with them and capitalizing on their ability. Successfully negotiating and zealously teaching, they traded and acquired five more talents. Indeed, no one readily benefits from another's ability unless he has that ability to begin with. A wise man grows in wisdom, a trustworthy man in trust.

"He brought five talents more." Note this: What each man knows, he can teach to another, up to the level of as much as he knows. This he can teach to another and no more. Therefore whatever someone has in himself, by teaching this to another, he gains it in the other, making that person have what he too has. Consequently he who had received the "five talents" is said not to have gained more than the five which he had and "he who had received the two talents" not more than the two which he had. COMMENTARY ON MATTHEW 66.[22]

---

[14]Jer 4:22. [15]PL 76:1106-7; CS 123:128 (Homily 18). [16]GCS 38.2:157. [17]Mt 25:20. [18]PG 58:713-14; NPNF 1 10:472. [19]PL 76:1107; CS 123:128 (Homily 18). [20]Jer 4:19. [21]Heb 5:14. [22]GCS 38.2:154-55.

WELL DONE, GOOD AND FAITHFUL SERVANT.
ORIGEN: The first servant stepped forward in
confidence, because he had gone to work and
made a profit. That confidence now made him
bold, for he was the first one to approach the
master and declare to him, "Master, you delivered to me five talents; here I have made five talents more." The master replied in words
favorable to us all, even as our master will reply
when he settles with us: "Well done, good and
faithful servant." These words run counter to
what he said to the third man: "You wicked and
slothful servant." COMMENTARY ON MATTHEW
67.[23]

SET OVER MUCH. CHRYSOSTOM: What then
does the master say? "Well done, good and faithful servant." For it is good to see the neighbor's
benefit. "You have been faithful over a little, I
will set you over much; enter into the joy of your
master." He means by this expression, enter into
the realm of all blessedness. THE GOSPEL OF
MATTHEW, HOMILY 78.2.[24]

25:22-23 Rewarding Faithfulness

YOU GAVE TWO TALENTS. ORIGEN: Concerning the two talents, those who did not stay with
the original sum given but sought to excel—
though unable to surpass the measure of two talents—are those who had imbibed worldly
know-how. Two seems to be an average or mundane number. Having received the two talents
from the one who knew their ability, he gained
two talents more. This can be viewed either
with respect to worldly knowledge or to a higher
knowledge. COMMENTARY ON MATTHEW 66.[25]

TWO TALENTS. GREGORY THE GREAT: The servant who returned with two talents was praised
by his master. He was led to his eternal reward
when his master said to him, "Well done, good
and faithful servant. Because you have been faithful about a few things, I shall put you in charge of
many." FORTY GOSPEL HOMILIES 9.2.[26]

ETERNAL JOYS. GREGORY THE GREAT: All the
good deeds of our present life, however many
they may appear to be, are few in comparison
with our eternal recompense. The faithful servant is put in charge of many things after over-
coming all the troubles brought him by
perishable things. He glories in the eternal joys
of his heavenly dwelling. He is brought completely into the joy of his master when he is
taken into his eternal home and joined to the
company of angels. His inner joy at his gift is
such that there is no longer any external perishable thing that can cause him sorrow. FORTY
GOSPEL HOMILIES 9.2.[27]

25:24-25 Hiding the One Talent

YOU REAPED WHERE YOU DID NOT SOW. ORI-
GEN: They exemplify the very words of the servant who answers and says, "I knew you to be a
hard man" and one who was able to reap "where
you did not sow and gather where you did not
winnow."

The master answered him and reproached
him as a wicked and lazy servant. Note that he
did not call himself a hard man. But he agreed
with the servant when he went on to say, "You
knew that I reap where I did not sow and gather
where I did not winnow."

How are we to understand the phrase that
our Lord truly reaps where he did not sow and
gathers where he did not winnow? In this way, it
seems to me: The righteous man "sows in the
Spirit," from which he will also "reap eternal
life."[28] Everything that is sown and reaped for
eternal life by the righteous man, God reaps.
The righteous man belongs to God, who reaps
where not he but the righteous man has sown.
So we may say that the righteous man has "scattered and given to the poor."[29] The Lord, however, gathers to himself whatever the righteous

---

[23]GCS 38.2:157-58. [24]PG 58:714; NPNF 1 10:472. [25]GCS
38.2:155. [26]PL 76:1107; CS 123:128 (Homily 18). [27]PL 76:1107;
CS 123:128-29 (Homily 18). [28]Gal 6:8. [29]2 Cor 9:9.

man has "scattered and given to the poor." Reaping what he has not sown and gathering where he has not winnowed, he counts as having been done to himself whatever the faithful have sown or winnowed for the poor. He says to those who have done good to their neighbors: "Come you, blessed of my Father, inherit the kingdom which was prepared for you. I was hungry and you gave me to eat . . ."[30]

And since he wishes to reap where he did not sow and to gather where he did not winnow, when he does not find anything, he says to those who failed to reap and gather: "Depart from me, you wicked, into everlasting fire, which my Father has prepared for the devil and his angels. For I was hungry and you did not give me to eat."[31] COMMENTARY ON MATTHEW 68.[32]

ONE TALENT. ORIGEN: Then there was another servant who showed less ability. Because of it, the master of the household gave him "one talent" as though to the servant less capable. "Receiving" it, the servant went away and "hid the talent in the earth." Instead he should have entrusted the money to the bankers. COMMENTARY ON MATTHEW 66.[33]

I WAS AFRAID. CHRYSOSTOM: But not so that other one, but how? "Master, I knew you to be a hard man, reaping where you did not sow, and gathering where you did not winnow. I was afraid. I hid your talent. Here it is. It belongs to you." THE GOSPEL OF MATTHEW, HOMILY 78.2.[34]

I HID YOUR TALENT. GREGORY THE GREAT: But the third servant was unwilling to work with his talent. He returned to his master with words of excuse: "Master, I knew that you are a hard man, reaping where you have not sown, gathering where you have not scattered; being afraid, I went away and hid your talent in the earth. Here it is; see, you have what is yours." The useless servant called his master hard, and yet he neglected to serve him for profit. He said

that he was afraid to invest the talent for interest, when he should have been afraid only of bringing it back to his master without interest. For many people in the church resemble that servant. They are afraid to attempt a better way of life but not of resting in idleness. When they advert to the fact that they are sinners, the prospect of grasping the ways of holiness alarms them, but they feel no fear at remaining in their wickedness.

Peter is a good example. When he was still weak, he saw the miracle of the fishes and said, "Depart from me, O Lord, because I am a sinful man."[35] If you regard yourself as a sinner, it is only right that you not drive God away from you! But those who see that they are weak and are for this reason unwilling to improve their habits or way of life are like people admitting that they are sinners and at the same time banishing God. They flee him whom they ought to hallow in themselves; even in the agony of death they do not know where to turn and cling to life. FORTY GOSPEL HOMILIES 9.3.[36]

25:26-27 A Wicked and Lazy Servant

SLOTHFUL SERVANT. GREGORY THE GREAT: The Lord answered, "You wicked and lazy servant! You knew that I reap where I have not sown and gather where I have not scattered. Therefore you ought to have given my money to the moneylenders. On my return I would at least have received what was mine with interest." The servant was trapped by his own words when his master confirms, "Yes, I reap where I have not sown and gather where I have not scattered. I expect something of you that I have not given. I expect much more than merely what I gave you to trade with." FORTY GOSPEL HOMILIES 9.3.[37]

---

[30]Mt 25:34-35. [31]Mt 25:41. [32]GCS 38.2:159-60. [33]GCS 38.2:155. [34]PG 58:714; NPNF 1 10:472. [35]Lk 5:8. [36]PL 76:1107; CS 123:129* (Homily 18). [37]PL 76:1107-8; CS 123:129-30* (Homily 18).

YOU OUGHT TO HAVE INVESTED MY MONEY. CHRYSOSTOM: What then does the Master say? "You ought to have invested my money with the banker." You ought to have spoken to someone and received his advice and been admonished. Are the bankers bad people? That is not for you to say.

What could be more gentle than this? Those who give money at interest keep close accounts on its repayment. But you have not done anything with it. You ought to have given it to someone else to work with and required them to report to you. I require it back with increase, that is, with some good works to boot. You ought to have done the easy part and left with someone else the part that is more difficult. THE GOSPEL OF MATTHEW, HOMILY 78.2-3.[38]

I SHOULD HAVE RECEIVED INTEREST. GREGORY THE GREAT: To give money to moneylenders means to lay out knowledge of preaching to those who can practice it. As you perceive my danger, if I hold the Lord's money, so carefully consider your own, dearly beloved. What you have will be required of you with interest. The point about interest is that more comes back than was laid out. FORTY GOSPEL HOMILIES 9.3-4.[39]

25:28-29 Giving and Taking Away

TO THE ONE WITH TEN TALENTS. ORIGEN: Note that the talent is taken away from the wicked and slothful servant and is given "to him who has ten talents." It is not easy to explain how what has been given to a person can be taken away and given to another who does good, so he may have it in addition to what he gained. It is possible, however, since God, who invariably makes good sense in the teaching of truth, by his divinity can take away the corresponding amount from him who made poor use of it and give it to him who multiplied his own.

"For to everyone who has will more be given, and he will have abundance; but from him who

has not, even what he has will be taken away." Furthermore, whatever someone has from natural creation, when he has exercised it, he receives that very thing also from the grace of God. In this way he may have abundance and be stronger in what he has. Concerning not only wisdom but also every good quality, we should reflect on the words of Solomon: "And if there is anyone perfect among the children of men, if your wisdom is taken away from him, he will be counted as nothing."[40] COMMENTARY ON MATTHEW 69.[41]

SO TAKE THE TALENT. CHRYSOSTOM: "Since he did nothing with his one talent, even that one is to be taken from him and given to the more productive partner. For to every one who has will more be given, and he will have abundance, but from him who has not, even what he has will be taken away." What does this mean for us? One who is given a gift of preaching or teaching is given it so others may profit from it. If one does not use this gift, he will lose it. But one who uses the gift diligently will gain even more of the gift in abundance, even as the inactive recipient will lose what he received. The penalty is not, however, limited to this. The punishment in addition is intolerable, and the sentence is filled with heavy accusation. THE GOSPEL OF MATTHEW, HOMILY 78.3.[42]

SCRIPTURAL EXAMPLES OF THOSE TO WHOM MORE WAS GIVEN. ORIGEN: If someone should wish to peruse Scripture elsewhere to hear from his Master the word *faithful*, I believe Abraham is a good instance: "Abraham believed God; and he reckoned it to him as righteousness."[43] Then there is the man who heard from his master the words "faithful servant." Without doubt his faith was reckoned as righteousness to him, like the faith of him who was faithful in little things, so

---

[38]PG 58:714; NPNF 1 10:472. [39]PL 76:1108; CS 123:130* (Homily 18). [40]Wis 9:6. [41]GCS 38.2:162. [42]PG 58:714; NPNF 1 10:472. [43]Gen 15:6.

that every mystery of the resurrection and the administration of godly affairs may be entrusted to him. Everything in this life, by the way, consists of little things.

Let us note also where that good and faithful servant is going who was faithful in the little things of this life. "Enter into the joy of your master," he is told. Every delight and every joy will be there when those who weep here below will be merry hereafter and those who righteously mourn will receive a worthy consolation. He says this in effect both to the one "who had received the five talents" and to the one "who had received the two." He says, "Enter." Know what it is to approach me and to pass from this world to the next. Notice also that the master said to the second servant what he said to the first: "Well done, good and faithful servant; you have been faithful over a little, I will set you over much."

I wonder also, since the same words were said to both servants, whether by chance the one who had less ability and exercised it fully would be regarded less by God than the one who had more ability. I wonder if this is in fulfillment of what was said elsewhere: "He that gathered much had nothing over, and he that gathered little had no lack."[44]

Such is indicated also concerning the commandment of love for God or for one's neighbor, according to the words "You shall love the Lord your God with all your whole heart and with all your soul and with all your strength."[45] Without doubt, when someone has loved God with all his heart and with all his soul and with all his strength, he has the same reward of love as the person with a bigger heart or with a more gifted soul or with greater ability. This alone is required: At whatever level one has received a gift from God, one should use it for God's glory.

It seems to me that "he who had received the one talent" was indeed among the believers, even though he was not among those who acted boldly in faith. He is among those who scatter their energies in trying to do everything but

have nothing to show for it.[46] Perhaps their behavior in other respects is not blameworthy. What they received they guard carefully, but they do not add to it, nor do they trade or faithfully transact with it. For that reason, the word does not bear any fruit in them, nor did anyone else gain from it. They even seem to be the type of people who fear God. They often see God as harsh and hard and implacable. COMMENTARY ON MATTHEW 67.[47]

THE THREE SERVANTS DISTINGUISHED. ORIGEN: The master had three servants. After they believed and became his servants, they were given a task to do. They received money from their master. One of them "traded" with it and "gained." The second one "gained," but not as much. And the third, out of fear and being insufficiently faithful, "went away and hid" his master's money. From his defensiveness it appears that he feared the master. He was in awe of the master even as the other had "zeal for God but not according to knowledge."[48] Diffidently, he "hid" his talent in the ground. Such are those who neither exert themselves nor question what has been said nor extend themselves to benefit souls, but they scatter their energies on what they have received and have been entrusted with. COMMENTARY ON MATTHEW 66.[49]

FROM ONE WHO HAS NOT. CHRYSOSTOM: Let us therefore, knowing these things, contribute whatever we have—wealth, diligence or care giving—for our neighbor's advantage. For the talents here are each person's abilities, whether in the way of protection, or in money, or in teaching or in whatever thing you have been given. Let no one say, "I have but one talent and can do nothing with it." You are not poorer than

---

[44]2 Cor 8:15; Ex 16:18. [45]Mt 22:37. [46]To evaluate this judgment of Origen, keep in mind that in his time the Christian religion, though in fact widely tolerated, had not yet become legally accepted and thus remained the subject of pagan hostility. Origen himself was soon to suffer the rigors of the Decian persecution. [47]GCS 38.2:158. [48]Rom 10:2. [49]GCS 38.2:155.

the widow. You are not more uninstructed than Peter and John, who were both "unlearned and ignorant men."[50] Nevertheless, since they demonstrated zeal and did all things for the common good, they were received into heaven. For nothing is so pleasing to God as to live for the common advantage.

For this end God gave us speech, and hands, and feet, and strength of body and mind and understanding, that we might use all these things both for our own salvation and for our neighbor's advantage. Our speech not only is useful for hymns and thanksgiving, but it is profitable also for instruction and admonition. And if indeed we used it to this end, we should be imitating our Master; but if for the opposite ends, the devil. THE GOSPEL OF MATTHEW, HOMILY 78.3.[51]

VIGILANCE IN GUARDING LOVE. GREGORY THE GREAT: And immediately a general thought is added: "For to everyone who has, more will be given, and he will have more than enough; but from everyone who has not, even what he seems to have will be taken away from him." To the one who has, more will be given, and he will have more than enough. Whoever has love receives other gifts as well. Whoever does not have love loses even the gifts he appeared to have received. Hence it is necessary, my friends, that in everything you do, you be vigilant about guarding love. True love is to love your friend in God and your enemy for the sake of God. Whoever does not have this loses every good that he possesses;

he is deprived of the talent he received, and according to the Lord's sentence he is cast into external darkness. External darkness comes as a punishment to one who has fallen voluntarily into internal darkness through his own sin. The one who freely enjoyed pleasurable darkness in this world will be constrained to suffer punishing darkness in the next. FORTY GOSPEL HOMILIES 9.6.[52]

25:30 Cast into Outer Darkness

THE WORTHLESS SERVANT CAST INTO DARKNESS. CHRYSOSTOM: "The unprofitable servant is to be cast into outer darkness, where there shall be weeping and gnashing of teeth." Do you see how sins of omission also are met with extreme rejection? It is not only the covetous, the active doer of evil things and the adulterer, but also the one who fails to do good.

Let us listen carefully then to these words. As we have opportunity, let us work to cooperate with our salvation. Let us get oil for our lamps. Let us labor to add to our talent. For if we are backward and spend our time in sloth here, no one will pity us any more hereafter, though we should wail ten thousand times. . . . Remember the virgins who again entreated and came to him and knocked, all in vain and without effect. THE GOSPEL OF MATTHEW, HOMILY 78.3.[53]

---

[50]Acts 4:13. [51]PG 58:714-15; NPNF 1 10:472. [52]PL 76:1108-9; CS 123:131 (Homily 18). [53]PG 58:714; NPNF 1 10:472.

25:31-46 THE FINAL JUDGMENT

[31]"When the Son of man comes in his glory, and all the angels with him, then he will sit on his glorious throne. [32]Before him will be gathered all the nations, and he will separate them one from another as a shepherd separates the sheep from the goats, [33]and he will place the sheep at

his right hand, but the goats at the left. ³⁴*Then the King will say to those at his right hand, 'Come, O blessed of my Father, inherit the kingdom prepared for you from the foundation of the world;* ³⁵*for I was hungry and you gave me food, I was thirsty and you gave me drink, I was a stranger and you welcomed me,* ³⁶*I was naked and you clothed me, I was sick and you visited me, I was in prison and you came to me.'* ³⁷*Then the righteous will answer him, 'Lord, when did we see thee hungry and feed thee, or thirsty and give thee drink?* ³⁸*And when did we see thee a stranger and welcome thee, or naked and clothe thee?* ³⁹*And when did we see thee sick or in prison and visit thee?'* ⁴⁰*And the King will answer them, 'Truly, I say to you, as you did it to one of the least of these my brethren, you did it to me.'* ⁴¹*Then he will say to those at his left hand, 'Depart from me, you cursed, into the eternal fire prepared for the devil and his angels;* ⁴²*for I was hungry and you gave me no food, I was thirsty and you gave me no drink,* ⁴³*I was a stranger and you did not welcome me, naked and you did not clothe me, sick and in prison and you did not visit me.'* ⁴⁴*Then they also will answer, 'Lord, when did we see thee hungry or thirsty or a stranger or naked or sick or in prison, and did not minister to thee?'* ⁴⁵*Then he will answer them, 'Truly, I say to you, as you did it not to one of the least of these, you did it not to me.'* ⁴⁶*And they will go away into eternal punishment, but the righteous into eternal life."*

OVERVIEW: When someone is brought into the presence of a king or a judge, on the spot where he is ordered to stand he will learn whether he has been brought in because of the good he did or the evil (INCOMPLETE WORK ON MATTHEW). He who knows our thoughts, who foresees all human works and knows how to judge rightly, will separate them according to the merits of each person, as a shepherd separates the sheep from the goats (EPIPHANIUS THE LATIN). The sheep signify righteous people by reason of their gentleness, because they harm no one, and by reason of their patience, because when they are harmed by others, they bear it without resistance. Jesus refers to sinners as goats, however, because these vices characterize goats: capriciousness, pride and belligerence (INCOMPLETE WORK ON MATTHEW). If Jesus has appeared in a lowly role, he now appears in an entirely different role, in which he reproaches, confronts and sits on his throne of glory (CHRYSOSTOM).

Even as Christ is healthy in souls that are healthy, he is ailing in souls that are ailing. They welcome Christ himself and clothe, by teaching righteousness, those who are naked and even

without a garment of righteousness (INCOMPLETE WORK ON MATTHEW). They have woven a garment for the cold and shivering Christ (ORIGEN). But he curses the works of those at his left hand. "I prepared the kingdom for you," he says, "but the fire I did not prepare for you but for the devil and his angels." But you have cast yourselves in it. You have imputed it to yourselves. Even when you see a dog hungry, you feel sympathy. But when you see the Lord hungry, you ignore it. You are left without excuse (CHRYSOSTOM).

25:31 The Son of Man Coming in Glory

WHEN HE COMES IN HIS GLORY. CHRYSOSTOM: In his previous parables when he speaks of two persons he is referring to two portions of humanity, the disobedient and the obedient. Here he speaks out more fearfully and with fuller clarity.

He does not say that the coming kingdom is compared to this or that, as he has been speaking previously, but now openly shows himself to be the Son of man, who "shall come in his glory."

If he has up to now appeared in a condition of dishonor, now he appears in a different role. He reproaches. He confronts. He sits upon his throne of glory.

And he continually mentions glory. For his cross was drawing near, a thing that seemed to be a matter of reproach. So he lifts his hearers up and brings before their sight the judgment seat, with all the world gathered around him. The Gospel of Matthew, Homily 79.1.[1]

The Son of Man. Jerome: Jesus rightly promises that the glory of the triumphant one [would follow] after two days in which he would celebrate the Passover and be consigned to the cross, mocked by humanity and given wine and gall to drink. Thus he will offset with the promised reward the blameworthy actions to follow. Clearly he who is to be seen in majesty is the Son of man. Commentary on Matthew 4.25.33.[2]

All the Angels with Him. Chrysostom: And not in this way only does he make his discourse awesome but also by showing the heavens opened. For all the angels will be present with him. They are there to bear witness to the many ways they had served when sent by the Lord for the salvation of humanity. Everything spoken of that day shows that it is fearful. Then "shall be gathered together," he says, "all nations," that is, all humankind.[3] The Gospel of Matthew, Homily 79.1.[4]

25:32-33 Gathering and Separating

Gathered Before Him. Epiphanius the Latin: How can he be the Son of man when he is God and will come to judge all nations? He is the Son of man because he appeared on earth as a man and was persecuted as a man. Therefore this person who they said was a man will raise all nations from the dead and judge every person according to his works. Every race on earth will see him, both those who rejected him and those

who despised him as a man. They will see him then, but not everyone in the same way: some will see him in punishment and others in heavenly bliss.[5] All nations will be gathered together by the angels from the foundation of the world, beginning first with Adam and Eve down to the last person on earth—whoever experienced human birth. "And he will separate them one from another as a shepherd separates the sheep from the goats." He, our Lord, who knows our thoughts, who foresees all human works and knows how to judge righteously, will separate them according to the merits of each person, as a shepherd separates the sheep from the goats. Interpretation of the Gospels 38.[6]

He Will Separate Them. Incomplete Work on Matthew: "And he will separate them one from another as a shepherd separates the sheep from the goats." So then, people on earth are intermingled, and not only intermingled in that the righteous live side by side with the wicked, but they are also indistinguishable. Between the righteous and the wicked there is no apparent difference. Even as in wintertime you cannot tell the healthy trees apart from the withered trees but in beautiful springtime you can tell the difference, so too each person according to his faith and his works will be exposed. The wicked will not have any leaves or show any fruit, but the righteous will be clothed with the leaves of eternal life and adorned with the fruit of glory. In this way they will be separated by the heavenly shepherd and Lord. The earthly shepherd separates animals by their type of body, whereas Christ separates people by their type of soul. The sheep signify righteous people by reason of their gentleness, because

---

[1]PG 58:717; NPNF 1 10:475. [2]CCL 77:243. [3]Chrysostom refers to the parable of the talents, in which the figures of the individual servants represent entire categories of humanity. He extends his observation to the pericope of the judgment of nations as well, observing immediately afterward that Jesus speaks no longer in parables but directly so as to cause greater fear. [4]PG 58:717; NPNF 1 10:475. [5]Dan 12:2. [6]PL Supp 3:899.

they harm no one, and by reason of their patience, because when they are harmed by others, they bear it without resistance. He refers to sinners as goats, however, because these vices characterize goats: capriciousness toward other animals, pride and belligerence. Homily 54.[7]

Right and Left. Incomplete Work on Matthew: "And he will place the sheep at his right hand but the goats at the left." When someone is brought into the presence of a king or a judge, on the very spot where he is ordered to stand he will learn whether he has been brought in because of the good he did or the evil. If he has been brought in because of the good, he is immediately made to stand close; if because of the evil, he is ordered to stand at a distance. So too God will place the righteous at his right hand but the goats at the left. Each one will know what his merits are, then and there. When judgment is passed, the punishment of shame will follow. He will justly place the righteous at his right hand, because they never knew the left side; he will justly place the wicked at the left, because they never wanted to know the right side. Homily 54.[8]

25:34 Blessed by My Father

Inherit the Kingdom. Chrysostom: He commended them for doing what was right. He reveals how great is his bond of love for them and has been from the beginning. "Then the king will say to those at his right hand, 'Come, O blessed of my Father, inherit the kingdom prepared for you from the foundation of the world.'" To what other blessedness could this blessedness be compared? To be blessed of the Father! Why were they counted worthy of such a great honor? "I was hungry and you gave me food, I was thirsty and you gave me drink." What honor! What blessedness!

He did not say "take" but "inherit" as one's own, as your Father's, as yours, as due to you from the first. "For before you were," he says,

"these things had been prepared and made ready for you, because I knew you would be such as you are." The Gospel of Matthew, Homily 79.2.[9]

First the Right Hand. Incomplete Work on Matthew: "Then he will say to those at his right hand . . ." And why will he not address first those at his left? Because God is always more willing to praise than to denounce. For he gives good things to those who are good according to his intentions because he is good; but to those who are bad, he reluctantly gives bad things against his intentions because he is a judge. Whatever humanity does against his nature, he does rather hesitantly. If indeed Christ delighted in the punishment of sinners, he never would have delivered himself up for them. "Come, O blessed of my Father," he says, "inherit the kingdom prepared for you from the foundation of the world." You who sowed one seed on earth will deservedly have a hundredfold in heaven. Indeed, the kingdom of heaven has not been created according to what human righteousness deserves but according to what God's power can prepare. "I was hungry, and you gave me food; I was thirsty, and you gave me drink." And many other acts of mercy, as we pointed out. Homily 54.[10]

25:35-40 Fed, Clothed, Welcomed

You Gave Me Food. Chrysostom: Then, in order that you may see in another way also the justice of the sentence, he first praises those who have done right: "Come, O blessed of my Father, inherit the kingdom prepared for you from the foundation of the world; for I was hungry, and you gave me food," and all that follows. Note that the judgment is in effect made by their fellow servants. This has happened before, when the virgins are judged by the virgins[11] and in the

---

[7]PG 56:942. [8]PG 56:943. [9]PG 58:719; NPNF 1 10:476. [10]PG 56:943. [11]Mt 25:1-13.

case of the drunken and gluttonous servant who was judged by the faithful servant. It happened once again in the case of the man who buried his talent, [who was judged] by the actions of those who produced more.[12] . . . This is said to bring them to the point of answering, "When did we see you hungry?" THE GOSPEL OF MATTHEW, HOMILY 79.2.[13]

TEACHING AS FEEDING AND CLOTHING.
INCOMPLETE WORK ON MATTHEW: This can also be said of teachers who gave the food of learning to those hungry for righteousness, so they might be fed and grow healthy in good actions; who administered the drink of truth to those thirsty for the knowledge of God. Teaching in the Word, they certainly fed them and also gave to drink, baptizing in the Holy Spirit those who are strangers in the world. For all souls are truly strangers on this earth who can say, "For I am your passing guest, a sojourner, like all my fathers."[14] Preaching the word of faith, they welcome souls from the spreading of error and make them fellow citizens and family members of the saints. They welcome Christ himself and clothe, by teaching righteousness, those who are naked and even without a garment of righteousness. As is written: "Put on, then, compassion, faith, peace and kindness."[15] That is to say, they clothe Christ and baptize them in Christ, as is written: "For as many of you as were baptized into Christ have put on Christ."[16] HOMILY 54.[17]

A STRANGER OR NAKED? ORIGEN: In the same way, we have woven a garment for the cold and shivering Christ. We have received the fabric of wisdom from God that we may impart knowledge to some and clothe them with "compassion, chastity, kindness, lowliness" and the other virtues. All these virtues are the spiritual garments of those who have listened to the words of those who teach these virtues, according to him who says, "Put on, then, compassion, kindness, lowliness, gentleness" and so forth, more so Christ

himself, who is all these things to the faithful, according to him who said, "Put on the Lord Jesus."[18] Therefore, when we have clothed with garments of this type "one of the least" who believe in Christ, we have apparently clothed the Lord himself, so that the word of God in the world will not go naked. But we must also welcome the Son of God who became a stranger and the members of his body who are strangers in the world, untainted by all mundane actions, even as he says about himself and his disciples: "They are not of the world, even as I am not of the world."[19] And Christ asks the Father to permit them to be with him where he is. COMMENTARY ON MATTHEW 72.[20]

SICK OR IN PRISON? INCOMPLETE WORK ON MATTHEW: He who visits the sick and those languishing with the disease of earthly vices, who heals them with the medicine of good doctrine, heals Christ in them. Even as Christ is healthy in souls that are healthy, he is ailing in souls that are ailing. But he is also the one who comes to those who have gone down to the world of the dead alive and are doing infernal work—that is, they are in prison and under guard of the devil. As Scripture says, "Let them go down to the world of the dead alive."[21] Coming through his word, he leads them out of that infernal prison and frees them from the guard of the devil. They give thanks to him, saying, "O Lord my God, I cry to you for help, and you have healed me. O Lord, you have brought up my soul from the world of the dead."[22] HOMILY 54.[23]

THE LORD HUNGERS IN HIS SAINTS. EPIPHANIUS THE LATIN: "I was hungry, and you gave me something to eat; I was thirsty, and you gave me something to drink."[24] [Jesus mentions]

---

[12]Mt 25:14-30. [13]PG 58:718-19; NPNF 1 10:475-76. [14]Ps 39:12 (38:13 LXX). [15]Col 3:12. [16]Gal 3:27. [17]PG 56:944. [18]Rom 13:14. [19]Jn 17:14. [20]GCS 38.2:169. [21]Ps 55:15 (54:16 LXX). [22]Ps 30:2 (29:3 LXX). [23]PG 56:944. [24]Mt 25:35.

many other things, which we have recited. Having been given the faith, the righteous say, "Lord, when did see you hungry and fed you, thirsty, and gave you something to drink, naked and clothed you?"[25] Other things also follow. What then, my most beloved? Does our Lord hunger and thirst? Is he who himself made everything in heaven and on earth, who feeds angels in heaven and every nation and race on earth, who needs nothing of an earthly character, as he is unfailing in his own nature, is this one naked? It is incredible to believe such a thing. Yet what must be confessed is easy to believe. For the Lord hungers not in his own nature but in his saints; the Lord thirsts not in his own nature but in his poor. The Lord who clothes everyone is not naked in his own nature but in his servants. The Lord who is able to heal all sicknesses and has already destroyed death itself is not diseased in his own nature but in his servants. Our Lord, the one who can liberate every person, is not in prison in his own nature but in his saints. Therefore, you see, my most beloved, that the saints are not alone. They suffer all these things because of the Lord. In the same way, because of the saints the Lord suffers all these things with them. INTERPRETATION OF THE GOSPELS 38.[26]

25:41-44 Depart from Me

YOU IMPUTED IT TO YOURSELVES. CHRYSOSTOM: But to the others he says, "Depart from me, you cursed." He does not say they are cursed by the Father, for the Father had not laid a curse upon them, but only their own works. He does not say that the eternal fire is prepared only for you but "for the devil and his angels." For concerning the kingdom indeed, when he had said, "Come, inherit the kingdom," he added, "prepared for you before the foundation of the world."[27] But concerning the fire, he does not say this but "prepared for the devil." I prepared the kingdom for you, he says, but the fire I did not prepare for you but "for the devil and his angels."

But you have cast yourselves in it. You have imputed it to yourselves. THE GOSPEL OF MATTHEW, HOMILY 79.2.[28]

I WAS HUNGRY. CHRYSOSTOM: "For I was hungry, and you gave me no food." For even though you should meet your enemy, is not his suffering enough to overcome and subdue your resistance to being merciful? And what about his hunger, cold, chains, nakedness and sickness? What about his homelessness? Are not these sufferings sufficient to overcome even your alienation? But you did not do these things for a friend, much less a foe. You could have at once befriended and done good. Even when you see a dog hungry you feel sympathy. But when you see the Lord hungry, you ignore it. You are left without excuse. THE GOSPEL OF MATTHEW, HOMILY 79.2.[29]

YOU DID NOT VISIT ME. ORIGEN: He could have said to the unrighteous, "I was sick, and you did not visit me; I was in prison, and you did not come to me." Instead he abbreviated his discourse and compressed both phrases into one, saying, "I was sick and in prison, and you did not visit me," for it was proper for a merciful judge to embellish the good deeds of people but to skim over their evil deeds. The righteous, however, dwell on each word, saying, "When did we see you hungry, and feed you; or thirsty, and give you drink?" And "when did we see you a stranger, and take you in; or naked, and clothe you?" Or "when did we see you sick or in prison, and come to you?" For it is characteristic of the righteous, out of humility, studiously to make light of each of their good deeds held up to them. It is as though to the Lord's words, "This, that and the other good thing you did to me," they disavowingly reply, "Neither this, that nor the other thing did we do to you." The unrighteous do not treat each item individually but are quick to say, "When did we see you hungry, or

---

[25]Mt 25:37-38. [26]PL Supp 3:900-901. [27]Mt 25:34. [28]PG 58:719; NPNF 1 10:476. [29]PG 58:719-20; NPNF 1 10:476.

thirsty, or a stranger, or naked, or sick or in prison, and did not minister to you, for we ministered the word to you." They refer to everything they did and tend to play down their evil actions, which might appear worse if enumerated one by one, for it is characteristic of wicked people to mention their faults, by way of excuse, as being either nonexistent or few and far between. COMMENTARY ON MATTHEW 73.[30]

WHEN DID WE SEE YOU HUNGRY? INCOMPLETE WORK ON MATTHEW: "Then they will answer him, 'Lord, when did we see you hungry . . . or thirsty?'" Oh, the invariable disobedience of sinners! Who does not realize that every evil we do is done not because we are corruptible but because we have a bad intention? Plainly then the corruptible flesh of sinners will die, but wickedness will live on. Did they not hear the Lord saying to the righteous, "As you did it to one of the least of these my brothers, you did it to me?"[31] Certainly they should have understood that what they fail to do to people, they fail to do to Christ. But those who hear, remain adamant; those who understand, pretend they do not understand. They stand in judgment, and yet they keep on sinning. This applies also to bad teachers . . . who did not clothe the naked, either by teaching justice or by baptizing in Christ; who did not welcome strangers in the world through the word or introduce them into the house of the church through faith; who did not heal the sick by their words; who did not lead out, through penance, those who were sitting in the prison of ungodliness. If it is ungodly not to offer material things to bodies, which cannot live forever even if they accept these things, can you imagine how ungodly it is not to administer spiritual things to souls that are in danger and could live forever if only these things

were administered to them? Since the soul is more precious than the body, it is all the more sinful not to give spiritual alms to troubled souls rather than material alms to bodies. HOMILY 54.[32]

25:45-46 Eternal Punishment or Eternal Life

ETERNAL PUNISHMENT, ETERNAL LIFE. EPIPHANIUS THE LATIN: You see, my beloved, there is no excuse for it. They knew what they had to do in this world. But greed and ill-will prevented them, so they laid up for themselves not treasures for the future but the world of the dead. Neither were they condemned because of the active wrong they did, nor did the Lord say to them, Depart from me, you wicked, because you committed murder or adultery or theft. But instead: because I was hungry and thirsty in my servants, and you did not minister to me. If those who did no wrong are thus condemned, what must be said of those who do the works of the devil? Will not the prophecy of blessed David come upon them: "The wicked will not stand in the judgment, nor sinners in the congregation of the righteous?"[33] Not that they will not rise, but that neither in judgment [nor in] the congregation of the righteous do they deserve to enter. They will stand, however, so that from punishment they may enter into punishment. "And they will go into eternal punishment, but the righteous into eternal life." Whatever will be is everlasting. Sinners will have everlasting punishment; and the righteous, everlasting life. INTERPRETATION OF THE GOSPELS 38.[34]

---

[30]GCS 38.2:173. [31]Mt 25:40. [32]PG 56:946. [33]Ps 1:5. [34]PL Supp 3:902.

26:1-5 THE PLOT TO KILL JESUS

¹*When Jesus had finished all these sayings, he said to his disciples,* ²*"You know that after two days the Passover is coming, and the Son of man will be delivered up to be crucified."*

³*Then the chief priests and the elders of the people gathered in the palace of the high priest, who was called Caiaphas,* ⁴*and took counsel together in order to arrest Jesus by stealth and kill him.* ⁵*But they said, "Not during the feast, lest there be a tumult among the people."*

Overview: The Father had set the hour of Christ's Passion (ORIGEN), where a feast and celebration were being kept for the salvation of the world. This foreknowledge prepares Jesus for his suffering (CHRYSOSTOM). What Ezekiel said to Jerusalem—that "it will be more tolerable for the land of Sodom than for you"—can be said more rightly of Jerusalem at Jesus' time (ORIGEN). The priests' counsel remained steadfast that he should be killed not on the feast but on another day (ORIGEN). Yet though they had said, "Not at the feast time," on Jesus' arrest they could not wait to kill him (CHRYSOSTOM).

26:1-2 Jesus Speaks of His Crucifixion

When He Had Finished These Sayings. ORIGEN: We know that the Father had set the hour of his Passion. For he said to his mother at one point, "My hour has not yet come."[1] In another place, "Now is my soul troubled; and what shall I say? Father, save me from this hour! No, this is why I came to this hour."[2] And elsewhere, "Father, the hour has come! Glorify your Son, that your Son may glorify you."[3] Since the Father set the hour of his Son's Passion, he could not suffer anything from the time the devil had departed from him until his Passion.[4] COMMENTARY ON MATTHEW 74.[5]

After Two Days the Passover Is Coming. JEROME: Let them[6] blush with shame who think the Savior dreaded death and said out of fear of suffering, "Father, if it be possible, let this cup pass from me." After two days, about to celebrate the Passover, he knew that he was to be betrayed and crucified. However, he did not turn away from the snares or take flight in fear. While the rest were unwilling to proceed, he remained unruffled when Thomas said, "Let us go that we may die with him."[7] Wishing to put an end to the earthly festivity and to declare the truth in the passing shadow of Passover, he said, "I have earnestly desired to eat this Passover with you before I suffer."[8] Indeed, "Christ, our paschal lamb, has been sacrificed" if we eat it with "the unleavened bread of sincerity and truth."[9] Furthermore, because he says, "After two days the Passover will be here" and omits a simple explanation, we should seek what is holy. After two days of the brilliant light of the Old and New Testaments, the Passover is celebrated for the world. This Passover, called *pesaḥ* in Hebrew, is not named after Christ's suffering as many believe.[10] It refers to the "passing over," when the destroying angel saw the blood on the

---

[1]Jn 2:4. [2]Jn 12:27. [3]Jn 17:1. [4]Origen frequently cites Wisdom 11:21 to indicate the progression through which the design of the divine economy is worked out with regard to the world. [5]GCS 38.2:174-75. [6]The adversaries confronted here by Jerome are the pagans, who used Jesus' request that his cup be taken from him to maintain that he could not have been of a divine nature. Specifically Jerome probably has in mind the anti-Christian polemic of Porphyry. [7]Jn 11:16. [8]Lk 22:15. [9]1 Cor 5:7-8. [10]The etymology *Pascha* = Passover (taken from the Hebrew) was common in Alexandrian circles, while in the West as in the Asiatic East, the faulty etymology *Pascha* = Passion (drawn from the Greek *paschein*) was commonplace.

doors of the Israelites, passed by and did not strike them down.[11] In other words, the Lord, giving help to his people, came down from above. Our passing over—that is to say, *pesah*—will be celebrated if we put behind us both earthly things and Egypt and move on to heavenly things. COMMENTARY ON MATTHEW 4.26.8-9.[12]

HE WILL BE DELIVERED UP. ORIGEN: He therefore used the verb impersonally—that is, "he will be delivered up." He did not say by whom, because the words apply to all those who delivered him up. But not everyone delivered him up in the same way. God delivered him up out of mercy for the human race: he "has not spared even his own Son but has delivered him for us all."[13] But the rest delivered him up for a bad reason, each one according to his own malice:[14] Judas out of greed, the priests out of jealousy and the devil out of fear—lest the human race be plucked from his hands because of Christ's teaching, little knowing that the human race would be plucked away more through his death than through his teaching and miracles. He was in fact delivered up "to be crucified" so that, "disarming the principalities and powers,"[15] he might triumph over them on the cross. COMMENTARY ON MATTHEW 75.[16]

TO BE CRUCIFIED. CHRYSOSTOM: When he had reminded them of the kingdom, he spoke again of the season of his suffering and of final judgment. It was as though he had said, "Why are you afraid of the dangers that are only for a season when such good things await you?" Notice how he has thrown into the shade what was most painful to them. For he does not say, "You know that after two days I am betrayed," but "You know that after two days is the Passover feast," to show that what is done is a mystery. A feast and celebration is being kept for the salvation of the world. With foreknowledge he is prepared to suffer all. So then, as though this were sufficient consolation for them, he did not even

say anything to them now about a resurrection. He had already spoken about it, and did not need to speak about it again. And moreover, as I said, he shows that even his suffering itself is a deliverance from countless evils, having by the Passover reminded them of the ancient benefits received in Egypt. THE GOSPEL OF MATTHEW, HOMILY 79.2-3.[17]

26:3-5 The Chief Priests and Elders Gather

THE PALACE OF THE HIGH PRIEST. CHRYSOSTOM: They are coming to the high priest with the desire to obtain their authority from him, by whom they ought to have been hindered.

How many high priests were there? For the law wills there should be one, but then there were many. From this it is beginning to be evident that the Jewish structure of governance had begun to collapse. For Moses, as I said, commanded there should be one and that when he was dead there should be another. THE GOSPEL OF MATTHEW, HOMILY 79.3.[18]

THEY TOOK COUNSEL. ORIGEN: The words of the prophet, "And the rulers took counsel together against the Lord and his anointed,"[19] were fulfilled[20] when "the chief priests and elders of the people gathered in the court of the high priest" and took counsel together "against the Lord and his anointed." They were not true priests but "of the people" and "elders." They only seemed to be the people of God but were after all the people of Gomorrah. It was they who would say, "Crucify him! Crucify him!" and "Away from the earth with such a one!"[21] Fur-

---

[11]Ex 11:1—12:36. [12]CCL 77:244-45. [13]Rom 8:32. [14]The Greek *paradidōmi*, like the Latin *tradere*, meant "to give over" both in the positive and in the negative sense. Thus the passive form, which does not specify the person by whom Jesus was to be given over, is subject to various interpretations in that different people gave Jesus over with different intentions: good (God) and evil (Judas, the priests). [15]Col 2:15. [16]GCS 38.2:176. [17]PG 58:720; NPNF 1 10:477. [18]PG 58:720; NPNF 1 10:477. [19]Ps 2:2. [20]Already in Acts 2:25-26 the Passion of Christ is indicated as the realization of Psalm 2:12. The psalm was traditionally considered messianic. [21]Lk 23:18.

thermore, what Isaiah said, "Hear the word of the Lord, O leaders of Sodom; pay heed to God's law, O people of Gomorrah,"[22] applies to the Jewish leaders who lived at the time of Christ. And what Ezekiel said to Jerusalem, "It will be more tolerable for the land of Sodom than for you,"[23] can be said more rightly of Jerusalem, over which the Lord wept, than of the time of the prophet. The chief priests sinned more greatly than Sodom. They did not recognize God's high priest but plotted against him. The elders of the people, not knowing the "firstborn of every creature"[24] and the one who is older than all creatures, took counsel against him. Jerusalem was forsaken at that so-called court where "they took counsel together how they might seize Jesus by stealth." Unfortunately this was the city that first killed the prophets and then the Lord of the prophets. That city took action against the founder of the whole world. COMMENTARY ON MATTHEW 76.[25]

BY STEALTH. CHRYSOSTOM: What did they consult together? That they might seize him secretly, or that they might put him to death? Both, for they feared the people. Thus they waited for the feast to be past, for they said, "Not on the feast day," lest he should make the Passion conspicuous. They were afraid of causing an uproar. Note that they never were afraid of the judgment of God but only the judgment of people. THE GOSPEL OF MATTHEW, HOMILY 79.3.[26]

THEY FEARED A RIOT. ORIGEN: They took counsel "in order to arrest Jesus by stealth." The prophet had aptly said about them, "May the Lord cut off all deceitful lips." "By stealth" they wanted to seize him and to kill him. But they said, "Not during the feast, lest there be a riot among the people," for they had seen Jesus performing many signs and wonders. Many indeed were those who sided with Jesus. They proclaimed that "a great prophet has arisen in Israel."[27] But others were against him, and they said, "It is only by Beelzebub, the prince of demons, that this man casts out demons."[28] Many had come to see the Lord. The people showed great eagerness for him. They either loved Christ or hated him. They either believed in him or did not believe in him. The priests' counsel remained steadfast (while they themselves who took counsel would not remain steadfast) that he should be killed not on the feast but on another day. "Christ our Passover"[29] was soon to be sacrificed so that, leaving behind the unleavened bread of the Jews, we might feast on the spiritual and true unleavened bread. COMMENTARY ON MATTHEW 76.[30]

NOT DURING FEAST TIME. CHRYSOSTOM: Yet for all this, boiling with anger, they changed their purpose again. For though they had said, "Not at the feast time," when they found the traitor, they did not wait but killed him at the feast. THE GOSPEL OF MATTHEW, HOMILY 79.3.[31]

---

[22]Is 1:10. [23]Ezek 16:51-52. [24]Col 1:15. [25]GCS 38.2:177. [26]PG 58:721; NPNF 1 10:477. [27]Lk 7:16 [28]Mt 12:24. [29]1 Cor 5:7. [30]GCS 38.2:177-78. [31]PG 58:721; NPNF 1 10:477.

26:6-16 JESUS IS ANOINTED AT BETHANY AND BETRAYED BY JUDAS

^{6}*Now when Jesus was at Bethany in the house of Simon the leper,* ^{7}*a woman came up to him with an alabaster flask of very expensive ointment, and she poured it on his head, as he sat at table.* ^{8}*But when the disciples saw it, they were indignant, saying, "Why this waste?* ^{9}*For this ointment might have been sold for a large sum, and given to the poor."* ^{10}*But Jesus, aware of this, said to them, "Why do you trouble the woman? For she has done a beautiful thing to me.* ^{11}*For you always have the poor with you, but you will not always have me.* ^{12}*In pouring this ointment on my body she has done it to prepare me for burial.* ^{13}*Truly, I say to you, wherever this gospel is preached in the whole world, what she has done will be told in memory of her."*

^{14}*Then one of the twelve, who was called Judas Iscariot, went to the chief priests* ^{15}*and said, "What will you give me if I deliver him to you?" And they paid him thirty pieces of silver.* ^{16}*And from that moment he sought an opportunity to betray him.*

OVERVIEW: About to suffer for the whole world and to redeem all nations by his blood, Jesus rests in Bethany, in the house of Simon the leper (JEROME). A woman with an alabaster jar came to him. Leprosy was considered a most unclean disease, yet the woman saw that Jesus had both healed the man and had gone into his house. She did not come to him on the premise that he was a mere man. If he were only human, she would not have wiped his feet with her hair (CHRYSOSTOM). This woman prefigures the Gentile people, who would give glory to God through the passion of Christ.

Special thanks are due to the whole female gender for the care they take of the body. Jesus would soon transfer all care of his body and all affection for his soul to the honor and praise of God (HILARY OF POITIERS). Various narratives tell of different women. Some pour out precious ointment over the head of Jesus; others do not anoint the head but only the feet. Others do not pour out abundantly but anoint only so much. Some of them anoint with ointment, leaving the whole house filled with the odor of his divinity (ORIGEN). The various narratives also differ as to whether the apostles were indignant for the sake of the poor or Judas for the sake of his own gain (JEROME). When the woman's action was challenged on the grounds of wastefulness, the Lord reminded them they would have much time to look after the poor. The Gentiles would be buried with him in the outpouring of ointment by this woman, for rebirth is given only to those who have died with him (HILARY OF POITIERS). She was praised by the Lord for having announced beforehand his Passion by bringing to him what is needed for a funeral. Far from condemning her as having erred, Jesus promises that what has been done will not go unnoticed. The world would remember openly that which was done in that house and in secret (CHRYSOSTOM).

26:6-7 Jesus Anointed at Bethany

THE HOUSE OF SIMON THE LEPER. JEROME: About to suffer for the whole world and to redeem all nations by his blood, Jesus tarries in

Bethany at the home of obedience.[1] It was once the house of Simon the leper—but he was no longer a leper. After he had been cured by the Savior he was still known by his original name, that the power of the healer might appear. In fact, one of the apostles listed with his original occupation and vice is Matthew the publican, though he certainly ceased to be a publican. There are those who want the house of Simon the leper to be known as that part of the people who believed in the Lord and were cured by him. Simon himself, moreover, is termed the obedient one.[2] His name can be interpreted also as "the clean one" in whose house the church was healed. COMMENTARY ON MATTHEW 4.26.6.[3]

JESUS WAS AT BETHANY. CHRYSOSTOM: It may seem that this woman is the same in all the Gospel narratives. But I doubt it. In John she is another person, one much to be admired, the sister of Lazarus.[4]

But not without purpose did the Evangelist mention the leprosy of Simon. He did this in order to show how the woman gained confidence and came to Jesus. Leprosy seemed a most unclean disease and to be abhorred. Yet she saw that Jesus had both healed the man and had gone into his house. This is why he remained with the leper. She grew confident that he could also easily wipe away the uncleanness from her soul.

It is significant that the city is named Bethany, that we might learn that it is of his own free will that he comes to suffer. If before he was fleeing from their envy, now he comes near, within about fifteen furlongs from Jerusalem. His former pattern of withdrawing himself now belongs to a past dispensation. THE GOSPEL OF MATTHEW, HOMILY 80.1.[5]

A WOMAN WITH AN ALABASTER FLASK. CHRYSOSTOM: The woman therefore having seen him, and having become extraordinarily confident, came directly to him. This was wholly unlike other women in the narrative, for example, the woman with the issue of blood. She was conscious of her uncleanness and approached him with fear and trembling, slowly and shrinking back.[6] And so it was with many women, the Samaritan,[7] the Canaanite[8] and others. This woman is conscious of her impurity. She comes to him in a private house, not publicly. And whereas all of these other women came to him for the healing of the body alone, this woman came to him to honor him only, and for the amendment of the soul. She was not at all afflicted in body. This is what makes her especially remarkable. And she does not come to him on the premise that he is a mere man. If that were so, she would not have wiped his feet with her hair. Her action was directed to one greater than man. Therefore she brings to Christ that part which is the most honorable member of the whole body, her head, and lays her hair over his feet. THE GOSPEL OF MATTHEW, HOMILY 80.1.[9]

AN EXPENSIVE OINTMENT. HILARY OF POITIERS: This woman prefigures the Gentile people, who gave glory to God in the suffering of Christ. She thoroughly anointed his head. Recall that Christ's head is God.[10] Ointment represents the fruit of good works. And special thanks are due to the female gender for the care of the body. So then, he transferred all care of his body and all affection for his precious soul to the honor and praise of God. But the disciples, keen on saving Israel, become quickly upset as usual: "This ought to have been sold to help the poor." But the ointment the woman carried was

---

[1]"Home of obedience" is the etymology of *Bethany*. As for Simon the leper, in the Gospels Jesus is not said to have cured him, but it is considered implicit that this occurred. [2]"Obedient" is the meaning of the name Simon. [3]CCL 77:246. [4]Jn 12:1-3 also tells of the anointing of Jesus by Mary sister of Lazarus, but in Matthew the woman anoints the head of Jesus, and in John the feet. Hence Chrysostom believes that there were two distinct episodes. See also p. 241 n. 13. [5]PG 58:723-24; NPNF 1 10:480. [6]Mk 5:25-34. [7]Jn 4:4-42. [8]Mt 15:21-28. [9]PG 58:724; NPNF 1 10:480. [10]1 Cor 11:3.

not for sale. ON MATTHEW 29.2.[11]

SHE POURED OINTMENT ON HIS HEAD. ORIGEN: With good reason, therefore, when Luke spoke of the woman who was a sinner, he introduced her as weeping copiously. She thus washed the feet of Jesus with her tears . . . only "anointing," and not his head but his feet.[12] This woman, however, who was not described as a sinner, did not anoint but "poured" ointment, and not on his feet but "on his head."[13] As to what is written about Mary, the sister of Lazarus, she too "anointed" the Lord's "feet." Note what the Gospel says: The whole "house was filled with the odor of the ointment."[14]

Perhaps the differences in these women therefore may signify the differences in the faithful. Some of them pour out precious ointment "over the head" of Jesus, others do not anoint the head but only the feet, and others do not pour out abundantly but anoint only so much. Some of them anoint with ointment, leaving the whole house filled with the odor of his divinity. Then there are others, also acceptable to Christ, for they anoint his feet with ointment, which the Pharisees did not even anoint with "oil." COMMENTARY ON MATTHEW 77.[15]

26:8-11 The Disciples' Indignation Rebuked

WHY THIS WASTE? JEROME: I know that some people criticize this passage because one Evangelist said only Judas became indignant since he kept the money purse and was a thief from the beginning,[16] whereas Matthew wrote that all the apostles were indignant. Some may be unaware of the figure of speech called *syllepsis*, customarily termed "all for one and one for all." The case is somewhat similar with Paul the apostle, who wrote in his epistle to the Hebrews (though many Latins have doubts about this),[17] describing the sufferings and merits of the heroes of faith, inferring: "They were stoned, they were sawn in two, they were tempted, they were put to death by the sword."[18] The Jews assert that

only one person, Isaiah the prophet, was tortured. We may also point out that the apostles were indignant for the sake of the poor but Judas for the sake of his own gain. Hence his grumbling was also mixed with his misdeeds, because he had no concern for the poor but only wanted to be able to steal. COMMENTARY ON MATTHEW 4.26.9.[19]

A BEAUTIFUL THING. CHRYSOSTOM: And why was it Jesus did not merely say, "She has done a good work," but before this he said, "Why do you trouble the woman?" He does not want to require too much of the woman. He takes into account her person. He said this that they might not mar her budding faith but rather cherish it. THE GOSPEL OF MATTHEW, HOMILY 80.2.[20]

YOU ALWAYS HAVE THE POOR. HILARY OF POITIERS: The Lord told them they would have much time to look after the poor. Further, it is only at his command that salvation can be given to the Gentiles buried with him in the outpouring of ointment by this woman, for rebirth is given only to those who have died with him in the profession of baptism.[21] ON MATTHEW 29.2.[22]

26:12-13 Preparing Me for Burial

THE PRECIOUS OINTMENT. ORIGEN: The ointment with an agreeable odor represents what

---

[11]SC 258:218-20. [12]Lk 7:36-38. [13]Luke 7:36-50 also tells of the anointing but in a context different from both Matthew (with Mark) and John, defining the woman who anoints the feet of Jesus (as in John) as a sinner. The anointing of the feet links Luke with John as opposed to Matthew, which speaks of the anointing of the head, but Origen does not think it possible that Mary the sister of Lazarus could have been defined a sinner. He is inclined to believe that there were three distinct women, uniting the accounts of Matthew and Mark only. [14]Jn 12:3. [15]GCS 38.2:181-82. [16]Jn 12:6. [17]In antiquity various doubts were expressed regarding the attribution to Paul of the epistle to the Hebrews. While in the East these doubts did not impede the acceptance of the letter into the New Testament canon, in the West this acceptance came later, toward the beginning of the fifth century. [18]Heb 11:37. [19]CCL 77:246-47. [20]PG 58:726; NPNF 1 10:481. [21]Rom 6:4; Col 2:12. [22]SC 258:220.

the faithful do for God. This very work of the faithful of God, which is ointment, becomes something else for the good of humanity—for instance, almsgiving, visits to the sick, welcoming strangers, humility, gentleness, pardon, and so forth. These are things that benefit human beings. He who does them to Christians anoints the Lord's feet with ointment, for they are the Lord's feet with which he will always walk. . . . This is the ointment which also anoints Christ's head and flows down over his whole body, that is, it pours down on the whole church. This is the precious ointment that fills the whole house with its odor, that is, the church of Christ. This is the work that is proper not for penitents but for the preeminently holy people. Certainly the teaching necessary for people which feeds those who are poor in spiritually good things or those who are perhaps weak in avoiding sin—this is the plain ointment with which the Lord's feet are anointed. However, the knowledge of the true faith which pertains to God alone—this is the precious ointment that anoints God, Christ's head. COMMENTARY ON MATTHEW 77.[23]

DONE TO PREPARE ME FOR BURIAL. CHRYSOSTOM: He said, "She has done it for my burial," that they might not be perplexed. See how he consoles her with what follows, saying, "What she has done shall be spoken of in the whole world."

And this was at once consolation to his disciples and comfort and praise to her. "For all the world will celebrate her hereafter. Now she has announced beforehand my suffering by bringing to me what is needed for a funeral. So let no one reprove her. For I am so far from condemning her as having done wrongly or from blaming her as having not acted rightly that I will not permit what has been done to lie unnoticed. The world will know that which has been done in this house and in secret. It is in truth the deed of a reverential mind and fervent faith and a contrite soul." THE GOSPEL OF MATTHEW, HOMILY 80.2."[24]

26:14 Judas Iscariot Went to the Priests

THE TWO JUDASES. ORIGEN: Judas means "confessor." Luke the Evangelist numbers both "Judas the son of James and Judas Iscariot" among the twelve apostles.[25] Since two of Christ's disciples were given this same name and since there can be no meaningless symbol in the Christian mystery, I am convinced that the two Judases represent two distinct types of confessing Christians. The first, symbolized by Judas the son of James, perseveres in remaining faithful to Christ. The second type, however, after once believing and professing faith in Christ, then abandons him out of greed. He defects to the heretics and to the false priests of the Jews, that is, to counterfeit Christians, and (insofar as he is able) delivers Christ, the "Word of truth," over to them to be crucified and destroyed. This type of Christian is represented by Judas Iscariot, who "went out to the chief priests" and agreed on a price for betraying Christ. COMMENTARY ON MATTHEW 78.[26]

THEN ONE OF THE TWELVE. CHRYSOSTOM: Then. When? It was when it had been made clear that he was being prepared for burial, that the Gospels would be preached everywhere and that he had been shown honor. Then Judas did the devil's deed.

But what can be the reason they mention his surname? Because there was also another Judas.

And why do they specifically say that "he was one of the twelve"? They have opted entirely to hide none of those things which seem to be matters of reproach. And yet they might have merely said that he was one of the disciples, for there were others besides. But now they add, "of the twelve," as though they had said, of the first company of those selected as the best, of those alongside Peter and John. THE GOSPEL OF MATTHEW, HOMILY 80.2.[27]

---

[23]GCS 38.2:185-86. [24]PG 58:726; NPNF 1 10:482. [25]Lk 6:16. [26]GCS 38.2:186. [27]PG 58:726-27; NPNF 1 10:482.

26:15-16 Betrayal for Thirty Pieces of Silver

THIRTY PIECES OF SILVER. ORIGEN: Let us consider what Judas said to the Jewish priests: "What will you give me if I hand him over to you?" He was willing to take money in exchange for handing over the Word of God. They do the same thing who accept sensual or worldly goods in exchange for handing over and casting out from their souls the Savior and Word of truth who came to dwell with them. Indeed, it would be fitting to apply Judas's example to all who show contempt for the Word of God and betray him, as it were, by committing sin for the sake of money or for any selfish motive. People who behave in this way appear openly to be calling out to the powers of the enemy who offer worldly gain in return for the sin of betraying God's Word, saying, "What will you give me if I hand him over to you?"

"And they gave him thirty pieces of silver." The number of coins they gave Judas was equivalent to the number of years the Savior had sojourned in this world. For at the age of thirty, he was baptized and began to preach the gospel, like Joseph was thirty years old when he began to gather grain for his brothers.[28] Just as at that time the grain was prepared by God for the sons of Israel but given also to the Egyptians, so also the gospel was prepared for the saints but preached also to the unfaithful and wicked. COMMENTARY ON MATTHEW 78.[29]

WHAT WILL YOU GIVE ME? CHRYSOSTOM: The Romans had set the Jews over the people in order that they should provide for their good order.[30] But by this time the Jews were becoming insurgent. Their government was now undergoing a change according to prophecy.

To these priests Judas went "and said, 'What will you give me if I deliver him to you?' And they paid him thirty pieces of silver. And from that moment he sought an opportunity to betray him." Judas was by now afraid of the multitude and desired to seize him alone.

O madness! The covetousness of Judas altogether blinds him! He had often seen Jesus when he went through the midst and did not betray him. Jesus had afforded many demonstrations of his Godhead and power, and no one had laid hold on him. Even at the supper Judas did not cease to talk with him and receive his care. This could have put an end to his evil thought. But all this profited nothing. THE GOSPEL OF MATTHEW, HOMILY 80.3.[31]

THE OPPORTUNITY TO BETRAY. ORIGEN: "From then on he sought an opportunity to betray him." Luke's Gospel shows most clearly the kind of opportunity for which Judas was looking when it says, "And he sought an opportunity to betray him in the absence of the crowds,"[32] that is, when the people were not with him but when he was alone with his disciples. His betrayer did the deed after supper, when Christ was alone in the garden of Gethsemane. For once Judas reached his agreement with the Jews, he determined that his opportunity would come when Jesus was not with the crowds. Notice how even today the betrayers of Jesus Christ, Word of truth and Word of God, see their best opportunity to hand him over at a time when Christians are being persecuted.... They are at their worst when the number of his faithful is at its fewest. And since there is a time for all things, for Solomon said "there is a time to be born and a time to die,"[33] the time for betraying the Word of truth was specifically when very few of the faithful were with Christ. COMMENTARY ON MATTHEW 78.[34]

---

[28]Gen 41:46. This is the patriarch Joseph, with reference to the events recounted in Genesis 41—50. The connection is explained by the fact that Joseph was, among the figures of the Old Testament, one of those considered a symbolic and prophetic prefiguration of Christ. [29]GCS 38.2:187-88. [30]Luke 22:4 says that Judas went to the priests and the *stratēgoi*, a term that here signifies the heads of the Jewish people in general terms. Chrysostom uses the term in the sense that these men would have been identified by the Romans. [31]PG 58:727; NPNF 1 10:482. [32]Lk 22:6. [33]Eccles 3:2. [34]GCS 38.2:188.

26:17-25 THE PASSOVER MEAL
WITH THE DISCIPLES

¹⁷*Now on the first day of Unleavened Bread the disciples came to Jesus, saying, "Where will you have us prepare for you to eat the passover?"* ¹⁸*He said, "Go into the city to a certain one, and say to him, 'The Teacher says, My time is at hand; I will keep the passover at your house with my disciples.' "* ¹⁹*And the disciples did as Jesus had directed them, and they prepared the passover.*

²⁰*When it was evening, he sat at table with the twelve disciples;^e* ²¹*and as they were eating, he said, "Truly, I say to you, one of you will betray me."* ²²*And they were very sorrowful, and began to say to him one after another, "Is it I, Lord?"* ²³*He answered, "He who has dipped his hand in the dish with me, will betray me.* ²⁴*The Son of man goes as it is written of him, but woe to that man by whom the Son of man is betrayed! It would have been better for that man if he had not been born."* ²⁵*Judas, who betrayed him, said, "Is it I, Master?"^f He said to him, "You have said so."*

e Other authorities omit *disciples*   f Or *Rabbi*

OVERVIEW: The first day of Unleavened Bread is the evening before the feast day. Even though they owned no home in which to observe the feast, Jesus and the disciples observed the Passover in order to show that Jesus was willing to suffer (CHRYSOSTOM). The owner of the house where Jesus and the disciples observed the Passover is the same as the one more clearly defined in Mark and Luke (CYRIL OF ALEXANDRIA). Origen likens this man to Moses, who bears the law, while Jerome likens the room in which they ate to the spiritual law.

When Jesus announced that one of the disciples would betray him, the disciples were sorrowful because they knew how quickly human nature can change (ORIGEN). At first Jesus withheld Judas's identity in order to allow him time to repent. The other disciples, however, were distraught. Jesus therefore revealed Judas's identity (CHRYSOSTOM). Jesus' ultimate betrayer is the devil (ORIGEN). Judas condemned himself by calling Jesus "teacher" instead of "Lord" (JEROME).

26:17-19 *Preparing for the Passover*

THE FIRST DAY OF UNLEAVENED BREAD.
CHRYSOSTOM: By "the first day of the feast of unleavened bread," he means the day before that feast. For it is customary always to reckon the day from the evening.[1] He mentions this with regard to the evening of the Passover. It was on the fifth day of the week they came to him. Hence on the day before the feast of unleavened bread they came to him. As to the time, Mark says, "On the first day of the Feast of Unleavened Bread, when they sacrificed the Passover lamb."[2] THE GOSPEL OF MATTHEW, HOMILY 81.1.[3]

I WILL KEEP THE PASSOVER. CHRYSOSTOM: The disciples came to him then on the first day, that is, the evening, when the Passover was drawing very near, and said, "Where will you have us prepare for you to eat the Passover?" Even from this it is clear that he had no house, no place in which to live, and I suppose neither had they. For surely they would have asked him

---

[1]To begin the day with the evening was a widespread practice in antiquity. [2]Mk 14:12. [3]PG 58:729-30; NPNF 1 10:485.

to come there. But none of them had anything, having given away all their worldly possessions. Why did he keep the Passover? To indicate in every way and until the last day that he was not opposed to the law. And for what possible reason does he send them to an unknown person? To also show by this that he might have avoided suffering. For he had the power to change the minds of those who crucified him. So it is once again clear: He is willing to suffer. THE GOSPEL OF MATTHEW, HOMILY 81.1.[4]

GO TO A CERTAIN ONE. CYRIL OF ALEXANDRIA: Saying "a certain person" does not reveal a name but indicates any one of the saints. For the Word governs over every saint. The disciples of the Lord are the first he receives—evangelists, apostles foreordained in their souls even in the same way as the Christ. He does not exclude; rather, unbidden, the Holy Spirit dwells within each from the hour of holy baptism. So this "certain man" is the one with the "earthen pot washed with water" as described by Mark and Luke.[5] FRAGMENT 285.[6]

THE BEARER OF WATER. ORIGEN: I think that the man "carrying a jar of water"[7] whom the disciples met when they entered the city and whom Jesus wanted them to follow into his house was bringing it into the house not only that the house might be clean but also more richly endowed. He was serving the head of the household (that is, the intellect),[8] bearing purifying water in an earthen vessel "that the heights of power might belong to God."[9] Or perhaps he was supplying potable water in the earthen vessel so that the Son of God could provide new growth to the vine, for the servant of the intellect is the water of the Law and the Prophets, which must be mixed with the wine of the evangelical word. But we who wish to belong to the church and to celebrate the Passover with Jesus follow that man, whom I believe to be Moses, giver of the law, who bears this kind of water, carrying spiritual doctrine about in historical

vessels. COMMENTARY ON MATTHEW 79.[10]

THE DISCIPLES PREPARED THE PASSOVER. JEROME: The other Evangelist writes that they found a large upper room furnished and ready and they made preparations there for him. It seems to me that the room symbolizes the spiritual law which, emerging from the restraints of the written record, receives the Savior in a lofty place. Paul says that what he formerly counted as gain, he now despised as loss and refuse, that he might prepare a worthy guest chamber for the Lord. COMMENTARY ON MATTHEW 4.26.19.[11]

26:20-22 At Table with the Twelve Disciples

READINESS FOR COMMUNION. ORIGEN: Perhaps someone will ask: If the twelve apostles all had clean consciences (that is, if they were all innocent of any act of betrayal against the teacher), why were they "sorrowful" at the news that he would be betrayed, as though it could have been one of them to whom he was referring? I believe that each of the disciples knew from the things Jesus had taught them that human nature is unstable and vulnerable to be turned toward sin and that in struggling "against the principalities and powers and rulers of this world of darkness"[12] a man can be besieged and fall or be so weakened by the power of the enemy that he becomes evil. Aware of these things, then, each disciple was "very sorrowful"

---

[4]PG 58:730-31; NPNF 1 10:485. [5]Mk 14:13; Lk 22:10. [6]MKGK 284. [7]Lk 22:10. [8]This complex allegory is based on the detail omitted by Matthew, that the man whom the disciples of Jesus met was carrying a jar of water (Mk 14:13; Lk 22:10). The head of the household to whom the water was being brought symbolizes the intellect; the water, which was to be used for the Eucharistic consecration, symbolizes the Old Testament doctrine (with the man carrying the jar symbolizing Moses); the wine given directly by Jesus signifies his spiritual doctrine. [9]2 Cor 4:7. [10]GCS 38.2:190-91. Origen, like Irenaeus, believes that the Old and New Testaments present the same spiritual doctrine, but the New Testament expresses it in a direct manner, whereas the Old Testament suggests it symbolically under the veil of the literal meaning. [11]CCL 77:249. [12]Eph 6:12.

because Christ had said "one of you will betray me." And each disciple, not knowing what he might do in the future, began to inquire one by one: "Is it I, Lord?" Yet, if the apostles had good reason to fear that they might betray him, we who have not yet tasted of perfection must also be afraid of falling victim to future weakness. This is why the apostle said, "I am certain that neither death nor life . . . is able to separate us from the love of God in Christ Jesus."[13] But whoever is not yet perfect should remain aware that he is still capable of falling. COMMENTARY ON MATTHEW 81.[14]

ONE OF YOU WILL BETRAY ME. CHRYSOSTOM: "When it was evening, he sat at table with the twelve disciples; and as they were eating, he said, 'Truly, I say to you, one of you will betray me.' " Even before the supper he had washed the feet of Judas. See how he spares the traitor. He did not say, "Judas, you will betray me," but only "one of you will betray me." This was again to offer time for repentance by keeping his identity concealed. He was willing to allow all the others to be alarmed, just for the sake of redeeming this one. All the others, whose feet he had washed and who had accompanied him everywhere and to whom he had promised so many things, were alarmed unnecessarily because of the one. THE GOSPEL OF MATTHEW, HOMILY 81.1.[15]

IS IT I, LORD? CHRYSOSTOM: Intolerable sorrow then seized that holy company. John says, "The disciples looked at one another, uncertain of whom he spoke."[16] Each of them asked in fear concerning himself, although conscious to themselves of no such imagination. But Matthew writes, "They were very sorrowful and began to say to him one after another, 'Is it I, Lord?' " He answered, "He who has dipped his hand in the dish with me will betray me." Note precisely at what time Jesus revealed his identity. It was when it was his will to deliver the rest from this trouble. For they were horri-

fied with fear and pressing in their questions. He wanted to give Judas time to change his mind, but he wanted also to relieve the others from their distress. But Judas continued to be incorrigible and past any hope of change. So now he is unmasked. THE GOSPEL OF MATTHEW, HOMILY 81.1.[17]

26:23-25 Woe to the Betrayer

BY WHOM THE SON OF MAN IS BETRAYED. ORIGEN: According to all appearances, Jesus departed and was about to suffer on the cross. In reality, however, he both departed and remained in the world with his disciples, keeping them in the faith, for they would not have been able to abide in his faith, especially once they saw him dead, if he had not been guarding their hearts invisibly. Christ didn't say "woe to that man by whom he is betrayed" but "woe to that man through whom he is betrayed," showing that Judas was only the means of his betrayal, whereas the agent of his betrayal was another, that is, the devil. The woe, however, is not only for Judas but for every betrayer of Christ, for whoever betrays one of Christ's disciples betrays Christ himself. Even though he is betrayed by the devil, nevertheless woe to those through whom his betrayal comes. COMMENTARY ON MATTHEW 83.[18]

THEY WERE SORROWFUL. JEROME: The others were grieved and very much saddened as they questioned Christ: "Surely, Lord, you don't mean me?" Lest he seem to betray himself by keeping silent, he too, whose conscience was troubling him and who had boldly placed his hand in the dish, questioned him: "Surely, teacher, you don't mean me?" To this he added lip homage and a show of incredulity. The others, who were not traitors, said, "Surely, Lord, you don't mean me?" He who was the traitor did

---

[13]Rom 8:38-39. [14]GCS 38.2:192-93. [15]PG 58:731; NPNF 1 10:486. [16]Jn 13:22. [17]PG 58:731; NPNF 1 10:486. [18]GCS 38.2:195.

not call him Lord but teacher, as if to have an excuse, upon rejecting the Lord, for having betrayed at most a teacher. "Jesus answered, 'You have said so.'" The traitor was put to shame by the same response Christ would later give to Pilate.[19] COMMENTARY ON MATTHEW 4.26.25.[20]

---

[19]Mt 27:11. [20]CCL 77:250.

26:26-30 THE LORD'S SUPPER

[26]*Now as they were eating, Jesus took bread, and blessed, and broke it, and gave it to the disciples and said, "Take, eat; this is my body." [27]And he took a cup, and when he had given thanks he gave it to them, saying, "Drink of it, all of you; [28]for this is my blood of the[g] covenant, which is poured out for many for the forgiveness of sins. [29]I tell you I shall not drink again of this fruit of the vine until that day when I drink it new with you in my Father's kingdom."*

[30]*And when they had sung a hymn, they went out to the Mount of Olives.*

g Other ancient authorities insert *new*

OVERVIEW: In the Lord's Supper, Christ's own presence in body and blood brings salvation from death and sin (CYRIL OF ALEXANDRIA). The bread is broken and the wine poured as a sacrament to God the Word (ORIGEN). The sacrament of bread and wine prefigured Jesus' giving of his own body and blood (JEROME). Jerome interprets "the blood of the covenant" as the spiritual fruit, that is, the belief of Israel, God's choice vine. The timing of Jesus' ordination of the sacrament is important. Through the sacrament of Passover, Christ willingly becomes the fulfillment of the Old Testament law (CHRYSOSTOM). Christ partakes in the sacrament with us (ORIGEN).

God did not will the death of Christ, but God did allow it (CYRIL OF ALEXANDRIA). Christ's resurrection was indeed a bodily resurrection; the disciples ate and drank with Christ after he was raised. Nonetheless his was a spiritual body that was not dependent on food and drink (CHRYSOSTOM).

26:26-27 The Bread and the Cup

HIS BODY AND BLOOD. CYRIL OF ALEXANDRIA: After Judas the betrayer had gone out, the Savior revealed the saving mystery to the Eleven. Now Christ was about to be raised within a short time in order to come and appear before the Father with his own body. So that we could have his body present, he has given us his own body and blood that it might ruin the power of decay. For without the presence of Christ, salvation from death is not possible and humanity is unable to be freed from sin which dwells along with us in this life. He dwells with us in our souls through the Holy Spirit, and we become sharers in holiness, heavenly people and spiritual name bearers. FRAGMENT 290.[1]

JESUS TOOK BREAD. ORIGEN: The bread which God the Word revealed to be his own body is

---

[1]MKGK 256.

the Word of the sustainer of souls. What was set upon the table was the Word proceeding from God the Word, bread from heavenly bread, as it is written: "You have prepared a table before me in the presence of my enemies."[2] And the wine which God the Word revealed to be his blood is the Word filling and wondrously inebriating the hearts of all who drink it. It is the Word contained in that chalice about which it is written: "My cup overflows."[3] This wine is the fruit of the true vine who said, "I am the true vine."[4] It is blood of grapes processed in the winepress of his Passion. Likewise the bread is the Word of Christ ground from that grain of wheat which "falls into the earth" and "bears much fruit."[5] It was not the visible bread that he held in his hands which God the Word called his body, but it was the Word in whose sacrament the bread was to be broken. Nor was it the visible drink that he identified as his blood, but it was the Word in whose sacrament the libation was to be poured out. COMMENTARY ON MATTHEW 85.[6]

BREAD AND WINE. JEROME: After the typical Passover meal was over and he had eaten the flesh of the lamb with his apostles, he took the bread that strengthens human hearts[7] and moved on to the true sacrament of the Passover. Thus even as Melchizedek, the priest of the most high God, had prefigured Christ by offering bread and wine,[8] so Jesus would exemplify this with his real body and blood. COMMENTARY ON MATTHEW 4.26.27.[9]

HE TOOK BREAD. CHRYSOSTOM: But the evening is a sure sign of the fullness of times and that the things were now come to the very end. [He took bread] and gave thanks to teach us how we ought to celebrate this sacrament and to show that he does not unwillingly come to the Passion. He is teaching us so that whatever we may suffer, we may bear it thankfully. So it is a sign of good hope. If the [Mosaic] type pointed to deliverance from bondage, how much more will the truth he embodies set free the whole

world. He is being delivered up for the benefit of our whole human race. This is why he did not ordain the sacrament before this time. But from then on, when the rites of the law were no longer in effect, Jesus ordained it. THE GOSPEL OF MATTHEW, HOMILY 82.1.[10]

HE TOOK THE CUP. ORIGEN: If therefore we wish to receive the bread of blessing from Jesus, who is eager to give it, we should enter the city and go into the house, prepared beforehand, where Jesus kept the Passover with his disciples. We ascend to the "large, furnished upper room"[11] where he "took the cup" from the Father and, "when he had given thanks, he gave it to them" who had gone up there with him and said, "Drink this, for this is my blood of the new covenant." The cup was both consumed and poured out. It was consumed by the disciples. It was "poured out for the remission of sins" committed by those who drink it. If you want to know in what sense it was poured out, compare this saying with what was written [by Paul]: "God's love has been poured into our hearts."[12] If the blood of the covenant was poured into our hearts for the remission of our sins, then by the pouring of that potable blood into our hearts all the sins we have committed in the past will be remitted and wiped clean. He who took the cup and said "drink this all of you" will not depart from us who drink it but will drink it with us (since he himself is in each of us), for we are unable alone or without him either to eat of the bread or to drink of the fruit of the true vine. You should not marvel that he who is himself the bread also eats the bread with us or that he who is himself the cup of the fruit of the vine also drinks it with us. This is possible because the Word of God is omnipotent and is at once the bearer of many different names, for the multitude of his virtues are innumerable, since he is

---

[2]Ps 23:5 (22:5 LXX). [3]Ps 23:5 (22:5 LXX). [4]Jn 15:1. [5]Jn 12:24. [6]GCS 38.2:196. [7]Ps 104:15 (103:15 LXX). [8]Gen 14:18. [9]CCL 77:251. [10]PG 58:738; NPNF 1 10:491. [11]Lk 22:12. [12]Rom 5:5.

himself every virtue. COMMENTARY ON MATTHEW 86.[13]

26:28 Poured Out for the Forgiveness of Sins

MY BLOOD OF THE COVENANT. JEROME: From material things he moves on to spiritual things—namely, the vine transplanted from Egypt is the people of Israel to whom the Lord speaks through Jeremiah: "Yet I planted you a choice vine. . . . How then have you degenerated and become a wild vine?" Isaiah the prophet also celebrates this in his lovely canticle, and Scripture bears witness to it in different places. Therefore the Lord says that he will not drink of this fruit of the vine except in the kingdom of his Father. I believe the kingdom of the Father is the faith of the believers, which the apostle confirms when he says, "The kingdom of God is within you."[14] Therefore, when the Jews have received the kingdom of the father—note that he says "of the father" and not "of God" (every "father" is the name of the son)—when, as I say, they have believed in God the Father and the Father has led them to the Son, the Lord will drink of their wine, like Joseph reigning in Egypt, who will drink and be merry with his brothers. COMMENTARY ON MATTHEW 4.26.29.[15]

WHAT WAS FORESHADOWED. CHRYSOSTOM: Why was this sacrament ordained at the time of the Passover? That we might learn that he is the giver of the law and that the things that are foreshadowed in the law are fulfilled in him. The Old Testament was a type of the things to come. He is the truth of those things. THE GOSPEL OF MATTHEW, HOMILY 82.1.[16]

26:29-30 In My Father's Kingdom

WHETHER THE FATHER WILLED THE SON'S DEATH. CYRIL OF ALEXANDRIA: The disciples were not merely confused; rather the matter greatly disturbed them, and the knowledge of this mystery was hard to grasp. How could one be raised from the dead, or one with countless signs done on behalf of the people be handed over to death and dishonor? Yet this agrees with what the prophet said: "Strike the shepherd."[17] David also says to the Father, "Therefore those whom you struck, they will persecute."[18] However, not all this occurred at the will of the Father; he did not desire for him [the Son] to suffer, if only the Jews would have accepted him. So one cannot say he willed a murder. The Father consented with the Son's choice to suffer this. So it is written that the Father struck "the shepherd." He permitted him to suffer yet had the power to prevent the suffering. Something like this is at work in the passage that says Pilate was "over" Christ. "You would have no power over me if it were not given to you from above,"[19] that is, "if the Father had not permitted me to suffer." FRAGMENT 292.[20]

I SHALL NOT DRINK AGAIN OF THIS VINE. CHRYSOSTOM: For because he had discoursed with them concerning his Passion and cross, he again introduces what he has to say about his resurrection. Here he speaks of "my Father's kingdom," which was his way of speaking of his own resurrection.

And in what sense did he drink after he was raised again? We must answer carefully to guard against those of low mind who might suppose the resurrection was merely an appearance. The apostles understood themselves after the resurrection to have eaten and drunk with him. He said this to show them that they would see him manifestly risen and that he would be with them once more. They themselves were to be witnesses to these events, in that they both saw them and experienced them. So he says, I will not drink the fruit of this vine again with you "until that day when I drink it new with you in

---

[13]GCS 38.2:199-200. [14]Lk 17:21. [15]CCL 77:251-52. [16]PG 58:738; NPNF 1 10:491. [17]Zech 13:7. [18]Ps 69:26 (68:27 LXX). The text here agrees best with LXX. [19]Jn 19:11. [20]MKGK 257.

my Father's kingdom." You will see me rise again. You will bear witness to my resurrection. THE GOSPEL OF MATTHEW, HOMILY 82.2.[21]

WHEN I DRINK IT NEW. CHRYSOSTOM: But what is "new"? He will drink it new as having an immortal and incorruptible body, a spiritual body. He will not drink out of need for drink. For it is not a body that suffers or has bodily needs. It was not because he needed to eat and drink after the resurrection that he spoke in this way of that which is new but in order to give them full assurance of his resurrection. THE GOSPEL OF MATTHEW, HOMILY 82.2.[22]

SINGING A HYMN. ORIGEN: After the disciples celebrated the feast with their teacher and received the bread of blessing and ate the body of the Word and drank the cup of thanksgiving, Christ taught them to sing a hymn to the Father for these gifts and to pass from one height to another height, for the faithful are never able to do anything in the valley. So they went up to "the Mount of Olives," where each one of them, like a fruitful olive tree, was able to say, "I am like a green olive tree in the house of God."[23] And those who had not yet become "like a green olive tree in the house of God" but were still "like olive shoots around the table" of their spiritual father,[24] were also able to be present on the Mount of Olives, about which Zechariah prophesied.[25] And how fitting it was that this mount of mercy be chosen as the place where the disciples would be forewarned of their future weakness. It is fitting because Christ did not wish upon them what he only foretold, for he was then already preparing to receive converts, not to banish defectors. COMMENTARY ON MATTHEW 86.[26]

---

[21]PG 58:739-40; NPNF 1 10:492. [22]PG 58:740; NPNF 1 10:492. [23]Ps 52:8 (51:10 LXX). [24]Ps 128:3 (127:3 LXX). [25]Zech 14:4. [26]GCS 38.2:199-200.

26:31-35 JESUS PREDICTS PETER'S DENIAL

[31]*Then Jesus said to them, "You will all fall away because of me this night; for it is written, 'I will strike the shepherd, and the sheep of the flock will be scattered.'* [32]*But after I am raised up, I will go before you to Galilee."* [33]*Peter declared to him, "Though they all fall away because of you, I will never fall away."* [34]*Jesus said to him, "Truly, I say to you, this very night, before the cock crows, you will deny me three times."* [35]*Peter said to him, "Even if I must die with you, I will not deny you." And so said all the disciples.*

OVERVIEW: Those who fell away from Christ on the night he was betrayed did so because they had not yet received the staying power of the Holy Spirit (ORIGEN). Jesus stresses the fact that they fell away as a fulfillment of prophecy. This fulfillment of Old Testament prophecy increases the faith of the community (CHRYSOS-TOM). Jesus, the shepherd, was killed in order to bring unity among the many wandering sheep (JEROME).

Why did Christ say he would "go before you to Galilee" after he was raised? Cyril of Alexandria claims that this indicated that Jesus left the Jews in order to lead the Gentiles. Chrysostom, however, says that it was in order that the Jews might believe in him. Peter not only fell away from Christ but abandoned him. Through his denial, Peter demonstrates the wickedness of human nature. The other disciples accepted Jesus' word that they would fall away. Perhaps Peter was hungry for recognition (ORIGEN).

26:31 You Will All Fall Away

YOU WILL FALL AWAY THIS NIGHT. ORIGEN: They didn't fall away in the daytime but at night, and it was on the night in which Jesus was betrayed. Peter also denied Christ at night, not during the day. Moreover, it was still in the middle of the night, since the cock had not yet crowed. Anyone who questions how the disciples could have fallen away after seeing such great signs and wonders and after hearing words of equal power (for the signs and wonders were performed by his words) should realize that Christ wanted to demonstrate through this warning that just as "no one can say that Jesus is Lord except by the Holy Spirit,"[1] so also no one is able to keep from falling away except by the Holy Spirit. When what Jesus had foretold came to pass, "You will all fall away from me this night," it was still true that "the Holy Spirit had not yet been given because Jesus had not yet been glorified."[2] If we . . . who have already professed Jesus to be Lord by the Holy Spirit (for "all who are led by the Spirit of God are sons of God"),[3] then fall away or deny him, we will not have an excuse like those who fell away or denied him without the Holy Spirit. COMMENTARY ON MATTHEW 87.[4]

I WILL STRIKE THE SHEPHERD. CHRYSOSTOM: Then he said to them, "You will all fall away because of me." After this he mentions a prophecy: "For it is written, 'I will strike the shepherd, and the sheep of the flock will be scattered.' "[5] He was urging them to be attentive to what has been prophetically predicted of his death and resurrection, and at the same time he wanted to

make it plain that he was indeed crucified according to God's purpose. All of this was to show that he was no alien from the old covenant or from the God who preached it. What was done in the Old Testament was a dispensation. All the prophets proclaimed all things beforehand from the beginning that are included in this salvation event. All this was to increase faith.

And he teaches us to know what the disciples were before the crucifixion and what they did after the crucifixion. For indeed they who were not able so much as to stand their ground when he was crucified, after his death became mighty and stronger than adamant. THE GOSPEL OF MATTHEW, HOMILY 82.2.[6]

THE FLOCK WILL BE SCATTERED. JEROME: "For it is written, 'I will smite the shepherd, and the sheep of the flock will be scattered.' " Zechariah the prophet says the same thing, only differently; and if I am not mistaken, God is addressed in the person of the prophet: "Strike the shepherd that the sheep may be scattered."[7] In harmony with these words is the psalm, which is recited in its entirety to the Lord: "For they persecute him whom you have struck."[8] The good shepherd is struck, however, that he may lay down his life for his sheep and that out of many flocks of wandering sheep there may be one flock and one shepherd. COMMENTARY ON MATTHEW 4.26.31.[9]

26:32 I Will Go Ahead of You to Galilee

AFTER I AM RISEN. CYRIL OF ALEXANDRIA: He did not leave the disciples with sad expressions but proclaimed the resurrection to them ahead of time, freeing them from grief, and he promised to go ahead of them into Galilee. In this way he shows that he is about to desert the

---

[1] 1 Cor 12:3. [2] Jn 7:39. [3] Rom 8:14. [4] GCS 38.2:200. [5] Zech 13:7. [6] PG 58:740; NPNF 1 10:493. [7] Zech 13:7. [8] Ps 69:26 (68:27 LXX). [9] CCL 77:252.

Jews and go to the Gentiles. FRAGMENT 293.[10]

GIVING COMPLETE ASSURANCE. CHRYSOSTOM: He does not permit them to become sorrowful but immediately says, "But after I am risen again, I will go before you into Galilee." For he does not immediately appear from heaven on a single occasion and then depart to a distant country. Rather, he promises to come in resurrected form to the same nation in which he had also been crucified, and nearly to the same place. All this was to give complete assurance that he had indeed been crucified and that he indeed rose again, thereby to comfort them more abundantly when in sorrow. Therefore also he specified "to Galilee," in order that being freed from the fears of the Jews they might believe his saying. This is why he indeed appeared there. THE GOSPEL OF MATTHEW, HOMILY 82.2.[11]

26:33-35 You Will Deny Me

I WILL NEVER FALL AWAY. ORIGEN: The other disciples only fell away from Jesus, but Peter, who thought that he could begin with deceit and end up with the truth, both fell away from Jesus and also denied him because of the audacious promise he made that he would never fall away.

It was not only out of carelessness but almost also out of wickedness that he said, "Even if all fall away because of you, I will not fall away." He made a rash promise because he did not know the deceitfulness of human nature. This is why Peter didn't simply fall away from Jesus or even deny him once but abandoned him so completely that he denied him three times. COMMENTARY ON MATTHEW 88.[12]

YOU WILL DENY ME THREE TIMES. ORIGEN: It seems to me that Jesus' other disciples had the foresight and wisdom (when it was first said "you will fall away because of me tonight") not to profess that they would never fall away, for they saw the truth of Jesus' prediction. But because only to Peter alone was it said, "Truly I tell you, before the cock crows you will deny me three times," they eventually promised along with Peter, "Even if we have to die with you, we will not deny you." The difference between Peter and the other disciples is this: Peter did not acquiesce even after Jesus prophesied that he would deny him three times before the cock crowed. The others, however, who were not included in this prophecy or in things said only to Peter, responded with a promise which did not seek to make a liar out of the Lord, as Peter's promise did. COMMENTARY ON MATTHEW 88.[13]

PETER'S BRAVADO. CHRYSOSTOM: Peter then spoke confidently and lifted himself up over the rest, saying, "Though they all fall away because of you, I will never fall away." It may be that in some degree his bravado sprang from jealousy. For at supper they were all talking about which one of them was the greater.[14] This passion for recognition was still troubling them. Therefore Jesus resisted Peter, not compelling him to a future denial—God forbid! But he left him destitute of his help, convicting human nature. THE GOSPEL OF MATTHEW, HOMILY 82.3.[15]

---

[10]MKGK 257-58. [11]PG 58:740; NPNF 1 10:493. [12]GCS 38.2:202. [13]GCS 38.2:203. [14]Lk 22:24. [15]PG 58:742; NPNF 1 10:494.

26:36-46 JESUS PRAYS IN GETHSEMANE

³⁶*Then Jesus went with them to a place called Gethsemane, and he said to his disciples, "Sit here, while I go yonder and pray." ³⁷And taking with him Peter and the two sons of Zebedee, he began to be sorrowful and troubled. ³⁸Then he said to them, "My soul is very sorrowful, even to death; remain here, and watch*[b] *with me." ³⁹And going a little farther he fell on his face and prayed, "My Father, if it be possible, let this cup pass from me; nevertheless, not as I will, but as thou wilt." ⁴⁰And he came to the disciples and found them sleeping; and he said to Peter, "So, could you not watch*[b] *with me one hour? ⁴¹Watch*[b] *and pray that you may not enter into temptation; the spirit indeed is willing, but the flesh is weak." ⁴²Again, for the second time, he went away and prayed, "My Father, if this cannot pass unless I drink it, thy will be done." ⁴³And again he came and found them sleeping, for their eyes were heavy. ⁴⁴So, leaving them again, he went away and prayed for the third time, saying the same words. ⁴⁵Then he came to the disciples and said to them, "Are you still sleeping and taking your rest? Behold, the hour is at hand, and the Son of man is betrayed into the hands of sinners. ⁴⁶Rise, let us be going; see, my betrayer is at hand."*

b Or keep awake

OVERVIEW: Gethsemane was known as a holy place, a place of prayer (ORIGEN). To spare the disciples greater sorrow, Jesus prayed alone in the garden (CHRYSOSTOM). Jesus was sorrowful too, not from fear of death but from fear that his disciples would no longer believe in him after his death (HILARY OF POITIERS, JEROME). In the garden, then, Jesus asks the disciples to "keep watch" (ORIGEN).

Jesus asked that God remove the cup from him. Origen centers this request on God's justice. Jesus' request shows his full humanity (CHRYSOSTOM). Ultimately following God's will, however, shows Jesus' higher will (LEO THE GREAT), which is in harmony with God's (CHRYSOSTOM). In spite of the sleeping disciples, Jesus models perseverance in prayer (ORIGEN). He is concerned that the disciples not fall into temptation (HILARY OF POITIERS, JEROME), and he especially admonishes Peter to be contrite of heart while acknowledging the limits of humanity (CHRYSOSTOM). To one's ability, however, one can be alert. The prayers of those who "watch

and pray" will be heard, but it is appropriate to sleep when the Lord commands us to sleep (ORIGEN).

Jesus' betrayal came at a time appointed by God, and Jesus did not flee from it even though he was guiltless (CHRYSOSTOM). As Jesus was "delivered into the hands of sinners" in the garden at that appointed time, so is Christ betrayed by those who fall away from him in the present day. Likewise, all who betray Jesus also "deliver him up" (ORIGEN).

26:36 A Place Called Gethsemane

GETHSEMANE. JEROME: Gethsemane is interpreted as the "very fertile valley" where the Lord ordered his disciples to sit down and wait for him to return while he prayed alone for everyone. COMMENTARY ON MATTHEW 4.26.37.[1]

---

[1]CCL 77:253.

WHILE I PRAY. ORIGEN: Jesus brought his disciples from the upper room to a garden which was called Gethsemane because, after he was betrayed, he did not want to be arrested in the same place where he and his disciples had eaten the Passover. Even before he was betrayed, however, he thought it fitting to choose to pray in places devoted purely to prayer, for he knew that some locations are holier than others, as it is written: "The place where you are standing is holy ground."[2] COMMENTARY ON MATTHEW 89.[3]

26:37 Jesus Was Sorrowful and Troubled

HE TOOK THREE WITH HIM. CHRYSOSTOM: His disciples were clinging to him inseparably. So he said to his disciples, "Sit here, while I go over there and pray."[4] For it was usual with him to pray apart from them. He did this to teach us how to pray, how to use silence and solitude to pray for great matters. And taking with him the three, he said to them, "My soul is very sorrowful, even to death; remain here, and watch with me"[5] Why does he not take all of them with him? That they might not be more sorrowful. He took only those who had been spectators of his glory.[6] THE GOSPEL OF MATTHEW, HOMILY 83.1.[7]

HE BEGAN TO BE SORROWFUL. HILARY OF POITIERS: When we read that the Lord was sad, we must examine everything that was said to find out why he was sad. He previously warned that they would all fall away. Brimming with confidence, Peter responded that even though all the others might be alarmed, he would not be moved[8]—he who the Lord predicted would deny knowing him three times.[9] In fact, Peter and all the other disciples promised that even in the face of death they would not deny him.[10] He then proceeded on and ordered his disciples to sit down while he prayed.[11] Having brought with him Peter, James and John, he began to grieve. Before he brought them along with him, he did not feel sad. It was only after they had accompanied him that he grew exceedingly sad. His sadness thus arose not from himself but from those whom he had taken with him. It must be realized that the Son of man brought with him none but those whom he showed that he would come into his kingdom at that time when, in the presence of Moses and Elijah on the mountain, he was surrounded by all the splendor of his eternal glory. But the reason for bringing them with him both then and now was the same. ON MATTHEW 31.4.[12]

26:38 Remain and Watch with Me

THE PROCESS OF DEATH IS FEARED. HILARY OF POITIERS: Then he said, "My soul is sad, even to death." Did he say, My soul is sad because of death? Certainly not. For if death were the reason for his fear, he certainly ought to have said so. But the reason for his fear lies elsewhere. Actually we have no indication, since the reason for what begins in another person may differ from what it is at the end. He had just said before, "You will all fall away this night because of me."[13] He knew that they would be frightened, that they would run away and deny knowing him. And since blasphemy against the Holy Spirit is forgiven neither here nor in eternity, he feared they might deny that he is God, once they looked upon him beaten and spat upon and crucified. This was the reason that prompted Peter, who, in betraying Christ, denied him in this way: "I do not know the man,"[14] for anything said against the Son of man will be forgiven. Christ is therefore sad even to death. So it is not death itself but the process of death that is feared, for after his death the faith of the believers would be strengthened by the power of the resurrection. ON MATTHEW 31.5.[15]

---

[2]Ex 3:5; Acts 7:33. [3]GCS 38.2:204. [4]Mt 26:36. [5]Mt 26:38. [6]In the transfiguration. [7]PG 58:745; NPNF 1 10:497. [8]Mt 26:33. [9]Mt 26:34. [10]Mt 26:35. [11]Mt 26:36. [12]SC 258:230. [13]Mt 26:31. [14]Mt 26:72. [15]SC 258:230-32.

KEEP WATCH WITH ME. ORIGEN: "Stay here and keep watch with me." It is as though Jesus had said, "Although I told the other disciples to 'sit here while I go and pray' but brought you three along with me, I don't want you to come any further, for you are not yet able. So, stay here keeping watch as I keep watch, knowing that the others were commanded to sit over there because they are weaker and need to be protected from this agony. [But] I have brought you who are stronger with me to labor with me in watching and praying. Nevertheless, you remain here, that each one stand firm in the state of his calling,[16] for every grace (however great it may be) has a superior." What Jesus meant when he said "remain here" is explained by what was said next: "going a little farther, he fell on his face." Therefore let us remain where Jesus commanded us to remain, as the apostle also admonished: "Everyone should remain in the state in which he was called."[17] And let us do everything in our power to keep watch with him who "neither slumbers nor sleeps, who keeps Israel."[18] COMMENTARY ON MATTHEW 91.[19]

MY SOUL IS VERY SORROWFUL. JEROME: What we said before about Christ's suffering and what took place before it is also brought out in this chapter.[20] It shows that the Lord, to test the fidelity of the human nature he had taken on, truly felt sorrowful. However, lest the suffering in his soul be overwhelming, he began to feel sorrowful over the events taking place just before his suffering. For it is one thing to feel sorrowful and another thing to begin to feel sorrowful. But he felt sorrowful, not because he feared the suffering that lay ahead and because he had scolded Peter for his timidity but because of the most unfortunate Judas and the falling away of all the apostles and the rejection by the Jewish people and the overturning of woeful Jerusalem. Jonah too became sad when the plant or ivy had withered, unwilling to have his booth disappear.[21] COMMENTARY ON MATTHEW 4.26.37.[22]

26:39 Let This Cup Pass from Me

IF IT BE POSSIBLE. ORIGEN: His words "if it be possible" referred not only to God's power but also to his justice. As to God's power, whatever is just or unjust is possible. As to his justice, which is not only powerful but also just, not everything is possible—only that which is just. COMMENTARY ON MATTHEW 95.[23]

NOT AS I WILL, BUT AS YOU WILL. CHRYSOSTOM: By saying then, "If it be possible, let it pass from me," he showed his true humanity. But by saying, "Nevertheless not as I will, but as you will," he showed his virtue and self-command. This too teaches us, even when nature pulls us back, to follow God. In order to make clear that he is truly God and truly human, words alone would not suffice. Deeds were needed. So he joined deeds with words in order that even those who have been highly contentious may believe that he both became man and died. Admittedly some still do not believe that this was so. But many more would have been unable to have believed if his face had not been seen at Gethsemane. See in how many ways he shows the reality of the incarnation. He demonstrates both by what he speaks and by what he suffers. THE GOSPEL OF MATTHEW, HOMILY 83.1.[24]

LET THIS CUP PASS. LEO THE GREAT: The disciples were admonished, and the Lord beseeches the Father that they might confront the force of

---

[16]The physical continuation indicates the spiritual condition. First the more imperfect disciples stop; then Peter, James and John, who are less imperfect. Jesus continues alone. [17]1 Cor 7:20. [18]Ps 121:4 (120:4 LXX). [19]GCS 38.2:207. [20]To explain Jesus' agitation, Jerome resorts to the medical distinction between *pathos* (*passio*, "disease") and *propatheia* (*propassio*, "beginning/anticipation of disease"). *Pathos* in the moral sense is considered evil, while *propatheia* signifies the beginning of the agitation, not yet morally wrong because voluntary assent is lacking. [21]Jon 4:8. The lament of Jonah for the shadow of the ivy plant that withered (Jon 4:6-8), since Jonah is the prefiguration of Christ, prefigures the sorrow of Christ for the contrariness of the Jews, for the weakness of the disciples and for the future destruction of Jerusalem. [22]CCL 77:253-54. [23]GCS 38.2:213. [24]PG 58:746; NPNF 1 10:497.

the present temptation with watchful prayer: "My Father, if it be possible, let this cup pass from me; nevertheless not as I will, but as you will." The first petition arises from weakness, the second from strength: He desired the former based on our nature and chose the latter based on his own. Equal to the Father, the Son knew that all things were possible to God; rather, he descended into this world to take up the cross against his will so that he might suffer through this conflict of emotions with a disquieted mind. But in order to show the distinction between the receiving nature and the received nature, what was proper of humanity desired divine intervention and what was proper of God looked upon the human situation. The lower will yielded to the higher will, and this demonstrated what the fearful person may pray for and what the divine healer should not grant. "For we do not know how to pray as we ought,"[25] and it is good for us that what we want, for the most part, is not granted. God, who is good and just, shows mercy toward us by denying us those things we ask for which are harmful. SERMON 43.2.[26]

26:40-43 Stay Awake and Pray

HE FOUND THEM SLEEPING. ORIGEN: But notice that after the first prayer "he came to the disciples and found them sleeping." Likewise after the second prayer "he came and found them sleeping, for their eyes were heavy." On this, I believe they were the eyes not so much of their bodies as of their souls. Besides, he had not yet removed the heaviness from their eyes, "because he was not yet glorified." And just as "the Spirit had not been given, because Jesus was not yet glorified," so too the heaviness had not yet been removed from their eyes "because Jesus was not yet glorified." Therefore he does not rebuke them, but "leaving them again, he went away and prayed for the third time, saying the same words." He also teaches us through those "same words," that we may not grow faint

in prayer but persist in the very words of our prayer until we obtain those things we have begun to pray for. COMMENTARY ON MATTHEW 95.[27]

PRAY THAT YOU MAY NOT ENTER INTO TEMPTATION. HILARY OF POITIERS: After that, he returns to the disciples and finds them sleeping. He asks Peter why he could not watch with him one hour—Peter, indeed, was one of the three, for he had boasted in front of the others that he would not fall away. And he indicates the cause of his greater fear, saying, "Pray that you may not enter into temptation." He wanted then to prevent temptation (so he included in his prayer the words "lead us not into temptation"),[28] lest anything in us cater to the weakness of the flesh. He also makes it clear why he urged them to pray in order to avoid temptation, saying, "The spirit indeed is willing, but the flesh is weak." These words did not apply to himself but were aimed at them. For that matter, how is it that now his spirit is willing, whereas before his soul was sad even to death?[29] At any rate, he orders them to watch and pray lest they give in to temptation and succumb to the weakness of the body. He therefore prays that, if possible, the cup may pass from himself, for when it comes to drinking from it, all flesh is weak.[30] ON MATTHEW 31.9.[31]

THE FLESH IS WEAK. JEROME: "Watch and pray that you may not enter into temptation." It is impossible for the human soul to avoid temptation. Hence we say in the Lord's Prayer, "Lead us not into temptation,"[32] which we are unable to withstand. We do not refuse to face temptation entirely but pray for the strength to bear up under it. Therefore he does not say, "Watch and pray that you may not be tempted" but "that you may not enter into temptation," that is, that temptation may not overwhelm you and hold

---

[25]Rom 8:26. [26]SC 74:43. [27]GCS 38.2:214-15. [28]Mt 6:13. [29]Mt 26:38. [30]Mt 26:39. [31]SC 258:236. [32]Mt 6:13.

you in its grip. For example, a martyr who has shed blood by professing faith in the Lord was certainly tempted but was not ensnared in the net of temptation. One who denies the faith, however, has fallen into the snares of temptation.

"The spirit indeed is willing, but the flesh is weak." This is aimed at those rash people who think that whatever they believe, they can obtain. Therefore, as much as we trust in the ardor of our spirit, so too should we fear the weakness of the flesh. And yet, according to the apostle, the works of the flesh are mortified by the Spirit. COMMENTARY ON MATTHEW 4.26.41.[33]

WATCH AND PRAY. ORIGEN: As long as Jesus was present, his disciples did not sleep. After he had walked away a short distance, they were unable to watch for even one hour in his absence. For this reason we should pray that Jesus will not leave us for even a short while but will fulfill what he promised when he said to us, "And I am with you all days, even to the end of the world."[34] In this way will we keep watch as he banishes sleep from our souls, to make it possible for us to fulfill his command: "Do not give sleep to your eyes or slumber to your eyelids, that you may escape as a doe from the nets and a bird from the snare of the fowlers."[35] But coming to the disciples and finding them asleep, he arouses them with a word and tells them to listen, so he may as it were say to those who are listening: "How is it that you were not able to watch with me for even one hour?"

He orders us then to be wakeful so we may keep watch and pray. Now that person watches who does good works, that person watches who diligently attends to the truth of the faith lest he be ensnared by any shady teaching. He who watches and prays in this way will have his prayer heard. This is what the Lord means when he says, "Watch and pray." We should first watch and, while watching, we should pray. COMMENTARY ON MATTHEW 93.[36]

THEIR EYES WERE HEAVY. HILARY OF POITIERS: The fact that, after returning and finding them asleep, he first reproves them, secondly is silent and thirdly orders them to rest, can be explained in this way: First, after the resurrection, he scolded them for scattering and for being apprehensive and restless;[37] second, once the Holy Spirit had been sent, he came and found them sleeping, since their eyes were too heavy for them to discern the freedom of the gospel—having been held back by the love of the law for some time, their faith was still sleeping; and third, with the return of his radiance, he restored them to restfulness and peace of mind. ON MATTHEW 31.11.[38]

26:44 Thy Will Be Done

COULD YOU NOT WATCH WITH ME ONE HOUR? CHRYSOSTOM: After that he returns and says to Peter, "So, could you not watch with me one hour?"[39] They all were sleeping. He admonishes Peter. He is hinting at him in what he said, especially in the words "with me." They are not employed without reason. It is as though he had said, "So you are the one who is ready to lay down your life for me, and you could not watch with me for one hour!"[40] What follows also suggests the same admonition: "Watch and pray that you may not enter into temptation." He is again instructing them not to be self-confident but contrite in mind, to be humble and to refer everything to God. THE GOSPEL OF MATTHEW, HOMILY 83.1.[41]

PRAY THAT YOU NOT ENTER INTO TEMPTATION. CHRYSOSTOM: And at one time we find him addressing them all together and at another time Peter. He says, "Simon, Simon, Satan has desired to have you, that he may sift you as wheat, but I have prayed for you."[42] Then he

[33]CCL 77:255-56. [34]Mt 28:20. [35]Prov 6:4-5. [36]GCS 38.2:210-11. [37]Mk 16:14. [38]SC 258:238. [39]Mt 26:40. [40]Mt 26:41. [41]PG 58:7546; NPNF 1 10:497-98. [42]Lk 22:31-32.

says to all in common, "Watch and pray that you may not enter into temptation."[43] He is in every way encouraging them to be resolute and strong in these convictions. Then, that he might not seem to make his language altogether condemnatory, he says, "The spirit indeed is willing, but the flesh is weak."[44] For no matter how much you might wish to despise death, you will not be able to do so until God extends his hand. For the carnal mind draws you down.

And again he prayed in the same way, saying, "My Father, if this cannot pass unless I drink it, your will be done."[45] It is clear here that his human will is in full harmony with God's will. This harmony is what we must always seek after and follow. The Gospel of Matthew, Homily 83.1.[46]

26:45-46 My Betrayer Is at Hand

TAKE YOUR REST. ORIGEN: Then, undoubtedly after the third prayer, he came to the disciples. But the sleep he now orders them to sleep is not that which, as is written, came upon the disciples twice before. For at first "he found them sleeping" but not at rest, and "again he came and found them sleeping, for their eyes were heavy." But now he orders them not simply to sleep but to take their rest. Indeed, there is a big difference between the sleep implied in Christ's second command to "sleep now and take your rest" and the sleep that is against his will after he orders them to "remain here and watch one hour with me." There was nothing contradictory between his words "watch with me" and later, "Sleep on and take your rest." He simply kept a certain order, so that first indeed we should watch and pray that we do not enter into temptation, and then we should sleep and take our rest according to Christ's command. COMMENTARY ON MATTHEW 96.[47]

BETRAYED INTO THE HANDS OF SINNERS. CHRYSOSTOM: Then he came to the disciples and said to them, "Are you still sleeping and taking your rest? Behold, the hour is at hand, and the Son of man is betrayed into the hands of sinners." All this belongs to the divine economy. "Into the hands of sinners" is said to make it clear that he was not liable to any charge but that this course of events was due to human wickedness. Finally he says, "Rise, let us be going; see, my betrayer is at hand." By all these means he was teaching them that this course of events was not something that happens of necessity, without human willing or out of human weakness. It is all unfolding, without denying freedom, as God's own secret dispensation. Even though he foreknew that Judas would come, so far was he from fleeing, he even went to meet him. THE GOSPEL OF MATTHEW, HOMILY 83.1-2.[48]

THE HOUR IS AT HAND. ORIGEN: "Look! The hour is approaching, and the Son of man will be delivered up into the hands of sinners." It is also in view of this hour, I believe, that he said to his mother, "My hour has not yet come."[49] And now he declares that with the hour approaching, "the Son of man will be delivered up into the hands of sinners." Would that only into the hands of those sinners had Jesus been delivered up! But now I believe that he is delivered up always "into the hands of sinners" when they who seem to believe in Jesus have him in their hands since they are sinners. Indeed, as often as a righteous person indwelt by Jesus has fallen under the sway of sinners, Jesus is delivered up "into the hands of sinners."

"Rise, let us be going; see, my betrayer is approaching." After he has awakened them from that sleep we spoke about, he says to his disciples, "Rise, let us be going." And seeing Judas in his mind, who was approaching him to deliver him up and who was not yet seen by his disciples, he says, "See, the one who will deliver me up is approaching." I believe, however, that "see, he is approaching" and "see, the one who will

---

[43]Mt 26:41. [44]Mt 26:41. [45]Mt 26:42. [46]PG 58:746-47; NPNF 1 10:498. [47]GCS 38.2:215. [48]PG 58:747; NPNF 1 10:498. [49]Jn 2:4.

deliver me up is approaching" are not equivalent. Furthermore, the traitor, who had separated himself from Jesus by his sins and his betrayal was not simply "approaching" Jesus, but "he is approaching" to deliver up the Son of God, whom he already betrayed. Plainly, all wrongdoers first betray Jesus; then they deliver him up.[50] COMMENTARY ON MATTHEW 97-98.[51]

---

[50]The allegorical interpretation is founded on the observation that Jesus merely says of Judas "he approaches" without adding "toward me." The detail, insignificant for the literal meaning, symbolically signifies that he who works evil against Jesus cannot be near him spiritually. [51]GCS 38.2:216.

26:47-56 JESUS IS ARRESTED

[47]*While he was still speaking, Judas came, one of the twelve, and with him a great crowd with swords and clubs, from the chief priests and the elders of the people.* [48]*Now the betrayer had given them a sign, saying, "The one I shall kiss is the man; seize him."* [49]*And he came up to Jesus at once and said, "Hail, Master!"[i] And he kissed him.* [50]*Jesus said to him, "Friend, why are you here?"[j] Then they came up and laid hands on Jesus and seized him.* [51]*And behold, one of those who were with Jesus stretched out his hand and drew his sword, and struck the slave of the high priest, and cut off his ear.* [52]*Then Jesus said to him, "Put your sword back into its place; for all who take the sword will perish by the sword.* [53]*Do you think that I cannot appeal to my Father, and he will at once send me more than twelve legions of angels?* [54]*But how then should the scriptures be fulfilled, that it must be so?"* [55]*At that hour Jesus said to the crowds, "Have you come out as against a robber, with swords and clubs to capture me? Day after day I sat in the temple teaching, and you did not seize me.* [56]*But all this has taken place, that the scriptures of the prophets might be fulfilled." Then all the disciples forsook him and fled.*

i Or *Rabbi*   j Or *do that for which you have come*

OVERVIEW: Those who gathered at Jesus' betrayal with clubs in hand did so because they thought that he could disappear from their midst (ORIGEN), which indeed he could have done; nevertheless Jesus submitted quietly to his betrayers. By contrast the betrayers were enraged, especially Judas (CHRYSOSTOM). Accepting the kiss of betrayal, Jesus grants power to his adversaries (HILARY OF POITIERS). All adversaries of truth betray God's Word in the same way that Judas betrayed Jesus (ORIGEN).

The disciple severed the slave's ear because it was closed to truth in the first place (HILARY OF POITIERS). Jesus commands that the sword be sheathed in order that he remain true to his commitment to God's will (ORIGEN, CHRYSOSTOM). The disciples' possession of swords symbolizes Jesus' betrayal. In spite of swords and clubs on both sides, Jesus was not forced to submit to his adversaries; he willingly submitted to them according to the Scriptures. The disciples, however, fled because they realized that Jesus would not attempt to escape (CHRYSOSTOM). Origen suggests they fled because they had not yet received the Holy Spirit.

26:47 Judas and a Large Crowd

A GREAT CROWD WITH CLUBS. ORIGEN:
Someone may question why "a great crowd" gathered "with swords and clubs" against him. According to John, this large crowd consisted of a band of soldiers and officers sent by the chief priests. And someone may say that because of the multitude of believers from the people, so many came against him lest a large crowd of believers snatch him out of their hands. But I think there may be another reason why the crowd had gathered against him. Those who believed that he exorcised devils in the name of Beelzebub thought that out of a kind of black magic he could escape from the midst of those who wanted to take hold of him. And perhaps some of them had heard that once when he was to be thrown down from a mountaintop he escaped from the hands of those who were holding him, not by simple human flight but by some preternatural force.[1] COMMENTARY ON MATTHEW 99.[2]

26:48-49 Judas Had Given a Sign

THEY SEIZED HIM. CHRYSOSTOM: For having shown his own strength, at once he yielded himself. But the other Evangelist says that even at that very moment he continued to reprove him, saying, "Judas, would you betray the Son of man with a kiss?"[3] Are you not ashamed even of the form of your betrayal? Nonetheless he submitted to be kissed and did not even resist this shameless act. He gave himself up willingly. They laid their hands on him. They seized him that night on which they ate the Passover. To such a degree did they boil with rage and madness. They, however, would have had no strength against him unless he had permitted it. Yet this did not deliver Judas from unspeakable punishment. He even more exceedingly condemns himself by the manner of his betrayal, by the Lord's meekness and leniency and gentleness. He became fiercer than any wild beast. THE GOSPEL OF MATTHEW, HOMILY 83.2.[4]

BROKEN TRUST. JEROME: It was shameless indeed and a sign of broken trust to call him master and to plant a kiss on the one he betrayed. But Judas still has something of the modesty of a disciple, for he does not deliver up Christ to his persecutors openly but with the sign of a kiss. This is the mark which God put on Cain lest anyone who came upon him should kill him.[5] COMMENTARY ON MATTHEW 4.26.49.[6]

THE BETRAYER KISSED HIM. CHRYSOSTOM:
How fitting are the instruments of the priests! They came against him "with swords and clubs."[7] Judas himself was with them, one of the Twelve. In the interest of fair disclosure the Evangelist still calls him "one of the Twelve," unashamedly. "Now the betrayer had given them a sign, saying, 'The one I shall kiss is the man; seize him.'" O with what depravity had the traitor's soul been inflamed! With what kind of eyes did he then look at his Master? With what mouth did he kiss him? O accursed purpose! What sign did he devise? What did he dare? What sort of clue of betrayal did he give? Whoever I kiss! He was emboldened by his Master's gentleness. Yet it by itself was sufficient to shame him. The kiss deprived him of all excuse, for he was betraying one incomparably meek.

But why does he say ["Seize the one I kiss"?] Often when Jesus had been under attack and possible seizure, he had gone out from the crowd, through the middle of it, without their even knowing it.[8] THE GOSPEL OF MATTHEW, HOMILY 83.2.[9]

JUDAS KISSED HIM. HILARY OF POITIERS:
There is a certain order to the different facets of Christ's suffering. But the reason for Judas's kiss was that we might discern all our enemies and those who we know would delight in raging

---

[1]Lk 4:28-30. [2]GCS 38.2:217. [3]Lk 22:48. [4]PG 58:748; NPNF 1 10:499. [5]Gen 4:15. [6]CCL 77:257. [7]Mt 26:47. [8]Cf. Lk 4:30. [9]PG 58:747-48; NPNF 1 10:498.

against us. The Lord does not resist his kiss. ON MATTHEW 32.2.[10]

26:50-51 *Jesus Arrested*

AUTHORIZING HIS BETRAYAL. HILARY OF POITIERS: As to what he tells Judas, "Do what you have to do," he authorizes his own betrayal by that very statement. For he who had it within his power to call upon twelve thousand legions of angels[11] against his betrayers would have found it so much easier to oppose the plans and artifices of one man. At length he says to Pilate, "You would have no power over me unless it had been given you."[12] He thus gives power against himself when he says, "Do what you have to do." In other words, because the crime of what is willed is counterbalanced by what is perpetuated, Judas would accomplish in deed what he had already done in his will. ON MATTHEW 32.2.[13]

WHY ARE YOU HERE? ORIGEN: But I think that all betrayers of the truth, pretending to love the truth and using the sign of a kiss as a mark of affection, betray the Word of God. Cloaked in belligerence, brandishing clubs and the swords of battle and proffering insults, his enemies desire to take hold of him. And the traitor says to Jesus, "Master." Indeed, all heretics, like Judas, address Jesus in the same way, "Master." They kiss him even as Judas did. Jesus speaks peacefully to them all, since they are all Judases who betray him: "Judas, is it with a kiss that you betray the Son of man?" As for Judas, he is reproached by Christ for his false friendship. "Friend, why are you here?" We hear of no one who is good called by that name in the Scriptures. Moreover, to the wicked and the one not wearing a wedding garment he says, "Friend, how did you get in here without a wedding garment?"[14] Wicked too is that man in the parable of the denarius who hears the words, "Friend, I am doing you no wrong; did you not agree with me for a denarius? Take what belongs to you,

and go. I choose to give to this last as I give to you."[15] COMMENTARY ON MATTHEW 100.[16]

HEARING WITH THE LEFT EAR. ORIGEN: Perhaps what Peter did[17] was a mystery, for the right ear of the Jewish people had to be cut off because of their malice toward Jesus. Though they seem to hear the law, they now hear with their left ear the shadowy tradition of the law but not the truth, since they are enslaved by words that profess the service of God but do not serve him in truth. The mystery of these words against Christ is found in the person of Christ's adversary, the high priest Caiaphas. Now it seems to me, since all the Gentile believers were made one people in Christ, the very fact that they believed in Christ was the reason why the right ear of the Jews was cut off, according to what had been prophesied about them: "Make the ears of this people heavy, and shut their eyes; lest they see with their eyes, and hear with their ears . . . and turn and be healed."[18] COMMENTARY ON MATTHEW 101.[19]

CUTTING OFF HIS EAR. HILARY OF POITIERS: The apostle cuts off the ear of the slave of the high priest; that is, a disciple of Christ cuts off a disobedient ear from a man in the priesthood. What was once incapable of hearing the truth is now cut off. ON MATTHEW 32.2.[20]

26:52-54 *How Would the Scriptures Be Fulfilled?*

PUT YOUR SWORD AWAY. ORIGEN: He said to Peter, "Put your sword back into its place" (which is one of patience). After restoring the amputated ear, as the other Evangelist says (which was a sign of both supreme kindness and divine power),[21] he spoke these words that they might ring true to what he had said and done

---

[10]SC 258:240. [11]Mt 26:53. [12]Jn 19:11. [13]SC 258:240. [14]Mt 22:12. [15]Mt 20:13-14. [16]GCS 38.2:220. [17]Jn 18:10. [18]Is 6:10. [19]GCS 38.2:221. [20]SC 258:242. [21]Lk 22:51.

before. Although they might not remember the good things done in the past, they might acknowledge the good things done in the present. COMMENTARY ON MATTHEW 103.[22]

THE SERVANT OF THE HIGH PRIEST. CHRYSOSTOM: Who was this "one" who cut off the ear? John says it was Peter.[23] For this was an act of fervor. Another point deserves inquiry: Why were the disciples bearing swords? That they indeed bore swords is evident from the text both here and in the other accounts. But why did Christ even permit them to have swords? For Luke affirms also that "one of them struck the servant of the high priest, cutting off his right ear,"[24] remembering that in Luke Jesus had said to them, "When I sent you without purse, traveling bag and shoes, did you lack anything?" And when they said, "Nothing," he said to them, "But now, he that has a purse, let him take it, and a bag, and he that has no sword, let him sell his garment, and buy one." And when they said, "Here are two swords," he said to them, "It is enough."[25] So why did they have swords? Because he had said to them, "Let him buy a sword." Yet this was not meant that they should arm themselves, far from it, but to indicate that he was to be betrayed. The swords had prophetic rather than military purpose. They indicated his being forcefully seized and betrayed. THE GOSPEL OF MATTHEW, HOMILY 84.1.[26]

NO MORE OF THIS. CHRYSOSTOM: Peter is rebuked for using his sword and for his severe threat. He was resisting the servant who came indeed with hostility. He was not defending himself but doing this on behalf of his Master.

Christ however did not permit any harm to ensue. For he healed [the servant] and manifested a great miracle, enough to indicate at once both his forbearance and his power and the affection and meekness of his disciple. Peter had acted from affection. Now he acts from duty. For when he heard, "Put your sword back into its place," he obeyed immediately. THE GOSPEL OF MATTHEW, HOMILY 84.1.[27]

PERISHING BY THE SWORD. CHRYSOSTOM: One of his followers, in another account, asked, "Lord should we strike with our swords?"[28] But it is clear in all accounts that he rejected it and healed the man and rebuked his disciple in such a way that he might move him to acquiescence. "For all who take the sword will perish by the sword." Then he adds, "Do you think that I cannot appeal to my Father, and he will at once send me more than twelve legions of angels? But how then should the Scriptures be fulfilled, that it must be so?" By these words he quenched their anger, appealing to holy Scripture. He prayed that the disciples might accept meekly whatever befell him when they had learned that this also is occurring according to God's will. His response is twofold: He is able to appeal to his Father, and he is able to resist the angry passions of his supposed defenders with these words: "All who take the sword will perish by the sword." THE GOSPEL OF MATTHEW, HOMILY 84.1.[29]

26:55-56 The Disciples Fled

JESUS YIELDS VOLUNTARILY. CHRYSOSTOM: Then he also adds, "Day after day I sat in the temple teaching, and you did not seize me." By this he makes it clear that the seizure was of his permission. He passes over the miracles and mentions only his teaching, that he might not seem to boast.

When I taught, you did not seize me. Why now, when I hold my peace, do you come against me? I was in the temple every day, and no one seized me. Now you come to me late and at midnight with swords and staves! What need is there of these weapons? I have been around daily. Thus he was teaching them that unless he

---

[22]GCS 38.2:224. [23]Jn 18:10. [24]Lk 22:50. [25]Lk 22:35-38. [26]PG 58:751; NPNF 1 10:501-2. [27]PG 58:752; NPNF 1 10:502. [28]Lk 22:49. [29]PG 58:752; NPNF 1 10:502.

had voluntarily yielded, not even then would they have succeeded. Even then those who were holding him with their hands would not succeed in doing so if he were not willing. THE GOSPEL OF MATTHEW, HOMILY 84.2.[30]

THE SCRIPTURES FULFILLED. CHRYSOSTOM: After this, he solves also the difficulty of why he willed it at this time. "All this has taken place that the Scriptures of the prophets might be fulfilled."[31] See how even up to the last hour and in the very act of being betrayed, he did everything he did seeking their amendment and healing, employing prophecy and argument and admonition. Those who take up coercion will perish by their coercion. To show that he is suffering voluntarily, he says, "I was daily with you teaching." All this was to show his accord with his Father's will and "that the Scriptures of the prophets might be fulfilled."

But why did they not lay hold on him in the temple? Because they would not have dared to do so in the temple on account of the people. This is why he continued teaching at all times and places, even to the last hour, taking away their excuse. In order to obey the prophets, he gave up even his very life. In no way did he teach contrary to the prophets.

"Then all the disciples forsook him and fled." Up until the time he was seized, they remained.

But when he had said these things to the multitudes, they fled. For from then on they could see that escape was no longer possible. So he gave himself up to them voluntarily, saying that this was done according to the Scriptures. THE GOSPEL OF MATTHEW, HOMILY 84.2.[32]

THEY FLED. ORIGEN: There is now much to choose from the prophets, such as their sayings that were fulfilled when Christ said he had to suffer these things. Moveover, it is customary for scholars to collect prophetic words that were fulfilled. And in the psalm[33] you may find a number of things reflected in those who came with Judas to seize Jesus, even as you may find things said about Judas in that psalm. "Then all the disciples forsook him and fled." Fearing the crowds and Judas at their head, they fled because they did not yet have the Spirit ("since Jesus had not yet been glorified")[34] and the "Spirit of power and love." If they had the Spirit, they would not be weak nor would they need anything besides divine love. COMMENTARY ON MATTHEW 104.[35]

---

[30]PG 58:753; NPNF 1 10:502-3. [31]Chrysostom holds that Jesus recalled the fulfillment of the Scriptures in order to strengthen his disciples in that critical moment. [32]PG 58:753; NPNF 1 10:503. [33]Ps 109:2-4, 22-25 (108:2-4, 22-25 LXX). [34]Jn 7:39. [35]GCS 38.2:224-25.

26:57-68 JESUS IS QUESTIONED BY THE COUNCIL

[57]*Then those who had seized Jesus led him to Caiaphas the high priest, where the scribes and the elders had gathered.* [58]*But Peter followed him at a distance, as far as the courtyard of the high priest, and going inside he sat with the guards to see the end.* [59]*Now the chief priests and the whole council sought false testimony against Jesus that they might put him to death,* [60]*but they found none, though many false witnesses came forward. At last two came forward* [61]*and said, "This fellow said, 'I am able to destroy the temple of God, and to build it in three days.'"*

62And the high priest stood up and said, "Have you no answer to make? What is it that these men testify against you?" 63But Jesus was silent. And the high priest said to him, "I adjure you by the living God, tell us if you are the Christ, the Son of God." 64Jesus said to him, "You have said so. But I tell you, hereafter you will see the Son of man seated at the right hand of Power, and coming on the clouds of heaven." 65Then the high priest tore his robes, and said, "He has uttered blasphemy. Why do we still need witnesses? You have now heard his blasphemy. 66What is your judgment?" They answered, "He deserves death." 67Then they spat in his face, and struck him; and some slapped him, 68saying, "Prophesy to us, you Christ! Who is it that struck you?"

OVERVIEW: Caiaphas, the scribes and the elders were all disreputable (ORIGEN). Peter is to be commended, however, for at least he followed Jesus rather than fleeing like the other disciples (JEROME). The council found no false witness against Jesus at first because Jesus was blameless (ORIGEN). The testimony finally presented was false because those speaking twisted what Jesus had said regarding the temple (JEROME). Caiaphas, working on behalf of the devil in more ways than one, trespasses Jesus' previous command not to swear by commanding Jesus to swear. By contrast Jesus will sit enthroned in power at God's right hand. The "clouds of heaven" represent the prophets and apostles of Christ (ORIGEN). What Caiaphas called blasphemy was Christ's way of saying that he was in accordance with God's will (CHRYSOSTOM).

Why did Caiaphas tear his robes? Caiaphas was furious because he could not find sufficient charges against Jesus (JEROME). He tore his robes in order to underscore his accusation of blasphemy (CHRYSOSTOM, LEO THE GREAT). It is customary for Jews to rend their garments when they hear blasphemy (JEROME). In so doing, Caiaphas broke the rule of high priests that they are not to tear their clothes (LEO THE GREAT).

Jesus shows great perseverance as he was persecuted (CYRIL OF ALEXANDRIA, CHRYSOSTOM). His persecution also highlights his adversaries' corruption (CHRYSOSTOM). He endured persecution for us and was in turn exalted by God (ORI-

GEN). Christ's persecution fulfills Old Testament prophecy (CYRIL OF ALEXANDRIA, CHRYSOSTOM, ORIGEN). Those who strike another in the church strike Christ (ORIGEN).

26:57 Jesus Led to Caiaphas the High Priest

THEY LED HIM TO CAIAPHAS. JEROME: In accordance with God's command, Moses ordered that high priests should succeed their fathers and a line of descent should be woven among priests. Josephus relates that the disreputable Caiaphas purchased the high priesthood from Herod for one year only.[1] No wonder, then, the dishonorable high priest judges dishonorably. COMMENTARY ON MATTHEW 4.26.57.[2]

THE SCRIBES AND ELDERS HAD GATHERED. ORIGEN: I believe the word for Jewish slavery whereby poor and abandoned persons now profess to be slaves is "Caiaphas." He is known as the high priest who, at odds with the truth, rails against Jesus. But Jesus according to the truth is a priest, the Word of God; under him are established all who worthily and zealously serve God the Father. Where the high priest Caiaphas is found, however, there the scribes come together, that is, learned men who preside over the perishing written word. While being scribes, they are also elders who preside not over the truth but over the classic usage of a

---

[1]Josephus *Ant.* 18.2.2, 4.3. [2]CCL 77:259.

mere word.[3] They are unwilling to consider anything beyond that. COMMENTARY ON MATTHEW 105.[4]

26:58 Peter Followed at a Distance

LOVE OR CURIOSITY. JEROME: Either out of a disciple's love or out of human curiosity, Peter wanted to know what judgment the high priest would make concerning the Lord: whether he would have Christ put to death or beaten with whips. There is a difference between the eleven apostles and Peter at this point. They fled, whereas he followed the Savior from a distance. COMMENTARY ON MATTHEW 4.26.58.[5]

26:59-62 Seeking False Testimony

THEY FOUND NO FALSE TESTIMONY. ORIGEN: From this it is clear that Jesus "committed no sin; no guile was found on his lips."[6] His life was unimpeachable and completely blameless, leaving his enemies no opportunity for provocation. Clearly they found nothing to say against him or to insinuate by shading the truth ("the chief priests and the whole council sought false testimony," but they could find none). There is room for false testimony when it is given with a shading of the truth; however, no shading of the truth was found which could further their lies against Jesus—although there were many who wished to find favor with Caiaphas and the chief priests and the scribes and the elders and the whole council. These avidly sought that testimony. COMMENTARY ON MATTHEW 107.[7]

DESTROY AND REBUILD THE TEMPLE. JEROME: How can they be false witnesses if they said what we read the Lord had said before? Because a false witness takes the truth and twists its meaning. The Lord had spoken of the temple of his body,[8] but they falsely accused him with those very words. With a few things added or changed, they made it into an understandably false accusation. The Savior had said, "Destroy

this temple." They changed his words to say, "I can destroy God's temple." . . . But the Lord, indicating the living and breathing temple, had said, "And in three days I will raise it up."[9] It is one thing to build and another to raise up. COMMENTARY ON MATTHEW 4.26.61.[10]

26:63-64 Jesus' Silence and Answers

I ADJURE YOU BY THE LIVING GOD. ORIGEN: We find in the law several cases of swearing. And now, on this occasion, the priest commands Jesus to swear "by the living God." In this regard, I believe it is improper for one who wants to live by the gospel to command someone to swear.[11]

Likewise, the Lord himself says in the Gospel: "But I say to you, 'Do not swear at all'"[12] and do not command someone else to swear at all. So, according to Christ's Gospel command, if it is not permissible to swear, neither is it permissible to command someone else to swear. Therefore it is clear that the high priest unlawfully ordered Jesus to swear, even though he may have ordered him to swear "by the living God." COMMENTARY ON MATTHEW 110.[13]

YOU HAVE SAID SO. ORIGEN: It was not fitting for our Lord to respond to the high priest's command to swear. . . . For this reason, he neither denied that he was Christ, the Son of God, nor did he openly declare it. Instead, as though accepting to be a swearing witness . . . he replied, "You have said so."

---

[3]As is his habit, Origen stresses the inability of the Jews to understand the spiritual sense of the Old Testament, which has prevented them from accepting Christ. The mention in the Gospels of the elders of the people recalls the antiquity and thus insufficiency of the literal meaning of the Scriptures, which by now are superseded by the newness of the spiritual meaning revealed by Christ. [4]GCS 38.2:225. [5]CCL 77:259. [6]Is 53:9. [7]GCS 38.2:226. [8]Jn 2:21. [9]Jn 2:19. [10]CCL 77:259-60. [11]The high priest adjured (*exorkizō*) while Jesus had forbidden people to take oaths (*omnyō*, Mt 5:34). Origen points out the difference between the two verbs, but he considers them at bottom to have the same meaning, so that Jesus' prohibition would extend also to adjuration. [12]Mt 5:34. [13]GCS 38.2:229.

And since "everyone who commits sin is of the devil,"[14] the high priest also committed a sin in plotting against Jesus. Therefore he was of the devil, and, being of the devil as it were, he imitated his very father, who doubtingly asked the Savior twice, "If you are the Son of God," as is written concerning his temptations. Similar in fact are the words "If you are the Son of God" and "if you are the Christ, the Son of God."[15] Someone may rightly say in this regard that to doubt whether Christ is the Son of God is the work of the devil and of the high priest who plotted against our Lord. COMMENTARY ON MATTHEW 110.[16]

AT THE RIGHT HAND OF POWER. ORIGEN: It seems to me that the Son of man seated "at the right hand of Power" signifies enthronement and empowerment. He was seated therefore next to Power—the only power properly so called—and at the right hand. He received all power from the Father "in heaven and on earth."[17] His adversaries too will see his enthronement, sometime after the blessed have seen him with joy.

Now the passage according to Mark does not say "hereafter." It reads simply, "You will see the Son of man seated at the right hand of Power."[18] This does not imply anything contrary to what we have said. However, in light of Matthew's words, "hereafter you will see" and Luke's words, "so will the Son of man be in his day,"[19] one may ask whether since the time the Savior had said these things, they were fulfilled to those who heard his words. . . . Our reply is that they appear to have been fulfilled, since from that time, that is, from the time of the dispensation, the Son of man has been seated "at the right hand of Power,"[20] and his disciples witnessed his resurrection from the dead. For this reason, as we noted before, they saw him seated "at the right hand of Power." COMMENTARY ON MATTHEW 111.[21]

ON THE CLOUDS OF HEAVEN. ORIGEN: The prophets of God and the apostles of Christ are those living clouds which Jesus orders to rain down or not to rain down, as he sees fit, upon the fruitless vineyard. Now if anyone does not wish to become these clouds upon which and with which the Son of man will appear, Christ will know this. For God the Word and wisdom and truth and justice will always come upon these clouds and be with them, manifesting his coming to those worthy of himself. Furthermore, we speak of these clouds as though they bear a "sign from heaven," heavenly clouds that do not pass away. They have been made worthy of the throne of God and the kingdom of God as "heirs of God and coheirs of Christ."[22] And they will reign with him. COMMENTARY ON MATTHEW 111.[23]

26:65 He Has Blasphemed

THE HIGH PRIEST TORE HIS ROBES. JEROME: Blind anger and impatience, bereft of grounds for a false accusation, dislodged the high priest from his seat, and he displayed the rabid state of his mind with a vehement bodily gesture. The more Jesus kept silent over the false witnesses and dishonorable priests indignant at his response, all the more did the high priest, overcome with rage, provoke him to give an incriminating reply. Still Jesus kept quiet, because as God he knew that whatever he replied would be twisted into grounds for accusation. COMMENTARY ON MATTHEW 4.26.63.[24]

BLASPHEMY. CHRYSOSTOM: Then the high priest rent his clothes, saying, he has spoken blasphemy. He did this to add force to the accu-

---

[14]1 Jn 3:8. [15]Mt 4:3, 6. [16]GCS 38.2:230. [17]Mt 28:18. [18]Mk 14:62. [19]Lk 22:69. [20]In Matthew, Jesus says that in a short time the Son of man will be sitting at the right hand of God, while Luke 22:69 says that from this moment he will be sitting at the right hand of God. Origen resolves the difficulty by explaining that from the beginning of the economy of the incarnation, Christ sits at the right hand of God. [21]GCS 38.2:231-32. [22]Rom 8:17. [23]GCS 38.2:233. [24]CCL 77:260.

sation and to aggravate what he said by a symbolic action. What had been said moved the hearers to fear. They did in this case what they would later do in the case of Stephen: they stopped their ears.[25] The high priest does the same thing.

Yet what kind of blasphemy was this? For indeed he had said before, when they were gathered together, that "the Lord said unto my Lord, sit thou on my right hand."[26] And he had interpreted the saying, and they dared to say nothing. They held their peace and from that time forward did not challenge him further. Why then did they now call the saying a blasphemy? And why did Christ now answer them? He did so to take away all their excuses. Even to the last day he taught that he was the Christ, and that he would sit at the right hand of the Father and that he would come again to judge the world. All this was the language of one manifesting his full accordance with the will of the Father. THE GOSPEL OF MATTHEW, HOMILY 84.2-3.[27]

THE FURY OF CAIAPHAS. JEROME: The one whom fury had lifted out of his priestly throne[28] was impelled by that same fury to tear his garments. When Caiaphas tore his robes, he demonstrated that the Jews had lost the glory of the priesthood and that the seat of the high priest was now vacant. But it is the custom of the Jews to tear their clothes when they hear any blasphemy against God. We read that Paul and Barnabas did this when they were honored and worshiped as gods in Lycaonia.[29] COMMENTARY ON MATTHEW 4.26.65.[30]

RENDING GARMENTS. LEO THE GREAT: To emphasize his alarm over the words he had just heard, Caiaphas "tore his garments." Unaware of his own madness, he deprived himself of priestly honor. Caiaphas, where does reason reside in your mind? . . . You are oblivious to the command you read concerning high priests: "Do not let the hair of your heads hang loose, and do not rend your clothes."[31] But you, who have now for-

feited your dignity, are the very object of disgrace. And in token of the end of the old regulation, the same rending that rips your priestly attire will soon also tear apart the veil of the temple. SERMON 44.2.[32]

26:66-68 He Deserves Death

THEY STRUCK HIM. CYRIL OF ALEXANDRIA: This is clearly a reflection of the holy prophet's words, "Be appalled at this, O heavens, and shudder with great fear," says "the Lord,"[33] the one true God, the king of kings and Lord of lords. He was dishonored by us: first he endured blows, and then he endured laughter from the impious, exemplifying the highest forbearance yet presented to us. How can the one who "examines heart and mind," the one who illumines prophets, not know "who strikes you"? FRAGMENT 301.[34]

THEY SPAT IN HIS FACE. CHRYSOSTOM: Note with admiration the self-restraint of the disciples. Observe how carefully they relate these things. This clearly shows their disposition to love the truth. They relate with all truthfulness the things that seem to be opprobrious. They disguise nothing. They are not ashamed of anything. Rather, they account it as a very great glory, as indeed it was, that the Lord of the universe should endure to suffer such things for us. This shows both his unutterable tenderness and the inexcusable wickedness of those men who had the heart to do such things to him that was so mild and meek. His words were such as to change a lion into a lamb. . . . All of these things the prophet Isaiah had foretold. He had proclaimed it beforehand: "Like as many were astonished at you, so shall your form be held inglorious of men, and your glory of the sons of

---

[25]Acts 7:57. [26]Mt 22:44; Ps 110:1 (109:1 LXX). [27]PG 58:754; NPNF 1 10:504. [28]Jerome refers to Matthew 26:62: "And the high priest stood up and said . . ." [29]Acts 14:10-14. [30]CCL 77:261. [31]Lev 21:10. [32]SC 74:46. [33]Jer 2:12. [34]MKGK 261.

men."[35] THE GOSPEL OF MATTHEW, HOMILY 85.1.[36]

THEY SLAPPED HIM. ORIGEN: It was necessary for him to teach these things by example, "giving his back to whips and his cheeks to fists" and not turning his face away "from insults and spitting."[37] Thus would he, by suffering these things in our place, deliver us (as I believe) who were worthy to suffer all that disgrace. Truly he did not "die for us"[38] that we might not die but that we might not die for ourselves. And he was spat upon and beaten for us, so that we who were worthy of all these things because of our sins might not just suffer them but, suffering them for the sake of justice, we might gratefully accept them. Paul makes it clear that the Savior "humbled himself becoming obedient all the way to death, even to the death of the cross."[39] ..."On account of all this, God exalted him."[40] God not only exalted him because of the death he underwent for our sake but also because of the buffeting and the spitting and all the rest.

Christ did not turn his face away "from insult and spitting,"[41] so his face might be glorified more than the face of Moses[42]—with so much glory that comparatively the glorification of Moses' face was outshone, even as the light of a lamp is outshone by that of the sun and even as knowledge, which knows in part, is outshone "when that which is perfect has come."[43] But they also buffeted the holy head of the church. Because of this, they will be beaten by Satan, not that they may not be extolled or may have their power brought to an end but that, once in the hands of the enemy and punisher, they may receive just punishment for the sin they committed in buffeting Jesus.

Not content with spitting in his face and buffeting him, they even struck his face with the palms of their hands, and, mocking him, they said, "Prophesy to us, O Christ! who is it that struck you?" On account of this ... they have been struck and punished. Yet they were unwilling to accept any discipline, as Jeremiah had prophesied about them: "You chastened them and they did not grieve; they were unwilling to receive correction."[44] And now whoever harms anyone in the church and does these things to him spits on the very face of Christ, and, buffeting Christ, they slap him with the palms of their hands. COMMENTARY ON MATTHEW 113.[45]

---

[35]Is 52:14. [36]PG 58:757; NPNF 1 10:506. [37]Is 50:6. [38]Rom 5:8. [39]Phil 2:8. [40]Phil 2:9. [41]Is 50:6. [42]Ex 34:29. [43]1 Cor 13:10. [44]Jer 5:3. [45]GCS 38.2:235-36.

26:69-75 PETER DENIES JESUS

[69]*Now Peter was sitting outside in the courtyard. And a maid came up to him, and said, "You also were with Jesus the Galilean."* [70]*But he denied it before them all, saying, "I do not know what you mean."* [71]*And when he went out to the porch, another maid saw him, and she said to the bystanders, "This man was with Jesus of Nazareth."* [72]*And again he denied it with an oath, "I do not know the man."* [73]*After a little while the bystanders came up and said to Peter, "Certainly you are also one of them, for your accent betrays you."* [74]*Then he began to invoke a curse on himself and to swear, "I do not know the man." And immediately the cock crowed.* [75]*And*

Peter remembered the saying of Jesus, "Before the cock crows, you will deny me three times." And he went out and wept bitterly.

OVERVIEW: In spite of his zeal, Peter denied Jesus out of fear. Matthew and Mark differ on the exact time the cock crows; however, there is no real discrepancy (CHRYSOSTOM). Peter not only denied Jesus' humanity, he denied Jesus' divinity as well (JEROME). One may excuse Peter because the Holy Spirit was not given before Peter's denial. All the while Peter was inside Caiaphas's courtyard, he was unusually influenced by false teachings and was under the influence of darkness. The accusers also represent adverse forces to acknowledgment of truth (ORIGEN).

26:69-75 Peter Remembered and Wept Bitterly

I DO NOT KNOW THE MAN. CHRYSOSTOM: Oh strange and wonderful acts! When indeed he saw his master seized, Peter was so fervent as both to draw his sword and to cut off the man's ear! But when it was natural for him to be more indignant and to be inflamed and to burn, hearing such revilings, then he became a denier. For who would not have been inflamed to indignation by the things that were then done? Yet the great disciple, overcome by fears, so far from showing indignation, even denies and cannot even stand the threat of a tiny and lowly servant girl.

This happens not only once but a second and third time. He denies the Lord. In a short period and even before judges, he denies him. For it was "when he went out to the porch" that they asked him whether he was the man who "was with Jesus of Nazareth." And he was not even aware of his own lying. Luke says that Christ looked upon him,[1] and this made it clear that he had denied him and was not even aware of how far he had fallen into forgetfulness. This happened even though the cock had crowed. He needed a further remembrance from his Master.

Jesus' look was greater than any voice. Peter was so full of fear. Mark says that when he had once denied the Lord,[2] then first the cock crowed, but then it did so for a second time and a third time. He shows us more particularly the weakness of the disciple, that he was utterly dead with fear. Mark had learned these things from the eyewitnesses, for he himself was a follower of Peter. One marvels at Mark in that, so far from hiding his teacher's faults, he declared them more distinctly than the rest. On this very account he was a true disciple.

Why does Matthew affirm that "Peter remembered the saying of Jesus, 'Before the cock crows, you will deny me three times,' " while Mark declares after the third denial that "the cock crew the second time"?[3] Both are in harmony. At each crowing the cock is inclined to crow both a third and a fourth time. Mark showed that not even the sound of the rooster checked him and brought him to recollection. So that both things are true. For before the cock had finished the one crowing, Peter had denied a third time. And not even when reminded of his sin by Christ did he dare to weep openly, lest he should be betrayed by his tears. Then "he went out and wept bitterly." THE GOSPEL OF MATTHEW, Homily 85.1-2.[4]

PETER DENIED CHRIST WITH AN OATH. JEROME: "And again he denied it with an oath, 'I do not know the man.' " I know that some people with a soft spot in their hearts for the apostle Peter have interpreted this passage to the effect that Peter did not deny God but man, and what he meant was "I do not know the man, because I know God." The wise reader realizes how frivolous this interpretation is, for those who thus

---

[1]Lk 22:61. [2]Mk 14:68-72. [3]Mk 14:72. [4]PG 58:758-59; NPNF 1 10:507.

defend the apostle make the Lord guilty of a lie. If Peter did not deny him, then the Lord lied in saying, "Truly, I say to you, this very night, before the cock crows twice, you will deny me three times." Notice what he says: "You will deny me"—not "the man."

"Certainly you are also one of them, for your accent betrays you." Not that Peter spoke a different language or belonged to a foreign nation . . . but since each province and region had their own characteristics and vernacular, one could not help having a certain sound to his speech. For instance, the Ephrathites in the book of Judges cannot pronounce the word *synthema*.[5]

"Then he began to invoke a curse on himself and to swear that he did not know the man. And immediately the cock crowed." In the other Gospel we read that after Peter's denial and the crowing of the cock, the Savior looked at Peter and, by his very gaze, aroused bitter tears in him.[6] It could not be that Peter, on whom the light of the world had gazed, should remain in the darkness of denial. COMMENTARY ON MATTHEW 4.26.72-75.[7]

YOU WERE ONE OF THEM. ORIGEN: Upon examining Peter's denial, we note that "as yet the Spirit had not been given, because Jesus was not yet glorified."[8] For this reason, neither was it possible for Peter at the time to profess belief in Jesus nor was he to be criticized for not professing belief in him, since it is said to those who profess belief: "It is not you who speak, but the Spirit of your Father speaking through you."[9] We . . . since the Spirit of the Father has the power to speak in us and since it is in our power to "make room" in us for the Holy Spirit and not "for the devil,"[10] if we should deny Christ, we would have no excuse.

It may be that whoever is in the courtyard of Caiaphas "the high priest" cannot admit knowing the Lord Jesus unless he has gone outside his courtyard and has been brought outside of every teaching contrary to Jesus and outside of Jewish traditions handed down, not according to the

Spirit of the Scriptures but according to the "commands and teachings of men."[11] Consider how Peter, seated outside at a distance from Jesus and in the high priest's courtyard, denied Jesus before them all; and again, for the second time, going out to the porch and wishing to leave but not yet outside the gateway, he denied the Lord.[12] Then, for the third time, "while the bystanders came and said, 'Certainly you are also one of them,'" when "he began to invoke a curse on himself and to swear 'I do not know the man,'" he was not yet outside. Furthermore, all the denials were made at night and in the darkness, before the break of dawn and the sign of the new day, that is, the crowing of the cock that bestirs the early risers. And if, by way of hypothesis, Peter had denied after the crowing of the cock, as was said, "The night is far gone, the day is at hand . . . let us conduct ourselves becomingly as in the day,"[13] he would have had no excuse for his actions.

Perhaps all people when they deny Jesus . . . seemingly deny him before the crowing of the cock, when the sun of justice has not yet risen for them and its rising is not yet at hand. But if upon the rising of the sun for the soul "we sin deliberately after receiving the knowledge of the truth, there no longer remains a sacrifice for sins but a fearful prospect of judgment and a fury of fire which will consume the adversaries."[14] COMMENTARY ON MATTHEW 114.[15]

THE ACCUSERS. ORIGEN: I believe that the first servant girl who caused Christ's disciples to deny him stands for the synagogue of the Jews "according to the flesh," who have frequently coerced the faithful to deny him. The second

---

[5]Judg 12:6. *Shibboleth* in the Hebrew. [6]Lk 22:61-62. [7]CCL 77:261-62. [8]Jn 7:39. [9]Mt 10:20. [10]Eph 4:27. [11]Mk 7:7. [12]Peter denies Jesus when he is "outside (*exō*), in the courtyard" of the palace where the assembly had gathered. He repents when he goes outside (*exō*) of the courtyard. Origen interprets the first "outside" in the sense of being far from Jesus and "in the courtyard" as a symbol of the evil of the world. Overcome by this, Peter renounces Christ. The second "outside" refers to being far from the dangers of the world, and thus Peter repents. [13]Rom 13:12. [14]Heb 10:26-27. [15]GCS 38.2:236-38.

maidservant stands for the assembly of Gentiles, who also in persecuting Christians has forced them to deny the Lord. And third were the bystanders in the courtyard, who are ministers of the different heresies and who also compel others to deny the truth of Christ. COMMENTARY ON MATTHEW 114.[16]

---

[16]GCS 38.2:240.

27:1-10 THE DEATH OF JUDAS

[1]When morning came, all the chief priests and the elders of the people took counsel against Jesus to put him to death; [2]and they bound him and led him away and delivered him to Pilate the governor.

[3]When Judas, his betrayer, saw that he was condemned, he repented and brought back the thirty pieces of silver to the chief priests and the elders, [4]saying, "I have sinned in betraying innocent blood." They said, "What is that to us? See to it yourself." [5]And throwing down the pieces of silver in the temple, he departed; and he went and hanged himself. [6]But the chief priests, taking the pieces of silver, said, "It is not lawful to put them into the treasury, since they are blood money." [7]So they took counsel, and bought with them the potter's field, to bury strangers in. [8]Therefore that field has been called the Field of Blood to this day. [9]Then was fulfilled what had been spoken by the prophet Jeremiah, saying, "And they took the thirty pieces of silver, the price of him on whom a price had been set by some of the sons of Israel, [10]and they gave them for the potter's field, as the Lord directed me."

OVERVIEW: Out of this day would emerge the overthrow of the temple and its altars, the surpassing of the Law and the Prophets, the undoing of the kingship and priesthood. Due to their persistent shouts, Pilate chose to pardon a man who was a murderer and demanded the crucifixion of the Savior of the world (LEO THE GREAT). They bound him with chains, but these fetters would be broken (ORIGEN, JEROME). The religious leaders make clear their complicity and guilt by buying the piece of land for burial (CHRYSOSTOM). The potter is the one who brought us to life with his own hands and who is refashioning us to glory through Christ. Christ's blood purchased the field of the potter for us, travelers in this world (MAXIMUS OF TURIN).

Having betrayed innocent blood, Judas hanged himself—a disgraceful death (CHRYSOSTOM). Although Judas repented his sin, he could not change its consequence (ORIGEN, JEROME).

27:1-2 The Religious Leaders Confer

WHEN MORNING CAME. LEO THE GREAT: O religious leaders [of the Jews], this morning was far from your time of ascendency, as it might have seemed to you. Your sun was in fact beginning to set. The dawn you expected did not come. A night of blackest darkness was brooding over your spiteful hearts. Out of this morning would come the overthrow of the temple and its altars, the surpassing of the law and the prophets, the undoing of the kingship and priesthood, turning youth to continual lament.[1] For you set out that morning on a mad and bloody course. You offered up to die the Author of life, the Lord of glory. Pilate—that terror-stricken judge—was overcome by your shouts, so that he chose a man for pardon who was a murderer and demanded the crucifixion of the Savior of the world. SERMON 41.5.[2]

BREAKING FETTERS. ORIGEN: Anyone who demands from me a scriptural text concerning the breaking of those fetters with which the chief priests and elders bound Jesus should understand that it was on account of this very event that Jesus said through the prophet, "Let us break their bonds."[3] It was just as though Jesus had said this of the chief priests and elders, or even more so of those rulers who operated through them and of the kings of the world who "set themselves," and of those rulers who "take counsel together against the Lord and against his anointed," who also said, "let us cast their cords from us."[4]

Our inquirer will be satisfied still more with scriptural demonstration that Jesus broke the chains of those who "took counsel" against him and led him away, bound, if he understands the meaning of what was written concerning Samson, who also broke the fetters of those foreigners who bound him, for he was a Nazirite of God and had power in his uncut head of hair.[5] If therefore he whose power came from the hair on his head was able to break the chains of the oppressors who bound him, how much more will Christ decisively break those chains binding him, who, after performing great signs and miracles, freely delivered himself to be bound (the power of his divine nature lay dormant and still, allowing him to be captured). Samson's bonds were but a type of Christ's. COMMENTARY ON MATTHEW 115.[6]

THEY BOUND HIM. JEROME: The Lord was led not only to Pilate but also to Herod so that he could be mocked by both. Notice the solicitude

with which the priests carried out their evil doing; they remained vigilant throughout the night in preparation for committing murder. "And they delivered him bound to Pilate." It was their customary practice to bind a man who had been condemned to death and to hand him over to his judge. COMMENTARY ON MATTHEW 4.27.1-2.[7]

27:3-5 Judas Hangs Himself

I HAVE SINNED IN BETRAYING INNOCENT BLOOD. CHRYSOSTOM: This was a charge both against him and against these others. Against Judas, not because he repented but because he did so late and slowly and became self-condemned. For that he gave himself up, he himself confessed. And it was a charge against the others, in that having the power to reverse the verdict, they did not repent. But observe when it is that Judas feels remorse. When his sin was completed and had been fully accomplished. The devil is like this. He does not permit those that are inattentive to see the evil in due time, lest they might repent. At least when Jesus was saying so many things, Judas was not influenced. But when his offense was completed, then repentance came upon him. And then it was too late to be profitable. For to condemn it and to throw down the pieces of silver and not to regard the Jewish people were all acceptable things. But to hang himself, this again was unpardonable and a work of an evil spirit. For the devil led him out of his repentance too soon, so that he should reap no fruit from it, and carried him off by a most disgraceful death, and one manifest to all, having persuaded him to destroy himself. THE GOSPEL OF MATTHEW, HOMILY 85.2.[8]

---

[1]The death of Jesus has signified the exhaustion of the function of the temple. [2]SC 74:35; NPNF 2 12:166**. [3]Ps 2:3. On the messianic significance of Psalm 2 mentioned by Origen, see p. 265 n. 3. [4]Ps 2:2-3. [5]Judg 16:4-22. [6]GCS 38.2:242-43. [7]CCL 77:263. [8]PG 58:759; NPNF 1 10:507

HE BROUGHT BACK THE SILVER. JEROME: The weight of Judas's impiety overshadowed the magnitude of his avarice. Seeing the Lord condemned to death, he brought the money to the priests as if it were in his power to change the sentence of Christ's persecutors. Although he would change his mind eventually, he could not change the consequence of his first decision. Yet if he sins who betrays innocent blood, how much more do they sin who purchase innocent blood and provoke a disciple by offering a reward for his apostasy. Those who deny the apostle's free will and attempt instead to explain Judas's betrayal by attributing to him an evil nature will need also to explain how a person of evil nature can repent.[9] COMMENTARY ON MATTHEW 4.27.4.[10]

HE REPENTED. ORIGEN: Let us see whether or not, by the grace of God, we can explain the meaning of the following verse, which still remains hidden to many: "When Judas his betrayer saw him condemned, he repented and returned the thirty pieces of silver to the chief priests" and so on.[11]

If this were written after Jesus had been sentenced by Pilate, scourged and delivered to the Jews for crucifixion,[12] we would not need to inquire any further into the meaning of the report that "Judas . . . saw him condemned" because we know that Judas was a party to those events.

But how is it that Judas saw Jesus condemned before Jesus had either been sentenced or interrogated by Pilate? Some perhaps will answer that Judas was anticipating in his mind the final result of Jesus having been handed over by the chief priests and elders of the people, which he did witness. Others, however, will say that one whom Judas "saw condemned" was not Jesus but Judas himself. According to this account, when the chief priests and elders of the people handed Jesus over to Pilate, Judas then realized the evil he had done and understood that such an audacious act was already under the judgment and condemnation of God. Perhaps also Satan, who

had entered Judas after the dipping of the morsel of bread, remained present in him until Jesus was delivered to Pilate but "departed from him"[13] after he finished accomplishing Satan's will. Judas then sensed the devil's departure and at once saw and understood that "betraying righteous blood" is condemned by God, which he was able to understand only after the devil had ceased working in him. Only then, free from Satan's influence, was Judas capable of penitence by returning the thirty pieces of silver to those who had paid him. When the devil had left him, he could then say what he had not been able to say earlier, for when his heart was still full of Satan he was unable to confess, "I have sinned in betraying righteous blood." We are not saying, however, that the devil ceases to prey upon anyone whom he may have left. Rather, he waits and watches for an opportune moment to apply himself again. Even after his victim has sinned and come to recognize the devil's influence, he still waits and watches for yet a third opportunity to deceive. COMMENTARY ON MATTHEW 117.[14]

THE CONSEQUENCES OF SIN REMAIN. JEROME: It profits nothing to do an act of penance which is incapable of correcting the sin. If a man sins against his brother in such a way that the wrong he committed can be amended, it is possible for him to be forgiven. If the consequences of his sin remain in force, however, in vain does he attempt to do penance. The psalmist applies this truth to our most miserable Judas when he says, "Let his prayer be counted as sin."[15] Not only

---

[9]On the various human natures identified by Gnostics and Manichaeans, see *Matthew 1-13* (ACCS), p. 155 n. 18. To the affirmation that Judas was evil by nature, Jerome objects that he would not thus have repented. [10]CCL 77:263. [11]Matthew says that Judas repents upon seeing Jesus condemned, but when he repents Jesus has not yet been condemned. The second of the two explanations adopted by Origen to resolve the apparent anomaly is based on the fact that grammatically the subject of "was condemned" can be either Jesus *or* Judas. Origen forces the interpretation of the passage into this second sense. [12]Mt 27:26. [13]Lk 4:13. [14]GCS 38.2:245-47. [15]Ps 109:7 (108:7 LXX).

was Judas unable to repair the damage of his sinful betrayal, but he even continued to compound the evil of that initial crime by committing suicide. Of such things the apostle speaks in his second epistle to the Corinthians: "Let not a brother be overwhelmed by greater sorrow."[16] COMMENTARY ON MATTHEW 4.27.5.[17]

27:6-8 Buying a Field with Blood Money

NOT LAWFUL TO PUT INTO THE TREASURY. CHRYSOSTOM: If they had put the blood money into the treasury, their deed might have remained relatively more hidden. But the religious leaders make clear their guilt to all subsequent generations by buying the piece of land for burial. They thereby unconsciously declare their guilt.

So do not imagine that someone might do a good work through murder and use the reward for some supposed good purpose. Such alms are satanic. Such reasoning is twisted. Do not be naive about this. There are still many who imagine that they are permitted to violently take countless things that belong to others. Then they make an excuse for their violence if they give some ten or a hundred gold pieces to charity. Of these the prophet has said, "You have covered my altar with tears."[18] Christ is not willing to be fed by covetousness. He does not accept these gifts. Why do you insult your Lord by offering these unclean things? It is better to leave people to pine with hunger than to feed them from these polluted sources. THE GOSPEL OF MATTHEW, HOMILY 85.3.[19]

PROOF OF TREASON. CHRYSOSTOM: Once again they are self-condemned by their own conscience. Don't you see this? They knew that they had been paying straightaway for a murder. They even bought a field for the burial of strangers. They did not even put the silver into a treasury. So this directness itself became a witness against them and a proof of their treason. THE GOSPEL OF MATTHEW, HOMILY 85.3.[20]

TO BURY STRANGERS. ORIGEN: Because the quality of resting places for the dead varies (for many are buried in their ancestral tombs which were secured by a pledge, but those who suffer misfortune are often buried in the graves of the homeless), those who received payment in exchange for the blood of Jesus used it to acquire a potter's field for the purpose of having a place in which to bury those foreigners who could not supply a pledge to secure a proper tomb. If it is suitable to interpret these foreigners typologically, we can consider those persons to be foreigners who remained strangers to God until the end and alien to his covenants. Vagabonds such as these meet their end buried in a potter's field acquired with blood money. The righteous are able to say, "We are buried with Christ in a new tomb cut from the rock in which no dead body had yet been laid," but those foreigners who remain finally estranged from Christ and alien to God will have to say, "We are buried with strangers in the field which is called the 'Field of Blood.'" COMMENTARY ON MATTHEW 117.[21]

THEY TOOK COUNSEL. CHRYSOSTOM: They did not make these decisions randomly but took counsel together. This indicates that no one is innocent of the deed. All are guilty. So it is in cases of conspiracy. THE GOSPEL OF MATTHEW, HOMILY 85.3.[22]

THE FIELD OF BLOOD. CHRYSOSTOM: Even the very name of the place proclaims more sharply than a trumpet their guilt of murder. THE GOSPEL OF MATTHEW, HOMILY 85.3.[23]

27:9-10 Fulfilling Jeremiah's Prophecy

SPOKEN BY THE PROPHET. CHRYSOSTOM: All these things had been foretold from ancient times by prophecy. It was not the apostles alone

---

[16]2 Cor 2:7. [17]CCL 77:263-64. [18]Mal 2:13. [19]PG 58:761; NPNF 1 10:509. [20]PG 58:760-61; NPNF 1 10:508. [21]GCS 38.2:248-49. [22]PG 58:761; NPNF 1 10:509. [23]PG 58:761; NPNF 1 10:508-9.

but the prophets who were also declaring these events precisely as they occurred. Don't you see how they foresaw in every way the suffering of Christ? How they knew of its chastisement beforehand? THE GOSPEL OF MATTHEW, HOMILY 85.3.[24]

ON THE SOURCE OF MATTHEW'S QUOTATION. JEROME: This prophecy does not come from Jeremiah but from a similar passage in Zechariah,[25] who is almost the last of the twelve prophets. Although the meaning does not differ much, Zechariah's word order and vocabulary do conflict with Matthew's quotation.[26] In a copy of the Hebrew Scriptures given to me by a member of the Nazarene sect, I recently read an apocryphal edition of the book of Jeremiah in which this quotation from Matthew appeared word for word. Nevertheless it still seems more likely to me that Matthew took this prophecy from Zechariah, since it was the ordinary practice of the Evangelists and apostles to communicate only the meaning of texts from the Old Testament while neglecting to observe their word order. COMMENTARY ON MATTHEW 4.27.10.[27]

THE POTTER'S FIELD. MAXIMUS OF TURIN: This field then is this entire world, in which we who have been dispersed and scattered bear the fruit of good work for the Lord.

Yet perhaps you would inquire of me, if the field is the world, who the potter might be who could have the ownership of the world. Unless I am mistaken, the potter is the one who made the vessels of our body from clay. Scripture says of him, "Then the Lord God formed the man from the dust from the earth."[28] The potter is the one who, with the warmth of his own breath, made alive the slimy clay of our flesh and with fiery heat put together the fluid and earthly matter of our bodies.

The potter, I say, is the one who fashioned us unto life with his own hands and who is refashioning us unto glory through his Christ. The apostle says, "We are being changed into his likeness from one degree of glory to another."[29] That is to say, we who from our previous condition have broken to pieces because of our own misdeeds are restored in a second birth through the loving kindness of this same potter. We who have been struck by death because of Adam's transgression rise anew through the grace of the Savior. Clearly this potter is the one of whom the blessed apostle says, "Will what is molded say to its molder?" And again, "Has the potter no right over the clay to make out of the same lump one vessel for beauty and another for menial use?"[30] For from the same clay of our body God preserves some persons for the kingdom on account of their individual merits and keeps others for punishment.

The field of this potter, then, was bought with Christ's blood for travelers. For travelers, I say, who were without home or country and were cast about as exiles throughout the earth, rest is provided by the blood of Christ, so that those who have no possession in the world might have a burial place in Christ. Who do we say that these travelers are if not very devout Christians who, renouncing the world and possessing nothing in the world, rest in the blood of Christ? For the Christian who does not possess the world utterly possesses the Savior. Christ's burial place then is promised to travelers so that the one who preserves himself from fleshly vices like a traveler and stranger may merit Christ's rest. For what is Christ's burial place if not the Christian's rest? We therefore are travelers, in this world, and we sojourn in this life as passersby, as the apostle says: "While we are in this body we are away from the Lord."[31] We are travelers, I say, and a burial place has been bought for us at the price of the Savior's blood. "We have been buried with him," the apostle says,

---

[24]PG 58:761; NPNF 1 10:509. [25]Zech 11:12-13. [26]In reality the citation corresponds in part to Jeremiah 32:6-9 and in part to Zechariah 11:12-13. On the apocryphal book of Jeremiah mentioned here by Jerome, the information is limited and unclear. [27]CCL 77:264-65. [28]Gen 2:7. [29]2 Cor 3:18. [30]Rom 9:20-21. [31]2 Cor 5:6.

"through baptism in his death."[32] Baptism therefore is Christ's burial place for us, in which we die to sins, are buried to evil deeds and are restored to a renewed infancy, the conscience of the old person having been dissolved in us for

the sake of another birth. Sermons 59.3-4.[33]

---

[32]Rom 6:4. [33]CCL 23:237-38; ACW 50:142-44*.

27:11-14 PILATE QUESTIONS JESUS

[11]*Now Jesus stood before the governor; and the governor asked him, "Are you the King of the Jews?" Jesus said, "You have said so."* [12]*But when he was accused by the chief priests and elders, he made no answer.* [13]*Then Pilate said to him, "Do you not hear how many things they testify against you?"* [14]*But he gave him no answer, not even to a single charge; so that the governor wondered greatly.*

Overview: Jesus appears before Pilate in fulfillment of Old Testament prophecy (Cyril of Alexandria). Jesus' response to Pilate's question about kingship was one of humility (Origen). Jesus, and later the apostles, is charged with political disloyalty. Jesus' accusers wanted some charge against him worthy of the death penalty. While Jesus remains silent to their accusations, he does confess to being a heavenly king (Chrysostom). His silence is not avowal to the charge; rather, he despises it by not refuting it. One who needs no defense does well to keep silent (Maximus of Turin). The Word of God remains silent to them (Origen).

27:11-12 Jesus Questioned

Jesus Before Pilate. Cyril of Alexandria: They led Jesus to Pilate. And they handed him over to the Roman soldiers. Thus the things announced beforehand by the holy prophets were fulfilled to them. For it says, "Woe to the lawless man. Evil will be his lot according to his works."[1] Just "as you have done, so shall it be done to you. Your retribution will be paid back

upon your own head."[2] Fragment 302.[3]

Pilate's Question. Origen: Truly Jesus "did not consider equality with God something to be grasped"[4] and not once but often humbled himself on behalf of humanity. See now, "having been made judge of every creature"[5] by the Father, the King of kings and Lord of lords, to what extent he humbled himself. He compliantly stood before the governor of the land of Judea, who asked him perhaps deridingly or doubtingly, "Are you the king of the Jews?" Jesus thought this question was proper, and he replied, "It is as you say." Before that, having been adjured by the chief priest to say whether he was the Christ, the Son of God, he answered, "You have said it yourself."[6] Notice the two questions. The first one, "If you are the Christ the Son of God," was germane to Christ as a Jew. The Roman governor did not state his question by saying, "Are you the Christ?" but rather, "Are you the king of the Jews?" Com-

---

[1]Is 3:11. [2]Obad 15. [3]MKGK 261. [4]Phil 2:6. [5]Acts 10:42. [6]Mt 26:64.

MENTARY ON MATTHEW 118.[7]

ARE YOU THE KING OF THE JEWS? CHRYSOSTOM: Do you see what he is asked first? Is this the same charge that they had been continually bringing forward in every circumstance? They could see that Pilate was not ready to take into account subtle matters of Jewish law. So they directed their accusation outwardly to state charges of political disloyalty. They did the same later with the apostles, always charging them with political motivations, always bringing forward some trumped-up idea that they were after worldly power.[8] They were treating Jesus now as if he were a mere man and as if he were under suspicion of treason. . . . What they were really interested in was finding some charge that would put him to death. THE GOSPEL OF MATTHEW, HOMILY 86.1.[9]

YOU HAVE SAID SO. CHRYSOSTOM: What does Christ answer to Pilate's question? "You have said so." He confessed that he was [indeed] a king, but a heavenly king. This would be made clearer elsewhere when he replied more specifically to Pilate, "My kingship is not of this world."[10] He gives a reason that cannot be doubted: "If my kingship were of this world, my servants would fight, that I might not be handed over."[11] There was, of course, no excuse for even making such accusations, either from the governor or priests. For in order to refute this suspicion he paid a tax and taught others to pay it.[12] And when others wanted to make him a king, he fled.[13] THE GOSPEL OF MATTHEW, HOMILY 86.1.[14]

RESPONSE TO PILATE'S QUESTION. HILARY OF POITIERS: To Pilate's question as to whether he was king of the Jews, he answered, "It is as you say." How different was the statement he had made to the priest! When the latter asked him whether he was the Christ, he said, "You have said it yourself."[15] This answer is given to the priest as though pertaining to the past, for in

many places the law had foretold the coming of the Christ. ON MATTHEW 32.7.[16]

NO REPLY TO FALSE ACCUSATIONS. CHRYSOSTOM: So why then did he not defend himself reasonably by recalling these acts when he was under accusation of being a usurper of power? Because his acts themselves proved his meekness and gentleness and spiritual power. They were beyond number. The judicial process was corrupt, and his accusers were willfully blind and dealt unfairly. So he chose to reply to nothing. He held his peace. He answered briefly to the authorities so as not to appear arrogant from continuing silence. But he did not say anything in reply to these false accusations. He knew he was not likely to persuade them. THE GOSPEL OF MATTHEW, HOMILY 86.1.[17]

27:13-14 Pilate Amazed

HIS SILENCE. MAXIMUS OF TURIN: It might seem remarkable to you, brothers, that the Lord should be accused by the chief priests before the procurator Pilate and should be silent and that he should not refute their wickedness by his response, since indeed a defense which follows quickly is the only way to refute a persistent accusation. It might seem remarkable, I say, brothers, that the Savior should be accused and should remain silent. Silence is occasionally understood as avowal, for when a person does not wish to respond to what is asked of him he appears to confirm what is raised against him. Does the Lord then confirm his accusation by not speaking? Clearly he does not confirm his accusation by not speaking; rather he despises it by not refuting it. For one who needs no defense does well to keep silent, but let one who fears to

[7]GCS 38.2:250-51. [8]Chrysostom refers to the hostility of the Jewish authorities toward the disciples of Jesus in general, as described in many passages in Acts. [9]PG 58:763; NPNF 1 10:511. [10]Jn 18:36. [11]Jn 18:36. [12]Mt 22:17. [13]Jn 6:15. [14]PG 58:763; NPNF 1 10:511. [15]Mt 26:64. [16]SC 258:246-48. [17]PG 58:763; NPNF 1 10:511.

be overcome defend himself and one who is afraid of being vanquished hasten to speak. When Christ is condemned, however, he also overcomes, and when he is judged he also vanquishes, as the prophet says: "that you should be justified in your words and should vanquish when you are judged."[18] Why was it necessary for him therefore to speak before being judged, when for him judgment was a complete victory? SERMONS 57.1.[19]

HE WAS ACCUSED. ORIGEN: The ministers and elders of western Jewish literature, who are the sons of those chief priests and elders who accused Jesus, still today adopt and repeat these same allegations against him. On this account, since the sins of their forebears go before them and remain in them, their works suffer "[God's] wrath forever,"[20] and they are forsaken along with their entire people "like a tent in the vineyard, like a lodge in a cucumber field and like a city besieged."[21] Just as Jesus "gave no answer"[22] then, neither does he give an answer now to the accusations of the Jewish priests and elders. The Word of God remains silent toward them. Still today they turn a deaf ear to the Word of God, as they previously did to the prophets and to him at the consummation of the ages when he "was made flesh and dwelt among us."[23] COMMENTARY ON MATTHEW 119.[24]

---

[18]Ps 51:4 (50:6 LXX). [19]CCL 23:228; ACW 50:137. [20]1 Thess 2:16. [21]Is 1:8. [22]Mt 27:12. [23]Jn 1:14. [24]GCS 38.2:252. Origen was writing long before the development of modern ethnic anti-Semitism. He had a profound appreciation of the rabbinic tradition and knew that tradition well enough to know that its main complaint against Jesus in the third century had remained the same accusations implied in Mt 27:11-12.

27:15-26 JESUS IS SENTENCED TO DEATH

[15]Now at the feast the governor was accustomed to release for the crowd any one prisoner whom they wanted. [16]And they had then a notorious prisoner, called Barabbas.[k] [17]So when they had gathered, Pilate said to them, "Whom do you want me to release for you, Barabbas[k] or Jesus who is called Christ?" [18]For he knew that it was out of envy that they had delivered him up. [19]Besides, while he was sitting on the judgment seat, his wife sent word to him, "Have nothing to do with that righteous man, for I have suffered much over him today in a dream." [20]Now the chief priests and the elders persuaded the people to ask for Barabbas and destroy Jesus. [21]The governor again said to them, "Which of the two do you want me to release for you?" And they said, "Barabbas." [22]Pilate said to them, "Then what shall I do with Jesus who is called Christ?" They all said, "Let him be crucified." [23]And he said, "Why, what evil has he done?" But they shouted all the more, "Let him be crucified."

[24]So when Pilate saw that he was gaining nothing, but rather that a riot was beginning, he took water and washed his hands before the crowd, saying, "I am innocent of this man's blood;[l] see to it yourselves." [25]And all the people answered, "His blood be on us and on our children!" [26]Then he released for them Barabbas, and having scourged Jesus, delivered him to be crucified.

k Other ancient authorities read *Jesus Barabbas*   l Other authorities read *this righteous blood* or *this righteous man's blood*

OVERVIEW: The practice of releasing a prisoner was due to leniency until conviction. Barabas, whom they released, represents opposition to Christ within anyone who does evil (ORIGEN, HILARY OF POITIERS). He was a known murderer and therefore a great contrast to Jesus, whose guilt was disputed. Pilate's wife suffered over convicting Jesus in a dream sent by God, perhaps in order to persuade Pilate not to convict him (CHRYSOSTOM). In spite of her dream, Jesus was convicted out of jealousy. The people followed the Jewish leaders in calling for the release of Barabbas (ORIGEN), although it seems that Pilate thought they might choose the release of Jesus out of shame and generosity (CHRYSOSTOM). Both Pilate and the people are guilty of condemning Jesus (LEO THE GREAT, CHRYSOSTOM). Jerome suggests that Pilate puts the blame on the people. Christ is the ultimate victor, however, or he was proven innocent even in his conviction (MAXIMUS OF TURIN). Jesus did not condemn the people; rather, he received those among them and their children who repented (CHRYSOSTOM). He endured whipping so that others would not be whipped (JEROME, APOLLINARIS).

27:15-17 Whom Do You Want?

ANY ONE PRISONER. ORIGEN: You should not be surprised that shortly after Roman rule had begun [in Palestine], the Jews who came under their yoke were granted the privilege of asking for [the release of] "one [prisoner] whom they wanted," even though he appeared to be guilty of a thousand murders; the pagan nations granted a certain amount of leniency to their subjects until the yoke had been firmly secured around them. COMMENTARY ON MATTHEW 120.[1]

DISSENSION OR PEACE. ORIGEN: I believe that these events reveal something of a mystery. Barabbas represents the one who enacts dissension, war and murder in human souls, but Jesus is the Son of God who works peace, reason, wis-

dom and everything good. When the two of them were bound humanly and bodily, the people requested that Barabbas be released. Because of this act, they suffer continual dissention, murder and robbery. Such things afflict the pagans from without but the Jews, who do not believe in Jesus, from within their very souls. Where Jesus is absent, there is dissention and strife and war. Where Jesus is present, however, in such a way that the people can say "if Christ is in us, although the body is dead on account of sin, the spirit is alive on account of righteousness,"[2] there is everything good: spiritual riches beyond measure and peace, for "he is our peace who has made us both one."[3] Anything contrary to this should be recognized as the mark of Barabbas struggling to be set free from his bondage within human souls, that is, not only in the historically sinful Israel, considered according to the flesh, but in all who teach like it and live like it. Within everyone who does evil, then, Barabbas is set free and Christ is bound. Within everyone who does good, however, Christ is set free and Barabbas is bound. COMMENTARY ON MATTHEW 121.[4]

BARABBAS OR JESUS? CHRYSOSTOM: Note how far Pilate goes to give the crowd a chance to relieve themselves from blame. Observe how they did not leave themselves so much as a shadow of an excuse. Here was their choice: Let an acknowledged criminal go free, or free one whose guilt was still disputed. If they should choose to let the known offender go free, would it not be even more fitting to allow the innocent to go free? For surely Jesus did not seem to them morally worse than acknowledged murderers. But they instead chose a robber. This was not just any robber but one who was infamous for wickedness in many murders. THE GOSPEL OF MATTHEW, HOMILY 86.2.[5]

---

[1]GCS 38.2:253-54. [2]Rom 8:10. [3]Eph 2:14. [4]GCS 38.2:256-57. [5]PG 58:765; NPNF 1 10:512

27:18-19 *I Have Suffered in a Dream*

The Dream of Pilate's Wife. Chrysostom: This dream was no small event. It should have been enough to stop them in their tracks when viewed in relation to the other proofs seen in other things that occurred. Why didn't the dream come to Pilate? Perhaps she was more worthy. Or perhaps because, even if he had seen it, he would not have equally believed or perhaps would not have even mentioned it. So it was providentially arranged that the wife should see it, in order that it might become more commonly known. And note that she does not only behold the dream but also suffers from it. One might imagine that Pilate might have been made more reluctant to participate in this murder, even from a feeling of sympathy toward his wife. The time of the dream also is significant, for it happened on that very night. The Gospel of Matthew, Homily 86.1.[6]

She Suffered in a Dream. Origen: Jesus was delivered up out of jealousy, and plainly out of jealousy. Even Pilate could not ignore it. Furthermore, the Evangelist did not overlook the matter of divine providence regarding the praise of God, who desired to convert Pilate's wife in a dream. The woman took it upon herself to prevent her husband from passing sentence against Jesus. But Matthew did not explain the dream. All he said was that she had "suffered many things in a dream" because of Jesus. Therefore she "suffered in a dream" and did not suffer beyond that, so we may say that Pilate's wife was fortunate. She "suffered many things in a dream" because of Jesus and she received "in a dream" what she would suffer. Hence you may say it is better for someone to receive bad things in a dream than to receive them in life. Who indeed would not choose to receive bad things "in a dream" [rather than receive them] in life [unless one deserved such things, and it were better to receive bitter things in life than to receive minor troubles in a dream]? He finds comfort indeed

and peaceful repose "in the bosom of Abraham"[7] who receives bad things in his life (and not those bad things which he receives in his dreams), and because of them he will also be consoled. As to whether he will also have the beginning of conversion to God for having "suffered many things in a dream" because of Jesus, God only knows. Commentary on Matthew 122.[8]

27:20-23 *Let Him Be Crucified*

Which of the Two? Origen: It is evident how the elders and the mentors of Jewish worship have stirred up the Jewish people and incited them against Jesus, that they might destroy him and have Barabbas released. For the crowds put their belief in their leaders and priests. For his part, the procurator addressed the people and said to them, "Which of the two do you wish that I release to you?" The crowd— a truly sizable crowd walking, as it were, on the "broad path that leads to destruction"[9]—sought and kept crying out to have Barabbas released to them. Commentary on Matthew 123.[10]

The Name Barabbas. Hilary of Poitiers: When Pilate offered to release Jesus, following the customary practice wherein the people were granted the privilege of gaining the freedom of one prisoner per solemn feast day, they were persuaded by their priests to choose Barabbas instead. Here already the mystery of their future infidelity is contained in Barabbas's very name, which means "son of the father." They preferred this "son of the father" to Christ. At the instigation of their leaders, they chose the Antichrist, a man of sin and son of the devil.[11] They chose the one elected for damnation over the author of life. On Matthew 33.2.[12]

What Shall I Do with Jesus? Chrysostom: Since the crowd asked for the other, Pilate said,

---

[6]PG 58:764; NPNF 1 10:512. [7]Lk 16:23. [8]GCS 38.2:257-58. [9]Mt 7:13. [10]GCS 38.2:258. [11]2 Thess 2:3. [12]SC 258:248-50.

"What shall I do then with the Christ?" In this way he was trying to make them embarrassed, by giving them the power to choose, that at least out of shame they might release him and their generosity could be expressed. It made them contentious to hear it said that he had done no wrong. Yet they were being given an opportunity to save him out of humanity. Surely this is an offer whose plausibility cannot be disputed. THE GOSPEL OF MATTHEW, HOMILY 86.2.[13]

27:24 See to It Yourselves

PILATE'S ACQUIESENCE. LEO THE GREAT: By what law is it, my Jewish friends, that what is unlawful to do is lawful to desire? By what standard is it that what defiles the body does not taint the heart? You fear to be contaminated by the shedding of his blood that you would take upon yourselves and your children. Since your wickedness will not commit so great a crime, allow the procurator to pass judgment. But, prevailing upon him impetuously, you do not allow him to swerve from that goal you deceitfully abstain from.

Pilate sinned by doing what he did not want to do. He acquiesced in your judgment, doing whatever your rage wrought by force. Such was your observance of the law that you eschewed placing into the treasury the money which the seller of Christ returned to you, wary lest the blood money pollute the sacred coffers. Whose heart is guilty of this pretense? The conscience of the priests accepts what the money box does not receive. Thus with untold shades of deceit you cover yourselves, and a deal is made with the traitor. SERMON 44.3.[14]

HE WASHED HIS HANDS. CHRYSOSTOM: Why then did Pilate allow him to be sacrificed? Why didn't he rescue him, like the centurion had rescued Paul?[15] For that man too was aware that he could have pleased the Jews and that a sedition may have taken place and a riot; nevertheless he stood firm against all these. But not so Pilate.

He was extremely cowardly and weak. He joined in their corruption. He did not stand firm against the bullying crowd or against the Jewish leadership. In every way he allowed them an excuse. For they "cried out exceedingly," that is, cried out the more, "Let him be crucified." For they desired not only to put him to death but also that it should be on a trumped-up charge of iniquity. And even though the judge was contradicting them, they continued to cry out against him. THE GOSPEL OF MATTHEW, HOMILY 86.2.[16]

INNOCENT OF THIS MAN'S BLOOD. MAXIMUS OF TURIN: For Christ conquers when he is judged, because in this way he is proven innocent. Hence Pilate says, "I am innocent of the blood of this just man." It is a better case which is not defended and still is proved. It is a fuller righteousness that is not supplemented by words but is still supported by the truth. It must be that the tongue should keep silent when justice itself is present to itself. Let the human tongue keep silent in a good affair, inasmuch as it has also been accustomed to speak out in favor of bad causes. I do not want righteousness to be defended in the same manner that wickedness is usually excused. It is not by reason of speech but because of virtue that Christ vanquishes, for the Savior, who is wisdom, knows how to vanquish by keeping silent and how to overcome by not responding. Therefore he prefers to establish the truth of his case rather than to speak about it. What in fact would compel him to speak when silence is enough to conquer? But perhaps fear would compel him, lest he lose his life. Yet this was precisely the reason for his victory. He lost his own life in order to gain life for all; he preferred to be conquered in himself in order to be the victor in everyone. SERMONS 57.1.[17]

A CHANCE TO DO RIGHT. CHRYSOSTOM: Do

---

[13]PG 58:765; NPNF 1 10:512. [14]SC 74:47. [15]Acts 27:1-44. [16]PG 58:765; NPNF 1 10:512. [17]CCL 23:228; ACW 50:137-38.

you see how many things Christ did in order to give them a chance to do right? Do you remember how many times he had checked Judas? So likewise did he restrain these men too, both throughout all his ministry and at the very time of his condemnation. For surely when they saw the governor and judge washing his hands of it, saying, "I am innocent of this man's blood," they should have been moved to compassion both by what was said and by what was done. The same is true when they saw Judas had hanged himself as when they saw Pilate himself offering them the choice of another in the place of Christ. THE GOSPEL OF MATTHEW, HOMILY 86.2.[18]

BLAMING THE PLAINTIFFS. JEROME: Pilate accepted the water in line with that prophetic saying, "I will wash my hands among the innocent,"[19] that he might cleanse the works of the Gentiles by the washing of his hands and in some way separate us from the wickedness of the Jews who cried out "Crucify him!" What he intimated was this: I truly wanted to release an innocent man, but a riot is breaking out and the charge of treason against Caesar has been brought against me. So "I am innocent of the blood of this just man."

The judge who was induced to pass judgment against the Lord does not condemn the defendant but puts the blame on the plaintiffs. He declares him to be a just man who was meant to be crucified. "See to it yourselves," he says. "I am the administrator of the laws. It is according to your word that his blood is being shed." COMMENTARY ON MATTHEW 4.27.24.[20]

27:25 On Us and on Our Children

ALL THE PEOPLE ANSWERED. CHRYSOSTOM: Look how high the contrary evidence is piling up. The accuser and traitor condemns himself. The judge who sentences tries to absolve himself of guilt. The dream of warning comes that very night. Even at the point of his condemnation Jesus is evidently innocent. What kind of

plea will his murderers have? Even if they were not willing to let him be acknowledged as innocent, at least they should not have preferred a robber to him, and especially a notorious robber, known to be such. THE GOSPEL OF MATTHEW, HOMILY 86.2.[21]

AND ON OUR CHILDREN. CHRYSOSTOM: What then did they do? When they saw the judge washing his hands and saying, "I am innocent," they cried out, "His blood be on us and on our children." They were rendering a sentence against themselves. He was yielding himself up that all should be done.

Note how great is their madness. For passion and evil desire work on us like this. They did not permit anyone to see anything of what was right. They not only curse themselves, they draw down the curse upon their own children as well. They acted with unutterable madness. They acted both against themselves and against their children!

Yet this lover of humanity did not hold their own sentence against them. He did not confirm it upon their children or even upon them. Rather he received both from them and from their children those who repented. He counted them worthy of good things beyond number. Think of who might have been among them! Even Paul perhaps. Even some among the thousands that believed in Jerusalem, for it is said, "You see, brothers, how many thousands there are among the Jews of those who have believed."[22] And if some continued in their sin, to themselves let them impute their punishment. THE GOSPEL OF MATTHEW, HOMILY 86.2.[23]

27:26 Pilate Hands Over Jesus to Be Crucified

---

[18]PG 58:765; NPNF 1 10:512-13. [19]Ps 26:6 (25:6 LXX). [20]CCL 77:266-67. [21]PG 58:765-66; NPNF 1 10:513. [22]Acts 21:20. [23]PG 58:766; NPNF 1 10:513.

THEY SCOURGED JESUS. CHRYSOSTOM: Why did Pilate have Jesus whipped? Either as one presumably condemned, or to please the crowd, or as if he were willing to give their judgment some sort of standard legal expression. And yet he ought to have resisted them. For indeed even before this he had said, "Take him yourselves and judge him by your own law."[24] There were many reasons that Pilate and the others might have held back: the signs and the miracles, the great patience of the one who was suffering these things, and above all his benign silence. For since both by his defense of himself and by his prayers, he had shown his humanity, again he now shows his glory and the greatness of his nature, both by his silence and by his indifference to what they said. This might have led them to marvel. But neither Pilate nor the crowd takes sufficient note of these evidences. THE GOSPEL OF MATTHEW, HOMILY 86.2.[25]

HE RELEASED BARABBAS. JEROME: Barabbas the robber, who had provoked a riot among the crowds and committed murder, was released to the Jewish people. . . . Now Jesus, having been delivered up by the Jews, was absolved of guilt by Pilate's wife and was called a just man by the governor himself. Moreover, the centurion declared that he was truly the Son of God.[26] The learned reader may be hard pressed to explain the fact that Pilate washed his hands and said, "I am innocent of the blood of this just man,"[27] and later handed over the scourged Jesus to be crucified. It is important to realize that Jesus was dealt with according to Roman law, which decreed that whoever is to be crucified must first be beaten with whips. Thus Jesus was handed over to the soldiers for scourging, and their whips did their work on that most sacred body and that bosom which held God. This came about so that, in keeping with the words "many cords of sins"[28] and with the whipping of Jesus, we might be free from scourging. As holy Scripture says to the just man: "The whip did not draw near to your tabernacle."[29] COMMENTARY ON MATTHEW 4.27.24.[30]

THEY STRUCK HIM. APOLLINARIS: The floggings [are] for the sins of the world, because the sinner is flogged many times, according to the prophecy that says, "I gave my back to the whips."[31] And so is fulfilled [the saying] that the righteous [will give himself] for sinners. The height of goodness is also fulfilled when "the righteous [suffered] for the unrighteous,"[32] so that "by his wounds we might be healed," as Isaiah says.[33] FRAGMENT 138.[34]

---

[24]Jn 18:31. [25]PG 58:766; NPNF 1 10:513. [26]Mt 27:54. [27]Mt 27:24. [28]Ps 32:10 (31:10 LXX). [29]Ps 91:10 (90:10 LXX). [30]CCL 77:267-68. [31]Is 50:6. [32]1 Pet 3:18. [33]Is 53:6. [34]MKGK 49.

27:27-43 THE SOLDIERS MOCK AND CRUCIFY JESUS

[27]*Then the soldiers of the governor took Jesus into the praetorium, and they gathered the whole battalion before him.* [28]*And they stripped him and put a scarlet robe upon him,* [29]*and plaiting a crown of thorns they put it on his head, and put a reed in his right hand. And kneeling before him they mocked him, saying, "Hail, King of the Jews!"* [30]*And they spat upon him, and took the reed and struck him on the head.* [31]*And when they had mocked him, they stripped*

him of the robe, and put his own clothes on him, and led him away to crucify him.

[32]*As they went out, they came upon a man of Cyrene, Simon by name; this man they com-pelled to carry his cross.* [33]*And when they came to a place called Golgotha (which means the place of a skull),* [34]*they offered him wine to drink, mingled with gall; but when he tasted it, he would not drink it.* [35]*And when they had crucified him, they divided his garments among them by casting lots;* [36]*then they sat down and kept watch over him there.* [37]*And over his head they put the charge against him, which read, "This is Jesus the King of the Jews."* [38]*Then two robbers were crucified with him, one on the right and one on the left.* [39]*And those who passed by derided him, wagging their heads* [40]*and saying, "You who would destroy the temple and build it in three days, save yourself! If you are the Son of God, come down from the cross."* [41]*So also the chief priests, with the scribes and elders, mocked him, saying,* [42]*"He saved others; he cannot save him-self. He is the King of Israel; let him come down now from the cross, and we will believe in him.* [43]*He trusts in God; let God deliver him now, if he desires him; for he said, 'I am the Son of God.'"*

OVERVIEW: Christ is adored even while he is mocked (HILARY OF POITIERS). He bears shame that was due to us (APOLLINARIS). Each of Jesus' vestments has spiritual significance (HILARY OF POITIERS, APOLLINARIS, ORIGEN, CHROMATIUS). Simon of Cyrene, an outsider who carried Jesus' cross, represents the spread of faith to the Gen-tiles (LEO THE GREAT). To another, Simon repre-sents compulsory service due for our salvation (ORIGEN). For yet another, Simon participates in Christ's great triumph over death by bearing the ultimate emblem of victory, the cross (CHRO-MATIUS).

In contrast to Adam, who tasted the sweet-ness of the apple but experienced the bitterness of death, Christ tasted the bitterness of gall but experienced the sweetness of life over death (CHROMATIUS). Gall also contrasts with the wine Jesus drank with his disciples at the Last Sup-per. Jesus' garments are the words of Scripture. Those who shook their heads as they passed by blasphemed Jesus but are as transient as heresies (ORIGEN). Christ suffered for all persons (CHRY-SOSTOM). He did not come down from the cross so that he might destroy the devil (JEROME). Neither was he willing to save himself by some extraordinary act (ORIGEN).

27:27-31 Beaten and Mocked

THEY MOCKED HIM. HILARY OF POITIERS: The beaten Lord is dressed in a scarlet robe, a purple cloak and a crown of thorns, and a reed is placed on his right hand. Bending their knees before him, they mock him. Having taken upon himself all the infirmities of our bodies, he is covered with the scarlet blood of all the mar-tyrs destined to reign with him, and he is cloaked with the high honor of the prophets and patriarchs in purple cloth. He is also crowned with thorns, that is, with the former sins of the remorseful Gentiles, so that glory might derive from the destructive and useless things, plaited on his divine head, which they contrive. The sharp points of the thorns aptly pertain to the sins from which a crown of vic-tory is woven for Christ. The reed symbolizes the emptiness and weakness of all those Gen-tiles, which is held firm in his grasp. His head, moreover, is struck. As I believe, not much harm was done to his head from being struck with the reed; however, the typical explanation for this is that the bodily weakness of the Gen-tiles that was previously held in Christ's hand finds comfort now in God the Father, for he is the head.[1] But amid all this, while Christ is mocked, he is being adored. ON MATTHEW 33.3.[2]

STRIPPED OF THE ROBE. APOLLINARIS: It was not as though those men had the power [to do these deeds]. Rather, it seemed good to God that these events occur for the redemption of humanity. The "Lord of glory" was treated shamefully for us because of the dishonor due to us. He is now glorified while the day of the righteous is always mocked by the ignorant. Since the cloak was tinged with the color of blood, those murdering him dressed him with it, though they did not realize the significance of what they were doing. Instead, they clothed Jesus . . . in scarlet cloth and bound his hand with the symbol of one of the sons of Tamar and Judah.[3] The cloak itself [represents] the blood shed by the world and by the people in it. The Savior was put to death for the salvation of all. But they who are choked by "worries, wealth and pleasure" have received the word of God but have not borne fruit.[4] They weave thorns together and crown Jesus with them, dishonoring him. . . . Those who deemed his kingdom to be of little value placed a reed in his right hand. FRAGMENT 139.[5]

THE SCARLET ROBE. ORIGEN: That scarlet robe was prefigured by the scarlet sign mentioned in Joshua the son of Nun, which Rahab used for her safety,[6] and mentioned in Genesis,[7] which was placed on the hand of one of Tamar's newborn sons in token of the future Passion of Christ. So now, in taking up the "scarlet robe," he took upon himself the blood of the world, and in that thorny "crown" plaited on his head he took upon himself the thorns of our sins. As to the robe, it is written that "they stripped him of the scarlet robe."[8] But as to the crown of thorns, the Evangelists mention nothing further. Apparently they wanted us to determine what happened to that crown of thorns placed on his head and never removed. My belief is that the crown of thorns disappeared from the head

of Jesus, so that our former thorns no longer exist now that Jesus has removed them from us once and for all on his own distinguished head. COMMENTARY ON MATTHEW 125.[9]

THE REED. ORIGEN: What can be said about the reed they placed "in his right hand"? Here is my explanation: The reed embodied the hollow and fragile scepter that we all were leaning on before we saw it was a bad scepter, for we were trusting in the reed-shaped rod of Egypt or Babylon or some other kingdom opposed to God's kingdom.[10] Then he took that reed and rod of the fragile kingdom from our hands, to subdue it and break it to pieces on the cross. In place of that reed we once were leaning on, he gave us the scepter of the heavenly kingdom and the rod mentioned in Scripture: "The rod of justice, the rod of your kingdom."[11] In other words, the rod that chastens those who need to be chastened, as the apostle notes: "What do you want, that I come to you with a rod?"[12] He also gave us a staff that we might celebrate the paschal feast (as Scripture says, "Let your staff be in your hand"),[13] laying down that reed-shaped rod we once had before we celebrated the Lord's paschal feast.

Then they took this fragile, hollow reed and struck the honorable head of Jesus with it, for that ever-adverse kingdom reviles and scourges God the Father, the head of the Lord and Savior. And amid all this, the only-begotten goodness itself was unharmed, nor did he suffer anything, "being made a curse for us,"[14] since by nature he is a blessing. But since he is a blessing, he destroyed and took away and dispelled all human malediction. COMMENTARY ON MATTHEW 125.[15]

---

[1]1 Cor 11:3. [2]SC 258:250-52. [3]Gen 38:1-30. The reference is to the scarlet rope of Rahab (Josh 2:18) and Tamar (Gen 38:27), both traditionally considered symbolic prefigurations of the Passion of Christ. The two examples also appear in the comment to follow (Origen "The Scarlet Robe"). [4]Lk 8:14. [5]*MKGK* 49. [6]Josh 2:18. [7]Gen 38:28. [8]Cf. Mk 15:20. [9]GCS 38.2:261-62. [10]See Is 36:6. [11]Ps 45:6 (44:7 LXX). [12]1 Cor 4:21. [13]Ex 12:11. [14]Gal 3:13. [15]GCS 38.2:262.

THE MYSTERY OF HIS KINGSHIP. CHROMATIUS: These things were done to mock Jesus. But now we know these things happened through a heavenly mystery. Wickedness was at work among the former; among the latter, the mystery of faith and the light of truth. In the purple tunic Christ is dressed as king; and in the scarlet robe, as prince of martyrs, he is resplendent as precious scarlet in his sacred blood. He receives the crown as conqueror, for crowns are usually bestowed upon conquerors. He is adored as God by people on bended knees. Therefore he is vested in purple as king, in scarlet as prince of martyrs; he is crowned as conqueror, is hailed as Lord and is adored as God.

We can recognize in the purple cloak also the church, married to Christ the king and resplendent with regal glory. Hence it is called by John in the Revelation a "royal nation."[16] As to this purple cloth, we read in the Song of Solomon: "His whole bed is purple."[17] For Christ rests on that bed where he is able to find purple cloth, that is, royal faith and a beautiful spirit. . . .

The crown of thorns which the Lord received on his head stands for our community, which came to faith from the Gentiles. At one time we were thorns—that is to say, sinners. Believing now in Christ, we have become a crown of righteousness, for we no longer cause pain or harm to the Savior. Rather, we surround his head with our profession of faith while we praise the Father in the Son, because the head of Christ is God, as the apostle says.[18] This is the crown foretold by David in a psalm: "You placed a crown of precious stones on his head."[19] We were thorns at one time, but after we were included in the crown of Christ, we became precious stones. For he, who raised up children of Abraham from stones, made precious stones out of thorns.[20]

This scriptural passage did not consider of trivial importance the fact that a reed was placed in the Lord's right hand. Note what David says about Christ in the psalm: "My tongue is the pen of a ready writer."[21] As he was about to suffer,

therefore, he took up the reed in his right hand, so that with a heavenly notation he might pardon us our misdeeds or inscribe his law in our hearts with divine letters. As he says through the prophet: "I will put my law within them."[22] . . . We may also infer other things about the reed, for it has many spiritual meanings. A reed that is hollow and without pith connotes the Gentile people, who were once without the pith of God's law, empty of faith and devoid of grace. Therefore this type of reed, that is, the Gentile people, is put in the Lord's right hand, for his left hand already contained the Jewish people who were persecuting him. TRACTATE ON MATTHEW 19.1-4.[23]

27:32 Simon Compelled to Carry the Cross

A MAN OF CYRENE. LEO THE GREAT: But as the multitudes went with Jesus to the place of punishment, a certain Simon of Cyrene was found on whom to lay the wood of the cross, instead of the Lord. Even this act signified that faith would come to the Gentiles, to whom the cross of Christ was not to be shame but glory. It was not accidental therefore but symbolic and mystical, that while the Jewish rulers were raging against Christ, a foreigner was found to share his sufferings. Thus the apostle would say, "If we suffer with him, we shall also reign with him."[24]

Note that it was not a Hebrew or an Israelite but a foreigner who was drawn into service for the Savior in his most holy humiliation.[25] By this transference the propitiation of the spotless Lamb and the fulfillment of all mysteries passed from the circumcision to the uncircumcision, from the sons according to the flesh to the sons according to the spirit. Hence the apostle would

---

[16]Rev 1:6; cf. 1 Pet 2:9. [17]Song 3:10. [18]1 Cor 11:3. [19]Ps 21:3 (20:4 LXX). [20]Mt 3:9. [21]Ps 45:1 (44:2 LXX). [22]Jer 31:33. [23]CCL 9a:89-91. [24]2 Tim 2:12; Rom 8:17. [25]That Simon was a foreigner is not mentioned in the Gospels; Leo assumes this because Simon was from Cyrene.

say, "Christ our Passover is sacrificed for us."[26] He offered himself to the Father as a new and true sacrifice of reconciliation. He was slain not in the temple, whose worship was now at an end, and not within the confines of the city which for its sin was doomed to be destroyed, but beyond the walls of the city, "outside the gate."[27] Thus with the cessation of the old symbolic victims, a new victim was being placed on a new altar. The cross of Christ was to become the altar not of the temple but of the world. SERMON 46.5.[28]

THE GOVERNMENT UPON HIS SHOULDERS. CYRIL OF ALEXANDRIA: The Savior is led to the suffering that brings salvation. They laid his cross on Simeon of Cyrene. Another of the holy Evangelists said that Jesus himself carried the cross.[29] Now surely both [accounts] are correct. For the Savior carried the cross, and, having met the Cyrene about half way, they transferred the cross to him. It is said about him through the voice of Isaiah that "a child has been born to us, and a son has been given to us, and the government shall be upon his shoulders."[30] Now the cross has become the means by which he governs, through which he continues to rule over all heaven, since it is true that even as "far as death" he has become "obedient, even to death of a cross. Therefore God has exalted him."[31] FRAGMENT 306.[32]

SIMON OF CYRENE. ORIGEN: "As they went out, they came upon a man of Cyrene, Simon by name; they compelled this man to carry the cross" of Christ. It was fitting not only for the Savior to take up his cross but also for us to carry it, doing compulsory service for our salvation. Furthermore, we did not benefit by taking up his cross then as much as we benefit by it now, since he takes it upon himself and carries it. COMMENTARY ON MATTHEW 126.[33]

COMPELLED TO CARRY THE CROSS. CHROMATIUS: Finally, the Gospel reports in the present

reading that as the Lord was being led to his Passion, "they found a certain man of Cyrene named Simon and compelled him to carry the cross." The cross of Christ is the triumph of virtue and a trophy of victory. How blessed is Simon, who deserved to be the first to bear so great a sign of victory! He was compelled to carry the cross before the Lord because the Lord wanted to demonstrate his cross to be a singular grace of that heavenly mystery which is himself: God and man, Logos and flesh, Son of God and Son of man. He was crucified as man but triumphed as God in the mystery of the cross. His suffering was of the flesh, but his glorious victory was divine. Through his cross, Christ defeated both death and the devil. Through the cross, Christ mounted his chariot of victory and chose the four Evangelists, as though horses for his chariot, to announce so great a victory to all the world. Simon of Cyrene therefore was carrying the instrument of this great triumph in his arms. He was a partaker of the Passion of Christ so that he might be a partaker of his resurrection, as the apostle teaches: "If we die with him, we will also live with him. If we endure with him, we will also reign with him."[34] Similarly the Lord himself says in the Gospel: "He who does not take up his cross and follow me cannot be my disciple."[35] TRACTATE ON MATTHEW 19.5.[36]

27:33-34 When They Came to Golgotha

WINE MINGLED WITH GALL. CHROMATIUS: When they had come to Golgotha, the Gospel says, "They gave him vinegar mixed with gall, but when he tasted it, he refused to drink." This event was foretold by David when he wrote, "They gave me gall for food, and they gave me vinegar to slake my thirst."[37] Take note of the mystery revealed here. Long ago, Adam tasted

---

[26]1 Cor 5:7. [27]Heb 13:12. [28]SC 74:59-60; NPNF 2 12:172. [29]Jn 19:17. [30]Is 9:6. [31]Phil 2:8-9. [32]MKGK 262-63. [33]GCS 38.2:263. [34]2 Tim 2:11-12. [35]Lk 14:27. [36]CCL 9a:91-92. [37]Ps 69:21 (68:22 LXX).

the sweetness of the apple and obtained the bitterness of death for the whole human race. In contrast to this, the Lord tasted the bitterness of gall and obtained our restoration from death's sting to the sweetness of life. He took on himself the bitterness of gall in order to extinguish in us the bitterness of death. He received acrid vinegar into himself but poured out for us the precious wine of his blood. He suffered evil and returned good. He accepted death and gave life. The location of his death is also not without significance, for it is reported that the body of Adam is buried in that very ground.[38] Christ was crucified there where Adam was buried, that life might arise where death once entered. Death comes through Adam, but life comes through Christ, who deigned to be crucified and to die so that by the wood of the cross he might erase the sin of the tree and by the mystery of his own death he might cancel the punishment of our death. TRACTATE ON MATTHEW 19.7.[39]

THE WINE NOT WITH GALL CONTRASTED. ORIGEN: Just as it sufficed for the Lord only to taste "vinegar mixed with gall,"[40] so also was it sufficient for our benefit that he only taste death, which lasted no longer than three days. The other wine, however, which was not "mixed with gall" or with anything else, he took and drank, and "when he had given thanks,"[41] he gave it to his disciples, promising that he would drink it "anew in the kingdom of God."[42] COMMENTARY ON MATTHEW 127.[43]

27:35-38 Jesus Crucified

THEY CAST LOTS FOR HIS GARMENTS. ORIGEN: There are those who to this day do not have the Lord with them but do have his "garments"—namely, the words contained in Scripture. They do not have them in full but only in part. Nonetheless the prophet had spoken that prediction which was now fulfilled.[44] Now, as to whether any of his clothes were torn apart when they divided his garments or whether any of

them remained intact and just what those items were, nothing is said by the first three Evangelists. But in John we read that "when the soldiers had crucified Jesus they took his garments and made four parts, one for each soldier; also his tunic. But the tunic was without seam, woven from top to bottom; so they said to one another, 'Let us not tear it but cast lots for it.'"[45] Therefore not all but only one of the soldiers who had cast lots received it. Now anyone debating the differences between those who have the Lord's "garments" will doubtless find some people who, although they do not have the Lord in their teachings, do have the "tunic" that was "woven from top to bottom."[46] COMMENTARY ON MATTHEW 128.[47]

WHY THE ROBE WAS NOT DIVIDED. HILARY OF POITIERS: That they distributed his clothes by casting lots for them rather than by cutting them up signifies the eternal incorruptibility of Christ's body. The life and salvation of all things was hung from the tree of life with a thief on his left and a thief on his right. This demonstrates that the entire human race is called to the mystery of the Lord's suffering. ON MATTHEW 23.4-5.[48]

THIS IS JESUS, THE KING OF THE JEWS. ORIGEN: "Whether in pretense or in truth, Christ is proclaimed,"[49] and all literature—whether Greek, Roman or Hebrew—gives evidence of his kingdom. And in place of a crown, "over his head" is written "This is Jesus king of the Jews." There is no other reason for his death (nor was

---

[38]The evidence is nil. The reasoning comes from the typology of Rom 5. [39]CCL 9a:93. [40]Origen indicates that Jesus tasted the vinegar mixed with gall but did not drink it, interpreting the gesture as indicative of the transitory nature of his Passion, as opposed to the perennial quality of eschatological rest symbolized by the wine he was to drink with his disciples in the kingdom of heaven. [41]Mt 26:27. [42]Mt 26:29. [43]GCS 38.2:265. [44]Ps 22:18 (21:19 LXX). [45]Jn 19:23-24. [46]The tradition is that the garment was seamless. "Have some part of the garments of Jesus" signifies allegorically participating in his doctrine in different ways, depending on the various pieces of clothing. [47]GCS 38.2:265-66. [48]SC 258:252. [49]Phil 1:18.

there) than that he was the "king of the Jews." He spoke about this when he said, "I have been made king by him on Zion, his holy mountain."[50] And while the chief priest, in keeping with the letter of the law, wore on his head a type of sign with a petal bearing the inscription "the holiness of the Lord,"[51] the true chief priest and king—Jesus on the cross—has a sign that reads "This is the king of the Jews." Rising up to the Father and receiving him in himself, he has for his inscription and title the Father of renown and has the Father as his crown. He has been made worthy of him as a house worthy of God the Father, and he alone can fully possess the Father. COMMENTARY ON MATTHEW 130.[52]

27:39-40 Come Down from the Cross

THEY SHOOK THEIR HEADS. ORIGEN: No one standing still or directly approaching him blasphemes Jesus. "Those who passed by blasphemed him,"[53] and those who stayed behind plucked food from the vineyard wall demolished by God. Concerning this it is written, "Why then have you broken down its walls, so that those who pass along the way pluck its fruit?"[54] Therefore, as long as one does not pass along the way or avoid it and can say to God while standing, "You have set 'my feet upon a rock,'"[55] one does not blaspheme Jesus. But if one should fall or pass by or cross over or turn away, one blasphemes God. Likewise, those who have fallen into evil works and those who have abandoned the "everlasting statutes"[56] and the way of the heavenly church "are tossed to and fro and carried about with every wind of doctrine, by the cunning of men, by their craftiness in deceitful wiles."[57]

Now, if anyone should say that all heresies are "passing along" and turning away, that one will not be wrong. For this reason also those are held to be "passing along" and blaspheming Jesus who do not keep their head steady but are "wagging" it up and down. For they are not wise, nor do they have their eyes in their head where they

belong, as we read in Ecclesiastes: "The wise man has his eyes in his head."[58] Therefore those who pass by and turn away have need to blaspheme Jesus the Son of God, for "no one speaking by the Spirit of God ever says 'Jesus be cursed.'"[59]

There are various forms of blasphemy. One of them is uttered by those who do not understand or hear what is being said or acknowledge what is true. Now Jesus had said, "Destroy this temple, and in three days I will raise it up."[60] But those who were passing along, like "false witnesses"[61] against Jesus, related what he had not said, attacking him: "Aha, you who would destroy the temple and build it in three days, save yourself." The truth is, he will not destroy the temple, but what others destroy he will build, whether it be the "temple of his body," which the Jews delivered up to death, or the temple of his witnesses and all those who had God's word in them and who, because of the snares of the wicked, died out of love for God (for "the hour is coming, and now is, when the dead will hear the voice of the Son of God, and those who hear it will live").[62] And they lied not only when they said, "You who would destroy the temple," but also when they said, "And I will build it in three days." For he did not say that he would build the temple but raise it up. The verb *build* does not designate a sudden action, but "raise up" does. COMMENTARY ON MATTHEW 132.[63]

THEY DERIDED HIM. CHRYSOSTOM: O cross most abominable, most execrable! Did not God rescue the prophets from their dangers? Did God not save the righteous? Why not him? What could equal this folly? The coming of dan-

---

[50]Ps 2:6. [51]Ex 28:36. [52]GCS 38.2:267. [53]Origen reveals that Jesus was blasphemed by those who were passing and who therefore did not stand still. Passing or being in motion symbolizes a negative spiritual condition, whereas standing still or stable is a positive condition. [54]Ps 80:12 (79:13 LXX). [55]Ps 40:2 (39:3 LXX). [56]Prov 22:28. [57]Eph 4:14. [58]Eccles 2:14. [59]1 Cor 12:3. [60]Mt 26:61; Mk 14:58; Jn 2:19. [61]Mt 26:60. [62]Jn 5:28-29. [63]GCS 38.2:268-69.

gers upon the prophets and saints did not injure their honor before God. But what happened to this incomparable person? By what he said and what he did he offended all our expectations to the utmost. He was forever correcting beforehand our assumptions about him. Even when all these ignominies were said and done, they could not prevail, even at that time. The thief who had lived depraved in such great wickedness, who had spent his whole life in murders and house breakings, when these things had been said, only then confessed him. When he made mention of his kingdom, the people bewailed him. These things that were done seemed to testify the contrary in the eyes of many who knew nothing of the mystery of God's dispensations. Jesus was weak and of no ostensible power; nevertheless truth prevailed even by the contrary evidences.

So hearing all these things, let us arm ourselves against all temptations to anger and outrage. Should you perceive in your heart a swelling of pride, seal your breast against it. Set your hopes only upon the cross. Call to mind the humbling things that were then taking place. Then you will cast out as dust all rage by the recollection of the things that were done to him.

Consider his words. Consider his actions. Remember that he is Lord and you are his servant. Remember that he is suffering for you, and for you individually. You may be suffering only on your own behalf. He is suffering on behalf of all by whom he had been crucified. You may be suffering in the presence of a few. He suffers in the sight of the whole city and of the whole people of the covenant, both of strangers and those of the holy land, to all of whom he spoke merciful words.

Even his disciples forsook him. This was most distressing to him. Those who previously paid him mind suddenly deserted him. Meanwhile his enemies and foes, having captured him and put him on a cross, insulted him, reviled him, mocked him, derided him and scoffed at him. See the Jews and soldiers rejecting him

from below. See how he was set between two thieves on either side, and even the thieves insulted him and upbraided him. The Gospel of Matthew, Homily 87.2.[64]

The Sign of Jonah. Chrysostom: This is the sign which previously Jesus had promised to give them when they asked for it, saying, "An evil and adulterous generation seeks for a sign, but no sign shall be given to it, except the sign of the prophet Jonah."[65] The sign of Jonah is Christ's cross, death, burial and resurrection. And again, declaring in another way the efficacy of the cross, he said, "When you have lifted up the Son of man, then you will know that I am he,"[66] which has this meaning: When you have crucified me and think you have overcome me, then, above all, you shall know my power.

For after the crucifixion, the city was destroyed. The Jewish state came to an end. They lost their political order and their freedom. Meanwhile the gospel flourished. The word was spread abroad to the ends of the earth, by both sea and land. Both the inhabited earth and the desert would thereafter perpetually proclaim its power. These are the things Christ pointed to which began to occur at the very time of the crucifixion. For indeed it was much more marvelous that these things should be accomplished when he was nailed to the cross than when he was walking on earth. The Gospel of Matthew, Homily 88.1.[67]

27:41-43 Let God Deliver Him Now

Let Him Come Down from the Cross. Jerome: "Let him come down from the cross, and we will believe in him." What a deceitful promise! Which is greater: to come down from the cross while still alive or to rise from the tomb while dead? He rose, and you do not believe. Therefore, even if he came down from the cross,

---

[64]PG 58:771; NPNF 1 10:517. [65]Mt 12:39. [66]Jn 8:28. [67]PG 58:775; NPNF 1 10:520.

you would not believe. Further, it seems to me that this would usher in the evil spirits. As soon as the Lord was crucified, they sensed the power of the cross and realized their own strength was broken. They were acting in this way to get him to come down from the cross. But the Lord, knowing the snares of his adversaries, remained on the cross that he may destroy the devil. COMMENTARY ON MATTHEW 4.27.42.[68]

HE CANNOT SAVE HIMSELF. ORIGEN: "So also [as others were passing along and blaspheming him] the chief priests and the scribes" were passing along. Thwarted by his power and authority, they said to him, "He saved others; he cannot save himself." In other words, they did not believe that he who was able to save others was much more able to save himself. They promised that they would "believe in" him as the king of Israel if they saw him "come down from the cross." But he had no mind to do anything unworthy of himself out of revenge or to do what they considered beyond belief and extraordinary. COMMENTARY ON MATTHEW 132.[69]

---

[68]CCL 77:272. [69]GCS 38.2:270.

27:44-56 THE DEATH OF JESUS

[44]And the robbers who were crucified with him also reviled him in the same way.

[45]Now from the sixth hour there was darkness over all the land[m] until the ninth hour. [46]And about the ninth hour Jesus cried with a loud voice, "Eli, Eli, lama sabach-thani?" that is, "My God, my God, why hast thou forsaken me?" [47]And some of the bystanders hearing it said, "This man is calling Elijah." [48]And one of them at once ran and took a sponge, filled it with vinegar, and put it on a reed, and gave it to him to drink. [49]But the others said, "Wait, let us see whether Elijah will come to save him."[n] [50]And Jesus cried again with a loud voice and yielded up his spirit.

[51]And behold, the curtain of the temple was torn in two, from top to bottom; and the earth shook, and the rocks were split; [52]the tombs also were opened, and many bodies of the saints who had fallen asleep were raised, [53]and coming out of the tombs after his resurrection they went into the holy city and appeared to many. [54]When the centurion and those who were with him, keeping watch over Jesus, saw the earthquake and what took place, they were filled with awe, and said, "Truly this was the Son[x] of God!"

[55]There were also many women there, looking on from afar, who had followed Jesus from Galilee, ministering to him; [56]among whom were Mary Magdalene, and Mary the mother of James and Joseph, and the mother of the sons of Zebedee.

m Or earth   n Other ancient authorities insert And another took a spear and pierced his side, and out came water and blood   x Or a son

---

OVERVIEW: At first each thief blasphemed. But after the sun had fled, the earth shook, rocks split apart and darkness fell, one of the thieves believed in Jesus and recanted his initial denial by a subsequent confession (ORIGEN, JEROME). The light of the world held back its beams so that the Lord would not be seen hanging (JEROME). To his last breath Jesus honored God as his Father. He cried out on the cross in the voice of Scripture. He turned even their wickedness to use for our salvation (CHRYSOSTOM). Those who attribute to the lips of Christ doctrines that are alien to the truth turn the metaphor of the sponge around: they fill the sponge with vinegar, place it on a reed and drink it themselves (ORIGEN). By his own power Jesus laid down his life (CHRYSOSTOM). To cry out with a loud voice and give up the spirit, which is equivalent to committing the spirit to the hand of God, is reserved only for the saints who, like Christ himself, have prepared themselves for God through good works (ORIGEN).

The earth could not hold this dead man. Rocks were split, for the Word of God and the power of his eternal goodness rushed in, penetrating every stronghold and principality. Graves were opened, for the gates of death had been unlocked (HILARY OF POITIERS). In the Passion of the Lord the outer curtain was torn from the top, which represents the beginning of the world, to the bottom, representing the end of the world. Thus by the tearing of the curtain the mysteries that with good reason had been hidden until the coming of Christ were being disclosed (ORIGEN). Certain women had followed him, ministering to him wherever he went. They were present even amid these dangers. These women were first to express compassion toward Jesus in his death and burial. The sex that was most disparaged was first to enjoy the sight of his resurrected blessings. Even when the disciples had fled in the darkness, these women were still present (CHRYSOSTOM).

27:44 The Robbers Jeer

ONE CONVERTED. ORIGEN: It is appropriate that both thieves be understood to have blasphemed the Lord at first. Afterwards, however,

one of them converted and believed because of the wonders he heard performed by the Lord and also, perhaps, because he saw miraculous changes in the heavens and the falling of an untimely darkness. COMMENTARY ON MATTHEW 133.[1]

MOCKED IN THE SAME WAY. JEROME: Here, through a figure of speech called syllepsis,[2] instead of only one thief, both are described as having mocked Jesus. According to Luke, however, after one thief blasphemed, the other thief confessed his faith and rebuked the first.[3] The Gospels do not disagree with each other. At first each thief blasphemed. But after the sun had fled, the earth shook, rocks split apart and darkness fell, one of the thieves believed in Jesus and recanted his initial denial by a subsequent confession. Along with the two thieves each crowd of both the Gentiles and the Jews at first mocked the Lord. COMMENTARY ON MATTHEW 4.27.44.[4]

27:45 Darkness on All the Land

DARKNESS FELL. ORIGEN: It is my opinion that just as the other signs which accompanied Christ's Passion were performed only in Jerusalem, so also the darkness which covered the land until the ninth hour occurred only in Judea. For in Jerusalem alone was the veil of the temple rent asunder and the earth shook and rocks split apart and graves opened.[5] . . . By the power of Christ, however, darkness fell upon all the land of Judea for three hours, but the light which illumines every church of God in Christ shone upon the rest of the land. Although darkness fell upon Judea until the ninth hour, it is clear that the light shone on it again, "until the full number of Gentiles come in, and so all Israel will be

---

[1]GCS 38.2:271. [2]Resorting to the trope of syllepsis (a grammatical construction used to perform two syntactic functions such as a free agreement between two elements of a phrase), Jerome explains the divergence of Matthew from Luke. [3]Lk 23:39-40. [4]CCL 77:272-73. Here, as is typical, Jerome follows and expands upon Origen. [5]Mt 27:51-52.

saved."[6] The fact that darkness fell upon the land of Judea for three hours demonstrates that it was because of its sins that Judea was deprived of the light of three moments, that is, the light of God the Father, the splendor of Christ and the illumination of the Holy Spirit. COMMENTARY ON MATTHEW 134.[7]

ALL THE LAND. ORIGEN: Certain believers, wishing to offer some defense of the gospel in a few brief words, have said that if no new miracle had been performed at the time of Christ's Passion but everything happened in the normal manner,[8] then it would also have to be believed that the eclipse of the sun occurred as usual. Since it is agreed, however, that other prodigies which happened at that time were not customary events but new and wondrous (for the veil of the temple was torn in two from top to bottom and the earth shook and rocks were split apart and graves were opened and many bodies of the saints rose from the dead),[9] it follows that neither did the eclipse of the sun happen as it normally does. COMMENTARY ON MATTHEW 134.[10]

FROM THE SIXTH HOUR. JEROME: Those who write against the Gospels[11] suppose that it is out of ignorance that the disciples of Christ have interpreted the eclipse of the sun (a phenomenon which usually happens at certain, established times) in accordance with the resurrection of the Lord, whereas an eclipse of the sun normally occurs only at the rising of a new moon. Now there is no doubt that at the time of the Passover the moon was full.[12] Lest we believe that the shadow of the earth or the movement of the moon's orb across the sun had produced a brief twilight, a duration of three hours is specified in order to preclude all other explanations. I am persuaded that this happened in fulfillment of the prophecies: "The sun will set at noon, and the light in the day will become dark over the earth,"[13] and in another place, "The sun set when it was still the middle of the day."[14] And it seems quite clear to me that

the light of the world (this is a greater heavenly body) had held back its beams so that neither would the Lord be seen hanging nor would the wicked blasphemers take any delight while the sun was still shining. COMMENTARY ON MATTHEW 4.27.45.[15]

REPORT OF AN ECLIPSE. APOLLINARIS: Now a certain Phlegon,[16] a philosopher among the Greeks, recollects this darkness as an incredible occurrence in the fourteenth [night] of the moon, when an eclipse should not have appeared . . . for eclipses occur at the time when these two stars [the sun and the moon] draw near to one another. An eclipse of the sun happens at the conjunction of the sun and the moon as it runs into its way. This is not the time of the full moon, when the sun is diametrically opposed to the moon. But the eclipse occurred as creation mourned over what had happened, signifying that the drunken behavior of the Jews was linked to a darkened mind. The sunshine of the intellect had departed from them. For if they had been considering him—for that darkness found its source in the wrathful one and was evidence of what was about to overtake the murderers. FRAGMENT 142.[17]

27:46 Why Have You Forsaken Me?

THE CRY IN THE NINTH HOUR. HILARY OF POITIERS: Night following day marks a division of times. Thus is fulfilled the triad of days and nights, and the hidden mystery of God's work is perceived with astonishment by all of creation.

---

[6]Rom 11:25-26. [7]GCS 38.2:274-75, 278. [8]These were pagans who maintained on the basis of astronomical calculations that at the time of Jesus' death no eclipse could have occurred. [9]Mt 27:51-52. [10]GCS 38.2:272-73. [11]Cf. p. 236 n. 6. [12]Easter was celebrated on the fourteenth of Nisan, according to the lunar calendar in use then among the Jews. On that day the moon was full. [13]Amos 8:9. [14]Jer 15:9. [15]CCL 77:273-74. [16]Phlegon of Tralles wrote a work on various marvels, long-lived people and the Olympics at the time of Hadrian (mid-second century), of which only a very few fragments are extant. He displayed a certain curiosity about the Christian religion. [17]MKGK 50-51.

The cry to God in truth is the voice of a body departing, having declared the separation of the Word of God from itself. He wonders why he is being abandoned when he exclaims, "God, my God, why have you forsaken me?" But he was forsaken because his humanity had to pass even through death. It must be considered carefully that he gave up the spirit with a loud cry after he drank from the sponge full of vinegar offered to him on a reed.[18] Wine is the honor and power of immortality, but it soured through the fault of the vessel or through carelessness. Therefore, since this wine had soured in Adam, he himself accepted it and drank from the nations. The fact that it was offered to him to drink from a sponge on a reed signifies that he took from the bodies of the Gentiles the sins which had ruined eternity and transferred our sins to himself, uniting them to his immortality. On Matthew 33.6.[19]

WHO IS FORSAKEN? ORIGEN: Certain people, in an outward display of piety for Jesus, because they are unable to explain how Christ could be forsaken by God, believe that this saying from the cross is true only as an expression of his humility. We, however, who know that he who was "in the form of God"[20] descended from the greatness of his stature and emptied himself, "taking the form of a servant"[21] according to the will of the one who sent him, understand that he was indeed forsaken by the Father inasmuch as he who was the form of the invisible God and the image of the Father "took the form of a servant." He was forsaken for people so that he might shoulder so great a work and come "even to death" and "the death of the cross,"[22] a work which seems thoroughly shameful to most people. For it was the height of his abandonment when they crucified him and placed above his head the disdainful inscription "This is Jesus, king of the Jews."[23] It was the height of his abandonment when they crucified him with thieves and when "those who passed by blasphemed him and wagged their heads."[24] The chief priests and scribes said, "He saved others but cannot save

himself."[25] At that time "even the thieves reviled him" on the cross.[26] Clearly then you will be able to understand the saying "Why have you forsaken me?" when you compare the glory Christ had in the presence of the Father with the contempt he sustained on the cross, for his throne was "like the sun in the presence of God and like the moon established forever; and he was his faithful witness in heaven."[27] Afterwards, he also added with regard to those reasons for which he said "why have you forsaken me?" "But now you have cast off and rejected, you are full of wrath against your anointed. You have renounced the covenant of your servant, you have defiled his crown in the dust."[28] COMMENTARY ON MATTHEW 135.[29]

TESTIMONY FROM THE PSALM. JEROME: Jesus appropriated the beginning of the twenty-first psalm.[30] That which is read in the middle of the verse,[31] "Look at me," is superfluous. For in the Hebrew it reads, "My God, my God, why have you forsaken me?" They are impious therefore who say that the psalm is written in the person of David or Esther or Mordecai, since the Evangelists understand that other testimony taken from the same psalm is to be applied to the Savior, as for example, "they divided my garments and cast lots for my clothing" and "they pierced my hands and my feet."[32] COMMENTARY ON MATTHEW 4.27.46.[33]

STILL YOU ARE MY GOD. CHRYSOSTOM: Why does he speak this way, crying out, "Eli, Eli, lama sabach-thani?" That they might see that to his last breath he honors God as his Father and is

---

[18]Mt 27:48, 50. [19]SC 258:254. [20]Phil 2:6. [21]Phil 2:7. [22]Phil 2:8. [23]Mt 27:37. [24]Mt 27:39. [25]Mt 27:42. [26]Mt 27:44. [27]Ps 89:36-37 (88:37-38 LXX). [28]Ps 89:38-39 (88:39-40 LXX). [29]GCS 38.2:279. [30]Ps 22:1 (21:1 LXX). Jerome means that Jesus willingly applied the beginning of the psalm to himself with the exception of "look at me," the intermediate phrase between "My God, my God" and "why have you abandoned me?" He therefore contests the Jewish interpretation, which in disagreement with the Christians denied the messianic nature of the psalm. [31]See LXX. [32]Ps 22:18, 16 (21:19, 17 LXX). [33]CCL 77:274.

no adversary of God. He spoke with the voice of Scripture, uttering a cry from the psalm.[34] Thus even to his last hour he is found bearing witness to the sacred text. He offers this prophetic cry in Hebrew, so as to be plain and intelligible to them, and by all things Jesus shows how he is of one mind with the Father who had begotten him. THE GOSPEL OF MATTHEW, HOMILY 88.1.[35]

27:47-49 Will Elijah Save Him?

CALLING ELIJAH. CHRYSOSTOM: But observe here also their wantonness, intemperance and folly. They thought, it is said, that it was Elijah whom he called. Right away they gave him vinegar to drink. But another came to him and "pierced his side with a spear."[36] Who could be more lawless, who more brutal, than these men? How could they have carried their madness to so great a length, offering insult at last even to a dead body? But note well how he turned even their evil deeds to use for our salvation. For after the blow the fountains of our salvation gushed forth. THE GOSPEL OF MATTHEW, HOMILY 88.1.[37]

THE SPONGE FILLED WITH VINEGAR. ORIGEN: One can use the spiritual sense of this text profitably against those who write malicious things against Christ.[38] Concerning them Isaiah says, "Woe to those who write wickedness."[39] (I say that they who publish such things are speaking "iniquity in the highest."[40]) Some will use this text with a view toward those who, constructing a narrative gathered from pagan tongues, fill the sponge not with the word that is drinkable or with the wine which "gladdens the heart"[41] or with the water of restoration[42] but, on the contrary, with poisonous, undrinkable, unwise vinegar. They place this sponge on the reed of their writing and (as far as they are able) seem to offer a swallow of these diatribes for Jesus to drink. Others give Jesus "to drink of wine mixed with gall," which Jesus the Son of God does not want. Others offer him vinegar instead of wine.

Others offer him "wine mixed with gall" when they, having understood the doctrine of the church, live unworthily of it. Those who attribute to the lips of Christ doctrines that are alien to the truth turn the metaphor around. They fill the sponge with vinegar, place it on a reed and drink it themselves. COMMENTARY ON MATTHEW 137.[43]

27:50 Jesus Breathed His Last

HE GIVES UP HIS SPIRIT. ORIGEN: If giving up the spirit or (according to John) handing over the spirit were simply tantamount to dying, it would be easy to understand the passage which states "he gave up his spirit." However, since discerning minds define death to be nothing other than the separation of the soul from the body, we can see that yielding up one's spirit is something more than simply dying physically. It is quite something else to "cry out with a loud voice and give up the spirit" (as in Matthew) or to commit one's spirit to the hand of God (as in Luke)[44] or to bow one's head and hand over his spirit (as in John).[45] It is for all people to die, including the evil, because the soul of every person, including the unrighteous, will be separated from the body.

But to cry out with a loud voice and give up the spirit, which is equivalent to committing the spirit to the hand of God, or to bow the head and hand over the spirit is reserved only for the saints who, like Christ himself, have prepared themselves for God through good works so that when they leave this world they might with confidence commit themselves to the hand of God, or hand over their spirits.

If therefore we now understand what it means to cry out with a loud voice and thus to give up the spirit, that is, to commit oneself to

---

[34]Ps 22:1 (21:2 LXX). [35]PG 58:776; NPNF 1 10:521. [36]Jn 19:34. [37]PG 58:776; NPNF 1 10:521. [38]Cf. p. 236 n. 6. [39]Is 10:1. [40]Ps 73:8 (72:8 LXX). [41]Ps 104:15 (103:15 LXX). [42]Ps 23:2 (22:2 LXX). [43]GCS 38.2:281-82. [44]Lk 23:46. [45]Jn 19:30.

the hand of God (as we have explained above in accordance with Luke's Gospel), and if we understand what it means to bow the head and hand over the spirit, let us hasten to guard the conduct of our lives so that, upon our deaths, we also, like Jesus, might be able to cry out with a loud voice and thus to give up our spirit to the Father. COMMENTARY ON MATTHEW 138.[46]

HE LAID DOWN HIS LIFE. CHRYSOSTOM: "When Jesus had cried out with a loud voice, he yielded up the spirit." This refers to what he had earlier said: "I have power to lay down my life, and I have power to take it again," and "I lay it down of myself."[47] So for this cause he cried with the voice, that it might be shown that the act is done by his own power. THE GOSPEL OF MATTHEW, HOMILY 88.1.[48]

SOULS BEING RECEIVED IN HEAVEN. APOLLINARIS: This is also the beginning of the translation of souls into the heavens. For whatever souls follow Christ are translated. Stephen made this plain when he said, "Lord Jesus Christ, receive my spirit."[49] Paul also writes, "It is better to depart and be with Christ."[50] Such was not the case with those of ancient times. It was said concerning the dead that each was handed over "to his people."[51] This proceeding was below, as was the detention of souls. The Lord changes the direction of the journey from below to above by means of himself. FRAGMENT 143.[52]

27:51-52 The Temple Curtain Torn

THE CURTAIN TORN IN TWO. ORIGEN: Anyone who searches the Scriptures with some diligence will see that there were two curtains, an inner curtain which covered the Holy of Holies and another curtain exterior to either the tabernacle or the temple. These two curtains are figures of the holy tabernacle which the Father prepared from the beginning.[53] Of the two curtains, one "was torn into two parts from the top all the way to the bottom." This happened at the

time when Jesus "cried out with a loud voice and gave up his spirit."[54] Thereby the divine mystery was revealed that in the Passion of the Lord our Savior the outer curtain was torn from the top, which represents the beginning of the world, to the bottom, representing the end of the world. Thus by the tearing of the curtain the mysteries were disclosed, which with good reason had been hidden until the coming of Christ. Both the outer curtain and inner curtain would have been torn if it had not been the case that we still know only "in part"[55] and if it had not been the case that everything were already revealed to the beloved disciples of Christ who constitute his body. As it is, however, because we are being brought gradually to the knowledge of new things, only the outer curtain is "torn from top to bottom." But "when the perfect comes"[56] and the other things which now remain hidden are revealed, then the second curtain may also be removed. We will then see even the things which were hidden within the second curtain: the true ark of the covenant, the cherubim, the true mercy seat and the storehouse of manna in a golden bowl, and all these clearly[57]—and even things greater than these. All of this has been revealed through the law of Moses when God said to him, "Make everything according to their forms which were shown to you on the mountain."[58] COMMENTARY ON MATTHEW 138.[59]

THE TEMPLE VEIL TORN. HILARY OF POITIERS: Immediately thereafter the curtain of the temple was torn. After that the people were split into factions. The glory of the curtain along with the protection of its defending angel was taken away.[60] ON MATTHEW 33.7.[61]

---

[46]GCS 38.2:283-84. [47]Jn 10:18. [48]PG 58:776; NPNF 1 10:521. [49]Acts 7:59. [50]Phil 1:23. [51]Gen 25:8. [52]MKGK 51. [53]Origen refers to Exodus 25:9, 40, in which God tells Moses to set up the tent (a model of the future temple) after the shape of the celestial model shown to him on Mount Sinai. [54]Mt 27:50. [55]1 Cor 13:9. [56]1 Cor 13:10. [57]Heb 9:35. [58]Ex 25:40. [59]GCS 38.2:285-86. [60]This may be a reference to Ezekiel 10, wherein the glory of the Lord is carried away by the cherubim. [61]SC 258:256.

The Earth Shook. Origen: "And the earth shook," that is, all flesh trembled when the new word, the realities of the new covenant, the new song and all new heavenly things came upon them. This is what the prophet wrote concerning this very event: "All [namely, the disciples of Christ] who saw these things trembled and every one was afraid."[62] Commentary on Matthew 139.[63]

The Rocks Were Split. Jerome: The literal meaning of the great signs is undoubtedly that both heaven and earth and all things within them wished to acclaim their crucified Lord. It seems to me, however, that the trembling earth and other signs also represent a type of believers, namely, those who once were comparable to a graveyard but who, having abandoned the errors of their former ways and having softened their once stony hearts, have come to acknowledge the Creator. Commentary on Matthew 4.27.51.[64]

Graves Were Opened. Hilary of Poitiers: The earth shook. For the earth could not hold this dead man. Rocks were split, for the Word of God and the power of his eternal goodness rushed in, penetrating every stronghold and principality. Graves were opened, for the gates of death had been unlocked. And a number of the bodies of the saints who had fallen asleep arose. Dispelling the shadows of death and illuminating the darkness of hell, Christ destroyed the spoils of death itself at the resurrection of the saints, who saw him immediately. The centurion and the guards who witnessed this disturbance of the entire natural order confessed him to be the Son of God. On Matthew 23.7.[65]

27:53-54 Truly This Was the Son of God

Coming Out of the Tombs. Apollinaris: The raising up of the saints' bodies was announcing that the death of Christ was actually the cause of life. They certainly were not made visible prior to the Lord's resurrection, since it was necessary that the resurrection of the Savior first be made known. Then those raised through him were seen. It is plain that they have died again, having risen from the dead in order to be a sign. For it was not possible for only some of the firstborn from the dead to be raised to the life of the age to come, but the remainder [must be raised] in the same manner. Now Luke says that the crowd passing by "beat their breasts and went away."[66] Thus the divine superiority did not escape the notice of the Jews, either in the Passion itself or in the obscurity of the Savior. But habitual human forgetfulness held them fast, and the deceit of the teachers led many astray. Fragment 144.[67]

Truly the Son of God. Jerome: Another Gospel[68] demonstrates more clearly the cause of the centurion's astonishment after the shaking of the earth. It wasn't until after he had seen Christ give up the spirit that he said, "Truly this was the Son of God," for no one has the power to give up the spirit except he who is the Creator of souls. Here we can understand "soul" for "spirit" because the soul animates the body and makes it spiritual and because the spirit is the substance of the soul itself, as it is written: "You take away their spirits and they cease to be."[69] Commentary on Matthew 4.27.54.[70]

27:55-56 Many Women Had Followed Jesus

Many Women Were There. Chrysostom: Certain women were notably present as these things occurred. They were most inclined to feel for him, to grieve over his sufferings. Note how great is their constancy. They had followed him, ministering to him wherever he went. They were present even to the time of the dangers. They had seen all these events—how he wept,

---

[62]Ps 64:9 (63:9 LXX). [63]GCS 38.2:286. [64]CCL 77:275. [65]SC 258:256. [66]Lk 23:48. [67]MKGK 51. [68]Lk 23:47. [69]Ps 104:29 (103:29 LXX). [70]CCL 77:276.

how he yielded up his spirit, how the rocks were split, and all the rest.

These women were first to be attentive to Jesus at his death and burial. The sex most likely to be disparaged was first to enjoy the sight of his resurrected blessings. They most steadily showed their courage. Even when the disciples had fled in the darkness, these women were still present. Among these women was his mother. She is called Mary the mother of James.[71] They lamented over the things that had occurred. They beat their breasts. Meanwhile the religious leaders were glorying in those very things for which the others were grieving, neither moved by pity nor checked by fear. Indeed, the things that had been done showed their great wrath. These women were there all along, to behold the darkness over the land, the split rocks, the veil of the temple torn, the shaking of the earth. THE GOSPEL OF MATTHEW, HOMILY 88.2.[72]

THE WOMEN HAD MINISTERED TO HIM. JEROME: Women attended to the food and clothing for their masters from their own possessions. This was according to Jewish custom. This practice did not proceed from Gentile law and even could have been a scandal among the Gentiles. Paul himself mentions that he was unable to continue this custom: "Can it really be said that we do not have the ability to lead the sisters around the women just as the other apostles also do?"[73] These women waited on the Lord out of

their own resources. He reaped from their physical support as they benefited from his spiritual blessing. It was not because the Lord of all creatures was out of necessity looking for food but rather that he might present a model of teaching and discipleship for them. Note carefully, though, what sort of attendants he had: Mary Magdalene from whom he cast out seven demons. Mary the mother of James and Joseph, and her own aunt, the sister of Mary, the mother of the Lord. The mother of Zebedee's sons, a woman who had sought to care for her children in the kingdom. And there were other women present. COMMENTARY ON MATTHEW 4.27.55.[74]

WOMEN BEATIFIED. ORIGEN: Isaiah is said to have prophesied concerning these women when he wrote, "Women are coming to the spectacle, for this is not a wise people."[75] He calls women who had been distant and were looking upon Jesus from afar. He calls them to the Word, that they might abandon a foolish, forsaken people and come to the new covenant. I consider these women blessed who were elevated to beatitude by their vision of the Word and by the bodily death of Jesus; for everything in Christ, if seen truly, beatifies the beholder. COMMENTARY ON MATTHEW 141.[76]

---

[71]Chrysostom wrongly identifies Mary mother of James and Joseph (Mt 27:56) with the mother of Jesus. [72]PG 58:777-78; NPNF 1 10:522. [73]1 Cor 9:5. [74]CCL 77:277. [75]Is 27:11. [76]GCS 38.2:293.

27:57-66 THE BURIAL OF JESUS

[57]*When it was evening, there came a rich man from Arimathea, named Joseph, who also was a disciple of Jesus.* [58]*He went to Pilate and asked for the body of Jesus. Then Pilate ordered it to be given to him.* [59]*And Joseph took the body, and wrapped it in a clean linen shroud,* [60]*and laid it in his own new tomb, which he had hewn in the rock; and he rolled a great stone to the door of*

the tomb, and departed. ^{61}Mary Magdalene and the other Mary were there, sitting opposite the sepulchre.

^{62}Next day, that is, after the day of Preparation, the chief priests and the Pharisees gathered before Pilate ^{63}and said, "Sir, we remember how that imposter said, while he was still alive, 'After three days I will rise again.' ^{64}Therefore order the sepulchre to be made secure until the third day, lest his disciples go and steal him away, and tell the people, 'He has risen from the dead,' and the last fraud will be worse than the first." ^{65}Pilate said to them, "You have a guard^o of soldiers; go, make it as secure as you can."^{p} ^{66}So they went and made the sepulchre secure by sealing the stone and setting a guard.

o Or *Take a guard*   p Greek *know*

OVERVIEW: Joseph of Arimathea exposed himself to death, taking upon him the enmity of all, due to his affection for Jesus. He not only dared to ask for the body but also did not desist until he obtained it. Let us men imitate the noble spirit and courage of the women who were near to Jesus in his time of trial! Even as they had ministered to him when he was alive, now they exposed their lives to danger when he was dead. Since the sepulcher was sealed, there could be no unfair dealing. So then the proof of Jesus' resurrection has become incontrovertible precisely by what his enemies themselves have secured (CHRYSOSTOM). The Gospel writer speaks of Joseph's wealth not to boast but to explain how Joseph was able to obtain the body of Jesus. The tomb in which he was placed could represent the virgin womb of Mary (JEROME). Both the linen in which the body of Jesus was wrapped and the new tomb in which he was laid were preserved by the power of the body of Jesus (ORIGEN). The linen in which Christ was wrapped represents the church, which was expanded to include the Gentiles in the revelation given to Peter where clean and unclean animals are lowered before him on a linen sheet (HILARY OF POITIERS).

27:57-60 Joseph of Arimathea Buries Jesus

JOSEPH TOOK THE BODY TO HIS OWN NEW TOMB. CHRYSOSTOM: This was Joseph of Arimathea, who had been hiding his discipleship up to this time. Now, however, he had become very bold after the death of Christ. Joseph was not an obscure person. He was highly visible, a member of the council and highly distinguished. From this it becomes clear that he was a man of special courage. For he exposed himself to death, taking upon him the enmity of all by his affection for Jesus. He not only dared to ask for the body, but he did not desist until he obtained it. He did more than receive it and bury it in a splendid manner. He even laid it in his own new tomb. Joseph thereby showed both his love and his courage. This did not occur randomly or without purpose. It occurred so that there should not be any unsupported suspicion that one had risen instead of another. THE GOSPEL OF MATTHEW, Homily 88.2.[1]

OBTAINING THE TOMB. JEROME: Joseph of Arimathea is referred to as a rich man not because the writer of the Gospel wanted to boast that very wealthy and noble men were disciples of Jesus but rather in order to show why he was able to obtain Jesus' body from Pilate. For the poor and obscure did not have the right to approach Pilate, the representative of Roman power, and obtain the body of the Crucified. In another Gospel, this same Joseph is called *bouleutēs*, which means "councilor" or "senator."[2]

---

[1]PG 58:778; NPNF 1 10:522.   [2]Mk 15:43; Lk 23:50.

Some think that the first psalm was composed with him in view: "Blessed is the one who does not walk in the counsel of the impious,"[3] and so on. Commentary on Matthew 4.27.57.[4]

The Clean Linen Shroud. Origen: "He wrapped it in a clean linen shroud and put it in a new tomb" where no one was buried, thus preserving the body of Jesus for its glorious resurrection. But I think that this shroud was much cleaner from the time it was used to cover Christ's body than it ever had been before. For the body of Jesus retained its own integrity, even in death, so that it cleansed everything it touched and renewed even the new tomb which had been cut from rock. Commentary on Matthew 143.[5]

The New Tomb. Jerome: We are able to discern from the spiritual sense of Scripture that the body of the Lord must not be covered in gold nor in jewels and silk but in pure linen. This may also mean, however, that the one who wrapped Jesus in clean linen is he who received him with a pure mind. . . . His body was placed in a new tomb lest it be imagined after the resurrection that one of the other interred bodies had arisen. The new tomb, however, may also signify Mary's virginal womb. The great stone was placed at the entrance to the tomb in order to show that it could not be opened without the help of several persons. Commentary on Matthew 4.27.59-60.[6]

The Acts of Joseph of Arimathea. Hilary of Poitiers: Joseph of Arimathea, having asked Pilate to return Jesus' body, wrapped it in a shroud, placed it in a new tomb carved out from a rock and rolled a stone in front of the entrance to the tomb. Although this may indeed be the order of events and although it was necessary to bury him who would rise from the dead, these deeds are nevertheless recounted individually because each of them is not without some importance. Joseph is called a disciple of the Lord because he was an image of the apostles, even though he was not numbered among the twelve apostles. It was he who wrapped the Lord's body in a clean linen shroud; in this same linen we find all kinds of animals descending to Peter from heaven.[7] It is perhaps not too extravagant to understand from this parallel that the church is buried with Christ under the name of the linen shroud.[8] Just as in the linen, so also in the confession of the church are gathered the full diversity of living beings, both pure and impure. The body of the Lord, therefore, through the teaching of the apostles, is laid to rest in the empty tomb newly cut from a rock. In other words, their teaching introduced Christ into the hardness of the Gentile heart, which was uncut, empty and previously impervious to the fear of God. And because he is the only one who should penetrate our hearts, a stone was rolled over the entrance to the tomb, so that just as no one previous to him had been introduced as the author of divine knowledge, neither would anyone be brought in after him. On Matthew 33.8.[9]

The Great Stone. Origen: We say, therefore (lest this passage be understood crudely), that he who said "we were buried with Christ through baptism" and we have risen with him[10] is himself buried after Christ and with Christ in the new, spiritual tomb cut from rock. Furthermore, all who are buried with Christ in baptism, so that they may also rise with him from the new tomb, belong to the "firstborn from the dead who holds primacy in all things."[11] Joseph did not roll many stones over the entrance to the tomb but only one "great" stone. [This stone] was greater than the power of those who lay in wait but not greater than the power of the

[3]Ps 1:1. [4]CCL 77:277-78. [5]GCS 38.2:296. [6]CCL 77:278. [7]The sheet full of animals of all sorts that is shown to Peter in a vision (Acts 10:11-12) symbolizes, according to Hilary, the church that takes into itself people of all races and conditions. By analogy, the sheet that wraps Jesus is a symbol of the church. [8]Rom 6:4; Col 2:12. [9]SC 258:256-58. [10]Rom 6:4; Col 2:12. [11]Col 1:18.

angels who descended from heaven and removed the stone and sat on it.[12] For all things which surround the body of Jesus are thereby clean and new and not simply "great" but surpassingly great.[13] COMMENTARY ON MATTHEW 143.[14]

27:61 Mary Magdalene and the Other Mary

THE NOBLE SPIRIT OF THE WOMEN. CHRYSOSTOM: For what purpose do the two Marys wait beside the sepulcher? As yet they did not fully know his greatness. They had brought ointments. They were waiting at the tomb, so that if the madness of the civil authorities should relax, they might go and care for the body. Do you see these women's courage? See their depth of affection? See their noble spirit in providing? See their noble spirit even to death?

Let us men imitate these women! Let us not forsake Jesus in times of trial! These women exposed their lives so much for him even when he was dead, even as they had spent so much for him when he was alive. But we men, I repeat, neither feed him when hungry nor clothe him when naked. Seeing him begging, we pass him by. And yet if we might really behold him in the neighbor, we would divest ourselves of all our goods. THE GOSPEL OF MATTHEW, HOMILY 88.2-3.[15]

27:62-63 The Priests and the Pharisees Go to Pilate

WE REMEMBER WHAT THE IMPOSTOR SAID. CHRYSOSTOM: But note carefully the disciples' love of truth. They do not conceal from their reader what was said by their enemies. They call Jesus an impostor. Note the contrast between the savagery of the authorities and the simple and truthful disposition of the disciples. Not even at his death did the authorities surrender their anger. THE GOSPEL OF MATTHEW, HOMILY 89.1.[16]

I WILL RISE AGAIN. CHRYSOSTOM: But is it

worthwhile to inquire concerning that point also where he said, "After three days I rise again"? His detractors clearly understood this saying. Even if they did not grasp the metaphor of Jonah, they remembered this.[17] THE GOSPEL OF MATTHEW, HOMILY 89.1.[18]

27:64-66 Securing the Tomb

THE SECURED SEPULCHER PROVES THE RESURRECTION. CHRYSOSTOM: Everywhere deceit recoils upon itself and against its will supports the truth. Observe: It was necessary to believe that he died, and that he rose again, and that he was buried and that all these things were brought to pass by his enemies. Note, at any rate, these words bearing witness to every one of these facts. "We remember that that deceiver said, when he was yet alive" (he was therefore now dead), "'After three days I rise again.' Command therefore that the sepulcher be sealed" (he was therefore buried), "lest his disciples come and steal him away." Since the sepulcher was sealed, there could be no funny business. So then the proof of his resurrection has become incontrovertible by what they themselves have put forward. For because the tomb was sealed, there was no deceitfulness at work. But if there was no sleight of hand and the sepulcher was found empty, it is clear that he has risen, plainly and incontrovertibly. Do you see how even against their will his enemies contend for the proof of the truth? THE GOSPEL OF MATTHEW, HOMILY 89.1.[19]

MAKE IT AS SECURE AS YOU CAN. CHRYSOSTOM: What then does Pilate reply? "You have a

---

[12]Mt 28:2. [13]Mk 16:4. [14]GCS 38.2:296-97. [15]PG 58:778; NPNF 1 10:522. [16]PG 58:781; NPNF 1 10:525. [17]Chrysostom's affirmation is surprising at first sight, given that in Matthew 16:21 Jesus preannounces his resurrection after three days. It is explained with reference to *saphōs* ("openly, publicly"). In fact, Jesus had on other occasions spoken of his resurrection, addressing only his disciples, and only with regard to Jonah had he publicly preannounced the resurrection (Mt 12:40). [18]PG 58:781; NPNF 1 10:525. [19]PG 58:781; NPNF 1 10:525.

guard of soldiers; go, make it as secure as you can." Then what? "So they went and made the sepulcher secure by sealing the stone and setting a guard." Pilate takes every precaution to ensure the seal, so that even the soldiers could not commit fraud. His orders say, "Seal it as secure as you can, so that even you may not have it in your power to blame others." For if the soldiers were not checked by their sealing, someone might have claimed that the soldiers themselves could have given up the body to be stolen. Although this would have been highly improbable, yet nevertheless, since they had earlier cast aside shame, so in this case they might have done so. Thus even this possibility was cut off, which might have otherwise given the disciples opportunity to feign the history concerning his resurrection. But now having themselves made it sure, they are not able to say so much as this. THE GOSPEL OF MATTHEW, HOMILY 89.1.[20]

HISTORICAL EVIDENCE ENHANCED. JEROME: It would not have sufficed for the chief priests, scribes and Pharisees to have crucified the Lord our Savior if they had not also guarded the tomb, called in the military, sealed the entrance and, as far as they were able, resisted the resurrection. Their concern for these details serves only to advance our faith; the greater their precautionary care, the more fully is revealed the power of the resurrection. Thus he was buried in a new tomb cut from rock. If the tomb had been constructed from a mound of stones, it could have been said that his body was excavated from underneath the stones and secretly removed. That he had to be buried in a sepulcher is also shown by the prophecy which says, "He will dwell in a deep cave cut from the strongest rock," and again, two verses further: "You will see the king in his glory."[21] COMMENTARY ON MATTHEW 4.27.64.[22]

I WILL RAISE IT UP. ORIGEN: It is reasonable to ask the chief priests who approached Pilate the following line of questions. Tell us, for what purpose do you think Jesus said, "Destroy this temple and in three days I will raise it up"?[23] Was he speaking about the death and resurrection "of his body"[24] or about the destruction and reconstruction of the temple? If you thought that he was speaking of his resurrection, why did you testify against him because he had said, "I am able to destroy this temple and in three days to rebuild it"?[25] If, however, you thought that he was speaking of the temple, as you have testified, then how do you know that he meant "after three days" he would be raised from the dead? See then how Christ exposes their impiety with their own words.[26] Through their words, the chief priests condemn their own testimony, for understanding truly that Christ was speaking of his resurrection, they deliberately twisted his meaning to make it seem like he was speaking of the destruction and reconstruction of that inanimate temple. COMMENTARY ON MATTHEW 145.[27]

THAT IMPOSTER. ORIGEN: What do you say, chief priest? Do you really think that Christ said to his men "after three days I will rise again"[28] and then secretly commanded them to steal his body during the night and to tell everyone that he had risen from the dead after three days?[29] Yet it is manifestly incredible that after giving such great moral instruction to all peoples and after demonstrating such great power throughout all of Judea, he would then turn and deceive his disciples. Even they would find fault with

---

[20]PG 58:781-82; NPNF 1 10:525. [21]Is 33:16-17. [22]CCL 77:279. [23]Jn 2:19. [24]Jn 2:21. [25]Mt 26:61. [26]Origen recognizes a contradiction in the actions of the chief priests in that they first used the words of Jesus regarding the destruction and rebuilding of the temple to accuse and condemn him without taking into account that Jesus, speaking of the temple, had alluded to his death and resurrection, and then employed precisely this meaning of his words with Pilate. One could object that, as we have seen on p. 301, n. 17, the priests could have drawn Jesus' prophecy regarding his resurrection from his words about Jonah rather than those of the temple. [27]GCS 38.2:297-98. [28]Mk 8:31. [29]This consideration of Origen also appears ill-fitted because the priests warned Pilate that Jesus' body may be stolen by the disciples without instruction from Jesus.

their commander and therefore refuse to do his bidding, most especially in view of the danger which would have threatened them from the people if they had confessed the man just crucified to be both their teacher and the Messiah. But if it is hardly believable for him to have said such a thing to his disciples, see if it is not more logical to believe that just as he performed great miracles and predicted that his gospel would be preached "to the ends of the earth,"[30] that his disciples "would stand before rulers and kings"[31]

and that "Jerusalem would be destroyed by an army,"[32] so also did he predict his resurrection when he said "destroy this temple and in three days I will raise it up." Indeed, it was for that reason that the chief priests and Pharisees said to Pilate, "That imposter said, while he was still alive, 'after three days I will rise again.'"[33] COMMENTARY ON MATTHEW 145.[34]

[30]Mt 26:13. [31]Mk 13:9. [32]Lk 21:20, 24. [33]Mt 27:63. [34]GCS 38.2:298.

28:1-10 THE RESURRECTION

[1]*Now after the sabbath, toward the dawn of the first day of the week, Mary Magdalene and the other Mary went to see the sepulchre. [2]And behold, there was a great earthquake; for an angel of the Lord descended from heaven and came and rolled back the stone, and sat upon it. [3]His appearance was like lightning, and his raiment white as snow. [4]And for fear of him the guards trembled and became like dead men. [5]But the angel said to the women, "Do not be afraid; for I know that you seek Jesus who was crucified. [6]He is not here; for he has risen, as he said. Come, see the place where he[q] lay. [7]Then go quickly and tell his disciples that he has risen from the dead, and behold, he is going before you to Galilee; there you will see him. Lo, I have told you." [8]So they departed quickly from the tomb with fear and great joy, and ran to tell his disciples. [9]And behold, Jesus met them and said, "Hail!" And they came up and took hold of his feet and worshiped him. [10]Then Jesus said to them, "Do not be afraid; go and tell my brethren to go to Galilee, and there they will see me."*

q Other ancient authorities read *the Lord*

OVERVIEW: The two women precede the apostles in their ministry to the Lord in his death and resurrection. It is significant that this occurred on the first day of the week (PETER CHRYSOLOGUS). The angel came to roll back the stone, to bear witness to the women of the resurrection. The angel delivers the women from fear and announces to them the resurrection of the one who was crucified, pointing to the evidence of the empty tomb (CHRYSOSTOM). The

Lord rises in his same body, his wounds bearing witness to the resurrection (PETER CHRYSOLOGUS). The women were first to see and gladly declare not only what had been said to them but also what they had seen (CHRYSOSTOM). When Jesus meets the women, he binds them by the covenant of the bridegroom, not by the right of the ruler (PETER CHRYSOLOGUS). As they take hold of his feet, they thereby received by his touch an irrefutable proof of his resurrection. Just as the women embraced him then, so we too can embrace the risen Lord (CHRYSOSTOM).

28:1 The Dawn of the First Day

RESOLVING THE CHRONOLOGY OF THE WOMEN'S VISIT. AUGUSTINE: One must not dismiss lightly the question concerning the exact hour at which the women came to the tomb. For if Matthew says, "In the evening of the sabbath, at the dawn of the first day of the week, Mary Madgalene and other Mary came to see the tomb," what then does it mean that Mark says, "And early in the morning on the first day of the week, they came to the tomb at the rising of the sun"?[1] The other two Gospels, Luke and John, do not disagree with Mark; Luke says "early in the morning,"[2] and John says "in the morning when it was still dark."[3] Both statements are consistent with Mark's declaration that it was "early in the morning at the rising of the sun," that is, when the heavens in the east were brightening. But this doesn't occur except when the sun is very close to rising, a phenomenon which customarily is called the dawn. Therefore Mark does not oppose John, who says "when it was still dark," for as day is breaking the remaining shadows of darkness diminish only in proportion to the sun's rising. And Luke's phrase, "early in the morning," need not be understood to imply that the sun had already appeared above the horizon but rather is the kind of expression we normally use when we want to signify that something must be done earlier. For when we say "in the morning," lest we are understood to mean that the sun is already visible, we usually add "very early," so that we will be understood to refer to the dawn.

Thus it is said "in the evening of the sabbath," as if he had said "in the night of the sabbath," that is, in the night which follows the day of the sabbath. Matthew's words themselves, however, are sufficient, for he says, "In the evening of the sabbath, at the dawn on the first day of the

week." This would be impossible if we understood "in the evening" to signify only the first part of the night. For it is not the beginning of the night which "dawns on the first day of the week" but the night which begins to be terminated by the coming of the light. Now the end of the first part of the night is the beginning of the second part, but the end of the whole night is the light. Thus we cannot say that the evening is "at the dawn of the first day of the week" unless by "evening" we intend "night," which the light brings to an end. In addition, it is divine Scripture's customary way of distinguishing the whole from the part.[4] Therefore by saying "evening" it signifies the whole night, the end of which is the dawn. Thus the women came to the tomb at dawn, and therefore they came at night, which is signified in Scripture by the designation of evening. For, as I have said, the whole night is included under that name. Therefore, in whatever part of the night they may have come, they came at night; even if they came at the very end of the night, the fact remains without a doubt that they came at night. HARMONY OF THE GOSPELS 3.65.[5]

TOWARD THE DAWN. PETER CHRYSOLOGUS: "In the evening toward the dawn." Behold, with the Lord's resurrection the evening does not grow dark, it becomes light. What was normally the beginning of night now becomes the break of day. "In the evening of the sabbath toward the dawn of the first day of the week." Even as mortality is transformed into immortality, corruption into incorruption and flesh into the Word of God, the darkness is transformed into light, so that the night itself rejoices that it did not die but is transmuted. . . .

"In the evening of the sabbath toward the dawn of the first day of the week." The sabbath

---

[1] Mk 16:2. [2] Lk 24:1. [3] Jn 20:1. [4] Augustine applies the trope of synecdoche: at times the Scriptures name a part instead of the whole, and at other times the whole instead of a part. [5] PL 34:1197-98; NPNF 1 6:210-11.

rejoices that it now has a subservient effect. Under the yoke of the law the sabbath had become smugly apathetic and alienated from life-giving power. Through the primacy of the Lord's Day the sabbath is now wonderfully awakened to works of divine power. To paraphrase the Lord: Is it not permitted to heal the sick on the sabbath, to give aid to the afflicted, sight to the blind and life to the dead? SERMONS 77.2-3.[6]

AFTER THE SABBATH. SEVERUS: The sacred authors of the Gospels did not say whether the Savior was raised "after the sabbath," or when most of the night had passed, or at the dawn or when the sun had already begun to shine. Indeed, it would be contradictory for the authors to say that the same event transpired at different times. However, they did write that some of the women arrived at the tomb at one time and some of the women at another time, but not all at the same time—how could that be possible, since they came separately?—and that each of the women heard the angels say similar things regarding the Savior: "He is risen, he is not here," without adding when his resurrection occurred. It follows that if the resurrection had taken place on that divine night, as all of the Evangelists aver and agree, no one has specified the hour. [That hour] is unknown to the entire world except for the God who was raised and for the Father—who alone knows the Son as he is known by the Son—and except for the Spirit, who "searches everything, even the depths of God."[7] ...

As for the expression "after the sabbath," it does not refer to the evening which follows the setting of the sun at the end of the sabbath, for Matthew did not use the singular *opse sabbatou* but the plural *opse sabbatōn*. The Jews were accustomed to call the entire week *sabbata*. Thus the Evangelists call the first day *opse sabbatōn* when they mean the first day of the week. We also use a colloquial expression when we call the second and third days of the week the second

and third of the *sabbata*. Matthew then did not say *opse sabbatou*, that is, the evening of the sabbath, because he did not intend to denote the evening of that very day. Rather, he used *opse sabbatōn* so as to indicate that it was very late and well after the end of the week. Similarly, I think, we are in the habit of saying "you came *opse tou kairou* [well after the time], *opse tēs hōras* [well after the hour], *opse tēs chreias* [well after the need]" not in order to indicate the evening or the time after the setting of the sun but in order to suggest that the person arrived too late for the event. In a similar fashion, *opse sabbatōn* means that the women arrived very late and well after the end of the week. Now each week ends at the setting of the sun after the sabbath. CATHEDRAL SERMONS, HOMILY 77.[8]

THE WOMEN WANT TO SEE. PETER CHRYSOLOGUS: The apostles are preceded in ministry by women, who follow the men by gender and the disciples by order.[9] The apostles are not thereby made masters by these women. These women are bringing to the sepulcher the form and appearance of women, but they together symbolize the wholeness of the Lord's churches. Mary and Mary: one as herself, and herself as the other. Mary, the single maternal name of Christ, is duplicated in two women.[10] Here is symbolized the church coming from two peoples yet made into one from two peoples—that is, from the Gentiles and the Jews. For "the first shall be last and the last shall be first."[11] SERMONS 75.3.[12]

28:2-3 An Angel Rolls Back the Stone

---

[6]CCL 24a:470. [7]1 Cor 2:10. [8]PO 16:796-98, 802-4. [9]That is, the two women were first to become attentive to the Lord in his death and resurrection, followed by the apostles later. They did not seek to usurp the leadership roles assigned to the apostles. They followed the disciples in their ordering of their lives toward service. [10]In a single name, Mary, both the Jewish and Gentile streams are symbolically brought into the oneness of the church. The Jewish stream is "herself," and the Gentile stream is "the other." The otherness of the Gentiles is poetically and typologically symbolized in the "other Mary." [11]Mt 19:30; Mk 10:31. [12]CCL 24a:459-60.

WHY THE ANGEL ROLLED AWAY THE STONE.
CHRYSOSTOM: After the resurrection the angel
appeared. But for what purpose did he come? To
roll back the stone. Why? To attest to the
women of the resurrection so that they might
believe. The women themselves had earlier witnessed him in the sepulcher. Now they behold
an empty tomb. This is why the angel rolled the
stone away and why an earthquake took place:
that they might be thoroughly aroused and
awakened to the resurrection. THE GOSPEL OF
MATTHEW, HOMILY 89.2.[13]

WHY WAS THE STONE ROLLED BACK? PETER
CHRYSOLOGUS: An angel descended and rolled
back the stone. He did not roll back the stone to
provide a way of escape for the Lord but to show
the world that the Lord had already risen. He
rolled back the stone to help his fellow servants
believe, not to help the Lord rise from the dead.
He rolled back the stone for the sake of faith,
because it had been rolled over the tomb for the
sake of unbelief. He rolled back the stone so that
he who took death captive might hold the title
of Life. Pray, brothers, that the angel would
descend now and roll away all the hardness of
our hearts and open up our closed senses and
declare to our minds that Christ has risen, for
just as the heart in which Christ lives and reigns
is heaven, so also the heart in which Christ
remains dead and buried is a grave. May it be
believed that just as he died, so was he transformed. Christ the man suffered, died and was
buried; as God, he lives, reigns, is and will be
forever. SERMONS 75.4.[14]

RESOLVING DISCREPANCIES. AUGUSTINE: According to Matthew, the angel sat upon the
stone which had been rolled from the tomb,
whereas Mark says that upon entering the tomb
the women were astounded to see a young man
sitting on the right, dressed in a white robe.[15]
This discrepancy would be troubling unless we
understand that Matthew remained silent concerning that angel whom they saw when they

entered the tomb and Mark remained silent concerning that angel whom they saw sitting on the
stone outside the tomb. If this be the case, the
women saw two angels and heard from them
about Jesus progressively; first from the one
who sat on the stone outside the tomb and then
from the one whom they saw sitting on the right
when they entered the tomb. They went into the
tomb then because they had been exhorted to do
so by the angel sitting outside, when he said,
"Come and see where the Lord was placed."[16]
Upon entering, as it is written, they saw and
heard similar things from the angel sitting on
the right side of the tomb, who is mentioned by
Mark but ignored by Matthew.

If this explanation fails to satisfy, we certainly ought to understand that when they
entered the tomb they were in some sort of
walled enclosure which, it is reasonable to
believe, had been established as a secured location in front of the rock from which the tomb
was cut. According to this scenario, the angel
whom they saw sitting on the right side of the
tomb would have been in the same space as the
angel who Matthew says was sitting on the stone
which, at the time of the earthquake, had been
rolled back from the entrance to the tomb, that
is, from the sepulcher cut from the rock. HAR-
MONY OF THE GOSPELS 3.63.[17]

HIS FACE AND HIS CLOTHING. PETER
CHRYSOLOGUS: "His appearance," says the Evangelist, "was like lightning, and his raiment white
as snow." The brightness of his countenance is
distinguished from the brilliance of his clothing.
His face is compared with lightning from heaven
and his garment to snow falling upon the earth.
Listen to the prophet as he says, "Praise the
Lord from the earth, you fire, hail and snow!"[18]
In the angel's face, then, heaven's brilliance
adapts to nature. His clothing symbolizes the
grace of human fellowship, and the appearance

---

[13]PG 58:783; NPNF 1 10:527. [14]CCL 24a:460-61. [15]Mk 16:5.
[16]Mt 28:6. [17]PL 34:1197; NPNF 1 6:209-10. [18]Ps 148:7-8.

of this angel as he speaks is so tempered that physical eyes can withstand the peaceful brilliance of his raiment. As they look upon the lightning of his appearance, they tremble and revere the messenger of their Maker. SERMONS 75.6.[19]

28:4-5 Do Not Be Afraid

THE ANGEL'S PURPOSE. CHRYSOSTOM: For what intent and purpose does the angel say to the women, "Do not be afraid; for I know that you seek Jesus"? First to deliver them from dread and then to announce to them the resurrection. He addresses them personally: "I know you seek Jesus who was crucified." By this he treated them with great honor. To be afraid is not for you but for those that crucified Jesus. The contrast here is between the extreme punishment that awaits those who dared to crucify Jesus and the freedom from fear for those who, having repented, sought after him. It was both by his words and by his appearance that the angel brought them deliverance from fear. The brightness of his appearance was such as to bring good news. He went on to say, "I know that you seek Jesus the crucified." Note that he is not ashamed to call him "the crucified." For it is chiefly by his crucifixion that he blesses. THE GOSPEL OF MATTHEW, HOMILY 89.2.[20]

YOU SEEK JESUS WHO WAS CRUCIFIED. PETER CHRYSOLOGUS: The angel mentions the name of Jesus, alludes to his cross, speaks about his Passion and refers to his death. He then proclaims his resurrection and confesses his lordship. After all the punishment and after the sepulcher, the angel heralds the Lord, speaks of his subjection and sees that the full offense of the Passion has been transmuted into the glory of the resurrection. How could anyone judge that God was lessened by becoming human? Or believe that his power was demeaned by the Passion? Or think that his sovereignty was diminished by his servanthood? The angel speaks

worthily of the crucified one. He shows the very place where the Lord's body was laid, lest someone else and not he is believed to have risen from the dead. SERMONS 76.1.[21]

28:6 He Has Risen, As He Said

HE HAS RISEN. PETER CHRYSOLOGUS: The Lord rises in the same flesh. He brings back the wounds, takes on again the holes from the nails and bears witness by his very body with the signs of his resurrection, which were the ravages of his suffering. If so, how could anyone imagine that he might return in some other body? How could anyone fail to believe that he will return in his own flesh? It is fanciful to think that the servant would by chance disdain his own flesh. Rest assured, my friend, when you arise from the dead it will be you in your own body. Otherwise it would not be you if you should rise in the flesh of another. SERMONS 76.1.[22]

HE IS NOT IN THE TOMB. CYRIL OF ALEXANDRIA: So the angel became an evangelist and herald of the resurrection to the women. "Do not seek," he says, "the one who" always "lives," who in his own nature is life, "among the dead. He is not here," that is, dead and in the tomb, "but he has been raised." He has become a way of ascent to immortality not only for himself but also for us. For this reason he made himself nothing and put on our likeness, that "by the grace of God," just as the blessed Paul says, "he might taste death on behalf of all."[23] And so he has become the death of death. FRAGMENT 317.[24]

OBSERVE THE PLACE OF HIS BURIAL. CHRYSOSTOM: What evidence demonstrates that he has risen? "As he said"—that is, the event is known on the testimony of the angelic visitor. And if you refuse to believe the angel, then remember Jesus' own words, and you will not

---

[19]CCL 24a:461-62. [20]PG 58:784; NPNF 1 10:527. [21]CCL 24a:464-65. [22]CCL 24a:465. [23]Heb 2:9. [24]MKGK 268.

hesitate to believe me. The evidence, however, is further presented: "Come and see the place where he lay." For this purpose the angel had rolled away the stone: that they might see the evidence of his resurrection. THE GOSPEL OF MATTHEW, HOMILY 89.2.[25]

28:7-8 Tell His Disciples

TELL HIS DISCIPLES HE HAS RISEN. CHRYSOSTOM: He calls upon them not only to behold the evidence but to attest it further to others: "Then go quickly and tell his disciples that he has risen from the dead, and behold, he is going before you to Galilee; there you will see him." The angel here is preparing the women to take the good news to the other disciples. They are to tell of the evidence that made them believe—the empty tomb. Furthermore, "he is going before you to Galilee." He says this to relieve them from anxieties and the fear of danger, that their faith not be hindered. THE GOSPEL OF MATTHEW, HOMILY 89.2.[26]

BEFORE YOU INTO GALILEE. PETER CHRYSOLOGUS: The angel goes on to say, "Go quickly and tell his disciples that he has risen; and behold, he goes before you into Galilee; you will see him there." The angel here sends not merely the women but the church in the two women. He sends the one so that by sending her he may spread the news far and wide. Here the angel is sending the bride to the bridegroom. SERMONS 76.2.[27]

THEY RAN TO TELL THE DISCIPLES. CHRYSOSTOM: Why "with fear and great joy"? They had seen an amazing event. It was beyond all their expectations. The tomb had been empty where they had just before seen him laid. The angel led them to the tomb that they might become witnesses both of his tomb and his resurrection. It is evident that no one could have stolen his body, when so many soldiers were sitting nearby him. Hence he raised up himself. For this reason

they rejoiced and stood in awe. The women received the reward of continuing with him. They were first to see and gladly declare not only what had been said to them but also what they themselves had seen. THE GOSPEL OF MATTHEW, HOMILY 89.2.[28]

BOTH FEAR AND JOY. AUGUSTINE: It may be asked how Mark could say, "And going out, they fled from the tomb, for trembling and astonishment had come upon them; and they said nothing to anyone, for they were afraid,"[29] whereas Matthew says, "They departed quickly from the tomb with fear and great joy, running to tell his disciples." The apparent discrepancy between the two accounts is resolved if we understand that the women dared to say nothing either to the angels (that is, to respond to what they had heard from them) or to the guards whom they had seen lying on the ground. For the joy of which Matthew speaks is not opposed to the fear which Mark recounts. We ought to understand that both fear and joy were at once awakened in their minds, even if Matthew had failed to speak of fear. But the question is settled when he says, "They departed quickly from the tomb with fear and great joy." HARMONY OF THE GOSPELS 3.64.[30]

28:9-10 Jesus Met Them

FIRST TO RECEIVE THE WORD OF LIFE. HILARY OF POITIERS: The events during which the small band of women first saw the Lord, were greeted by him, fell to their knees and were commanded to announce the good news to the apostles reverse the order present at the beginning of the world. The gender through which death entered the world would also be the first to receive the glory, vision, fruit and news of the resurrection. The guards, who had seen every-

---

[25]PG 58:784; NPNF 1 10:527. [26]PG 58:784; NPNF 1 10:527. [27]CCL 24a:465-66. [28]PG 58:784; NPNF 1 10:527. [29]Mk 16:8. [30]PL 34:1197; NPNF 1 6:210.

thing, spurned the glory of the resurrection when they accepted a bribe to lie about the theft of Christ's body.[31] They sold their silence regarding the resurrection in exchange for the honor and pleasure of this world, for its honor is in money. ON MATTHEW 33.9.[32]

EVE'S CURSE UNDONE. JEROME: Two different feelings occupied the minds of the women: fear and joy. Fear came from the magnitude of the miracle they had witnessed and joy from their desire for the resurrection. Nevertheless both feelings impelled their steps. They continued on to the apostles so that through them the seed of faith would be scattered.

"And behold, Jesus met them, saying 'Hail!'" They who sought him out and ran to him deserved to be the first to meet the risen Lord and to hear him say, "Hail." Thus it happened that Eve's curse was undone by these women. COMMENTARY ON MATTHEW 4.28.8-9.[33]

JESUS MET THEM. PETER CHRYSOLOGUS: While they were going, the Lord "met them" and said, "Hail!" When he meets them, he does not frighten them with his power but comes before them with the ardor of his love. He does not startle them with his authority but greets them warmly. He binds them by the covenant of the bridegroom, not by the right of the ruler. He honors them with the love of a brother. He greets them with a gracious salutation. At one time he had said to his disciples, "Salute no one on the road."[34] So why is it that here along the way this visitor is so quick to salute them? He does not wait to be recognized. He does not demand to be understood. He does not allow himself to be questioned. Rather, he extends this greeting immediately, enthusiastically. He did this because the force of his love overcomes and surpasses all. Furthermore, by doing so Christ himself greets the church. He makes its very heart to be his own and thus receives its body into his own, as the apostle says, "And he is the head of the body, the church."[35] This greet-

ing itself evidently shows that the full figure of the church abides in these women. They are contrasted with those disciples whom Christ scolds who were wavering over the resurrection. He quells their fears by showing his side and the deep holes from the nails.[36] By taking food,[37] he now restores their faith. SERMONS 75.2.[38]

THEY WORSHIP HIM. CHRYSOSTOM: After they had departed with fear and joy, Jesus met them, saying, "Hail!" They ran to him with great joy and gladness. They "took hold of his feet." Thus they received by his touch an irrefutable proof of his resurrection, with full personal assurance of it. And they "worshiped him."

What does he then say? "Do not be afraid." Again, Jesus himself casts out their fear, making room for faith: "Go and tell my brothers to go to Galilee, and there they will see me." Note well how he himself sends good tidings to his disciples by these women. He thereby brings honor to women, as I have so often said, honor to that sex which is most prone to be dishonored. Through these women he brings good hope and the healing of that which was diseased.

Some among you may desire to be like these faithful women. You too may wish to take hold of the feet of Jesus. You can, even now. You can embrace not only his feet but also his hands and even his sacred head. You too can today receive these awesome mysteries with a pure conscience. You can embrace him not only in this life but also even more fully on that day when you shall see him coming with unspeakable glory, with a multitude of the angels. If you are so disposed, along with him, to be compassionate, you shall hear not only these words, "All hail!" but also those others: "Come, you blessed of my Father, inherit the kingdom prepared for you before the foundation of the world."[39] THE GOSPEL OF MATTHEW, HOMILY 89.3.[40]

---

[31]Mt 28:12-13. [32]SC 258:260. [33]CCL 77:280-81. [34]Lk 10:4. [35]Col 1:18. [36]Lk 24:39; Jn 20:27. [37]Lk 24:42-43. [38]CCL 24a:465-66. [39]Mt 25:34. [40]PG 58:784; NPNF 1 10:527.

28:11-15 THE REPORT OF THE GUARD

[11]*While they were going, behold, some of the guard went into the city and told the chief priests all that had taken place.* [12]*And when they had assembled with the elders and taken counsel, they gave a sum of money to the soldiers* [13]*and said, "Tell people, 'His disciples came by night and stole him away while we were asleep.'* [14]*And if this comes to the governor's ears, we will satisfy him and keep you out of trouble."* [15]*So they took the money and did as they were directed; and this story has been spread among the Jews to this day.*

OVERVIEW: Truth is proclaimed even by its adversaries. For when the soldiers came forward to attest these events, the priests gave them money in order that they might pretend that a fraud had occurred. Yet they could not produce a plausible lie. Remember that a mandated seal had been placed upon the tomb. How could it be ignored that there were many watchmen and soldiers stationed around the sepulcher? And how could they have removed the huge stone that had made the burial secure? Even if they had moved it somehow, how could they have escaped the observation of so many? The entire premise is implausible (CHRYSOSTOM). Having bought out Judas, the priests tried to purchase silence and entomb faith (PETER CHRYSOLOGUS, JEROME). If the disciples had any thought of stealing his body away, they would have done it before he was buried and sealed away in the tomb. But remember on that night none of the disciples were present at the tomb. They were all hiding (CHRYSOSTOM, JEROME)!

28:11 The Guard Told the Priests

THE REPORTS TO THE CHIEF PRIESTS. CHRYSOSTOM: The earthquake occurred for the sake of the soldiers, in order to terrify them and that they might bear testimony to "all that had taken place." This in fact occurred. They reported to the chief priests everything that had happened. The testimony came from the guards themselves. As such it was free from suspicion. THE GOSPEL OF MATTHEW, HOMILY 90.1.[1]

28:12-13 Paying for a Lie

THE BRIBERY OF THE SOLDIERS. CHRYSOSTOM: Some of these signs were displayed publicly to the world, others privately to those present on the spot. Some of these events were displayed publicly for the world that was in darkness. Some were displayed privately, as the appearance of the angel. So truth shines forth, proclaimed even by its adversaries. For when the guards came forward to attest these actual events, the priests gave them money, so that they might pretend that a fraud had occurred. "Tell people, 'His disciples came by night and stole him away while we were asleep.'" THE GOSPEL OF MATTHEW, HOMILY 90.1.[2]

THE PURCHASE OF A LIE. CHRYSOSTOM: How could they have stolen him? O most foolish of all men! They can't even lie plausibly! The conspicuousness of the truth highlights their falsehood. For indeed what they said after the bribe was extremely farfetched. Their falsehood did not even have the ring of plausibility.

For how, I ask, could the disciples have stolen him? They were poor and unlearned. They were hiding out at this time, not even ventur-

---

[1]PG 58:787; NPNF 1 10:530. [2]PG 58:787; NPNF 1 10:530.

ing to show themselves.

Remember that a mandated seal had been placed upon the tomb. How could it be ignored that there were many watchmen, soldiers and Jewish authorities stationed around the sepulcher? These very authorities were already suspicious of just such a thing happening! They themselves had sought to prevent this very contingency! They were anxious to avoid just this! THE GOSPEL OF MATTHEW, HOMILY 90.1.[3]

SAY, "THEY STOLE HIS BODY WHILE WE WERE ASLEEP." CHRYSOSTOM: Further, for what motive might these poor disciples have stolen the body? That they might feign the doctrine of the resurrection? On what premise might it have entered into their minds to pretend such a thing? These were men were hiding out to simply stay alive.

And how could they have removed the huge stone that had made the burial secure? Even if they had somehow moved it, how could they have escaped the observation of so many? The premise is implausible. They would not have attempted such a desperate move. Such a venture would have proved fruitless.

In fact, the disciples were themselves quite afraid; they were far from bold. The evidence shows that they had all rushed away from Jesus the moment they saw him seized. If then at that time they did not dare so much as to stand their ground when they saw him alive, how when he was dead could they have had the courage to withstand such a number of soldiers? Do you think they might have escaped notice? How could they have burst through the circle of defenders? It would have taken many hands to remove such a great stone that had sealed the tomb. THE GOSPEL OF MATTHEW, HOMILY 90.1.[4]

28:14 Satisfying the Governor

IF THIS COMES TO THE GOVERNOR'S EARS. CHRYSOSTOM: They were correct in saying ear-

lier that "the last fraud will be worse than the first."[5] They were in effect making this declaration against themselves. After so much violent conduct they ought to have repented, but rather they strove to outdo their former lunacies, feigning absurd fictions. When he was alive, they purchased his blood. When he was dead and risen again, they again by money were striving to undermine the evidence of his resurrection. THE GOSPEL OF MATTHEW, HOMILY 90.1.[6]

WE WILL KEEP YOU OUT OF TROUBLE. PETER CHRYSOLOGUS: Among these misdeeds, we find the priests bribing people and, what is worse, deceiving them by pointing falsely to the misdeeds of others. Meanwhile they were putting a price on sin. They paid money to cover up their manipulations. They buy out Judas who betrayed his Lord. They compensate with money the blood of the Savior of the world. They try to shut up faith in the empty tomb by purchasing silence. With petty theft they deal in the greater crime of denying the resurrection. "They gave a sum of money to the soldiers and said, 'Tell people, "His disciples came by night and stole him away while we were asleep." And if this comes to the governor's ears, we will satisfy him and keep you out of trouble.' So they took the money and did as they were directed; and this story has been spread among the Jews to this day." Among the Christians too. What they covered up with gold in Judea would shine brightly and intensely over the whole world. The disciples received Christ; they did not steal him. You purchased treachery, but you did not steal the truth. Christ rose from the dead. You lost money. SERMONS 76.4.[7]

28:15 Spreading the Story

THEY TOOK THE MONEY. JEROME: The guards acknowledged the miracle, returned to the city

---

[3]PG 58:787; NPNF 1 10:530. [4]PG 58:787-88; NPNF 1 10:530. [5]Mt 27:64. [6]PG 58:788; NPNF 1 10:530. [7]CCL 24a:468.

quickly and described to the chief priest what they had witnessed. Those who should have turned, repented and sought out the resurrected Jesus continued instead in their wickedness. They converted the money which had been given to the temple into a bride for their falsehood, just as they had earlier given thirty pieces of silver to Judas, the betrayer. Everyone therefore who diverts the offerings given to the temple or to the church for other purposes, namely, the satisfaction of his own will, is like these scribes and chief priests who purchased a lie and bought the blood of the Savior. COMMENTARY ON MATTHEW 4.28.14.[8]

TO THIS DAY. CHRYSOSTOM: See how their own actions trap them everywhere in their own devices. For if they had not come to Pilate or asked for the guard, they would have been more able to act in this impudent fashion. But as it was, they did ask for a guard. Indeed, as though they were laboring to shut their own mouths, they took these precautions themselves. If the disciples did not even have the fortitude to watch with him for an hour while he prayed, even when he scolded them, how would they then have had the strength to venture upon such a desperate enterprise? Don't be foolish. If the disciples had any thought of stealing his body, they would have done so before he was buried and sealed in the tomb. They would have acted before a guard was placed at the tomb on the first night, when it might have been done in greater security and with less danger. . . . But remember on that night none of the disciples were present at the tomb. They were scattered in hiding! THE GOSPEL OF MATTHEW, HOMILY 90.1.[9]

---

[8]CCL 77:281-82. [9]PG 58:788; NPNF 1 10:530.

28:16-20 THE RISEN LORD APPEARS TO HIS DISCIPLES

[16]Now the eleven disciples went to Galilee, to the mountain to which Jesus had directed them. [17]And when they saw him they worshiped him; but some doubted. [18]And Jesus came and said to them, "All authority in heaven and on earth has been given to me. [19]Go therefore and make disciples of all nations, baptizing them in the name of the Father and of the Son and of the Holy Spirit, [20]teaching them to observe all that I have commanded you; and lo, I am with you always, to the close of the age."

OVERVIEW: Having put into their hands a summary of Christian teaching, which is expressed in the form of baptism, the risen Lord commanded the disciples to go forth into the whole world. With Jesus' resurrection his own proper glory is again restored, following his humiliation. Jesus reminded his disciples of the consummation of all things, so that they would not look at the present dangers only but also at the good things to come that last forever. He promised to be not only with these disciples but also with all who would subsequently believe after them (CHRYSOSTOM).

28:16-17 The Disciples See Jesus in Galilee

BUT SOME DOUBTED. CHRYSOSTOM: This

seems to me to be the last appearance in Galilee, when he sent them out to baptize. And if "some doubted," herein again admire the Evangelists' truthfulness. Even up to the last day, they were determined not to conceal even their own short-comings. Nevertheless even these are assured by what they see. THE GOSPEL OF MATTHEW, HOMILY 90.2.[1]

28:18-20 *I Am with You Always*

THE GREAT COMMISSION. JEROME: "Jesus approached them and said, 'All authority in heaven and earth has been given to me.'" This authority was given to one who had just been crucified, buried in a tomb, laid dead and afterwards had arisen. Authority was given to him in both heaven and earth so that he who once reigned in heaven might also reign on earth through the faith of his believers.

"'Go therefore and teach all nations, baptizing them in the name of the Father and of the Son and of the Holy Spirit.'" First they teach all nations; then they baptize those they have taught with water, for the body is not able to receive the sacrament of baptism before the soul has received the truth of the faith. They were baptized in the name of the Father and of the Son and of the Holy Spirit so that the three who are one in divinity might also be one in giving themselves. The name of the Trinity is the name of the one God.

"'Teach them to observe all that I have commanded you.'" What a marvelous sequence this is. He commanded the apostles first to teach all nations and then to baptize them in the sacrament of faith and then, after faith and baptism, to teach them to observe all that he had commanded. Lest we think these commandments of little consequence or few in number, he added "all that I have commanded you," so that those who were to believe and be baptized in the Trinity would observe everything they had been taught. COMMENTARY ON MATTHEW 4.28.18-20.[2]

GO, MAKE DISCIPLES OF ALL NATIONS. CHRYSOSTOM: What does he finally say to them when he sees them? "All authority in heaven and on earth has been given to me." He is still speaking to them according to his humanity, for they had not yet received the Spirit which was able to raise them to higher things. "Go therefore and make disciples of all nations, baptizing them in the name of the Father and of the Son and of the Holy Spirit, teaching them to observe all that I have commanded you; and lo, I am with you always, to the close of the age." He gives them one charge with a view toward teaching and another charge concerning his commandments. He makes no mention of the future of the Jews. He does not scold Peter for his denial or any one of the others for their flight. Having put into their hands a summary of Christian teaching, which is expressed in the form of baptism, he commands them to go out into the whole world. THE GOSPEL OF MATTHEW, HOMILY 90.2.[3]

AS IF TO ONE BODY. CHRYSOSTOM: After that, because he had enjoined on them great things, to raise their courage he reassures them that he will be with them always, "even to the end of the world." Now do you see the relation of his glory to his previous condescension? His own proper power is again restored. What he had said previously was spoken during the time of his humiliation.

He promised to be not only with these disciples but also with all who would subsequently believe after them. Jesus speaks to all believers as if to one body. Do not speak to me, he says, of the difficulties you will face, for "I am with you," as the one who makes all things easy. Remember that this is also said repeatedly to the prophets in the Old Testament. Recall Jeremiah objecting that he is too young and Moses and Ezekiel shrinking from the prophet's office.[4] "I am with

---

[1]PG 58:789; NPNF 1 10:531. [2]CCL 77:282-83. [3]PG 58:789; NPNF 1 10:531. [4]Jer 1:6, 8; Ex 4:10, 12; cf. Ezek 2—3.

you" is spoken to all these people. THE GOSPEL OF MATTHEW, HOMILY 90.2.[5]

TO THE CLOSE OF THE AGE. CHRYSOSTOM: Observe the excellence of those who were sent out into the whole world. Others who were called found ways of excusing themselves. But these did not beg off.

Jesus reminds his disciples of the consummation of all things. He seeks to draw them further on, that they may not look at the present dangers only but also at the good things to come that last forever. He is in effect saying, "These difficult things that you will undergo are soon to be finished with this present life. For this world will come to an end. But the good things you are to enjoy are immortal, as I have often told you before." Having invigorated and roused their minds by the remembrance of that coming day, he sent them out. Those who live faithfully, with good works, should strangely desire that day even as those who lack good works should fear it.

So let us not fear and shudder. Let us repent while there is opportunity. Let us rise out of our sins. We can by grace, if we are willing. THE GOSPEL OF MATTHEW, HOMILY 90.2.[6]

---

[5]PG 58:789-90; NPNF 1 10:531. [6]PG 58:790; NPNF 1 11:531-32.

APPENDIX
Early Christian Writers and the Documents Cited

The following table lists all the early Christian documents cited in this volume by author, if known, or by the title of the work. The English title used in this commentary is followed in parentheses with the Latin designation and, where available, the Thesaurus Linguae Graecae (=TLG) digital references or Cetedoc Clavis numbers. Printed sources of original language versions may be found in the bibliography.

Apollinaris of Laodicea
Fragments on Matthew (*Fragmenta in Matthaeum*) — TLG 2074.037

Augustine
Harmony of the Gospels (*De consensu evangelistarum libri iv*) — Cetedoc 0273
Sermon (*Sermones*) — Cetedoc 0284

Chromatius of Aquileia
Tractates on Matthew (*Tractatus in Matthaeum*) — Cetedoc 0218

Cyril of Alexandria
Fragments on Matthew (*Fragmenta in Matthaeum*) — TLG 4090.029

Epiphanius the Latin
Interpretation of the Gospels (*Interpretatio Evangeliorum*)

Eusebius of Emesa
Homilies (*Homiliae*)

Gregory the Great
Forty Gospel Homilies (*XL Homiliarum in Evangelia*) — Cetedoc 1711

Hilary of Poitiers
[Commentary] On Matthew (*In Matthaeum*)

Incomplete Work on Matthew (*Opus imperfectum in Matthaeum*)

Jerome
Commentary on Matthew (*Commentariorum in Matthaeum libri iv*) — Cetedoc 0590

John Chrysostom
The Gospel of Matthew (*Homiliae in Matthaeum/Commentarius in sanctum Matthaeum evangelistam*) — TLG 2062.152

Leo the Great
Sermons (*Sermones*)   Cetedoc 1657

Maximus of Turin
Sermons (*Sermones*)   Cetedoc 0219a

Origen
[Commentary on] The Gospel of Matthew
   (*Commentariorum in Matthaeum libri 10-17*)   TLG 2042.029-030

Peter Chrysologus
Sermons (*Sermones*)   Cetedoc 0227+

Severus of Antioch
Cathedral Sermons (*Homiliae cathedrales*)

Theodore of Heraclea
Fragments on Matthew (*Fragmenta in Matthaeum*)   TLG 4126.002

Theodore of Mopsuestia
Fragments on Matthew (*Fragmenta in Matthaeum*)   TLG 4135.009

BIOGRAPHICAL SKETCHES & SHORT DESCRIPTIONS OF SELECT ANONYMOUS WORKS

This listing is cumulative, including all the authors and works cited in this series to date.

Acacius of Caesarea (d. c. 365). Pro-Arian bishop of Caesarea in Palestine, disciple and biographer of Eusebius of Caesarea, the historian. He was a man of great learning and authored a treatise on Ecclesiastes.

Alexander of Alexandria (fl. 312-328). Bishop of Alexandria and predecessor of Athanasius, upon whom he asserted considerable theological influence during the rise of Arianism. Alexander excommunicated Arius, whom he had appointed to the parish of Baucalis, in 319. His teaching regarding the eternal generation and divine substantial union of the Son with the Father was eventually confirmed at the Council of Nicaea (325).

Ambrose of Milan (c. 333-397; fl. 374-397). Bishop of Milan and teacher of Augustine who defended the divinity of the Holy Spirit and the perpetual virginity of Mary.

Ambrosiaster (fl. c. 366-384). Name given by Erasmus to the author of a work once thought to have been composed by Ambrose.

Ammonius (c. fifth century). An Aristotelian commentator and teacher in Alexandria, where he was born and of whose school he became head. Also an exegete of Plato, he enjoyed fame among his contemporaries and successors, although modern critics accuse him of pedantry

and banality.

Andreas (c. seventh century). Monk who collected commentary from earlier writers to form a catena on various biblical books.

Aphrahat (c. 270-350 fl. 337-345). "The Persian Sage" and first major Syriac writer whose work survives. He is also known by his Greek name Aphraates.

Apollinaris of Laodicea (310-c. 392). Bishop of Laodicea who was attacked by Gregory of Nazianzus, Gregory of Nyssa and Theodore for denying that Christ had a human mind.

Apostolic Constitutions (c. 381-394). Also known as *Constitutions of the Holy Apostles* and thought to be the work of the Arian bishop Julian of Neapolis. The work is divided into eight books, and is primarily a collection of and expansion on previous works such as the *Didache* (c. 140) and the *Apostolic Traditions*. Book 8 ends with eighty-five canons from various sources and is elsewhere known as the *Apostolic Canons*.

Arius (fl. c. 320). Heretic condemned at the Council of Nicaea (325) for refusing to accept that the Son was not a creature but was God by nature like the Father.

Athanasius of Alexandria (c. 295-373; fl. 325-373). Bishop of Alexandria from 328, though often in exile. He wrote his classic polemics against the Arians while most of the eastern bishops were against him.

Athenagoras (fl. 176-180). Early Christian philosopher and apologist from Athens, whose only authenticated writing, *A Plea Regarding Christians,* is addressed to the emperors Marcus Aurelius and Commodius, and defends Christians from the common accusations of atheism, incest and cannibalism.

Augustine of Hippo (354-430). Bishop of Hippo and a voluminous writer on philosophical, exegetical, theological and ecclesiological topics. He formulated the Western doctrines of predestination and original sin in his writings against the Pelagians.

Babai the Great (d. 628). Syriac monk who founded a monastery and school in his region of Beth Zabday and later served as third superior at the Great Convent of Mount Izla during a period of crisis in the Nestorian church.

Basil the Great (b. c. 330; fl. 357-379). One of the Cappadocian fathers, bishop of Caesarea and champion of the teaching on the Trinity propounded at Nicaea in 325. He was a great administrator and founded a monastic rule.

Basil of Seleucia (fl. 444-468). Bishop of Seleucia in Isauria and ecclesiastical writer. He took part in the Synod of Constantinople in 448 for the condemnation of the Eutychian errors and the deposition of their great champion, Dioscurus of Alexandria.

Basilides (fl. second century). Alexandrian heretic of the early second century who is said to have believed that souls migrate from body to body and that we do not sin if we lie to protect the body from martyrdom.

Bede the Venerable (c. 672/673-735). Born in Northumbria, at the age of seven he was put under the care of the Benedictine monks of Saints Peter and Paul at Jarrow and given a broad classical education in the monastic tradition. Considered one of the most learned men of his age, he is the author of *An Ecclesiastical History of the English People.*

Benedict of Nursia (c. 480-547). Considered the most important figure in the history of Western monasticism. Benedict founded many monasteries, the most notable found at Montecassino, but his lasting influence lay in his famous Rule. The Rule outlines the theological and inspirational foundation of the monastic ideal while also legislating the shape and organization of the coenobitic life.

Book of Steps (c. 400). Written by an anonymous Syriac author, this work consists of thirty homilies or discourses and which specifically deal with the more advanced stages of growth in the spiritual life.

Braulio of Saragossa (c. 585-651). Bishop of Saragossa 631-651 and noted writer of the Visigothic renaissance. His *Life* of St. Aemilianus is his crowning literary achievement.

Caesarius of Arles (c. 470-543). Bishop of Arles renowned for his attention to his pastoral duties. Among his surviving works the most important is a collection of some 238 sermons that display an ability to preach Christian doctrine to a variety of audiences.

Callistus of Rome (d. 222). Pope (217-222) who excommunicated Sabellius for heresy. It is very probable that he suffered martyrdom.

Cassian, John (360-432). Author of a compilation of ascetic sayings highly influential in the development of Western monasticism.

Cassiodorus (c. 485-c. 540). Founder of Western monasticism whose writings include valuable histories and less valuable commentaries.

Chromatius (fl. 400). Friend of Rufinus and Jerome and author of tracts and sermons.

Clement of Alexandria (c. 150-215). A highly educated Christian convert from paganism, head of the catechetical school in Alexandria and pioneer of Christian scholarship. His major works, *Protrepticus, Paedagogus* and the *Stromata,* bring Christian doctrine face to face with the ideas and achievements of his time.

Clement of Rome (fl. c. 92-101). Pope whose *Epistle to the Corinthians* is one of the most important documents of subapostolic times.

Commodian (c. third or fifth century). Poet of unknown origin (possibly Syrian?) whose two surviving works focus on the Apocalypse and Christian apologetics.

Constitutions of the Holy Apostles. *See Apostolic Constitutions.*

Cyprian of Carthage (fl. 248-258). Martyred bishop of Carthage who maintained that those baptized by schismatics and heretics had no share in the blessings of the church.

Cyril of Alexandria (375-444; fl. 412-444). Patriarch of Alexandria whose strong espousal of the unity of Christ led to the condemnation of Nestorius in 431.

Cyril of Jerusalem (c. 315-386; fl. c. 348). Bishop of Jerusalem after 350 and author of *Catechetical Homilies.*

Cyril of Scythopolis (b. c. 525; d. after 557). Palestinian monk and author of biographies of famous Palestinian monks. Because of him we have precise knowledge of monastic life in the fifth and sixth centuries and a description of the Origenist crisis and its suppression in the mid-sixth century.

Diadochus of Photice (c. 400-474). Antimonophysite bishop of Epirus Vetus whose work *Discourse on the Ascension of Our Lord Jesus Christ* exerted influence in both the East and West through its Chalcedonian Christology. He is also the subject of the mystical *Vision of St. Diadochus Bishop of Photice in Epirus.*

Didache (c. 140). Of unknown authorship, this text intertwines Jewish ethics with Christian liturgical practice to form a whole discourse on the "way of life." It exerted an enormous amount of influence in the patristic period and was especially used in the training of catechumen.

Didymus the Blind (c. 313-398). Alexandrian exegete who was much influenced by Origen and admired by Jerome.

Diodore of Tarsus (d. c. 394). Bishop of Tarsus and Antiochene theologian. He authored a great scope of exegetical, doctrinal and apologetic works, which come to us mostly in fragments because of his condemnation as the predecessor

of Nestorianism. Diodore was a teacher of John Chrysostom and Theodore of Mopsuestia.

Dionysius of Alexandria (d. c. 264). Bishop of Alexandria and student of Origen. Dionysius actively engaged in the theological disputes of his day, opposed Sabellianism, defended himself against accusations of tritheism and wrote the earliest extant Christian refutation of Epicureanism. His writings have survived mainly in extracts preserved by other early Christian authors.

Dorotheus of Gaza (fl. c. 525-540). Member of Abbot Seridos's monastery and later leader of a monastery where he wrote *Spiritual Instructions.* He also wrote a work on traditions of Palestinian monasticism.

Epiphanius of Salamis (c. 315-403). Bishop of Salamis in Cyprus, author of a refutation of eighty heresies (the *Panarion*) and instrumental in the condemnation of Origen.

Epiphanius the Latin. Author of the late fifth-century or early sixth century Latin text *Interpretation of the Gospels.* He was possibly a bishop of Benevento or Seville.

Ephrem the Syrian (b. c. 306; fl. 363-373). Syrian writer of commentaries and devotional hymns which are sometimes regarded as the greatest specimens of Christian poetry prior to Dante.

Eucherius of Lyons (fl. 420-449). Bishop of Lyons c. 435-449. Born into an aristocratic family, he, along with his wife and sons, joined the monastery at Lérins soon after its founding.

Eunomius (d. 393). Bishop of Cyzicyus who was attacked by Basil and Gregory of Nyssa for maintaining that the Father and the Son were of different natures, one ingenerate, one generate.

Eusebius of Caesarea (c. 260/263-340). Bishop of Caesarea, partisan of the Emperor Constantine and first historian of the Christian church. He argued that the truth of the gospel had been foreshadowed in pagan writings but had to defend his own doctrine against suspicion of Arian sympathies.

Eusebius of Emesa (c. 300-c. 359). Bishop of Emesa from c. 339. A biblical exegete and writer on doctrinal subjects, he displays some semi-Arian tendencies of his mentor Eusebius of Caesarea.

Eusebius of Vercelli (fl. c. 360). Bishop of Vercelli who supported the trinitarian teaching of Nicaea (325) when it was being undermined by compromise in the West.

Euthymius (377-473). A native of Melitene and influential monk. He was educated by Bishop Otreius of Melitene, who ordained him priest and placed him in charge of all the monasteries in his diocese. When the Council of Chalcedon (451) condemned the errors of Eutyches, it was greatly due to the authority of Euthymius that most of the Eastern recluses accepted its decrees. The empress Eudoxia returned to Chalcedonian orthodoxy through his efforts.

Evagrius of Pontus (c. 345-399). Disciple and teacher of ascetic life who astutely absorbed and creatively transmitted the spirituality of Egyptian and Palestinian monasticism of the late fourth century. Although Origenist elements of his writings were formally condemned by the Fifth Ecumenical Council (Constantinople II, A.D. 553), his literary corpus continued to influence the tradition of the church.

Fastidius (c. fourth-fifth centuries). British author of *On the Christian Life. He* is believed to have written some works attributed to Pelagius.

Faustinus (fl. 380). A priest in Rome and supporter of Lucifer and author of a treatise on the Trinity.

Filastrius (fl. 380). Bishop of Brescia and author of a compilation against all heresies.

Fulgentius of Ruspe (c. 467-532). Bishop of Ruspe and author of many orthodox sermons and tracts under the influence of Augustine.

Gaudentius of Brescia (fl. 395). Successor of Filastrius as bishop of Brescia and author of numerous tracts.

Gennadius of Constantinople (d. 471). Patriarch of Constantinople, author of numerous commentaries and an opponent of the Christology of Cyril of Alexandria.

Gnostics. Name now given generally to followers of Basilides, Marcion, Valentinus, Mani and others. The characteristic belief is that matter is a prison made for the spirit by an evil or ignorant creator, and that redemption depends on fate, not on free will.

Gregory of Elvira (fl. 359-385). Bishop of Elvira who wrote allegorical treatises in the style of Origen and defended the Nicene faith against the Arians.

Gregory of Nazianzus (b. 329/330; fl. 372-389). Bishop of Nazianzus and friend of Basil and Gregory of Nyssa. He is famous for maintaining the humanity of Christ as well as the orthodox doctrine of the Trinity.

Gregory of Nyssa (c. 335-394). Bishop of Nyssa and brother of Basil, he is famous for maintaining the equality in unity of the Father, Son and Holy Spirit.

Gregory Thaumaturgus (fl. c. 248-264). Bishop of Neocaesarea and a disciple of Origen. There are at least five legendary *Lives* that recount the events and miracles which led to his being called "the wonder worker." His most important work was the *Address of Thanks to Origen*, which is a rhetorically structured panegyric to Origen and an outline of his teaching.

Gregory the Great (c. 540-604). Pope from 590, the fourth and last of the Latin "Doctors of the Church." He was a prolific author and a powerful unifying force within the Latin Church, initiating the liturgical reform that brought about the Gregorian Sacramentary and Gregorian chant.

Hesychius of Jerusalem (fl. 412-450). Presbyter and exegete, thought to have commented on the whole of Scripture.

Hilary of Arles (c. 401-449). Archbishop of Arles and leader of the Semi-Pelagian party. Hilary incurred the wrath of Pope Leo I when he removed a bishop from his see and appointed a new bishop. Leo demoted Arles from a metropolitan see to a bishopric to assert papal power over the church in Gaul.

Hilary of Poitiers (c. 315-367). Bishop of Poitiers and called the "Athanasius of the West" because of his defense (against the Arians) of the common nature of Father and Son.

Hippolytus (fl. 222-245). Recent scholarship

places Hippolytus in a Palestinian context, personally familiar with Origen. Though he is known mostly for *The Refutation of All Heresies,* he was primarily a commentator on Scripture (especially the Old Testament) and other sacred texts.

Ignatius of Antioch (c. 35-107/112). Bishop of Antioch who wrote several letters to local churches while being taken from Antioch to Rome to be martyred. In the letters, which warn against heresy, he stresses orthodox Christology, the centrality of the Eucharist and unique role of the bishop in preserving the unity of the church.

Irenaeus of Lyon (c. 135-c. 202). Bishop of Lyons who published the most famous and influential refutation of Gnostic thought.

Isaac of Nineveh (d. c. 700). Also known as Isaac the Syrian or Isaac Syrus, this monastic writer served for a short while as bishop of Nineveh before retiring to live a secluded monastic life. His writings on ascetic subjects survive in the form of numerous homilies.

Isho'dad of Merv (fl. c. 850). Nestorian commentator of the ninth century. He wrote especially on James, 1 Peter and 1 John.

Isidore of Seville (d. 636). Youngest of a family of monks and clerics, including sister Florentina and brothers Leander and Fulgentius. He was an erudite author of comprehensive scale in matters both religious and sacred, including his encyclopedic *Etymologies.*

Jacob of Nisibis (d. 338). Bishop of Nisibis. He was present at the council of Nicaea in 325 and took an active part in the opposition to Arius.

Jacob of Sarug (c. 450-c. 520). Syriac ecclesiastical writer. Jacob received his education at Edessa. At the end of his life he was ordained bishop of Sarug. His principal writing was a long series of metrical homilies, earning him the title "The Flute of the Holy Spirit." His theological views are not certain, but it seems that he expressed a moderate monophysite position.

Jerome (c. 347-420). Gifted exegete and exponent of a classical Latin style, now best known as the translator of the Latin Vulgate. He defended the perpetual virginity of Mary, attacked

Origen and Pelagius and supported extreme ascetic practices.

John Chrysostom (344/354-407; fl. 386-407). Bishop of Constantinople who was famous for his orthodoxy, his eloquence and his attacks on Christian laxity in high places.

John of Damascus (c. 650-750). Arab monastic and theologian whose writings enjoyed great influence in both the Eastern and Western Churches. His most famous writing was the *Orthodox Faith.*

John the Elder (c. eighth century) A Syriac author who belonged to monastic circles of the Church of the East and lived in the region of Mount Qardu (north Iraq). His most important writings are twenty-two homilies and a collection of fifty-one short letters in which he describes the mystical life as an anticipatory experience of the resurrection life, the fruit of the sacraments of baptism and the Eucharist.

Josephus, Flavius (c. 37-c. 101). Jewish historian from a distinguished priestly family. Acquainted with the Essenes and Sadducees, he himself became a Pharisee. He joined the great Jewish revolt that broke out in 66 and was chosen by the Sanhedrin at Jerusalem to be commander-in-chief in Galilee. Showing great shrewdness to ingratiate himself with Vespasian by foretelling his elevation and that of his son Titus to the imperial dignity, Josephus was restored his liberty after 69 when Vespasian become emperor.

Justin Martyr (c. 100/110-165; fl. c. 148-161). Palestinian philosopher who was converted to Christianity, "the only sure and worthy philosophy." He traveled to Rome where he wrote several apologies against both pagans and Jews, combining Greek philosophy and Christian theology; he was eventually martyred.

Lactantius (c. 260-c. 330). An eloquent writer known to us through Jerome. He is acknowledged more for his technical writing skills than for his theological thought.

Leander (c. 545-c. 600). Latin ecclesiastical writer, of whose works only two survive. He was instrumental is spreading Christianity among the Visigoths, gaining significant historical influence in Spain in his time.

Leo the Great (regn. 440-461). Bishop of Rome whose *Tome to Flavian* helped to strike a balance between Nestorian and Cyrilline positions at the Council of Chalcedon in 451.

Letter of Barnabas (c. 130). An allegorical and typological interpretation of the Old Testament with a decidedly anti-Jewish tone. It was included with other New Testament works as a "Catholic epistle" at least until Eusebius of Caesarea (c. 260/263-340) questioned its authenticity.

Letter to Diognetus (c. third century). A refutation of paganism and an exposition of the Christian life and faith. The author of this letter is unknown, and the exact identity of its recipient, Diognetus, continues to elude patristic scholars.

Lucifer (d. 370/371). Bishop of Cagliari and vigorous supporter of Athanasius and the Nicene Creed. He and his followers entered into schism after refusing to acknowledge less orthodox bishops appointed by the emperor Constantius.

Luculentius (fifth century). Unknown author of a group of short commentaries on the New Testament, especially Pauline passages. His exegesis is mainly literal and relies mostly on earlier authors such as Jerome and Augustine. The content of his writing may place it in the fifth century.

Macarius of Egypt (c. 300-c. 390). One of the Desert Fathers. Accused of supporting Athanasius, Macarius was exiled c. 374 to an island in the Nile by Lucius, the Arian successor of Athanasius. Macarius continued his teaching of monastic theology until his death.

Macrina the Younger (c. 327-379). The elder sister of Basil the Great and Gregory of Nyssa, she is known as "the Younger" to distinguish her from her paternal grandmother. She had a powerful influence on her younger brothers, especially on Gregory, who called her his teacher and relates her teaching in *On the Soul and the Resurrection*.

Manichaeans. A religious movement that originated circa 241 in Persia under the leadership of Mani but was apparently of complex Christian origin. It is said to have denied free will and the universal sovereignty of God, teaching that kingdoms of light and darkness are coeternal and that the redeemed are particles of a spiritual man of light held captive in the darkness of matter (*see* Gnostics).

Marcion (fl. 144). Heretic of the mid-second century who rejected the Old Testament and much of the New Testament, claiming that the Father of Jesus Christ was other than the Creator God (*see* Gnostics).

Marius Victorinus (b. c. 280/285; fl. c. 355-363). Grammarian who translated works of Platonists and, after his late conversion (c. 355), used them against the Arians.

Mark the Hermit (c. sixth century). Monk who lived near Tarsus and produced works on ascetic practices as well as christological issues.

Martin of Braga (fl. c. 568-579). Anti-Arian metropolitan of Braga on the Iberian peninsula. He was highly educated and presided over the provincial council of Braga in 572.

Maximus of Turin (d. 408/423). Bishop of Turin who died during the reigns of Honorius and Theodosius the Younger (408-423). Over one hundred of his sermons survive.

Maximus the Confessor (c. 580-662). Greek theologian and ascetic writer. Fleeing the Arab invasion of Jerusalem in 614, he took refuge in Constantinople and later Africa. He died near the Black Sea after imprisonment and severe suffering. His thought centered on the humanity of Christ.

Methodius of Olympus (d. 311). Bishop of Olympus who celebrated virginity in a *Symposium* partly modeled on Plato's dialogue of that name.

Minucius Felix of Rome (second or third century). Christian apologist who flourished between 160 and 300 (the exact dates are not known). His *Octavius* agrees at numerous points with the *Apologeticum* of Tertullian. His birthplace is believed to be in Africa.

Montanist Oracles. Montanism was an apocalyptic and strictly ascetic movement begun in the latter half of the second century by a certain Montanus in Phrygia, who, along with certain of his followers, uttered oracles they claimed were inspired by the Holy Spirit. Little of the authentic oracles remains and most of what is known of Montanism comes from the authors who wrote against the movement. Montanism was formally condemned as a heresy before by Asiatic synods.

Nemesius of Emesa (fl. late fourth century). Bishop of Emesa in Syria whose most important work, *Of the Nature of Man,* draws on several theological and philosophical sources and is the first exposition of a Christian anthropology.

Nestorius (c. 381-c. 451). Patriarch of Constantinople 428-431 and credited with the foundation of the heresy which says that the divine and human natures were associated, rather than truly united, in the incarnation of Christ.

Nicetas of Remesiana (fl. second half of fourth century). Bishop of Remesiana in Serbia, whose works affirm the consubstantiality of the Son and the deity of the Holy Spirit.

Novatian of Rome (fl. 235-258). Roman theologian, otherwise orthodox, who formed a schismatic church after failing to become pope. His treatise on the Trinity states the classic western doctrine.

Oecumenius (sixth century). Called the Rhetor or the Philosopher, Oecumenius wrote the earliest extant Greek commentary on Revelation. Scholia by Oecumenius on some of John Chrysostom's commentaries on the Pauline Epistles are still extant.

Origen of Alexandria (b. 185; fl. c. 200-254). Influential exegete and systematic theologian. He was condemned (perhaps unfairly) for maintaining the preexistence of souls while denying the resurrection of the body, the literal truth of Scripture and the equality of the Father and the Son in the Trinity.

Pachomius (c. 292-347). Founder of cenobitic monasticism. A gifted group leader and author of a set of rules, he was defended after his death by Athanasius of Alexandria.

Pacian of Barcelona (c. fourth century). Bishop of Barcelona whose writings polemicize against popular pagan festivals as well as Novatian schismatics.

Palladius of Helenopolis (c. 363/364-c. 431). Bishop of Helenopolis (400-417) and then Aspuna in Galatia. A disciple of Evagrius of Pontus and admirer of Origen, Palladius became a zealous adherent of John Chrysostom and shared his troubles in 403. His *Dialogus de vita S. Johannis* is essentially a work of edification, stressing the spiritual value of the life of the desert, where he spent a number of years a monk.

Paschasius of Dumium (c. 515-c. 580). Translator of sentences of the Desert Fathers from Greek into Latin while a monk in Dumium.

Paterius (c. sixth-seventh century). Disciple of Gregory the Great who is primarily responsible for the transmission of Gregory's works to many later medieval authors.

Paulinus of Nola (355-431). Roman Senator and distinguished Latin poet whose frequent encounters with Ambrose of Milan (c. 333-397) led to his eventual conversion and baptism in 389. He eventually renounced his wealth and influential position and took up his pen to write poetry in service of Christ. He also wrote many letters to, among others, Augustine, Jerome and Rufinus.

Paulus Orosius (b. c. 380). An outspoken critic of Pelagius mentored by Augustine. His *Seven Books of History Against the Pagans* was perhaps the first history of Christianity.

Pelagius (c. 354-c. 420). Christian teacher whose followers were condemned in 418 and 431 for maintaining that a Christian could be perfect and that salvation depended on free will.

Peter of Alexandria (d. c. 311). Bishop of Alexandria. He marked (and very probably initiated) the reaction at Alexandria against extreme doctrines of Origen. During the persecution of Christians in Alexandria, Peter was arrested and beheaded by Roman officials. Eusebius of Caesarea described him as "a model bishop, remarkable for his virtuous life and his ardent study of the Scriptures."

Peter Chrysologus (c. 380-450). Latin archbishop of Ravenna whose teachings included arguments for the supremacy of the papacy and the relationship between grace and Christian living.

Philoxenus of Mabbug (c. 440-523). Bishop of Mabbug (Hierapolis) and a leading thinker in the early Syrian Orthodox Church. His extensive writings in Syriac include a set of thirteen *Discourses on the Christian Life*, several works on the incarnation and a number of exegetical works.

Poemen (c. fifth century) One-seventh of the sayings in the *Sayings of the Desert Fathers* are attributed to Poemen, which is Greek for shepherd. Poemen was a common title among early Egyptian desert ascetics, and it is unknown whether all of the sayings come from one person.

Polycarp of Smyrna (c. 69-155). Bishop of Smyrna who vigorously fought heretics such as the Marcionites and Valentinians. He was the leading Christian figure in Roman Asia in the middle of the second century.

Potamius of Lisbon (fl. c. 350-360). Bishop of Lisbon who joined the Arian party in 357, but later returned to the Catholic faith (c. 359?). His works from both periods are concerned with the larger Trinitarian debates of his time.

Procopius of Gaza (c. 465-c. 530). A Christian Sophist educated in Alexandria. He wrote numerous theological works and commentaries on Scripture (particularly the Hebrew Bible), the latter marked by the allegorical exegesis for which the Alexandrian school was known.

Prudentius (c. 348-c. 410). Latin poet and hymn-writer who devoted his later life to Christian writing. He wrote didactic poems on the theology of the incarnation, against the heretic Marcion and against the resurgence of paganism.

Pseudo-Dionysius the Areopagite (fl. c. 500). Author who assumed the name of Dionysius the Areopagite mentioned in Acts 17:34, and who composed the works known as the *Corpus Ar-*

eopagiticum (or *Dionysiacum*). These writings were the foundation of the apophatic school of mysticism in their denial that anything can be truly predicated of God.

Pseudo-Macarius (fl. c. 390). An imaginative writer and ascetic from Mesopotamia to eastern Asia Minor with keen insight into human nature and clear articulation of the theology of the Trinity. His work includes some one hundred discourses and homilies.

Quodvultdeus (fl. 430). Carthaginian deacon and friend of Augustine who endeavored to show at length how the New Testament fulfilled the Old Testament.

Rufinus of Aquileia (c. 345-411). Orthodox Christian thinker and historian who nonetheless translated Origen and defended him against the strictures of Jerome and Epiphanius.

Sabellius (fl. 200). Allegedly the author of the heresy which maintains that the Father and Son are a single person. The patripassian variant of this heresy states that the Father suffered on the cross.

Sahdona (fl. 635-640). Known in Greek as Martyrius, this Syriac author was bishop of Beth Garmai for a short time. His most important work is the deeply scriptural *Book of Perfection* which ranks as one of the masterpieces of Syriac monastic literature.

Salvian the Presbyter of Marseilles (c. 400-c. 480). An important author for the history of his own time. He saw the fall of Roman civilization to the barbarians as a consequence of the reprehensible conduct of Roman Christians.

Second Letter of Clement (c. 150). The so-called *Second Letter of Clement* is the earliest surviving Christian sermon probably written by a Corinthian author, though some scholars have assigned it to a Roman or Alexandrian author.

Severian of Gabala (fl. c. 400). A contemporary of John Chrysostom, he was a highly regarded preacher in Constantinople, particularly at the imperial court, and ultimately sided with Chrysostom's accusers. His sermons are dominated by antiheretical concerns.

Severus of Antioch (fl. 488-538). A monophysite theologian, consecrated bishop of Antioch in 522. Severus believed that Christ's human nature was an annex to his divine nature and argued that if Christ were both divine and human, he would necessarily have been two persons.

Shepherd of **Hermas** (second century). Divided into five *Visions,* twelve *Mandates* and ten *Similitudes,* this Christian apocalypse was written by a former slave and named for the form of the second angel said to have granted him his visions. This work was highly esteemed for its moral value and was used as a textbook for catechumens in the early church.

Sulpicius Severus (c. 360-c. 420). An ecclesiastical writer born of noble parents. Devoting himself to monastic retirement, he became a personal friend and enthusiastic disciple of St. Martin of Tours. His ordination to the priesthood is vouched for by Gennadius, but no details of his priestly activity have reached us.

Symeon the New Theologian (c. 949-1022). Compassionate spiritual leader known for his strict rule. He believed that the divine light could be perceived and received through the practice of mental prayer.

Tertullian of Carthage (c. 155/160-225/250; fl. c. 197-222). Brilliant Carthaginian apologist and polemicist who laid the foundations of Christology and trinitarian orthodoxy in the West, though he himself was estranged from the main church by its laxity.

Theodore of Heraclea (d. c. 355). An anti-Nicene bishop of Thrace. He was part of a team seeking reconciliation between Eastern and Western Christianity. In 343 he was excommunicated at the council of Sardica. His writings focus on a literal interpretation of Scripture.

Theodore of Mopsuestia (c. 350-428). Bishop of Mopsuestia, founder of the Antiochene, or literalistic, school of exegesis. A great man in his day, he was later condemned as a precursor of Nestorius.

Theodoret of Cyr (c. 393-466). Bishop of Cyr (Cyrrhus), he was an opponent of Cyril, whose doctrine of Christ's person was finally vindicated in 451 at the Council of Chalcedon.

Theophilus of Antioch (late second century). Bishop of Antioch. His only surviving work is *Ad Autholycum,* where we find the first Christian commentary on Genesis and the first use of the term *Trinity.* Theophilus's apologetic literary heritage had influence on Irenaeus and possibly Tertullian.

Theophylact of Ohrid (c. 1050-c. 1108). Byzantine archbishop of Ohrid (or Achrida) in what is now Bulgaria. Drawing on earlier works, he wrote commentaries on several Old Testament books and all of the New Testament except for Revelation.

Valentinus (fl. c. 140). Alexandrian heretic of the mid-second century who taught that the material world was created by the transgression of God's Wisdom, or Sophia (*see* Gnostics).

Valerian of Cimiez (fl. c. 422-439). Bishop of Cimiez. He participated in the councils of Riez (439) and Vaison (422) with a view to strengthening church discipline. He supported Hilary of Arles in quarrels with Pope Leo I.

Victorius of Petovium (d. c. 304). Latin biblical exegete. With multiple works attributed to him, his sole surviving work is the *Commentary on the Apocalypse* and perhaps some fragments from *Commentary on Matthew.* Victorinus expressed strong millenarianism in his writing, though his was less materialistic than the millenarianism of Papias or Irenaeus. In his allegorical approach he could be called a spiritual disciple of Origen. Victorinus died during the first year of Diocletian's persecution, probably in 304.

Vincent of Lérins (d. 435). Monk who has exerted considerable influence through his writings on orthodox dogmatic theological method, as contrasted with the theological methodologies of the heresies.

Timeline of Patristic Authors

Location	British Isles	Gaul	Spain, Portugal	Italy	Africa
2nd century		Irenaeus of Lyons, c. 135-c. 202 (Greek)		Clement of Rome, fl. c. 92-101 (Greek)	
				Justin Martyr (Ephesus, Rome), c. 100/110-165 (Greek)	
				Valentinus the Gnostic, fl. c. 140, (Greek)	
				Marcion, fl. 144 (Greek)	
3rd century					Clement of Alexandria, c. 150-215 (Latin)
				Callistus of Rome, regn. 217-222 (Latin)	Tertullian of Carthage, c. 155/160-225/250 (Latin)
				Minucius Felix of Rome, fl. c. 218-235 (Latin)	Origen (Alexandria, Caesaria of Palestine), 185-254 (Greek)
				Novatian of Rome, fl. 235-258 (Latin)	Cyprian of Carthage, fl. 248-258 (Latin)
				Marius Victorinus (Rome), fl. 355-362 (Latin)	Dionysius of Alexandria, d. 264 (Latin)
4th century		Lactantius, c. 260-330 (Latin)			
					Arius (Alexandria), fl. c. 320 (Greek)
					Alexander of Alexandria, fl. 312-328 (Greek)
					Pachomius (Egypt), c. 292-347 (Coptic/Greek?)
				Eusebius of Vercelli, fl. c. 360 (Latin)	Athanasius of Alexandria, c. 295-373; fl. 325-373 (Greek)
		Hilary of Poitiers, c. 315-367 (Latin)	Potamius of Lisbon, fl. c. 350-360 (Latin)	Lucifer of Cagliari (Sardinia), fl. 370 (Latin)	Macarius of Egypt, c. 300-c. 390 (Greek)
			Gregory of Elvira, fl. 359-385 (Latin)	Faustinus (Rome), fl. 380 (Latin)	
				Filastrius of Brescia, fl. 380 (Latin)	Didymus (the Blind) of Alexandria, 313-398 (Greek)
			Prudentius, c. 348-c. 410 (Latin)	Ambrosiaster (Italy?), fl. c. 366-384 (Latin)	
				Gaudentius of Brescia, fl. 395 (Latin)	
				Ambrose of Milan, c. 333-397; fl. 374-397 (Latin)	
				Rufinus of Aquileia, c. 345-411 (Latin)	Augustine of Hippo, 354-430 (Latin)

Greece	Asia Minor	Syria	Mesopotamia, Persia	Palestine	Location Unknown
	Polycarp of Smyrna, c. 69-155 (Greek)	Ignatius of Antioch, 35- d. 107/112 (Greek)			
		Theophilus of Antioch, c. late 2nd cent. (Greek)			
Athenagoras, fl. 176-180 (Greek)					
				Hippolytus (Palestine?), fl. 222-245 (Greek)	
	Gregory Thaumaturgus (Neocaesarea), fl. c. 248-264 (Greek)				
	Methodius of Olympus (Lycia), d. c. 311 (Greek)		Aphrahat c. 270-350 (Syriac)	Eusebius of Caesarea (Palestine), c. 260/263-340 (Greek)	Commodian, c. 3rd or 5th cent. (Latin)
Epiphanius of Salamis (Cyprus), c. 315-403 (Greek)		Eusebius of Emesa, c. 300-c. 359 (Greek)		Acacius of Caesarea (Palestine), d. c. 366 (Greek)	
	Basil the Great, b. c. 330; fl. 357-379 (Greek)	Ephrem the Syrian, c. 306-373 (Syriac)		Cyril of Jerusalem, c. 315-386 (Greek)	
	Macrina the Younger, c. 327-379 (Greek)				
	Apollinaris of Laodicea, 310-c. 392 (Greek)				
John Chrysostom (Antioch, Constantinople), 344/354-407 (Greek)	Gregory of Nazianzus, b. 329/330; fl. 372-389 (Greek)				
	Gregory of Nyssa, c. 335-394 (Greek)				
	Evagrius of Pontus, c. 345-399 (Greek)			Diodore of Tarsus, d. c. 394 (Greek)	
		Nemesius of Emesa (Syria), fl. late 4th cent. (Greek)		Jerome (Rome, Antioch, Bethlehem), c. 347-420 (Latin)	
	Theodore of Mopsuestia, c. 350-428 (Greek)				

Timeline of Patristic Authors

Location	British Isles	Gaul	Spain, Portugal	Italy	Africa
5th century	Fastidius, c. 4th-5th cent. (Latin)	John Cassian (Palestine, Egypt, Constantinople, Rome, Marseilles), 360-432 (Latin) Sulpicius Severus, c. 360-c. 420 (Latin) Vincent of Lérins, d. 435 (Latin) Valerian of Cimiez, fl. c. 422-439 (Latin) Eucherius of Lyons, fl. 420-449 (Latin) Hilary of Arles, c. 401-449 (Latin) Salvian the Presbyter of Marseilles, c. 400-c. 480 (Latin)		Chromatius (Aquileia), fl. 400 (Latin) Pelagius (Britain, Rome), c. 354 c. 420 (Greek) Maximus of Turin, d. 408/423 (Latin) Paulinus of Nola, 355-431 (Latin) Peter Chrysologus (Ravenna), c. 380-450 (Latin) Leo the Great (Rome), regn. 440-461 (Latin)	Cyril of Alexandria, 375-444 (Greek) Quodvultdeus (Carthage), fl. 430 (Latin) Palladius of Helenopolis, c. 363/364-c. 431 (Greek) Ammonius of Alexandria, 5th cent. (Greek)
6th century		Caesarius of Arles, c. 470-543 (Latin)	Paschasius of Dumium (Portugal), c. 515-c. 580 (Latin) Leander of Seville, c. 545-c. 600 (Latin) Isidore of Seville, c. 560-636 (Latin) Martin of Braga, fl. c. 568-579 (Latin) Braulio of Saragossa, c. 585-651 (Latin)	Benedict of Nursia, c. 480-547 (Latin) Cassiodorus (Calabria), c. 485-c. 540 (Latin) Gregory the Great, c. 540-604 (Latin)	Fulgentius of Ruspe, c. 467-532 (Latin)
7th century					
8th century	Bede the Venerable, c. 672/673-735 (Latin)				

Greece	Asia Minor	Syria	Mesopotamia, Persia	Palestine	Location Unknown
Nestorius (Constantinople), c. 381-c. 451 (Greek)	Basil of Seleucia, fl. 444-468 (Greek)	Severian of Gabala, fl. c. 400 (Greek)		Hesychius of Jerusalem, fl. 412-450 (Greek)	
		Theodoret of Cyr, c. 393-466 (Greek)			
	Diadochus of Photice, c. 400-474 (Greek)				
Gennadius of Constantinople, d. 471 (Greek)					
		Philoxenus of Mabbug, c. 440-523 (Syriac)			
			Jacob of Sarug, c. 450-c. 520 (Syriac)		
				Procopius of Gaza (Palestine), c. 465-530 (Greek)	
		Severus of Antioch, fl. 488-538 (Greek)			
	Mark the Hermit (Tarsus), c. 6th cent. (Greek)			Dorotheus of Gaza, fl. c. 525-540 (Greek)	Pseudo-Dionysius the Areopagite, fl. c. 500 (Greek)
	Oecumenius (Isauria), 6th cent. (Greek)			Cyril of Scythopolis, c. 525-d. after 557 (Greek)	
					(Pseudo-) Constantius, before 7th cent. ? (Greek)
Maximus the Confessor (Constantinople), c. 580-662 (Greek)					Andreas, c. 7th cent. (Greek)
		Sahdona, fl. 635-640 (Syriac)			
		John of Damascus, c. 650-750 (Greek)	Isaac of Nineveh, d. c. 700 (Syriac)		
			John the Elder, 8th cent. (Syriac)		

BIBLIOGRAPHY

This bibliography refers readers to original language sources and supplies Thesaurus Linguae Graecae (=TLG) or Cetedoc Clavis (=Cl.) numbers where available.

Apollinaris of Laodicea. "Fragmenta in Matthaeum." Pages 1-54 in *Matthäus-Kommentare aus der griechischen Kirche*. Edited by Joseph Reuss. Berlin: Akademie-Verlag, 1957. TLG 2074.037.

Augustine. "De consensu evangelistarum libri iv." Cols. 1011-1230 in *Opera omnia*. Patrologiae cursus completus, Series Latina, vol. 34. Edited by J.-P. Migne. Paris: Migne, 1861. Cl. 0273.

———. "Sermones." In *Opera omnia*. Patrologiae cursus completus, Series Latina, vol. 38. Edited by J.-P. Migne. Paris: Migne, 1861. Cl. 0284.

Chromatius of Aquileia. "Tractatus in Matthaeum." Pages 185-498 in *Chromatii Aquileiensis opera*. Edited by R. Étaix and J. Lemarié. Corpus Christianorum, Series Latina, vol. 9a. Turnhout, Belgium: Typographi Brepols Editores Pontificii, 1974. Cl. 0218.

Cyril of Alexandria. "Fragmenta in Matthaeum." Pages 153-269 in *Matthäus-Kommentare aus der griechischen Kirche*. Edited by Joseph Reuss. Berlin: Akademie-Verlag, 1957. TLG 4090.029.

Epiphanius the Latin. "Interpretatio Evangeliorum." Cols. 834-964 in Patrologiae cursus completus, Series Latina, Supplementum, vol 3. Edited by Adalberto Hamman. Paris: Édition Gernier Frères, 1963.

Eusebius of Emesa. "Homiliae." In *Eusèbe d'Émèse discours conservés en latin*, vol. 2. Edited by É.M. Buytaert. Spicilegium Sacrum Lovaniense, vol. 27. Louvain: Spicilegium Sacrum Lovaniense Administration, 1957.

Gregory the Great. "XL Homiliarum in Evangelia." Cols. 1075-1312 in *Opera omnia*. Patrologiae cursus completus, Series Latina, vol. 76. Edited by J.-P. Migne. Paris: Migne, 1857. Cl. 1711.

Hilary of Poitiers. "In Matthaeum." In *Sur Matthieu II*. Edited by Jean Doignon. Sources chrétiennes, vol. 258. Paris: Cerf, 1979.

Jerome. "Commentariorum in Matthaeum libri iv." In *Sancti Hieronymi presbyteri opera: Pars 1.7*. Edited by D. Hurst and M. Adriaen. Corpus Christianorum, Series Latina, vol. 77. Turnhout, Belgium: Typographi Brepols Editores Pontificii, 1969. Cl. 0590.

John Chrysostom. "Homiliae in Matthaeum." In *Opera omnia*. Patrologiae cursus completus, Series Graeca, vol. 58. Edited by J.-P. Migne. Paris: Migne, 1862. TLG 2062.152.

Leo the Great. "Sermones." In *Sermones Tome 3*. Edited by Dom René Dolle. Sources chrétiennes, vol. 74. Paris: Cerf, 1961. Cl. 1657.

Maximus of Turin. "Sermones." In *Maximi episcopi Taurinensis sermones*. Edited by Almut Mutzenbecher. Corpus Christianorum, Series Latina, vol. 23. Turnhout, Belgium: Typographi Brepols Editores Pontificii, 1962. Cl. 0219a.

Opus imperfectum in Matthaeum. Cols. 611-946 in *Opera omnia*. Patrologiae cursus completus, Series Graeca, vol. 56. Edited by J.-P. Migne. Paris: Migne, 1862.

Origen. "Commentariorum in Matthaeum libri 10-17." In *Origenes Werke*, vol. 10. Edited by Erich

Klostermann. Die griechischen christlichen Schriftsteller der ersten drei Jahrhunderte, vol. 40. Leipzig: J. C. Hinrichs, 1935. TLG 2042.030.

———. "Commentariorum series in evangelium Matthaei." In *Origenes Werke*, vol. 11. Edited by Erich Klostermann. Die griechischen christlichen Schriftsteller der ersten drei Jahrhunderte, vol. 38.2. Leipzig: J. C. Hinrichs, 1935. TLG 2042.028.

Peter Chrysologus. "Sermones." In *Sancti Petri Chrysologi collectio sermonum: pars 2*. Edited by Alexander Olivar. Corpus Christianorum, Series Latina, vol. 24a. Turnhout, Belgium: Typographi Brepols Editores Pontificii, 1981. Cl. 0227+.

———. "Sermones." In *Sancti Petri Chrysologi collectio sermonum: pars 3*. Edited by Alexander Olivar. Corpus Christianorum, Series Latina, vol. 24b. Turnhout, Belgium: Typographi Brepols Editores Pontificii, 1982. Cl. 0227+.

Severus of Antioch. "Homiliae cathedrales." In *Les homilae cathedrales de Sévère d'Antioch: Homilies 18-25*. Edited and translated by Maurice Briere and Françoise Graffin. Patrologia Orientalis, vol. 37.1. Turnhout, Belgium: Typographi Brepols Editores Pontificii, 1975.

———. "Homiliae cathedrales." In *Les homilae cathedrales de Sévère d'Antioch: Homilie 77*. Edited and translated by Marc Antoine Kugener and Edg. Triffaux. Patrologia Orientalis, vol. 16.5. Paris: Firmin-Didot et Cie, 1922.

———. "Homiliae cathedrales." In *Les homilae cathedrales de Sévère d'Antioch: Homilies 104-112*. Edited and translated by Maurice Briere. Patrologia Orientalis, vol. 25.4. Paris: Firmin-Didot et Cie, 1943.

Theodore of Heraclea. "Fragmenta in Matthaeum." Pages 55-95 in *Matthäus-Kommentare aus der griechischen Kirche*. Edited by Joseph Reuss. Berlin: Akademie-Verlag, 1957. TLG 4126.002.

Theodore of Mopsuestia. "Fragmenta in Matthaeum." Pages 96-135 in *Matthäus-Kommentare aus der griechischen Kirche*. Edited by Joseph Reuss. Berlin: Akademie-Verlag, 1957. TLG 4135.009.

Author/Writings Index

Apollinaris of Laodicea, 56, 64-65, 75, 87, 93, 96, 98, 146-47, 176, 184, 200, 202, 283, 285, 293, 296-97

Augustine, 11, 13-14, 27, 29, 31, 54, 61, 71, 77-79, 83, 98, 100, 119, 132, 145-47, 161, 215-20, 304, 306, 308

Chromatius of Aquileia, 12, 15, 18, 22-24, 39, 72-74, 80, 85-86, 286-87

Chrysostom. *See* John Chrysostom

Cyril of Alexandria, 7, 9, 24, 34, 45, 50, 55-56, 62, 66, 80, 84-85, 99, 102, 105, 108-10, 156-57, 168, 175, 180-81, 185, 187, 196, 201, 213-14, 220, 222, 245, 247, 249, 251, 267, 276, 287, 307

Epiphanius the Latin, 27-29, 43, 45-46, 68, 75, 95, 120-21, 141, 194-95, 198, 216, 219, 231, 233, 235

Eusebius of Emesa, 9

Gregory the Great, 110-11, 144-46, 222-27, 229

Hilary of Poitiers, 3-5, 7-9, 11-12, 14-15, 27-28, 33-34, 36, 39-40, 44, 51, 53, 61, 64-65, 68-69, 82, 95, 99, 101-2, 104, 115, 123, 125, 127, 133, 136, 171-72, 175, 180, 187, 194-95, 203, 207, 209-10, 213, 215, 217-18, 220, 240-41, 254, 256-57, 260-61, 277, 280, 284, 288, 293, 296-97, 300, 308

Incomplete Work on Matthew, 89-91, 93-95, 98, 101, 104-5, 107, 109, 112-13, 115-17, 121, 124, 126, 131, 133-38, 142, 148-50, 152-56, 159-60, 163-65, 169, 172, 176-77, 180-81, 184, 188-89, 191, 198, 201, 204-5, 207-8, 210, 213, 231-33, 235

Jerome, 3, 5, 7-8, 13, 23, 25, 29, 38, 42, 46, 53-57, 61-62, 64-

65, 67-68, 70, 74, 77, 92, 94, 101, 105, 115-16, 120, 134, 143, 152-54, 162, 164, 166-67, 171-72, 182, 191, 193, 197, 199, 231, 236, 239, 241, 245-46, 248-49, 251, 253, 255-56, 260, 264-67, 269, 272-73, 275, 282-83, 290, 292-94, 297-300, 302, 309, 311, 313

John Chrysostom, 2, 5-9, 11, 13-15, 17, 20-23, 25-26, 28, 30, 32, 34-35, 38, 40-41, 43-46, 48-49, 51, 53-54, 56-58, 60, 62, 64-65, 67, 70-71, 74, 76, 79, 84-87, 90-93, 98-99, 102-4, 108-11, 114-15, 117-21, 123, 128-29, 131, 133, 137, 139-40, 142, 152-54, 159, 165-68, 171-72, 178-80, 182-84, 188, 190-91, 193-97, 201-2, 204-5, 207-9, 212, 222, 224-32, 234, 237-38, 240-44, 246, 248-52, 254-55, 257-58, 260, 262-63, 266-67, 269, 272, 274, 277, 279-83, 289-90, 294-97, 299, 301, 306-14

Leo the Great, 55-56, 255, 267,

271, 281, 286

Maximus of Turin, 275, 277, 281

Origen, 2, 17-19, 21-23, 25, 33, 35, 39-41, 44, 48-50, 53, 55, 57-61, 63, 66-67, 70-71, 73-74, 78-79, 83-84, 90, 92, 100-101, 103, 153, 156-58, 160-61, 163-67, 169, 171, 173-77, 179, 182, 186-88, 190, 194, 197, 199, 202, 204, 207-8, 211-12, 222-28, 233-34, 236-38, 241-43, 245-48, 250-52, 254-58, 260-61, 263-66, 268, 270, 272-74, 276, 278-80, 285, 287-89, 291-98, 300, 302

Peter Chrysologus, 3-4, 80, 304-9, 311

Severus of Antioch, 125, 127, 149-50, 305

Theodore of Heraclea, 2, 34, 36, 43, 49, 73, 105, 173, 199

Theodore of Mopsuestia, 2, 18, 30, 36, 38, 44-45, 47, 59, 79